How to Write for the World of Work

Seventh Edition

Donald H. Cunningham
Auburn University

Elizabeth O. Smith
Auburn University

Thomas E. Pearsall
Emeritus, University of Minnesota

THOMSON

WADSWORTH

Australia   Canada   Mexico   Singapore   Spain   United Kingdom   United States

How to Write for the World of Work, Seventh Edition
Cunningham • Smith • Pearsall

Publisher: *Michael Rosenberg*
Acquisitions Editor: *Dickson Musslewhite*
Director of Development: *Karen Judd*
Development Editor: *Edward L. Dodd, III*
Production Project Manager: *Brett Palana-Shanahan*
Marketing Manager: *Katrina Byrd*
Print Buyer: *Mary Beth Hennebury*

Compositor: *ATLIS Graphics*
Project Manager: *Laura Horowitz*
Photography Manager: *Sheri Blaney*
Cover Designer: *Diane Levy*
Text Designer: *Julia D. Gecha*
Printer: *RR Donnelley*

Cover Images: Front: left to right: © Dan Lim/Masterfile,
© Orion Press/Index Stock Imagery,
© Larry Williams/Masterfile;
Spine: © Chuck Burggraf/Index Stock Imagery

For more information contact Thomson Wadsworth,
25 Thomson Place, Boston, Massachusetts 02210 USA,
or you can visit our Internet site at http://www.thomson.com

For permission to use material from this text or product,
submit a request online at http://www.thomsonrights.com.

Any additional questions about permissions can be
submitted by email to thomsonrights@thomson.com.

ISBN-13: 978-1-4130-0194-5
ISBN-10: 1-4130-0194-7

Library of Congress control number: 2004105084

For Pat, Robert, and Anne

Brief Contents

Contents

Chapter 20 Research Sites and Sources: Field Research 563

Chapter 21 Documenting Sources 584

Unit V   Writer's Guide 607

Preface

Because professional workplace practices and your needs as a student preparing to enter the workplace have undergone vast and rapid changes since 2000, the year our previous edition was published, this seventh edition in many ways is a new book. We have added a new chapter, extensively revised six chapters, and have made numerous changes and additions to update all remaining chapters. Our aims in revising the book, as they have been in all previous editions, are

1. to incorporate up-to-date research and communication practices and other current developments in the workplace.
2. to provide clear, detailed, and realistic suggestions for communicating in the workplace.

The revisions—as those in past editions—continue to reflect the increased diversification and professionalism of the workforce, the globalization of the workplace, and the expansion of computers and electronic media into a web of overlapping practices that have influenced all aspects of communication and have led to new perspectives on research, document design, visuals, writing, reading, speaking, and the storage, retrieval, and transmittal of information.

The organization of the book remains essentially the same as in earlier editions. It is divided into five major units. Unit I, consisting of Chapters 1 though 7, covers the basic principles of communication that relate to all the other chapters. Unit II, consisting of Chapters 8 through 12, gives advice and practice for creating short messages, documents and presentations. Unit III, consisting of Chapters 13 through 17, covers somewhat more specialized and complex documents. Unit IV, consisting of Chapters 18 through 21, explains how to conduct research efficiently and to document sources correctly. Unit V is our handbook—a succinct guide to the style and conventions of writing.

New in the Seventh Edition

In addition to updating many of the writing samples for this seventh edition, we have made significant revisions by adding information about trends and developments that have been around for a decade or so but which have accelerated during the past three or four years.

- In Chapter 1, "The Process of Workplace Communication," we continue to focus on setting objectives, organizing material, planning visuals; and researching, drafting, revising, documents and presentations; and communicating ethically. We have expanded our comments on collaborative work.

- We have revised Chapter 4 to expand on the cultural differences among writers and readers and speakers and listeners, emphasizing the need to think internationally to help reduce the potential for miscommunication when writing or speaking to audiences whose primary language is other than English. The principles presented in this chapter will also help you prepare documents and presentations so those who have to translate them will understand more clearly what you intend to say. The revisions are so extensive that we have retitled the chapter "Creating World-Ready Documents and Presentations: Style and Tone."

- Our new Chapter 8, "Workplace Correspondence: Letters, Memos, and E-mail," replaces Chapters 8 and 9 of the sixth edition. The result, we believe, brings decisions about format and content closer together.

- Chapter 11, "Communicating News: News-Release Publications, Brochures, and Web Sites," is a new chapter. We briefly describe documents you may be called upon to write to describe or promote your organization's activities, products, and services.

- Chapter 12, our chapter on oral presentations, has changed significantly to reflect the increasing reliance on computers and presentations software. You will find yourself making informal reports in meetings with colleagues and giving reports using multimedia for large audiences. The principles of oral communication have adapted to the increasing use of different media for presenting reports.

- Chapter 13, "Principles of Workplace Reports," illustrates the elements of workplace reports using two reports published by the U.S. Environmental Protection Agency: the *Draft Report on the Environment 2003* and *EPA's Draft Report on the Environment: Technical Document*. (The word *draft* is included in the titles of these reports to indicate an ongoing national dialogue on the environment.) The *Draft Report* is written for widespread distribution; the *Technical Document's* target audience is scientists. We encourage you to compare the documents.

- Increased use of computers and searches on the World Wide Web have created a major shift in research strategies and the documentation of research.

The Core of the Book

Although no chapter in this seventh edition remains unchanged, we have maintained the core of the book to which students and teachers have responded enthusiastically through several editions: We focus on the research, writing, reading, and speaking that goes on in the professional workplace and on the basic triad of workplace communication—information, audience, and purpose.

- We break these workplace activities into their day-to-day tasks, such as basic correspondence (including e-mail, oral and multimedia presentations, electronically scannable resumes, and professional portfolios), reports (including proposals, recommendation reports, and instructions), and research (including library, field, and internet searches).

- We explain as carefully and precisely as we can how to accomplish each of these activities. We use real examples, most reproduced as they originally appeared in some work situation. Several examples are produced by students. And while we designed the book for the classroom, we want it to have the feel of the world when one day the classroom tasks will become the real thing.

- We continue to regard our audience as the student who is being educated for a specific vocation or profession. We visualize you as practical and industrious, willing to work when shown what needs to be done, and one who wants to continue to develop verbal, visual, and computer literacy. Our purpose, as in previous editions, is to lead you from the simpler forms of correspondence to the challenging complexities of reports and other kinds of documents, including oral presentations and professional portfolios.

- We continue to believe that carefully integrated visuals should be a part of nearly every assignment. We regard visuals not as merely aids in writing and speaking but as equal to written and spoken language in documents and presentations. The choice of the appropriate medium should be made on the basis of subject, purpose, audience, and cost.

- We provide planning checklists to guide you through the discovery and organizing stages of the writing process. The revision checklists provide you with an organized approach to revision for both when you write as an individual and when you collaborate with others. The checklists also provide useful evaluation criteria for peer evaluators and the teacher.

- Where appropriate, we have added to the activities at the end of chapters, suggestions not only for individual activities but also activities for collaborative assignments and activities that emphasize multicultural considerations. These activities, along with the planning checklists, meet the needs of varied educational situations and help you organize your efforts and encourage diligence and thoroughness in your work habits.

The unifying theme of this book continues to be that workplace writing and speaking presents specific information to a specific audience for a specific purpose. To put it another way, an occasion for a piece of workplace writing or for a workplace presentation always exists.

Workplace writing and speaking is usually generated by a specific piece of information that must be presented: *In answer to your query about the pricing of the Maltrex 5540. . . . We are on time with the computer conversion. . . . This is how you build the 86204 Heat Exchanger.* In the workplace, you write or make an oral presentation when you have something to say.

When you present your information, you must think of your audience. You must always be concerned with questions about how the occasion and the audience's expectations and needs shape your report or presentation: *Who will read my report? Who will hear my presentation? Why will they read or listen? What will they want from the report or presentation? What do they already know about the subject? What is left to tell them?*

Purpose is usually closely meshed with the audience's expectations and needs. You write and speak a certain way for bankers so that the bankers can get the information they need. But you go to bankers in the first place because your purpose is to get a loan. Often you will have multiple purposes for writing or speaking. Suppose, for example, you were writing to policyholders of an insurance company to tell them their rates for automobile insurance are to be increased. If your purpose were only to announce the new rates, you could send out a printed table showing the increase. But you would have an additional purpose: keeping the policyholders with the company. Therefore you would justify the increase, showing how circumstances beyond the company's control forced the increase. For good measure, you would remind the policyholders of the good service they have received from the company in the past.

Information . . . audience . . . purpose . . . the basic triad of workplace writing and speaking. We will remind you of it often in these pages, because the bringing together of all these elements is really what this book is all about.

Acknowledgments

This book represents our cumulative experiences and knowledge as we have learned in the workplace and the classroom and from our colleagues and students. We are pleased to acknowledge several people, by name or group.

As in previous editions, we thank Professor Frederick H. MacIntosh of the University of North Carolina and John A. Walter of the University of Texas. We thank Professor MacIntosh for his phrase "writing for the world's work," which in modified form has become part of our title. Professor Walter we thank again for his statement that "Scientists and engineers are concerned, when they write, with presenting information to a specific body of readers for a specific purpose." We think all professionals in the workplace have these basic concerns, and we believe they should permeate every portion of writing and speaking—from word to sentence to paragraph to the entire document or presentation. Our version of Professor Walter's statement— *workplace communication presents information to a specific audience for a specific purpose*—is stated and illustrated frequently throughout this book.

We owe a great deal of thanks to teachers across the country and in other countries who have used earlier editions of this book in their classes. Many have been kind enough to pass on comments from their students or encouraged their students to write us about how helpful they found the book. We view this book as a collaborative effort of ourselves and the many teachers and students who have written to us. We have especially benefited from the thoughtful suggestions of the following: O. Jane Allen, Joan Buckley, William G. Clark, Mary C. Cosgrove, Janet Forsman, Kyle Gearhart, Albert Geritz, Hal Gilstad, Susan J. Griffiths, Joan Grimm, Robert C. Grotius, Loren Gruber, Margot A. Haberhorn, John S. Harris, James Helvey, Jeffrey M. Johnson, Betsy Goebel Jones, Michael Keene, Shannon Kiser, Joel Kowalski (for the Canadian edition), Carol Lipson, Allison McCormack, Frances Blosser Maguire, Marianne Micros (for the Canadian edition), James Miles, Barbara Murray, Brian O'Meara (for the Canadian edition), Michael E. Petty, Randal L. Popken, L. Dan Richards, Lolita Rodman (for the Canadian edition), Ellen M. Scanlin, Joan Sherman, Maureen Schmid, Arlo Stoltenberg, Michael Stugrin, Thomas Warren, and Hilbert B. Williams.

We also thank the following reviewers for their candid and useful advice in our preparing this seventh edition: Hal Gilstad, *Grays Harbor College;* Sydney Gingrow, *Pellissippi State Technical Community College;* Clay Spinuzzi, *University of Texas at Austin,* and Bill Williamson, *University of Northern Iowa.*

Further thanks go to the Thomson Wadsworth employees who were involved in the publication of this edition, as well as those individuals and companies that have kindly given us permission to use materials. We are also thankful for the opportunities we have had to work with hundreds of students in our classrooms and, by extension, with thousands of other students who have used earlier editions of this textbook in classes around the world.

Finally, our warmest thanks are to our spouses—Pat Cunningham, Robert Smith, and Anne Pearsall—for their love, understanding, and encouragement.

Donald H. Cunningham
Elizabeth Overman Smith
Thomas E. Pearsall

How to Write for the World of Work

Basic Principles

The Process of Workplace Communication

our previous writing courses may have dealt with personal or literary writing. You will find workplace writing considerably different. Read a few lines of John Donne's "The Bait":

Come live with me, and be my love,
And we will some new pleasures prove,
Of golden sands, and crystal brooks,
With silken lines, and silver hooks.

Donne is making a personal artistic statement with a skill and beauty quite beyond most of us.

Look now at the piece of workplace writing in Figure 1.1. The writer who wrote these two short paragraphs was making an impersonal statement to convey a specific piece of information. The style is not particularly artistic, but it is competent. The paragraphs are easily understandable by their intended readers. To make sure the information would be understood, the writer also included a visual (a bar chart in this instance). The passage represents a style and a method of writing within the grasp of most of us.

Workplace communication is a craft, not an art form. As a craft, workplace communication is a rational process that can be learned. The process grows out of the underlying theme of this book that workplace communication presents specific information to a specific audience for a specific purpose. We will take you through the steps of the process. As you add the skills of workplace communication to your existing writing skills, you may find some tasks easier and some harder. The process is a bit like learning how to find your way in new territory, as the following metaphor suggests.

You probably know the neighborhood you live in quite well. Whether you walk or drive to school or work, the journey may take you several blocks or a few miles down several streets with several turnings. For these frequently traveled trips, you need no map other than the one in your head. You know the way. As you stray farther afield, you may glance at a map before you start to confirm the route. For a trip to a totally new destination, you obtain a map and prepare an itinerary from it. You keep the itinerary and map close at hand as you travel.

But suppose you are traveling into strange territory for which you have no map. All of us have done that on occasion, perhaps in a city new to us or in rough back country. Here we may make many false starts and turns. We may start in one direction and walk or drive on bravely until we realize that we are not moving any closer to our goal. We back up and start over again. The strange territory not only may be geographically unfamiliar, but also might be culturally quite different. We may need to learn much about issues of ethnicity and ideology in which the unfamiliar culture plays a defining role. Along the way, we may meet someone who gives us better directions for at least part of the way. So we proceed by trial and error and by gathering additional information until we reach our goal.

Workplace communication is a craft, not an art form.

FIGURE 1.1
Passage using both prose text and a visual to convey ideas.

Source: From *A New Look Through the Glass Ceiling: Where Are the Women?*, by U.S. General Accounting Office, 2002, January. Retrieved October 7, 2003, from www.gov/dingel/dingelmaloneyreport.pdf

Were Women Managers Better Off in 1995 Than in 2000?

In both 1995 and 2000, women managers earned less than their male counterparts in all ten industries studied. In seven of the ten industries, women managers' salaries actually declined relative to men managers' between 1995 and 2000. For example, in 1995 a full-time female manager in the communications industry earned $.86 for every $1.00 earned by a full-time male manager. Five years later, a full-time female manager in the same industry earned $.73 for every $1.00 earned by a full-time male manager.

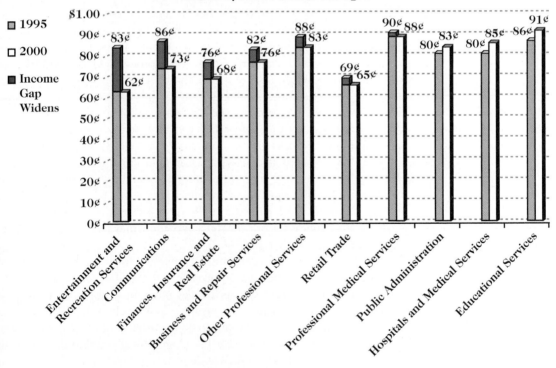

These seven industries are largely private sector industries. In contrast, the three industries where the salary gap narrowed are in the public sector, or are heavily regulated: education, hospitals and medical services, and public administration.

We hope the map metaphor is clear. Sometimes communication is easy. Writing and speaking about familiar subjects and in familiar ways—perhaps writing a letter to a friend, filling in a frequently used laboratory report, or giving a routine oral briefing—resemble our walks and drives to familiar places.

Sometimes the communication may be more difficult, but we use "maps"—patterns for organization and format. For example, in creating a resume, you already have the information about your education and work experience, and you can find an acceptable pattern for the resume in Chapter 9 of this book. Throughout the book, we present many such patterns to help you find your way.

But sometimes, in communicating, as in traveling, you enter unexplored territory without a map. This situation presents the highest level of difficulty. A competent writer or speaker will attempt to learn as much as possible about the situation, make some conjectures about what the communication must accomplish, and then write or prepare the oral presentation material. The last step is to double-check everything to be sure no important points or considerations have been overlooked. In short, you must become a strategic thinker when you write or speak.

> The communication process can be complex and is not easily reduced to a formula.

In the rest of this chapter, we summarize a process that you can use at every level of difficulty. The process involves analyzing your audience, setting objectives, discovering and gathering information, planning organization, planning visuals, writing and revising, writing and planning collaboratively (sometimes), and communicating ethically. The communication process can be complex and is not easily reduced to a formula. You can write using paper and pencil or using word-processing software on a computer. You may make notes before composing on the computer, or you may compose directly on the computer. Everyone develops his or her own productive process. However, if you are not yet writing on a computer, we encourage you to begin. Computer technology has removed most of the laborious work from drafting, revising, and making corrections. In Chapter 2 and throughout the rest of this book, we discuss the use of computers in workplace communication, and we provide suggestions for using them. Sections in Chapter 2 discuss the process as it takes place online (see especially pages 48–50).

Depending on the level of difficulty, you may need to follow all of the steps only some of the time, but you will need to follow some of the steps all of the time. What is important is to check each step to see whether it is applicable to your project. If you do not do that, you risk overlooking some basic aspect that can cause a lot of difficulty later. To give you even more specific guidance, at the end of every chapter that deals with a written or oral product, such as correspondence and reports, we provide a Planning and Revising Checklist. Use of these checklists will help you to consider those key items important to the success of your work. They also help to keep a collaborating group on track.

Analyzing Your Audience

Because workplace writing and speaking deal with audience, purpose, and information, you should start with one of the three. We suggest that you start with your audience for four reasons:

1. Shared communication relies on a shared view of the world, and you usually have to look for ways to adjust your communication to accommodate readers and listeners (in the workplace, you are expected to make meaning clear). There will be unwritten, yet nevertheless significant, cultural and organizational requirements concerning your audience that you must know and follow when you communicate, whether in writing or orally.

2. Having readers or listeners in mind helps to keep you grounded in reality, focused on why they are reading or listening to your presentation and on how and where the audience will use the document or receive the presentation. In the workplace, readers are not always sitting uninterrupted in comfortable chairs in a well-lighted office, and listeners are not always in a quiet, calm environment. At times, you have to adjust your communication to those conditions. Although you cannot always anticipate the conditions, you must try keep those possibilities in mind as you plan.

3. Identifying your audience, its needs, and the environment or circumstances in which they will read your document or hear your presentation helps you decide on content, purpose, organization, media, and format. What media and format are best for presenting your information? What medium does the audience prefer? Will you need to design for print or screen? Will the document be put on a CD or on the Web in HTML or as a PDF document, or will it be print? The answers will depend a lot on your audience. It is their convenience, not yours, that you must keep in mind.

4. Your document or presentation may fit into a larger system or context of information in which secondary audiences and purposes are important and need to be defined. Identifying all the predictable audiences helps you see more clearly all requirements of the communication.

Your audience is usually made up of individuals or groups with specific reasons for reading or listening.

In workplace communication, you can usually define your audience rather narrowly: an executive with a college degree, a group of technicians with good knowledge of the field, a homeowner installing a lock, a farmer with an associate degree in animal technology, a team of health-care specialists who need to know how to perform a specific task on a new piece of software, your boss. They are all intelligent and well educated, but they are uninformed about some aspect of their work, or they need certain information to do their jobs. You can define your audiences by experience, occupation, education, and relationship to you. You know to some degree their general knowledge and the special knowledge they already possess about your subject.

The main question is what information the readers or listeners need to understand what you are attempting to convey. For the most part, you can assume intelligent readers and listeners (otherwise, how could you communicate with them?) who are uninformed about some aspects of the issues or subjects about which you are writing or speaking (otherwise, why would you communicate with them?). If they already know the specifics of what you have to say, you need not write or speak unless it is a means to get on record your shared understandings or for other archival purposes. You may also know their attitude about your subject: friendly, neutral, hostile, or apathetic. Are they predisposed to accept your ideas? Are some of your readers and listeners likely to accept some of your ideas but resist others? Jot down everything you can think of about your audience—what you think they know, what you think they want or need to know, what kinds of evidence they are likely to accept, and their reasons for reading the document or listening to your presentation or what you can do to motivate them to read it or listen attentively.

Anticipating Readers' and Listeners' Questions

Audience analysis continues throughout the entire process. Keep your real or imagined reader or listener in the forefront of your mind. You need to be on the lookout for the many instances when you suspect that your audience will not fully understand your statements or points. As you plan and write or speak, imagine yourself carrying on a dialogue with your audience. What are some of the questions they might ask you? These questions are not just theoretical; readers and listeners may actually be asking themselves these questions as they attempt to understand your document or presentation fully.

You have new ideas to offer your audience. Make sure your ideas are presented in such a way that your audience can grasp them, for they are trying to synthesize your ideas into their own thinking. Your audience will be reading and listening, but they will also be questioning. We suggest a few of those questions here and some of the ways you might respond to them.

As they read or listen, your audience is silently asking such questions as "Why?" "What for?" "How do I know your information is credible?" You must try to anticipate these questions and answer them.

Readers' and Listeners' Questions

So what?	A key question. Always be sure your reader or listener knows the significance and implications of the information you present. After you have researched, analyzed, synthesized, and clarified your own thinking about some matter, you may have a tendency to assume that everybody else understands matters as well as you do and shares your viewpoint. Such assumptions are among the most frequent traps into which writers and speakers fall.
Why is this important to me?	Show where the readers' or listeners' self-interests are involved. Most readers and listeners will not read a document or listen to a

presentation attentively unless they believe it contains information that is relevant to them. If you demonstrate that what you are saying is in the audience's best interest, you are likely to motivate them to read or listen.

How do you know what you are saying is true?	Provide the needed evidence. Do you have either experience or research to back up what you are saying? What kinds of evidence and what kinds of sources will your audience accept as credible or authoritative?
How does it work exactly?	A relevant and simple example or a comparison can help readers or listeners. Most people think better in concrete terms. Give examples, illustrations, anecdotes, narrations, and comparisons.
How is the task accomplished? Why should I do the task your way and not mine?	Provide clear instructions for the work to be done. If your readers or listeners believe they have legitimate reasons for continuing as usual or in some way other than the one you propose, justify your methods and techniques. Many people are hostile to new ways of doing things or at least resist them. They do not necessarily discourage innovation and are not envious of your ideas, but they often have to be persuaded to change the way they do things.
How come?	Tell your readers or listeners why you are asking that something be done. There is a term in physics, *hysteresis,* which refers to a body's resistance to change or to an extremely slow response to changes that affect it. Many people will also display symptoms of hysteresis, especially if they think they will have to change their ways of doing or thinking. Do not count on the new way being immediately accepted as a better way.
What does this word or phrase mean?	Provide a definition to ensure that your readers and listeners understand your words in the same sense that you do. Not considering that others might interpret your words and statements differently from the way you intend can be a major obstacle to clear communication
How does this idea tie to that one?	If you suspect that some readers will not see how one idea or point relates to another, provide a transition—a bridge of some sort—to link them together. The journey through your document or presentation should be smooth. Do not force readers to go back and forth through your document to pick up the thread of your thought. Listeners will not even have the opportunity to review earlier statements. There is another term in physics that is applicable here: *entropy.* Entropy refers to a tendency toward becoming formless and disorganized. Every communication, regardless of what it is about or whom it is for, is subject to entropy. Imposing a structure or organization on your thoughts—and sharing that structure with your audience—enables them to follow your explanations and ideas much easier and much quicker.
Now that I understand you, what do you want me to do?	Make sure all conclusions and recommendations are firmly stated.

Do not overlook the journalist's always useful questions: Who? What? When? Where? Why? How? Providing answers to these questions helps to clarify and explain more fully your ideas.

Setting Objectives

In the beginning of the process, when you have your reader or listener firmly in mind, set your objectives—both yours and your audience's—in terms of achieving professional and career goals and solving workplace problems. This is a major step in working toward getting their thinking parallel to yours.

Reviewing your objectives in light of who your audience is helps to prevent major problems. You and your organization have a serious problem if your document or oral presentation lacks a clear sense of exactly whom and what it is intended for.

Communicating to Achieve Professional and Career Goals

Whatever your professional work—agronomist, accountant, biotechnician, highway engineer, financial planner, fire control specialist, manufacturing engineering manager, forester, systems analyst, interior designer, nutritionist—you make your living by solving problems. You report your findings, express your opinions, and attempt to persuade your readers and listeners that your expertise will contribute to solving the problem. Much of your work comes out in the form of memos, letters, reports, proposals, manuals, and oral presentations. However, the ability to write and speak well comes not merely by doing it, but by working at it intelligently. In fact, writing and speaking are not favorite activities for many professional people, particularly those who see themselves as already having a full agenda.

Doing a good job of writing and speaking is important. But communicating well requires hard, painstaking work. To help motivate yourself to do your best, identify how you think the documents and presentations related to the project you are working on will benefit you personally and professionally. For example, you and your group may be part of a major project that strategic planners in your organization regard as extremely important to future business. All kinds of correspondence, reports, and presentations will be required as the project team is formed and organized into working groups. Documents and presentations will be required throughout the project, and they must be done well.

Your ideas will compete with those of others, both inside and outside your organization. You and your group will compete with others for budget, salary increases and bonuses, facilities, more desirable assignments, higher rank and position, and, of course, job security. Realizing these potential payoffs should motivate you to create effective workplace documents and presentations. Listing the specific professional and career objectives you wish to achieve with a particular piece of writing or presentation will motivate you to do the job well.

Communicating to Solve Problems

What do you hope to accomplish with this piece of writing or this presentation? Is that goal for you and for your organization? What does your reader hope to accomplish by reading it? What does your listener hope to accomplish by listening to your presentation? Usually, these questions are two sides of the same coin. You may be trying to sell a certain kind of building material to a contractor. The contractor's purpose is to discover whether your product is worth buying. Or you may be explaining to someone how to assemble a device ordered by mail. The reader or listener needs to assemble it. Having a clear sense of your intentions and your audience's expectations is critical to the success of your communication.

Write down your objectives. Nothing clarifies thought as much as forcing yourself to set the thought down on paper or to open a new document on the computer and make notes. The process is more than a means of reporting thought. Often it is thought itself. Putting ideas in writing helps you clarify your own thinking. When you compare what you had thought with what you have written down and with what you are now thinking, you gain insight into where your thoughts are leading you. Your objectives as stated should be measurable. That is, they should be stated in a way that allows you to know if they have been accomplished.

An objective such as *the reader will understand how to assemble the device* or *my audience will be able to increase their productivity* is not measurable as stated. How do you plan to test the understanding? The objective stated as *the reader will be able to assemble the device in a half hour* is measurable. You could give the reader the unassembled device and the instructions. If the reader, using your instructions, assembles the device in a half hour, your instrumental objective is met. Much workplace communication lends itself to such measurable goals. For example, the objective for the resume and letter of application used in a job campaign could be that at least 10 percent of the people receiving them grant you an interview.

Of course, some pieces of writing or oral presentations have understanding rather than action as their objective. However, even when understanding is your objective, you can still present actions that the reader or listener should be able to take after reading your work or hearing your presentation. Think of yourself as a teacher who wants to check students' comprehension and understanding. The teacher would devise a test of some sort. You can do the same. If you could go with your document, what questions would you ask the reader about it? What questions would you ask the listener? In essence, you are continuing the dialogue described earlier, only now you are asking the questions. For example, a writer or speaker whose objective is for readers or listeners to understand how prejudice develops and operates in society could ask them to

- Define prejudice from a behavioral perspective (by describing how prejudiced people behave).

- Cite examples of how our culture often teaches prejudice toward old people, children, women, men, and minorities.

- Illustrate behavior that acts to include people in groups or to exclude them.

Obviously, the writer or speaker as teacher must present the information in such a way that the audience as students could answer the questions.

Writing down, first, your analysis of your audience and, second, your objectives fixes them in your mind. You have started the process that, partly through cold rational thought and partly through intuitive insights, will lead you to a complete piece of writing—one that will help achieve common understandings between you and your audience.

Discovering and Gathering Information

Three ways to search for information: brainstorming, consulting other persons and similar documents, and conducting more formal research.

The first step in discovering and gathering information is to inventory the information you already have available in your head to satisfy your objectives. If your subject is one with which you are thoroughly familiar, you may already know much or all that you need to know to do the task. At other times, your own knowledge is not enough.

Brainstorming

Write down what you do know about the subject. Use a method known as *brainstorming*. In brainstorming, you set aside thoughts of organization and critical evaluation and write down everything that comes to mind pertinent to the subject. Be as imaginative as you can be at first. Later you can subject your ideas to scrutiny and critique. You may use a pad of paper or start a file in your word-processing software. You might name the file *notes1*. Only by doing some brainstorming can you truly tell what resources you have available to you.

You have probably engaged in some form of brainstorming as part of a group problem-solving effort, such as compiling a list of possible speakers for your club or organization's meetings, a list of potential ways to raise money, or a list of possible sites for your company's holiday party. Even though brainstorming was originally developed for small-group activities, you can use brainstorming by yourself to focus on a topic. To guide your brainstorming and, later, to evaluate what it has produced, use the knowledge you generated about the needs and attitudes of your audience. To what person or people should your writing or presentation be directed? Do they need any particular information to carry out some process? If you are proposing to perform work or research for your reader or listener, what information is relevant? What information would persuade an employer to hire you?

Consulting Other People and Similar Documents

Writers and speakers in the workplace consult with their colleagues during this discovery stage of generating information. Just having somebody with whom you can discuss your writing or presentation or can exchange points of view can be extremely helpful. In addition, writers and speakers look at previous documents and presentations that they or others in their workplace have produced that are similar to the one they are planning. Such documents not only may provide useful information, but also may guide the discovery process; that is, they may suggest information you need to prepare your own document or presentation. Writers and speakers sometimes go online and browse the World Wide Web for information or access a library's online catalog for resources. In the same way, the writer's or speaker's knowledge of highly evolved and widely used organization patterns is also useful in the discovery process. We discuss many of these throughout this book.

Your friends, coworkers, acquaintances, and fellow students form a network of free consultants. Use them.

Conducting More Formal Research

For more information on research strategies and sources, see Chapters 18, 19, and 20.

Obviously, you will rely on your own thoughts based on your own experiences and knowledge. But if your information is thin, the next stage of the discovery process is formal research. You will often need to use other people's ideas and information from other sources to elaborate on your own thinking. We have a good deal to say about research in Chapters 18, 19, and 20. You may combine library research or investigation of resources on the World Wide Web with empirical research, such as experimentation or polling or surveying, using techniques taught in your own discipline. Or you may interview experts in the field.

Planning Your Organization

As you gather information, your thoughts may leap ahead to organizing your presentation. You may suddenly see in clear outline how your information can best be presented. You may even find yourself writing out drafts of paragraphs that you will later include in your letter or report. Or you may add another slide to your oral presentation. Your mind will be making connections among all the parts of the composing process. Such connections are part of the intuitive creative process of the mind that no one thoroughly understands as yet. But what is clear is that the composing process, like any other creative process, is often *not* an uninterrupted straight path from beginning to end. We leap ahead on the path, and then we double back on our previous tracks. If those who lack knowledge about writing or planning oral presentations were to see our back-and-forth movements at this stage, they might regard us as sloppy or inept writers. However, knowledgeable and experienced writers and presenters know that our process taps, rather than stifles, our skill and creativity.

Use the process; do not fight it. When such connections do occur, write them down; otherwise, you will lose them. Many will later prove to be worthless, but one or two of them could be the keys to your report or presentation.

At some point in your research, you must turn your attention to the planning chores before you. Now is the time to evaluate your material and to find the coherent organization that will satisfy you and your audience. Sit down with your notes, or print out your computer file. Once again review your audience and objective statements. Revise them if necessary.

Although your organizational plan will be more or less tentative as you begin, you must have a deliberate plan, or several difficulties could emerge. You might become so overwhelmed by the material you have gathered that you experience writer's block. Or even if you are able to begin, you might quickly find that your draft or your plan for your presentation is in serious trouble. Developing an organizational plan will help you feel more confident of your grasp of your materials.

Standard Organizational Plans

For more information on standard organizational plans for correspondence and reports, see Chapters 3, 8, 9, 14, 15, 16, and 17.

In your review of audience and objectives, assess what expectations your readers and listeners might have about how particular documents or oral presentations are organized. Check to see whether any of the organizational patterns that you know or that are presented in this book would be useful. Just a partial list of such patterns includes such general ones as the time or chronological approach, cause and effect, and scientific argument with its use of induction, deduction, and comparison. In addition, there are more specific patterns, such as application letters, sets of instructions, proposals, and oral briefings and presentations. Many readers and listeners are familiar with these patterns. When you write or plan your oral presentation, take advantage of their familiarity.

If a pattern fits, use it, but recognize that patterns, even at their best, are still rather incomplete maps. In writing all but the most obvious kinds of correspondence and reports, you are usually entering unexplored territory to some extent. And you should relate the map to the audience as well as to the territory. For example, the general outline for most sets of instructions is fairly clear: (1) an introduction that provides an overview of the process to be done, (2) a list of tools and equipment to be used in the process, and (3) a step-by-step account of the process. The same holds true for oral presentations. Only the impromptu talk, in which you speak off the cuff briefly, has no preparation. But even in impromptu speaking, you quickly resort to fairly well-known standard patterns.

Your task is to relate this general outline to what you know about your audience. Will readers or listeners need to be persuaded to perform the procedure? If so, you must figure out the reason for resistance and address it. If your audience is ready to accept your instructions, you can dispense with the persuasion. Do the members of your audience already know all about the tools to be used—what they are and how to use them? If so, you need only give them a list of the tools. But what if some of the tools are not familiar to your audience? Then you would explain the tools and instruct your audience in their use. Does your audience know where to obtain the needed equipment? If not, you must supply that information. Does the audience know the significance of all the steps in the process itself? If so, you can run through the steps with little explanation. If not, you will need to take time for some explanation. In effect, you are carrying on the dialogue with your audience that we recommended earlier (see pages 7–8).

Other Organizational Plans

Sometimes no ready-made pattern, complete or otherwise, is available. At such times, you may organize best by returning to your objectives and breaking them up into subobjectives. As you do so, you should once again keep your audience and its needs in mind. For instance, a psychologist was planning a one-day workshop in which her objective was to teach her audience how to cope with stress and keep it from turning into harmful distress. Her audience was primarily individuals with high school educations. She thought that they would probably know what stress and distress are but have little real knowledge of how to deal with them. Also, they were rural people who, for the most part, would have little contact with psychologists unless a problem became serious. They would be, the psychologist reasoned, most interested in practical self-help advice and not much interested in theory. Building on that analysis, the psychologist organized her workshop around the following series of subobjectives:

- Identify stress in daily life.

- Identify symptoms of distress and causes of distress.

- Recognize a stressful situation and know at what point to take action to prevent stress from becoming distress.

- Learn and apply tension-releasing techniques.

- Learn problem-solving techniques for decision making.

- Identify sources of expert help if needed.

Frequently, as they did in this case, the subobjectives become the topics that make up the organizational plan.

Just how complete you make your organizational plan depends to some extent on how well you know the territory. If you know the territory well, a sketchy plan of the major headings of the report or presentation may be all you need to begin. Sometimes, you may want to go a step further and break the topics down into subtopics. For example, for her rural audience, the psychologist divided her first topic, "identify stress in daily life," into two subtopics: (1) problems and pressures of farming and ranching and (2) problems and pressures of basic human needs. To organize the considerable amount of information to be presented on the fourth topic, which explains how to develop a few stress-reducing skills, the psychologist further divided the topic into specific techniques:

- Adopting old-fashioned remedies such as drinking certain kinds of vegetable juices or teas and bathing in botanical oils such as lavender and jasmine.

- Practicing body/mind exercises such as meditation or yoga, which reduce respiratory and pulse rates and lessen the amount of stress hormones that the adrenal gland must secrete.

- Exercising regularly and getting sufficient rest and sleep.

- Avoiding caffeine and other substances that overexcite the body's metabolism.

- Eating fresh fruits and unprocessed foods that contain magnesium and potassium.

When the territory is really unfamiliar, you may want even more of a map. One useful technique is to write summaries of all the major parts of the report. Another is to construct a rough outline.

Whether you begin by deliberately constructing an organizational plan or by intuiting a workable sequence of ideas, you should at some point pause and evaluate your plan critically. This is the time to catch flaws in your plan. It is easy to throw away an outline and start over again. By contrast, it is painful to discover a fatal organizational flaw when you are well into the writing stage and are forced to scrap hours of work.

Planning Visuals

Visuals are equal partners with words. For more information on using visuals, see chapters 6 and 7.

While you are still in the planning stage, consider what visuals—photographs, drawings, tables, and graphs, and such—may be available to you or that you can construct yourself. In the workplace, writers and speakers rely on visuals of all sorts to help them deliver their message. They see no particular virtue in saying something in words if an illustration or graph will make the concept clear. Also, tables that display needed statistical information will usually save the writer or speaker words and save the audience time.

The bar chart in Figure 1.1 (page 4) provides side-by-side comparisons of salary differences between male and female full-time managers and the change between the two earnings from 1995 to 2000—all virtually at a glance. Think of all the words and sentences it would take to express this information in traditional prose paragraph form and the immediate comparisons that would be lost. And even the proverbial thousand words would not describe your authors as well as the photographs in Figure 1.2 do.

FIGURE 1.2
Your authors. (That's Cunningham with the beard.)

The line graph in Figure 1.3 shows the annual production of corn in the United States from 1993 through 2003 in a way that would be difficult to communicate in prose. The table in Figure 1.4 makes the information it displays far more accessible than would a prose passage giving the same information. Putting your information in a table frees you to comment on the material that is important to your purpose. For example, in Figure 1.4, you

FIGURE 1.3
Line graph.

Source: From *Crop Production* (p. 5), by U.S. Department of Agriculture, National Agriculture Statistics Service (NASS), Agricultural Statistics Board, 2003. Retrieved October 7, 2003, from www.jan.mannlib. cornell.edu/reports/nassr/field/ pcp-bb/2003/crop0903/pdf

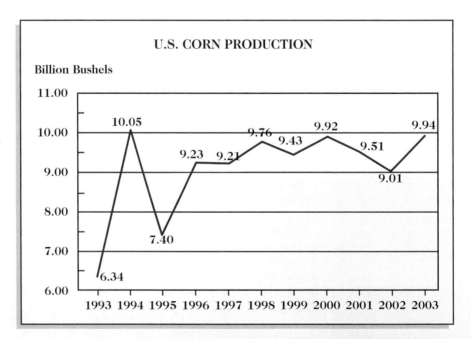

FIGURE 1.4

Tables are especially effective in displaying comparative data.

Source: From *Air Travel Consumer Report* by U.S. Department of Transportation, January, 2003, Washington, DC: GPO. Retrieved October 7, 2003, from www.airconsumer.ost.gov/reports/2003/0301atcr.pdf

Office of Aviation Enforcement and Proceedings
U.S. Department of Transportation

NOVEMBER
MISHANDLED BAGGAGE REPORTS
FILED BY PASSENGERS
U.S. AIRLINES*

		NOVEMBER 2002			NOVEMBER 2001		
RANK	AIRLINE	TOTAL BAGGAGE REPORTS	REPORTS ENPLANED PASSENGERS	TOTAL PER 1,000 PASSENGERS	BAGGAGE REPORTS	REPORTS ENPLANED PASSENGERS	PER 1,000 PASSENGERS
1	ALASKA AIRLINES	2,018	897,241	2.25	2,625	936,336	2.80
2	CONTINENTAL AIRLINES	6,382	2,579,816	2.47	9,848	2,766,375	3.56
3	NORTHWEST AIRLINES	9,500	3,441,206	2.76	11,448	3,311,311	3.46
4	SOUTHWEST AIRLINES	16,670	5,783,947	2.88	22,514	5,863,537	3.84
5	US AIRWAYS	8,870	3,066,605	2.89	12,056	3,705,748	3.25
6	DELTA AIRLINES	20,686	6,845,808	3.02	19,478	6,380,477	3.05
7	UNITED AIRLINES	14,672	4,718,178	3.11	20,289	4,607,250	4.40
8	AMERICA WEST AIRLINES	4,960	1,574,233	3.15	4,483	1,361,573	3.29
9	AMERICAN AIRLINES	22,040	6,130,402	3.60	18,761	4,735,945	3.96
10	AMERICAN EAGLE AIRLINES	7,810	927,242	8.42	7,953	864,972	9.19
	TOTALS**	113,608	35,964,678	3.16	129,455	34,533,524	3.75

For simplicity, statistics are displayed to two decimal places. Actual ranking order is based on our computer carrying out the number of decimal places to nine.

TOTAL BAGGAGE REPORTS—For the domestic system only. These are passenger reports of mishandled baggage, including those that did not subsequently result in claims for compensation.

ENPLANED PASSENGERS—For the domestic system only.

*U.S Airlines with at least one percent of total domestic scheduled-service passenger revenues.
**TransWorld Airlines (TWA) ceased operating December 2001. Effective January 2002, TWA is no longer ranked in this table. Totals for November 2001 reflect the deletion of TWA's data for that month.

might point out that although there were 1,431,154 more airline passengers in November 2002 than in November 2001, the number of reports of mishandled baggage decreased by 15,847—a notable improvement.

Remember, though, that just as you choose words and write paragraphs in a context, you choose and use visuals in a context. We discuss visuals in Chapters 6 and 7. In our chapters on various kinds of reports, we frequently draw your attention to where you can profitably employ visuals. We urge you to always be alert to the possibility of using a visual to carry part of your message. With word processing and computer graphics, you can now easily incorporate visuals into all your documents, from memorandums and letters to proposals and instructions, and into your oral presentations.

Writing and Revising

For some experienced writers and speakers, the organizational stage merges almost without their realizing it into the writing or final oral presentation preparation stage. For less-experienced writers and speakers, the two stages may be quite separate. In either case, you must move beyond planning and write something. If possible, find a quiet place where you will not be disturbed. Use a large desk or table where you can lay your notes, visuals, and plans around you. Plant your feet firmly under the table and begin. (Sometimes *chain your feet* might be the more appropriate metaphor.) Write as rapidly as you can. Use whatever technology you are comfortable with, whether it is a pencil and a pad of paper or a computer.

Do not worry about writing well yet or having your oral presentation polished, and pay no particular attention to such considerations as style and spelling. Just get something on paper or on the screen. Follow your organizational plan, but do not be a slave to it. If in writing and thinking about your writing or oral presentation, a clearer, less obstructed path to your objectives opens before you, follow it. Also, if one segment of your letter or report or oral presentation seems easier to you than another, begin with that. You can always put elements in proper order later. The copy, cut, and paste features in your word-processing or presentation software make rearranging easy. If you are using research material, note in your draft the source so that you can cite it correctly later. Most word-processing software enables you to insert footnotes or endnotes relatively easily.

Write or work on your document or presentation for about two hours at a time. In two hours, you can produce about a thousand words. After resting and getting your mind off your project, work for another two hours if need be. Four hours of writing or preparing an oral presentation in a day is a lot of work, usually enough for most people. If your writing is going to carry over to another time, quit when you are in full rush and know exactly what you are going to say next. It makes beginning again much easier. When you have finished your work, leave it for at least a day. Letting your work "cool off" for a day or so will help you achieve a little necessary detachment. When you come back to it, the revision process begins.

Revision is difficult to plan and organize into specific aims—just as it is a challenge to separate hydrogen from oxygen in water or to separate eggs from milk in a cake, it is challenging to separate revision into specific steps. But you can begin planning revision by dividing it into two major stages: substantive revision and mechanical revision.

Substantive Revision

Make the most significant revisions first.

Begin by revising for clarity and meaning. At this point, do not spend time checking spelling and punctuation or even making fine distinctions of word choice. You might find yourself changing a lot of relatively minor elements that will be deleted or changed substantially later.

Reviewing the Material Yourself

If you feel compelled to give your text a light edit, searching for typos, spelling errors, inconsistent capitalizations and abbreviations, do so. But do not get bogged down in details when you need to focus on generating and sharpening content. Attend to big considerations—the *substantive* matters—first.

Check your document or presentation materials in terms of both clarity and meaning:

- Have you achieved your purpose? Have you merely described how something occurs when you actually needed to explain how to perform a procedure? Have you provided data but failed to explain the significance of the data? Have you followed through on your purpose? Does everything in your document or presentation speak to your purpose? Are there any gaps or digressions in your writing or presentation where you lose sight of your subject as you have defined and limited it? Revisit your analysis of the audience and its needs and purposes. Make sure that everything in the document or presentation contributes to your and your audience's purposes.

- If you are writing or speaking to solve a problem (and you usually will be), readers and listeners must be able to grasp what you want to say the first time they read or hear it; the problem, no matter how complex, must be defined well, and the solution or solutions must be clear. Look at how clearly you state your intention and purpose in the title, the introduction, the conclusion, and, if there is one, the abstract or executive summary. Are they clearly stated either explicitly or implicitly early in the text of your document or presentation?

- If your document or presentation requires a full-scale introduction, have you clearly defined and limited your subject? Perhaps you are responding to a complaint. Is your opening sufficiently friendly? Will it calm a tense situation or make more trouble? Perhaps you are explaining how to perform a crucial step that must be carried out precisely as you direct. Will some readers or listeners understand your intention and meaning in a way different from the one you intend? Perhaps you are defining a problem and offering a solution. Will readers and listeners understand your recommendations and how you arrived at them?

- Now examine the body of your document or presentation. Are the purpose and subject of each paragraph or screen or slide clear? Have you focused on a manageable number of ideas and organized your discussion so that your audience can follow easily? Organization—as we emphasize throughout this book—is paramount. Most readers and listeners can hold in their heads only four or five major ideas at a time. Be sure you inform them of how the material is organized. Providing that framework will enable them to attend to and retain more information.

- Are you sure of all your facts? Double-check them. It is easy to miscopy, make mathematical and computational errors, and uncritically accept the data of others.

- Are your sentences well structured? Are there sentences that just do not make sense? Sometimes cutting and pasting errors can create gibberish or fragments.

- Is your diction appropriate to the occasion? For most workplace communication, diction should be straightforward and unembellished—well-mannered, neither heavy nor slangy. Good writing and speech have a good sound to them. Read your work aloud. Does it sound right? For help with some of these revisions, see the entries on diction (page 627), paragraphs (pages 637–638), and sentences (pages 649–652) in Unit V, "Writer's Guide."

- Could you replace or supplement some of your writing or talking with photographs, drawings, graphs, or tables?

Put yourself in the reader's or listener's place and carry on a dialogue, with your writing or presentation notes before you. Some readers and listeners will understand quite clearly the points you intend to make. Others will not. Ask the questions we suggest on pages 7 and 8. Are all the so-whats answered? Is your work believable? Have you provided evidence where it is needed? Are conclusions and recommendations furnished? Be hard on yourself. Everything is for the reader's or listener's convenience, not yours. Where you find fault, reorganize and rewrite. If you are working with a word processor, you can quickly move and rearrange words, sentences, and paragraphs and insert headings or new items of information. A faulty phrase or sentence can be deleted and a better one substituted with a few keystrokes. Although revision is never thoughtless work, it has become increasingly less painful with the word processor.

You should save different versions of your revisions. You can easily go back to a previous version if you decide it is better. If you are working with a document or presentation you have typed or written with pen or pencil, cut it up. Literally, cut it up. Take a pair of scissors to it, rearrange it for better organization, and tape it all back together on a new sheet of paper.

Having Others Review Your Material

It is fair for you to show your work to others to make sure that what you say makes sense to others as well as to yourself. Of course, it helps if those who comment on your writing or oral presentation are able to play the role of your intended audience. And, of course, this kind of critique can be painful if you cannot take criticism of your work. But it is better to catch the problems early, before your real audience sees a mistake. You must be prepared for criticism. See pages 23–27 for more information on cooperative writing.

Conducting Usability Tests on Your Material

We always hope that our documents and presentations are useful to our readers and listeners—that people can use the information efficiently, effectively, and successfully to accomplish whatever they need to do. However, it is not safe to assume that our words and statements (which are so clear to us) can have only one meaning or that our design of pages or computer screens (which are so clear to us) are easy to follow. If the document or presentation is important enough to merit testing by people who are reasonably representative of the intended audience, then conduct some form of usability testing. Usability tests, when designed properly, can show how well your audience understands and can use the information in your document or presentation. Keep in mind, though, that usability testing is very expensive, and it should be reserved for only those documents or presentations that management of the organization or company regards as extremely important. Some such documents might be instructions that provide client support on important processes, services, or products; a proposal that is going after a multi-million-dollar contract; or a new Web site that is scheduled to be launched soon.

For more information on usability testing, see Chapter 17.

The design of the usability test will depend on the nature of the information and what you want your audience to be able to do. If you want to test how well an audience understands your communication, you might conduct interviews or design questionnaires that help to determine ease of reading, retention of material, speed of reading, error of interpretation issues, or user's overall satisfaction. If you want to test whether readers or listeners can make correct decisions or perform tasks by following your instructions, you should consider directly observing them performing those things. See pages 513–516 for information about user testing sets of instructions.[1]

Mechanical Revision

Check for mechanical accuracy and consistency.

When you have the major issues of purpose, organization, format, content, and style controlled to your satisfaction, it is time to get really picky about surface flaws. Begin by reading your document or viewing your presentation for continuity. There should be no large gaps in information. Insert better

---

[1]Usability testing has become a thriving industry over the past 15 years. Four books that will introduce you to the basics of usability testing are Carol M. Barnum, *Usability Testing and Research* (New York: Longman, 2002); Joseph S. Dumas and Janice C. Redish, *A Practical Guide to Usability Testing* (Norwood, NJ: Ablex, 1993); Steve Krug, *Don't Make Me Think! A Common Sense Approach to Web Usability* (Indianapolis: New Riders Publishing, 2000); and Jeffrey Rubin, *Handbook of Usability Testing: How to Plan, Design, and Conduct Effective Tests* (New York: Wiley, 1994).

transitions or more cohesive sentences. Refer to a dictionary or style guide as you go through your document or presentation materials.

- Check all the spellings you are doubtful about, even if you have used the spell checker or thesaurus on your computer.

- If your document or presentation is a typical piece of workplace communication, it probably contains numbers, abbreviations, and quotations. Have you handled them correctly and consistently?

- Do you have a consistent system for capitalization?

- Look out for grammatical problems you know you tend to have—faulty comma placement, dangling modifiers, or faulty grammatical parallelism, for instance. See Unit V, "Writer's Guide," for help in such matters.

- Check for cutting and pasting errors that can result in mixed-up titles or headings; shifts in font style and size; and inconsistent margins, spacing, bullets, or numbering.

When you are completely satisfied with your document or presentation materials, once again check to make sure they are in the necessary format required by the situation. In Chapters 5, 6, and 7, we discuss layout and design principles. In Chapter 8, we describe letter and memorandum formats. In Chapter 13, we describe the formal elements of workplace reports, such as title pages and tables of contents. Consult these chapters as needed.

Before sending your letter or report on its way or before packing your slides or disks for your talk, look at them one more time. Proofread for those little errors that may have slipped through despite all your care. Make whatever corrections are necessary. Then, and only then, send your work to your readers. Then, and only then, are you ready to make that oral presentation.

And good luck!

Writing and Planning Collaboratively

In today's professional workplace, organizations and companies thrive, languish, or perish depending on their ability to create opportunities to solve complex problems and communicate clearly with those who need information. The complexities of today's problems require mobilizing employees from different areas of expertise and backgrounds to bring to bear different viewpoints and insights into the problems. Because working in a group enables members to pool their labor and take on larger projects, collaborative writing and collaboratively preparing and delivering oral presentations are common in the world of work. Effective collaboration is the hallmark of top-performing organizations and companies, and their employees know how to tap into the collective intelligence of their coworkers. Here we discuss writing. In Chapter 12, "Oral Presentations," we discuss collaboration in making group oral presentations.

Collaborative writing takes three basic forms: interactive writing, cooperative writing, and coauthoring.[2]

Interactive writing is by far the most common. In interactive writing, the writer discusses the work with someone else at some or all of the major steps of writing from analyzing audience through revising. Interactive writing may be something as simple as saying, "Hey, Mary, look this draft over for me, would you?" It can also be a fairly rigid review process in which a supervisor or review panel, right or wrong, has the last word. Beyond knowing how to give and take criticism gracefully, you need no special skills for interactive writing.

> Of the three types of collaborative writing, cooperative writing is the most significant.

Cooperative writing is the next most common method. The cooperative writing process follows essentially the same steps as the individual writing process described earlier in this chapter. The major difference is that except for the writing step, the group carries out the steps together. The work is divided into major segments to be written by individual writers. These individual writers will likely have to repeat at least some of the steps to plan and write their individual segments. When the writing is done, the group reconvenes to integrate the pieces and prepare a final version. This is the method your authors used to write this book. To help you with this process, we later provide some principles to follow in cooperative writing. Following that, we point out some problems you may encounter and suggest solutions for them.

Coauthoring is the least common method in the workplace. In coauthoring, as defined here, two or more people sit down together to draft a piece of writing. Although working at a personal computer, where everyone can see what is going on, eases the process, writing in this way normally consumes more time than one person writing alone. Because it is so time consuming, this method is typically reserved for short, important pieces of writing. Although you may think of its three authors as "coauthors," only a few paragraphs in this book have been coauthored in the sense of this definition. Because this method is so seldom used, we do not discuss it further.

Fifteen Principles for Cooperative Writing

You must learn how to work on a team or in a group. There will be times when you will work with a mix of men and women, some of whom are more experienced than others in collaborating. Some will be from more technical areas than others. Some will be more enthusiastic about the project. Most will

---

[2]For a useful anthology on collaborative writing, see *Collaborative Writing in Industry: Investigations in Theory and Practice,* edited by Mary M. Lay and William M. Karis (Amityville, NY: Baywood, 1991). Some of the terminology we use comes from this anthology, in particular from Barbara Couture and Jone Rymer, "Discourse Interaction between Writer and Supervisor: A Primary Collaboration in Workplace Writing," 87–108; and William Van Pelt and Alice Gilliam, "Peer Collaboration and the Computer-Assisted Classroom: Bridging the Gap Between Academia and the Workplace," 170–206.

have different reasons for being on the team. Some will be more mature. Sometimes you will be involved in a group project that has clear instructions; sometimes not. Regardless of the situation, your group must create instant commitment to the project and to the group, maintain that commitment, agree on the division of work and a work schedule, and reach consensus on priorities.

Focus on these principles of cooperative writing.

To help you work as a member of a group with common goals, interests, and direction and to help you develop strategies to manage nonproductive or destructive conflict and to encourage productive conflict, we offer the following principles to guide your behavior:

1. Understand the advantages of group work. The diversity of a group widens the breadth of skills and knowledge the group possesses. Each member knows how to address a particular issue and where to go for additional information or help if he or she or the group needs it.

2. Create an environment in which group members can share what they know. Show respect for one another. Each member of the group brings some strengths to the project. To be effective, the group must create a spirit of equality and mutual respect. The strength of collaboration comes in bringing different viewpoints, backgrounds, and perspectives to bear on complex problems, questions, and issues that require interdisciplinary approaches.

3. Leave your ego at the door of the conference room. Be prepared to listen to criticism of your work and to respond to the criticism cheerfully. Defend your position when necessary, but when it becomes clear that change is needed, agree to the change gracefully and move on. Criticize other people's work constructively. Be as positive as you can be in praising what is good and in pointing out changes that you think are needed. Always criticize the work, never the person who did the work.

4. Confrontation over major points, such as audience analysis and content, is appropriate, even sometimes necessary, to reach solutions to problems. Intellectual disagreements occur among people with different perspectives. But do not waste group time and energy agonizing over less important matters. For example, if a word chosen by one of the writers is objectively wrong, perhaps *infer* when *imply* is meant, reference to a dictionary can quickly straighten out the matter. If the chosen word is not one you would have used but is still appropriate, perhaps *upon* for *on,* do not insist on your choice, particularly if the rest of the group does not support you.

5. Make sure every member of the group understands (a) the common purposes and objectives, (b) the relationship of their work and writing to the purpose and completion of the project, and (c) how the report relates to the overall project and to other related projects, if any. Do not leave the planning steps of the process, such as analyzing the audience and setting objectives, until everyone has reached a com-

mon vision of the work. Steps poorly conceived early in the process will come back to haunt you later.

6. Coordinate format matters before anyone starts to write. Agreeing early on such matters as the level and style of headings, documentation style, margins, spacing, typeface, and layout of the text and visuals will greatly ease the final revision. Also, agreement on which computer environment and software package your group will use will help.

7. Establish a firm timetable for completing steps in the process, such as rough draft completion, visuals in final form, and meeting for final revision. Everything will take longer than you think it will, so leave plenty of time for all the steps leading up to report completion and submittal.

8. Put the plan in writing, and make sure that every member of the group gets a copy. It is important that all members of the group have the same understanding.

9. Keep everybody informed about matters, especially if something changes or if new people join the group either as additional personnel or as replacements.

10. Even with all the planning done, do not lock in the specifications of the project so much that the group cannot adapt to a change in conditions. However, there must be an overwhelming reason to change some part of the plan. Reviewing the plans and suggesting changes is everybody's job, but the group may want to appoint one or two members to occasionally step back and review the group's progress and work and to report to the group any concerns about the project.

11. If in writing your draft segment, you think work you have done will substantially affect another writer's draft, notify the other writer at once. Do not put people through unnecessary work.

12. When the drafts are brought together for integration and revision, the group must be alert for redundancies and for gaps in the content. Everything should blend together smoothly in the final draft.

13. Revise thoughtfully and seriously but not excessively. All writing can be revised almost without limit, but the workplace will not allow you time for such a luxury. When the group is in general agreement that enough is enough, it usually is.

14. As in interactive writing, either as a group or as an individual within a group, share your work with people outside the group. This can be done at any step that seems appropriate.

15. Use the planning and revision checklists available in this book. Supplement them if you can from your own experience. Such checklists help tremendously in bringing everyone in the group together.

Problems and Solutions in Cooperative Writing

The following are some common problems in cooperative writing and suggestions for solving them:

- People sometimes take critiquing badly. They may grow hostile. If time allows, divert attention for a while to some other subject to allow them time to cool off. When you return to your criticism, relate it to some criterion—for example, to some of the points made about style in this book. It may be that the writer has simply refused to subordinate his or her tone to the tone agreed on by the group. Perhaps a review of why that tone was chosen will bring the writer around.

  When everything else fails, consider how serious the differences are between the writer and the rest of the group. If the differences do no vital harm to the group's intention, perhaps you should move on. If the differences are serious, the group must make the necessary changes. Remember that it is a group project, not an individual one.

  Another possible solution may exist if the group includes someone whose writing skills are clearly superior to those of others in the group. In such a case, the group can designate this person as the lead writer. The group grants the lead writer the right to make final decisions that the group fails to make for itself. Such a method often works well in the world of work, though it may create problems in classroom work. If you do appoint a lead writer, do not second-guess him or her when you disagree.

- Some people simply do not know how to give constructive criticism. They react negatively to anything that is not their own idea and attack people personally, often causing great friction in the group. It is usually better not to correct such people during a group session. It is sometimes effective to take them aside privately and attempt to make them see the dissension they are causing. If this does not work, the group may have to ignore such individuals as best they can.

  Sometimes, if such an individual seems able to work better with one person than with the rest of the group, it may be effective to split the group, at least temporarily, to take advantage of this. In a classroom situation, when everything else fails, the group may have to bring the problem to the instructor and ask for relief.

- Some people seem never to finish their work on time or forever have questions about format, documentation, and such. Such people are hard to deal with in a group. One solution is for the group to appoint a coordinator. The coordinator's job is to see that work is completed according to schedule. The coordinator also serves as a central point to collect finished work and to answer questions about what the group has already decided.

- Some people—either from inexperience or personal inclination—do not understand or value the nature of collaborative work or do not see

FIGURE 1.5
Suggested procedure for beginning a new group project.

At the beginning of a collaborative project, plan a meeting in which your group works through the following steps. Steps 1, 4, and 8 are to be completed by each group member. Steps 2, 3, 5, 6, 7, and 9 are to be completed by the group. Distribute a copy of the statements produced in steps 3, 6, and 7 to each member of the group. This activity should take a little over an hour.

1. *For each individual:* Define in your words and in writing what you think a successful collaborative effort is. (5 minutes)
2. *For the group:* Share your definition with others in your group. Take turns reading your definitions with each other. (5 minutes)
3. *For the group:* Arrive at a consensus of what a successful collaboration is. Select a group member to put the statement in writing. (10 minutes)
4. *For each individual:* Describe in your own words and in writing four attitudes or situations that you believe prevent successful collaboration. (5 minutes)
5. *For the group:* Share your list of these four attitudes or situations with others in your group. (10 minutes)
6. *For the group:* Arrive at a consensus of which four attitudes are the ones that most adversely affect collaboration. Select a group member to put the list in writing. (10 minutes)
7. *For the group:* Select one of the difficulties and identify ways to prevent or solve it. Select a group member to put the statement in writing. (10 minutes)
8. *For each individual:* State in your own words and in writing what you believe are the strongest abilities that you bring to a collaboration. (5 minutes)
9. *For the group:* Share individual statements with the group. (5 minutes)

the benefits of group efforts as opposed to individual efforts. But the success of collaborative projects depends on every member making a commitment and maintaining that commitment to the project. Use the questions and procedure outlined in Figure 1.5 to get everybody into a unified group with a shared perspective.

Communicating Ethically

The three major ethical systems are utility-based, rules-based, and rights-based.

Communication skills are powerful tools. They can be used for good or ill, ethically or unethically. In your everyday workplace activities, you will encounter situations in which you make ethical decisions: whether to forward to somebody else an e-mail message that deals confidentially with a sensitive issue, whether to include but suppress or downplay data that does not support your position, or whether to use your employer's system to send a strictly social and personal e-mail message to a friend. In many of these situations, the correct thing to do is clear. But other situations—regardless of how well developed your own personal sense of ethics is—offer no clear-cut category of right or wrong acts, only gray areas. This is especially true in multicultural contexts. Decisions that are clear in one cultural context will not work for all cultural contexts. What may be considered expected and justifiable compensation in one country may be considered illegal bribery in another. In some cultures, it is considered more ethical to save face than to tell an unpleasant truth. In some cultures, it is acceptable to transact business on the golf course or in a sauna. In other cultures, the only acceptable place to transact business is in the office.

As a workplace professional, you need to have a practical working knowledge of ethics. Many ethical systems exist, but most are either utility-based, rule-based, rights-based, or some combination of the three. We describe each of these systems and present two cases in which we draw everything together.[3]

Utility-Based

In a utility-based ethics system, you judge whether your act is ethical by weighing its consequences—how the act impacts those affected by it. An ethical act should have utility, that is, it should work for the general good of whatever group it concerns. One common expression of this system is that an ethical act will do the greatest good for the greatest number of people. Conversely, an unethical act will harm more people than it helps.

For example, suppose you were asked to write cigarette advertisements. Successfully marketing cigarettes is a positive good for certain members of the community, such as tobacco farmers, cigarette manufacturers, and stockholders in cigarette companies. However, evidence clearly shows that far more people are harmed than are helped by the successful marketing of cigarettes. Smokers suffer cigarette-related illnesses and die prematurely. The high health costs associated with cigarette-related illnesses burden health insurance companies and government Medicare programs. Thus most people have higher insurance premiums and taxes whether they smoke or not. Using a utility-based ethical test, it is clear that writing ads to market cigarettes is an unethical act.

---

[3]In this section on ethics, we drew on the following works: William K. Franken, *Ethics* (Englewood Cliffs, NJ: Prentice-Hall, 1963); H. Lee Shimberg, "Ethics and Rhetoric in Technical Writing," *Technical Communication* 25.4 (1978): 16–18; Arthur E. Walzer, "The Ethics of False Implicature in Technical and Professional Writing," *Journal of Technical Writing and Communication* 19 (1989): 149–160; and Mark R. Wicclair and David K. Farkas, "Ethical Reasoning in Technical Communication," *Technical Communication* 31.2 (1984): 15–19. More recent books discuss many ethical dilemmas and challenges and present case studies that will help you apply the abstract concept of ethics to specific situations. Here are a few of them: Lori Allen and Dan Voss, *Ethics in Technical Communication: Shades of Gray* (New York: Wiley, 1997); Paul Dombrowski, *Ethics in Technical Communication* (Boston: Allyn and Bacon, 2000); and Michael H. Markel, *Ethics in Technical Communication: A Critique and Synthesis* (Westport, CT: Ablex, 2001).

Rule-Based

In a rule-based ethical system, the ethical test judges the acts themselves rather than the consequences of the acts; that is, acts are measured against rules. The rules themselves may come from religion, for example, the Ten Commandments. They may simply come from commonly accepted principles. Most people, for example, generally accept the principles that it is unethical to lie, cheat, or steal. In a strict rule-based system, lying is unethical even if the consequences of the lie are beneficial. In a more flexible rule-based system, lies such as "white lies" might be acceptable, but most other lies would be considered unethical.

Lies, incidentally, need not be outright lies. You can lie by promoting false inference even when technically telling the truth. For example, you could write, "Our engineers designed the 100X drive shaft to operate safely between 4,000 and 10,000 rpm." If the drive shaft was indeed so designed, technically, you have not lied. However, if, despite the design, the shaft operates safely only between 4,000 and 9,000 rpm, you have lied because you have falsely led your reader to infer that the shaft operates safely at the designed speeds.

Let us use marketing cigarettes again as an example. In the United States and certain other countries today, cigarette ads must carry a warning that cigarette smoking may be hazardous to health in various specific ways. In that sense, a cigarette ad may be technically telling the truth. However, if the ad shows healthy, attractive models smoking, leading readers to infer that smoking is a healthy activity, the ad may be lying by false inference. Depending on the rules in the rules-based system and the statements made or implied in the ad, the cigarette ad may or may not be unethical.

Other legal and ethical considerations concern using ideas, writing, drawings, and research generated by someone else—either people with whom you work or people whose publications you have read. Many of these are intellectual properties protected by legal and ethical rules. Legal requirements related to copyright and patents require you not only to acknowledge and credit others for their work, but also to get their permission to use their work. Even if the work is not protected by law, there exist unwritten cultural and professional conventions to which you must adhere. You must acknowledge your sources.

Rights-Based

A rights-based system of ethics assumes that everyone has certain rights that, except under certain strictly defined circumstances, cannot be taken away. For example, as the Declaration of Independence states, all Americans have the rights to "life, liberty, and the pursuit of happiness." To protect society at large, convicted criminals may lose all three of these rights, but in general, the rights are assumed to be, as the Declaration states, "unalienable." That is, our rights cannot be taken away.

By the extension of such basic rights as "life, liberty, and the pursuit of happiness," we can devise such rights as the right to expect the tools we use, the cars we drive, and the airplanes we fly in to be safe and not subject our life to unsought dangers.

Another way of looking at rights-based ethics is to say that we must treat our fellow human beings with dignity and not use them solely for our own self-interest or the interest of our organization. We all use people, obviously. We use mechanics to repair our cars, police to protect us, pilots to fly us, customers to provide us profits, and so forth. But a rights-based ethical system implies a fair exchange, such as appropriate payment for a safe and worthwhile product. Cigarette ads clearly fail the rights test. Cigarettes may rob the smoker of life and the pursuit of happiness. By raising health-care costs, cigarette use curtails the rights of nonsmokers. Cigarette ads manipulate people to buy a harmful product solely to benefit those involved in cigarette production.

Acknowledging people who have contributed to your work can be a sensitive ethical subject. Certainly, those who hold patents or copyrights on ideas you make use of have a legal right to be credited. Others who contribute in substantive ways are ethically entitled to acknowledgment as well.

A Case Analysis

Mary Saylor works in a cancer research laboratory that is funded totally by grants from federal agencies and large funding organizations. Her job is to write and edit proposals to such agencies and organizations to obtain money for research that the laboratory wants to do. Often, such proposals are for new lines of research suggested by previous research. The more successful the previous research has been, the more likely that the laboratory will be granted the money to proceed with the new research.

Saylor is a writer and not a cancer researcher. However, she has a good background in biology and statistics, and she has worked at the laboratory for five years. Therefore she has acquired a good knowledge of the way cancer research is conducted and reported. Her current assignment is to edit and polish a draft proposal prepared by Dr. Sam Gregory. Gregory wants to pursue a new line of research based on his earlier work. He has supplied Saylor with his laboratory notes as well as the rough draft.

In working with the draft proposal, Saylor notices that some of the graphs are unusually smooth and regular. Checking the data in the lab notes, she finds that Gregory has manipulated his data to make his findings appear more precise and accurate than they really are. Looking further, Saylor finds that Gregory has highlighted the data that supports his research and has buried the data that does not. Furthermore, she finds one successful experiment reported that has no lab notes to support it. When she calls Gregory to tell him this, he says he has misplaced his notes but to proceed anyway.

How does Gregory's work stand up when scrutinized according to the three ethical systems?

Utility-Based

If Gregory's proposal is accepted for funding, what will be the consequences? It seems clear that Gregory is fudging his data. Therefore his past research is not as good as it should be, indicating that future research, too, may be less good than it should be. Money may go to Gregory's potentially inadequate research that could have gone for more successful research in some other laboratory.

Because Gregory's research is likely to waste limited research funds, cancer research will suffer, and potential progress in cancer cures will be stymied. Clearly, Gregory's proposal runs a high risk of doing harm to cancer research and cancer patients. Only Gregory himself benefits. By the utility test, the writing and submission of Gregory's proposal is an unethical act.

Rule-Based

Gregory's proposal clearly fails the rules test. His smoothing of his graphs and burying of his unfavorable data are both forms of lying, either outright or by false inference. Given both these actions, a high probability exists that the reported successful experiment for which no lab notes can be found is an outright lie. In general, rule-based systems prohibit lying. Gregory's proposal is essentially a lie and therefore unethical.

Rights-Based

Taxpayers have a right to expect their tax dollars spent on cancer research will go for worthwhile research. Funding organizations have a right to expect their money will be well used. By manipulating his data, Gregory is, in fact, attempting to manipulate the people who control cancer research funding. Therefore he is using them without offering them the fair exchange of adequate research. Once again, Gregory's research appears unethical.

Acting Ethically

Once you have decided an act is unethical, the hard part begins. What to do about it? In this case, once Mary Saylor has determined that to submit Gregory's proposal would be unethical, she has to decide what to do next. Obviously, she can decide to be a party to an unethical act and edit and submit the proposal. If she decides this is impossible for her to do, she has several other options.

She can go to Gregory, tell him what she has determined, and ask him to either rewrite his proposal in an ethical way or withdraw it. If this fails, she can go to the laboratory directors, lay the facts of the matter before them, and let them decide what to do. If they decide in Gregory's favor, she is in a bind with limited options. She can protect herself with documentation and say, "I wash my hands of this," and go about her work. She can look for work elsewhere, in a more ethical environment. She can blow the whistle on Gregory with the funding agencies.

Clearly, these options, perhaps even the first, have the potential of causing Mary Saylor grave problems, possibly even injuring her own career. It is really not enough to have the ability to determine whether something is unethical. One also has to have the moral sense to know what to do about it. Sometimes, it takes enormous courage to be ethical.

A Case for Analysis

Read the following case. Decide whether Bob Davis is being asked to act unethically. If so, what action do you think he should take?

Bob Davis works in the human resources division (HR) of a small corporation. Bob, who has a degree in organizational psychology, has been in HR for five years and is well thought of by his fellow employees, particularly for his writing abilities. He has a new boss, Margaret Tucker, who came on board three months ago as head of HR. Learning about Davis's writing abilities, she asks him to edit for final publication a draft report she has written for the corporate chief executive officer (CEO) and the chief financial officer (CFO) recommending that the corporation expand HR office space and add new employees. The initial cost of the expansion would be $250,000. The ongoing cost of future operations would increase by $350,000 a year, mostly for salary and employee benefits.

The rationale for the expansion is that the increasing complexity of dealing with government regulations, employee health care insurance, and employee pensions has increased HR's workload. The department needs additional employees and space for them.

Davis takes the report and goes to work on it at once. He notices that Tucker does not refer to available HR employee work surveys but rather uses vague and imprecise language such as "Large new demands upon employee time brought about by an ever-increasing workload in the areas of government regulations, health care, and pensions lead me to conclude that additional employees and space for them is justified." Thinking to improve her precision, Davis checks out the hourly workload figures reported in the surveys. To his surprise, they justify less than half of what Tucker is requesting in her recommendation report. Davis takes his misgivings about the figures to Tucker.

Tucker considers his comments and says, "Bob, in a recommendation report, we're dealing with probable truths, not hard facts. My projection may be as good as yours."

"No," Davis says. "My projection is based on the facts in the surveys, and they seem solid and accurate to me. In any case, we should report the data so the CFO and CEO can judge the figures for themselves."

"No," says Tucker. "We won't do that. Anyway, we need to build for future expansion, and this increase will give us a head start. We'll get in ahead of other departments who would do the same to us if they could." Tucker looks at Davis thoughtfully. She says, "Do it my way, Bob, or I'll get someone else who will." Davis leaves her office, wondering what to do.

Suggestions for Applying Your Knowledge

Any textbook can supply only a limited number of examples to illustrate its subject matter. Yet for most of us, an ounce of example is worth a pound of theory. Therefore we urge you to begin gathering examples of workplace writing that will help you grasp the concepts in this book. Examples bring the use of patterns and visuals to life. Examine them to see how they have been written to meet a specific purpose for a specific audience. Not all the examples you find will be equally good, so they will provide you with ample material for discussion as well as instruction. There are many potential sources of examples.

Government Publications

The federal government pumps out thousands of publications every year on a vast number of subjects. The government publishes a wide array of material ranging from scholarly articles to self-help books such as *Find and Fix the Leaks,* which shows how to reduce air leaks in a home without reducing air quality. Your local or school library probably has a collection of government publications you can use.

If your school is a U.S. government depository, its library receives publications issued by the U.S. Superintendent of Documents, the Department of Energy, the National Aeronautics and Space Administration (NASA), the U.S. Geological Survey, the Defense Mapping Agency, and the National Oceanic and Atmospheric Agency. These government agencies are excellent sources for samples of workplace documents.

Your state land-grant university almost certainly has an extension service. This service prints fact sheets, pamphlets, and booklets on a wide variety of subjects, such as choosing insecticides, detecting oak wilt, choosing a television set, and planning a meeting. Other state agencies, such as the department of transportation, also publish informational pamphlets of many kinds.

Magazines and Professional Journals

Your library should have a good collection of magazines and professional journals. These publications represent an enormous reservoir of examples. The advertisements in professional and trade journals, for instance, are often fine examples of high-level persuasion and also process and mechanism description. A magazine such as *Consumer Reports* contains numerous examples of analytical essays written to compare various kinds of consumer goods.

Company Sources

Companies of any significant size must publish a good deal of material. They can often provide you with examples of handbooks, sales literature, proposals, and so forth. Business and government agencies depend for their very existence on the kinds of correspondence we describe in this book. If you have legitimate access to such correspondence, it will provide you with both good and, unfortunately, bad examples for evaluation and discussion.

Internet and Intranet Resources

The Internet offers ready access to information on any topic. Companies, governments, organizations, educational institutions, and individuals establish Web sites to provide information about their activities. For example, many companies have developed huge knowledge databases to provide information on the company, its products, and its services. Frequently, they include an e-mail address if you want to contact them. You may have access to company documents, such as business plans, mission statements, employee handbooks, and procedures of all kinds. Many organizations also have internal electronic sources (an intranet) for document sharing and employee resources. You will find an abundance of good (and bad) information and examples of documents from electronic sources.

A Note About the Suggestions

We have not supplied the traditional exercises at the ends of chapters. We believe that only the classroom instructor, perhaps in collaboration with the students, can design the exact exercises needed to fit the needs of any particular class. This belief stems directly from our basic principle that successful communication presents specific information to a specific audience for a specific purpose. Therefore we have provided not exercises but "Suggestions for Applying Your Knowledge," addressed to both student and instructor. In these sections, we suggest a wide range of possible methods and sources that can be used to construct the out-of-class and in-class exercises needed. When appropriate, we designate the suggestions as individual activities, collaborative activities, or multicultural activities.

Computers and Workplace Communication

Employers want you to come with the ability to communicate. Read the want ads. One of the most common qualifications you will see is "strong communication skills." Employers look for workers who write well and have strong oral communication skills. Our purpose is to help you develop successful communication that presents specific information to a specific audience for a specific purpose. In this chapter, we discuss computer-mediated communication—the ways the computer helps you communicate.

The computer environment opens up opportunities to

- communicate with members of your organization or colleagues at other locations on collaborative projects.

- maintain files of documents easily accessible and easily revised or printed.

- share documents instantly and without generating a hard copy.

- access library databases from your office or home so that you are more efficient in locating information in the library when you get there.

- locate information on the World Wide Web.

The computer environment provides numerous opportunities to develop effective, well-researched documents, but you control the environment and the activities. You must write solid, well-thought-out texts. Your reader must have confidence that you provide accurate, complete information.

In this textbook, we supply guidelines for incorporating computer technology into your communication activities. You must adapt the guidelines to your writing and oral communication habits and to the available software and hardware. The examples we give are from current software, hardware (Macintosh, IBM, Gateway, Dell, and so on), and operating systems (Windows or Unix, for example). No matter whether you are using a personal computer or a handheld device such as a Palm Pilot or are a part of a network of computers, you must adjust to rapid development of new technologies.

Employers no longer ask whether you can use a computer; they assume you can. In most jobs, you will need a good working knowledge of word-processing and presentation software such as Corel WordPerfect, Microsoft Word, and Microsoft PowerPoint. You might also need to know other software that may be used in your profession. For example, accountants must know how to use spreadsheet programs such as Lotus 1-2-3 or Excel.

Many companies have software designed specifically for them (proprietary software). Employers will train you or give you a few days to learn the software. However, you need a basic understanding of computers and the capabilities of the software, and you must show confidence in your knowledge of computers. You will then be ready for the ever-changing environment.

Be flexible and change with your work environment.

In fact, *change* is the word to remember as you read this chapter. As the computer technology changes, and along with it come changes in the writing and reading environment, you must change. You must be flexible and adapt to the changes technology brings to your workplace setting.

The computer has changed the communication environment. You will find yourself composing e-mail messages online that you will write quickly and send. You will read messages you receive quickly. You will follow links on the World Wide Web for information and sometimes not remember where you started or how you arrived at the information. You have to read material efficiently so that you can locate the information you seek. You depend on the cues the writer gives you (such as headings or bulleted lists) and the document design features on the Web (links shown as underlined terms or icons).

The computer is a tool that aids in the writing and reading process. You must know how to use it and control it, just like any other tool. Keep in mind what Jay Bolter, a scholar studying electronic writing, says about computers: "Computers are intelligent only in collaboration with human readers and writers."[1] You may be amazed occasionally, particularly as you surf the World Wide Web. You probably will not use all of the capabilities of the computer, and you may even resist some of the changes that come with each new version of familiar hardware and software. But you use the tool, and you control the tool; and as with any tool, the more you use it, the more proficient you will become.

We will focus on the capabilities of word-processing software. For example, you might use Microsoft Word, Corel WordPerfect, or Lotus Word Pro to produce documents that are predominantly made up of words. These and other word-processing programs are frequently integrated with other features that allow you to include graphics and information from database and spreadsheets, to create presentations, or to convert a document to the format needed for publication on the World Wide Web (a document using hypertext markup language—HTML). You will see that their menus are similar, the commands or keystrokes for performing tasks are identical for the common actions (such as copy, cut, and paste), and they have similar capabilities. You must know their capabilities and explore the software to discover how to activate the feature. Word-processing software coordinates directly with other software in a suite of software.

Word-processing software

- Lets you type information once. You can revise documents easily without having to retype information.

- Makes it easier to move text around. You can cut and paste within a document or across documents to build a new document.

- Searches for errors that are repeated and lets you replace the text with correct information.

- Opens up lots of possibilities for document design. You can format a document on your own or use existing company templates.

---

[1]From *Writing Space: The Computer, Hypertext, and the History of Writing* (p. 193) by Jay Bolter, 1991, Hillsdale, NJ: Erlbaum.

- Offers many features that enhance the presentation of your document. For example, you can easily add a bulleted list, bold important information, or insert a box to highlight a warning in a set of instructions.

- Automates repetitive tasks so that you have more time for writing the document. For example, if you must complete forms repeatedly, you can construct the form once and then use the form as a template as often as you need it.

- Includes tools such as a spell checker, grammar checker, and thesaurus so that you can check your work easily. You still must carefully read and edit your text; the software takes care of only the errors that require no decisions, such as *recieve/receive*. It does not catch errors such as *there/their.*

- Allows you to save a document so that you can send it electronically to someone in your office or at another location. It also saves a document so that you can publish it on the Web.

Good word-processing software contains features that allow you to increase your writing productivity. That is, you can spend more time actually writing and less time retyping the text.

In addition to word-processing software, we will discuss ways to incorporate visuals into your documents using the graphics feature of commonly available software (Chapters 6 and 7). In Chapter 12, we discuss how you may use presentation software for effective oral presentations. Again, learning the software is the easy part. Creating effective visuals and presentations means providing text and visuals to support your document or oral presentation. The computer cannot write the text or describe the topic—only you can.

Computers mediate communication. That is, they provide an effective and efficient environment for quick, easy exchange of information. Computers range in size from desktops and laptops to tablets and handhelds. Handhelds include pagers, cellphones, and personal data assistants (for example, Palm Pilots and pocket PCs such as Dell Axim and iPAQ). The small screen environment of the handhelds offer additional challenges to the writer and reader.

Your employer will train you in the specifics of communications within your organization. You bring to the training curiosity and flexibility to adapt your communication skills to the current software and computer environment. In this chapter, we describe the computer environments in which you may find yourself and suggest ways to help you write in those environments. First, we discuss not only your responsibilities as a writer to your reader, but also your reader's responsibilities in using a document. We then overlay the writing process discussed in Chapter 1 with suggestions for incorporating computers into the process. Finally, we look at several online communication environments that require writing and reading strategies somewhat different from those needed in working with hard-copy documents.

Writers' and Readers' Responsibilities

Review Chapter 1.

As a writer, you are responsible for providing your readers with accurate information so that they can use the information for their purposes to solve a problem, perform a task, or gather information. You have the responsibilities, discussed in Chapter 1, of presenting ethical and legally sound documents for decision makers. Medical lab technicians depend on accurate instructions to operate the electron microscope or to handle blood samples safely; personnel directors rely on clearly worded benefit policies to present to employees.

Review Chapters 4, 5, 6, and 7.

Chapters 4 ("Creating World-Ready Documents and Presentations: Style and Tone"), 5 ("Design and Development of Documents"), and 6 and 7 ("Visuals and Document Design, I and II") provide basic principles for effective writing. The principles apply whether you write a document in longhand or type it using a computer. You must present specific information to a specific audience for a specific purpose. The information must be organized and easy to access. The reader must be able to navigate through the document easily and locate the information needed. In this section, we look at writing and reading online material. Online material is written directly on the computer and is read from the computer. A hard copy of the document may or may not be generated. In fact, frequently, the information is gathered from the online document, incorporated into another document electronically, and published electronically.

For example, you may receive an e-mail from your supervisor requesting you to recommend the best computer for the office. You first go to the Web sites for several of the computer manufacturers to get the latest specifications and prices. You copy the information, including a picture of the latest system, into a word-processing document. However, because you want to check with others in your field regarding state-of-the-art equipment, you send e-mail messages to several colleagues at other companies. Your colleagues respond with suggestions that you also incorporate into your report. You may even access your local library in search of a recent article in a computer magazine that compares the latest equipment. You now have a collection of information that you have saved in a word-processing file. You spend a few days organizing the material and drafting the report. You send an electronic copy to a coworker to double-check your report and make suggestions before you revise and print a copy of the report. You proofread the report carefully, make corrections, and print a final version for your supervisor—or, in some offices, you may send the final report in its electronic form.

Writing Online

We encourage you to compose online.

We encourage you to begin your writing on the computer. You will write e-mail online, so you might as well get in the habit of starting all of your documents on the computer. Often, you will not have time to draft a document in longhand and then type it into a computer before revising and sending the document out. Why not type the document on the computer and revise it from the screen? You will save time transcribing from handwritten notes to computer-generated documents. You can generate a hard copy (or, better yet, exchange copies across the office network) for others to comment on before you send the final version of the document. Because you will most likely gather, write, and share information using a computer and you will be working under deadlines, you will need to be efficient. Any tool—in this case, the computer—should help the process, not get in the way.

Collaboration is easier if you have your document ready on a disk or in a file to send across the network to give to the project coordinator. Following file-naming conventions and document formats established by your office will make the process easier. You will want to establish file-naming conventions that allow you and others to find and work on the document and create a series of versions of the document (for example, *report1* for the first version, *report2* for the second version, . . . , *finalreport* for the final version). The *Save As* feature of your software lets you change the name of the file. By saving different versions of a document, you may find that you like all or portions of an earlier version rather than the revised document. Also, you will not have to recreate an entire document if it is lost. Of course, you should always save your document in at least two places (on the hard drive, at a network location, and on a disk).

You also may find that your company has certain templates or boilerplate material available on the office network for you to use in your documents. For example, you can open the template for the office memo and fill in the Date, To, From, and Subject as prompted before writing the body of your memo. You will then know your memo meets the guidelines set by the company. Or you may need to use a block of information that states the company's affirmative-action policy. Commonly used statements, known as *boilerplate material,* can easily be inserted into your document from the file on the office network or from a company-provided disk.

Figure 2.1 illustrates how a document might develop electronically. While you may do most of the writing, you may also coordinate with others as you gather information and produce the document. For some of the information you gather, you may have to acknowledge your source (see Chapter 21); other information that belongs to your company does not have to be acknowledged.

Readers will read documents that are inviting to read, easy to follow, and easy to use (Chapter 5). Word-processing software helps you develop and write such documents. However, you must provide solid information or lose credibility with the reader. Here are a few suggestions that will help.

- **Provide correct and accurate information.** Review the purpose of the document to make sure you have provided what the reader requires. For example, you recommend which computer to purchase, or you give the time, date, and location of the meeting. Readers depend on you to accurately describe the situation and give the needed information.

    You have ethical and legal responsibilities (Chapter 1) to provide complete, truthful information. If you use information from sources

Save frequently and save different versions.

Review Chapter 21 guidelines for acknowledging your sources.

FIGURE 2.1
How a document might develop electronically.

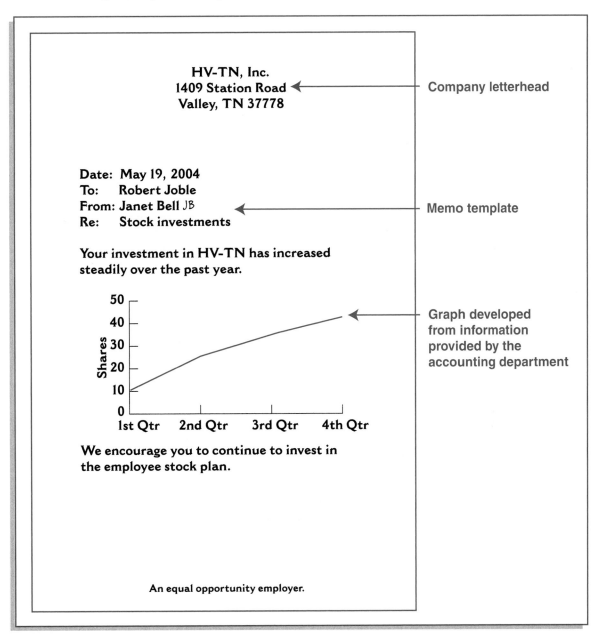

outside of your company, you will need to acknowledge your sources (Chapter 21). Word-processing software makes it easy to insert footnotes (notes that appear at the bottom of the page, like those we use in this book) and endnotes (notes that appear at the end of the document). You can establish links between information in a spreadsheet and in a word-processing document so that the changes made on the spreadsheet will also change in the word-processing document. Computers make correcting and updating information easy.

- **Place the most important information where the reader will see it immediately.** Do not force the reader to search for the answer to a problem. Few will come to a meeting if they must search for its time and location. Online text needs even closer attention because readers will spend even less time looking for information. (Readers generally spend 7 seconds or less looking for information on a Web page.) A screen full of text provides little visual orientation for the reader. Keep in mind that readers of online material can move back and forth (following links) or mark pages they visit frequently using the bookmark feature of their Web browser, but they do not always know where they are in the entire work, as in a book.

Review Chapters 6 and 7 guidelines for developing visuals.

- **Use visuals to display the information in another form.** (See Chapters 6 and 7.) Large blocks of text may intimidate or bore your reader. If you have information that can be shown in a visual, you should seriously consider doing so. You can create graphs of data or drawings of products and import files with the *.gif* or *.jpg* extensions and other graphic files from the Web or other sources. If you create a line graph and decide a bar graph would better display the data, you can change the style with a click of the mouse. You have no excuse for avoiding inserting visuals in your documents—it's easy to do!

Review Chapter 5 guidelines for document design.

- **Use the appropriate document format—for example, memo, letter, report, or instructions—to help the reader.** (See Chapter 5.) Word-processing software makes formatting your document easy. You will want to establish the format at the beginning of the document. If necessary, consult with group members and company guidelines. When you begin a document, set the margins and tabs, select the font and point size, and insert features such as page numbers, headers and/or footers, and other features. You can always adjust the format.

  If you routinely create the same document but change the data (for example, your monthly expense report or periodic memos on safety), consider establishing a style sheet or template that creates the format and keeps it the same for each routine report. Check your word-processing package; many include commonly used templates and style sheets for documents such as memos, calendars, or sales reports that can save you time. Another way to save time is to put frequently used addresses, signature blocks, and blocks of information (boilerplate material) into macros, separate files, or the address book tool so that you can easily retrieve the information into the document you are working on. Such time savers can help you spend more time on the content.

- **Establish and display the material's organization.** Headers and footers supply information at the top (head) or bottom (foot) of every page. Most headers include the document or section title and page number, and sometimes the date. This textbook uses a header to identify the chapter and page number. Well-designed Web sites have navigation bars to guide the reader through the site (see the Environmental Protection Agency Web site in Figure 2.2, pages A and B in the first color insert).

- **Check spelling and grammar.** You lose credibility with each spelling or grammar error, especially if the errors are easily caught and corrected by a spell checker or grammar checker.

Reading Online

As you write, think about how you read.

As you read, think about how you write.

Readers have responsibilities too, but they might need to be enticed into looking at your document. As you write a document, think about how you read and what makes a document easier for you to follow. If you think about your experiences as a reader, you can incorporate some of the successful sentence structures, document features, and information into your documents. As you read online material, traveling from link to link, you also become an author. Bolter notes that "electronic writing emphasizes the impermanence and changeability of text, and it tends to reduce the distance between author and reader by turning the reader into an author."[2] Readers construct the document they read as they follow links to information they need.

Readers share the following common characteristics:

- **They come to the document to gather information.** The writer wants a reader to find the information.

- **They actively seek information.** A writer's cues reveal the organization and point the reader to pertinent information. Readers must know how the author uses arguments and persuasion to present information. They also need the source of the information.

- **They use the document to help complete a task.** A writer's cues, such as headings, bolded text, and summary statements, point the reader to the information.

- **They follow paths through the document to reach needed information.** Readers do not always read workplace documents from front to back as they would a novel. Instead, readers go to the knowledge database of a printer manufacturer's Web site and enter a keyword to search for the action needed to correct a printer error, or they might look for the anticipated cost for materials and equipment in a proposal for updating a cooling system for a storage facility. Readers may use the table of contents, index, or Web site map to locate requirements for getting a daycare center licensed.

Reading online material requires the reader to follow paths or links to gather information. For example, Figure 2.2 (see pages A and B in the first

---

[2]From *Writing Space: The Computer, Hypertext, and the History of Writing* (p. 3) by Jay Bolter, 1991, Hillsdale, NJ: Erlbaum.

color insert) illustrates a reading path that begins with the Environmental Protection Agency home page (Figure 2.2a). The left navigation bar provides access, for example, to the EPA Newsroom, Educational Resources, and more. If readers want to read the *Draft Report on the Environment,* they click on that link. The report's home page (Figure 2.2b) identifies the major areas (themes) of the report and provides links to each area across the top of the re- port page as well as in the center of the report's home page (Introduction, Air, Water, Land, Human Health, Ecological Condition, Working Together, Appendices). The link Browse EPA Topics (Figure 2.2c) identifies 18 areas on the Environmental Protection Agency Web site to link to for more information. Figure 2.2d expands the Browse topics to an alphabetical list of all the topics.

Some of the links lead to more information than the reader wants; oth- ers go to material that is not of interest to the reader. Keeping track of the paths and the information is a challenge for most readers. Reading hypertext material such as that on the Web challenges the reader. Bookmarks, the Back key, Return to Home Page links, bread crumbs, site maps, and other features help but do not completely solve the problem of orienting the reader. A header and a footer appear on each page of the Environmental Protection Agency Web pages to orient the reader. For example, U.S. Environmental Protection Agency is in the header, and links to the EPA Home | Privacy and Security Notice | Contact Us as well as the last update date and the site's URL are in the footer.

The writer's and reader's responsibilities are interrelated. As you write, imagine being the reader and how you would gather information from the document. When you are a reader, observe techniques the writer uses to lead you to information. Consider using some of the same techniques in docu- ments you write.

The Writing Process Online

Now that you know your responsibilities as a writer and you know the ex- pectations of readers, you must produce the document. The writing process described in Chapter 1 adapts easily to the computer. You can generate ideas into a new file, you can develop the ideas, you can revise and edit the docu- ment, and you can send or print the document. Additionally, you can easily share the document with others within the office or at locations around the world. We urge you to use the computer; it simplifies setting up the document features and gives you more time to work on the content.

In this section, we review the writing process discussed in Chapter 1 and suggest ways the computer helps you in the writing process. Focus on the portion of the process that seems to give you the most trouble. Maybe the computer can help. For example, if you have trouble getting organized, you might start with an outline. Open a new document, and from the menu in Microsoft Word, select View—Outline, or in Corel WordPerfect, select

Insert—Outline/Bullets, Numbering. If you press Tab, you can add subsections to the outline. You can rearrange your outline until you are comfortable with it. Or if you need a visual to show what you are trying to say, open a new document and create a chart or graph. You can easily move back and forth between the visual and the text so that you describe the point you are making. Remember—you are not locked into one outline or a particular visual. You might try creating different versions to see what meets the purpose of your document and best presents the information to your audience.

Discovering and Gathering Information

Record all your ideas. You will select the best ones later.

Open a new word-processing document. Do not worry about format or sentence-level issues such as spelling and grammar. Instead, type in your ideas. You might call the file *ideas1*. You are not usually ready at this point to create an outline, but if you want, you can use the outline feature of your word-processing software to organize your ideas. Your main purpose is to gather all of the ideas you have for the document in one place. You are making notes to get you started.

As you work, you will find that you need more data or information. The power of computers moves to the forefront when you begin consulting with others and sharing information. E-mail lets you send a message to someone else within the office or at another location almost instantly. Networked computers let you send a file to another location, or you can transfer the file using a disk. You can exchange ideas and gather information without leaving your desk. Bear in mind, however, that a walk down the hall to ask the computer programmer about a software feature you are writing about may be more effective, especially when you need to ask several questions to clarify the problem. Likewise, a trip to the company library or local library often yields information you might overlook when you gather information only from an electronic database.

Attaching a file to an e-mail message and simply saving a file to the company's network are the most frequently used means for sharing documents. You can work through the occasional problems with sharing files across platforms and with different software. You do not have to worry about time zones or playing phone tag.

For example, one of your authors served on a committee that did a feasibility study for an organization looking into holding a conference. The committee members were located at universities in Alabama, Georgia, Iowa, Michigan, North Carolina, Ohio, Pennsylvania, and Wisconsin. The committee formed at a national convention and did not meet as a group again until the next annual convention. All meetings were conducted through a mailing list on the Internet. The document outlining the options for the conference was sent via e-mail. A year later, the committee met in person and reported its findings at the organization's open meeting, where more discussion occurred. The ad hoc committee fulfilled its purpose without meeting face to face. It researched the feasibility of holding a conference and reported back to the organization.

Planning Your Organization

Develop the organization based on the needs of the reader and the purpose of the document.

After you brainstorm and make notes about the topic, you must organize the material so that the readers can find the information they need. Decide the order in which you want to present the information. The order probably does not match the order in your notes, but word-processing software gives you the flexibility to move text to an effective location. You may want to use the outline feature of your word processor to structure the outline. Just remember—you probably will deviate from the outline as you write. The structured outline or a set of notes in a file should guide you through the writing. You developed the organization; you can change it as well.

The organization you choose for the document provides the reader with a map of the information. Whether you plan to use comparison and contrast or chronology to set the order of your document, you must make the plan clear to the reader. As you move text in from your notes, consider establishing section headings for placing the information. The headings may be taken directly from your outline, if you developed one. Within each section, you can then arrange the information following the organizational plan you have established. Figure 2.3 illustrates how the text moved into different sections of a draft for this chapter.

Keep in mind that the organization depends on the needs of the reader and the purpose of the document. The purpose establishes the format the reader expects—a one-page letter, for example, or a report that can be read in 30 minutes. The time and space allotted for a document determine its organization. For example, fitting a set of instructions on the product's side panel will control how much you write and the organization of the information.

Planning Visuals

Plan to incorporate visuals in your documents.

Including visuals in your document gets easier with each new version of software. If you are using an integrated software package such as Microsoft Office, Lotus SmartSuite, or Corel WordPerfect Suite, you have several options for graphics: constructing tables; drawing visuals; charting data in line, bar, or pie graphs; and importing graphics created in another software package.

One suggestion may make your document more manageable as you write: Create the visuals in a separate file and create each visual on a separate page. You can keep the file open and easily go between the text document in one window and the visual document in another window as you work. When you have the text fairly stable, you can move the visual in. The software packages allow you to easily create, label, insert, resize, and format the visuals for your document. Even after you have inserted the visual into your text, you can edit it. Adjusting the size or position of the visual is easy. We describe the features of visuals in Chapters 6 and 7.

FIGURE 2.3
How text moves from notes into the draft of a document.

In the *ideas1* file collect your notes and ideas in one file. You can easily copy notes into the draft of the document as you need the information.

For example, the notes shown below moved into sections of this chapter. Your notes provide

- reminders of what to cover in the document.
- record the quotes from other sources that you plan to use.
- identify terms you need to define.

NOTES	DRAFT OF DOCUMENT
7 seconds or less looking for information on a Web page	**Introduction** . . . Keep in mind what Jay Bolter, a scholar studying electronic writing, says about computers: "Computers are intelligent only in collaboration with human readers and writers."[1]
"Computers are intelligent only in collaboration with human readers and writers." (Jay Bolter, *Writing Space*, 193)	**Place the most important information where the reader will see it immediately. Do not force the reader to search for the answer to a problem.** . . . Readers generally spend 7 seconds or less looking for information on a Web page.
include figure illustrating reading path	Word-processing software • Lets you type information once. You can revise documents easily without having to retype information. • Makes it easier to move text around. You can cut and paste within a document or across documents to build a new document.
need source that explains copyright laws for web material	You must assume that any material you find, whether or not it bears ©, C, or "Copyright (date) by (source)" is copyrighted material. The U.S. Copyright Office identifies what you need to know when using copyrighted material (www.loc.gov/copyright).
list useful word processing features	Reading online material requires the reader to follow paths or links to gather information. For example, Figure 2.2 (see the first color insert) illustrates a reading path that begins with the Environmental Protection Agency home page (Figure 2.2a).

FIGURE 2.4
Checklist for setting up your word-processing document.

Checklist for Formatting Your Documents

To create professional documents, you need to know how to control your word-processing software.

Get in the habit of setting up your document first. That is, set the tabs, font, page numbers, and other features; save the document; and then begin writing. You can always adjust the settings.

_____ Select the page orientation and paper size.

_____ Insert headers and footers. Headers place information at the top of each page; footers, at the bottom of the page.

_____ Set tabs. To align text, you must use the tab instead of the space bar. You may need to move tabs to get the appropriate spacing. Decimal tabs make it easy to align columns of numbers (and other items).

_____ Select the font. A serif font works best when you give your reader a lot of text to read. Sans serif fonts work best in headings, in presentation slides, and in documents without a lot of text.

_____ Set justification. Only the left justification needs to be set. Readers find it easier to read text with a ragged right margin, particularly when there is a lot of text.

_____ Add page numbers. If your document goes beyond one page, you need to add page numbers to help orient the reader.

_____ Select the line space. Will the document be single-spaced, double-spaced, or spaced at 1-1/2 lines?

_____ Save the document. Be sure to save your document often. Save different versions of each document. You can return to an earlier version if you do not like the changes you have made.

Many of the items can be established as part of your preferences on your computer so that you do not change the items above for each document, but you should check as you begin a document to make sure the format matches the purpose of the document. Consider setting up style sheets if you use the same format for documents.

Writing Online

You should now have a computer file full of notes and information that you need to organize. Perhaps as you made notes on the computer, you grouped related information together. Open the *notes* file, and review the information or perhaps print out the *notes* to review them. Now you must begin writing.

Open a second document and establish the format—see the checklist in Figure 2.4. Do not forget to establish a file-naming convention that others working on the document will recognize. You might call this file *proposal1* (for the first draft of the proposal). Also, start a file for each visual (maybe, *fig1, fig2,* and so on). When you create a series of versions of the document, you can always go back to an older version if the changes you make do not work.

Every writer has a way that best suits his or her style of producing a document. You can copy notes from *ideas1* and paste them into *proposal1* following the organization you establish for the document. You may want to start writing a portion of the document that you are most comfortable with. You need not start with the introduction. In fact, the introduction may be one of the last things you write. Or you may write the introduction first to give you direction (an outline) of what is to follow. For example, if you cannot clearly state the problem in the introduction, then you probably will have difficulties in the body of the feasibility study presenting relevant findings and supporting your conclusions. You will adjust the introduction as you finish the document.

As this chapter was written, we developed tricks to get more writing done. When stuck, we switched to the file with the visuals and created or edited the figures or worked on the references. We worked on what was fun or easy to do before returning refreshed to the document and ready to add more.

You may produce most, if not all, of the document electronically before you print the final version. Or you may periodically want to print the document to see how it looks and reads in hard-copy form. Of course, if you are producing a document that will remain electronic, you probably will not want to print it at all. We are getting better with editing material that we read online; however, if the document will appear in hard copy, you *must* at some point edit on the hard copy to protect against spacing problems, unreasonable breaks in the text across pages, and so on. You want to see what the reader will see.

Computers give us much more flexibility in where we start and how we move text until we find the best place for the information in the document. With a document developed cooperatively, one member of the group might establish the overall organization and format for the project and then insert the information from electronic documents from other group members. Of course, the final report must be seamless (that is, a reader should not be able to identify where one writer's contribution ends and another's begins), and the format, including visuals, must be consistent throughout.

The document's purpose and its readers will determine how much time you spend writing. Frequently, deadlines determine when a document is finished. Memos generally are written and sent out quickly because they are internal documents that address immediate problems. Letters to clients, however, may need more planning, drafts, and approval from others in the office before they go out.

Revising Online

The ease with which we can revise computer-generated documents has both advantages and disadvantages. The advantage is that copying, cutting, and pasting within a document, between documents, or across several documents and workstations provides flexibility in providing accurate information. You can change the format to meet the needs of readers and the purpose of the document. You can do this almost endlessly. In the workplace, a deadline frequently limits the revision period. The writer's job is to allow enough time before the deadline to write and revise.

The importance of substantive revision does not change. That is, you must organize the document and work with the information to develop a clear, concise document. The content must satisfy the reader's purpose for coming to the document. If readers cannot easily follow instructions for putting a gas grill together, they will return the grill to the store. If the proposal for highway repairs does not clearly state the cost estimates, the company bidding on the job will not receive serious consideration. No matter how good the computer and software make a document look, if the reader does not understand the text or find the information needed, the document has failed. Bad writing is still bad writing no matter how good it looks. Effective document design invites the reader into the document, but only good, available information will keep the reader there.

Software available on computers, however, does help with some of the mechanical revision—spelling, grammar, and formatting. Spell checkers and grammar checkers are available as part of the word-processing software you use. We cautioned earlier, however, not to rely on the spelling and grammar checkers. You still must proofread the document.

Additionally, if you set the format features early in the document, you will have a consistent document design throughout the document. The checklist in Figure 2.4 will help you establish the look of the document and the way the information is presented.

Writing Collaboratively

The principles of cooperative writing remain the same whether you are writing online, creating a computer-generated document, or writing in longhand. And the problems and solutions in cooperative writing also remain unchanged whether writing is done on or off the computer. What does change is the environment. We have easier access to each other through e-mail and network connections. More and more companies use local-area networks or wide-area networks to connect computers to each other and share information. The phone, fax, video conferencing, and online discussions through such features as Lotus Notes give us more options for incorporating ideas from others into a project. Although a writer and team have access to information online through the Web and online libraries, they still must cull the important information, interpret it, and present it effectively—not an easy task. Your critical thinking skills are key here. Your ability to work with others is essential.

Writing Ethically

In Chapter 1 and throughout this textbook, we describe the importance of writing ethically. You accept responsibility for the information you provide your reader when you publish the document in hard copy form, electronically, or orally. You represent yourself and your company or client through the text you produce. In this section, we discuss your responsibilities as you gather information from electronic sources—in particular, the World Wide Web.

Evaluating and using information on the Web differs little from evaluating and using information found in print sources such as an environmental impact statement or an insurance contract. Ease of access to a seemingly endless supply of information, speed of copying material, and the appearance of up-to-date information make the Web an attractive source of information. But do not let the ease of access, speed, or recency deceive you. As with information from a report, article, book, or speech, you must evaluate the source of the information, the content for accuracy and completeness, and the timeliness and stability of the Web site.

Use these questions to guide your evaluation of Web sites.

Source	Who developed the site? What are their credentials? Whom do they represent? How might you verify the information on the page? Can you contact the author(s) to request more information? Does the author provide an objective viewpoint? Is the information free of advertisements or other indications that the writer is presenting a biased view?
Content	How was the information obtained? Are the sources for information clearly listed so that you can verify them in another source? Is the statistical data easy to understand, are graphs accurate, and is the method explained? Is there a print version of the material? Is the complete version on the Web? Is the information copyrighted?
Site	Is the information current and kept up to date? When was the page written? When was the page first placed on the Web? When was the page last revised?
Navigation	Is the site easy to move around in? Is there a site map?

Figures 2.5a and 2.5b (see pages D and E in the first color insert) show an example of a Web site developed by the U.S. National Library of Medicine and the National Institutes of Health Medlineplus Health Information (www.medlineplus.gov) and questions for critiquing the Web site. Note—the site is available in English and Spanish.

Acknowledging Sources

After you evaluate an information source, you may find you want to include some of the information in, say, your report on improved methods of asphalt repair or in a memo to your boss asking for a new computer workstation. What information do you have to acknowledge?

Let us take the computer workstation request first. You visited two local computer stores and Web sites for three manufacturers, and you read reviews in *PC Magazine* and cdnet.com You also checked with your company's information technology specialist to ensure that what you request will be compatible with the company's network. The specialist also gave you a range of prices and identified the sources the company has purchase agreements with. How do you present your findings to your supervisor? Your supervisor wants you to identify the computer you want and the total cost of the workstation. How much acknowledgment must you give to the sources you consulted? Very little.

Let us assume, too, that your boss wants assurance that the workstation will help you be more productive, so you must justify the cost. You must focus on how each feature (RAM, hard drive space, monitor size, CD read/write drive, software, and so on) will improve your output. Depending on your department's budget and how costly your request is, you might offer two or three configurations and the costs for each. Assuming you priced several sources and are confident in your request, you might strengthen your request by adding a sentence or two to review how you arrived at the workstation configurations that you did. Consider the following:

> I tested the computer at our local computer store, ABComputing, and met with Sally Jones (the company's information technology specialist). I checked the Web sites for IBM, Dell, and Gateway as well as read reviews in *PC Magazine* and the cdnet.com web site. The prices for each configuration are guaranteed for 30 days.

Spend most of your time describing the computer and how each feature meets your needs. For example:

> Because the multimedia presentations I create for the department activities frequently exceed 250 MB of disk space, I need to burn the presentation onto a DVD. I will then distribute the DVD to the company's sales representatives.

You need not provide formal bibliographic citations. Your supervisor trusts you to do the research and report the prices accurately.

However, in certain situations, you must document sources in greater detail. For instance, you may be writing a report on the latest research on asphalt repair materials for a panel of civil engineer and highway supervisors. They need to evaluate the options before approving the repairs. The report may also go to the state legislature's subcommittee on highways. Your sources include interviews with civil engineers and asphalt contractors, research published in professional journals such as *Public Works* or *Concrete International,* several government reports on highway maintenance, and Web sites for asphalt suppliers. You might include a sentence such as the following in your report:

> In a study done by the National Center for Asphalt Technology, Gudimettla, Cooley, and Brown found that "mixes containing the crushed gravel had a much lower torque value (more workable) than mixes containing the granite and limestone aggregates at a given temperature" (51).

You will have a reference section at the end of the report with an entry such as the following:

> Gudimettla, J. M., Cooley, L. A., & Brown, E. R. (2003, April). *Workability of hot mix asphalt* (NCAT Report No. 2003-03). Auburn, AL: National Center for Asphalt Technology. Retrieved August 30, 2003, from www.eng.auburn.edu/center/ncat/reports/rep03-03.pdf

Discuss with class members the different reasons for citing and not citing sources.

Citing your sources is important when you are using information gathered by another individual or organization. The information is copyrighted. Acknowledging your sources strengthens your report. You show that the information presented has been studied by reliable sources and the findings lend support and credibility to your conclusions.

You must assume that any material you find, whether or not it bears a notation such as ©, C, or "Copyright (date) by (source)" is copyrighted material. The U.S. Copyright Office identifies what you need to know when using copyrighted material (www.loc.gov/copyright).

To sum up, you must acknowledge your sources. You may quote sources and paraphrase information from sources as long as you identify the source. If you borrow more than what is considered fair use (less than 5 percent of the source), you must get permission from the author. This applies to linking to Web sites, too. If you create a link to a site, you should get permission first. We discuss the issue of citing print and electronic sources in more detail in Chapter 21.

Writing Environments

The writing environment has expanded beyond the boundaries of a quiet corner with a desk and a few select readers. The quiet corner and desk may still be where you initiate a document, but you send your electronically produced documents into environments that can reach anyone or any machine—for example, astronauts on a space station or a land rover on Mars. The global network of satellites and computers links virtually everyone.

Banks, for example, rely on internal networks (intranets) for their employees to conduct the daily communication activities of the business. Most banks have branches, sometimes located across several states. Colonial Bank (www.colonialbank.com), for example, has offices in several cities in the Southeast that circulate money electronically, not by sending an armored truck. Likewise, many of us can telephone our bank to access account information and make transactions.

The *Internet* is a collection of computers networked (connected together) through locations around the world. The global network sends and receives information almost instantaneously. *Intranet* refers to computers networked locally and linked to the Internet. *E-mail* and the *World Wide Web* rely on Internet connections. *Groupware* most frequently relies on intranet connections for collaborative activities.

In this section, we describe three widely used writing environments: electronic mail; mailing lists, groupware, and online chat sessions; and the World Wide Web. These writing environments change constantly, requiring you to develop as a flexible writer who can adapt to the different environments and their changes.

Electronic Mail (E-mail)

Companies and individuals now rely on electronic mail (e-mail) as a quick and easy way to get a message to someone. We no longer play phone tag; we send messages. We can even send *instant messages,* which allow us to have a conversation with someone when we are online at the same time.

The writing environment for e-mail requires as careful and thoughtful writing as your other writing (see also Chapter 8). Consider e-mail writing as similar to writing an office memo or a letter to a client. You generally will spend little time composing an e-mail message. Consider your reader's needs and expectations: e-mail readers and writers expect prompt replies. Identify the purpose of your message early and provide the information immediately.

However, do not let timeliness get in the way of producing a succinct, error-free message. E-mail readers might overlook one or two typing errors, but they will not overlook repeated errors. For example, the representative of a firm hiring several recent college graduates explained that one applicant contacted her via e-mail as she had requested. However, the applicant misspelled *receive* in several places in the message. The representative was willing to overlook the first error, but when the error was repeated, she could not consider the e-mail writer as a potential employee. Because of repeated small errors, the writer lost credibility as an applicant for the position.

As with any other professional document, you must know the reader, the purpose, and the circumstances behind the e-mail message. Some messages require only a quick one- or two-line response; others may require drafting in your word-processing software before you copy the message into e-mail.

Many companies now ask job applicants to send an electronic version of their resume. Keep in mind that readers associate your writing with the quality of your work. Remember, too, that companies have the right to monitor their employees' e-mail just as they do their other work. You may delete a message from your computer, but the company's server more than likely retains a copy. E-mail appears to be fleeting but in fact is permanent. The host server archives all activity and the activity can be retrieved.

Few people keep a hard copy of e-mail messages. Many use folders within the e-mail system to keep messages that they may want to refer back to or hold until they have time to respond. Know that others may keep a copy of your message or forward it on for other people to read.

Review guidelines in Chapter 8.

Here are some suggestions for writing effective, readable e-mail messages (see also Chapter 8):

- **Keep your messages relatively short and to the point.** Many professionals receive more than 100 messages daily in addition to their other work. They will read their messages quickly.

- **When possible, have your main point appear on the first screen of the message.** That is, write the message so that your main point is seen first. You can follow up with more detail in the message. Between 20 and 30 lines of e-mail text show at one time. The reader should see your main point as early as possible in the first 20 to 30 lines.

- **Include a short description of the e-mail topic in the subject line.** Readers frequently will scan their inbox to see who they have mail from and what the mail is about. Your subject line should signal the content of your e-mail. Be as brief and concise as possible. Tell your readers what they want to know with little interference.

- **Use short paragraphs.** Readers lose their place in long electronic paragraphs.

- **Use uppercase and lowercase letters.** The variety in the letters' shape help readers' eyes follow the text.

- **Respond within a reasonable amount of time.** If you cannot give an appropriate response quickly, send a short e-mail acknowledging the message and explaining that you will get back to the sender after you have thought about your answer. Keep in mind, however, that, like most workplace correspondence, the writer had a reason for writing and in many cases needs a reasonably quick response.

- **Reread your message before you send it.** Check for grammar and punctuation errors. Use the spell checker if one is available for your system. Readers of e-mail are generally fairly forgiving of errors and typos, but you do not want to appear sloppy. Know your reader and your relationship with the reader. You might take more care in writing to your boss than to a colleague on a mailing list.

- **Understand e-mail addresses to prevent errors and delays in sending and receiving messages.** Internet addresses have two major parts: the username and the address of the host computer, *username@hostcomputer.* Similar to the Web addresses, Internet addresses contain an extension that indicates the type of institution with which the user is associated: .edu (education), .org (nonprofit organization), .com (commercial organization), .mil (military), and .gov (government) are common extensions.

- **Build a signature block for yourself so that you can add it to e-mail messages when needed.** In addition to your name, a signature block frequently identifies your position, company, address, phone, and fax numbers. You do not always have to use it if your reader knows the information, but a signature block makes it easier for someone to recognize you and contact you.

- **Write straightforward messages as you would in a memo, letter, or other workplace document.** Humor and satire rarely are successful electronically because the reader cannot hear your tone of voice or see your face. Some writers use combinations of symbols such as :) for a smile to indicate emotion. Reserve this for informal messages to friends and family. Personal attacks, called *flaming,* also are inappropriate.

- **Keep your inbox organized to avoid overlooking or forgetting to respond to an important message.** Create folders to hold mail you need to keep but remember to periodically clean your folders, as you do with electronic and hard-copy versions of other documents.

- **Think twice before forwarding a message written to you.** Writers know that once they send their e-mail message, they lose control of it, but you must consider the original writer's purpose before forwarding the message. Forwarding a job announcement to a friend or other members of a list is fine; forwarding a discussion about your company's budget probably is not.

- **Select carefully e-mail that you forward to others.** Sending e-mail such as jokes and other trivia that clutters a reader's inbox is not an acceptable business practice. Sending e-mail messages (particularly promoting your business or service) to multiple addresses, called *spamming,* is also inappropriate.

Mailing Lists, Groupware, and Online Chat Sessions

Check with organizations you belong to for online discussion group information.

The communication environment becomes truly dynamic in mailing lists, groupware, and online chat sessions. Mailing lists (sometimes referred to as listservs, for one type of software used to manage them) are e-mail lists that you subscribe to. Many professional organizations have established such electronic forums for their members to discuss issues. Mailing lists and Web-based discussion forums have grown in popularity. Organizations and individuals form groups to discuss almost any issue you can think of. In most cases, you subscribe by sending a one-line message to the address: subscribe *youremailaddress.* Members of a business can discuss a problem, collaborate on projects, and share and write documents using *groupware,* such as Lotus Notes or proprietary software on a company's server. Meetings may be held online with participants in different locations.

IRC (Internet Relay Chat), *MOOs* (MUD Object Oriented), and *MUDs* (Multi-User Dimension) create environments for online chat sessions. Internet access providers such as America Online (AOL) and others also provide rooms for meeting and instant messaging. And more and more businesses are using Web-based discussion software for live online discussions during meetings within the company and with clients. You may have experience with online discussions or chats in WebCT and Blackboard (two course management systems used on many college campuses).

The discussion sessions frequently are *synchronous* discussions—that is, members are online at the same time much like a face-to-face conversation. (E-mail is *asynchronous;* it cannot be read until it is sent and received.) Online discussions give everyone equal opportunity to talk and read each others comments. Such forums provide a writing environment for discussions on any topic imaginable. New forums are created daily—you might even need to create one as part of work on a committee.

Suggestions for effective e-mail messages apply to the messages you send to mailing lists or through groupware, and they even apply to chat sessions, although chat sessions frequently have their own rules. On any list, or as you participate in group discussions online, you must know who the readers and writers are. You may want to monitor the conversation on a mailing list for a couple of days before you enter the conversation. List members who join but do not enter into the conversation are called *lurkers.* Lurkers read the messages as one way to stay attuned to issues in the field, but they do not respond. You want your comments and questions to be appropriate for the forum. Frequently, new members ask questions or raise issues that have already been addressed. Most members are patient with such questions, but if you lurk for a few sessions, you may have a better idea of the discussions of the group.

The environments just described are online conversations, and like conversations, they change constantly. The conversations you have online as part of your workplace activities follow the rule of oral workplace conversations: present well-thought out ideas in a professional manner.

World Wide Web

The World Wide Web presents an ever-changing communication environment. You know which sites you find easiest to read and to locate information on. You know that keeping track of where you are on the Web as you follow links can be confusing. You have followed links and probably forgotten where you were on the site or whether you even stayed on the site. In this section, we describe some of the ways you may find the Web useful in your work. The Web may help you do your job and provide information to support research you do for school or work, or you may use it to present information about yourself and your work. The Web can serve as a resource for issues that come up daily at work. If, for example, you are in charge of scheduling deliveries, weather may be a factor, and you may consult www.weather.com or www.mapquest.com before you schedule and route the deliveries. If you have a question about your company's benefits, your company's Web site might contain a copy of the policy statement. Say, for example, that your company plans to relocate some personnel to the Pacific Northwest, and you have been asked to find cost-of-living information and attractions in the area.

When you find the answers on the Web, remember to check the last update of the Web site and evaluate the source to make sure it provides accurate and up-to-date information. Depending on your line of work, the Web might help you locate current pricing and the specifications for an oscilloscope, manufacturers of digital cameras, or background information on copyright laws before you consult a lawyer.

Many of you may have Web sites. You may have developed one for business or just for fun. Perhaps you have developed a Web site to advertise a student organization on campus and link it with a professional organization, for example the Society for Technical Communication (www.stc.org). Now may be the time to review your Web site and develop it into a solid example of your writing. If you list your Web address on your resume, companies you are applying to will likely look at the site. Use this to your advantage. The site lets you show your work to others—an electronic portfolio that potential employers can easily access to see your work (discussed in Chapter 10). Because your Web site is so public, you want to represent yourself in text and graphics as you would most like to be seen and in a form appropriate for the work you are doing or plan to do. Showing your interests, your work, class projects, links to sources you find important, and so on gives the reader an idea of who you are. Be sure to represent yourself as you want to be known.

If you have not developed a Web site yet, you will be surprised at how easy it is to do. Word-processing software such as Microsoft Word and Corel WordPerfect can convert a document to *HTML code* (hypertext markup language, the code for Web pages). Or you can use software created specifically for Web development such as Dreamweaver or FrontPage. More complicated features, such as custom graphics, must be written in more flexible code such as JavaScript or using software such as Macromedia's Flash. Web documents are becoming easier to create.

We began the chapter by suggesting that you be flexible and open to changes in the communication environment. Our description of the writing process includes suggestions for effectively using the computer—and word-processing software in particular—to be a more productive writer. The writing environments we have described illustrate some of the situations you will encounter. If you are flexible and adapt easily to the changes, you will continue to succeed as the technology and the communication environment change. For example, the use of handheld computers has increased, and users are adapting their reading and writing to the small screen environment. Think of the changes as opportunities!

Suggestions for Applying Your Knowledge

1. Interview a member of the profession you want to join. Ask this person how much time he or she spends using the computer and what tasks he or she uses it to perform. Ask the person to describe how he or she composes a letter or a report to someone outside the company and how he or she writes an e-mail to a colleague within the company but at another location. Compare the writing processes the person describes for each of these activities.

2. Evaluate the Web site of a company you would like to work for. Apply the criteria discussed on pages 50–51 of this chapter.

3. Write and send an e-mail to a company asking a question about one of its products. Before you write the e-mail, review the company's Web site to make sure the answer is not found on the site.

Persuasion and Scientific Argument

I n persuasion, you are trying to sell somebody something—from a piece of merchandise to an idea. In scientific argument, the notion of selling is gone or at least greatly subdued. Rather, you are trying in an emotion-free way to convey to the reader the accuracy of your information and the reasonableness of your interpretation of it. In truth, of course, emotional persuasion and the completely scientific argument are but two ends of a continuum. In the workplace, you will operate most of the time toward the middle of the continuum rather than at the extremes. Figure 3.1 illustrates the continuum and the locations of a few typical pieces of workplace writing on it. When writing or speaking in the workplace, you must be aware of this continuum and position your piece of writing or oral presentation on it in accordance with your audience and purpose.

Persuasion

We make daily use of persuasion, and we are daily exposed to it from others. We engage in persuasion when we try to convince someone to lend us money, to vote for our political candidate, to hire us, or to accept bad news gracefully. We cannot pick up a magazine or turn on the television without being exposed to hundreds of persuasive advertisements. One could make a good case that persuasion is our most frequent use of language. Having the right answer or solution to a question or problem is only half our work. To be successful, we also must persuade others to believe that we have the right answer or solution.

Persuasion is a double-edged sword.

Despite its pervasive nature, or perhaps because of it, persuasion sometimes has a bad name. Perhaps we are merely nervous in the presence of so powerful a force. In truth, persuasion is a tool for good or evil. Winston Churchill's powers of persuasion helped the world survive an evil time in World War II. Unfortunately, Adolf Hitler's powers of persuasion had helped to bring on that evil time. Somewhat like the parent who teaches a child how to use a hammer and then hopes the child will use the hammer to hit nails and not people, teachers of persuasion hope for a moral use of persuasion from their students. In any event, because we use and are exposed to so much persuasion, it is well that we understand it.

FIGURE 3.1
The emotional persuasion–scientific argument continuum.

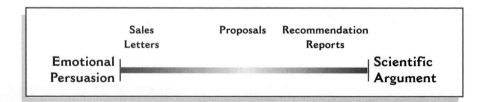

Unless we are in the unusual situation of working alone on a one-person project in which nobody else is particularly interested, we will be faced with the necessity of persuading others that our assertions, findings, answers, solutions, and viewpoints are correct. We cannot assume other people will think and act as we wish or that the merits of our decisions and work speak sufficiently for themselves. To be persuasive, we must be credible, we may use emotional appeals, and we should use facts and logical analysis.[1]

Credibility

For you to be believed, your audience must have confidence in you.

You have credibility if your readers and listeners perceive you, the writer or speaker, as someone reliable in whom they can trust and believe. Many factors can make your credibility rise or fall in the minds of your readers. Cheap stationery, unorganized documents, and poor spelling can bring you down. Conversely, good stationery, organized documents, and correct spelling can bring you up. Evidence of impracticality brings you down—for example, a letter of application for a position that your experience fails to justify. Being seen as open and honest will bring you up, as will having a good grasp of your subject matter. Be careful of extremes. Excessive humility or arrogance brings you down; confidence in your knowledge, ability, or authority brings you up.

In some instances, your credibility may be a major component of your persuasive strategy, for example, in employment letters and interviews and in written or oral proposals. You may have to spend a good deal of time detailing your education and experience to convince the interviewer or reader that you are suited for some position or task. In attempting to persuade managers, investors, or customers to approve your new engineering design or business plan, relying on the technical merits of your proposal may not be sufficient. It is not necessarily true that if you invent a better mousetrap, the world will beat a path to your door. You may also have to show that you are credible in dealing with such nontechnical, judgmental matters as budget allocations, long-range marketing plans, possible customer prejudices, or the tendency of an organization to resist certain new ideas or change.

Perhaps most important of all, your readers and listeners must see you as a person of goodwill who has their interests at heart. You must have a "you attitude"; that is, you must consider your audience's needs and viewpoints at all times. This is easier said than done. We all view the world through our own eyes, filtered through our own concerns. The writer of the successful letter or report or the speaker in an oral presentation must be sensitive in the extreme. If you know the people you are writing or speaking to, try to anticipate their reactions. Think about what pleases them and what annoys them. If you do not know them, you probably will not go too far wrong by asking yourself how you would react in a similar situation. Statements that would

---

[1]Knowledgeable readers will see in all this our debt to Aristotle, a debt that we cheerfully acknowledge.

make you feel abused or annoyed are likely to do the same to someone else. Also, think about the reader's or listener's technical knowledge and whether your information will be self-evident or should be supplemented with analogies and illustrative examples.

Show that your ideas benefit the audience. Remember that we all respond most favorably when we are convinced that our own interests are being served. Every company is in business to turn a profit, yet to stay in business, the company must provide a service or product that people need or desire. You should emphasize the service, the product, the need, or the desire and not the profit. You need not say,

> Pay your bill because we need the money.

Rather you say,

> Prompt payment of bills protects your good credit rating.

Less obviously, we are often misled by our own skill and hard work into making statements of no concern to our readers. Consider this approach:

> We have created, at considerable expense in money and time, a new fire detector for use in private homes.

This is all wrong. Readers and listeners do not care about your time and money. Also, although they may live in "private homes," they will not relate to such a nonspecific term. Compare this approach:

> You'll sleep more easily tonight and every night when you and your family are protected from smoke and flame by our new battery-operated fire detector.

In the second example, you deal directly with your audience's concerns, not yours. When writing or speaking, always remember to define your audience's needs and problems. Use that knowledge to give your message from their point of view, not yours.

We have discussed here some of the tactics used to achieve credibility, and indeed, good tactics will help and bad ones will hurt. Furthermore, although all people are different and you will have to adjust your persuasive tactics to the person you are persuading, you will also do well to remember the three major characteristics that Aristotle believed underlie true credibility: good sense, good moral character, and goodwill.

Emotional Appeals

The use of emotion may be the aspect of persuasion we distrust the most. Partially, this distrust comes from our fear that use of emotional appeals can distort the truth. For this reason, we take emotion out of scientific argument and insist instead on a logically organized array of facts and well-reasoned opinions. In truth, the use of emotion in many situations in which the readers and listeners expect logic and factual evidence would probably fail as a persuasive device. Also, our distrust of emotion likely stems from our belief that emotion may persuade us to act against our better judgment. Each of us can point to times in our lives when we have used our intellect to rationalize a choice that had actually been dictated by our emotions—sometimes to our later sorrow.

Nonetheless, the very power of emotion makes it a force that we are unlikely to avoid using when it can be helpful. You can legitimately appeal to your audience's emotions, especially by showing how your ideas will benefit them, their group, or their organization. Try to fit the appeal to the interests of specific readers and listeners. This is easier said than done, but let us examine a few tactics.

An example used earlier shows the use of an emotional appeal, in this case, fear:

> You'll sleep more easily tonight and every night when you and your family are protected from smoke and flame by our new battery-operated fire detector.

It may or may not amuse you to know that advertising copywriters know this kind of appeal as "backing the hearse up to the door."

Notice the use of emotion-laden words in this ad for a man's leather vest:

> Team this vest with a turtleneck sweater or an Eddie Bauer chamois shirt, and you have the ultimate in handsome defiance of winter chill.

The word *handsome* appeals to the reader's vanity, *defiance* adds a macho touch, and *winter chill* suggests the discomfort we wish to avoid while being handsome and macho.

Emotional appeals are not restricted to advertising, of course. They also have their place in serious writing and speaking. For instance, a passage in an environmental impact study that describes the buildup of debris on a floodplain and wetlands area is likely to include a quantitative table or chart that indicates the type of litter (for example, plastic containers, Styrofoam cups, Styrofoam pieces, small plastic items, glass containers, aluminum cans, tires). Such data will likely be effective in communicating with scientists and engineers who specialize in environmental work. However, a photograph of the area showing plastic jugs, glass bottles, dead cats and dogs, and old tires is likely to affect citizens and government officials in a more directly emotional way, appealing to their anger, disgust, fear, and pride. Such an emotional appeal elicits more sympathetic responses and creates more emotional commitment than tables and charts full of abstract numbers are likely to do. Unless you are engaging in a strict and rigorous scientific argument, you should consider the use of emotional appeals as a persuasive device, but for most readers and listeners, you must use this device with subtlety and discretion. Of course, an argument cannot depend entirely on emotional appeal, but emotional appeal can gain your audience's interest and help you lead them to an analysis and interpretation of the data—an appeal to reason and logic.

Facts and Analysis

When we are being persuasive, our audience can often be categorized into three groups: those who are already persuaded, those who can be persuaded, and those who will never be persuaded. For the last group, nothing you can do or say will have any effect. For the first group, perhaps establishing your

Readers and listeners are motivated by emotions, perhaps more so than by logic.

Facts do not speak for themselves. You should analyze and interpret them.

credibility and making an emotional appeal will be enough to keep them persuaded. For the middle group, you are likely to need facts and analysis. In a political race, for instance, a candidate may mount a negative attack to persuade the voters that his or her opponent should not be elected. The attack might go something like this:

- My opponent is incompetent (examples of incompetence).

- My opponent would ruin the economy (examples of past economic blunders).

- My opponent would lead us into war (examples of warlike statements and actions).

A positive argument is similarly constructed, only now the statements are positive and in support of the candidate:

- I am competent (examples of competence).

- I have accomplished things (identify projects completed).

- (And so forth.)

Few readers or listeners will doubt the truth of your information. What will likely be at issue are not facts but such matters as meaning, value, significance, and possible consequences. Much of your analysis will consist of making clear the implications and meanings of your facts. That is, as your readers and listeners absorb your facts, they will want to know what our students and we have come to call the *so-whats*. The so-what principle is amply illustrated in descriptions of merchandise in catalogs. Read the following description of a bicycle helmet taken from a Recreational Equipment, Inc., catalog:

Bell Bicycle Helmet   High-strength *Lexan*® shell with polystyrene lining for greater shock absorption. Wide air scoops for ventilation, foam pads for comfort. Adjustable sizing by means of *Velcro*® pads assures a perfect fit.

The following two columns list the facts and so-whats of the description:

Facts	So-Whats
High-strength *Lexan*® shell with polystyrene lining	Greater shock absorption
Wide air scoops	Ventilation
Foam pads	Comfort
Adjustable sizing by means of *Velcro*® pads	A perfect fit

Read the description with the so-whats removed:

High strength *Lexan*® shell with polystyrene lining. Wide air scoops. Foam pads. Adjustable sizing by means of *Velcro*® pads.

People who know about bicycle helmets could no doubt provide their own so-whats. Those who are less knowledgeable may miss the true meaning of the facts presented. Even those who know may need to be reminded, and the so-whats will help to persuade even them.

The need for so-whats is not restricted to merchandise descriptions, advertising or even persuasion. They are a necessary part of many letters, memos, e-mails, reports, and oral presentations. Providing the so-whats, in fact, is where your professionalism comes into play. Only you may be able to see the implications and conclusions to be drawn from the facts. Suppose, for example, an accountant, after an organizational audit, reports to top company officials that the district office in Auburn, Alabama, is not following Company Accounting Procedure (CAP) 112 to the letter. Higher authority may or may not know the significance of being sloppy about CAP 112. The accountant might add the following:

> Despite the small irregularities in the observance of CAP 112, the records are in good order, and no significant problems are evident.

Higher authority relaxes.

But suppose the accountant adds this so-what instead:

> Although the irregularities in the observance of CAP 112 are small, they are significant because they are in an area to which the Internal Revenue Service pays a great deal of attention.

Higher authority is now alerted and, indeed, now probably expects a recommendation to solve the problem, perhaps something like the following:

> I recommend that the district manager at Auburn be brought to the home office for training in CAP 112 and related procedures.

Read over the drafts of your document or oral presentation material to see whether you have clearly stated the necessary implications and conclusions—the so-whats. Without them, you may not have done the job you intended to do. In stating conclusions and recommendations, you have a clear choice in whether you state them before or after your supporting evidence. The placement of your implications and conclusions can be of major importance. When the implications are important enough to be considered warnings, they should be stated early, perhaps as early as the introduction. When the reader or listener is likely to consider the implications good news, you should again state them early. But when the reader or listener is likely to consider the implications bad news, you might be wise to put them later.

In much workplace communication, factual analysis leading to conclusions and recommendations becomes your major mode of presentation. When such is the case, you are moving toward the scientific end of the continuum—toward scientific argument.

Scientific Argument

When is scientific argument your appropriate choice? An example may make the matter clear. Imagine for a moment that you are an employee of a small eyewear retail chain that is considering expanding from its present three-office operation in one city to a six-office operation in two cities. Your management gives you the job of gathering and analyzing the information about costs, available credit, markets, profits, and so forth. You analyze the data with no preconceived bias and reach the conclusion that, yes, to expand in the current economy would be profitable, although some risks are involved. When you make your report, you carefully and without emotion present your data and the analysis of that data that underlies your conclusions. You make sure that both the potential and the risks are clearly stated. In other words, you are not trying to sell management on the idea of expanding; rather, you are showing them what is involved in the decision. Because you are not trying to sell, you hide nothing from your audience. Any emotional bias or pressure at such a time might confuse the issue and lead to a bad decision.

> The scientific process is reflected in the major forms of argument. Scientific argument is objective and appeals to the rational side of readers and listeners.

In this section, we show you how to present such a scientific argument. We talk first about the form of argument itself and then about induction and deduction, comparison, and casual analysis.

The Form of Argument

In argument, we present the facts and the chain of reasoning about the facts that lead us to certain opinions, which we present as conclusions and sometimes as recommendations. (See also Chapter 14, "Recommendation Reports.") In its most basic form, an argument is a thesis supported by opinions that are in turn supported by factual data, something like this:[2]

Thesis: The cost of American health care is out of control.
Opinion:
- Health-care costs as a percentage of the gross national product (GNP) are too high.
     Support: From 1980 to 1998, health-care expenditures as a percentage of GNP rose from 8.9 percent to 13.5 percent.
Opinion:
- Medical expenses are rising too rapidly.
     Support: From 1980 to 1998, health-care expenditures in the United States rose from $247.3 billion to over $1.1 trillion. From 1980 to 1999, health-care costs had an average inflationary rise of 6.18 percent per year. During the same period, inflationary costs for all items on the Consumer Price Index increased on average only 3.85 percent per year.

---

[2]Data are from U.S. Bureau of Census, *Statistical Abstract of the United States, 2000*, tables 151 and 768, and *Statistical Abstract of the United States, 2001*, table 145 (http://census.gov.prod/2001/pubs/statab/sec15/pdf). Accessed 25 September 2003.

Opinion:

- Despite rising costs of health care, we are not getting our money's worth.

  Support: Other industrialized countries have lower infant mortality rates and longer life spans than the United States. In 1999, over 42 million people in the United States, including an estimated 10 million children, had no medical coverage whatsoever, private or governmental.

The example also illustrates why it is an argument and not merely a setting down of facts. Even this simple example interprets facts and reaches conclusions. Other interpretations or additional facts may bring about different conclusions. For example, some might argue that the increased costs are largely a result of improved medical technology, which in turn has improved medical care. Others might claim that the real fault lies with an unwarranted increase in malpractice suits, which result in unnecessary medical testing. Still others might argue that we simply are seeing the free enterprise system at work.

What does this disagreement mean for you other than that human affairs are complex and difficult to interpret? Most important, perhaps, it means that you cannot assume that a few supporting facts will make your case. Your facts must be relevant, of course, but you must also attempt to cover as many of the variables as seem to apply. You cannot, for various good reasons, always think of all the variables or find all the information needed. Therefore, you will find that moderation, open-mindedness, and caution are necessary virtues in most scientific arguments.

Induction and Deduction

In scientific argument, the basic methods of reasoning and presenting that reasoning are induction and deduction. Using induction, you analyze your data by generalizing from particular facts to reach your conclusion. Using deduction, you analyze your data by applying a known principle to your data to reach your conclusion.

Induction

The following paragraph, written with data from the *Statistical Abstract of the United States, 2000,* illustrates induction:[3]

fact

In 1980, infant deaths among whites in the United States per 1,000 live births were 10.9. In 1998, the ratio was 6.0. For the same years, infant deaths per 1,000 live births among blacks in the United States were 22.2 (1980) and 14.1 (1998). Therefore, from 1980 to 1998, infant mortality at birth was more than halved for both blacks and whites, but the death rate for black infants has remained more than twice as high as for whites.

Notice two things about this inductive presentation. First, the conclusion, although interpretive, does not exceed the data presented. Nothing in the data tells why the difference exists between white and black infants.

---

[3]Tables 122 and 125.

Therefore, the conclusion makes no attempt to generalize about causal factors. For causality to be explained, more information on such relevant factors as income, geography, medical assistance available, births at home, births in hospitals, and so forth would have to be gathered and analyzed.

Second, notice that in the presentation, the data is presented first, followed by the conclusion. You can reverse the presentation and still present the material inductively:

> From 1980 to 1998 in the United States, infant mortality at birth for both blacks and whites was more than halved, but the death rate for black infants was still more than twice as high as for whites. In 1980, infant deaths among whites in the United States per 1,000 live births were 10.9. . . .

Both methods are perfectly acceptable, and you should choose the one that presents your material more effectively. Presenting the conclusion first may help the readers' understanding by putting the facts in a better context for them. But by putting your conclusion last, you leave your readers with your main point in mind.

Deduction

When reasoning deductively, you apply a known or generally accepted principle to your data and draw a conclusion based on the application. For example, you may establish a characteristic of some class and then, after determining that something is in that class, conclude that the thing has the same characteristic, as in this famous syllogism:

> All men are mortal.
> Socrates is a man.
> Therefore, Socrates is mortal.

Often, in a presentation, you will not give all the terms of a syllogism; for a really well-established principle, you may assume the reader knows the principle without being told. Therefore, you might rewrite the syllogism this way: "Because Socrates is a man, he will die someday."

Whether you are using a fully stated principle or an implied one, be sure not to commit the error of applying the second and third terms in reverse, as in this statement:

> All men are mortal.
> Socrates is mortal.
> Therefore, Socrates is a man.

From this statement of the syllogism, we in fact do not know deductively that Socrates is a man. He could be, for instance, a dog or a goldfish, both of which are also mortal.

Deductive reasoning and presentation are useful as long as you begin with established principles, or at least principles that your readers accept, as in this example:

> Generally speaking, lower-income groups in the United States do not obtain medical care as good as that obtained by groups with higher incomes. According to the *Statistical*

Abstract of the United States, 2001, the median yearly income of black households in the United States in 1999 was $31,788 as compared to a median income of $51,224 for white households (Table 668, p. 437). We would expect, therefore, that blacks in general do not obtain as good medical care as do whites.

For the people who accept your principle about the positive correlation between money and medical care, this deductive argument would be acceptable. If need be, you could strengthen your argument by combining your deductive argument with an inductive one in this manner:

Possible evidence that blacks in general do not receive medical care as good as that received by whites can be seen in the comparative figures for the races in infant mortality. From 1980 through 1998, the infant mortality rate for blacks was more than double that of whites. In 1998, among whites, the infant mortality rate per 1,000 live births was 6. The comparable figure for blacks was 14.1.

Note that the infant mortality rate is given only as "possible" evidence. As we noted before, there may be other variables. Nevertheless, if you use induction and deduction carefully and in combination, you can present your data logically and reasonably.

Some pitfalls lie in wait for the user of induction and deduction. Probably the most common and perhaps the most dangerous is to generalize from insufficient information. We are all guilty of making this mistake from time to time. Perhaps we read in the newspapers about the scandalous conduct of a few members of Congress. We shake our heads and imagine Washington, D.C., as a hotbed of skullduggery. This would be generalizing from insufficient evidence. As Aristotle long ago pointed out, one swallow does not make a summer. Neither do a scandalous few indicate that all our representatives behave badly.

Walk carefully when you make conclusions, and make only those conclusions that are justified by your evidence. Do not attempt to fool others (or yourself) by building assumptions into the questions you ask about your material. The question "Why do men make better business executives than women?" assumes a proposition that will produce considerable disagreement.

Comparison

As we have seen, induction and deduction are the chief modes of logical thought and of presenting scientific argument. Comparison is a specialized form of induction and deduction. (*Comparison,* as we use the term here, is the examination of things to see both their differences and their similarities; therefore, contrast is also implied.) Comparison can form a piece of a longer argument or, in some instances, the organizational plan for an entire argument. It served as a piece of an argument in the earlier example that compared black infant mortality rates with white rates.

In comparison, we frequently look for *correlation.* For example, suppose we wanted further evidence to support the concept that, in general, lower-income groups in the United States do not obtain as good medical care as do upper-income groups. One test of that concept would be to see whether a positive correlation exists between per capita income in certain states and the numbers of doctors in the same states. After checking the data in the *Statistical Abstract of the United States, 2001,* and another source, we could express what we find in this comparison:

> Evidence that good medical care correlates positively with income can be found by comparing the numbers of physicians in states with the per capita incomes in the same states. We do not find a perfect positive correlation; for example, Alaska, with a per capita income of $33,839, has fewer physicians per 100,000 population than does Missouri, with a per capita income of $28,907. However, we do find, in general, a positive correlation between numbers of physicians and per capita income as shown in this table, which compares the states ranked top and bottom in per capita income:

States Ranked by per Capita Income	Average per Capita Income[a]	Average Number of Physicians per 100,000 Population[b]
States ranked 1–5 (CT, NJ, MA, MD, NY)	$38,748	498
States ranked 46–50 (UT, NM, WV, MS)	$23,563	198

> [a]From *U.S. Bureau of Economic Analysis.* News Release, 23 April 2003 (bea.gov.bea/newsreel/spi0403.htm). Accessed 13 October 2003.
> [b]From *Statistical Abstract of the United States, 2001,* Table 154.

In constructing this example, we paid attention to the principle of scrupulous honesty in scientific argument when we pointed out that the positive correlation was not perfect. Also, because we had fairly extensive statistical data to present, we used a table. Tables are great word savers that also often make a comparison more obvious to the reader. (See also pages 169, 171–173.)

Causal Analysis

Causal analysis is yet another specialized form of induction and deduction. In causal analysis, you use inductive and deductive reasoning to establish certain causal relationships. The organizational plans for causal analysis are easy enough to outline, but you must exercise great care when drawing inferences from the evidence presented. The basic plan is that X caused Y. Variations for the basic plan exist, such as this one:

> If X continues, Y will result.
> Y exists; its probable causes are U, W, X.
> In itself, X is not undesirable, but its probable effect, Y, will be.

Here is a fairly straightforward cause-and-effect statement. Notice that it operates on several levels:

> Vibration of the table causes the vials to be improperly positioned, which in turn blocks the passageway for insertion bags and jams the machine.
>
> During the past month, we have experienced several failures in the bag injections station at machine 5. These failures are a result of the 45-ml. vials being out of position for the insertion of the bags, thus jamming the machine. These jams are causing an average of 10 minutes of downtime on machine 5 during each 10-hour shift. The resulting loss in production is approximately 66 kits ($802.00 in lost revenue) per shift.
>
> The reasons the vials are not in the proper position at the insertion station are the vibration of the table during operation and the sudden stop at each station. . . .

Here, the writer is making a credible case; her causal analysis is really an induction drawn from quite direct evidence of many observations of the machine operating. Because the causal relationships among these occurrences have been discovered through direct observation, we have no trouble accepting the causal analysis.

Uses of Persuasion and Scientific Argument

You will find that much of your workplace writing, whether in correspondence, reports, or workplace presentations will be devoted to persuasion and scientific argument—trying to get others to think and act as you wish. Correspondence that attempts to sell ideas or merchandise, although it uses facts and analysis, is frequently closer to the persuasion end of the continuum than to scientific argument. In reports, proposals are often somewhere in the middle of the continuum. Recommendation reports generally fall farther along the continuum toward scientific argument. Different persuasion strategies and forms of arguments have their advantages and disadvantages. You must use your judgment in deciding which strategies and arguments are best in a specific situation. As in all workplace writing and speaking, your purpose and your audience will guide you to the appropriate place on the continuum.

Suggestions for Applying Your Knowledge

Individual Activities

1. Examine several pieces of writing to determine where they belong on the persuasion–scientific argument continuum. See what efforts the writer has made to establish credibility. What emotional appeals, if any, are made? At what level does the writer use factual analysis? You can find your examples in many places: advertisements; direct-mail solicitations; business and college correspondence and reports; Web sites; articles in magazines such as *Newsweek, Consumer Reports, Popular Science, Discover, Scientific American,* and *Business Week;* stories and editorials from newspapers; and technical and scientific articles from journals in your field. Report your findings orally or in writing.

2. Examine closely one of the pieces of writing from Suggestion 1. How well has the writer accomplished his or her purpose? How successful are the persuasive strategies? If you were the intended audience, would you be persuaded or satisfied with the scientific argument presented? How well has the writer handled credibility, emotional appeals, and factual analysis? Look for organizational patterns. Note any errors of logic, such as generalizing from insufficient evidence.

3. Write two advertisements for a technical product such as an automobile, camera, calculator, or computer printer. The first ad will be placed in a daily newspaper, the second in *Scientific American.* Be aware of how you attempt to appeal to credibility, emotion, and facts and analysis and how you suit your persuasive tactics to the responses of the different audiences.

Collaborative Activity

In collaboration with several other people, browse through a collection of statistics, such as the *Statistical Abstract of the United States* or the *Canada Yearbook,* for significant trends that interest you. For example, what is happening to the family farm? Are farms growing in size? Does this growth correlate with a drop in farm worker numbers and a rise in crop yields? Do these two trends correlate in some way with increases in the use of machinery and commercial fertilizer on the farm with a consequent rise in energy consumption? Could there be a causal relationship among all these trends?

For another example, are the numbers of women in the workforce increasing? Are more women marrying later in life? Is the birth rate dropping? Is there a correlation among all these trends? Is there evidence of causality?

Continuing the collaboration, write an interpretive report on the subject. Be careful not to press your conclusions beyond the supporting evidence. Also, in all such papers, be sure to establish a purpose and an audience before you begin.

CHAPTER 4

Creating World-Ready Documents and Presentations: Style and Tone

s businesses expand into other countries or plan to compete seriously in the global marketplace, they are learning that they must prepare information that can be readily understood by readers and listeners from other countries or that can be easily translated into other languages.

Even businesses that do not have international partners or clientele are faced with the need to communicate with a workforce that is increasingly diverse ethnically, culturally, and linguistically. In the United States, for instance, in the last decade of the 20th century, more than 9 million immigrants were lawfully admitted into the country. In 2001, the most recent year for which there is complete data from the U.S. Immigration and Naturalization Service, legal immigrants totaled over 1 million—nearly 200,000 receiving priority-worker visas (immigrants with advanced degrees or exceptional abilities or with needed skills).[1] These priority-workers hold important positions in U.S. companies and organizations. They are well educated and resourceful, have business acumen, and possess good language skills and some command of a variety of English: Australian, British, Canadian, Caribbean, South African, or Indian. For many, though, any variety of English is a second or third language. And while some may have studied Western cultures generally and American culture specifically, these are not their original cultures.

The development of multinational companies and organizations around the world and the migration patterns over the past few decades have created similar situations in most countries.

As a college-educated professional, you will be called on to write letters, e-mail, memos, and reports and to speak at conferences and in meetings. When you do, you will be expected to communicate clearly with everybody, including those whose ethnic, cultural, and linguistic backgrounds are different from yours.

The major objective of this chapter, and an important consideration throughout this book, is to help you prepare documents and presentations that are world-ready. World-ready documents and presentations are those that are designed to be as culturally neutral as possible so that they can be

- Understood easily by workers and business partners and clientele of other cultures who have some command of your native language but whose first language is other than your own

- Translated relatively easily into the language of the target audience

The task of making documents and presentations world-ready is a challenge, because conventions differ from one country to another and many of us know only one language and one culture. Even those of us who are bilingual have native cultural and linguistic practices so deeply ingrained in us

Today's workplace professionals must be aware of cultural and linguistic differences in writing and reading.

---

[1]U.S. Department of Justice. *Statistical Abstract of the Immigration and Naturalization Service, 2001.* Washington, DC: U.S. Immigration and Naturalization Service, 2003, pp. 10, 11, and 16.

that we usually are not even aware of them. We tend to think that what we understand also makes sense to everybody else.

We encourage you to learn as much as you can about other cultures and languages so that you become fully aware of the assumptions you make. The more you know about other languages and other cultures, the better prepared you will be to cross diverse cultural borders, and the more able you will be to communicate with users of those languages and members of those cultures. In Chapter 6, "Visuals and Document Design I," and Chapter 7, "Visuals and Document Design II," we present guidelines on preparing world-ready visuals. For now, we begin by providing advice on how to present routine information in documents and presentations for persons whose language and culture are other than your own.

Expressing Routine Information Mindfully

Globalization—the integration of the world economy into one large market—requires mindful use of language.

While conventions for expressing measurements, time, dates, and places might appear to be fairly important, they are used with little commonality across countries and can create confusion and misunderstanding. Readers and listeners from other countries will attempt to adjust to your writing and speaking. Your awareness of different conventions and values, and your willingness to adapt to international audiences will help you minimize their efforts.

The company or organization you work for may have clear requirements on how to express information to international audiences. Whether it does or not, reviewing the items that follow will be helpful in your own thinking about how to communicate with readers and listeners of cultures different from your own.

Currency Symbols

Types of currency range from Algerian dinars (DZD) to Zimbabwe dollars (ZWD). When you express sums of money, indicate the type of currency unless the context makes it clear. For example, $100 can refer to one hundred dollars in U.S., Hong Kong, or Singapore dollars. To clarify, you need to designate the currency as $100 US or $100 USD, $100 HK or $100 HKD, or $100 SGD.

Also important is the placement of the currency symbol. In some countries, the currency symbol precedes the sum, as in $100 US or £100 (for 100 pounds in Britain) or €100 (for 100 Euros); in others, it follows the sum, as in 100 F (for 100 francs in France) or 100 DM (for 100 deutsche marks in Germany).

Dates

To be clear about a date, write it out in long form. Although all dates contain the day, month, and year, their order differs widely around the world. In the

United States, the date is typically written as month-day-year: May 7, 2005 in long form and 5/7/05 in short form. In most other countries, the date is typically written as day-month-year: 7 May 2005 in long form and 7/5/05 in short form. As you can readily see, a short-form date such as 7/5/05 can be read as July 5, 2005 or 7 May 2005. Japanese express the date yet another way, as year-month-day: 2005 May 7 in long form and 05/5/7 in short form. Be clear and consistent in using dates.

Decimals

Know the method of punctuation your audience most likely uses to indicate the decimal point. In the United States, a period is used to indicate the decimal point in the sum ninety-seven and six-tenths: 97.6. In Britain, Germany, Chile, and other countries, the decimal is expressed with a comma: 97,6.

Geographic Place Names

Because geographic nicknames are culturally specific and difficult to translate, avoid using them unless the context makes them clear or you define them. Most Americans recognize The Big Apple, The Big Easy, Big D, and the Show-Me State as New York City, New Orleans, Dallas, and Missouri, respectively. Fewer know that the Keystone State refers to Pennsylvania. Many do not know that the Eternal City is Rome, Italy. By the same token, few Italians or Sri Lankans recognize Bean Town as a nickname for Boston or the Volunteer State as a reference to the state of Tennessee.

Holidays and Events

When referring to holidays and events, make the dates clear. Americans and Canadians celebrate Thanksgiving Day. However, in the United States, Thanksgiving Day is observed on the fourth Thursday of November. In Canada, it is observed on the second Monday in October. Likewise, both citizens of the United States and citizens of Mexico celebrate Independence Day. However, in the United States, it is observed on July 4. In Mexico, it is celebrated on September 16.

Boxing Day, primarily a British holiday that is unknown to many Americans, is observed on the first weekday after Christmas when presents are given to employees and other service workers, such as delivery persons and letter carriers. Without explanation, the French celebration of July 14 (Bastille Day) has little significance to Americans.

Metric and Imperial Units of Measure

There are two main standards of measure used around the world: the metric and the imperial systems. Almost every country except the United States has adopted the metric system of measurement. However, the United States is increasingly using the metric system, especially in workplace contexts. In research and writing, it is often necessary to be able to convert readily from the metric to the imperial (or U.S.) system and vice versa. When in doubt about which system to use, provide both:

An average adult Gekho is approximately 14 inches (36 cm) long.
The cylinder is 9 inches (22.860 cm) long.
The storage tank capacity is approximately 378 liters (approximately 100 U.S. gallons.)

It is important to designate U.S. gallons, for the British imperial gallon (which is a standard measurement in Canada) equals approximately 1.2 U.S. gallons.

Numbers in Thousands

Keep in mind that large numbers are expressed in several ways. In the United States, a comma is used to separate thousands: 3,215. In Britain and Germany, a period is used: 3.215. In Sweden and other countries, a space is used: 3 216.

Seasons

Instead of referring to a season of the year, refer to the appropriate months. The seasons for countries in the southern hemisphere are opposite the seasons for countries in the northern hemisphere. January is in the middle of the winter in the United States, Canada, and Europe; it is in the middle of the summer in South Africa, Brazil, Australia, and New Zealand.

Slang

Slang is so culturally dependent that it should be avoided except in rare instances. For example, most Americans would not understand the British term *argy-bargy,* a reference to a loud dispute or noisy argument. Likewise, nonnative speakers and readers of American English would probably have difficulty understanding the following slang:

- *glitch* (meaning a flaw), as in "A glitch in the software must be causing the problem."

- *humongous* (meaning large or very big), as in "The new depot is humongous."

- *quick-and-dirty* (meaning done quickly but not well), as in "We've done a quick-and-dirty design."

When communicating with nonnative speakers and readers of American English, use the phrases in the parentheses. They are much easier to translate.

Temperature Scales

There are several different scales for measuring temperatures: Celsius and Fahrenheit are the two most commonly used. The Celsius (or Centigrade) scale, which is widely used in countries that use the metric system, runs from 0 degrees (representing the point at which water freezes) to 100 degrees (representing the point at which water boils). The symbol C is used to represent Celsius degrees, as in 28°C.

On the Fahrenheit scale, which is used primarily in the United States, 32 degrees represents the point at which water freezes; 212 degrees represents the point at which water boils. The symbol F is used to represent Fahrenheit degrees, as in 55°F. An average temperature of 22° might seem cold. But if it were 22° Celsius, it would be a mild 71.6° Fahrenheit. To internationalize, always indicate both scales, as in 22°C (71.6°F).

Time (and Time Zones)

In the United States time is generally expressed in a 12-hour format, as in 9:30 a.m. or 9:30 p.m. to indicate whether the time is before noon (ante meridian) or after noon (post meridian). Sometimes the a.m. and p.m. are written as am or pm, A.M. and P.M., or A.M. and P.M. The U.S. military, however, always uses a 24-hour format, as in 09:30 or 0930 (for 9:30 a.m.) and 15:30 or 1530 (for 3:30 p.m.). Almost all other countries use the 24-hour format, separating the hour from the minutes by either a colon, a period, or no punctuation: 09:30, 09.30, or 0930, and 15:30, 15.30, or 1530.

In countries that have time zones, such as in the United States, it is best to indicate the zone to avoid confusion: 9:30 a.m. CST (indicating Central Standard Time). When time is adjusted seasonally, the zone designation becomes 9:30 a.m. CDT (indicating Central Daylight Time).

Achieving Clarity and Conciseness

Much research has been done in the last 50 years to find out what kinds of language make writing more readable and oral presentations more understandable. Much of this research has been concerned with clarity and conciseness. Conclusions from this research boil down to two simple principles: Use simple and familiar words, and keep sentences relatively short. This language style may at first seem to privilege American style, which often calls for clear and direct communication. However, striving for clarity and conciseness in almost any language will usually make it more easily understood by nonnative users and will also cut down on the efforts required to translate it.

Effective communication begins with these four principles.

In telling you how to make your writing and speaking more understandable, we will follow these four principles:

- Keep sentences at a reasonable length.

- Use familiar words when possible.

- Eliminate unneeded words.

- Put action in your sentences.

Keep Sentences at a Reasonable Length

One measure of whether a sentence is of reasonable length is its efficiency. Does it express the intended thought without a lot of extra words? Using this criterion prevents you from assuming, for example, that a sentence of 11 words is of a reasonable length and one of 35 words is too long. Look at this 13-word sentence:

> There is a direct telephone line that connects us with the Madrid office.

If we count only the number of words in the sentence—13—we might call this a short sentence. But if we count the number of words needed to express the thought, we can see that it contains three unnecessary words: *there is* and *that*. Only 10 words are needed to communicate the idea—a word reduction of 25 percent:

> A direct telephone line connects us with the Madrid office.

Compare the following two sentences. Each contain nine words:

> The high-quality type presentation was made by Glaser.
> Because Glaser made an effective presentation, he was promoted.

The first sentence uses nine words (counting the compound adjective *high-quality* as two words) to communicate a six-word thought:

> Glaser made a high-quality presentation.

Maybe even a three-word idea:

> Glaser presented well.

Or perhaps

> Glaser spoke well.

These two versions would not always be the best possible sentences for the situation, but they are certainly better than the original nine-word sentence. The second sentence, about Glaser's promotion, contains nine words, too, but it says twice as much in those nine words as does the first sentence.

Although efficiency is perhaps the best criterion to judge whether a sentence is of reasonable length, word count itself is a second criterion. The answer to when a sentence can be considered to have too high a word count is somewhat subjective. The complete answer depends on how well the sentence is constructed and on the reading and listening abilities of the audience. In good workplace communication, the sentences may range from several words to as many as 30 or 35. We do not give you these numbers as ironclad standards never to be violated, but the numbers do indicate what is a reasonable length in a sentence. You can check the average length of your sentences by using word processing software that provides counts of words, sentences, paragraphs, average word length, and average words per sentence.

Use Familiar Words When Possible

Few subjects lead to more disagreement among technical experts and businesspeople than the use of specialized language in their communication. Some insist that such language is absolutely necessary, the single most important thing they can do to achieve precision, accuracy, credibility, and legal security. On the other hand, just as many do not use technical and specialized language except when communicating with their professional peers.

We are not suggesting that you eliminate technical vocabulary. Our position is that unfamiliar language—whether it is technical and specialized or not—makes workplace writing and oral presentations confusing, ponderous and dull, and difficult to translate into other languages. We think it is important to remember the following points when you are writing or speaking about technical and unfamiliar concepts and you are unsure whether your readers and listeners understand them:

- Use technical or specialized language, but define it or also use familiar synonyms.

- Avoid using pseudo-technical language.

Define Unfamiliar Words and Use Synonyms

Occasionally, you will have to use words that are unfamiliar to your readers and listeners. Every professional and interest group has its own accepted and necessary language. Physicians, for example, need technical terms such as *coronary thrombosis* and *coronary sclerosis* to distinguish between two kinds of heart problems. In the first case, a heart artery is blocked by a clot. In the second case, a heart artery is blocked by a thickening and hardening of the artery walls.

The paradox of technical language is that while it provides an economical way to convey specialized information to those who understand the language, at the same time it blocks communication of information to those who do not understand it. The problem lies not in the technical words themselves but with technical people who use such words for a nontechnical audience without definition. In talking to a layperson, for example, a physician should either use familiar language, such as *heart attack,* or define the needed terms in familiar language as we have done here. In describing the problem to the patient, the physician may say "heart attack caused by a clot" or "heart attack caused by hardening of the artery walls."

The most difficult part of all is recognizing when words in our vocabulary are specialized and professional words known only to people who share our profession and interests. We customarily use such words so easily and frequently that we forget that most other people do not share our knowledge of them. As always in any writing or speaking, audience analysis is a prime factor here. For some audiences, you can write or speak about *Creutzfeld-Jakob disease.* For others, you can call it *bovine spongiform encephalopathy.* But most audiences will recognize the disease only when it is called *mad cow disease.*

Avoid Using Pseudo-Technical Language

A far worse problem than the use of true technical language is the use of pseudo-technical language. Pseudo-technical language is created by the writer or speaker needlessly substituting unfamiliar multisyllable words for good, everyday, familiar words, such as calling the area of a building where the elevators and stairs are a *vertical access area.* Another bureaucratic example we have seen refers to a person without a car as *transportation disadvantaged.* This kind of language is difficult for native speakers of English to understand. You can imagine how difficult it is for nonnative speakers.

Many people become addicted to such language, perhaps in the belief that they thus indicate their high educational attainments. For the most part, when you have a choice between complex words such as those in the left column below and their simpler synonyms in the right column, choose the simpler words.

Complex, Less Familiar Words	Simple, More Familiar Words
abate, abatement	drop, decrease, cut down
behest	request
cognizant	aware
facilitate	ease, help
hiatus	gap, interval
multitudinous	many
obviate	prevent, do away with
remuneration	pay
salient	important
terminate	end, conclude, stop
utilize	use
wherewithal	means

The list can be extended, but you get the idea. For maximum understanding, choose the familiar word. Every word, left and right, is an excellent word, but the steady use of words similar to those in the left column would convince readers not of your high intelligence but of your insensitivity—both to your readers and listeners and to the proper use of language.

Users of big words and unfamiliar words seldom stop at single words. Combinations of words to make hard-to-understand, perhaps even meaningless, phrases seem to have a special place in their hearts. But the impression made by such language is like that of pseudo-technical vocabulary—it is so much static. In fact, that is what is wrong with it. It is all noise and little, if any, meaning. Such phrase building is demonstrated ironically by Gerald Cohen's humorous Dial-A-Buzzword, a pseudo-technical vocabulary wheel that makes it easy to string words together until they register on the Richter earthquake scale.

The three dials rotate independently. From Figure 4.1, you might select combinations such as *functional input compatibility, operational systems environment,* or *sequential output approach.* A turn of the dials might result in the alignment shown in Figure 4.2, from which you could choose *overall*

FIGURE 4.1

Cohen's Dial-A-Buzzword.

Source: Gerald Cohen's Dial-A-Buzzword Wheel. Reprinted by permission from Gerald Cohen.

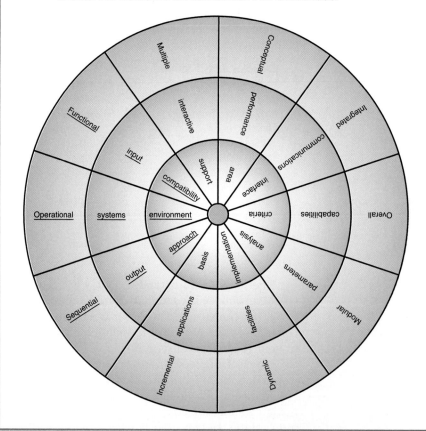

DIAL-A-BUZZWORD offers you a thousand impressive 3-word combinations.

Write your next proposal or technical manual in half the time.

Directions:

1. Turn the dials to line up the words.
2. Select the most pleasing 3-word combinations.
3. Join the selected combinations into sentences.

FIGURE 4.2
Cohen's Dial-A-Buzzword, set for a different combination.

Source: Gerald Cohen's Dial-A-Buzzword Wheel. Reprinted by permission from Gerald Cohen.

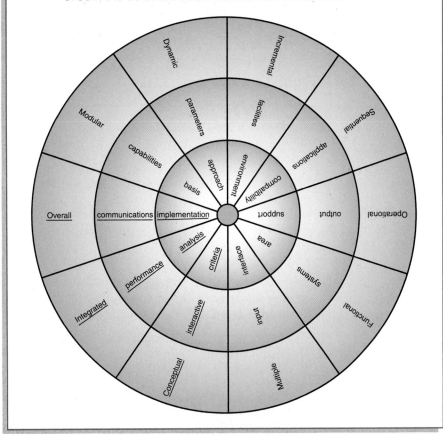

DIAL-A-BUZZWORD offers you a thousand impressive 3-word combinations.

Write your next proposal or technical manual in half the time.

Directions:

1. Turn the dials to line up the words.
2. Select the most pleasing 3-word combinations.
3. Join the selected combinations into sentences.

communications implementations, integrated performance analysis, or *conceptual interactive criteria.* By adding a few necessary structural words to the selected phrases, we can easily build prefabricated sentences that say nothing:

The *functional input compatibility* of the *operational systems environment* features a *sequential output approach.*

Overall communications implementation follows *integrated performance analysis* of the *conceptual interactive criteria.*

Try a couple of these sentences yourself:

The _____ _____ _____ is a _____ _____ _____ of the _____ _____ _____.

The _____ _____ _____, which is the result of a _____ _____ _____, is a _____ _____ _____.

If you did not know how these sentences were generated, you might think they mean something to somebody.

When unfamiliar language crowds out more familiar language, writing and speech become especially difficult to understand and to translate. The solution is to avoid technical vocabulary when your readers and listeners do not understand it (unless you define it) and to avoid pseudo-technical vocabulary at all times. Learn to live without it. You will avoid a lot of foolishness.

Eliminate Unneeded Words

Unneeded words create static and increase the length of sentences. To help limit your writing and speaking to necessary words, follow these three principles:

- Remove unneeded prepositional phrases.

- Remove fillers.

- Cut out unnecessary repetitious words.

Reduce Unnecessarily Long Prepositional Phrases

Overuse of complex prepositional phrases bogs down sentences. The following list shows typical complex prepositional phrases that should be replaced by simpler ones:

Do Not Use Complex Prepositional Phrases	Use Simple Prepositional Phrases
in accordance with	with
in the event of	if
due to the fact that	because
for the purpose of training	for training, to train
pursuant to	under
subsequent to	after, following
with regard to, in regard to	on, about
in order to	to
in view of the fact that	since, because
with reference to	about
at the present time	now
by means of	by
during the time that	that, while

Remove Fillers

It and *there* are often used as fillers, words that fill out a sentence until you think of what you are going to say. When a filler is the subject of a sentence, it is followed by a linking verb, such as *appear, seem,* or *be,* and a word that is actually the logical subject of the sentence:

There are three trusses the beam rests on.
There is a suitable airplane available at Sydney.
It appears six workers were absent from the night shift.
It is our plan to be in Chicago next Friday.
It seems obvious that we must meet the deadline.

Such constructions as *there are, there is, there were, it is,* and *it seems . . . that* take the place of the logical subject and verb and distract from the natural emphasis they should have. Since fillers take up space and delay the logical subject and verb, removing them replaces emphasis on the logical subject and verb, maintains the subject and verb in close proximity, shortens the sentence, and makes the sentence easier to read and to translate:

The *beam rests* on three trusses.
A suitable *airplane is* available in Sydney.
Six *workers were* apparently absent from the night shift.
We plan to be in Chicago next Friday.
Obviously, *we must meet* the deadline.

In some instances, a *there is* or *there are* opening is acceptable, such as when the *there is* can only be readily replaced by a verb like *exist.* An example would be "There is really no sure-fire rule to follow about using the active or passive voice." To get rid of this *there is* construction, we would have to substitute "No sure-fire rule to follow about using the active or passive voice really exists"—not necessarily an improvement.

In any case, go over your sentences carefully to be sure the *there is* and *there are* constructions are necessary.

Cut Out Unnecessary Repetitious Words

A word or phrase that is repeated or says the same thing twice is a redundancy. A redundant system in engineering is a backup system that provides alternative action if the primary system should fail. Redundant navigation systems in space vehicles are desirable. Certain principles of redundancy in writing and speaking are useful. For example, an overview gives the reader or listener a good mental picture of the content and arrangement of a document, a heading system identifies key topics that are restated and developed in detail in the document text, or a visual repeats what is described in words.

But many expressions are so redundant as to be pointless. Examples are *red in color, rectangular in shape, large in size, return back, combine together, descend down,* and *25 in number.* Only the first word in each phrase should be kept. Other redundancies come early in phrases: *the month of July, the city of Cairo, the field of biology,* and *a total of 10.* Only the last word should be kept.

Another source of unnecessarily repetitious words is the doublet: *any and all, each and every, revered and respected, unless and until, if and when, cease and desist,* and *give and convey.* Many such doublets and even triples are carryovers from legal language. Lawyers are very fond of such redundancies. Lawyers do not write contracts that merely sell property. Rather they "sell, transfer, and convey" not property but the "right, title, and interest" to the property. Lawyers drawing up wills do not merely leave an estate to someone. Rather the legal document "wills, devises, and bequeaths" the estate plus the "rest, residue, and remainder" to the heir. Lawyers, some of them, anyway, will argue that in law, as in a space vehicle, redundancy is necessary. The point is debatable, but the success of plain-language laws in the United States seems to be evidence that legal redundancy has been overdone. The problem lies not only with lawyers, however, but with those who imitate lawyers when there is no justification for redundancy.

Put Action in Your Sentences

Nouns used for verbs and use of the passive voice create unnecessary sentence length.

Avoid Nominalizations of Verbs

In using nouns for verbs, we substitute the noun form of a word for the verb itself. The process is referred to as *nominalization.* Nominalization often makes a sentence longer and less understandable. The following sentence has three nominalizations:

> *Failure* to perform an *adjustment* of the drain valve to the 4000 liters/minute level will result in a *closure* of the vacuum pump.

The three italicized nouns stand for the perfectly good verbs *to fail, to adjust,* and *to close.* Not only has nominalization resulted in a longer sentence, as used here it has also resulted in a vague one. For example, who is to adjust the drain valve? What causes the vacuum pump to close? One way to streamline the sentence and make it clearer is to change the nouns into verbs and furnish the subjects the verbs need:

> If you fail to adjust the drain valve to 4000 liters/minute, the waste water pressure will decrease, causing the vacuum pump to close.

Certain general verbs create nominalizations by drawing attention away from the perfectly good verb. Verbs such as *have, give, take, be, do, get,* and *make* are innocent enough by themselves, but when connected with nouns ending in *-ance, -ence, -ion, -ity,* and *-ment,* they change a perfectly good verb into a noun. Here are five such phrases that can be streamlined into single verbs:

Noun Phrases	Verbs
to be in agreement with	agree
to give assistance to	assist, help, aid
to have a preference for	prefer
to be desirous of	desire, want
to make application	apply

There is a correct use of nominalizations. Writers frequently use a nominalization to refer to an idea stated in a previous sentence:

> We *decided* to submit a bid for the new building project. This *decision* was part of our long-range business plan in that area.

However, when you write or speak a sentence like "It is our intention to submit the proposal by the deadline," think about it a bit. Is there a more important verb hiding away in the sentence somewhere? How about *intend* or *plan* for *intention?*

> We *intend* to submit the proposal by the deadline.

Use Active Voice

Another way to put action into your sentences is to use the active voice. You frequently have the choice of making a particular noun either the subject or the object in a sentence, with the resulting difference in verb form:

> Active voice: The company *gave* each employee a bonus.
> Passive voice: Each employee *was given* a bonus by the company.

In the active voice, the subject acts *(the company gave)*. In the passive voice, the subject is acted upon *(Each employee was given)*. The passive consists of some form of the verb *be* plus the past participle *(is given, was given, has been given)*.

Verb tense has nothing to do with whether the verb is active or passive. Nor does the subject in an active voice sentence have to be a person:

> Active voice: Mr. Sasakawa *gave* the book to Yoshi.
> Passive voice: Yoshi *was given* the book by Mr. Sasakawa.
> Active voice: The pump *pushes* the fluid into the third receptacle.
> Passive voice: The fluid *is pushed* into the third receptacle by the pump.
> Active voice: The mirror *reflects* the light.
> Passive voice: The light *is reflected* by the mirror.

An advantage of the active voice is that the actor is always identified because it is the subject of the sentence:

> The *company* gave . . .

In the passive voice, the actor, no longer the subject, may or may not be identified:

> Each employee was given a bonus *by the company.*
> Each employee was given a bonus.

You should use the active voice for a good reason: The logic of the active voice matches the grammar of the sentence. Whoever or whatever does the action is the subject of the sentence; whoever or whatever receives the action is the object.

At times, however, the passive voice is effective and preferred. When the doer of an action is obvious, it is often more efficient to write a passive voice sentence that refers only to the action and not to the doer. For example, in conducting an experiment, the experimenter may have performed all the procedures. To use the active voice while reporting the experiment, he or she would have to say things like "I tested the solution for titanic acid." In the passive voice, the experimenter can avoid the obvious and repetitive "I" and emphasize the procedure by stating "The solution was tested for titanic acid." At other times, the receiver of the action is more important than the doer. When this is the case, you can use the passive to emphasize the importance:

> The bricks were then moved to the cooling chamber.
> The letter has been filed.

And, of course, there will be times when you do not know the actor or agent:

> The office was burglarized during the night.

There is really no sure-fire rule about using the active or passive voice. In general, put what you want emphasized in the subject slot. If the passive voice buries your main idea the way nominalization and general verbs do, use the active voice.

Using Language That Does Not Offend

Effective communication is inclusive writing and speaking that is sensitive to audiences' social and cultural contexts.

Throughout this chapter, we discuss the importance of communicating with individuals who are different from you. They may be of a different gender; have a different racial, ethnic, cultural, or linguistic background; or in other ways belong to a different demographic group from you (for example, readers over the age of 50, readers who are teenagers, or readers who are primarily concerned with finances more than other matters). Or the difference may not be so visible, such as a difference in religion, position in an organization, or a disability. But the language we use reflects our awareness of individuals and our concern for referring to and representing the individual fairly. Following are guidelines for addressing this type of workplace diversity, using inclusive language, and avoiding language that will offend members of a group or single out individuals unfairly. We are not always aware of our ethnocentric biases and the attitudes behind our use of language.

Being Gender-Neutral

The English language has long been a male generic language. Today, we regard such terms as *chairman, businessman,* and *man-hours* as gender-biased; that is, the terms tend to indicate that men's experiences and activities are more valid and prominent than women's. Gender-biased terms single out men or women when there should be no distinction. For example, not everyone who reads a letter or e-mail is male, so *Dear Sir* is not appropriate as a catchall phrase. If you do not know who will read the letter, omit the greeting line or salutation. Another example that may not be so obvious is the italicized phrase within this sentence:

> We will need to *man the sales booth* during the hardware convention.

Not everyone in the sales force is male, so *man* is not appropriate. Instead you might use the phrase *staff the sales booth.*

Use gender-neutral words and phrases in general references to people. Use words and phrases such as *people, humanity, humans, humankind, human beings,* and *worker* instead of the masculine-based or masculine-sounding *mankind* and *workman; synthetic, artificial,* and *of human origin* instead of *man-made;* and *informal agreement* or *informal contract* instead of *gentleman's agreement.*

Be aware of possible gender bias in visuals that portray males in dominant roles or women in subordinate roles. In mixed-group photographs, show both standing or sitting or "random" placement to reinforce their equality. Portray a balanced representation of males and females in organizational photographs.

Avoiding Racial and Ethnic Bias

Racial and ethnic bias affects your working relationship with the individual you are communicating with. Respect requires you to be alert to how you refer to others. For example, very few situations require identifying someone by race or ethnicity:

> The Japanese computer technician quickly brought the network back on line.

Instead of singling out the technician as Japanese, you should refer to him or her by name (if necessary) or just remove the racial reference.

Be aware of the possible negative implications of color references, such as "a lily-white reputation" or "a black mark on the record." Such expressions are extremely offensive to some people, for they view these kinds of expressions as reflecting White European and American values.

Treating All Groups Equally

Referring to differences that cannot be seen or are unknown or irrelevant undermine good workplace communication. For example, in writing a procedures manual, you might include a list of points of contact. It is not appropriate to give the first and last name of the technical staff on the list but give only the first name of the secretaries or housekeeping staff (as in "Call George, Dr. Braunmuller's administrative assistant, to schedule an appointment with the advisory group.").You are not treating the two groups equally. Be consistent.

Also be careful about showing bias toward or against age groups. For example,

> We surveyed people walking in the mall about their use of the local hospital. They were asked to circle one of the following age groups: under 18; 18–20; 21–22; 23–24; 25–30; over 30.

The age groups listed obviously show bias toward 18–30 years old. Will the age breakdown provide an accurate and useful description of the age of those using the local hospital?

Achieving Proper Tone

The decision to adopt a certain tone is determined by purpose and audience.

Understanding tone is perhaps best approached first through analogy. We all know, for example, that the way we dress sets a certain tone. If we wake up on a day when we are not working at an office and put on jeans and a sweatshirt, we are saying this is a casual kind of day. If we put on a dark suit with formal accessories, we are saying this is a serious day. We have important things to do.

We also know that certain clothes have the proper tone for certain occasions and not for others. A well-cut business suit is appropriate in most offices but would look pretty silly at a picnic. A party dress suitable for an evening social event would look out of place at the office or at a football game or soccer match.

To move the analogy closer to writing and speaking, we all know that the words we use in conversation and the sound of our voice as we speak them set the tone for the conversation as serious, friendly, funny, angry, or otherwise. We might use one tone at a sporting event and another when talking to an authority figure such as a bank's lending officer.

So it is with writing and speaking. Many tones are available to you, from the casual to the most formal. The tone you choose depends on your purpose, audience, and material. You set the tone by the way you write and speak—the words, the sentence structures, and the format of the document you choose. For most workplace writing and speaking, you want to set a tone that is efficient yet friendly, crisp but not rude, serious but not too formal. Tone is clearly related to style. For the most part, if you follow our advice about achieving clarity and conciseness, you will be on your way to a good, businesslike tone.

However, when you are addressing people of another culture, you must always be aware that you and your audience may not have the same notion of what is acceptable in tone. Members of some cultures prefer a more formal tone and style than you might. For instance, writers in some cultures would make a request this way:

> I noted with interest your speech on computer-assisted instruction given recently in Los Angeles. Would you please be kind enough to send a copy to me at the above address?

Most American readers would regard this language to be too formal and obsequious. Most would never speak such sentences, and they would regard the tone as overly formal, perhaps even pretentious. But to many others, the tone is polite and appropriately formal, indicating the sincerity of the request.

Americans speak a great many things that they should not write. But when Americans write well, they usually do not get too far from what they regard as the tone of common, courteous, educated speech. Most would write, "Please send me a copy of your talk" or perhaps "I would appreciate your sending me a copy of your talk." The difference in tone is obvious. These latter versions are more informal and sound friendlier to Americans. However, they may sound pushy or rude, like a command, to readers and listeners from other cultures, even though words like *please* and *appreciate* are used. Keep in mind that what sounds polite and sincere to members of one culture might sound servile or submissive to members of another culture and still too brusque for others.

We certainly want to avoid sounding rude. We are not talking here about being deliberatively stern—as a business might be in telling a customer that an overdue debt is about to be turned over to a collection agency. Rather, we are referring to an inadvertent rudeness that results from carelessness on the part of the writer or speaker.

In conversation, we get immediate feedback from our listener. If we say something friendly, the listener smiles. If we say something rude, our listener frowns. We always know where we are. In writing, we lack this immediate feedback. We may write something that we think is crisp, efficient, and businesslike without realizing that we have fallen into a tone that is abrupt to the point of rudeness. The following letter is a case in point:

> Dear Ms. Cortez:
>
> Enclosed please find UPS Express Invoice #4-653-982436. Please let it be understood that it is not the policy of ITC Corporation to accept for payment any shipping charges for packages mailed to our attention.
>
> We request that you look into this matter at once.
>
> Sincerely,

Read this letter aloud. Imagine it being spoken to you or your speaking it to someone. No matter how you read it aloud, it sounds cold, rude, and unfriendly. The phrase *let it be understood* will sound too harsh for some readers. The writer, we can assure you, had no intention of being either. She simply wanted to be businesslike.

In writing such a letter, imagine that you are in conversation with the recipient. In your mind's eye, place her in front of you. Hear what you are saying, and imagine her response. Is she angry when you are hoping for a nod of understanding? If so, rewrite your letter. You have been inadvertently rude. The previous letter rewritten for proper tone might read as follows:

> Dear Ms. Cortez:
>
> With this letter we are returning UPS Express Invoice #4-653-98246 to you. It came with your April shipment of packages to us.
>
> Our policy is that the sender pays the cost of such shipments. Therefore, we are returning the invoice to you and ask that you pay it.
>
> Thank you for your shipment. If you have any questions regarding shipping costs, please write or call.
>
> Sincerely,

The rewritten letter is clear about who pays the cost, but the tone, although businesslike, is friendly. Notice also that it contains more useful information than the first letter.

Reports, when compared to letters, memos, and e-mail, are likely to be less personal in tone. Their tone, nevertheless, should still be courteous and should not be too formal or pseudo-technical. As in most writing and speaking, audience analysis helps decide the proper tone.

Suggestions for Applying Your Knowledge

Individual Activities

1. For each of the following words and phrases, substitute a more familiar word or phrase that means the same thing.
   assuage
   demeanor
   eschew
   germane
   inchoate
   nadir
   remuneration
   vitiate
   a natural geological protuberance
   totipalmated feet
   a sampling of fluid hydride of oxygen
   a member of the team precipitately descended

2. Streamline the following sentences by substituting verbs where appropriate for the nominalizations. Keep the same verb tense, and do not change the meaning of the sentence.
   a. We are in agreement that new circuit breakers should be installed.
   b. These payments are in excess of those specified by the contract.
   c. Mr. Aufranc was present when we conducted an inventory of unassembled equipment.
   d. Our staff has done a survey of health needs of the five surrounding counties.
   e. The night clerk is supposed to make a record of the daily activities.
   f. The committee will give consideration to alternatives.
   g. Figure 3 is a list of the centrifugal pump replacement parts.

3. Fillers weaken verb power and distract from the logical subjects of the following sentences. Strengthen these sentences by removing the fillers *it* and *there,* rewriting to emphasize the logical subjects and verbs.
   a. There are many service persons who own their own tools.
   b. It was noticed by the pilot that the air speed indicator was malfunctioning.

    c. There are two screws that fasten the cover to the wall box.

    d. There is a house at 212 Normal Avenue that is being converted into a daycare center.

    e. It is evident that the time needed to repair the hoses is still too long.

    f. There are two grooves that run the length of the handle.

    g. There are several different types of needles that can be used.

4. Delete the unnecessary words in these sentences. Rewrite where necessary, but do not change the meaning.

    a. This morning at 8:00 a.m. the prisoners were transferred away to the prison facility by means of a bus.

    b. In view of the fact that the two companies are not in agreement with each other about the important essentials, it is the consensus of the board that advance planning is of great importance.

    c. It is absolutely essential that the scalpels be sharp-edged in order to bisect the specimens in two.

    d. Prior to the conductance of these tests, we made a decision to make use of disposable culture plates in lieu of glass ones because of the cost factor involved.

    e. I am of the opinion that the city and county agencies are at this point in time cooperating together.

    f. A total of ten (10) registered nurses will be needed to staff the proposed new intensive-care unit.

    g. Either of these timetables are totally acceptable.

    h. The received message is decoded into two separate and distinct signals for correct and positive identification purposes.

5. Rewrite verbs in these sentences to make them active voice. Be sure to keep the same verb tense.

    a. A review of the case by the appeals board was requested by the representative.

    b. For the final test five dyes were used.

    c. At our Milan plant semiconductors are manufactured.

    d. The causes of wood warping are discussed in Part 4.

    e. A 1.5 percent earning tax is imposed by the new ordinance.

    f. The necessary equipment for constructing a battery eliminator is listed in Table I of this manual.

Collaborative Activity

Pair up with a student who is majoring in a field different from yours. Each of you develop a list of at least five terms or phrases that you believe are unfamiliar to people outside your field. Do you have a way to determine whether they are legitimate technical terminology, or are they examples of pseudotechnical terms? Ask your partner whether he or she is familiar with any of the terms or phrases. If so, do they have meanings different from how they are used in your field? If your partner is unfamiliar with the terms, define them for her or him. What types of definitions worked best?

Write a brief memo or prepare a brief oral presentation to the rest of the class reporting your findings.

Multicultural Activities

1. In his book *Beyond Culture* (New York: Doubleday, 1976), Edward T. Hall distinguishes between low-context and high-context cultures and their communication practices. Both cultures have complex unwritten ground rules (regarding customs, manners, and social interaction) within which members are accustomed and expected to operate. Consequently, their communication practices are sometimes so different that misunderstandings occur frequently when members of one culture attempts to communicate with members of the other culture.

   Members of low-context cultures communicate intention and meaning through direct and explicit statements. Americans are members of a low-context culture and tend to practice straightforward communication to create clear statements that readers and listeners can understand easily. In fact, members of low-context cultures (generally Western Europeans and North Americans) assume that it is their responsibility to communicate clearly, to make the content of their writing and oral presentations as clear as possible. They communicate more explicitly, less implicitly.

   In contrast, members of high-context cultures express intention and meaning primarily though less direct, more subtle ways. Most Middle Eastern, Asian, and South American professionals communicate in a less direct style, relying a lot more than those of a low-context culture do on using nonverbal signals, allusions, and nuances of meaning to convey intent and meaning. Their communication contains more expressions of respect and courtesy; they dislike direct assertions and disagreements and avoid them when possible.

   Low-context and high-context cultures do not exist in pure unadulterated forms. Individuals of each type of culture may have personal preferences that appear to be more characteristics of the other culture, and some members of either culture have learned some of the ways of the other. Nevertheless, communication between members of low- and high-context cultures are fertile fields for miscommunication.

   If you are a native speaker of English and there are nonnative speakers of English in your class, interview them about what communication difficulties they have experienced in the United States and as students on campus. If there are no nonnative speakers of English in your class, contact your school's administrative office that deals with international students to see if you can arrange to interview international students. Focus your interview on the kinds of communication difficulties these students have experienced as students at your school and as residents in the town. Are they members of low-context or high-context cultures?

If English is not your native language, interview native speakers of English in your class about the communication difficulties they have experienced when traveling abroad. If none have traveled abroad, interview them about their experiences in communicating with people who are not native speakers of English.

Prepare a brief written and oral presentation on your findings, and be ready to share them with the other students in your class.

2. Search your campus Web site for references to multicultural or international programs. Find out whether your school has an office or program that is concerned primarily with such programs. Do any colleges or departments offer courses in multicultural studies, including writing for multicultural audiences? Are any faculty members or administrators involved in such activities? Prepare a brief written and oral presentation to present your findings to the other students in the class.

3. Conduct an informal survey among the other students in your class about their experiences traveling or working in other countries or their experiences interacting with students from other countries. What kinds of communication difficulties, if any, did they experience? How did they solve the problems, if they did? Categorize your findings, comparing the findings with your own experiences interacting with students from other countries. Prepare a brief written and oral presentation to present your findings to other students in the class.

Design and Development of Documents

Chapters 5, 6, and 7 work as a unit to cover two components of document design: the text and the visuals. The text and visuals of any document (whether it be a letter to a client, an e-mail message, or a form from the post office) work together to convey the information to the reader. The rhetoric of text and visuals influences the reader's use and understanding of the text. Although we have divided the discussion into three chapters, you must coordinate the text and visual features when you write.

Writers can now create and arrange text and visuals to design a document within a single software package. Letters and reports follow document designs not only established by companies as part of their corporate image, but also the format readers expect to see. Electronic documents such as Web pages require the writer to understand design issues that influence how the reader moves through the hypertext environment. Even e-mail requires the writer to consider document design issues. As a writer, you want to present the document so that the reader can easily read the information. Readers will not read a document they must struggle with to find information they need.

There was a time when writers were concerned primarily with organizing content and expressing it in an appropriate style. Almost all considerations about the actual design of the finished piece of writing were the responsibilities of editors and graphic designers who would mark the writer's manuscript with symbols and abbreviations that would provide specific instructions for margins, typeface, spacing, headings, and so on. Following these instructions, the compositor (the person who set the type) and printer would actually produce the finished work. Today with computers, word-processing and desktop publishing software, and laser printers readily available, writers insert most of the design features without the assistance of production people.

You will find yourself responsible for making decisions about the design of your own documents simply because you can easily incorporate the components of document design using software on the computer on your desk. Although you can make these decisions before creating text, while creating text, and after creating text, you should make them as early as possible because they will influence the writing process. If the document is written in collaboration with others, everybody should be informed of its design. Whether you are writing solo or as part of a group, leave nothing to guesswork; much time can be lost in changing a design to make it consistent throughout the document.

All features of writing can be regarded as some aspect of the document's design, for example:

- capital letters and lowercase letters and the typeface (font)

- punctuation and special characters

- bulleted lists and paragraph length

- space between words and white space on the pages

- headers

- tables and graphics

In designing a document, you can use the special features of word-processing, presentation, and desktop publishing software to full advantage. However, the principles of design, not the technology, are important to remember and use. You may have been to Web sites that were difficult to navigate and read, or you may have tried to read paper documents that were difficult to follow. To help you make wise decisions, you need to know what graphics designers, production editors, and printers have known for decades about

- Making documents inviting to read
- Making the contents easy to follow
- Making documents easy to use

Knowing how to accomplish these goals will help you present your information and ideas in an attractive and professional manner. In a real sense, design is a partner with development (Chapter 1), organization (Chapter 3), and style in presentation (Chapter 4). The document's design coordinates the text and the visuals. In this chapter, we focus on the text and the visual presentation of the document. In Chapters 6 and 7, we discuss visuals and visual features of a document.

Making Documents Inviting to Read

Good document design helps the reader find the information. The information must be in the document.

Readers usually look at a document as a whole before they read it. If the text looks inviting to read, readers will probably find it easy to read. However, keep in mind that if the document does not provide information the reader needs, even a good design will not make the document useful.

Use Good Materials and Equipment

Paper

Many companies have style manuals with guidelines for writing company documents.

Print the document on good-quality paper that has a nonglare surface and is heavy enough to make the print stand out. Most companies have stationery, referred to as *letterhead*, to use for documents going outside the company. Letterhead usually has the company logo and address printed on good-quality (usually bond) paper. Internal documents frequently are printed on paper with no letterhead or on paper with a preprinted memo structure on a less costly paper. Check your company's guidelines for the paper to use and where to place the information on the page (particularly when you use company letterhead).

The better grades of paper are made of linen and cotton fibers (20-pound bond paper, for example). White paper or light shades of blue, tan, or gray provide good contrast between the typeface and the paper. You want the reader to see the print clearly.

Recycled paper and paper that is recyclable are common now. In fact, many readers check to see whether the document can be recycled or whether the publisher has used recycled paper as one small way to help the environment.

Paper Size

The standard page size for letters and reports in the United States is 8.5 × 11 inches. The page orientation can be either portrait (8.5 × 11 inches) or landscape (11 × 8.5 inches). Some organizations have letterhead available on half sheets (5.5 × 4.25 inches) for shorter notes. If you work for a company with sites in other countries, you will see paper measured in the metric system. For example, the closest to 8.5- × 11-inch paper measures 8.26 × 11.69 inches or 210 × 297 millimeters (referred to as *A4* paper).

Of course, the environment or circumstances in which a document will be used can have a significant influence on what size paper is most appropriate. For example, you have probably received a computer disk with instructions printed on the label for using the software on the disk. Someone working in a small space or in a constrained situation (such as an electronic technician working 100 feet above the ground on the superstructure of a wind turbine) probably prefers smaller page sizes. Word-processing software allows you to adjust margins and page size easily.

Screen Size

Readers can adjust their view of the document on the screen. For example, they can adjust the screen resolution (through the Control Panel in the Microsoft Windows environment) or the percentage of the document shown on the screen (a View menu item in most software packages). In a Web browser, they can adjust the window size and text size in most cases.

Learn about the environment the reader will be in when using the document.

As a writer and document designer, you must be aware of how these changes affect how the document is read and how the information is seen. The possibilities are too numerous to cover—just know that you can expect your document to change depending on the settings on the reader's computer. (Using tabs, a proportional spaced typeface, style sheets for Web pages, and other formatting features help to maintain the integrity of the document across platforms and software.)

The small screen environment of cell phones, pocket PCs, and other handhelds creates additional challenges to the writer that are not resolved by simply using shorter sentences and few graphics. You will need to explore this environment.

Printing

Laser printers are standard in the workplace. Laser printers produce a sharp, clean print and superior graphics. Top-end models print color as well. Ink-jet printers are also widely used and print in color. Color printers let you add emphasis to documents, which we discuss later in this chapter.

In choosing how to reproduce a document, you must consider how the document will be used. If you need only a copy for your files or copies for internal use, use the copier in your office. However, documents going outside the company, for example, a set of manuals for operating an oscilloscope or a proposal to a client, should be printed by a professional copy shop or by a properly equipped in-house department with adequate equipment and materials. Wherever you have the document reproduced, the printer used is important because it produces the final copy and determines what the text will look like.

Document Delivery

When you select the method of delivery, consider how the reader will use the document. How often will readers refer to the document? How will they access the document? You may consider putting longer documents on a CD, on a Web site, or in a binder—or deliver in all of the forms.

Identify other methods of delivering documents.

More and more documents are now delivered electronically via e-mail, network file sharing, or on CDs or a Web site. For example, city annual reports are distributed on a CD and posted on the city Web site (for example, see the Orlando, Florida, Web site www.cityoforlando.gov). Government reports are available on .gov Web sites, for example, www.epa.gov, shown in Figure 2.2b (see page A in the first color insert). The electronic file may be in any format; however, the Adobe Acrobat's PDF format is currently common, and the Acrobat Reader may be included on the CD. The Acrobat PDF file holds its original formatting and is not easily changed. CDs are inexpensive and easy to create. The paper and mailing costs are considerably less than those for a bound, 100-page report.

A three-ring notebook works well for paper documents that may be added to, such as a company's procedures manual. Notebooks hold up under repeated use, but this feature also makes them the most expensive type of binder. Spiral binding allows the user to fold the document back on itself so that one page shows at a time, but pages cannot be added to the document. Plastic binding works for documents that will be used only occasionally and when the user has enough room to open the document fully. Other types of binding are available. Check with your company's printing department or a local printing and copy shop for other options. Be sure to increase the left margin to 1.5 or 2 inches to allow room for the binding.

Use an Uncrowded Design

Dense or busy-looking pages and computers screens will put off all but the most committed readers, even though the document contains useful information and interesting ideas. Judicious use of white space and an attractive type (font) can encourage readers to read a document. You want to use white space—the space not used by the text and visuals—effectively.

White Space with Printed Documents

As shown in Figure 5.1, no more than 50 percent of the page of most letters, memos, and reports should be the text area (the part of the page where the text and visuals appear). The other 50 percent is white space (comprising the

FIGURE 5.1

A page consists of three basic areas: the white space, the text, and the visuals. On this page, the features combine to create an inviting page to read.

Source: Environmental Protection Agency. (2003). Purer water. In *Draft report on the environment 2003*. Retrieved October 24, 2003, from http://www.epa.gov/indicators/roe/pdf/roeWater.pdf. 2-17.

EPA's Draft Report on the Environment 2003

Consumption of Fish and Shellfish

Fish and shellfish are important and desirable sources of nutrition for many people. However, chemical and biological (bacteria, pathogens) contaminants can accumulate in fish and shellfish, making it unhealthy to consume them, especially in large quantities.

What is the condition of waters that support consumption of fish and shellfish?

Most states sample fish in their waters and then issue fish consumption advisories as a way of informing the public of risks associated with eating certain types and sizes of fish from certain waterbodies. Advisories are based on fish tissue monitoring data collected by states and tribes and are largely focused on areas of known or suspected contamination.

In the U.S., 14 percent of the river miles, 28 percent of lake acreage, and 100 percent of the Great Lakes and their con-

necting waters are under fish consumption advisories.[38] Those percentages have increased in recent years (Exhibit 2-10). The increases are most likely the result of more consistent monitoring and reporting and decreases in concentration criteria, and are not necessarily an indication that conditions are getting worse.

Fish advisories that limit or restrict consumption, especially of top-level predators (e.g., walleye and lake trout), are widespread across the U.S. Advisories are issued for various contaminants—mercury, dioxin, and PCBs are responsible for many of the advisories throughout the U.S. In January 2001, EPA and the U.S. Food and Drug Administration issued a nationwide advisory for women who are pregnant or may

Consumption of Fish and Shellfish Indicators

Percent of river miles and lake acres under fish consumption advisory

Contaminants in fresh water fish

Number of watersheds exceeding health-based national water quality criteria for mercury and PCBs in fish tissue

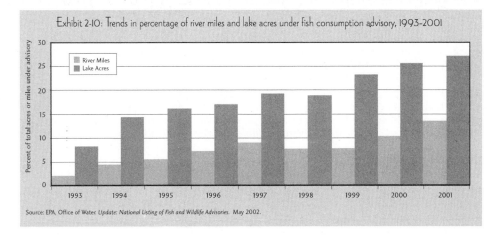

Exhibit 2-10: Trends in percentage of river miles and lake acres under fish consumption advisory, 1993-2001

Percent of total acres or miles under advisory

River Miles
Lake Acres

1993 1994 1995 1996 1997 1998 1999 2000 2001

Source: EPA, Office of Water. *Update: National Listing of Fish and Wildlife Advisories*. May 2002.

Chapter 2 - Purer Water

FIGURE 5.2

White space and headings in e-mail help the reader see the important information.

```
Date:      Friday, February 8, 2005
From:      Joanne Welsh (welshjh@ttu.com)
To:        Marie Housen (housenmm@ttu.com)
Re:        Training Sessions

Here are ideas for my portion of the computer training sessions. I
confirmed this morning the software available in the room with Internet
access. Not only is there Internet access, but there's also access to
presentation software such as PowerPoint—all on PCs, not Macs. The
Internet sessions will focus on sending and receiving e-mail and sending
a file via e-mail as an attachment. The class will meet Wednesday,
February 13 from 2-4 p.m. The Web session will cover evaluating Web sites
for accurate, reliable information and how to acknowledge the information
in company reports to clients. The class will meet Wednesday, February 20
from 2-4 p.m. The class for developing a computer-generated presentation
will meet Wednesday, February 27 2-4 p.m. We should send reminders to
everyone the day before the class.

Joanne
```

```
Date:      Friday, February 8, 2005
From:      Joanne Welsh (welshjh@ttu.com)
To:        Marie Housen (housenmm@ttu.com)
Re:        Training Sessions

Here are ideas for my portion of the computer training sessions.

I confirmed this morning the software available in the room with Internet
access. Not only is there Internet access, but there's also access to
presentation software such as PowerPoint—all on PCs, not Macs.

INTERNET SESSION
The Internet sessions will focus on sending and receiving e-mail and
sending a file via e-mail as an attachment. The class will meet
Wednesday, February 13 from 2-4 p.m.

WEB SESSION
The Web session will cover evaluating Web sites for accurate, reliable
information and how to acknowledge the information in company reports to
clients. The class will meet Wednesday, February 20 from 2-4 p.m.

PRESENTATION SESSION
The class for developing a computer-generated presentation will meet
Wednesday, February 27 2-4 p.m.

We should send reminders to everyone the day before the class.

Joanne
```

margins around the text area and visuals and the spaces between lines, between words in a line, and between letters and characters). There are, of course, exceptions: letters and memos that are shorter than a full page and bulletins, brochures, newsletters, and manuals often require more white space.

White Space with Online Documents

White space in e-mail, Web documents, or online help, such as company policy manuals, is as important as—maybe even more important than—it is in documents printed on paper because the reader's eyes must distinguish breaks in the text to move through the text on the screen. Readers cannot easily hold their place with their finger or mark the text with a pencil. They must rely on the cursor, the mouse, and the scroll bar to move through the text. Figure 5.2 compares an e-mail message that is one long paragraph and the same message with breaks in the text.

Margins

For 8.5 × 11-inch pages, maintain a minimum of a 1-inch margin (the white space outside the text area) all around. For most documents, do not justify the right margin. When the right margin is justified, the text edge along the right side of the page appears in a straight line. Readers may have trouble distinguishing between lines and may lose track of where they are reading. You want to avoid gaps in the text. The gaps interfere with the reader's eyes sweeping the line and do not present a professional-looking document. Figures 5.3 and 5.4 show an example of a right-justified document and the same document without justification. Notice the gaps and problems with hyphens on the right-justified document.

All text and visuals should be kept within the margins (see Figure 5.1) except for special effects. There are two exceptions: (1) headers or footers and page numbers, which usually lie two spaces above and below the text area, and (2) special texts—usually visuals—or other marks that extend beyond the text area. Such special texts, graphics, and marks are called a "bleed." Bleed graphics, such as the photo in the top left corner of Figure 5.1, are designed to look as if they continued beyond the edge of the text.

Line Spacing

Letters, memos, brochures, and most newsletters are single-spaced. Single-spaced, space-and-a-half, or double-spaced reports are common. For example, space-and-a-half is frequently used for engineering reports. Proposals are often single-spaced.

You need to check with the corporate style guide or other employees for your company's preferred style. Also, know what your readers expect and the purpose of the document. A one-page, single-spaced document may be appropriate for a meeting of 100 members of the sales team if you need to get some information to them quickly and inexpensively. The same document may be better presented on two sheets of paper, stapled and double-spaced, if you are asking the sales managers to write comments on the document

White space is key
to good document design.

FIGURE 5.3

Spacing problems occur in a document when full justification is on and when Web addresses are included. Fixed-width fonts such as Courier do not adjust. Each letter takes the same amount of space.

Web addresses create two problems: (1) in a document that is going to appear only in hard-copy form, remove the underlining (the link). The link cannot be followed, so the underlining serves no purpose. Underlined text tends to be harder to read because the underline interferes with the descenders (the part of the letter that falls below the line of text, for example, p, q, y). (2) the address is recognized as one word, so it will stay together and often move to the next line. If the link will not be used, then insert a space to break the address across lines. If the link is needed, then try to revise the text to avoid awkward line breaks.

The Facilities and Information Technology Committee (FITC) met on April 6, 2005, and developed a list of items which they would like for you to include in your presentation before the division managers. The list is given below.

1. Who and how many employees will be affected by your proposal?

2. How will the proposed renovation or purchase of new equipment save money and/or leverage resources?

3. Explain how your requests will support state-of-the-art research and development.

4. Have you addressed the accessibility of the proposed equipment for employees with disabilities including those who are in wheelchairs, visually impaired, hearing impaired, or disabled in another way?

5. Are the resources going to be shared with other departments?

6. Be prepared to provide information on specific items in your budget.

7. Indicate how your proposed request matches against the strategic initiatives of your division and the company.

Please submit your response online at www.university.edu/facilities.

---

before you give it to the sales team. Remember that the length of the document will determine costs for reproducing and binding.

- If the document is single-spaced, provide some eye relief and "breathing room" by double-spacing between paragraphs and above and below headings, indented lists, long quotations, displayed equations and formulas, and visuals.

- If the document is double-spaced, allow no extra line spaces between paragraphs, but indent the first line of each paragraph.

FIGURE 5.4

Selecting a proportionally spaced typeface takes care of most of the problems with spacing. In the example, the font was changed from Courier 12 to Times New Roman 12, right justification was removed, and the tab was moved closer to the number to eliminate the gap between the numbered item and the text. The link for the Web address was removed.

The Facilities and Information Technology Committee (FITC) met on April 6, 2005, and developed a list of items which they would like for you to include in your presentation before the division managers. The list is given below.

1. Who and how many employees will be affected by your proposal?

2. How will the proposed renovation or purchase of new equipment save money and/or leverage resources?

3. Explain how your requests will support state-of-the-art research and development.

4. Have you addressed the accessibility of the proposed equipment for employees with disabilities including those who are in wheelchairs, visually impaired, hearing impaired, or disabled in another way?

5. Are the resources going to be shared with other departments?

6. Be prepared to provide information on specific items in your budget.

7. Indicate how your proposed request matches against the strategic initiatives of your division and the company.

Please submit your response online at www.university.edu/facilities.

Figure 5.5 illustrates a passage that is crowded, uninviting, and difficult to read. Figure 5.6 shows a redesigned version of the same information that has much better visual appeal because it incorporates more white space that reduces the density of text, allowing for easier reading and providing room for readers to make their own notes. The trade-off of additional length for easier reading is worth it. The result, as you can see, is that the longer versions are much quicker to read and easier to remember because readers can quickly identify the points of discussion and the order in which the points are being made.

FIGURE 5.5

The writer uses very little spacing to indicate organization in this memo. Readers will have to read very carefully to identify the steps of the new procedure. They may overlook the important classification of contract charges.

Date: January 11, 2005
To: Sales Representatives
From: Ellen Gault *EG*
Re: External Short-Term Customer Contract

Effective February 1, 2005, we will implement the new procedure for approving external short-term customer contracts. Enclosed is the new External Short-Term Customer Contract Request form. We require the form be filled out and signed by the customer. However, we are also asking you to assist customers in filling out the form to ensure that all information needed to fulfill the request is included. We also require you to send a copy of the signature card you have on file for the customer. This is so we may verify the signature on the form. We will also have to have the customer's mailing address so we can send the contract to them. These steps are necessary in order that we may be in compliance with the directives related to our Total Quality Control Plan.

Charges for research are $15.00 an hour. The minimum charge will be $15.00 payable in advance. Charges for document preparation are $25.00 an hour. Additional copies are 20 cents per page. On requests where it appears several hours will be required to complete the work, we need to be contacted in advance so that we can estimate the charge and a 20 percent down payment can be forwarded with the contract request. The actual balance will be due upon completion of the work. The contract request form and the payment needs to be sent to my administrative assistant, Warren Thompson.

Please call Warren Thompson at 806-295-6841 or me at 806-295-6842 if you have any questions concerning this matter.

FIGURE 5.6

The writer revised the memo shown in Figure 5.5. The use of headings, numbered lists, overview statements, and grouping information into meaningful segments in a consistent manner enhances the layout of the text. The memo is longer but is much easier and faster to read.

Date: January 11, 2005
To: Sales Representatives
From: Ellen Gault *EG*
Re: External Short-Term Customer Contract

Effective February 1, 2005, we will implement the new procedure for approving external short-term customer contracts.

Enclosed is the new External Short-Term Customer Contract Request form. Below are explanations of the new procedure and contract charges.

New Procedure

The new two-step procedure is designed so that we can assure the shortest time possible in completing the contract work and be in compliance with our Total Quality Control Plan.

1. Have the customer fill out and sign the form. If necessary, assist customers in filling out the form to insure that all information needed to fulfill the request is included.

2. Send the completed, signed form to Warren Thompson for approval. Also attach a copy of the signature card you have on file for the customer so that we can verify the signature on the form.

   If appropriate, send the following:

   • The address to send the contract to if it is different from the customer's address listed on the form.

   • A 20% down payment of the total estimated charges for document preparation that may exceed 50 hours.

Contract Charges

We bill for two kinds of work: (1) research and (2) document preparation. Work is charged by the hour, and any fraction of an hour is charged at the full hourly rate.

Research: $15.00 an hour. The minimum charge will be $15.00 payable in advance.

Document Preparation: $25.00 an hour. Additional copies are 20¢ per page.

On requests where it appears that more than 50 hours of work will be required, contact Warren Thompson in advance so that he can estimate the charge. A 20% down payment is to be paid upon approval of the contract request form. The actual balance will be due upon completion of the work.

Please call Warren Thompson at 806-295-6841 or me at 806-295-6842 if you have any questions concerning this matter.

Use Typefaces Effectively

Use a legible, nondistracting typeface (referred to as a *font* in software programs) for body text. Although a wide variety of type styles, sizes, and special features are available in word-processing software, avoid unusual types with fancy lines and flourishes. Design a consistent look for each part of the document.

Frequently, writers use a *serif* font such as Times Roman for the body of a document and a *sans serif* font such as Univers for the headings. Random changes in type, or what appear to be random changes, will confuse or annoy readers. This advice applies not only to documents printed on paper, but also to documents published on the Web.

Roman and Italic Type

There are two basic styles of type: roman, and italic.

- Roman (roman) is an upright typeface that is most frequently used for body text because it is the most readable.

- Italic *(italic)* is a slanted typeface that is not as easy to read as roman and is used for special purposes, such as to designate titles of books, plays, and works of art and names of ships, aircraft, and spacecraft (for example, *Titanic* or *Challenger*); to indicate foreign words and other words that are referred to as words (as we used *font* above); and sometimes to emphasize important words or phrases.

Serif and San Serif Type

Type can also be classified as serif and sans serif.

- Serif (serif) contains small features that clearly mark the ends of letters and characters. Sometimes there are also uneven widths of lines that form the character. For instance, the little cross strokes on I, i, C, 1, 5 are serifs.

  Frequently, a serif type works best for a document's body text. Readers may have less trouble reading large blocks of text with serif fonts because the cross strokes and uneven lines in serif type make individual letters easier to distinguish and consequently speed up reading. You will see serif type commonly used in body text.

- Sans serif (**sans serif**) has no such features: I, i, C, 1, 5. The uncluttered and streamlined shape of sans serif type works well with shorter blocks of text and gives text a more modern appearance.

  Sans serif type used for special purposes, such as for headings or displayed passages where it is desirable to have the type contrast noticeably from the body text. Some recommend that a sans serif typeface be used on Web pages because readers will find it easier to read from the screen.

  A sans serif typeface is used effectively in the headings of Figures 5.1, 5.6, and 5.10.

Highlighting

Use restraint when highlighting text.

Use highlighting techniques consistently but sparingly. Draw the readers' attention by using italic, boldface (extra-dark type), underlining, ALL-CAPITAL LETTERS, sans serif type, or different colors.

- Do not use boldface one time and underlining another for the same purpose.

- Do not overuse highlighting or the document will look cluttered and confusing.

Passages consisting of words formed of all-capital letters should be kept to a minimum. They reduce reading speed and increase the chances that typographic errors and misspellings will be overlooked, partly because capital letters have fewer distinctive features than lowercase letters. It is overkill to combine special effects such as all-capitals, italic, bold, and shadow images. If many items are highlighted, those that really need emphasizing will not stand out. Use italics and boldface type more frequently than underlining. The underline interferes with the letters that descend (g, j, p, q, y, g, j, p, q, y)—that is, the line crosses through the portion of the letter that descends below the bottom of the letter. Use italics for titles. Boldface works well if you have a good printer and copy machine, but boldface type fades when multiple copies are made on lower-quality copiers.

Use standard type sizes. How large the type should be depends on the distance from which the document will be read. The standard type size for body text 18 to 24 inches away from the reader's eyes is 10 to 12 points as in these examples:

This is 10-point in Times Roman typeface.

This is 12-point in Times Roman typeface.

This is 10-point Univers typeface.

This is 12-point Univers typeface.

Use the same type size and font for all body text. Smaller type, perhaps 8-point, can be used for text that will be read only briefly, such as labels and captions on visuals, footnotes or endnotes, or legends accompanying visuals.

Unless a document is designed for readers who are visually impaired, do not use type that is larger than 12-point for body text. It wastes space and paper and does not have the professional look required in the workplace. Of course, there are exceptions: the most notable is typeface for overhead projector slides and computer-generated slideshows. The point size for presentations will be between 22 and 42 depending on the size of the room, the audience, and the equipment you are using. We discuss creating effective oral presentations in Chapter 12.

Use Color Effectively

Color cues help readers locate information.

Color, when used effectively, enhances the readability of a document. Readers use color cues to locate information in the text and to distinguish the importance of information. Writers use color to signal important information or to show relationships among items—for example, a warning in a set of instructions or the different colors used for bars in a bar chart. Almost all Web sites and other electronic documents incorporate color. The document appears more accessible to the reader. Elizabeth Keyes refers to color as an "information structure signal."[1] In this section, we describe several ways color may be used to signal the reader about the organization (structure) of the information.

The following guidelines are selected and adapted from Keyes's article:

- Use color to call attention to important information. Because you want to signal important information, use it only on the most important information. Often you will see the word WARNING in red to alert the users to read the warning that follows.

- Use color to help a reader navigate through a document. For example, color in this textbook indicates the start of a new chapter. Links on Web pages are another example. The links on Web pages appear in one color until the link is followed but changes color to indicate when the link has been followed. Readers find this helpful in keeping track of where they have been on a Web site.

- Use color to simplify information that contains many details and multiple relationships among the details. You can use it to separate the information but at the same time show that the information is related. In Figures 2.2a–2.2d (see pages A and B in the first color insert), for example, color is used on the Environmental Protection Agency Web site to help the reader navigate the Web site.

By now, you have used this textbook for a few weeks. Have you used the color of the headings and the typeface to help you understand the hierarchy of information in the textbook?

You have ready access to the color spectrum and more colors than you will ever use. Look for the color spectrum on the software package you are using. It is an option when you select font or insert a graphic. If you follow some simple guidelines, you can effectively coordinate the colors. If at all possible, have several colleagues review your document before you send it to clients or to others in your company. Here we provide some guidelines that

---

[1] Elizabeth Keyes, "Typography, Color, and Information Structure," *Technical Communication* 40 (1993): 638–54.

William Horton[2] and others suggest you follow when integrating color into a document.

- Use colors that your reader expects to see: blue, red, green, and yellow. Leave experimenting with color and color combinations to the marketing and entertainment departments. You have information to deliver to your reader; do not let color detract from the information.

- Use colors commonly associated with the action. For example, in the United States, red signals danger.

- Keep in mind that different cultures associate certain colors with different meanings. For example, black signifies death in the United States; white signifies death in China. Test the document with different audiences, particularly if it will be distributed internationally.

- Coordinate the colors selected with the company logo and colors in documents going to clients to look unified and well thought out.

- Use complementary colors. On the color spectrum, look for colors of the same hue, that is, shades of the same color. Complementary colors are next to each other on the color spectrum.

- Use low contrast and darker shades of colors across the pages of larger documents. For example, the color used for the headings in this textbook is not the brightest shade of red.

Remember two things if you use color in a document:

1. You can use any color imaginable for text and background for any document (especially Web documents); however, if your reader cannot read the information, you have not succeeded as a writer.

2. Adding color to a document may increase the cost of reproducing the document. You must decide if the cost increase is justified by the improvement in helping your readers find the information.

As you revise the content, you may need to revise the design of the document.

As you develop your documents, always keep your readers' needs in mind. When you write important documents (such as your resume or a report for a client) or any documents to be distributed to more than one reader, ask others to read and comment on not only the content but also the document's design. We have provided an overview of the most common document design features. As a writer, you must remain flexible and adjust to your readers' needs; as a reader, be alert to what text and document design features work for you and incorporate them into the documents you write. Know your audience, the purpose of your document, and the information you are providing.

---

[2]William Horton, "Overcoming Chromophobia: A Guide to the Confident and Appropriate Use of Color," *IEEE Transactions on Professional Communication* 34 (1991): 160–73.

Making the Contents Easy to Follow

In spite of the work you may have put into organizing and expressing your information as clearly and logically as you can, your document should be designed so that its organization is obvious to the reader. You want the reader to navigate quickly through a document, whatever the length—memos, e-mail messages, 40-page reports, online procedures manuals, or Web sites. As a writer, you must provide the navigation cues.

Readers expect related documents (such as instructions or letters) to have similar textual, visual, and document design cues. That is, readers look for numbered steps in instructions to find out where to start or the signature box in a letter to know who wrote the letter. Readers come with experience reading other documents. Readers are familiar with moving around hard-copy documents. They know the table of contents is in the front, the index is in the back. They can find each quickly. Readers know how much information is between the front and the back of a book or a report or a letter—they see it and they can flip through the pages. You can build on their experience while presenting your ideas.

Electronic documents have no fixed boundaries as do hard-copy documents. For this reason, navigation cues are perhaps more important with electronic documents. Although site maps, like those shown in Figures 2.2c and 2.2d (see page B in the first color insert), give us an overview of the Web site, we have no way of knowing how much material is a part of each page of the site as in hard copy. We can move around the site, but we can also lose our place there. If we do not understand the categories (topics in the index), we may have trouble.

Whether you are writing a document for publication in hard-copy form or electronic form, you need to transfer your organization to your readers. You must provide the reader with navigational cues and tools: cues such as headings, chapter breaks, or breadcrumbs on a Web site; tools such as Web site maps or table of contents. Layout and design cues help transfer this picture.

Good readers scan a document before they begin reading to understand the organization of the information. They then select where to start reading and how much reading to do. However, not all readers are good readers. Some may lack good reading strategies or may have a first language different from that of the document. You must provide navigation cues for all readers.

Many workplace documents are not read from beginning to end. Readers go to the document to find specific information. Headings, displayed lists, paragraphs to show organization, and Web site links will help them quickly understand the organization of large blocks of information.

Readers want their information highlighted. If your documents are to succeed, they must have the willing participation of these visual-minded readers. It is not so much a question of whether readers will *understand* what you have to say as of whether they will be willing to *read* what you have to say.

Make the organization obvious to readers.

Use Headings

Headings help fulfill the readers' assumptions that your information is shaped into an organized and meaningful whole. Without headings to display your plan of organization, the reading becomes tedious and the main ideas remain lost from view, buried in the mass of words and sentences that make up the document. The reader should be able to pick out the major ideas of your document. Note, for example, that the passages in Figures 5.5 and 5.7 makes the reader's work difficult for the very reasons we have just outlined.

To grasp the major ideas in Figure 5.7, you probably would have to read it and note the major ideas, separating them from subordinate ideas and details by bolding them or by reconstructing the outline of the material in brief notes or marks in the margin. Understanding the document would require considerable work.

Now look at another version of this memo in Figure 5.8. Notice how the headings make it easier to read and understand what the writer has written. In a single brief exposure, the reader sees immediately the writer's inner picture of organization. The more visible the content and arrangement, the greater the impact on the reader. Headings stand out best when they are slightly larger than the body text or printed in bold or italics.

The version in Figure 5.8 is longer than the version in Figure 5.7 because headings take up space. However, in spite of this, it is quicker to read and easier to understand and remember because the reader can quickly identify the points of discussion, the order in which they are made, and how much discussion is devoted to each.

Use levels of headings to show relationships in the information you are presenting.

Remember to make distinctions between the different levels of headings you use so that your reader will see the relation among the different sections of the text. We use many such design features in this book. Notice in particular the size and color of the various levels of headings and how we distinguish lists from normal text. Just as headings in your textbooks signal different sections and the relation of sections to each other, so do headings within documents you write. When you write, the purpose of the document, the information presented in the document, and the reader's expectations determine how many levels of headings you will need.

Find an example of a document without headings, and consider how you might add them. For example, you might include headings in a one-page memo (Figure 5.8) or in an e-mail message (Figure 5.2). You will probably need just one level of heading; you might use a sans serif font such as Univers and make the typeface bold. If your e-mail software does not let you use bold or a different font, then use all capitals.

Frequently, with proposals and other requests for information the headings are given to you. That is, the request for proposal (commonly called the RFP) identifies each area that must be addressed, or a request from another division in your company outlines what information is needed. The information needed determines the headings. In Figure 5.9, the boxed words can become the headings for each section of the proposal.

FIGURE 5.7

A document without headings or displayed lists, even in a short passage, does little to make the work of readers easier. To grasp the major ideas of this memo, readers will probably have to read it more than once to identify the major ideas and to separate them from subordinate ideas and details by underlining them or by constructing an outline of the material by brief notes in the margin.

```
Date: May 20, 2005
To:   T.Y. Lee, Supervisor, Greentree District #7 TYLee
From: Allen McClure, Area Chief, Reforestation Project

Subject: Recommendation of Replacement of Fire Suppression Tractor in Area 1

The purchase of a new fire supression tractor will give Area 1 the dependable
equipment needed for fire suppression, fire protection, and routine management
activities. This purchase will result in the continued maximization of fiber
yield and minimum loss to wild fire.

The potential loss of Area 1 plantations, due to fire, because of the downtime
is critical with the present unit. The area has 58,191 acres of timberland;
22,629 acres are in plantations one to 20 years old. To ensure development of
these plantations, fire suppression is essential.

The new fire suppression tractor is also essential in developing a road system
in these plantations to give better fire protection and aid in suppression.

Our commitment to maximum yield from our timberlands and the future dependency
of the DePhalant Mill to this commitment makes dependable equipment a must.
The fire suppression tractor is also used in minor road construction projects
and tree planting, which are also essential in the commitment to maximum
yield.

The present tractor had maintenance costs of $10,101 and $9,600 for the past
two years. In contrast, during this same period the 2-year-old tractor in Area
2 had maintenance costs of $1,500 and $3,000. These tractors are for the same
purposes and the hours of operation were essentially the same. The cost of
operating the present tractor in Area 1 is prohibitive.

The unit to be replaced is a D4D diesel crawler, purchased in May 1980, asset
no. M548, which is totally depreciated. This crawler has no book value and
will be traded in or sold.

The alternative to purchasing a new tractor would be to lease a tractor or
continued use of the present tractor. Experience indicates that this type of
equipment is more costly to lease than to own. Continuing to operate our
present tractor would be impractical due to extensive downtime, high
maintenance costs, and its potential unreliability.
```

FIGURE 5.8

Notice how the displayed list and the headings make this memo easy to read and understand. In a single brief pass, readers see immediately the writer's inner picture of organization. The more visible the content and arrangement, the greater the impact on the readers.

Date: May 20, 2005
To: T.Y. Lee, Supervisor, Greentree District #7 TYL
From: Allen McClure, Area Chief, Reforestation Project

Subject: Recommendation of Replacement of Fire Suppression Tractor in Area 1

I recommend the replacement of the fire suppression tractor in Area 1 for the following reasons:

- loss of production to downtime is critical
- the maintenance cost of the tractor is excessively high
- the tractor is completely depreciated

Loss of Production to Downtime

The potential loss of Area 1 plantations, due to fire, because of the downtime is critical with the present unit. The area has 58,191 acres of timberland; 22,629 acres are in plantations one to 20 years old. To ensure development of these plantations, fire suppression is essential.

The new fire suppression tractor is also essential in developing a road system in these plantations to give better fire protection and aid in suppression.

Our commitment to maximum yield from our timberlands and the future dependency of the DePhalant Mill to this commitment makes dependable equipment a must. The fire suppression tractor is also used in minor road construction projects and tree planting, which are also essential in the commitment to maximum yield.

Excessively High Maintenance Cost

The present tractor had maintenance costs of $10,101 and $9,600 for the past two years. In contrast, during this same period the 2-year-old tractor in Area 2 had maintenance costs of $1,500 and $3,000. These tractors are for the same purposes and the hours of operation were essentially the same. The cost of operating the present tractor in Area 1 is prohibitive.

Depreciation

The unit to be replaced is a D4D diesel crawler, purchased in May 1980, asset no. M548, which is totally depreciated. This crawler has no book value and will be traded in or sold.

Purchase of New Tractor

The alternative to purchasing a new tractor would be to lease a tractor or continued use of the present tractor. Experience indicates that this type of equipment is more costly to lease than to own. Continuing to operate our present tractor would be impractical due to extensive downtime, high maintenance costs, and its potential unreliability.

FIGURE 5.9

The Request for Proposal identifies the six areas of the proposal that the proposal writer must address. The writer can pull out a heading (shown within the boxes) for each area of the proposal. The proposal readers can quickly locate the information.

REQUEST FOR PROPOSAL

Nancy and Edward Grover Endowment
for Research in Teaching in the
Computer-Mediated Classroom

1. Describe the specific objectives of the proposed project for improving computer classroom teaching.

2. How do the project objectives relate to and promote the enhancement of teaching and accomplishment of the general objectives in course(s) taught in the computer classroom? How many students will be reached by the proposed project? Describe the rationale and significance of the proposed project.

3. Outline what you plan to do and how you plan to accomplish and evaluate the results.

4. Outline plans for dissemination of the project results and methods of assessment.

5. Explain any use of graduate student labor planned for this project. These funds may not be used to support a graduate student's thesis or dissertation; however, you may use graduate student labor on the project.

6. Provide a detailed budget for this project. List by major expenditure category: faculty salary and employee benefits (14% of requested salary, when appropriate), wages (provide hourly rate and number of hours requested), expendable supplies (include examples of this category), travel required to conduct project (number of trips planned, where, when, etc.), requested equipment (include estimates for each item).

Each document will be different. Some general guidelines include

- use a sans serif font such as Arial and using **bold** instead of <u>underline</u> to set off the heading.

- use *italics* sparingly and then only for sections within major sections.

- use all capital letters for short blocks of text only. Readers have a harder time distinguishing the letters when the block of text is uniform (no ascenders or descenders).

Look at the headings in Figures 5.1, 5.6, and 5.8. Figure 5.10 illustrates possible formats to distinguish levels of headings and to show the hierarchy of information in the document.

FIGURE 5.10

Two panels from a bank brochure on the Roth IRA show different formats for the headings. Select headings so that the reader can see quickly the organization of the information.

Title	bold, all caps, centered, sans serif font	**UNDERSTANDING THE ROTH IRA**
1st level heading	left margin, upper/ lowercase, bold, sans serif font	**Selecting the Account Holder** You want to select a financial institution that provides quarterly statements of your investments.
2nd level	part of the paragraph, upper/lowercase, italics, sans serif font	*Banks.* Banks provide services in addition to IRAs that you may want to use. For example, you can get cash when you need it from an ATM machine.

Title	bold, upper/lowercase, 14 point font, centered, sans serif font	**Understanding the Roth IRA**
1st level heading	left margin, upper/ lowercase, 12 point, bold, line space between heading and paragraph	**Selecting the Account Holder** You want to select a financial institution that provides quarterly statements of your investments.
2nd level	left margin, upper/ lowercase, 10 point (same as the text), bold, line space between heading and paragraph	**Banks** Banks provide services in addition to IRAs that you may want to use. For example, you can get cash when you need it from an ATM machine.

Use Displayed Lists

Present important information or other significant data in vertical list form instead of in sentence and paragraph form. Lists help break up long bodies of text and call attention to specific items. Readers find them useful for giving information in a concise, easy-to-read format. Readers of online text find lists helpful because lists provide shorter chunks of information that can be scrolled through and read with less chance of losing the location.

Readers of documents written in a language other than their first language find lists helpful for the same reason. The shorter chunks of information do not overwhelm the reader. In Figure 5.8, notice how the bulleted list at the beginning of the memo identifies the organization of the memo and the headings use terms from the list to signal the reader where the discussion for each point begins.

As you construct your list, consider the following guidelines:

- If the sequence of the items in a list is random or arbitrary, use a bullet (•).

- If the order is important, as in a set of instructions, use Arabic numerals (1, 2, 3, ...).

Most word-processing software will fill in the pattern (bullets or numerals) when you start the sequence. Be sure to change the tab so that you do not have a large gap between the bullet or the numeral and the text. You want the equivalent of 2 to 3 spaces between the bullet or number and the text. Use indent to align the lines following the first line of text.

Problem
-    Too much space

Solution
- Change the tab settings to move the text closer.

Problem
1.   Too much space. Large gaps make it more difficult for the reader and look unprofessional.

Solution
1. Proper spacing simplifies reading, looks more professional. And readers will see the numbers more clearly if you align (stack) all lines following the first.

- Use the same spacing for all lists throughout a document. Readers quickly determine the pattern and hierarchy of the information. If you are inconsistent, you will lose your reader. Figures 5.4, 5.6, and 5.8 show acceptable spacing.

- Use parallel sentences or phrases throughout the list. If the grammatical construction shifts, readers may slow down or stop reading. Consider the lists below:

Parallel (Acceptable)
- Use bullets to signal items in a list.
- Align the text in the list to help the reader see bullets and distinguish between items in the list.
- Insert lists to highlight a series of items that might otherwise be lost in a long paragraph.

Not Parallel (Unacceptable)
- Bullets signal items in a list.
- Aligning the text in the list helps the reader see bullets and distinguish between items on the list.
- If I want to call attention to a series of items that might otherwise be lost in a long paragraph, I use a list.

Use Text to Forecast

Stay alert to forecasting cues as you read.

As you write the document, you will provide the reader with cues as to what is coming. The text forecasts for the reader what comes in the section with transition statements and summary paragraphs that point to the next part of the document. For example, the following paragraph introduces Chapter 1: Literacy in the Older Adult Population. We have added italics to the words that signal statements that forecast the content of the chapter.

> *This chapter* profiles the prose, document, and quantitative literacy skills of older adults in the United States—those age 60 and older. *In addition* to examining differences in performance within the older adult population, we analyze the literacy proficiencies of older adults in comparison with those of younger adults. *The latter part* of the chapter compares older adults' self-assessed literacy skills with their demonstrated proficiencies. *Finally,* we examine the extent to which adults in various age groups receive assistance with various types of everyday literacy tasks, another indicator of their proficiencies.[3]

Paragraphs, frequently short and at the end of a section, signal transition to the next section of a document. Transition paragraphs tell the reader what will follow. Do not hide information in a document because readers frequently skim until they find the information they need. Transition paragraphs and headings that forecast what follows help the reader.

Making Documents Easy to Use

All the features of effective design and layout discussed so far in this chapter contribute toward creating documents that are easy to use. Chances are great that documents that look inviting to read and that are designed so that the progression of thought is easy to follow will also be easy to use. That is, readers will read the document with the purpose of locating information they need.

Here we discuss two strategies for making documents easy to use:

1. Matching the document design to the readers' purpose
2. Matching the document design to the readers' environment

Match the Document Design to the Readers' Purpose

To make a document easy to use, you must understand clearly the purpose of the document and how readers are likely to use it. That is, you must consider the document from the readers' points of view. Some readers will want to read a document from beginning to end. Others will want to read only the

---

[3]Helen Brown, Robert Prisuta, Bella Jacobs, and Anne Campbell, *Literacy of Older Adults in America: Results from the National Adult Literacy Survey,* NCES 97-576 (Washington, DC: U.S. Department of Education, National Center for Education Statistics, 1996) 15.

sections that are relevant to their needs. Still others will want to locate a specific piece of information that is crucial to their immediate need.

Figures 5.11, 5.12, and 5.13 show directions for claiming speaking and instructional fees and for claiming reimbursement for professional travel. The directions in Figures 5.11 and 5.12 are ineffective because the information is not presented in a way that helps readers gain access to the specific information they will need. At the least, document design should help readers perform any one of the tasks easily. The best design will help readers undertake several of the tasks, as necessary. The directions in Figures 5.11 and 5.12 force the reader to scan the document from beginning to end because there are few visual cues to what information is where. However, not all readers will want to start and finish at the same places, so the design is poor. Figure 5.12 has information paragraphed according to tasks, but that is still not enough.

Figure 5.13 contains the same information as in Figures 5.11 and 5.12 but in an extraordinarily different design. It uses self-contained blocks of information, judicious use of white space, and varied type styles to help readers understand the underlying logic of the document and how to find the specific information they need. It is straightforward, helpful, and friendly.

Match the Document Design to the Readers' Environment

How will the reader use the document?

When you consider your document's purpose and how the reader will use it, you should also consider the environment in which the reader will use the document. Although you cannot control the environment, you can create a design that will work well in most situations for which the document is intended.

Let us consider several examples:

- Golfers use a scorecard. Most of the cards have the scoring table for the first nine holes on one side and the second on the other side. A heavier paper, sized to fold and put in a pocket, provides golfers with something fairly substantial to write on and keep safely during play. Frequently, color is used, and the layout of each hole is given as well as a review of some of the basic rules of courtesy. The scorecard matches the needs of most golfers.

- The instructions on a cake mix fill one side of the box. The reader need not turn the box over to continue making the cake. Pictures show a measuring cup with the amount of water needed and the number of eggs. The text is easy to read, with white space and color to emphasize the easy steps to making a cake.

- A company's cleaning crews' carts have a set of laminated cards that give instructions for using cleaning supplies. The cards hang on the crews' cart for easy reference if a spill occurs. The cards have few words but a lot of visuals because the cleaners may not have time to read the warnings or may not be efficient readers.

FIGURE 5.11

Readers will find it difficult to locate the steps they need to take to claim expenses. See Figures 5.12 and 5.13 for revised instructions.

Central Business Office
Drawer 6000
Empire-Juniper Professional Consultants
Meyer Road and State Route 7
Sandpoint, ID 83864

Procedures for Claiming Expense Reimbursement
and Instructional or Speaker's Fee

Please use this sheet as a guide to assist you in providing us with the proper receipts for your professional travel expense reimbursement and fee payment. Following this guide will ensure payment with a minimum of difficulty and time.

To claim mileage, provide us with a memo requesting that you be reimbursed for personal auto mileage. Cite the purpose of the travel, the function of the meeting, dates, and round-trip mileage for each day at 30¢ per mile. Please include your mailing address. To claim lodging, provide us with the original hotel receipt. If you share a room with another person also participating in the meeting, ask the hotel to print two separate receipts. To claim airfare, provide us with the original receipts. To claim meals, provide us with the original receipts. To claim taxi fare, provide us with a signed receipt from the driver.

To be paid an instructional or speaker's fee, if your fee is to be paid directly to you, submit a bill stating the service you provided, the unit for which you provided the service, and the dates of the work in accordance with the letter or memorandum of agreement. Payments made to individuals will be made in accordance with the letter or memorandum of agreement by PAV (Payment Authorization Voucher) or DAV (Departmental Authorization Voucher). These are initiated upon completion of your service or work. Taxes are deducted from compensation paid to individuals.

FIGURE 5.12

The layout and design of this example helps the reader, but look at Figure 5.13 for further document design features that make the information easier to locate.

Central Business Office
Drawer 6000
Empire-Juniper Professional Consultants
Meyer Road and State Route 7
Sandpoint, ID 83864

Procedures for Claiming Expense Reimbursement
and Instructional or Speaker's Fee

Please use this sheet as a guide to assist you in providing us with the proper receipts for your professional travel expense reimbursement and fee payment. Following this guide will ensure payment with a minimum of difficulty and time. Please include your mailing address.

To claim mileage, provide us with a memo requesting that you be reimbursed for personal auto mileage. Cite the purpose of the travel, the function of the meeting, dates, and round-trip mileage for each day at 30¢ per mile.

To claim lodging, provide us with the original hotel receipt. If you share a room with another person also participating in the meeting, ask the hotel to print two separate receipts.

To claim airfare, provide us with the original receipts.

To claim meals, provide us with the original receipts.

To claim taxi fare, provide us with a signed receipt from the driver.

To be paid an instructional or speaker's fee, if your fee is to be paid directly to you, submit a bill stating the service you provided, the unit for which you provided the service, and the dates of the work in accordance with the letter or memorandum of agreement. Payments made to individuals will be made in accordance with the letter or memorandum of agreement by PAV (Payment Authorization Voucher) or DAV (Departmental Authorization Voucher). These are initiated upon completion of your service or work. Taxes are deducted from compensation paid to individuals.

FIGURE 5.13
The information is easier to locate in this example.

Central Business Office
Drawer 6000
Empire-Juniper Professional Consultants
Meyer Road and State Route 7
Sandpoint, ID 83864

Procedures for Claiming Expense Reimbursement
and Instructional or Speaker's Fee

Please use this sheet as a guide to assist you in providing us with the proper receipts for your professional travel expense reimbursement and fee payment. Following this guide will ensure payment with a minimum of difficulty and time. **NOTE:** Please include your mailing address with requests for reimbursement.

To claim **Mileage**	provide us with a memo requesting that you be reimbursed for personal auto mileage. Cite the purpose of the travel, the function of the meeting, dates, and round-trip mileage for each day at 30¢ per mile.
To claim **Lodging**	provide us with the original hotel receipt. If you share a room with another person also participating in the meeting, ask the hotel to print two separate receipts.
To claim **Airfare**	provide us with the original receipts.
To claim **Meals**	provide us with the original receipts.
To claim **Taxi Fare**	provide us with a signed receipt from the driver.
To be paid an **Instructional** or **Speaker's Fee**	if your fee is to be paid to your place of employment, submit a bill stating the service you provided, the unit for which you provided the service, and the dates of the work in accordance with the letter or memorandum of agreement.
	if your fee is to be paid directly to you, it will be made in accordance with the letter or memorandum of agreement by PAV (Payment Authorization Voucher) or DAV (Departmental Authorization Voucher). These are initiated upon completion of your service or work.
	Taxes are deducted from compensation paid to individuals.

FIGURE 5.14

A partial list of the documents received with the purchase of a new pocket PC. The list of features for each document identifies some of the document design elements, not all.

Document	Purpose	Some of the Features
Poster-size 16″ × 16″	Shows how to set up the pocket PC quickly	• Large typeface • Numbered steps • Visuals showing the parts of the pocket PC dominate • Color used to highlight key parts of the pocket PC and step numbers • 5 languages
5½″ × 8¼″ 180-page user's guide	Gives step-by-step instructions for setting up and troubleshooting the pocket PC	• Chapters with sections clearly signaled by headings; contents listed at the beginning of each chapter • Diagrams used to show parts of the pocket PC • Text and photographs bleed into the margin to emphasize the information • English
5½″ × 8¼″ 192-page system information guide	Provides instructions for setting up and safely using the pocket PC	• 8 pages of Cautions in bulleted lists • Diagrams of the pocket PC the chapter and topic • Black and white printing (no color) • Soft cover, perfect binding • 12 languages; 16 pages for each
5½″ × 8¼″ 12-page troubleshooting brochure	Provides instructions for troubleshooting the pocket PC	• Numbered steps for installation • Bulleted steps for troubleshooting • Black and white printing • 5 languages, 2 pages for each
5″ × 5″ envelope with CD	Contains software to install	• Clear envelope with warning on orange label about responsibilities once seal broken • Icon on envelope indicating Do Not Throw Away • No instructions on the CD
4¾″ × 4¾″ quick start guide	Gives instructions for installing flash card	• Numbered steps with screen captures • Color on glossy paper • 5 languages, 3 pages for each

- Figure 5.14 shows a list of documents you are likely to receive with a handheld device, in this example a pocket PC. Notice the range of formats the documents take, from a poster to a book of more than 100 pages to a CD-ROM and online documents to read. The information on most of the documents is given in several languages (for example, Arabic, English, French, German, Japanese, Korean, Russian, Spanish, and Swedish).

Electronic documents are no different. You must know how your reader will read the document. For example,

- The service representative goes to the online manual on his handheld to troubleshoot and repair an oscilloscope at a hazardous-waste-monitoring facility. The online manual you write will provide the instructions, but you must also consider the size of the computer screen, the amount of light, the amount of space to work in, and the power source as you write the instructions. An index or fast-search feature, white space, lines that do not run off the screen, visuals sized to fit the screen, and color that shows clearly on a screen in variable light are just a few of the choices you must consider.

As with printed documents, you have control over the text and visuals—to a point—in the electronic environment. The reader's environment and the computer environment (hardware and software) the reader uses will affect the presentation of the document. For example, the size of the screen may affect the amount of text the reader sees without having to move the scroll bar, the color may change, or the size of the print on the screen may be reduced, depending on how the user has the screen set. The Web browser or e-mail software the reader uses also may affect the presentation.

As you review the documents you develop, consider the purpose of the document and information it provides, but also consider how the reader will use the document. Your choices for the design of the document and the content will follow easily from a careful analysis.

PLANNING AND REVISING CHECKLIST: TEXT AND DOCUMENT DESIGN

Think about the following while planning and revising the design of your documents.

Planning

- Do you have access to and know how to use the computer, software, and printer available?
  _____ Software available (for example, spreadsheet to create budget report, Adobe Acrobat to create PDF files)?
  _____ Color printer?

- Will the document be read online or on paper?
  _____ What environment do most readers have for accessing and reading the documents?
  _____ How will the document be delivered to end-users:
    _____ Paper; binder needed?
    _____ E-mail, CD, Web, or other electronic delivery?

- Are there ways in which you can make your document more visually attractive and more inviting to read? Check the use of the following:
  _____ White space
  _____ Color
  _____ Balance between text and visuals

- What are the specifications for the document?
  _____ Size of paper or screen
  _____ Page orientation (portrait or landscape)
  _____ Size and style of font for the body text
  _____ Size and style of font for displayed passages
  _____ Size and style of font for headings and links
  _____ Single- or double-spaced text
  _____ Right margin unjustified
  _____ Width of margins
  _____ Position of page numbers
  _____ Text of header/footer

- What is the best way to present the information?
  _____ Text
  _____ Lists
    _____ Bulleted list (unordered)
    _____ Numbered list (ordered)
  _____ Tables
  _____ Visuals (for example, chart, graph, photograph, video)
  _____ Links to other documents

- What devices can you use to highlight the major ideas and important pieces of information and distinguish the major ideas from the subordinator ideas?
  - _____ Italics
  - _____ Bold
  - _____ Underline (only for web addresses)
  - _____ All caps (use sparingly)
- If others are also working on the document, do they know the specifications for the design?

Revising

- Does the document conform to the specifications for size of paper or screen, size and style of font, and so on?
- Is the overall design attractive?
- Are the pages (paper or Web) of the document broken up to avoid long stretches of solid text?
- Does the design of the document match the underlying logic and the use of the document?
- Do headings and subheadings mark main points and major sections of the document? Are major sections of the document visually distinct?
- Can readers make their way easily through the text? Can readers gain quick access to specific information?
- Is the overall design consistent throughout the document?
- Does the overall design work in the environment where the document will be used?

Suggestions for Applying Your Knowledge

Collaborative Activity

At the end of Chapter 1, "The Process of Workplace Communication," we suggest that you start gathering examples of writing found in the workplace. In a group, share the different examples class members have found. Examine the different design features. Write a memo or prepare an oral report for your instructor and classmates that explains the following:

- The types of documents found
- The intended audiences for each document

- What features aid or hinder a smooth reading of each document

- What features provide clues to each document's organization

Evaluate what the writer or writers have done well. What additional features could have been used?

Individual Activity

Revise the following memo using design principles discussed in this chapter to make its meaning as clear as possible to the reader. You will have to do more than rearrange the text. You may decide the information can be sent by e-mail to the reader. If so, be sure to send a copy to your instructor. The memo is part of the correspondence related to the inventory of a direct-mail marketing company specializing in gardening supplies. The warehouse manager identifies problems with returned merchandise and recommends solutions. Write a brief memo to your instructor explaining your reasons for the design features you used.

MEMO

September 15, 2004
To: Ruth J. Wades
Vice President, Operations

From: Jerome Dean
Warehouse Manager

Subject: Returns

The number of returns has doubled over the past six months. There are several reasons for this. We changed primary shippers. The new shipper has had repeated delays in picking up and delivering the merchandise in the time specified in the contract. Repeated phone calls and visits have not resulted in improved service. Customers do not accept delivery on items received after the promised delivery date. I recommend we use On-Time Shipping for all of our regional customers. The addition of crystal vases to our inventory has created problems. The foam packing material seeps through the gift boxes for the vases. We have not found a plastic wrap that will protect the box from the foam. We need to use bubble wrap. Machines for dispensing bubble wrap cost $55,000 for sheets 360 × 450; $75,000 for 450 × 600; $150,000 for adjustable sheet size. Currently the 360 × 450 sheets cover the crystal boxes, but if we carry larger vases, we will have problems. There is a two-day delay between the time an order is taken and when the warehouse receives the order. Incompatible computer systems in customer service and in the warehouse further delay the processing. Customer service and the warehouse need a direct link via computer.

Multicultural Activity

Compare the use of color and the provisions for different languages in a paper document and on a Web site. Locate a set of instructions for the paper document and use a commercial or government Web site for the electronic document.

- How does each use color to provide information-structure signals? What colors are used? How many colors are used?

- How many languages are incorporated in the document? Does the design or color change for each language?

Visuals and Document Design I

Think for a moment of anything that you have studied recently in one of your courses: the double-helix structure of DNA, the Federal Reserve Board, the hydrological cycle, how to add antibiotics to livestock feed, the relationship between exposure to carbon monoxide and human health, a method of predicting lateral pressure transmitted to nonyielding and rigid basement walls by swelling expansive soils, or what have you.

Some of these concepts and events can be difficult to understand in abstract language, but a visual may clarify them. They probably were illustrated in whatever you studied, whether textbooks, articles, reports, Web sites, or slides projected on a screen. The visuals helped you to understand the subject and later to recall and think about it. Visuals can remove language barriers and work across cultures. Signs in airports are an obvious example, but next time you put an ink cartridge in your printer, look at the instructions. The visuals show the user how to install the cartridge; the limited text is in several languages. Long after you have forgotten the words, you are probably able to recall the visual.

The visuals and the text should complement each other.

Visuals can make certain kinds of data and relationships more apparent than is possible in text and can emphasize or clarify information that might otherwise go unnoticed or be difficult to understand. Take, for instance, an idea that is primarily pictorial, such as the proper distribution of lawn fertilizer using a drop-type spreader. The reader can understand more easily how to distribute the fertilizer evenly by looking at the drawing in Figure 6.1 than by reading a statement such as "For even distribution, apply one lot of fertilizer lengthwise and the other crosswise over the lawn."

FIGURE 6.1

Almost any idea can be conveyed visually. This drawing shows the proper distribution of lawn fertilizer using a drop-type spreader.

Source: Texas Extension Service, The Texas A&M University System.

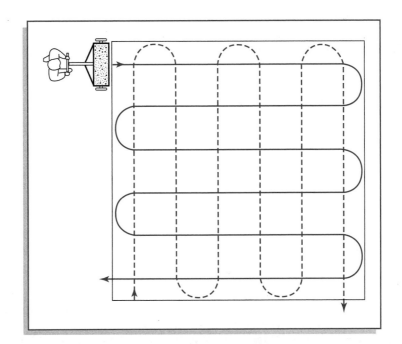

FIGURE 6.3

At a glance, the reader can see which months Alabama has the most tornadoes. The reader who wants to know the actual number of tornadoes can look more closely at the graph. Bar graphs such as this one show comparisons.

Source: Permission granted by the Alabama Cooperative Extension System to use publication as an example. Information may be out of date.

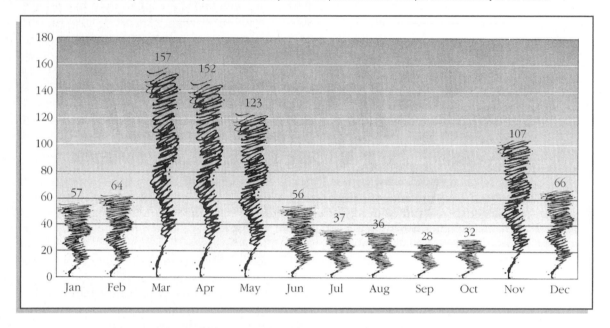

Even when the information is not normally regarded as primarily visual, visuals can succinctly present data that would otherwise take many words to explain. For example, Figure 6.2 (see the first color insert, page C) shows how text and visual combine to describe the water quality of U.S. coastal waters. Some readers will find the visual easier to understand; others, the text. The text and the visuals support each other, as in the bar chart in Figure 6.3, which shows almost at a glance the number of tornadoes in Alabama over 45 years.

Visuals have become an essential and conspicuous part of Web sites, presentations, reports, and even correspondence. The care with which they are created greatly affects readers' impressions of the value of information contained in our communication activities. Therefore, the choice, execution, and placement of visuals should not take a back seat when you plan your writing. You should strive to be as fluent in using visuals as in using words and sentences. There is a "symbiotic relationship between the visual and the verbal [what we are calling the text]."[1] The extra care in coordinating the visuals and the text will pay off by making the document easier to read and by making your work look professional.

---

[1] Charles Kostelnick and David D. Roberts, *Designing Visual Language: Strategies for Professional Communicators* (Boston: Allyn and Bacon, 1998) xix.

Incorporate meaningful visuals into your documents.

One cautionary note: Incorporate visuals in your document only when the reader needs the visuals, when the purpose of the document calls for a visual, and when the information is best conveyed in a visual. You omit unnecessary words to convey information; do the same with visuals. Omit any unnecessary clutter from the visual to present a clear, concise representation of the information you want the reader and listener to have.

In this chapter, we use examples from a variety of sources to illustrate factors that influence the reading of visuals. The quality of the visuals you create will affect how clear an understanding of the information readers gather from the visual. Also, you have a responsibility to your readers to present the information accurately and without intentionally misleading the reader. We provide several guidelines for using visuals to present information ethically. In Chapter 7, we provide guidelines for creating effective visuals. We assume that you will create the visuals for your document using a computer.

Factors Influencing Comprehension of Visuals

To use visuals, readers must be able to differentiate them from surrounding text, identify the important information in them, and comprehend the information. The following 7 factors determine the ease, speed, and accuracy with which visuals are read. The factors apply to hard copy as well as online documents. Chapter 11, "Communicating News: News-Release Publications, Brochures, and Web Sites," also discusses document design issues and the importance of good visual design.

Visuals Should Be Perceptible

perceptible

To aid readers in immediately recognizing visuals, separate visuals from the text around them with adequate white space. The defaults set by the software you use will take care of most spacing issues and placement of the labels and caption. Only occasionally will you have to adjust the spacing. You will want to select the most effective placement of the visuals within the text. The *text-wrapping* feature of the software controls the location.

You may also select a border for the visual that will define the area of the visual. Readers find borders helpful when distinguishing between the visual and the text. Again, the software lets you select a border. For most documents you will want a thin-ruled line (see Figure 6.2 on color page C and the visuals in the instructions in Chapter 17).

Size and place the visuals to meet the purpose of the document and to best display the information. You can easily change the size and placement of visuals through the software. When visuals are too large to fit on a page with text, put them on a page by themselves immediately following or facing the page on which you analyze their contents. Orient the visual on the page so that the reader does not have to turn the document to read the information. If the visual is too large and must be turned, place it so that the binding of the report is at the top of the visual. (Be sure to increase your top margin for any bound document.)

Visuals Should Be Accessible

accessible

Accessibility refers to the ease with which readers can locate individual visuals. Distinguishing visuals from text contributes to making them easy to find. Placement of visuals is equally important. Readers and listeners move back and forth between the text and visuals as they gather information. For example, when you are using a Send-N-Return Envelope (Figure 6.4), you probably look at the visual and then the corresponding text before you begin to reassemble the envelope. Place the visual at or near your discussion of it, as near as possible following the first reference to it (for example, the map in Figure 6.2 is on the page following the text identifying the seven coastal water conditions).

Think of the pages of your document as a collection of blocks of text and of visuals. Review how your reader will use the document, the reader's expectations for the document, and where the most important information should be placed to be seen. You also need to know the general design of the document. For example, if you are creating a brochure, you are limited to two sides of an 8.5- x 11-inch sheet of paper. You can make it a bifold or a trifold

FIGURE 6.4

Three visuals and the corresponding text fit on the back of the Send-N-Return envelope.

Source: The Send-N-Return envelope is a patented product of the Tension Envelope Corporation, headquartered in Kansas City, Missouri.

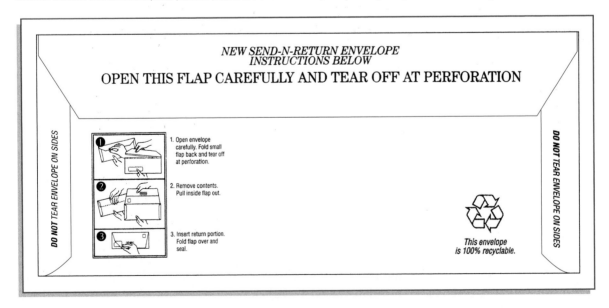

brochure. The information must fit in that area. If you are writing a report, your outline and the topic should give you an idea of how long the document will be. It is not at all unusual for a Request for Proposal (RFP) to specify the maximum length for the submitted proposal (see Chapter 15, "Proposals"). Once you have an overall idea of the plan for the document, you can lay out your text and visual blocks, as illustrated in Figure 6.5. The examples throughout this textbook illustrate some of the options.

FIGURE 6.5

Think of the text and visuals as blocks that must fit on a page. The purpose of the document, the information presented, and the amount of space available will determine how to arrange the blocks. These sketches give three possible arrangements.

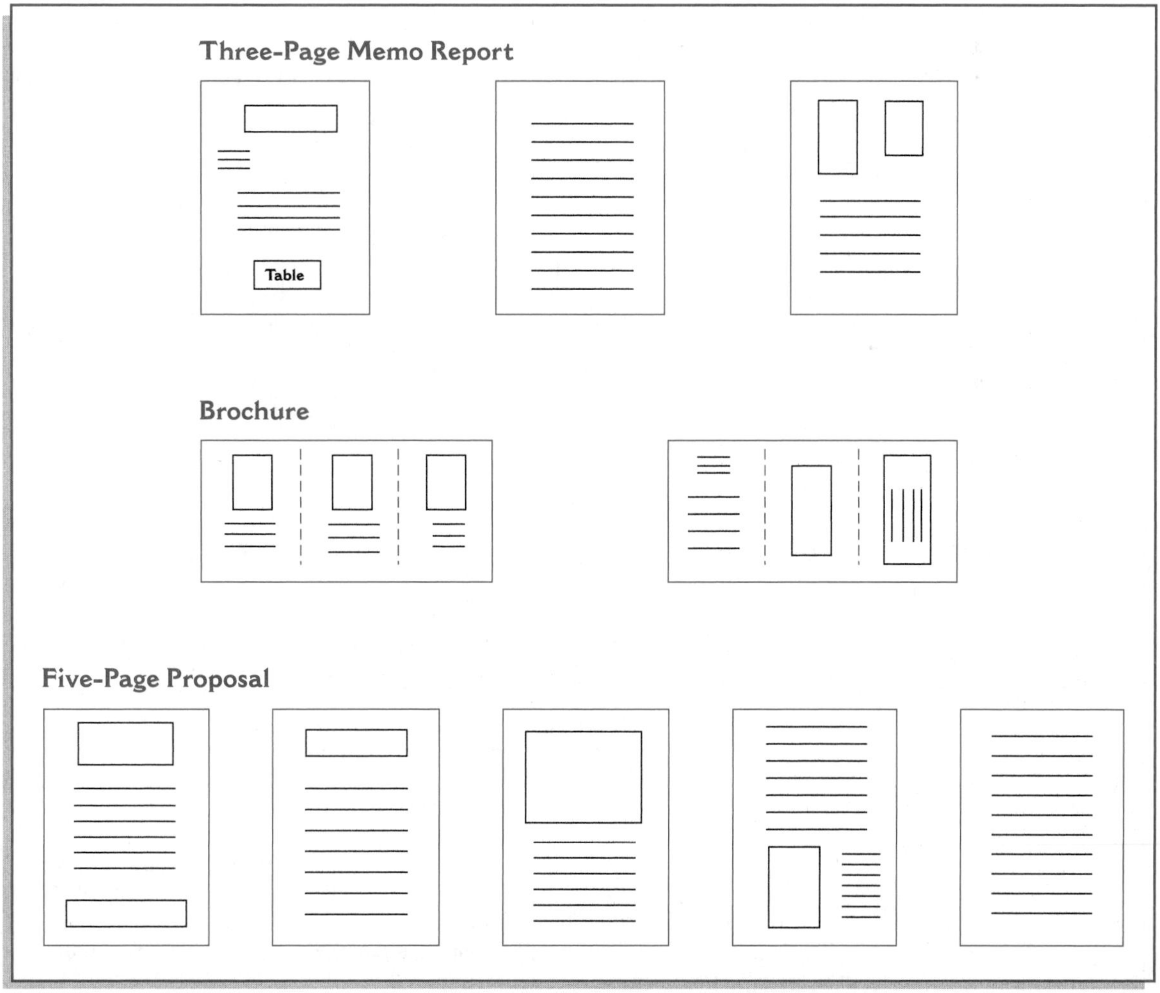

Three-Page Memo Report

Brochure

Five-Page Proposal

Sometimes, however, you may include visuals that have only indirect relevance to your discussion or that are relevant to only a portion of your audience. When this is the case, place them in an appendix so they do not interrupt the flow of your discussion.

A report that contains several visuals (more than five is a good guideline) should include a list of tables and figures in the prefatory elements (see the report in Chapter 13) to aid readers in selectively locating individual visuals.

Visuals Should Be Clearly Labeled

clearly labeled

Caption and label everything clearly so readers can scan visuals quickly and know exactly what they are looking at. Standardized labeling practices increase reading speed and comprehension. If possible, arrange all lettering to be read from left to right. If it is necessary to place labels on vertical scales, run the lettering so it can be read from bottom to top. Select the appropriate position using the features of the software program.

- Caption formal figures by arabic numerals and descriptive titles below the visual, as in

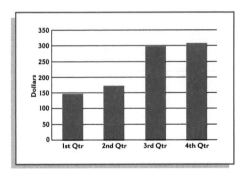

FIGURE 1   Growth of investment

All visuals are labeled as figures except information displayed in columns and rows. These visuals are referred to as *tables*.

- Caption formal tables by arabic numerals and descriptive titles above the table, as in the following table:

Table 1   Overview of Walsh Inc. Finances

	Income	Expenses
2003	$29,500	$25,375
2004	$35,000	$24,000

- Number figures and tables consecutively in the order of their reference in the text and refer to them as Figure 1, Table 1, and so on. Use your software's caption feature to identify the visuals. The software will also automatically number the visuals.

The suggested numbering system and placement of the caption have shifted over the past several years. Roman numerals no longer are required for captioning tables. And, frequently, all of the captions may be located above or all below the visual.

Our advice: Be consistent throughout the document. That is, if you label the first table with arabic numbers, you must use arabic numbers for all of the table captions. If you begin by putting the caption above tables and below the figures, do so throughout the document. Number tables and figures consecutively—but separately. If you have 5 tables and 10 figures in the same document, you would have Table 1, Table 2, Table 3, . . . , Table 5, and you would have Figure 1, Figure 2, Figure 3, . . . , Figure 10.

- Label by name or symbol the parts of objects and components of diagrams that you want readers to pay attention to. As you examine the sample visuals in this chapter and elsewhere in the book, notice how labels are used.

- Arrange labels neatly and straight in the background area of the visual.

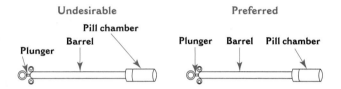

- Use right-hand justification of labels when the arrow comes from the right side of the label.

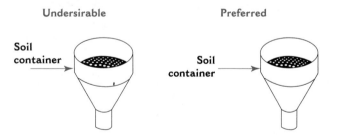

- Use left-hand justification for labels when the arrow comes from the left side of the label.

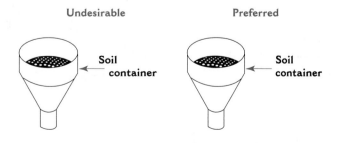

- Where there is adequate space, label the parts directly.

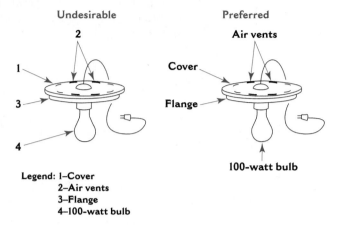

- If direct labeling results in a cluttered and crowded visual, use a key to identify the items.

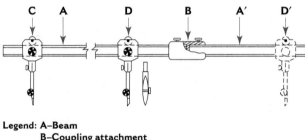

- If possible, center an arrow that comes from the top or bottom of the label.

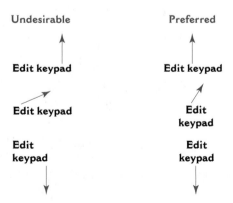

- Draw an arrow so that it does not touch the label.

- If possible, draw arrows so that they barely touch the items.

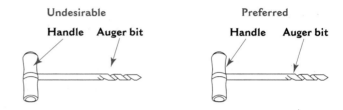

- In charts, graphs, and tables, label every column, row, axis, bar, and line. Use consistent terminology and symbols. Terms and symbols in a visual should be identical to those in the text, as shown in Figure 6.2b (color insert page C).

- If you borrow or adapt data or a visual from another source, give credit to the source below the visual. Review how we have identified the source for visuals used in this and other chapters in this textbook, for example, Figure 6.1, Figure 6.3, or the Web site in Figure 2.2 (see pages A and B in the first color insert).

Graphics software allows you to control the label. Spend a few minutes learning how to use the feature.

Visuals Should Be Integrated into the Document

integrated into the document

As we saw in Figure 6.2 (on page C in the first color insert), text wrapping integrates text and visuals. Other ways to integrate the information in visuals with the surrounding text are to (1) refer readers to the visuals, (2) use consistent nomenclature and symbols in visuals and text, (3) make the visual reflect the levels of organization in the related text, and (4) fully extract information from the visuals.

Refer Readers to the Visuals

If possible, introduce visuals before readers reach them. Such an introduction or reference to a visual written into the text of the report is known as a *call-out*. Place the call-out where you want readers to stop reading the text and to look at the visual, as we have done throughout this textbook. Among the options you have for pointing to a visual are

Figure 1 shows . . .
. . . as shown in Figure 1.
. . . (see Figure 1) . . .
Table 1 shows . . .
. . . as shown in Table 1.
. . . (see Table 1) . . .

If the visual is not near the call-out, include its location in the call-out, for example:

Recommended storage tanks (see Figure 12 on page 61) can be either buried or above ground.

An actual survey form sent to customers is found in Appendix B.

Make sure that everything about the visuals match:

- They are numbered or lettered consecutively.

- They appear in the proper order.

- They are referred to by call-outs.

- The visual referred to is the correct one.

- All this is reflected correctly in the list of visuals in the prefatory pages.

- Type fonts and sizes and border lines have been used consistently.

Maintain Consistency Between Text and Visuals

Do not call an antenna an *antenna* in the text and label it an *air terminal* on the visual. Such inconsistent terminology can easily confuse readers. Abbreviations in visuals should also follow the same style used in the text. Use the same standard symbols in text and in visuals.

Make the Visual Reflect the Organization of the Text

When a visual illustrates a hierarchically arranged concept in the text, make the levels distinctive in the visual through the labeling, as in Figure 6.6.

Discuss the Significance or Meaning of the Data in the Visual

Do not assume that a visual is clearly understandable in and of itself; therefore, do not include one unless you discuss it in the text. Point out the significance of the data or direct the reader's attention to particular relationships among the data presented in the visual. For instance, the discussion accompanying the bar graph in Figure 6.7 targets the time of day tornadoes frequently hit Alabama (see page 142):

Tornadoes occur with greater frequency during the late-afternoon to late-evening hours, according to National Weather Service records. In Alabama, five o'clock in the afternoon is the time of the maximum tornado incidence.

FIGURE 6.6

The labels on the preferred graphic cue the reader to the hierarchical arrangement of information. The highest level is the title of the graphic in oversized uppercase letters. The next highest level is the names of the main parts (EMISSION SECTION, FOCUSING SECTION, DEFLECTING SECTION, and ACCELERATING SECTION) in normal uppercase letters. The third level is the names of the subparts of the main sections in mixed uppercase and lowercase letters (Control Grid, Accelerating Grid, Focusing Grid, Deflecting Electrodes, and Screen). The lowest level is the names of the elements of the subparts in lowercase letters (the cathode and heaters are elements of the Control Grid). Type size and capitalization are only two methods of using labels to indicate hierarchy. Word-processing programs offer a wide range of type sizes and colors and type styles such as bold and italic.

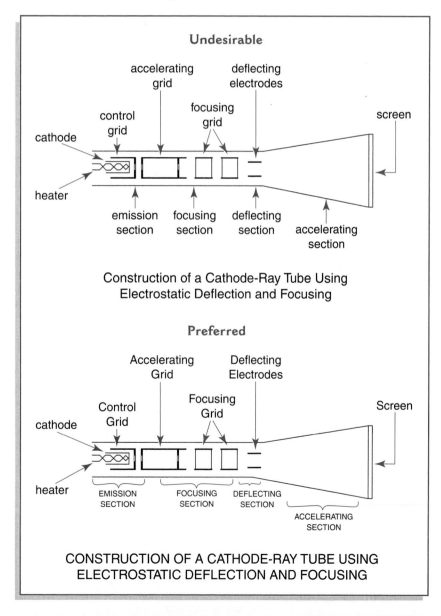

FIGURE 6.7

The writer makes sure the reader understands that tornadoes hit Alabama most frequently about 5:00 p.m.

Source: Permission granted by the Alabama Cooperative Extension System to use publication as an example. Information may be out of date.

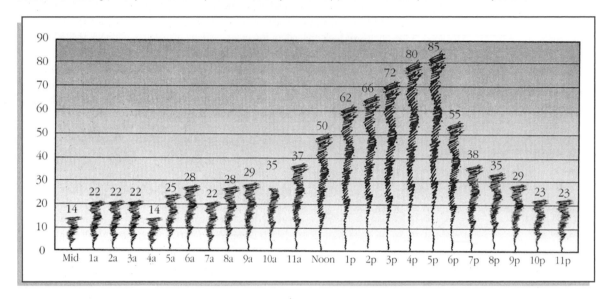

Providing both a bar graph and a description helps merge the information in the minds of readers and helps state your interpretation of the data explicitly. (Figure 6.7 and Figure 6.3 are found in the same brochure, *Tornado Safety in Alabama*. Notice the consistent format between bar graphs that helps the reader see the patterns.)

When you edit your manuscript, be sure you have not placed visuals amid unrelated text, you have left no apparent contradictions between visuals and the text, and the data in the visuals is easily understood or interpreted.

Visuals Should Be Easy to Understand

easy to understand

Visuals present abstract concepts visually and concisely. They concentrate into a relatively small space information that would otherwise require a great deal of text. However, because they are so succinct, they can be difficult to understand if they are not easy to read. Careful attention to captions and labels and to explaining the significance of the information helps make visuals almost self-explanatory. Here are four more tips for making visuals easy to read.

1. **Use digital images whenever possible.** Digital cameras provide images that are ready to insert into a document. Scanners convert images into digital form to allow you to copy existing artwork, including pho-

tographs, and incorporate them into your document. (Figure 7.1—see page E in the first color insert—was taken with a digital camera.)

You can easily copy an image off a Web site or from another electronic source. In fact, all the figures in this textbook that show Web sites were inserted into the textbook in digital form. Make sure you acknowledge your source. (See Chapter 21, "Documenting Sources," and review how we acknowledge our sources.)

If you must use an original hard copy of an image, make sure it is a sharp, clean image that will reproduce well. Images that are too dark, too light, or blurred will reproduce poorly and will be virtually useless. As long as the printer is working well, visuals that you create on a computer will probably reproduce well. If you reduce the size of a visual, make sure that labeling and any text or important features on the visual remain legible.

2. **Use specialized visuals and language only if readers can understand them.** A circuit diagram or other schematic drawing or a scatter diagram or logarithmic chart is not much good to readers who cannot read it. In such a case, choose another form of representation such as a block diagram, a photograph or drawing, or a bar chart or line graph that readers can interpret.

3. **When appropriate, accompany visuals with legends.** A legend adds to the information presented and makes the visual more understandable. Legends identify the color, shading, or line style used with the topic represented. For example, the legend identifies what each pattern represents in the pie chart below and the map in Figure 6.2b (color page C):

■ IRAs   ⊞ Cash
□ Savings   ▨ Retirement

4. **As a final check, ask another person whether he or she can understand the visual.** It helps to have another person look over the visuals, especially if that person's experience matches your reader's. You may want to conduct a usability test (see Chapter 17). Watch how representatives of the audience use the document. You may need to make adjustments.

Visuals Should Be Relatively Easy and Inexpensive to Prepare

easy to prepare

Not only do visuals provide information and illustrate relationships, they also improve the appearance of a page. Readers are quicker to review a document that does not overwhelm them with text. But readers also do not want visuals to detract from the text by appearing to clutter the page. Use visuals when they meet the identified purpose and provide the information needed.

Use Color Carefully

Review the guidelines in Chapter 5 on color combinations. Be aware that color affects how the reader interprets the information. Shading and patterns that fill in bars and other shapes you draw increase the attractiveness and readability of charts over those drawn in outline form. Using shading from black to various tones of gray or using different patterns of diagonal lines, cross-hatching, stippling, and other simple designs may be as effective as using color.

Visuals Should Be Appropriate for the Material and Purpose

appropriate for information and purpose

Determine what information you want to convey visually so you can choose the type of visual that best shows what you want to convey. Before you begin a visual, ask yourself such questions as

What is the purpose of this visual?
What am I trying to show in this visual?
What do I want the reader to see in this visual?
What should the reader understand after reading this visual?

Choose the visuals that best display the facts for the intended audience, and place them where they are most accessible, within the time and budget allowed.

Ethics of Visuals

Creating visuals requires more than following the suggested guidelines. You want to portray the information accurately and fairly to readers. Readers expect to read a visual quickly and interpret the information easily. Think about how you read visuals found in *USA Today* or on the Environmental Protection Agency Web site (Figures 2.2a and 2.2b on color insert page A and Figure 6.2 on color insert page C). If you are like most readers, you look at the relationship but do not read the scale or exact points on the graph unless you need exact numbers. Instead, you are looking for trends or getting an impression of the information the writer wants to convey. You probably trust the writer to present the information accurately.

Discuss these scenarios with class members.

Consider the following scenarios adapted from a survey of professional communicators by Sam Dragga.[2] We leave these descriptions for you to discuss in class; we encourage you to read the results of Dragga's survey.

- You want to show that your company encourages the disabled to apply for positions and provides an environment that accommodates the needs of the disabled. You want to show this on the company Web site; however, you do not have any employees who use a wheelchair. You ask one of the employees to sit in a wheelchair so you can get a photograph. Is this ethical? What might you do instead of photographing an employee who is not disabled to visually illustrate the company's accommodative environment?

- You have been asked to write a letter of recommendation for a colleague applying for promotion. To call attention to his good qualities, you list them in a bulleted list. You write a paragraph describing his weaker qualities. Is this ethical? If you list both sets of qualities either in a bulleted list or in paragraphs, will this take care of any ethical issues?

- In the annual report for the nonprofit organization you work for, you want to call attention to the activities of the organization. You use red to call attention to the money spent on activities, even though it is less than that spent on administrative costs (which you color in green because cool colors make things look smaller). Is this ethical? Do you think the readers will notice? What other color combinations might work better?

Did everyone agree?

As you see from these scenarios and the class discussion, you have decisions to make as a writer and reader. As a writer, you decide the best way to present the information so that it is a fair representation. As a reader, you must evaluate the visual carefully. The suggestions we give in the next two sections build on the discussion earlier in this chapter that visuals should be

- perceptible

- accessible

- clearly labeled

- integrated into the document

- easy to understand

- relatively easy and inexpensive to prepare

- appropriate for the material and purpose

---

[2]Sam Dragga, "'Is This Ethical?' A Survey of Opinion on Principles and Practices of Document Design," *Technical Communication* 43 (1996): 255–65.

Writer's Responsibilities

The writers Dragga surveyed believe that adjusting the design of the document to get more information on a page creates a problem only if the reader cannot read the information. However, these same writers think that distorting graphs and using inappropriate photographs and other pictorial representations is not acceptable workplace communication.[3] We have six suggestions to help you create visuals that present your information ethically:

- Do not use a scale that distorts the data.

- Do not distort the size using three dimensions or different thicknesses of pie segments or bars.

- Do not use different colors, shades of black and white, or fill patterns to distort the data. (Figure 6.8).

FIGURE 6.8
The third-quarter bar appears heavier and larger than the other bars. Readers might mistakenly see the third quarter as the most successful quarter, when the first quarter actually yielded more revenues.

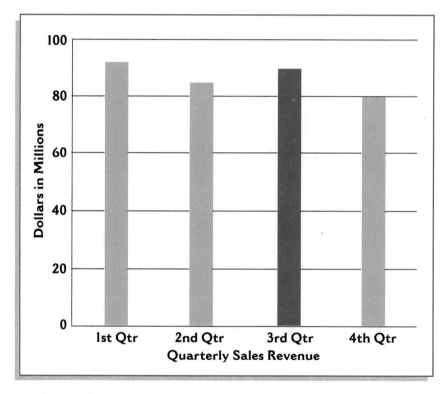

---

[3]Dragga 262.

- Do not go against commonly accepted practice to intentionally mislead the reader. For example, keep the years along the *x*-axis in chronological order (Figure 6.9) or use a drawing if a photograph cannot be taken of the actual situation.

- Do not clutter the visual with unnecessary information that will interfere with interpretation of the information.

- Do not combine types of visuals that interfere with interpretation of the information.

The American Psychological Association's *Displaying Your Findings: A Practical Guide for Creating Figures, Posters, and Presentations* is one of many resources with guidelines for working with visuals. Consult resources in your field if you will be presenting a lot of data in visual format to colleagues and clients.

FIGURE 6.9

The line graph climbs from left to right when the scale of widgets is shown in reverse chronological order. Will the reader see that sales have actually declined over the four-year period?

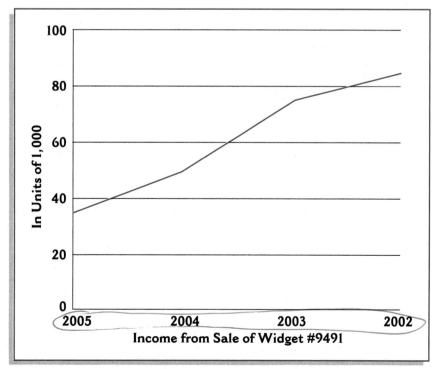

Reader's Responsibilities

How closely readers evaluate a visual depends on their purpose. The reader who intends to include the visual's information in a report to a client or to a colleague must confirm that the information is presented accurately. In revising your visuals, put yourself in the place of readers.

- Look at the scale to verify that the data is represented accurately.

- Evaluate three-dimensional pie segments or bars graphs carefully. If possible and appropriate, convert the visual to two dimensions.

- Confirm that the colors, shades of black and white, or patterns of fill do not interfere with evaluation of the data.

- Use commonly accepted formats. For example, keep the years along the x-axis in chronological order or use a drawing if a photograph cannot be taken of an actual situation.

- Make sure there is no unnecessary information that will interfere with interpretation of the information.

- Confirm and evaluate the source of the visual.

In Chapter 7, we provide guidelines and examples of effective, accurate, and ethically sound visuals. Use the Planning and Revising Checklist for visuals at the end of Chapter 7 to guide you through developing visuals for the documents you write.

Suggestions for Applying Your Knowledge

Collaborative Activities

1. Select a visual from a newspaper such as *USA Today*, a weekly magazine such as *Time*, or a Web site and bring both the visual and the accompanying article, if there is one, to class with enough copies for everyone to review it. First, have everyone look briefly at the visual and write two to three sentences stating the conclusion they can make about the topic of the visual. Share the conclusions.

   Next, evaluate the effectiveness of the visual—particularly if classmates disagreed about the information the visual was showing. Ask the following questions: Is the information perceptible? Accessible? Clearly labeled? Integrated into the article or self-contained? Easy to understand? Relatively easy and inexpensive to prepare? Appropriate for the material and purpose?

2. Locate a visual that you think misleads the reader. If you review a newspaper or a weekly magazine for a couple of weeks, you will probably find a visual you can discuss. Show the visual to others in your

class, but do not comment on what you consider questionable tactics by the developer of the visual. After the class has discussed the visual for a while, call attention to the problem you see if no one else has noticed it. Should this be considered a problem if most of the class does or does not notice the biased presentation?

Individual Activity

In a short memo, import a visual from the Web and write a two- to three-paragraph analysis of the visual. Be sure to cite the source of the visual. (Copying a visual from the Web is easy. Simply put the cursor on top of the visual and use the right mouse button on a PC or hold the mouse down on a Macintosh. Follow the menu prompts to save the visual. You can then open a word-processing document and insert the file with the visual.)

Multicultural Activity

Examine a set of instructions that provides the information in several languages. How are the visuals used? Do they supplement the set of instructions or are they the focus of the instructions? Can the task be performed without reading the instructions? Why types of visuals are used? For example, are the visuals icons, line drawings, photographs, or some other form? How is color used in the document? Is each language area designed the same? Discuss your findings in small groups.

CHAPTER **7**

Visuals and Document Design II

I n Chapter 6, we discussed the general factors that contribute to the quality of visuals. In this chapter, we tell you how to use specific types of visuals to explain objects and processes and to report totals, trends, and relationships. Throughout, we also discuss some of the ways that graphics software and high-quality printers have enhanced the production of visuals. You can accomplish the techniques we discuss in this chapter with any of the currently available office suites (integrated software packages that provide word-processing, spreadsheet, presentation, database capabilities, and Web development). Although you may need more specialized software for your workplace communication activities, the basic guidelines that follow will provide solid support for your communication activities.

Visuals contribute to the understanding of world-ready communication.

It is worth repeating our caution from Chapter 6:

Incorporate visuals in your document only when the reader needs the visuals, when the purpose of the document calls for a visual, and when the information is best conveyed in a visual.

Just as you select your words carefully to convey the information you want your reader or listener to gather from the text, you also must select the appropriate visual to convey the information. For example, will a photograph or a drawing better show the front panel on an oscilloscope? Or is the increase in the number of golfers using public courses best represented as a line graph or a bar graph? Or are the instructions for holding a tennis racquet best shown only as drawings with little or no text? You must decide which visual representation will best represent the information you want the reader and listener to have.

Review Chapters 5 and 6 as you combine text and visuals in your communication.

In this chapter, we describe the ease with which you can incorporate visuals into your communication activities using computer-generated visuals. We then describe different types of visuals you can use and suggest when you might select a particular visual. We have grouped the visuals as those that best explain objects, processes, and trends.

Computer-Generated Visuals

You no longer have an excuse for not including visuals in your communication when one is needed. Graphics software and hardware range from fairly simple and inexpensive drawing programs, color ink-jet printers, and laser printers to sophisticated and expensive computer-aided design (CAD) systems and large visual plotters. Most importantly, once a visual is created, you can make changes in a fraction of the time required with pencil, paper, and drafting tools. Visuals can be created, stored, retrieved, and edited on computers just as text is.

Using a graphics program is fairly simple and easy to learn. You create a visual on the computer screen and save it in a file (frequently with a file extension such as .jpg, .gif, or .bmp). You then insert the visual electronically into your text file. Or you create the visual within the program you are using (for example, WordPerfect, Word, Lotus, or Excel). The visual appears at the point where your cursor is in the document. Not only can you create graphs or line drawings, you can easily copy a visual from a Web site and paste it into your document. You can scan visuals or use a digital camera for photographs. The scanner or camera creates a digital image captured in a file that may easily be inserted into your document. Audio and video clips may also be incorporated into your communication.

Graphics programs and good-quality printers provide an impressive array of visuals and special effects that can make documents look like they are professionally typeset.

Drawing and paint programs enable you to use lines of various widths and styles and fill with color to create images. These programs also make it easy to create precise geometric shapes and manipulate them to make them larger, smaller, or skewed.

Chart and graph programs allow you to make a wide variety of charts and graphs, including bar, line, pie, and organizational. To create charts and graphs with most of these programs, you enter data on a spreadsheet and convert the spreadsheet to the desired chart or graph form. Programs have split-screen features that let you see the chart or graph and enter data at the same time. You can change the type of graph—for example, from a line graph to a bar graph—with a few keystrokes; you need not reenter the data.

Most graphics programs allow you to create visuals to import into a document or print or record on several types of output devices (black-and-white printers, color printers, and film recorders). Presentation software such as Microsoft PowerPoint or Lotus Freelance simplify creating slides for projection through an LCD projector.

In Chapter 12, we provide guidelines for giving professional oral presentations using a computer-generated slideshow.

Use clip-art images only when they are needed.

Clip-art programs allow you to reproduce ready-made electronic images. These programs contain from dozens to hundreds of clip-art files. Many of these programs are organized into thematic categories, such as business, leisure (such as sailing, basketball, or hiking), government, and education, which makes it easy to select images related to specific topics or themes.

Visuals from Web sites can be quickly and easily copied off the Web and incorporated into a document. However, before you use a visual from the Web, you should ask permission from the site manager. You must ask permission if you plan to use the visual in a document intended for publication. In any case, you must acknowledge your source. Note how we acknowledge the sources for figures used throughout this textbook.

Optical scanning programs and hardware copy line artwork and photographs, including video images, and format them for use in your own computer files. The copied artwork is actually a bit-map image (a series of black-and-white or color squares or dots) that can be displayed on a computer screen or printed. Many scanning software packages and desktop publishing systems allow the scanned images to be modified fairly easily, although editing images can be tedious.

Although word-processing software lets you combine text and visuals, **desktop publishing software** (Adobe PageMaker, for example) and **multimedia software** (Macromedia Studio, for example) give you more flexibility and are easier to use with larger documents. You can transfer word-processing and visual files into formatted pages, merging text and images, similar to those of newspapers and magazines. You can add animation and other dynamic features for Web-based documents. The visuals used in this textbook, including examples from other sources, were created with software commonly found in office-related software suites.

Web page design software (such as Microsoft FrontPage and Macromedia Studio) prepares files in *html* (hypertext markup language) for loading on to the Web. Effective Web sites blend text and visuals to present information to the readers.

These programs allow you to enlarge or reduce the size of the visual, to add special touches such as variations of shades and shadows and reverse type (white images on a black background), to fill in shapes with selected patterns or color, and even to tilt and rotate images. They also allow you to reproduce visuals or touch them up. The programs have similar features and follow many of the same keystroke conventions. If you learn one program, you can quickly learn another. Explore the options in the programs—just save different versions of your work so you can return to an earlier version if you do not like the changes you make.

You may want to create the text and visuals in separate files to make each file easier to manage. You will find it easier to edit text and visuals separately. You can move them together after the text and visuals are close to final form. For Web pages, the visuals and visual design are so closely related that you will want to create them together.

Using Visuals to Explain Objects

If you have ever tried to visualize something that you have never seen before or something that you cannot easily recall, you know the value of photographs and drawings. When you want readers to understand an object, pictorials (photographs and drawings) are the most exact method of communication. Although compressed in size and usually one-dimensional, pictorials closely resemble the objects they refer to and thus illustrate physical appearance and spatial relationships better than do words.

The following information on photographs and drawings should help you choose and prepare the appropriate pictorials for showing objects.

Photographs and Videos

Photographs and videos present the exact appearance of actual objects. Realism is their greatest asset. They are often essential in showing the appearance of newly created objects, objects readers have never seen before, objects at the end of a particular stage of development, and worn or damaged objects. Photographs are also useful in comparing sizes of objects by scaling them against more familiar objects, such as a hand or coin, or an actual scale such as a ruler.

Photographs, such as the one in Figure 7.1 (see page E in the first color insert), are indispensable in showing the exact appearance, in validating the existence or the condition of an object, and in presenting its actual appearance when it or a model is not available for direct observation. Drawings would not be suitable in these instances because they would not provide realistic appearances and would be time-consuming to prepare.

Whether you or somebody else takes the photograph or video, you need to be able to distinguish effective from ineffective photographs and videos. The most common problems are

- irrelevant material in the background

- overexposure of light objects and underexposure of dark objects

- lack of contrast between the main subjects and the background

- unintentionally out-of-focus areas or subjects

- poor camera angles

You can incorporate video clips into Web site pages and other online documents relatively easily—with the proper software.

You will use a digital camera or a scanner to import a copy of a photograph into your document. If necessary, you can *crop* (trim to eliminate unnecessary peripheral details), size, and enhance a photograph quickly and easily in most software with graphics capability.

Drawings

Like photographs, drawings show what objects look like. And though they are less realistic than photographs, they can better convey certain kinds of information. For example, they can depict objects (such as the International Space Station, as in Figure 7.2, on page F in the first color insert) or provide specific dimensions (such as showing the floor space needed for a wheelchair, as in Figure 7.3).

Because drawings are further removed from reality than are photographs, they allow much greater flexibility than do photographs and can be used to illustrate specific aspects of an object. As you examine Figures 7.4 through 7.8, you will see that this selectivity enables you to concentrate the reader's attention on particular features. Computer-aided design programs such as AutoCAD create professional-level drawings. The graphics components of office software such WordPerfect, Word, Excel, Lotus, or PowerPoint have enough features to create basic drawings.

The most commonly used views are external, cutaway, sectional, exploded, and phantom.

External Views

External views, like photographs, show the outside of an object to give readers an idea of its appearance. The outline drawing is a special kind of external view that shows, as the name suggests, an object in outline form. The clear, uncluttered appearance of outline drawings avoids the realistic clutter

FIGURE 7.3

The drawing gives a topdown view of the wheelchair and the amount of room it needs. No other view or photograph can so clearly show the wheelchair and the space needed.

Source: Equal Employment Opportunity Commission and the U.S. Department of Justice. (1992). *Americans with Disabilities Act handbook.* EEOC-BK-19. (App. C, 16). Washington, DC: U.S. Government Printing Office.

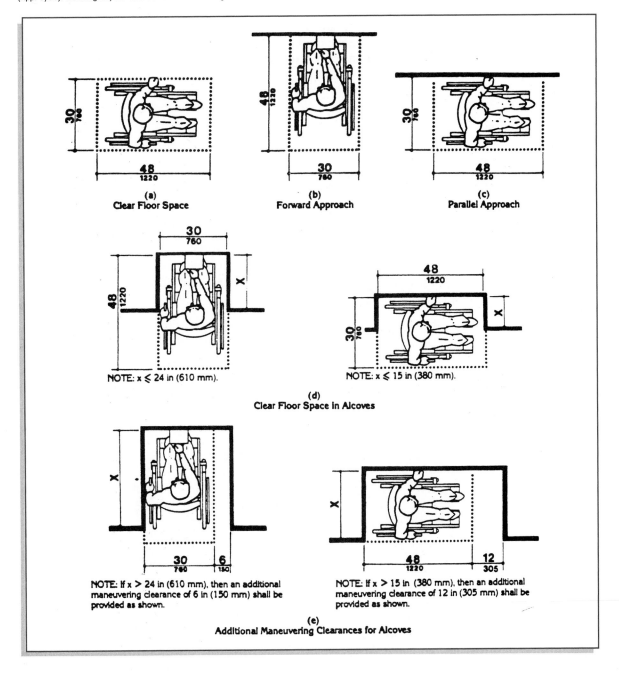

of photographs and makes them useful for selecting and emphasizing significant features. The outline drawing in Figure 7.4 shows different ways in which helicopters can lift heavy loads by various combinations of tether cables, spreader bars, and bridle cables. The drawing eliminates irrelevant material that would have been included in a photograph and allows the three different lifting methods to be depicted in the same illustration for easy comparison, which would be difficult to achieve in a photograph.

Photographs and external views do not show the inside parts of objects, how parts fit together, or the transportation of material through an object or device. However, hidden lines, which may be used with any kind of view, show features that ordinarily cannot be seen. The unseen features are repre-

FIGURE 7.4

Line drawings present views that are difficult, if not impossible, to show in photographs. Notice the legend at the top of the drawing that provides additional information.

Source: NASA. (1991, December). Calculating dynamics of helicopters and slung loads. *NASA Tech Briefs, PB91-924912, 970.*

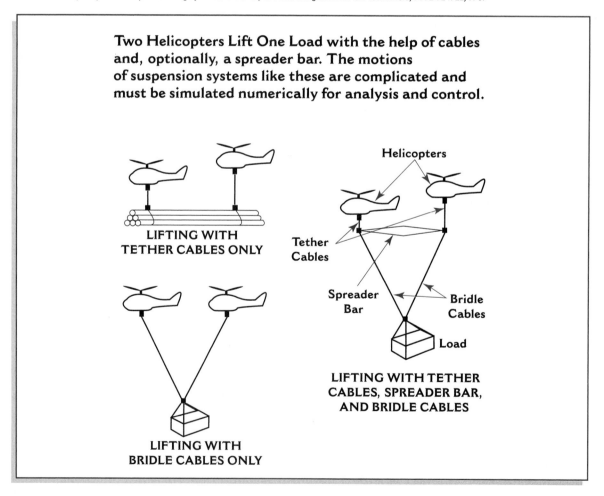

Two Helicopters Lift One Load with the help of cables and, optionally, a spreader bar. The motions of suspension systems like these are complicated and must be simulated numerically for analysis and control.

Helicopters

LIFTING WITH
TETHER CABLES ONLY

Tether
Cables

Spreader
Bar

Bridle
Cables

Load

LIFTING WITH TETHER
CABLES, SPREADER BAR,
AND BRIDLE CABLES

LIFTING WITH
BRIDLE CABLES ONLY

sented by short dashes, as in Figure 7.5. Interior parts that cannot be photographed or shown well by hidden lines can be illustrated by cutaway, sectional, and exploded views. These views are useful when objects contain so much housing that readers see only the exterior.

Cutaway Views

Cutaway views, as the name implies, show an object as if some part of its exterior nearest the viewer had been cut away. They are used to show both

FIGURE 7.5

In cutaway views, a portion of the exterior of the object is removed to reveal internal parts. In this drawing, the cutaway shows the loading spring of the ammunition magazine for the M-14 A-1 military rifle. Note also the use of hidden lines and exploded view to reveal the base plate.

Source: Courtesy Betty L. Bradford.

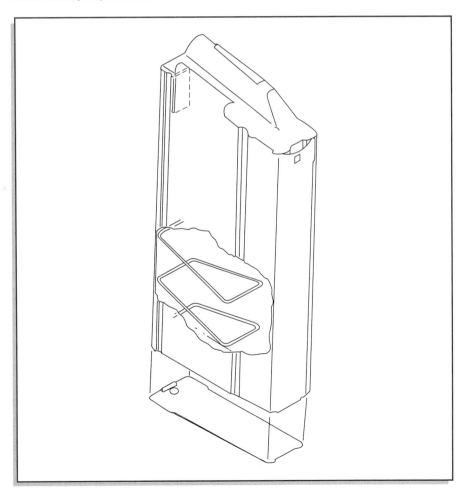

internal and external constructions in the same drawing. Figure 7.5 illustrates the use of hidden lines and a cutaway view to show unseen rear parts and interior parts of the ammunition magazine of an M-14 A-1 military rifle that would not be visible in an external view. Notice also the exploded view to show the bottom plate.

Sectional Views

Sectional views, as the name indicates, show an object as if some section of the object nearest the viewer had been removed. Similar to cutaway views, sectional views allow readers to "see" through the exterior cover almost as if they have X-ray vision. Sectional views may be partial or full; that is, the sectional cut may be through just a portion of the object or may run completely through it. In Figure 7.6, the door and the covering for the wave guide channel of a microwave oven have been removed. A cross-sectional view, which runs completely through the object, shows an object as if it had been split down the middle and the half nearest the viewer removed. In Figure 7.7, diagonal lines indicate the cut lines where the exterior cover has been removed to display the interior parts, including the specially designed electrode holder.

FIGURE 7.6

In this partial sectional view, the microwave oven's door to the oven cavity and housing for the wave guide channel are removed to illustrate the movement of microwaves.

Source: University of Minnesota Extension Service.

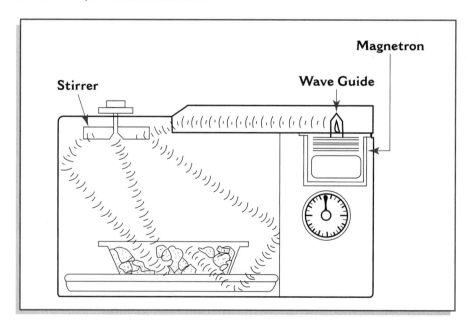

FIGURE 7.7

Diagonal lines in this sectional view represent where the external cover has been removed to reveal interior parts. Note the legend beneath the drawing that provides additional information.

Source: NASA. (1992, March). Jointed holder for welding electrode. *NASA Tech Briefs*, PB92-925903, 195.

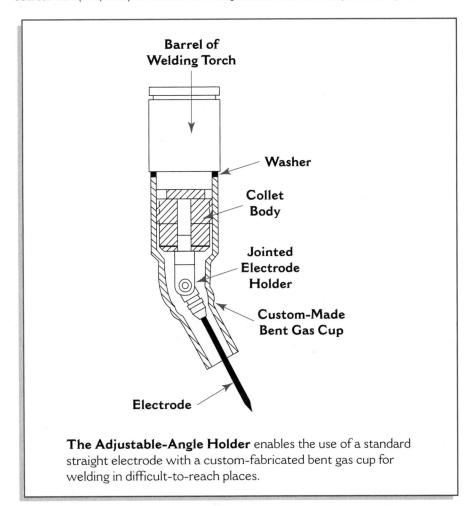

The Adjustable-Angle Holder enables the use of a standard straight electrode with a custom-fabricated bent gas cup for welding in difficult-to-reach places.

Exploded Views

Exploded views separate parts so readers can become familiar with the parts of an object or system or can see how the parts relate or fit together. They often are necessary in instructions to show readers how to assemble or disassemble complicated parts. The axis lines in Figure 7.5 (between the base plate and the main housing) and Figure 7.8 show how the parts are aligned.

FIGURE 7.8

Exploded views show parts of objects in a disassembled, but aligned, state. If necessary, axis lines illustrate how the components fit together.

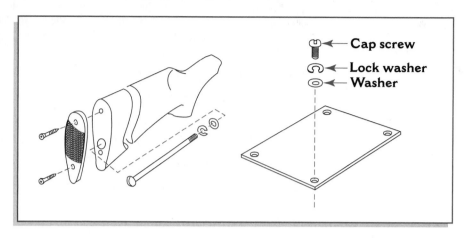

FIGURE 7.9

Phantom views show hypothetical or alternative images. The colored dashed lines denote the changing positions of the ratchet handle.

Source: Department of the Army. (1991, December). Preparation of freight for airlift transportation. Technical Manual TM 38-236. Washington, DC: U.S. Government Printing Office.

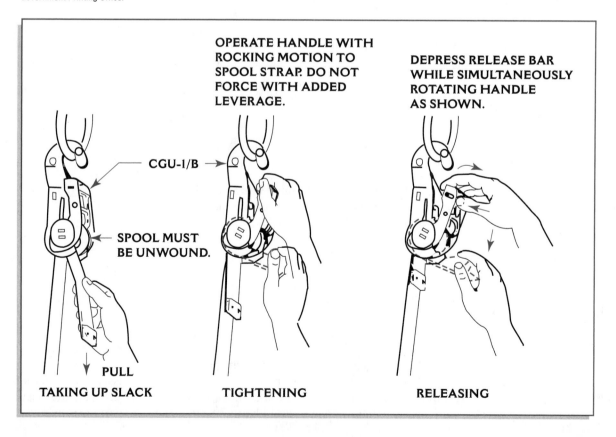

Phantom Views

Phantom views suggest the way objects would look in alternative positions. The drawing of the adjustable beam compass (page 138) illustrates many of the drawing techniques we've been discussing. Hidden lines indicate the existence of the beam inside the center pin and writing head. Break lines cut the beam in two to shorten the view. A partial sectional view shows the inside of the coupling device, indicating that the base beam and the extension beam are separated by a partition. A phantom view indicates where the writing head would be on the extension beam. In Figure 7.9, the colored dashed lines show the changing positions of the ratchet handle in tightening and releasing the cargo tie-down strap.

Using Visuals to Explain Processes and Show Relationships

You may find after you have explained a relationship verbally that you would like to show your reader the relationship visually. The visual may take the form of one of the flowcharts described below, or it may be a less formal drawing. The graphics features of your software give you unlimited options. The only caution we offer is to focus on getting the text in place before you start creating the visual. Often the visual will take more time to create than you have allotted for the project. On the other hand, occasions may arise in which, if you "see" the relationship, you can explain it better. We have emphasized throughout this book that your writing must be easy to understand. The same holds true for flowcharts: Draw them clearly, for they have a story to tell.

When you must describe a process, flowcharts can help readers visualize steps and activities that might otherwise take paragraphs of prose to explain and still be difficult to comprehend. Flowcharts may be prepared in different ways, ranging from simple block diagrams to pictorial flowcharts to specialized schematic diagrams. They may be single-level or multilevel. Software is available especially for drawing flowcharts, or you can use the draw feature of any of the software office suites to create a simple flowchart.

Most flowcharts are designed to be read from left to right and, if more space is needed, from first row to second row to third. A flowchart that illustrates a cyclical process might be best arranged as a circle, designed to be read clockwise. The circular flowchart in Figure 7.10 compares the gradual and complete metamorphic life cycles of insects.

Block Diagrams

The block diagram is the simplest of flowcharts. Simple block diagrams and their modifications are easy to draw, easy to read, and easy to understand. As

FIGURE 7.10

Circular pictorial flowcharts are appropriate to illustrate cyclical processes.

Source: Slack, K. V. (1982). Stream biology. In P. E. Greeson (Ed.), *Biota and biological principles of the aquatic environment.* Alexandria, VA: U.S. Geological Survey.

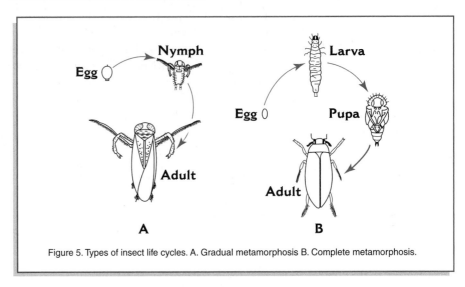

Figure 5. Types of insect life cycles. A. Gradual metamorphosis B. Complete metamorphosis.

shown in Figure 7.11, a block diagram represents the main stages of a process by means of labeled blocks connected by arrows. The arrows indicate the direction of the activity flow. Almost any simple geometric shape can be used as long as the shape is consistent.

Decision Trees

The decision tree (Figure 7.12) provides a concise description of the Green Community.

A decision tree is sometimes called a yes-no chart or an algorithmic chart. Figure 7.12 (see page F in the first color insert) shows a decision tree that uses the block and arrow-line features of block diagrams to assist readers in making decisions at specific points during a procedure.

Specialized shapes are used in certain kinds of flowcharts to indicate specific kinds of actions, such as the standard computer template symbols for computer documentation in Figure 7.13. Remember, though, the same symbol must be used consistently from one diagram to another. If start and end of a procedure are represented by ovals in one diagram, they should be ovals in the next. The shapes are part of the template found in software for creating flowcharts.

Constructing a Block Diagram or Decision Tree

You should know how to make block diagrams and decision trees because they are relatively easy to make and to read. Here is the way to make them using the graphics feature of a software package:

FIGURE 7.11

Block diagrams, the simplest of flowcharts, indicate the major steps of processes. The arrows represent the direction of activity in the process.

Source: Centers for Disease Control and Prevention. (2002). *Physical activity evaluation handbook*. Atlanta: U.S. Department of Health and Human Services. Retrieved October 12, 2003, from http://www.cdc.gov/nccdphp/dnpa/physical/handbook/pdf/handbook.pdf

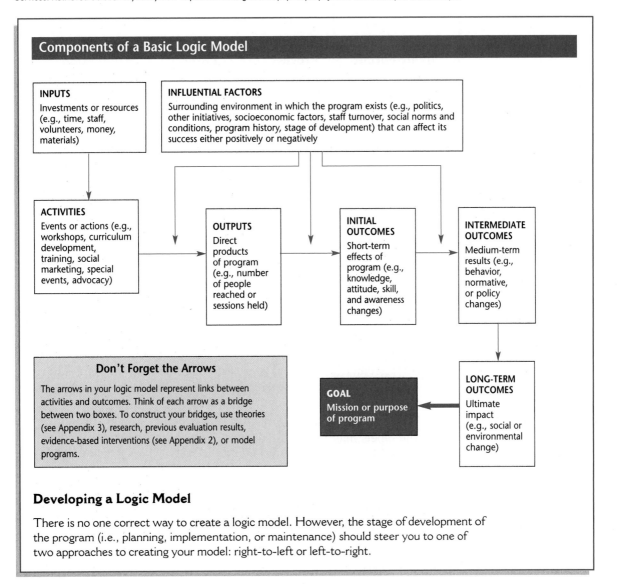

Developing a Logic Model

There is no one correct way to create a logic model. However, the stage of development of the program (i.e., planning, implementation, or maintenance) should steer you to one of two approaches to creating your model: right-to-left or left-to-right.

FIGURE 7.13
Some flowcharts use special shapes to indicate specific kinds of action. Illustrated here are several symbols used in computer documentation.

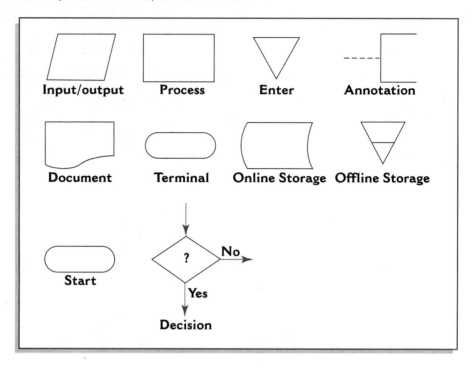

1. Draw geometric figures to represent stages in the process. Make each one large enough to contain the name of the stage it represents or other relevant information.

2. Label each geometric figure with the name of the stage it represents. The labels may be centered in the geometric figure (Figure 7.13) or aligned flush left (Figure 7.11).

3. Connect the geometric figures by using the line feature provided in the software. Add arrows as needed on the ends to indicate the direction of the activity flow.

4. If desired, put a border around the flowchart and use a caption.

Pictorial Flowcharts

Some flowcharts use pictorials or schematic symbols to indicate activity at specific points in the process. Instead of labeled blocks, you may use drawings of components. Pictorial flowcharts, such as that illustrated in Figure 7.14, are interesting ways to provide concrete images as well as a broad visual overview of a process. Imagine how many words and sentences it would take to describe these processes without using visuals such as these.

FIGURE 2.2

(a) Examples of online reading paths for the Environmental Protection Agency Web site, www.epa.gov. See pages 43–44 for discussion of reading online information. The home page offers multiple access points for navigating the Web site: the left column identifies major areas of the Web site, Key Topics on the right links to specific EPA topics, and Special Features and Top Stories provide links to the most recent information.

Source: U.S. Environmental Protection Agency (2003, December 29). Retrieved December 29, 2003, from www.epa.gov

FIGURE 2.2

(b) The EPA's *Draft Report on the Environment 2003* was listed on the home page under Special Features when it was first issued. The links (called breadcrumbs) at the top of the page identify the path to the report: EPA Home > Environmental Indicators Initiative > Draft Report on the Environment.

Source: U.S. Environmental Protection Agency. EPA's *Draft Report on the Environment 2003* (2003, July 2). Retrieved December 29, 2003, from www.epa.gov/indicators/roe/index.htm

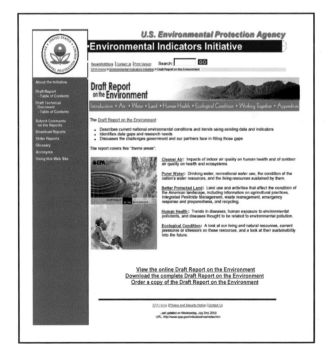

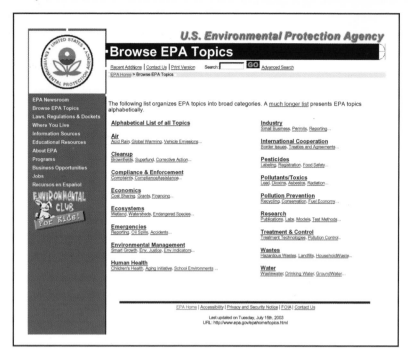

FIGURE 2.2

(c) The Browse EPA Topics page lists the major areas of information available on the EPA site.

Source: U.S. Environmental Protection Agency (2003, July 15). Retrieved December 29, 2003, from www.epa.gov/epahome/topics.html

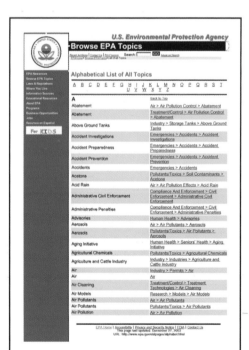

FIGURE 2.2

(d) The Alphabetical List of All Topics, reached by following the much longer list link on the Topics page, is updated frequently and takes readers directly to the selected topic.

Source: U.S. Environmental Protection Agency (2003, December 29). Retrieved December 29, 2003, from www.epa.gov/ebtpages/alphabet.html

FIGURE 6.2

The text and visual combine to describe the water quality of U.S. coastal waters. Some readers will find the visual easier to understand; others, the text. The text and the visuals support each other, and both provide information.

Source: U.S. Environmental Protection Agency (2003, December 29). Retrieved December 29, 2003, from www.epa.gov/indicators/roe/pdf/roeWater.pdf

(a)

(b)

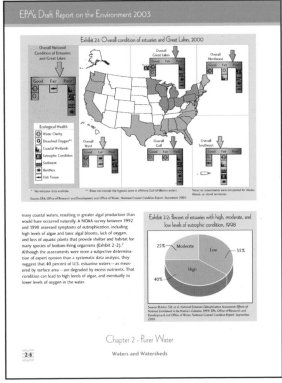

C

FIGURE 2.5

(a) Use the questions to evaluate a Web site, in this example, MEDLINEplus page.

Source: MEDLINEplus. U.S. National Library of Medicine and the National Institutes of Health. Department of Health and Human Services (2003, December 29). Retrieved December 29, 2003, from medlineplus.gov

Source
- Who developed the page?
- What are their credentials?
- Is there a way to verify the information on the page?
- Is the information free of advertisements or other indications that the writer is presenting a biased view?
- Does the author provide an objective viewpoint?

Site
- Is the information current and kept up-to-date?
- What are the dates on the page?

Navigation
- Is the site easy to move around in?
- Is there a site map?

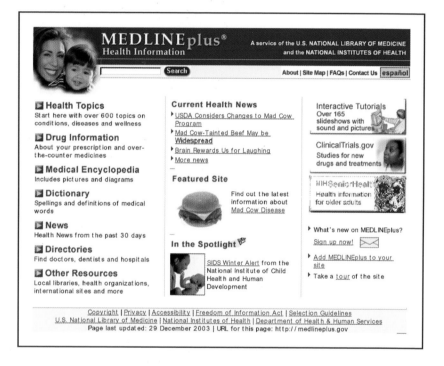

Content
- How was the information obtained?
- Are the sources for the information clearly listed so the reader can verify them in another source?
- Is the statistical data presented in easy to understand and accurate graphs and the method explained?
- Is there a print version of the information? Is the complete version on the Web?

FIGURE 2.5

(b) Compare the English and Spanish MEDLINEplus pages.

Source: MEDLINEplus. U.S. National Library of Medicine and the National Institutes of Health. Department of Health and Human Services (2003, December 29). Retrieved December 29, 2003, from www.nlm.nih.gov/medlineplus/Spanish/medlineplus.html

FIGURE 7.1

A color photograph best shows the effect of disease on this hedge. The photograph was taken with a digital camera and inserted electronically into the textbook. See pages 153–154 for a discussion of using photographs.

E

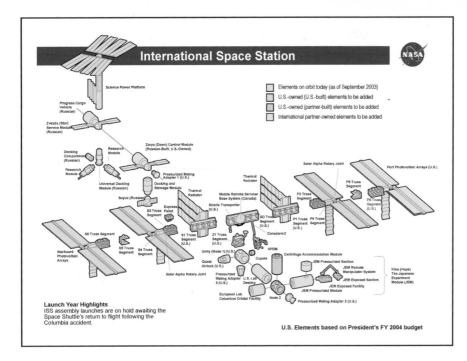

FIGURE 7.2

A drawing of the International Space Station showing the major parts of the space station. The color indicates the components by international partner.

Source: National Aeronautics and Space Administration. International Space Station (2003, October 18). Retrieved October 18, 2003, from http://www.hq.nasa.gov/osf/ISS_Core_Program.pdf

FIGURE 7.12

The decision tree maps out the activities of a Green Community. The different shapes and lines and the use of color on the Web site provide an overview of the activities and the relationship of each to the other.

Source: US Environmental Protection Agency. Green Communities (2003, October 12). Retrieved April 1, 2003, from http://www.epa.gov/greenkit/flow_chart.htm

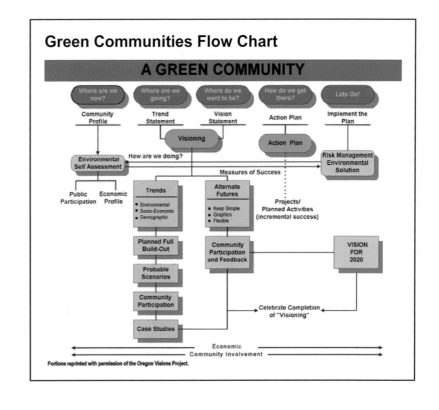

FIGURE 7.15

Map of Monthly-Average Streamflow for September 2003. At a glance, the reader can see the water conditions across the continental United States. Maps help readers associate information with an area. You can select one form of this map on the Web site and watch the information on the map change across the map.

Source: WaterWatch: Map of Monthly-Average Streamflow for the Month of the Year September 2003. (2003, September). Washington, D.C.: U.S. Department of Interior, U.S. Geological Survey. Retrieved October 17, 2003, from water.usgs.gov/waterwatch/

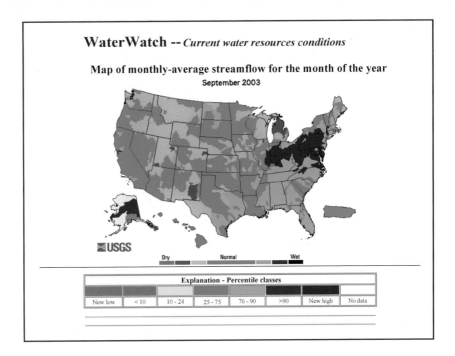

FIGURE 11.5

Amber Waves, a publication of the U.S. Department of Agriculture, is an example of a newsletter available online, in PDF format, and in hard copy. The Web page identifies the contents with a list of links on the left side, with headings, and with links to the information behind the short descriptions.

Source: *Amber Waves: The Economics of Food, Farming, Natural Resources, and Rural America.* Economic Research Service. U.S. Department of Agriculture (2003, November). Retrieved December 18, 2003, from www.ers.usda.gov/AmberWaves

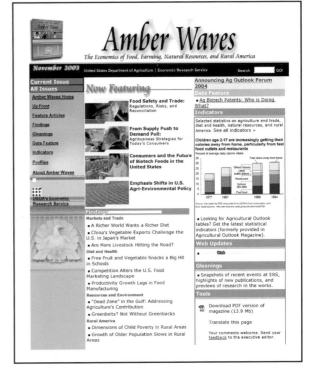

FIGURE 11.8

This trifold brochure provides parents with guidelines for using booster seats with their children. Each panel delivers useful information. (1) Front cover: Contains the title and an attractive cover to pull the reader into the brochure. *4 Steps for Kids* logo connects this brochure to the government campaign to increase child safety. This brochure focuses on the third step for children: the booster seat. (2) Back cover: Identifies the government organization that publishes the brochure. The *4 Steps for Kids* logo is repeated. (3) First panel: Seen when the brochure is opened, it answers the *why* for using booster seats. (4–6) Panels that show when the brochure is fully opened. The *4 Steps for Kids* logo is repeated with *3* highlighted to identify the children who should be using booster seats. The information on the panels is presented in clearly defined sections.

Source: National Highway Traffic Safety Administration (2003). *A Parent's Guide to Buying and Using Booster Seats.* Washington, D.C.: U.S. Department of Transportation. Retrieved September 27, 2003, from www.nhtsa.dot.gov/people/injury/childps/booster_seat/NewBoosterSeats/FINALCOR2.pdf

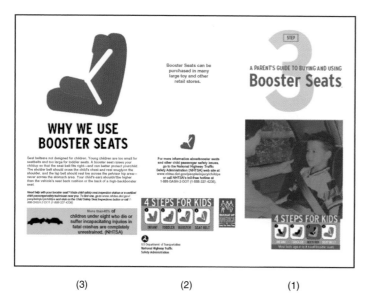

(3)   (2)   (1)

(4)   (5)   (6)

H

FIGURE 7.14
Pictorial flowcharts use drawings of components instead of geometric shapes or schematic symbols.

Source: Daellenback, C. B. (1981). Nickel-laterite pilot plant testing. In *Bureau of Mines Research, 1981.* Washington, DC: U.S. Department of the Interior.

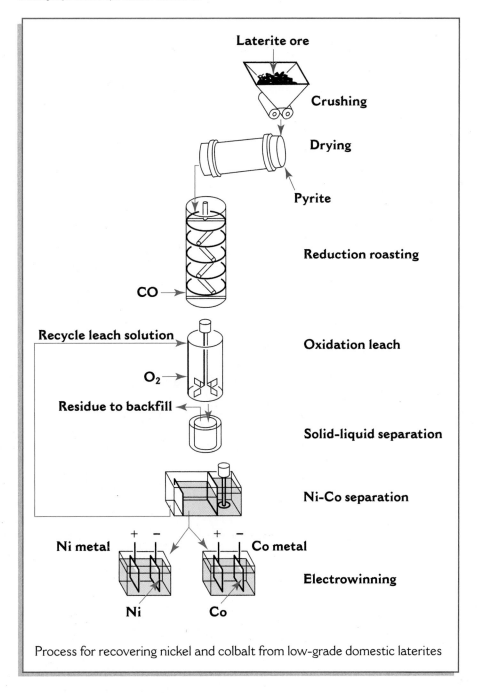

Process for recovering nickel and colbalt from low-grade domestic laterites

Maps

U.S. government Web sites are excellent resources for maps.

Maps provide helpful visuals for readers who are concerned with associating data with particular locations or regions. For example, the map of the United States in Figure 7.15 (see page G in the first color insert) clearly identifies the water conditions for regions of the country. The map in Figure 7.16a shows the percentage of adults across the United States diagnosed with diabetes. Figure 7.16b shows the same information in table format. Maps such as these can be downloaded from the Web and incorporated into a document. The maps shown in 7.15 and 7.16, typographical maps, and maps that show using animation are just a few of the informative maps you will find.

FIGURE 7.16

The map (a) shows adults with diagnosed diabetes. This information is also provided in table format (b). The Web-based map is found as a Web document (HTML) and as a PDF file. Much of the information found on government Web sites is provided in more than one form.

Source: Centers for Disease Control and Prevention. (2003). *Health risks in the United States: Behavioral risk factor surveillance system 2003.* Washington, DC: U.S. Department of Health and Human Services. Retrieved October 17, 2003 from http://www.cdc.gov/nccdphp/aag/aag_brfss.htm#4

(a)

Adults with Diagnosed Diabetes*

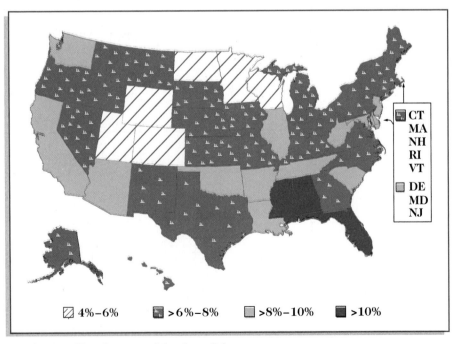

*People 18 or older who reported they have diabetes.

FIGURE 7.16
(continued)

(b)

Adults with Diagnosed Diabetes*

4%–6%	>6%–8%	>8%–10%	>10%
Colorado	Alaska	Arkansas	Alabama
Minnesota	Connecticut	Arizona	Florida
North Dakota	Georgia	California	Mississippi
Utah	Hawaii	Delaware	
Wisconsin	Idaho	Illinois	
Wyoming	Indiana	Louisiana	
	Iowa	Maryland	
	Kansas	New Jersey	
	Kentucky	Oklahoma	
	Maine	South Carolina	
	Massachusetts	Tennessee	
	Michigan	Washington	
	Missouri	West Virginia	
	Montana		
	Nebraska		
	Nevada		
	New Hampshire		
	New Mexico		
	New York		
	North Carolina		
	Ohio		
	Oregon		
	Pennsylvania		
	Rhode Island		
	South Dakota		
	Texas		
	Vermont		
	Virginia		

*People 18 or older who reported they have diabetes.

Using Visuals to Explain Trends and Relationships

We frequently rely on numerical data and statistical information in our problem solving and decision making. Consequently, tables, charts, and graphs showing such data and information are primary means of analyzing, interpreting, and presenting data. Each of the following sections begins with a model for the visual type. Keep in mind that models provide guidelines, but you must adjust the visual to meet the needs of the reader and the purpose of the document.

Graphics software allows you to change the features of the graphic easily. You can view the data as a bar graph, a line graph, a pie chart, or versions of these before deciding which to use in your document. If you follow these general guidelines and work through the options available on the software you are using, you should create an effective visual.

1. Enter the data carefully, including the data labels, in the order you want the information to appear. That is, if you want to show changes over several years, you must enter the years consecutively with the corresponding data. Once you have the data entered, you can view and modify the graph without having to adjust the data.

2. View the data in several forms (for example, as a bar graph and a line graph) and in horizontal and vertical orientation to see which is the best way to represent the data. Three-dimensional graphs are unsuitable for most information. The extra lines required to give the appearance of three dimensions interfere with the data.

3. Most software defaults to three-dimensional graphs, and many graphics packages create three-dimensional charts; change the default. Figure 7.17 (on pages 169 and 170) shows an example of a three-dimensional graph changed to two dimensions. Which do you think is easier to read?

4. The software adjusts the scale automatically. In most cases, you will not have to change the scale, but you can do so if necessary. Simply find the menu item for the adjustment.

Chapter 5 provides guidelines for coordinating colors.

5. Shade the bars or use color to better display the data. Use color if you have access to a color printer, if the information you are presenting will work best in color, and if color visuals will fit with the overall design of the document. We have selected several examples that use color effectively to display the information (see Figures 6.2, 7.1, 7.2, 7.12, and 7.15 [see the color insert pages C, E, F, and G). If you are using black-and-white imagery, select shades and patterns that will effectively set off the data.

6. Label each bar, line, or segment of the pie (what it represents) and each scale (quantities and units of measure). Again, if you entered the data correctly, the software will automatically place the information on the graph if you select the option to display the labels. Include a legend if necessary (for example, Figures 2.2, 7.2, 7.26, and 7.27).

7. Select a border that will help set off the visual from the text. Graphics software provides several options, including color. Our advice is to consider your audience and the purpose of the document but be conservative. You do not want to detract from the information or interfere with the reading.

8. Use a caption to identify the information in the visual.

Tables

Tables are word savers. They present simply and clearly large blocks of information without all the connecting devices needed in prose. They provide a lot of visibility to the main points presented, such as in Figure 7.18, which reports data on five crops. The column headings at the top of the table (Crop, District 1, District 2) project down the table. Only the captions in the first

FIGURE 7.17

Compare the data shown in the bar graphs. Most people find it easier to read the two-dimensional graph than the three-dimensional graph.

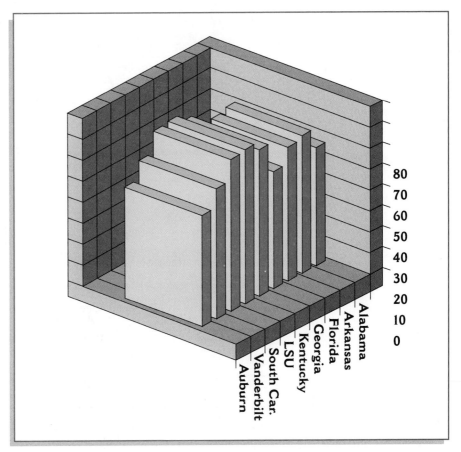

(*continued*)

FIGURE 7.17
(continued)

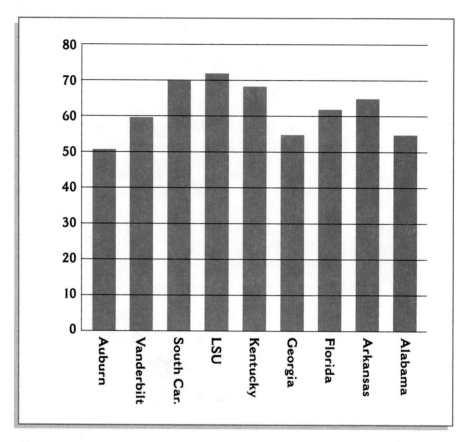

FIGURE 7.18
Tables display information arranged in columns and rows.

TABLE 1. DISTRICT CROP IRRIGATION REQUIREMENTS 10-YEAR AVERAGE		
Crop	**District 1**	**District 2**
Corn, grain	69	57
Corn, silage	13	12
Grain Sorghum	11	18
Alfalfa	5	7
Winter Wheat	2	6
Total	100	100

column project across the table. They may be used to present the data behind a graph (see Figures 7.16 and 7.23).

Tables are sometimes informal listings incorporated into the regular flow of the text, especially when the tabulation is simple and consists of only one or two columns. As such, they are part of the information within a paragraph—and generally part of the sentence structure—and are not set apart or identified by a number, a title, or a lined boundary.

More complicated, formal tables are often set apart from the text, either through the use of a lined border or by being placed on a separate page. When separated from the normal flow of the text, tables are usually given titles. If more than three or four tables are used in a report, they are usually numbered in the order of their appearance.

Tables have two primary uses:

1. Report totals for comparative purposes (as in Figures 7.18 and 7.19).

2. Serve as a ready reference, such as a timetable or schedule, or as instructions (as in Figure 7.20), and so on.

The table feature of your word-processing software makes creating tables easy. (The table feature is so easy that you can use the table structure to control the blocks of text and visuals on a page without showing the table lines.) Figure 7.21 illustrates how a table may be used to organize textual information—in this case, identifying the criteria for KidsWalk-to-School program.

The following general rules will help you set up tables properly:

- Whenever possible, orient the table so that it appears on the page in normal fashion, not turned sideways, forcing the reader to rotate the page to read it. Center the table between the left and right margins. White space around the table will help to set off the table for easier reading.

- Adjust each column or row as needed. The width of the row or column should be the same for like information. For example, in Figures 7.18 and 7.19, most of the data columns have the same width, but the first column is wider.

- Label each column and row to identify the data. If a column shows amounts, state the units in which the amounts are given, using standard symbols and abbreviations to save space. Center a column heading above the column.

- If columns are long, double-space after every fifth entry (Figure 7.19) or highlight every other row.

- Align the data, using expressed or implied decimal points as a guide. If the table is word- or phrase-based, align entries on an imaginary left margin in each column.

- If a particular column or row lacks data, use three periods or a dash in each space lacking data.

FIGURE 7.19

The reader can compare the literacy activities within each age group or across age groups using the information in this table. The tabular format, the white space between columns, the headings, and the explanation below the table contribute to the effectiveness of this table.

Source: Brown, H., Prisuta, R., Jacobs, B., & Campbell, A., (1996). *Literacy of older adults in America: Results from the National Adult Literacy Survey.* NCES97-576. Washington, DC: U.S. Department of Education, National Center for Education Statistics.

Table 1.6

Percentages of adults, by amount of help received with different literacy activities and by age

Activity/ age	n	WGT N (/1,000)	Row percentages			
			A lot	Some	A little	None
Filling out forms						
16 to 24	4,571	34,873	16 (0.9)	27 (1.0)	26 (1.1)	32 (1.1)
25 to 59	17,768	116,817	9 (0.3)	16 (0.4)	21 (0.5)	54 (0.6)
60 to 69	2,265	20,164	15 (0.9)	16 (1.0)	17 (0.9)	52 (1.6)
70 to 79	1,001	13,789	17 (1.2)	16 (1.4)	18 (1.3)	49 (1.6)
80 and older	440	5,413	32 (2.9)	12 (2.1)	18 (2.1)	37 (2.7)
Reading newspapers						
16 to 24	4,569	34,867	6 (0.5)	15 (0.9)	24 (0.8)	54 (1.1)
25 to 59	17,764	116,758	5 (0.2)	9 (0.3)	16 (0.4)	70 (0.5)
60 to 69	2,266	20,167	5 (0.6)	10 (0.9)	16 (1.0)	69 (1.4)
70 to 79	1,002	13,807	7 (0.9)	11 (1.3)	14 (1.0)	68 (1.5)
80 and older	440	5,413	14 (2.1)	11 (1.9)	12 (1.5)	62 (2.9)
Reading printed information						
16 to 24	4,561	34,780	11 (0.7)	22 (1.0)	28 (0.8)	39 (1.1)
25 to 59	17,745	116,681	7 (0.3)	14 (0.4)	23 (0.4)	56 (0.5)
60 to 69	2,262	20,155	9 (0.8)	15 (1.0)	21 (1.2)	55 (1.5)
70 to 79	1,000	13,785	13 (1.2)	13 (1.3)	19 (1.7)	55 (2.0)
80 and older	440	5,413	25 (2.3)	15 (2.3)	16 (2.1)	45 (3.0)
Writing letters						
16 to 24	4,560	34,821	4 (0.4)	8 (0.6)	14 (0.7)	73 (0.9)
25 to 59	17,744	116,683	4 (0.2)	7 (0.2)	11 (0.4)	77 (0.4)
60 to 69	2,262	20,132	6 (0.5)	6 (0.7)	9 (0.8)	79 (1.2)
70 to 79	999	13,756	7 (0.8)	7 (1.1)	7 (1.0)	79 (1.7)
80 and older	438	5,384	18 (2.1)	8 (1.9)	4 (0.9)	70 (2.8)
Using arithmetic						
16 to 24	4,570	34,856	5 (0.4)	9 (0.6)	14 (0.7)	73 (1.0)
25 to 59	17,765	116,796	4 (0.2)	6 (0.2)	8 (0.3)	83 (0.3)
60 to 69	2,266	20,167	5 (0.6)	6 (0.6)	7 (0.7)	82 (1.0)
70 to 79	1,002	13,807	8 (0.8)	7 (1.1)	6 (0.7)	78 (1.5)
80 and older	439	5,388	17 (2.1)	8 (1.3)	7 (1.1)	68 (1.9)

n = sample size; WGT N = population size estimate / 1,000. The sample sizes for subpopulations may not add up to the total sample sizes, due to missing data. Numbers in parentheses are standard errors. The true population values can be said to be within 2 standard errors of the sample estimates with 95% certainty.

Source: U.S. Department of Education, National Center for Education Statistics, National Adult Literacy Survey, 1992.

FIGURE 7.20

The table structure gives the cook an easy-to-read reference.

Oven Temperature	350°	350°	325°
Baking Time	25 min.	30 min.	40 min.
Pan to Use	round	13″ × 9″	glass

Compare the use of lines in the tables in Figures 7.19, 7.22, and 7.23. Which do you find easiest to read?

- Use lines sparingly. Your software may use a default of lines around each cell—change this. A thicker line at the top and bottom of the table set the information off from the text. Lines separating the column and row headings may be the only other lines you need. You can easily change this. If they improve legibility, use vertical lines to separate columns. See Figures 7.19 and 7.22 for examples of use of lines. Figure 7.23 illustrates data shown in bar graphs and in tables.

Graphs and Charts

Like tables, graphs and charts show relationships, save words, have strong visual impact, and help to break up what would otherwise be pages of solid text. Figure 7.24 is a page from EPA's *Draft Report on the Environment 2003.* Note that the title of the page is "Bioaccumulative Toxics in the Great Lakes: A Multimedia Look." The multimedia are two pie graphs, a combination bar graph and line graph, and a multiline graph that convey complex information in concise visuals. We describe the use of graphs and charts such as these below.

Bar Graphs

Bar graphs report totals and show trends in ways that simplify comparisons.

- They report amounts that exist at any one time. Figure 7.25 shows three simple bar graphs reporting the percentages of literacy level. Because the bars report comparable information, the literacy levels and proficiencies, and the scales for each bar graph are the same, the reader can also make comparisons among the bar graphs.

- They report changes over a period of time, with the horizontal axis representing time and the vertical axis representing the amount. Figure 7.24 shows a bar graph illustrating the deposits of PCBs and DDT from 1992 through 1998. (The trend lines emphasize the downward trend.)

- They can report more extensive information by subdividing each bar into increments. Figure 7.26 shows two charts with stacked bar graphs reporting coal-fired capacity: one using selective catalytic reduction

FIGURE 7.21

Tables do not have to be columns and rows of numbers. More and more, you will see tables used to condense and organize information. In this example, questions in the left column with criteria in the remaining columns guide the evaluation of a KidsWalk-to-School program.

Source: Centers for Disease Control and Prevention. (2002). *Physical Activity Evaluation Handbook.* Atlanta: U.S. Department of Health and Human Services. Retrieved October 12, 2003 from http://www.cdc.gov/nccdphp/dnpa/physical/handbook/pdf/handbook.pdf

KidsWalk-to-School Example: Focus the Evaluation and Gather Credible Evidence

Evaluation Questions	Indicators	Data Sources	Performance Indicators
To what extent does program implementation use community resources?	• Number of volunteers • Longevity of volunteers • Total volunteer time • Description of volunteer activities • School resources contributed to program	• Administrative records • Volunteer activity logs • Key informant interviews	• 25 volunteers total, including five core volunteers • Total volunteer time meets need • Volunteer activities meet need • School contributed to program
What effects has the program had on school-children?	• Number of days walked or biked to school in past week • Children's attitudes towards walking to school (three-question scale for parents and children) • Children's scores on traffic safety test	• Surveys of parents and children (before and after the program)	• 15% increase in number of days/week children walked or biked to school • 20% increase in Likert scale average of three attitude questions • 30% increase in children's traffic safety test scores from baseline
Has the program had any effect on other community members?	• Community members' knowledge of physical activity recommendations • Community members' intentions to exercise • Community members' exercise in past 7 days • Community cohesion scale	• Community household survey (before and after the program or after the program only) • Key informant interviews	• 50% increase in community members' knowledge of physical activity recommendations • 20% increase in community members' intentions to exercise • 10% increase in community members' exercise in past 7 days • 15% increase in community cohesion scale
How has the program affected the community's barriers to walking?	• Description of original barriers to walking • Description of barriers to walking after the program • Quantity and quality of advocacy efforts	• Walkability survey (observations) • Key informant interviews • Volunteer questionnaires	• Qualitative improvement in walkability barriers • Planned advocacy efforts were conducted

FIGURE 7.22

Baseball standings are easier to read when there are fewer lines and the column widths are adjusted to fit the information. Too many lines give the table a dense, cluttered look. White space gained with the removal of lines makes the table easier to read. Because every table is different, you will have to decide which lines are needed and which are not. Begin with three lines—a top and bottom line to frame the table and a line to separate column labels from the data. Consider carefully each line you add after those.

Example 1: Table With Interior Lines

	W	L	Pct	GB	L10	Str	Home	Away	Intr
New York	101	61	.623	—	7-3	Won 2	50-32	51-29	13-5
Boston	95	67	.586	6	6-4	Lost 2	53-28	42-39	11-7
Toronto	86	76	.531	15	7-3	Won 2	41-40	45-36	10-8
Baltimore	71	91	.438	30	3-7	Lost 2	40-40	31-51	5-13
Tampa Bay	63	99	.389	38	3-7	Won 2	36-45	27-54	3-15

Example 2: Table Without Interior Lines

	W	L	Pct	GB	L10	Str	Home	Away	Intr
New York	101	61	.623	—	7-3	Won 2	50-32	51-29	13-5
Boston	95	67	.586	6	6-4	Lost 2	53-28	42-39	11-7
Toronto	86	76	.531	15	7-3	Won 2	41-40	45-36	10-8
Baltimore	71	91	.438	30	3-7	Lost 2	40-40	31-51	5-13
Tampa Bay	63	99	.389	38	3-7	Won 2	36-45	27-54	3-15

(SCR), the other using scrubbers. The projections for each can be compared across 15 years (2005 through 2020), and differences between existing and retrofitting for SCR and for scrubbers can be compared. Report readers do not need the exact amounts; they see trends when reading bar graphs.

Many readers find bar graphs easier to understand than line graphs. Each bar represents a quantity; the height or length of the bar indicates the amount of the quantity. It makes little difference whether the bars run horizontally or vertically, but horizontal bar graphs are often used to report quantities of time, length, and distance; vertical bar graphs report heights, depths, and the like.

FIGURE 7.23

Readers can see trends and make comparisons easily with a well-constructed bar graph. This information is also provided in table format. The Web-based chart is found as a Web document (HTML) and as a PDF file. The Return to At-A-Glance link switches between the two forms. Much of the information found on government Web sites is provided in more than one form.

Source: Centers for Disease Control and Prevention. (2003). *Health risks in the United States: Behavioral risk factor surveillance system 2003.* Washington, DC: U.S. Department of Health and Human Services. Retrieved October 17, 2003 from http://www.cdc.gov/nccdphp/aag/aag_brfss.htm

Adults Who Are Physically Inactive,* by Race and Ethnicity†

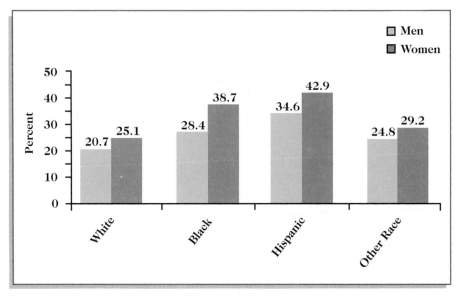

*People 18 or older who reported no leisure-time exercise or physical activity.
†White, black, and other race categories exclude Hispanics.

Adults Who Are Physically Inactive,* by Race and Ethnicity†

	White	Black	Hispanic	Other Race
Men	20.7%	28.4%	34.6%	24.8%
Women	25.1%	38.7%	42.9%	29.2%

*People 18 or older who reported no leisure-time exercise or physical activity.
†White, black, and other race categories exclude Hispanics.

Return to At-A-Glance

FIGURE 7.24

A page from *EPA's Draft Report on the Environment 2003* illustrates the use of different forms of visuals to convey information to the reader.

Source: U.S. Environmental Protection Agency. (2003). *EPA's draft report on the environment 2003.* Washington, DC: Authors. Retrieved October 17, 2003 from http://www.epa.gov/indicators/roe/pdf/roeWater.pdf or www.epa.gov/indicators/roe/html/roeWater.htm

---

EPA's Draft Report on the Environment 2003

Bioaccumulative Toxics in the Great Lakes: A Multimedia Look

Toxic chemicals enter the water of the Great Lakes (and therefore fish) from the atmosphere, tributaries, and sediments. These chemicals can be retained by plants and animals and increase in concentration though the food chain, a process called "bioaccumulation." Environmental data and modeling were used to estimate the relative contributions from each pathway to Lake Michigan. Total contaminant loads have decreased since the 1970s, and atmospheric deposition has increased in importance over time because of decreases in direct discharges to the lake and levels in sediments (Exhibit 2-11).

The Integrated Atmospheric Deposition Network (IADN) and the Great Lakes Fish Monitoring Program (GLFMP) monitor persistent bioaccumulative toxic (PBT) pollutants in the air and fish, respectively, of the Great Lakes. Both programs show decreases in PBTs over time (Exhibits 2-12 and 2-13). In spite of these downward trends, levels of PCBs and other PBTs in certain types of fish still exceed health protection levels in all five lakes. Air data from Chicago showing elevated PCB levels suggest that cities still contain significant sources of PCBs.

GLFMP samples are also being used to identify the presence of "new" bioaccumulating pollutants in the Great Lakes, such as certain brominated flame retardants.

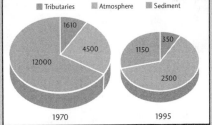

Exhibit 2-11: Lake Michigan polychlorinated biphenyls (PCBs) sources, 1970 and 1995
Values in kilograms per year

Note: This graphic was created for this report by the EPA Great Lakes National Program Office and the EPA, Office of Research and Development's Large Lakes Research Station using MICHTOX, a mass balance and bioaccumulation model, and air, water, and sediment data drawn from the Great Lakes Environmental Monitoring Database (GLENDA). The 1970 model run was based on available data and extrapolations. The 1995 model run was based on data collected during the Lake Michigan Mass Balance Study that collected over 25,000 samples at 200 locations in 1994-1995.

Source: EPA, Great Lakes National Program Office. *Great Lakes Environmental Monitoring Database (GLENDA).* 2002.

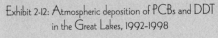
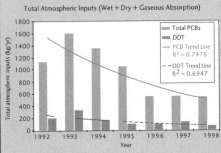

Exhibit 2-12: Atmospheric deposition of PCBs and DDT in the Great Lakes, 1992-1998

Note: Note: R^2 is the coefficient of determination. It gives a measure of the strength of the correlation.

Source: Buehler, S., et al. *Atmospheric Deposition of Toxic Substances to the Great Lakes: IADN Results through 1998.* 2001.

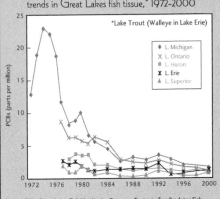

Exhibit 2-13: Polychlorinated biphenyls (PCBs) trends in Great Lakes fish tissue,* 1972-2000

Source: EPA, Great Lakes Fish Monitoring Program. Toxics in Top Predator Fish. February 24, 2003 (April 4, 2003: http://www.epa.gov/glnpo/glindicators/fishtoxics/topfishb.html).

Chapter 2 - Purer Water

Consumption of Fish and Shellfish

2-19

FIGURE 7.25

The three bar graphs have identical formats so that the reader can compare the information in each. Each axis is labeled; the scale is proportional; the title and subtitle clearly identify the data.

Source: Brown, H., Prisuta, R., Jacobs, B., & Campbell, A., (1996). *Literacy of older adults in America: Results from the National Adult Literacy Survey.* NCES97-576. Washington, DC: U.S. Department of Education, National Center for Education Statistics.

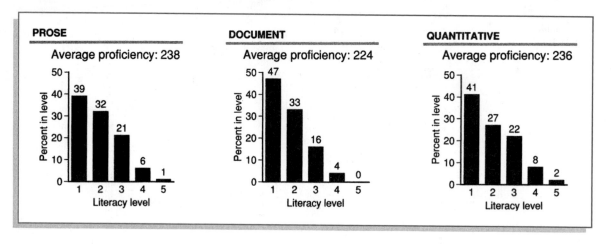

Divided- or Segmented-Bar Graph

Consisting of a bar divided into segments, a divided- or segmented-bar graph (Figure 7.27) effectively shows and compares percentages. The entire field of the bar represents 100 percent; each segment represents a portion of the 100 percent. The order of the segments should be the same in all bars. If a legend or key is used, its segments should be arranged like those in the bar. The bar can be presented vertically or horizontally.

Line Graphs

Like bar graphs, line graphs show comparisons between two or more quantities and trends. The curved line or lines help readers quickly grasp the results of comparative data because the fluctuation of the line or lines shows the variation in the data. Use a line graph when the emphasis is on a relationship between variables, as in the bottom right graph in Figure 7.24, or on a trend rather than on an actual amount in a combination line and bar graph (see Figure 7.24, bottom left).

Keep line graphs simple, particularly if your audience is unskilled in reading them.

Pie Charts

Like a divided- or segmented-bar graph, the pie chart (Figure 7.28) compares percentages of a whole. Each segment expresses a part of 100 percent.

FIGURE 7.26

Readers can see trends and make comparisons in the stacked bar graphs. The scale and labels for each graph are identical to make it easy for readers to compare the information.

Source: U.S. Environmental Protection Agency. (2003). *The Clear Skies Act: Technical support package.* Washington, DC: Author. Retrieved October 18, 2003 from http://www.epa.gov/air/clearskies/03technical_package_sectiond.pdf

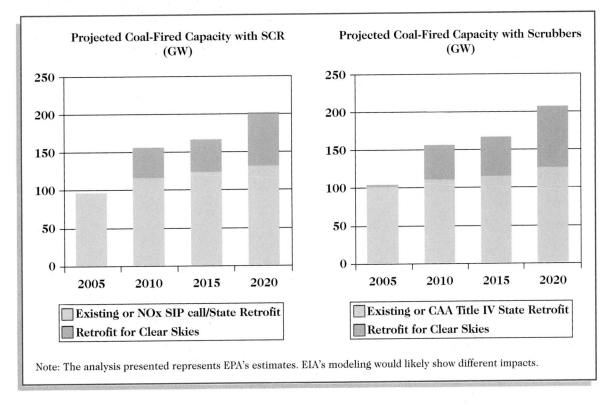

The practice of beginning at the 12 o'clock position and moving clockwise from the largest to the smallest slice has changed with the widespread use of graphics software. While it is possible to orient the segments to begin at 12, it is not easy in many of the packages to make the adjustments. If possible, organize the data in decreasing order so that the segments of the pie chart move from largest to smallest. However, some software packages do not follow this order.

If you are comparing in side-by-side pie charts, the segments in all charts should be in the same order. Group extremely small percentages (less than 2 percent) into one segment. The grouped segment may be labeled *miscellaneous* or *other*, with the individual groups and percentages given in parentheses or in a footnote.

FIGURE 7.27
Divided- or segmented-bar graphs are effective ways of showing and comparing percentages. The field of the bar graph represents 100 percent; each segment represents a portion of the whole. In this example, the bar graph illustrates the distribution of monthly expenses. The bar graph was created in Microsoft Word in approximately 10 minutes. The basic graph was created in less than a minute; adjusting the color, lines, legend and other features required 8 to 10 minutes.

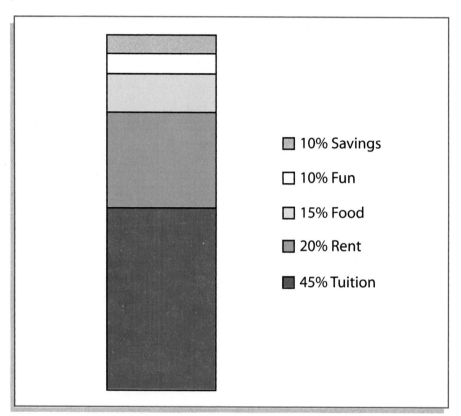

Study the side-by-side pie charts in Figure 7.24 and evaluate the presentation of the information. Check the order of the segments, the fill associated with each species, the use of three dimensions, and the different size of the charts.

Visual Combinations

With more sophisticated software, we can create visuals that combine features described in this chapter. That is, you overlay different data in the same

FIGURE 7.28

Readers can compare the information in the pie charts; the order of the slices, the scale, fill, and labels for each chart are identical to make it easy for readers to compare the information. Pie charts compare percentages of the whole.

Source: U.S. Environmental Protection Agency. (2003). *The Clear Skies Act: Technical support package.* Washington, DC: Author. Retrieved October 18, 2003 from http://www.epa.gov/air/clearskies/03technical_package_sectiond.pdf

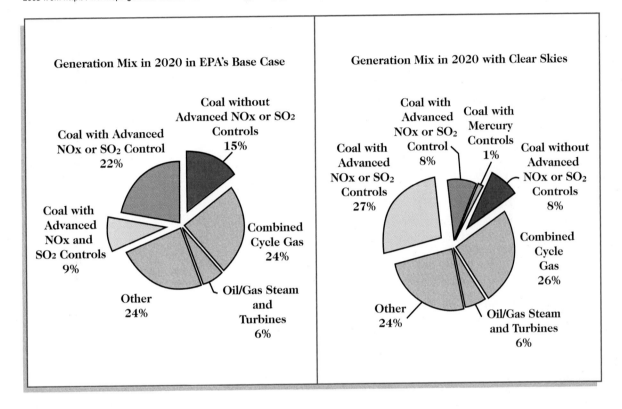

visual. Robert Harris defines a *combination graph* as a graph that "displays multiple data series using two or more different types of data graphics . . . to improve clarity and highlight relationships between the various data series" (97).[1] This definition encompasses visuals such as the combination of a bar graph and line graph in Figure 7.24 or the combination in Figure 6.2 (see page C in the first color insert).

We expand this definition to include drawings and other visual designs, not just data graphics such as bar or line graphs. Figure 7.29 provides examples of just such combinations. The visual supports the second point, size and

---

[1]Robert L. Harris, *Information Graphics: A Comprehensive Illustrated Reference* (Atlanta: Management Graphics, 1996) 97.

location, of three points in the article "Tree Factors to Consider." Note how the house and trees are placed across the *x*-axis in increasing size, similar to a bar graph. Each is labeled with examples of trees included in the height category. A scale on the right (the *y*-axis) gives the height the tree reaches when mature. The spacing guide is a 4-column table that provides suggested distances for planting the trees. The checklist at the left identifies other factors to consider when planting trees. Review other features of this visual and its relationship to the text surrounding it. Consider the white space, the amount of text, the placement of the visual and the text.

One final note: The visual in Figure 7.29 is found in a bulletin printed on recycled and recyclable paper using soy ink. The paper color is a light shade of grey, and the ink colors are black and green. The green is used for many of the headings, the fill in the trees, and to shade one box of text.

The selection of paper and ink reinforce the interests of the type of organization, The National Arbor Day Foundation, and the topic of the document, selecting the right tree to plant.

FIGURE 7.29

Combining visuals allows the writer to show a number of relationships in one visual. In this visual, the reader gets a comparison of tree height next to a house. In addition, the table identifies the space trees will need around a house.

Source: Visual from *Tree City USA Bulletin, no. 4*, reprinted by permission of The National Arbor Day Foundation.

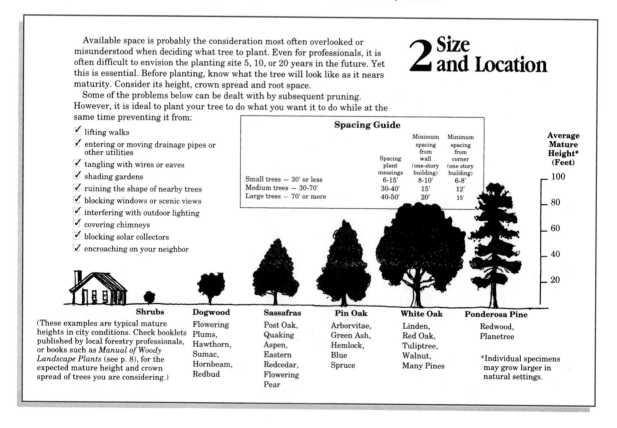

Visuals that combine different graphic features have become more prevalent because of the ease of creating them. Create them with your reader and your purpose in mind. They can easily become overloaded with details that hide the information. Edward Tufte calls this *chartjunk*, the unnecessary, unrelated data that interferes with the purpose of the visual.[2] Review your purpose, your reader, and the information you want the reader to gather from the visual.

---

[2]Edward Tufte, *The Visual Display of Quantitative Information* (Chesire, CT: Graphics Press, 1983).

PLANNING AND REVISING CHECKLIST: VISUALS

Planning

- What concepts or data in your document can be clarified by visuals? Keep in mind that visuals are important features of world-ready communication.
  - _____ Depict objects using photographs or drawings.
  - _____ Explain a process or procedure using block diagrams, pictorial flowchart, or decision trees.
  - _____ Show trends or relationships using tables, charts, or graphs.
  - _____ Show an area of a country using maps.
  - _____ Show action using a video clip or animation.

- How familiar is your audience with certain kinds of visuals? Do they understand specialized schematic drawings, charts, and formulas? Can they read topographic maps, for example?

- Have you planned your layout so that your visuals will be located in the best places?
  - _____ Will visuals that relate directly to information in the text be placed within the document?
  - _____ Will visuals that contain supplemental information be placed in an appendix?

- How much explanation will you provide for visuals? Do you need to provide
  - _____ legends?
  - _____ captions?
  - _____ explanations in the body of the text?

- What sources will you use to create the visuals?
  - _____ Available software
  - _____ Digital or video camera or other tool
  - _____ Source on the Web

Revising

- Are the visuals suited to your and your audience's purposes?
  - _____ Visuals and written text complement each other?
  - _____ Each visual introduced and discussed in the text?
  - _____ Most effective, appropriate visual used?

- Are the visuals well placed and easy to find?
  - _____ All visuals in the document?
  - _____ Visuals part of the page or section, not an afterthought?

- Are your visuals legible?
   _____ Legends provided?
   _____ All variables and values are clearly marked?
   _____ Captions identify purpose and source?
   _____ Numbered correctly and consecutively?

Suggestions for Applying Your Knowledge

1. Visuals are used to depict concepts, objects, processes, trends, and relationships. Either as an individual or as a member of a group, find examples of each use in reports, newspapers, magazines and professional journals, and textbooks and on the World Wide Web. Examine the strategies used in each visual and determine how well the visuals serve the writer's and readers' purposes. If your instructor makes such an assignment, photocopy the examples—making enough copies for the other students in your group or in the class—and be prepared to discuss the way each visual works in its document. If appropriate, explain how you would revise a visual for more effective format and placement and increased clarity.

2. Prepare both a line graph and a bar graph to show the closing volume of shares traded on the New York Stock Exchange from September 26 through September 30 (in millions of shares):

September 26	110
September 27	110
September 28	112
September 29	165
September 30	170

3. (a) Prepare a table and a bar graph to depict the following data about cigarette smokers who are at least 20 years old:

   In 1995, 34 percent had less than a high-school education; 38 percent were at least high-school graduates; 36 percent had some college education; and 28 percent were college graduates.

   In 2000, 36 percent had less than a high-school education; 37 percent were at least high-school graduates; 32 percent had some college education; and 24 percent were college graduates.

   In 2003, 34 percent had less than a high-school education; 33 percent were at least high-school graduates; 26 percent had some college education; and 16 percent were college graduates.

   (b) Write a paragraph interpreting the data presented about cigarette smokers who are at least 20 years old and their educational attainments. Incorporate the bar graph into your paragraph.

4. Either as an individual, with another student, or with a group designated by your instructor, analyze the following information about

applications for immigration amnesty in the United States from May 5, 1998, to April 28, 1999. The information is provided by the Immigration and Naturalization Service. Discuss the kinds of visuals that would be appropriate for displaying the information. Create the visuals.

(a) The number of regular and farm applications for amnesty:

Area	Regular	Farm
Eastern (VA, WV, PA, NY, MD, DE, NJ, RI, MA, NH, VT, ME, CT, PR)	126,608	25,452
Northern (WA, OR, ID, MT, ND, SD, MN, WI, CO, UT, IN, OH, AK, MI, WY, NE, IA, IL, MO, KS)	126,426	45,576
Southern (NM, TX, OK, LA, MS, AR, GA, TN, KY, FL, NC, SC, AL)	307,846	121,941
Western (CA, NV, AZ, HI)	750,204	256,379

(b) Percentage of applications for amnesty by country of citizenship:

Mexico	73.3%
All other countries	13.3
El Salvador	6.5
Haiti	2.7
Guatemala	2.2
Philippines	1.0
Colombia	1.0

5. Prepare a pie chart that depicts the following data about new entrants to the U.S. labor force in 1999.

Native white males	47%
Native white females	36%
Native nonwhite males	5%
Native nonwhite females	5%
Immigrant males	4%
Immigrant females	3%

6. Locate or write a letter or a report that contains a large amount of statistical data. Construct a table that will summarize the data. Alternatively, locate or write a letter or report that explains a process or procedure. Construct a flowchart or decision tree that will aid your audience in understanding your message.

7. Visit the Web site at http://spaceprojects.arc.nasa.gov/Space_Projects/pioneer/PN10&11.html#plaque. Study the drawing placed on the Pioneer Plaque. What is the purpose of the plaque? Who is the audience? Can you decipher the message in the visual?

Correspondence and Presentations

Workplace Correspondence: Letters, Memos, and E-mail

The most common forms of workplace writing are letters, memos, and e-mail.

Letters and memorandums (memos) travel by various routes ranging from the post office or interoffice mail to fax machines or electronic mail (e-mail). But no matter the route, letters, memos, and e-mail messages are by far the most common form of written communication in the workplace. Professionals—from human resources specialists to maintenance coordinators—spend much of their work day writing letters, memos, and e-mail like the ones illustrated in this chapter. They use these types of correspondence in many ways: to convey information, to request information, to describe procedures, to argue for change, to make and cancel appointments, to share drafts of documents, to report the results of work and research. Virtually every communication purpose is served at one time or another by letter or memo, whether hard-copy (printed on paper) messages or e-mail.

You might wonder why in an age of rapid telephone and telecommunication networks letters and memos are still so much in use. The answer is at least threefold:

- First, organizations need records that oral communication often does not provide. For example, two people may reach an agreement orally, and in a week each may have a different memory of the agreement. A letter, memo, or e-mail message on file can prevent such misunderstandings.

- Second, you can reach a wide audience with a letter, memo, or e-mail. You may, for instance, wish to send a set of instructions to 20 workers, each in a different location. One memo containing the instructions copied 20 times or an e-mail addressed to members in an address book is far more efficient than 20 telephone calls or holding a meeting. In addition, the memo or e-mail serves each worker as a constant reference for the instructions. It is a common practice in the workplace to send copies of correspondence to other people concerned with the subject matter—suppliers, clients, inspectors, and so forth. Some may need to be updated on progress, others may need to approve a payment, others may need to know when to order certain items or when to expect to receive them.

- Third, sometimes a situation is too sensitive to be handled in a phone conversation. You may be trying to satisfy an angry customer or tell someone he or she cannot have a desired job. Often such situations can be handled with less pain to all concerned in correspondence rather than a phone call.

In this chapter, we treat the planning and writing of hard-copy letters and memos and of e-mail equally—all as correspondence. Regardless of the type of correspondence you write, you should follow basically the same process we described in Chapter 1, "The Process of Workplace Communication": Analyze your audience, set objectives, discover and gather information, plan your organization, plan your visuals, and write and revise.

As was discussed in Chapter 1, you will want to be ethical in your correspondence; that is, you should present as complete and honest information as possible, considering the implications to your reader. And frequently, if the situation seems to call for it, you will collaborate with others in some manner. Because correspondence is usually shorter and sometimes more informal than reports, you may abbreviate all the steps to some degree, but you should not overlook any of them.

This chapter is organized into three major sections as follows:

1. A section on the basic principles of workplace correspondence
2. A section on the basic formats of workplace correspondence
3. A section on some typical situations that generate workplace correspondence, samples of the resulting correspondence, and analysis of the correspondence

In Chapter 9, "Resumes, Employment Letters, and Application Forms," we deal with subjects many of you will find helpful as you complete your education and look for a job. Chapter 10, "Portfolios and Interviews," includes a section on developing and organizing portfolios. In portfolios, you collect the best examples of your work (including workplace writing samples) to show to future employers or to your current employer at your job performance review.

Basic Principles of Workplace Correspondence

Three basic matters need special attention in producing correspondence: clarity and conciseness, clear organization, and good grammar.

When people in the workforce are asked to rank the writing skills needed on the job, clarity ranks number one, followed in order by conciseness, clear organization, and good grammar. In this section, we discuss ways to achieve these top-ranked skills in letters, memos, and e-mail and discuss the importance of courtesy in workplace correspondence.

Clarity and Conciseness

In part, you achieve clarity and conciseness by attention to style. As we discuss in Chapter 4, "Creating World-Ready Documents and Presentations: Style and Tone," you can make your writing more readable and easier to translate by following these basic principles: Be as culturally neutral as you can, keep sentences reasonably short, use familiar words when possible, eliminate unneeded words, and put action in your sentences.

Putting action in your sentences sometimes calls for you to use *I* or *we* in your sentences. Generally speaking, you should use *we* when you are speaking for your organization and *I* when you are speaking for yourself as a representative of the organization. For example, "Because company policy does not allow payment for transfers, we cannot refund your costs in this matter." But "I have reviewed your proposal carefully, and my reaction to it is favorable."

The more you know about your audience, the clearer you are likely to be. Many messages are unclear because the writers assume that information known to them is also known to their readers. Think carefully about your readers' knowledge of the language and concepts you are using. When need be, define and explain professional terminology. But think also about what has gone on before in relation to the issue being discussed. For instance, if there have been earlier meetings and correspondence about the issue, you will probably have to provide a context for your message by bringing your reader up to date. How much information you provide is a judgment call. Provide enough that your reader can understand the message, but do not re-hash irrelevant history.

Keep in mind that you may have more than one reader and that some readers may be members of a culture different from yours. You may be writing to a colleague and sending a copy to your supervisor. It may be that your supervisor does not know the past history of the project as well as you and your colleagues do. When such is the case, you will be wise to supply the information your supervisor needs. Or you may be writing to team members, some of whom are natives of Sweden and India and live and work in their home countries. When such is the case, you need to be clear about dates, times, places, units of measure, and other information that might be local knowledge for your local colleagues but would be confusing to your international partners.

Finally, although you may regard e-mail messages as informal notes, they have been accepted as legal documents. Therefore you should strive for absolute correctness and as much clarity as possible. You should minimize the use of such abbreviations as IMHO (in my humble opinion), IOW (in other words), and TIA (thanks in advance) and of emoticons, such as smileys :-) and frowns :-(and winks ;-). These abbreviations and emoticons may be acceptable in rapid responses to personal messages or to lighten the tone of personal messages, but they can be stylistic blunders in discussing substantive workplace matters that are more public and professional than private. Remember to use style and tone that are appropriate for the occasion.

Clear Organization

Throughout this book, we suggest many organizational patterns for such elements of correspondence as argument, persuasion, descriptions, and instructions. Mastering these patterns and applying them when appropriate will enhance your correspondence greatly. Often, as we demonstrate in Chapter 1, "The Process of Workplace Communication," a careful analysis of purpose, audience, and situation will suggest a suitable organization. Beyond such particular patterns and the value of analysis, several general principles of organization for letters, memos, and e-mail should prove helpful to you.

Introduce Your Letters, Memos, and E-mail

Begin by making your purpose clear and by providing any information your reader needs to understand what comes later. Sometimes making purpose and context clear may call for a full introduction, something like this one:

> In this memo, I provide the credit analysis of the H.C. Hunt Company that you requested on 6 May. The analysis covers three areas: customer evaluation, financial situation, and credit structure and pricing.

With such an introduction, the reader is reminded of the occasion for the memo and is given the outline that the memo will follow. Both reader and writer are off to a good start.

In other situations—for example, an e-mail written following a telephone conversation—the writer can plunge more swiftly into the body of the message, something like this:

> Thanks for the good suggestions about the problems with the visuals. Below is a list of the faulty visuals that need replacing.

The appropriate beginning is a matter of judgment. The major principles you should follow is that the reader (and any secondary readers) should be left in no doubt about the purpose of the correspondence and the context from which the correspondence comes.

Organize Your Letters, Memos, and E-mails for the Reader

Think about your reader's interests, and organize to satisfy those interests. For example, suppose you are arguing in a letter for a new procedure to be adopted. You could perhaps argue pro and con, explaining the advantages and disadvantages of the procedure. That's a better organization than none at all, but it is probably not the best plan. Perhaps a few moments of audience analysis might tell you that your reader is primarily interested in the cost, convenience, and timely introduction of the new procedure. If such is the case, organize your material into three sections that deal with those interests.

Display Your Organization for the Reader

In part, you can display the organization of your message in your introduction. You could, for instance, in your correspondence introducing the new procedure, forecast your organization for your reader by stating that the three reasons for adopting the new procedure are "low cost, greater convenience, and a short transition time." For additional suggestions for displaying organization, see Chapter 5, "Design and Development of Documents." In a letter, memo, or e-mail, you can also display your organization by using headings. In the example we are using, your headings could be Cost, Convenience, and Transition Time.

Good Grammar

Grammar, as business people use the term, is a catchall term for several different aspects of writing, including correct spelling, accurate punctuation, and clear sentence structure. Businesspeople want good grammar for at least two reasons.

First, faulty grammar may produce writing so unclear that the purpose and content of the correspondence remain indecipherable. At the very least, faulty grammar can delay the readers' understanding, thus annoying the readers by making them work harder than they should have to. This is especially true for readers who are non-native readers of your language or for translators who must translate your message into another language.

Second, even when clarity is not the issue, professionalism is. A difference exists between school and the workplace in this regard: School is more forgiving to those learning skills. An instructor may pass a letter that is good except for some sloppy grammar or punctuation. In business, the letter may be considered totally unsatisfactory.

To be an effective workplace correspondent, you must be proficient in grammar. Use Chapter 4, "Creating World-Ready Documents and Presentations: Style and Tone," and Unit V, "Writer's Guide," to help you. If they are not enough, ask your instructor to explain concepts you do not understand. Also consider having a colleague read your writing—a fresh set of eyes always helps.

If you master grammar to the point at which you can write without embarrassing errors, you will avoid the risk of seriously limiting your potential in any job you take that requires you to write.

Courtesy

Simple courtesy goes a long way in the workplace. Courtesy helps keep people working together toward a common goal. If you follow the advice we give you about tone in Chapter 4, "Creating World-Ready Documents and Presentations: Style and Tone," you will be well on your way to a courteous tone in your correspondence.

Be sensitive to people's feelings and to cultural differences. Memos to peers that sound like commands rather than recommendations will be resented. Brusquely stated requests will often fail to achieve the desired results. Refusing a request without adequate explanation is a discourteous act. Be positive in your statements, not negative. Do not say, "Your plan for reorganization will never work." Rather, say, "Here is an alternative plan that seems promising." Courtesy should work in all directions—peer to peer, supervisor to subordinate and vice versa, and organization to client and the reverse.

As important as courtesy is, sometimes it has limits. Usually, the implications, the so-whats, of your data can be stated courteously. However, when the stakes are high, do not allow courtesy to prevent you from stating the so-whats clearly and openly, sometimes even bluntly. As one researcher of the

For more information on providing the so-whats, see Chapter 1.

Challenger space shuttle disaster put it, "Politeness can be fatal when it is used for the wrong purposes."[1]

In the *Challenger* accident, a faulty rocket seal rendered inoperative by cold weather caused the fatal explosion. Months before the catastrophe, an engineer working for the rocket's manufacturer, Morton Thiokol, Inc. (MTI), wrote to NASA providing data about the seal's faulty performance in cold weather. He concluded as follows: "The conclusion is that the secondary sealing capability in the SRM field joint cannot be guaranteed."[2] He had expressed a so-what, but he had expressed it politely and somewhat vaguely. The engineers at NASA who received the letter later testified that they did not understand the significance of the stated conclusion. They may have understood it better if the MTI engineer had stated it more bluntly, something like this:

> Because the rubber O-rings lose their resiliency in cool weather, the secondary sealing of the SRM joint is likely to fail in cold weather. Data from our tests and the history of O-ring damage in previous cool-weather launches clearly support this conclusion. Such a failure would likely cause a catastrophic explosion with the resultant destruction of the space shuttle and the loss of the lives of all aboard.

Perhaps, just perhaps, such a direct statement would have changed the decision to launch the next morning, when the ambient temperature was 30 degrees Fahrenheit, and might have prevented the tragic explosion that killed seven people and nearly destroyed a multibillion-dollar program.

In a more recent space shuttle disaster, although the investigation into the possible causes of the *Columbia* explosion on 1 February 2003 is incomplete, it is possible that similar communication problems contributed to the failure to fully understand the damage to the exterior protective tile on the shuttle's left wing caused by portions of the foam panels of the fuel tank impacting it during takeoff.

As we tell you often, express the so-whats clearly. Although courtesy and politeness are important in day-to-day correspondence, when the situation is urgent, the need to be absolutely clear may take precedence.

Another matter of courtesy relates to the handling of both hard-copy and electronic correspondence. Frequently, messages that announce meetings and programs, changes in policy, and requests for information are considered public and are forwarded to interested readers. In certain instances, however, you must decide whether or not correspondence you receive is personal and private and should not be shared with others, either by making copies and giving them to others or by forwarding an e-mail message electronically to others.

---

[1]Patrick Moore, "When Politeness Is Fatal," *Journal of Business and Technical Communication* 6 (1992): 288.

[2]Dorothy A. Winsor, "The Construction of Knowledge in Organizations: Asking the Right Questions About the *Challenger*," *Journal of Business and Technical Communication* 4 (1990): 14.

Basic Formats of Correspondence

Workplace correspondence must be neat and follow consistent formats. Sloppiness and inconsistency indicate carelessness and lack of professionalism on your part. We comment first on letter and envelope formats (illustrated in Figures 8.1 through 8.4). We then demonstrate acceptable memo and e-mail formats illustrated in two-page spreads in Figures 8.5 and 8.6.

Letter Format

Our suggestions on letter format deal with such things as choice of stationery, fonts and printers, margins, and the parts of a typical business letter. As you will notice, much of our discussion also applies to memo and e-mail format. The letter in Figure 8.1 illustrates the format elements we discuss below. Take time to read it now. The bracketed letters next to features in the letter correspond to our comments that follow. We also discuss the format of continuation pages and envelopes.

Stationery [A]

The organization or company you work for will provide letterhead stationery. Use it when you are writing about company business. For personal use, choose a good-quality white bond paper of about 20-pound. weight—a paper that looks good and feels good in your hand. Do not buy cheap, lightweight paper. It is a false economy.

Fonts and Printers [B]

Choose a standard font such as Times Roman or Bookman. For workplace correspondence, do not choose a font style such as italic except for purposes of emphasis. Using an unusual font is considered unprofessional. In addition, be sure, for important work, to use a laser printer or ink-jet printer that prints darkly. If your printing is unevenly shaded or unacceptably light, replace the toner or ink cartridge in the printer.

Margins [C]

Letters should never look crowded or off balance on the page. Leave generous margins, at least 1 inch on either side and on top and bottom, or use margins appropriate for your company's or organization's letterhead stationery. For a short letter, come down farther on the page so that your letter does not hang at the top like a balloon on a string. The center of the body of a one-page letter should be just above the center of the page.

Writer's Return Address [D]

The writer's return address includes your complete mailing address but not your name. Do not abbreviate words such as Street or Avenue. You may

FIGURE 8.1

Basic letter format. Bracketed letters correspond to comments on pages 195, 197–198, and 200.

MOUNTAIN PIONEER TECHNICAL SERVICES, INC. (A and D)
605803 Twentieth Avenue South, Suite 210
Kellyville, CA 96002

15 February 2005   (B and C)

Ms. Linette D. Barton
242 Katie Lane   (E)
St. Louis, MO 63130

Subject: Request for Name Identification   (F)

Dear Ms. Barton: (G)

We have been retained by Karneth Production, Inc. to work on title requirements   (H)
on the Silver Valley Unit.

In the chain of titles on lands in Merced County (please see Exhibit G on Affidavit
of Identity), there is a Mike Barton and a Lin Barton. Also showing up in the chain
of title is a Michael D. Barton and a Linette G. Barton. What I am trying to do with
the two Affidavit of Identities that I am sending you is to ascertain that Mike Barton
and Michael D. Barton are one and the same and that Lin Barton and Linette G.
Barton are one and the same.

If you know they are one and the same people, would you have a disinterested party
who is knowledgeable about the facts execute the enclosed Affidavit of Identities in
front of a notary and return to me.

If you have any questions, please call me at 1-888-604-2918 between 8 a.m. and 5
p.m. (PST), Monday through Friday.

Thank you,   (I)

Hsu Tsing   (J)
Hsu Tsing   (K)
Contract Landman

Enclosures: 2 Affidavit of Identities   (L)

Copy: V.R. Natarajan   (M)

HT:jr   (N)

(A and D) Writer's address or organization/ company's letterhead (preprinted on paper)

(B) Standard font, such as Times Roman or Bookman

(C) 1-inch margins all around

(E) Inside address

(F) Reference or subject line

(G) Salutation

(H) Text body

(I) Complimentary close

(J) Writer's signature

(K) Writer's typed name and writer's position or title

(L) Enclosure notice

(M) Distribution notice

(N) Typist's initials

abbreviate the state or U.S. Territory, using the U.S. Postal Service's two-letter abbreviation. (See the list of abbreviations in Unit V, "The Writer's Guide," on page 612.) Your address may be incorporated into your company's or organization's letterhead stationery. The date is part of the heading. Write it in the long form, either *January 18, 2005* or *18 January 2005*. Do not write date number as ordinals (*9th* or *3rd*). Use the number by itself.

Inside Address [E]

Set up the inside address as you do your own address in the heading. Do, however, include your correspondent's name and any titles. The titles *Mr.*, *Mrs.* and *Dr.* are abbreviated. *Ms.* is the preferred form in the United States for most women in business. Most other titles are written out in full, such as *Professor* or *Sergeant*. Do not use a title after a name that has the same meaning as the title before the name. Write *Dr. Isadora Paludan* or *Isadora Paludan, M.D.*, but not *Dr. Isadora Paludan, M.D.*

For more information on writing for international audiences, see Chapter 4.

For international correspondence, use appropriate titles, such as *Sr.*, *Sra.*, and *Srta.* (for *Señor* [Mister], *Señora* [Mrs.], and *Señorita* [Miss] in Spanish) and *Herr* and *Frau* (for Mr. and Mrs. in German), *Monsieur*, *Madame*, and *Mademoiselle* (for Mr., Mrs. and Miss in French). Typically, *Herr*, *Frau*, *Monsieur*, and *Madame* are not abbreviated. Typically, *Mademoiselle* and *Fraulein* (Miss in German) are not used in professional correspondence. *Ms.*, so widely used in the United States, apparently has not become widely used in other countries. Attention to such details shows that you and your organization are culturally sensitive.

International business addresses look quite different from U.S. addresses, but they contain essentially the same information: building address, street address, city and province or region, country, and postal code (similar to the U.S. Postal Service zip code). Here is an example of a postal address for a businessperson in Japan:

Postal Address	Explanation
Mr. Horo Hayata	Name and title of addressee
Nakataka Exports	Name of company
10-93, 7-chome, Minamiazabu	Building number, area number, city district
TOKYO 110	City and postal code

Reference and Subject Lines [F]

A reference line is frequently used in workplace correspondence. Placed above or below the salutation, it is preceded by the term *Re* or *RE* followed by a colon. The reference line may refer to the correspondence that generated your correspondence or to a file number, for example "Claim #G4562." A reference line allows your correspondents or their secretaries or assistants to locate previous correspondence on the same subject. It also saves your readers from trite openers like "With reference to your letter of 7 July 2005."

A subject line identifies the subject of the letter. It is preceded by the word *Subject* followed by a colon. You may use both a subject and a reference line in the same letter.

Salutation [G]

Most of us are still slaves to convention in the salutation and use *Dear* _____ when we are writing to someone whose name we know. Most people accept the *Dear* as a convention and do not take it seriously, yet they would probably notice and even resent its absence. Therefore you should probably continue to use salutations such as *Dear Dr. Coney, Dear Ms. White,* and *Dear Professor Souther.* Use a first name only when you and the letter's recipient are on a first-name basis. Use a colon after the salutation.

The issue of what form of salutation to use when you do not know the name of the individual you are addressing has been complicated by the fact that exclusively male salutations such as *Dear Sir* and *Gentlemen* are no longer considered appropriate. No universally acceptable substitute has been found yet. Some people have begun to address a department directly, as in *Dear Credit Department* or *Dear Consumer Complaints.* In routine correspondence, it may matter little which of these alternatives you use, but in important correspondence, do everything you reasonably can to get a name to address. Usually, a quick call to the business or department in question will get you the name of the person who should receive the correspondence.

Text Body [H]

In the text body, single-space the paragraphs and double-space between paragraphs. In short letters of several lines, you may use double-space or space and a half for everything. In the block format (as shown in Figure 8.1), all elements begin on the left margin. In modified-block format, (shown in Figure 8.2) the beginnings of paragraphs are indented, and your address, date of the letter, complementary close, and signature block can be aligned to the right.

Keep sentences and paragraphs short. Average 14 to 17 words a sentence, and do not let paragraphs run more than six or seven lines. Generous use of white space in a letter invites readers in. Cramped, crowded spacing shuts them out.

Complimentary Close [I]

Use a conventional close such as *Sincerely* or *Sincerely yours* for people you do not particularly know. For people with whom you have some friendship, you may close with *Warm regards, With best wishes,* and so forth. Capitalize only the first word in the closing. Follow the close with a comma.

Writer's Signature [J]

Sign your name legibly in the space above your typed name.

Writer's Typed Name and Position or Title [K]

Type your name four line spaces below the complimentary close. A woman without an honorific title, such as *Colonel* or *Professor,* who prefers the title of *Miss* or *Mrs.* to *Ms.* should indicate the title preferred in parentheses to the left of her typed name: *(Mrs.) Alva Chen.* Below the typed name, put your business position or title if you have one.

FIGURE 8.2
Modified block-format letter.

1260 VanMeter Boulevard
Gallatin, IL 60404
30 August 2005

(2 line spaces)
Ms. Mary Bolt
Customer Service
Sunset Van Lines
2224 Wake Street
Contra Costa, CA 90233
(2 line space)
Re: Your letter of 23 August 2005
(2 line space)
Dear Ms. Bolt:
(2 line spaces)

_____
_____
_____

(2 line spaces)

_____
_____
_____

(2 line spaces)

_____
_____
_____

(2 line spaces)

                                        Sincerely,

(4 line spaces)   *Mary H. Palmer*

                                        Mary H. Palmer

(2 line spaces)
MHP:els
(2 line spaces)
Enclosure: Furniture inventory
(2 lines spaces)
Copy: United Services Automobile Association

Enclosure Notice [L]

The enclosure line tells the reader that something is enclosed with the letter. The format of the line and the amount of information given varies. Typical lines might be

Enclosure
Enclosures (2)
Enclosure: Medical examination form

Distribution Notice [M]

In most circumstances, you will use a distribution or copy line to inform your primary reader of others who have been sent copies of the letter. The notification requires a simple notation such as the following:

Copy: V.R.Natarajan   *or*   C: V.R. Natarajan

Identification of Typist [N]

When someone other than the writer types or keys in a letter, an identification line is used. Usually the writer's initials are in uppercase letters, and the typist's are in lowercase, as in HT:jr. Here, HT is the person who writes and signs the letter, and jr identifies the person who prepared the letter for the writer's signature.

Continuation Page

The format for one or more continuation pages is shown in Figure 8.3. Use plain bond paper for page two and beyond. Do not use letterhead stationery. Plan your spacing so that at least two or three lines of the body are carried over to the continuation page.

FIGURE 8.3
Continuation page.

Page 2
30 August 2005

_____
_____
_____

_____
_____
_____
_____

Sincerely,

Mary H. Palmer

Mary H. Palmer

MHP:els

Enclosure: Furniture inventory

Copy: United Services Automobile Association

FIGURE 8.4
Envelope.

```
MARY H. PALMER
1260 VANMETER BOULEVARD                              PLACE
GALLATIN, IL 60404                                   STAMP
                                                     HERE



                    MS. MARY BOLT
                    CUSTOMER SERVICE
                    SUNSET VAN LINES
                    2224 WAKE STREET
                    CONTRA COSTA, CA 90233
```

Envelope

The envelope format is shown in Figure 8.4. Notice that the address is in all capital letters. This is the form now preferred by the U.S. Postal Service and the postal services of most other countries.

Letters sent to business people will sometime quite legitimately be opened by their coworkers—for instance, when the person addressed is ill or on vacation. The assumption is that the letter concerns company business, and business goes on regardless of who is present to conduct it. Therefore if you are writing a personal or confidential letter to a person at a workplace address, mark it with the word *PERSONAL* or *CONFIDENTIAL,* directly under the address on the envelope.

Memo Format

Many organizations have preprinted memo forms that differ from the forms used for letters. Generally, these forms contain the organization's name or logo but not its address, the heading (consisting of guide words for *Date*, *To*, *From*, and *Subject*), the text body, and miscellaneous elements. See Figure 8.5 for an example of a typical memo layout.

A continuation page for a memo will look exactly like a continuation page for a letter (see Figure 8.3) except, of course, it will have no signature block at the end. Instead of signing the memo, you will write your initials or your signature next to your name in the heading.

E-mail Format

E-mail has grown so important in the workplace that it is now regarded as more than just a way to send brief notes that can be written quickly, with little planning, sloppy organization, and scant attention to revising and proofreading. As with regular letters and memos, you should present your ideas in readily understandable and useful ways when using e-mail. You should be as concerned about accuracy of information and completion of data, and organization, format, grammar, spelling, and punctuation as you would be with any professional document.

E-mail messages consist of four major parts: the heading, the text body, the signature block, and attachments, as shown in Figure 8.6.

FIGURE 8.5
Sample memorandum.

ELITE INSURANCE

Date: 15 November 2005

To: Frank Werner-Kramer
Claims Analyst
Mail Stop 362

From: Nancy Ingram   *N.J.*
Retirement Specialist
Mail Stop 465

Subject: Loan Information Requested

You are eligible to take out a loan from your company retirement account. We offer both general loans and residential loans. A general loan does not require explanation of purpose and must be repaid within five years. A residential loan does require explanation of purpose and must be repaid within ten years. I have enclosed an application in case you wish to request a loan.

All loans are subject to the following conditions:

Loan Amounts

- Minimum loan amount is $1000.
- Maximum loan amount is the lesser of $50,000 or 50% of the balance in your retirement account.

Interest Rate

- The interest rate will be set at prime rate at the time of the loan plus 1%.

Repayment of Loans

- Minimum loan payment is $50.00 per month, made through payroll deductions.
- Loans may be repaid in full without penalty at any time.

Enclosure: Loan application blank

Comments Concerning Memo Formats

Memos typically consist of three major sections: the heading, the body, and the miscellaneous elements at the end.

The Heading

Generally, the heading contains the organization's name or logo but not its address, and guide words for *Date, To, From,* and *Subject.* Because of the preprinted formats, memos require no salutation or complimentary close. Frequently, though, people provide job titles with their names and sign or initial next to their names on the *From* line.

The Text Body

The body of a typed or printed memo is spaced in the same way as the body of a letter, with similar margins. As in a letter or any other document, use headings when they are appropriate.

The Miscellaneous Elements

Memos may have notations for identification, enclosures, and copies, just as letters do. A continuation page for a memo will look exactly like a continuation page for a letter (see Figure 8.3) except, of course, it will have no signature block. Instead of signing the memo, you will write your initials or your signature next to your name in the heading of the memo.

FIGURE 8.6
Sample e-mail.

Date: Fri, 28 March 2005 14:01.1
From: Lee Callaway 〈calla@sunstor.com〉
To: Building G Personnel 〈abbettel@sunstor.com〉
             〈bbettle@sunstor.com〉
             〈kwang@sunstor.com〉
             〈lsoders@sunstor.com〉
             〈ntimmons@sunstor.com〉
Cc: 〈dmatthews@sunstor.com〉
Subject: Possible Defect in Storage Units 115-119

There is a possible defect in the panels of the storage units in which the files and sales displays for Building G are located. The defect might allow water damage during or after hard rains.

Would you please stop by my office Monday through Friday 9:00 a.m. to 5:30 p.m., at your earliest convenience so that we can arrange to inspect the panels of your storage unit(s).

If it is not convenient for you to come by, please use company mail service to send us a copy of your key and we will return it as soon as the inspection and repair (if needed) are made.

If you should have any questions, please contact me.

Thank you,

Lee Callaway
Maintenance Coordinator
114 Administration Building
255-3300

Comments Concerning E-Mail Formats

E-mail format is quite similar to memo format.

The Heading

The heading includes the *Date* and the *From* lines, which the e-mail software program automatically completes, and the *To, Subject,* and *CC* or *cc* (and some have a *BC* or *BCC*—both are abbreviations for "Blind Copy") lines. The *To, CC,* and *BC* lines must be carefully keyed in, for if they contain an error, the e-mail will not be deliverable.

The *To* line contains the e-mail address of the person or persons you are writing to. For your convenience, your e-mail program contains an address book in which you can enter abbreviations for long addresses. For instance, *abe* can be typed in and the entire e-mail address, *Abe_Lincoln@republic.UI.edu,* will be entered automatically.

The *Subject* line allows you to specify the topic of your message. Always fill in the subject line for two reasons: (1) Many people receive a lot of e-mail and have e-mail-filtering systems that automatically separate incoming e-mail into appropriate in-baskets, and (2) many people often choose whether to open an e-mail by what the subject line says. Many suspect that e-mail messages with blank subject lines are spammed messages and delete these messages without opening them.

The *CC* and *BC* prompts allow you to send other persons a copy of the e-mail message. CC (something of an outdated designation standing for *carbon copy*) lets the recipient of the e-mail know who else is receiving the message. Copy those who you think might have an interest in the e-mail, especially if they were included in the original e-mail. *BC* (standing for *Blind Copy*) indicates those persons who also receive the message but without the recipient knowing it. You need not copy yourself because the message will be automatically saved in your "Sent" folder.

The Text Body

The body of the e-mail contains the message, and it is typed the same way as that of a letter or memo, using paragraph indentations, lists, headings, and double-spacing between paragraphs. The style of e-mail messages ranges from the most informal (a message to a coworker, in which such informally personal touches as the abbreviations BTW [by the way], UFN [until further notice], and FYI [for your information] and emoticons are acceptable) to the more professional when discussing business-oriented topics (similar to the style discussed in Chapter 4). Most e-mail programs easily handle messages up to 20 to 25 pages long, although you will seldom write such lengthy e-mails.

The Signature Block

The signature block or closing consists of text that provides additional information about the author—name, title or position, telephone and fax numbers, and postal address—and the organization (such as a Web site address or a company slogan). Although you will not use the signature block for all e-mails, create one because you cannot assume that the reply address identifies you clearly.

Attachments

More and more, we now send whole documents in electronic files along with an e-mail message. The file (a proposal, a resume, a list of parts, a video or visual presentation, or any document that is too cumbersome to include in the e-mail message) is attached to the e-mail message. The receiver can open the attachment and use it as if it had been created on his or her machine. We have two suggestions about using attachments. First, attach files before you write your e-mail message, so you will not forget to attach it. It is very easy to write your e-mail message and just by habit hit the send button without remembering to attach the file you want to send. Second, if you are attaching an important file, test it with a friend to make sure that it can be opened.

Situations and Analyses of Typical Workplace Correspondence

Workplace correspondence can range from the simple to the complex, from informal to formal. In the workplace, there really is no rigid categorization of informal and formal. Rather, there is a continuum ranging from the very informal to the very formal. Where you place yourself on that continuum depends on audience and situation. For example, an e-mail message between two colleagues who know and trust each other might be as informal as this:

To: Emile

From: Ahsan

OK on 9 a.m. Tuesday meeting in your office. You make the coffee; I'll bring the doughnuts.

The formal might range from letters, memos, and e-mails that look like those in Figures 8.1, 8.5, and 8.6 on up to memos and letters that are really short formal reports.

Using the principles discussed in Chapters 1 through 7, you can generate almost any kind of correspondence you need. Those principles are summarized in the planning and revising checklist at the end of this chapter. To illustrate the process you would follow, we describe several typical workplace situations and then, in Figures 8.7 through 8.14, show the correspondence generated by those situations and explain how attending to checklist items produced the results achieved. When such is the case, we provide the additional information needed.

There are more types of workplace correspondence than can be adequately addressed here. In this chapter we discuss six major types.

A Routine Request

People in the workplace commonly request information from one another. For example, business thrives on potential buyers of a product requesting information about that product. See Figure 8.7.

A Special Request

You can be reasonably sure that people will answer a routine request either because it is easy to answer or because answering may benefit the answerer in some way. You will not have the same assurance with a special request. You will be making work for the person who responds to the request, and it may well be that there is no immediate benefit to the answerer. See Figure 8.8.

Informational Correspondence

Many letters, memos, and e-mails pass along information. Often they are in response to either a routine or special request. At other times, the information is something the writer thinks the reader or readers should know. We look at two such situations: a response letter (Figure 8.9, which answers the special request letter shown in Figure 8.8) and a set of instructions in e-mail format (Figure 8.10).

Good-News Correspondence

Most letters, memos, and e-mails—we are happy to say—carry good news. Any correspondence that moves business forward is good news, even a routine notice that a shipment is on the way. If your correspondence contains good news, announce the good news first. For example: We are pleased to tell you that we want you to come to work for us. Your bicycle is repaired and ready for pickup. Congratulations on your promotion to head of merchandising.

Following the good news, supply any needed details, explanations, and analyses. In some cases, you will resell the reader. You might not be familiar with the notion of reselling. Let us illustrate. We recently bought a fax machine. As we were completing the purchase, the salesperson said, "You will be happy with this machine. It speeds up the transmission of letters and documents in a way you'll really come to appreciate." He had already made the sale. What he was doing was reselling us. He wanted us to go away happy, convinced that we had not thrown our money away on an expensive gadget. You will frequently end good-news correspondence in the same way.

The memo in Figure 8.11 illustrates all three steps: (1) Report the good news first. (2) Supply the necessary information. (3) Resell the reader.

Bad-News Correspondence

In the workplace, a small number of letters, memos, and e-mail carry bad news. Examples would be memos telling someone an expected raise is not coming or that a proposed project will not be funded. Bad-news correspondence is tricky to write. Figure 8.12 illustrates a strategy that has served many businesspeople well: (1) Begin with a friendly opener. (2) Carefully and objectively explain and analyze the problem. (3) Clearly state the so-what—the bad news. (4) Offer the best alternative possible. (5) Close in a friendly way.

Persuasive Correspondence

Many letters, memos, and e-mails, even those we think of as informational, are at least partly persuasive. For example, in her informational e-mail to the department heads (Figure 8.10), Wangari Tupoloso has a goal of persuading the department heads to do position descriptions her way. But some correspondence has no goal other than persuasion. Most such correspondence in the workplace is somewhere in the middle of the emotional persuasion–scientific argument continuum (see Figure 3.1, page 60). We describe two situations in which persuasion is the goal: a fund-raising letter (Figure 8.13) and an e-mail requesting approval of a change in company policy (Figure 8.14), in which a more logical argument is used.

FIGURE 8.7
Routine request via e-mail.

Date: 3 Nov 2005 08:27.12 (CST)
From: sasinc@mindup.com
To: EngDyn@rockhill.com
Subject: Request for Information on Fuel Pump

Please send me the following information about your new adjustable-pressure electric fuel pump, type AK306J.

1. Can it be mounted anywhere and in any position?
2. Does it come with a mounting bracket?
3. Does it operate independently of the engine?
4. How many pounds of pressure does it adjust to?
5. Is the flow adequate for a Zephyr 0-470 engine?

If you have literature available that answers these questions, I would be pleased to receive it.

Thank you,

George Santiago
Owner/Manager
Santiago Auto Service
2089 Fair Oaks Boulevard
Bellflower, CA 90706

A Routine Request Via E-Mail

Situation

George Santiago owns a repair business that specializes in working with car hobbyists. In the magazine *Road & Track,* he has read about a new fuel pump that may serve a need he has. But the article he read does not provide all the information he needs. He decides to write to the manufacturer, whose e-mail address is included in the article, and request the information that he needs.

Analysis

George Santiago needs specific information. If his questions are vague, he knows that he will receive vague answers or no answers at all. He does not have to be particularly persuasive, because his address and title are in the signature block of his e-mail and the specific questions identify him as a potential customer who should be given a serious answer. He knows that his e-mail request will be read and answered by someone who is familiar with engine terminology.

Because he does not have a name to address at the company, he does not choose to use a salutation. His opening sentence provides all the context and purpose statement needed for such a routine request. He lists and numbers his questions for two reasons: He wants to make each question stand out so that it will be answered. His enumeration makes it easy for the receiver to answer each question.

Santiago's style is clear. He does not waste words or his reader's time, but his tone is courteous, not brusque. His grammar is correct, helping to demonstrate that he is someone the company should take seriously.

FIGURE 8.8
A special request letter.

86 Needham Hall
Melrose Technical Institute
Bailey Springs, MS 93920-1502
14 March 2005

Mr. Robert Bradley
Vice President of Human Resources
Ace South Transport, Inc.
1000 By-Pass I-440 East
Memphis, TN 31111

Dear Mr. Bradley:

I am an industrial technology student at Melrose Technical Institute. I am writing a report for my Transportation Management 3160 class on how firms such as yours screen for employment recent graduates of college programs.

I have done library and Internet research on the subject, but I want to augment them with information collected from some of the larger firms in the tri-state area. The results of my study will be shared with my classmates. I would also be happy to send a copy of my final report to you, should you want one.

Would you please spend a few minutes answering the following questions about the way your firm screens employees?

1. What priorities do you place on applicants' academic performance, experience, and on campus or in-plant interviews?

2. What do you expect of applicants' behavior and dress when they report for an interview?

3. How much importance do you place on recommendations from faculty, school officials, and previous employers?

4. Do you give any standard or in-house tests to applicants? If so, how much weight do you give to the scores?

My report is due 10 April. I appreciate your taking the time to read my letter and hope to receive a reply from you in early April.

Sincerely,

Jill Kehoe

Jill Kehoe

A Special Request Letter

Situation

Jill Kehoe is a student at Melrose Technical Institute, majoring in industrial technology. For a paper she is to write, she is researching how medium-sized companies screen recent college graduates. Using the *College Placement Annual,* she has obtained the names of the personnel directors of six such firms in her area. She will send similar letters to all six.

Analysis

Kehoe has to be persuasive in her letter. She has little she can offer Robert Bradley in return for his answer, so she has to depend largely on his goodwill. To encourage that goodwill, she identifies herself as a student and, without being obsequious about it, is particularly polite in her request. The purpose and context of the letter are clearly stated in the first two paragraphs. She offers Bradley what she can. She will share her paper with others, thus drawing Ace South Transport to the attention of students who may someday be potential customers or employees of the company. Further, she offers Bradley a copy of her report.

As in George Santiago's routine request (see Figure 8.7), Kehoe makes her questions quite specific and enumerates them for ease in answering. Because Bradley is an experienced personnel director, she can be sure that he will know the answers to her questions without the need for any research on his part.

Bradley is not likely to be hostile in any way, but he could well be somewhat apathetic and inclined to put off answering her letter. To help prevent that, Kehoe politely states the time when she must have an answer. She then builds goodwill with a courteous close. (But notice she avoids the trite expression "Thanking you in advance.")

Her good grammar, clarity of style, and courteous tone identify her as someone who should be taken seriously. Because her coherent organization and businesslike format smooth the way for an answer, they build goodwill for her with Bradley.

FIGURE 8.9
A response letter.

Ace South Transport, Inc.
1000 By-Pass I-440 East • Memphis TN 31111

24 March 2005

Ms. Jill Kehoe
86 Needham Hall
Melrose Technical Institute
Bailey Springs, MS 93920-1502

Dear Ms. Kehoe:

I am happy to answer your questions about how we screen applicants who are recent college graduates. I will take your questions in the order you ask them.

1. Our first priority is generally to consider whether the applicant's major field of study fits him or her for the job sought. For instance, we like to hire drivers who have been through an extensive training program, such as those now provided in many two-year colleges. In descending order, we consider academic performance, work experience, and interviews. The only exception to this priority order might be when someone's extensive work experience makes up for a lack of academic preparation.

2. We expect that applicants come prepared to ask good questions of us and to listen to us as we will listen to them. They should be clean and neat in appearance.

3. Recommendations from people who have worked with the applicant, either on the job or in school, serve primarily as a check on what we find out from an applicant's resume and records and from the interview process.

4. We give in-house tests to prospective drivers and clerical workers. As with recommendations, we use tests primarily as a check on education and experience. A good score on a test would not guarantee an applicant a job, but a bad score would put his or her employment by us in doubt.

A useful source you may not have run across in your library search is *The Fleet Owner*, which frequently publishes information about the hiring and training of employees in our industry. I would be pleased receive a copy of your report.

Sincerely,

Robert Bradley

Robert Bradley
Vice President for Human Resources

A Response Letter

Situation

Robert Bradley has received Jill Kehoe's request for information (see Figure 8.8). He is impressed by her coherence and businesslike approach. When he finds some time to spare from his busy schedule, he writes her a letter answering her questions (see Figure 8.9).

Analysis: A Response Letter

Bradley's purpose is to answer the questions posed by Kehoe. Because she has wisely enumerated her questions, he chooses to follow her order in answering. A reference to her letter will provide sufficient introduction and context for his reply. Because she has done her homework before writing him, he knows he does not have to go into lengthy explanations. By mentioning *The Fleet Owner,* he does provide another reference for her, always a good idea when possible. His letter is clear, courteous, and complete. The friendliness apparent in the tone will help to create goodwill for his company with both Kehoe and her classmates.

FIGURE 8.10

A set of instructions sent via e-mail.

Date: 7 June 2005 13:20.6 (EDT)
From: Wangari_Tupoloso@faircog.com
To: All Department Heads ⟨Jolene_Cramner@faircog.com⟩
             ⟨Reba_Miller@faircog.com⟩
             ⟨Toby_Anderson@faircog.com⟩
             ⟨William_Tuft@faircog.com⟩
Cc: ⟨Ansis_Lanyi@faircog.com⟩
Subject: DUTIES SECTION OF POSITION DESCRIPTIONS

Our new position description program is going well. You have all done an excellent job in working with your department staffs in gathering the information needed for useful descriptions.

The Duties sections of some position descriptions, however, have not covered the duties well enough to aid in training and evaluating new employees. Please look over the following material written to help with organizing and writing the Duties section. I have also attached three sample Duties sections. Please send me any comments that you think will help us achieve the goals we have set for our position descriptions.

Our purpose in the Duties section is to describe what someone in that position does to fulfill the function of that position. A good Duties section will have a useful introduction, a coherent organization, and plain, clear language.

Introduction:

Introduce a Duties section with a general description of what an employee in this position does. For example, you could write, "Serves as administrative assistant to the department head."

Organization:

Because duties vary from position to position, there is no set way to organize a Duties section. The following three organizational plans work well, however:

- Write a narrative describing in sequence what the employee does, hour by hour, day by day, or week by week, whichever fits the duties best.

- List the duties in order of their importance.

- In cases where employees perform several different functions, you can categorize the description into those functions. For example, in some of the smaller departments, administrative assistants have clerical, accounting, and managerial functions. Within the categories you could organize by sequence or order of importance.

Plain, Clear Language:

Use plain, clear language to describe duties. File clerks file, illustrators illustrate, janitors sweep, mop, and wax floors. Be specific, and don't gild the lily with statements such as "Provides organizational support for cleanliness activities within the facility."

Because you are describing activities, use active verbs, such as these:

- Maintains computerized department budget and provides department head with weekly budget status reports.

- Takes dictation and uses word-processing to type memos and letters free from spelling and grammatical errors.

Thanks,

Wangari Tupoloso, Director
Human Resources Department

Instructions Via E-Mail

Situation

Wangari Tupoloso is the director of human resources for a small but growing corporation. To help with the process of hiring, training, and evaluating new employees, the company has called for department heads to write descriptions for all the positions within their departments. The program has been in effect for some three months, and Tupoloso has the responsibility for seeing that it goes well. In reviewing recent position descriptions, she realizes that the department heads are having difficulty describing the duties of a position. Although Tupoloso's message will be a bit longer than most e-mail messages she sends or receives, she decides that an e-mail message to all of them may help correct the situation quickly.

Analysis

Good position descriptions are not easy or fun to write. Therefore Tupoloso realizes there may be some resistance to her e-mail message among the department heads. With too much resistance, she will not effect the changes she wants. The key to the success of this e-mail is getting off to a good start and having the department heads see it as useful information and not criticism. To that end, she begins her message with a compliment.

The first sentence in the second paragraph is the only criticism in the entire e-mail. In that sentence, Tupoloso states the problem and the so-whats of the problem clearly. She does so without a hint of sarcasm or hostility toward the department heads. The second and third sentences of the paragraph describe the material that is in a PDF file attached to the e-mail. By asking for comments in the final sentence of the paragraph, Tupoloso makes it clear that she is open minded about other ways of solving the problem.

In organizing her information, she separates it into three problem areas she sees in the position descriptions. She makes her plan of organization clear in her third paragraph and with her three headings. She uses a neutral tone in her instruction. She describes what needs to be done without dwelling on the mistakes of the past. She does not talk down in any way to her readers. Because most people learn well from examples, she provides them in her e-mail and provides three additional sample Duties sections as well.

FIGURE 8.11
A good-news memo.

Columbia Electronics Company

Date: 17 April 2006

To: Mark Johnson
DHR

From: Ann Manchester A. M.
CFO

Subject: Executive Council Approval of Company Childcare Center

Mark, I'm delighted to tell you that the Executive Council has approved your committee's recommendation concerning a company childcare center. The case your committee made for it was quite convincing. The Council was particularly impressed by your figures on the number of mothers working in the company with preschool children.

As you requested, Human Resources will be in charge of the project. The Council hopes you can have the center in place by August. I will be your coordinator with the Council for space and funding. Please schedule an hour's appointment with me at your earliest convenience.

Once again, congratulations to you and your committee. You have already put much time and enthusiasm into this project. The Council knows you will continue your good efforts in carrying your plans through to completion.

Good-News Letters, Memos, and E-Mails

Situation

Mark Johnson, chair of the employee benefits committee for Colombia Electronics, has been trying for some time to convince the executive council of the company that a company childcare center would pay for itself by reducing absenteeism, improving worker morale, and preventing rapid turnover among women employees. He has finally succeeded, and Ann Manchester, the company's Chief Financial Officer (CFO), has the pleasant task of writing a memo to Johnson to confirm the good news.

Analysis

Manchester has four major purposes in this memo. First, she wishes to convey the good news to Johnson. This she does, as she should, in her opening sentence.

Second, she wants Johnson to know how pleased the Council is with his and his committee's work on this project. She does this by telling him their case was "quite convincing" and that the Council was "impressed by their figures."

Third, she wants to set a deadline for the project and get Johnson and his committee started on it. Her next-to-last paragraph accomplishes that goal.

Finally, she resells Johnson on the project by once again complimenting him and his committee. Johnson and the committee members will be greatly pleased and ready to work on the project with great enthusiasm.

The Manchester memo is a good example of the importance of considering human values in correspondence. Johnson would have been satisfied with hearing that the project was approved and underway. However, Manchester's additional effort in the memo improves his self-esteem and recognizes the work of the committee and increases the efforts they will make in the matter of the daycare center and in other matters as well.

FIGURE 8.12
A bad-news letter.

AMBROSE APPLIANCES

2215 West Barnes Avenue • Denver, CO 80204

---

7 February 2004

Mr. John Rhodes
3295 West Avondale Drive
Denver, CO 80206

Dear Mr. Rhodes:

Thank you for your call about your dryer. As you know, following your call, our service representative Sophia Montana examined your dryer.

She found that the dryer's motor had been overheated so much that it is damaged beyond repair. She also noted that the lint filter was so clogged with lint that it was not functioning properly. As a result, the lint packed into the motor, causing the overheating. At that time, she showed you the warning in your operating manual that points out that failure to clean the lint filter after every use of the dryer may result in overheating and damage to the motor.

Your replacement guarantee covers only defects by the manufacturer and improper installation by us. Since neither was a factor in the motor's overheating, we cannot replace your motor free of charge as you have requested.

However, we are anxious to help you get your dryer working again. If you want our service representative to install a new motor, please call us. We can bill the installation as a continuing service call at $30 rather than the normal installation fee of $60, saving you $30. The cost of the motor itself is $170, so your total cost would be $200.

We value you as a customer, and we hope that our solution for replacing your motor will be acceptable to you.

Sincerely,

Willoughby Osgood

Willoughby Osgood
Service Manager

Bad-News Letters, Memos, and E-Mails

Situation

The motor on John Rhodes's clothes dryer has overheated and been damaged beyond repair. Rhodes has called the appliance store where he purchased the dryer and requested a new motor under the provisions of his replacement guarantee. A service representative sent to examine the motor finds that it was improper operation by Rhodes's part and not a defect that caused the overheating. Willoughby Osgood, the store's service manager, has the task of telling the bad news to Rhodes.

Analysis

Osgood has two goals in this letter. He wants to let Rhodes know that his service guarantee does not apply in this situation and at the same time keep as much of Rhodes's goodwill as possible. He has to be clear about the way in which Rhodes caused the problem and yet not insult or humiliate Rhodes in any way. He expects that Rhodes will be hostile. Because of Rhodes's expected hostility, Osgood chooses to write to him rather than to telephone. In a letter, Osgood can control the tone better than he might on the phone with an angry Rhodes. Also, the letter provides a record that could be useful in case of litigation at a later date.

Osgood maintains a neutral tone in the letter. He starts with a "thank you" and sets the context for the letter. In the second paragraph, he objectively points out the facts of the situation. In the third paragraph, he clearly states the so-what—the bad news that Rhodes will not get a free replacement motor. In the fourth paragraph, he offers an alternative solution that he hopes will be acceptable to Rhodes. Finally, he closes in a friendly way.

Most bad-news correspondence, like this letter, is ultimately persuasive; that is, the writers hope to persuade their readers that they cannot have what they want. If you have an alternative to offer, you hope to persuade the reader to accept that. To be persuasive, you have to delay the bad news until you have provided a rationale for it. A letter to Rhodes beginning with the blunt statement that because of his faulty use of the dryer, no free motor was forthcoming would make the problem worse, not better.

In writing his letter, Osgood followed a standard bad-news organization that has served many businesspeople well:

- Begin with a friendly opener.

- Carefully and objectively explain and analyze the problem.

- Clearly state the so-what—the bad news.

- Offer the best alternative possible.

- Close in a friendly way.

FIGURE 8.13
A persuasive letter.

The Village Library
16 Front Street
Fairfield, FL 33063

> The Village Library—What's in it for you?

Dear Neighbor:

Well, to begin with, the Village Library has more than 3,000 hardback books for you to borrow. The Village Library buys copies of the latest books, including those on the *New York Times* bestseller list, almost as soon as they are off the press. Right now on our shelves you can find the books you want to read, such as

> *The King of Torts*, by John Grisham
> *What Should I Do with the Rest of My Life?*, by Po Bronson
> *Late Bloomer,* by Fern Michaels
> *The Secret Life of Bees*, by Sue Monk Kidd

You'll find a fine stock of mysteries and a table full of paperbacks from which you can borrow without even checking them out. Simply bring back the paperbacks when you can, or swap your paperbacks for ours. Some titles currently on the table:

> *The English Assassin*, by Daniel Silva
> *#1 Ladies Detective Agency*, by Alexander McColl Smith
> *The Cottage*, by Danielle Steel
> *Dr. Atkins' New Diet Revolution*, by Robert C. Atkins
> *Rich Dad, Poor Dad,* by Robert T. Kiyosaki with Sharon L. Lechter
> *Nemesis,* by Isaac Asimov

Are you going on a long car trip? Before you leave, drop in to the library and, for a small fee, check out a few tapes and wile away the boring hours listening to a novel or a biography.

If you have been by the Village Library's new location at 16 Front Street, you know that our shelves are full, but we have room for many more shelves to be stacked with books for your reading pleasure.

In the next year, we will spend approximately $8,000 for shelving and $4,000 for books. When the Village Library reaches its full growth, it will be nearly self-sustaining, but for the moment, we need your help. When you contribute, dedicated volunteers will see to it that your money is spent in your best interest—to bring you the books and tapes you want.

Please use the attached form and enclosed addressed envelope to send your contribution to the Village Library today.

Yours for good reading,

Mary Powell

Mary Powell, President
Village Library

Enclosure

The Village Library

Yes! Count on my support. Enclosed is my check, fully tax deductible (made to The Village Library).

Donor $20 ( )   Patron $100 ( )
Sponsor $50 ( )   Angel $100 + ( )

Name _____

Address _____

Mail in the enclosed envelope or drop it off at the Village Library.

Donations entitle you to a complimentary family membership card and our great thanks.

Persuasive Letter

Situation

Mary Powell is the president of a small, newly established, nonprofit village library. She and everyone else who works for the library are unpaid volunteers. The library receives free space from the village but has to pay its own utilities and buy its own books. The library has no support other than yearly dues, rental fees, and donations from people who use it. When the library is finished and all the shelves are in, it should be self-sustaining, but for now it still needs help. Powell decides to raise money with a fund-raising letter to people in the village.

Analysis

Powell has one major goal: raising money for the library. Because she is sending her letter to every householder in the village, many of them will be unfamiliar with the library. Therefore, she has to tell them something about the library. Furthermore, she has to tell them about the library in a way that will get their attention and interest them and awaken their desire to use and, she hopes, support the library.

Her readers will not likely be hostile to her request, but it is all too easy to lay down a request for money and subsequently forget it. Therefore Powell knows that she has to ask for immediate action and make such action easy for the reader. Her letter meets all these requirements.

She begins with a boxed, attention-getting line above her salutation. For her attention-getter, she chooses a question directly aimed at her readers. She hopes their wish to see an answer to the question will encourage them to read on. Her question also appeals to the self-interest of her readers, another reason to continue.

The first part of her letter answers her question. She lists some of the books available in the library. She sets off the books she lists to draw attention to them and further draw the reader into the letter. She is careful to list the variety of books that will appeal to a variety of tastes. She mentions the tapes that are available and suggests a specific use for them.

After she awakens interest and desire in her readers, she begins her fund-raising effort. She tells specifically why the funds are needed. She reassures her readers that they will not be continually pressured for donations. She appeals again to her readers' self-interest, telling them that dedicated volunteers are working hard to meet their needs.

Finally, she asks for immediate action. With her attached form and enclosed envelope, she makes such action as easy as possible.

FIGURE 8.14
E-mail using a logical argument.

Date: 29 Mar 2005 10:20.15 MST
From: Varjuhh@sds.com
To: Hoveyb@sds.com
Subject: SOLUTION FOR SDS PRICING AND INVENTORY PROBLEMS

As discussed at the recent SDS Executive Council meeting, SDS is losing money because of poor pricing decisions and the need to carry excessive inventory. One suggestion at the meeting was to decentralize control over pricing and inventory and place more responsibility for both at the store level. I agree that our present centralized control system is inefficient. However, I believe the answer is not to decentralize, but to develop a new computerized central control system that works.

Many of our competitors are introducing technological innovations that are helping them in the very areas where we have problems. I'll describe one such major innovation (there are many others) and close with a recommendation for how SDS might proceed.

INNOVATION:

- Through the use of computer and space satellite systems already available, it is possible to collect complete sales data from every store every evening and transmit it to SDS headquarters for analysis.

ADVANTAGES:

- SDS can make immediate price corrections when needed to move an item and still maintain a profit margin.

- SDS will know when inventory of an item has reached the point where it needs to be replenished, removing the need to stock excessive inventory. Our competitors have cut their inventories by 30 percent using this technology.

- SDS will have precise knowledge of what items and what types and colors of items sell best in different stores. For example, if blue sweatshirts sell best in Charlotte and gray sells best in Ashville, we can stock accordingly. At the present time, we stock all stores with equal amounts of blue and gray. As a result, we have an excess of gray sweatshirts in Charlotte and a shortage of blue, and the reverse in Ashville.

With the right technology, SDS can get the right merchandise to the right stores at the right price and at the right time. To begin using such technology successfully, SDS has to make decisions at the highest levels of the company that affect all divisions of the company. To that end, I recommend that you form a Research and Development Committee composed of senior people from all the major divisions of SDS. Your charge to that committee should be to study information technologies useful to SDS and report back concerning their use to the Executive Council.

Failure to make use of technological resources available to us will lead inevitably to the failure of SDS to keep pace with its competitors.

I would like the opportunity to meet and discuss these issues with you at your earliest convenience.

Hans Varju-Hart
Vice President for Information Services
SDS, Inc.

E-Mail Using Logical Argument

Situation

Hans Varju-Hart is Vice President for Information Services for Southeastern Department Stores (SDS), a twelve-store chain located in small- and medium-sized cities in the Southeastern United States. SDS is struggling to stay solvent. Because it collects and uses sales information so poorly, it prices items badly and is forced to maintain excessive and costly inventories. Varju-Hart realizes that there are technological solutions to many of SDS's problems, and if they are not adopted soon, SDS may go under.

He decides that an e-mail message to SDS President Barry Hovey pointing out some of the technological advantages competitors have over SDS may initiate some of the changes needed. He chooses e-mail because it will reach Hovey much faster than a memo. Even though speed is an important advantage here, Varju-Hart also knows that Hovey expects recommendations to be carefully thought out and that he does not tolerate grammatical errors or misspellings. Varju-Hart is also aware that Hovey prefers to receive e-mail because he can forward messages electronically—with his comment—to others whose advice he seeks.

Analysis

Varju-Hart has a clear purpose in this email message. He wants to persuade his president, Barry Hovey, of the potential for SDS of technological developments in transmitting and processing information. He needs to grab Hovey's attention quickly in a way that a long memo or report might not do. Therefore he opts to describe one major technological innovation that could improve significantly the way SDS operates. Hovey understands department stores, but he does not speak computerese. Therefore computerese is notably absent from Varju-Hart's e-mail. There is no mention of local area networks or Unisys U6000/65 UNIX servers to boggle the mind. Instead, in plain English, Varju-Hart describes one major technological innovation and then gives three important so-whats, the significance of which Hovey will immediately grasp. Varju-Hart uses a format to make the so-whats, labeled *Advantages,* stand out.

Varju-Hart knows that Hovey will not immediately make expensive investments in technology without the input of major segments of the SDS management. Therefore rather than suggesting immediate action, he suggests the formation of a Research and Development Committee to investigate information technologies useful to SDS. However, to forestall needed changes getting bogged down in committee, he bluntly states his belief that SDS is headed for further failure if it does not take advantage of information technology.

In the discussion with Hovey that Varju-Hart hopes his e-mail will bring about, Varju-Hart can open Hovey's eyes to other innovations that will help SDS. Once on the R&D Committee, which as Vice President of Information Services he is sure to be, he can, he hopes, persuade others of the advantages of integrating information technology into every level of SDS.

Think about the following while planning and revising letters, memos, and e-mail.

Planning

In planning letters, memos, and e-mails, think about your purpose, content, and organization and your reader.

PURPOSE, CONTENT, AND ORGANIZATION

- What do you hope to accomplish?

- Is your guiding purpose informational, persuasive, or argumentative?

- What do you want your reader to know or do?

- What information will fulfill your purpose?

- What are the so-whats of your information?

- How can your information best be organized?

- Does any particular existing organizational pattern fit your purpose and content?

READER ANALYSIS

- What are your reader's interests and needs? How can you best organize to meet those interests and needs?

- How extensive is your reader's vocabulary in the subject area?

- Are there concepts you will need to explain to your reader?

- How much explanation of context will your reader need?

- Do you have secondary readers whom you must consider?

- What will be your reader's attitude?

- If your reader will be hostile or indifferent, how can you overcome such a barrier?

Revision

In revision, pay attention to content and organization, style and tone, and format and grammar.

CONTENT AND ORGANIZATION

- Is your purpose clear?
- Do your first few sentences provide the organizational and contextual information your reader needs?
- Is your organization clear and coherent?
- Have you displayed your organization with appropriate headings?
- Do your content and organization satisfy your purpose?
- Do your content and organization satisfy your reader's needs and interests?
- Have you stated clearly the so-whats of your information?
- Have you eliminated unneeded content?
- Is any action you want the reader to take clearly stated?

STYLE AND TONE

- Have you kept your sentences to a reasonable length?
- Are your word choices familiar to your reader?
- Have you eliminated unneeded words?
- Are your sentences active?
- Is your tone suitable to your purpose and for the occasion?
- Have you used personal pronouns such as *I, we,* and *you* appropriately?
- Have you avoided brusqueness and rudeness?

FORMAT AND GRAMMAR

- Have you followed a format suitable for the occasion and your purpose?
- Are your paragraphs a reasonable length, allowing for sufficient white space?
- Have you used good-quality bond paper?
- Is the letter or memo well typed or printed?
- Have you proofread carefully, eliminating all grammatical errors and typographical errors?
- Does your letter or memo present an overall good appearance?

Suggestions for Applying Your Knowledge

We suggest that you prepare for your study of workplace correspondence by gathering as many examples of real workplace letters, memos, and e-mails as you can. They will be invaluable in your study of correspondence. Most members of the class have probably received various kinds of sales letters. Many students generate correspondence with department stores, book clubs, and similar institutions. Some students already work and have legitimate access to both hard-copy and e-mail workplace correspondence.

The staff members of your school send and receive an enormous amount of correspondence. People such as the dean, bursar, placement officer, maintenance superintendent, and admissions officer do much of their business by mail—so much so that they often use form letters. Most may use e-mail more than postal mail. Some members of the class can go to these school officials and ask permission to reproduce some samples of their correspondence for classroom use. The names of people involved should be removed, of course, when letters and memos are reproduced.

When you have the letters, memos, and e-mails in class, use them as the basis for discussion. What is your honest opinion of them? Do they work? Are they clear, concise, and well organized? Is their information complete? Is their tone appropriate to their purpose? Have their writers sufficiently considered audience and purpose as well as the information they intended to convey? How successful are their persuasive strategies? How do the writers handle credibility, emotional appeals, and facts and analysis? Do any of the formats differ markedly from the norm? If so, do the differences help or distract? Have the writers avoided grammar and typographical errors?

Some suggested activities are given below: All involve collaboration with others at some point, usually in reviewing drafts. Some involve dealing with multicultural issues.

Collaborative Activities

1. Analyze and discuss in class the following inquiry letter. Is it a routine or special request? Will the reader be motivated to answer it? Why or why not? Does the reader receive enough information to provide the desired suggestions? If so, why do you think the information is sufficient? If not, what information do you think should be added? How do you think the letter should be answered?

WESTLAKE COMPUTER CENTER
UNION STATION PLAZA B
PORTLAND, OR 97201-9999

19 January 2005

Mr. Liam Markham
Technical Representative
Hughes Lighting Company
4420 Bear Creek Road
Raymond, MS 37703

Dear Mr. Markham:

Your firm was recommended to me as a possible supplier of lighting fixtures.

We are renovating our Mountain View plant and would like to install more powerful and intensive illumination to support the meticulous nature of the work that our production workers must perform in the production area.

Our production area is approximately 45,000 square feet and has no outside windows. The lighting system must be suspended from eighteen-foot ceilings.

We have looked through your latest catalog (Fall 2004), and we find nothing that seems to fit our basic lighting needs. However, the system featured on pages 23-24 of the catalog is, we think, similar to what we need. We look forward to receiving your suggestions.

Sincerely,

WESTLAKE COMPUTING SYSTEMS
Mae Norwood-Ramey
Assistant Procurement Specialist

2. If you believe Norwood-Ramey's letter needs to be revised, write the revised letter. Write a memo or e-mail to your instructor, your classmates, or both that identifies the nature of your revision and gives the rationale for the changes you made.

3. Assume that you are Liam Markham, and write a response to Norwood-Ramey's letter. Since Norwood-Ramey does not provide a telephone or fax number or an e-mail address, write a response letter. Give a copy of your letter to a classmate or your instructor or both for their comments.

4. The following are just a few opportunities that call for writing inquiry, request, and order letters, memos, or e-mail and writing responses to such correspondence. You may think of others.

   • Select an advertisement that invites you to send away for a free catalog, brochure, or sample product. Write a letter requesting the material. Give your letter to a fellow student or submit it to your instructor for comments. Include with your letter a photocopy of the advertisement so your instructor or fellow students can better evaluate your letter.

   • Select an advertisement in a nationally circulated publication or a Web site, and write a letter or e-mail asking for more information about the product or service advertised. Give your letter to a fellow student or submit it to your instructor for comments. Include a copy of the advertisement so your instructor or fellow students can better evaluate your letter.

   • If you are writing a research report for this course or another course, supplement material you have found locally by writing or e-mailing several companies or organizations for additional information. Ask for your instructor's or some of your classmates' opinions of your correspondence before you mail them.

5. Write a thank-you letter, memo, or e-mail to someone who has done something helpful for you. Be sure to be specific about the nature of the assistance and express your awareness of how you have benefited from the reader's help. Ask your instructor or classmates to critique the message before you send it.

6. Write a letter, memo, or e-mail persuading someone to take on a challenging job or to make a contribution. Ask your instructor or classmates to critique it.

7. Plan, write, and revise a letter on one of the following topics in collaboration with at least one but not more than two other classmates.

   Every school has problems of some sort. For example, many schools have registration practices that seem cumbersome and slow to students and faculty alike. Or perhaps there are problems such as inadequate access to computers or dimly lit parking lots, which are unsafe for both men and women. Choose such a problem. Find out who would be responsible for correcting the problem or at least who would consider your letter. Find out as much as you can about the person or group, and write them a letter about the situation. Make clear in your letter what the problem is and what you think the solution should be. Use methods of persuasion and argument that best suit the situation and your reader. If your instructor thinks it appropriate, send the letter.

8. In collaboration with at least one other student, interview the director of the local Better Business Bureau or an official who is responsible for handling customer inquiries or complaints. Identify the consumer's rights and the organization's or company's policy concerning these situations. Write a memo or e-mail to your classmates that summarizes your findings.

Multicultural Activities

1. Interview members of your class or other students at your school who are international students—members of cultures different from your own and whose native language is not English. Ask them about their experiences in writing or reading workplace correspondence written in American English, and have them identify problems they have experienced, what they think are the causes of those problems, how they were able to overcome them (if they did). Write a report that presents your findings to your fellow students and your instructor.

2. If you are a non-native speaker of American English, prepare a report in which you discuss the similarities and differences in the principles of letter writing in the United States and those of your own culture. Principles to consider might include the following:

   - style, tone, and voice (Americans tend to prefer common, everyday words except for necessary technical terms; use of *you* and other pronouns, active voice verbs, and short sentences and paragraphs)

   - format and layout

   - organization of information

   - amount of detailed information

   Prepare the report as both a written report and as an oral presentation addressed to your fellow students.

CHAPTER 9

Resumes, Employment Letters, and Application Forms

Every step of seeking employment is highly competitive. A letter from a former student to one of the authors illustrated this point rather painfully. He told us that in one instance, he and his staff were choosing between two recent graduates who seemed equal in every professional way. The decision was finally made by taking the person who had prepared the neatest application. As you read this chapter and Chapter 10, "Portfolios and Interviews," take note of the different communication activities you will engage in and the number of people you will encounter as you look for a job. Whether the deciding factor is a neat application, answering your home telephone in a professional manner, or showing respect for the receptionist who takes your application, you must have solid oral and written communication skills to present your credentials to a prospective employer.

You must enter the job market mentally prepared. Seeking employment will thrust you into many competitive communication situations, both written and oral. Your first contact with a potential employer may be by means of a letter of application and a resume showing your education and experience. Or a friend may tell you about an opening at the company she works for and suggest you send her supervisor an e-mail. Or the guest speaker at the student professional organization you belong to (for example, the Society of American Foresters or the Association of Nursing Students) may suggest that you send him your resume. If you present yourself effectively in the initial contact—frequently a spoken one—you will most likely be asked to send your resume. If your letter and resume succeed, you will probably be interviewed. If you obtain an interview, consider your resume and letter successful whether you receive a job offer or not. Remember those interviewing you are looking for someone who will contribute to their team's activities and work well with other members of the team.

The job search requires that you do more than write a resume to obtain an interview. You may also need to write requests for letters of recommendation and several follow-up letters, such as thank-you notes to those who interviewed you and those who wrote you letters of recommendation. You will also write letters of acceptance and refusal. You will likely complete an application form. To help you successfully reach your goal of getting a job, we discuss all these communication situations in this chapter. Read what we have to say about letters, resumes, and application forms, but also review library and Web resources and talk with your school's career placement advisers, a recent graduate, friends, and someone doing what you want to do. Some of the advice you gather may contradict other advice. You must decide what advice best fits your personal and career goals.

Applying for a job is a lot easier when you know what you are interested in and know what prospective employers are looking for. This chapter and Chapter 10 provide information on the job-hunting process. At the end of this chapter, we provide a self-inventory that will help you evaluate your interests and abilities. We describe the features of letters of application, resumes, and application forms and show you several examples. You must adapt the information to your needs. Keep in mind our definition of workplace writing: writing for a specific purpose, to a specific audience, to convey the information the audience needs. Your purpose is to find a job. You will need to evaluate what each employer wants and present your credentials (information about yourself) in such a way that employers (your audience) will see how you meet their hiring requirements.

Obtaining an interview and a job offer are your goals. In Chapter 10, we describe portfolios and interviews and suggest some techniques for having successful interviews. In an interview, employers want to see evidence of your expertise in your field (whether it is building houses, designing Web sites, or writing instructions or press releases). A portfolio contains samples of your communications and area-of-specialization activities to show potential employers during an interview.

Timing

Plan to devote three to six months to conducting your job search.

You should begin the job-search process early and allow enough time to research and apply for positions that best fit your personal and career goals. You also must add in the time it takes for companies and organizations to work through the hiring process. Looking for a position that is part of your career plans is not the same as looking for a part-time position to earn income while going to school. The more specialized the training needed for a position, the more time you may need to find a position.

It takes time to do everything right. Figure 9.1 provides a time line to help you plan your job search. You will fill in the dates that fit your plans. You cannot expect to graduate, look for a job for a week or two, and then start to work. If you want to start work shortly after you graduate, you need to begin looking three to six months ahead of time, depending on the current demand for workers in your field. Employment counselors, teachers, and friends working in the field have a pretty good idea of what the job market is like. Talk to them.

If you are interested in checking out employment possibilities in other countries, you will need to schedule even more time ahead. The procedure becomes lengthy when you consider the need to obtain a passport and possibly a special kind of work visa and other documentation that the target country might require of foreign workers. In addition, many prospective employers will request more information about you than U.S. employers want from domestic applicants.

Few companies can fill an opening immediately. They must advertise the position, review the applications, interview a select few of the applicants, and meet state and federal employment guidelines providing equal opportunities for employment before they can make a job offer. Companies invest a lot of time and money when they hire you (more than just the amount you receive in your paycheck). Training you, providing health insurance and other benefits, and equipping your workstation are just a few of the additional costs. They want to make sure their investment is going to be worthwhile. The process may take two weeks; it may take three months. Most likely, the time will be four to six weeks from the time the company first approaches you for an interview.

FIGURE 9.1

Construct a time line to help plan your job search. When you start your search will depend on the job market, your school schedule, your career goals, and your personal goals. The self-inventory, traditional resume, and portfolio should be your first activities.

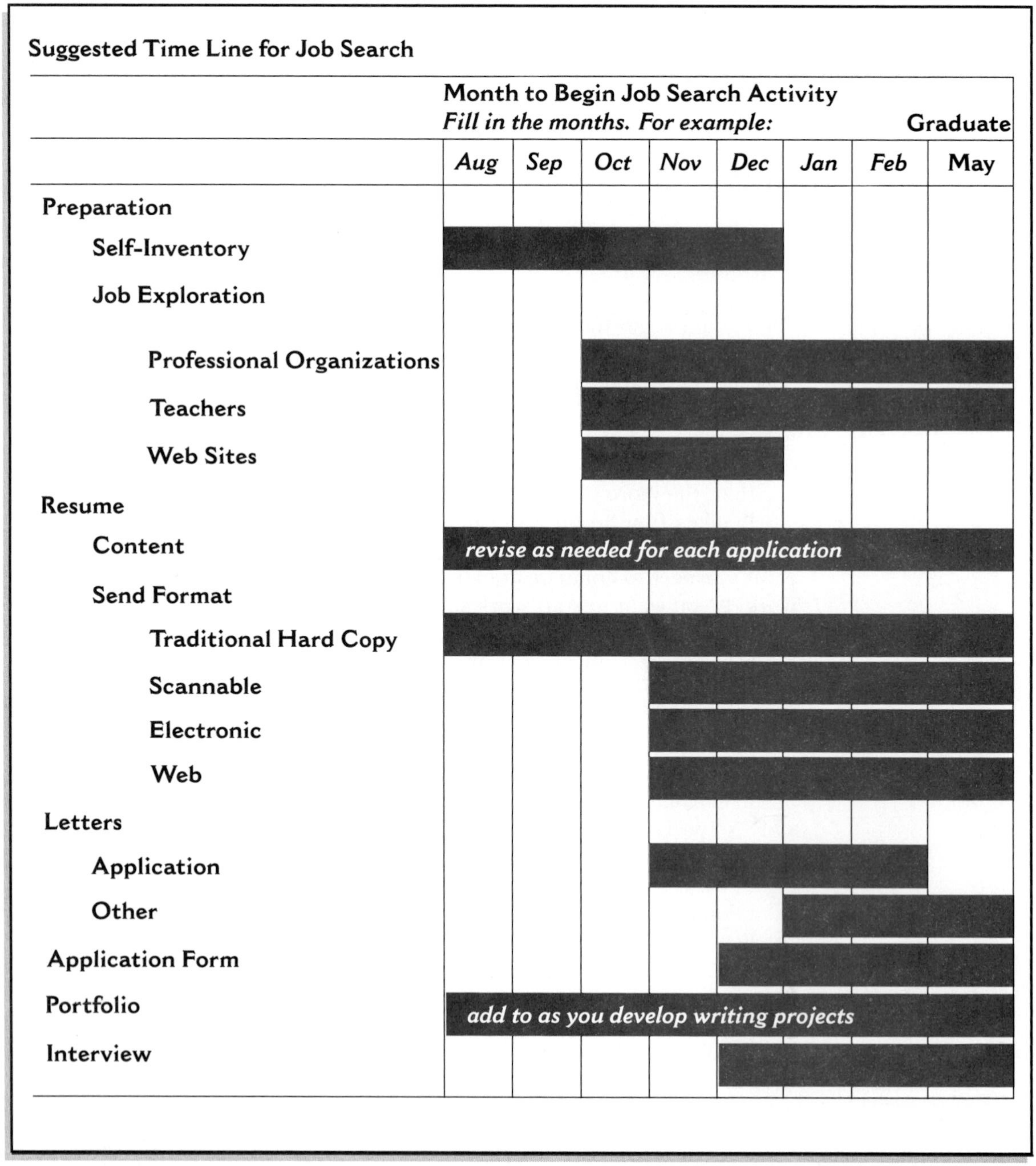

Suggested Time Line for Job Search

	Month to Begin Job Search Activity — Fill in the months. For example:							Graduate
	Aug	Sep	Oct	Nov	Dec	Jan	Feb	May
Preparation								
Self-Inventory	███	███	███	███	███			
Job Exploration								
Professional Organizations			███	███	███	███	███	███
Teachers			███	███	███			
Web Sites			███	███				
Resume								
Content	*revise as needed for each application*							
Send Format								
Traditional Hard Copy	███	███	███					
Scannable				███	███	███	███	███
Electronic				███	███	███	███	███
Web				███	███	███	███	███
Letters								
Application				███	███	███	███	
Other						███	███	███
Application Form					███	███	███	███
Portfolio	*add to as you develop writing projects*							
Interview					███	███	███	███

Preparation

Before the letter writing begins, you must prepare yourself in at least two ways. First, inventory your own interests, education, experience, and abilities. Second, explore the job market to find out what is available for you. What you discover about yourself and what the job market is looking for will help you see how well your credentials and interests match up with what prospective employers are looking for.

Self-Inventory

Socrates' axiom "know thyself" is important in preparing a list of skills and accomplishments.

Conducting the self-inventory enables you to understand more about yourself and to compile a complete record of your education and experience. So that you can organize the information you develop during your self-inventory, group similar information together.

A Self-Inventory Helps You Get in Touch with Your Own Identity

Consider the activities you have succeeded in and enjoyed. Which course did you enjoy more: computer programming or English? Do you prefer math to psychology or the other way around? Do you relate best to people or to working with equipment such as computers? Which would you rather do: read a book, go to a large party with music and dancing, or play charades with a few close friends? Never mind which you think you *should* like. Which do you *really* like? Have you ever sold merchandise in a store? Did you enjoy it? Is money extremely important to you or not? Do you stick to jobs? Do you see new ways to get an old job done? Do you find the most satisfaction in stability or in change? Do you work well independently, or would you rather have your tasks spelled out for you? Can you describe a time or two when you worked through a difficult situation? What did you learn from that experience? What goals have you set for yourself and how did you meet them? What teachers and supervisors do you believe would be willing to support your applications by providing you with a reference?

Be honest in your answers and analysis. It is your life. You would not want to spend it doing something you do not enjoy. And you are more likely to succeed at work you truly enjoy and have the capabilities for. A good sales representative might make a terrible horticulturist and vice versa.

The Self-Inventory Highlights Your Education and Experience

While you are analyzing yourself, be alert for evidence of those qualities employers value: loyalty, willingness to shoulder responsibility, ability to stick to a task until it is done, initiative, enough flexibility and a positive attitude to realize that things do not always go perfectly but that most problems can be solved. You must have a strong work ethic, have good analytical skills, be a good communicator, and work well with others no matter what job you have.

Organizing Your Self-Inventory

- **Schooling and Academic Preparation** Begin by reviewing relevant significant events in your school life. What did you accomplish in high school and college? What do you remember of your course work? Which courses did you enjoy? Which courses could you barely tolerate? Where did you earn your highest and lowest grades? Focus your attention on the most relevant part of your schooling. Rarely will you refer back to your high school activities if you have an associate or bachelor's degree, military experience, or other specialized training such as in heating and air conditioning installation or maintenance of a UNIX mainframe environment. If you are one of the many students these days who is declaring a double major, you will be bringing more interests to the table. Be sure to explain your varied interests and how your education combines them.

- **Extracurricular Activities** What were your extracurricular activities? Do you have any long-standing hobbies such as photography, needlepoint, rebuilding engines, or gardening? Have you been active in political, social, religious, or civic groups? Do you enjoy sports, music, or surfing the Web? Be sure to include appropriate activities that might set you apart from other applicants. For example, if you have a private pilot's license, include that information. Having the license says something about you—your personality, your level of ability, and so on. The employer sees a pilot as someone who invested considerable time in an activity that carries great responsibility for the safety of others. Childcare responsibilities have similar connotations for employers. If you took care of three children under the age of six, you were entrusted with a responsibility that not everyone can handle.

- **Work Experience** What has been your work experience? What was your first job? Your most recent? What have been your duties and responsibilities? Be specific here. Just noting down that you worked as a loader for delivery trucks does not get at the detail you need to record. Look at what you actually did and the significance of the work. For instance, "Loaded aluminum crates on delivery trucks, assured on-time delivery and an accident-free safety record during the loading" gives the kind of reflective detail you should record. Were you promoted or otherwise formally recognized for your work achievements? What sort of work have you enjoyed? Have you been in the military? What training and jobs did you have there? Did you work while going to school?

- **Interest in Working in Other Countries** If you are interested in seeking employment in another country, you should also ask such questions of yourself as these: Have you traveled or worked overseas? If so, what were your experiences? Do you know other languages? If so, how well? How familiar are you with the culture of other countries? Are you willing to provide more information about yourself than you would normally be expected to provide to U.S. employers? Employers in other countries are not subject to U.S. laws pertaining to the kinds of questions that can be asked during a job application.

In the planning and revising checklist at the end of this chapter, we provide a self-inventory—a series of questions you should ask yourself as a way of discovering the information you need. Open a file on your computer, and type in the answers to the questions.

You will be able to draw on the self-inventory information in all the communication activities of the job search, such as writing your resume and letters of application and filling in employers' application forms. Such information is particularly useful during an employment interview when you are expected to describe your qualities and abilities. Applicants who can speak easily about themselves and can show they know the company or organization they are interviewing with have a distinct advantage.

Job Exploration

As you begin the search for a job, first let everyone know that you are looking for a job and what type of job you would like. For some of the people we identify below, you may want to provide a short summary of your career goals and experiences, or you may want to give them a copy of your resume. For others, you may want to make an appointment to visit or take them to lunch so that you can describe your career plans to them without interruptions. Your self-inventory will provide you with the information to share.

Networking

Letting as many people as possible know that you are actively looking for work is important. Employers like to know a little bit about you before they contact you. They depend on formal and informal recommendations from others as they evaluate you. Your networking should include the following:

- Student chapters of professional organizations offer opportunities for you to meet members of the profession. Become active in such an organization. You may be surprised at how many doors this will open. More and more organizations also have Web sites with job listings.

- Career counselors at your school can be invaluable. Register with your school's career center. Employers routinely contact career centers and make campus visits to interview students. Career counselors have resources available to help you with your search and will help you target your search.

- College faculty and training instructors can be helpful networkers. Employers frequently call schools and ask about graduating students. Frequently, the employers have hired a graduate of the school who has done outstanding work, and they hope to find other graduates with similar abilities. Let your teachers know how to reach you. You also might want to ask them if you may list them as a reference.

- Friends and relatives can spread the word that may reach someone who is looking for a dependable worker. They work in places where you might want to work and can tell you a good deal about working conditions, opportunities for advancement, company policies, needed skills, and so forth. They are valuable sources of information.

Learning What Jobs Are Available

Once you get the word out, gather as much information as possible about potential jobs and potential employers. The Planning and Revising Checklist at the end of this chapter provides a series of questions in the Employer Inventory to help you gather the information you need. Where can you obtain such information?

- Use the World Wide Web to gather information from three sources. Type the name of a company or organization into a search engine, such as Google, and you will find a link to its Web site and probably links to dozens of articles related to the company or organization. Use the link to go to the Web site for the company or organization you want to work for. Such sites describe the activities of the company and frequently list job opportunities. For example, Hewlett Packard's homepage (www.hp.com) links to *Jobs at HP*. From there, you can follow numerous paths to find out about working at Hewlett Packard and how to apply. You may choose to follow links that use terms such as *college recruiting* or *recent graduates* and avoid wasting time reading about positions that require several years of experience.

  A second Web source you should review is the site for the professional organization that represents your field: for example, the American Public Health Association (www.apha.org), the Institute of Electrical and Electronics Engineers (www.ieee.org), and the National Agri-Marketing Association (www.nama.org).

  Companies that specialize in career information are a third source. These companies have Web sites for posting your resume and accessing job banks. You may find the amount of information overwhelming. Use the questions at the end of the chapter to help guide you with the information gathering. Figure 9.2 lists a few of the many career service and job bank sites on the Web. Some of these sites feature links to overseas jobs. If you are interested in working overseas, be sure to check them out.

- Register with your school's career placement office. We noted in the discussion of networking that you should contact your school's career placement office. Contact the office at least one semester or quarter before you plan to graduate—earlier is better.

  Many schools now have you enter items from your self-inventory into a database either on disk or across the Web. When they receive a call for an education major with experience in teaching kindergarten, piano, and computers, they will search the database using keywords such as *early childhood education, kindergarten, music, piano, word*

FIGURE 9.2

Companies, state governments, and the U.S. government provide career services across the World Wide Web. We have listed only a few of the many commercial and government sites. The Web site for your school library or career placement office probably links to some of these and to others. Many of these sites also include links to overseas job opportunities.

Web Resource	Web Address (http://)
Alabama Department of Industrial Relations	www.dir.state.al.us
America's Employers	www.americasemployers.com
America's Job Bank	www.ajb.dni.us
Careers in Ag	www.farms.com or www.agjobs.com
Career Mart	www.careermart.com
CareerMosaic	www.careermosaic.com
CareerPath.com	www.careerpath.com
Career Resource Center	www.careers.org
College Grad Job Hunter	www.collegegrad.com
Cool Works	www.coolworks.com
FlipDog	www.flipdog.com
HeadHunter.net	www.HeadHunter.net
HotJobs.com	www.hotjobs.com
JobGalleries.com	www.jobgalleries.com
JobTrak	www.jobtrak.com
JobWeb	www.jobweb.com
Monster.com	www.monster.com
Online Career Center	www.occ.com
Resortjobs	www.resortjobs.com
U.S. Office of Personnel Management	www.usajobs.opm.gov

processing, and *ClarisWorks*. Few students' resumes will match all of the keywords entered—that's expected. You will be notified if you meet a significant number of the requirements. You will also receive notices of upcoming job and career fairs.

- Read the newspaper, including the want ads. Not only will you keep up on the activities of your community, but you will also read about where the new bank will be located or when the local manufacturer is hiring. The want ads list specific openings. The weekend or Sunday issue usually has much more extensive listings of employment opportunities than do the weekday issues.

- Check with your state employment office or human resource department about state employment. The federal government also lists jobs.

You might begin with America's Job Bank (www.ajb.dni.us), a site developed by the U.S. Department of Labor and states' employment services, or www.usajobs.opm.gov, a site maintained by the U.S. Office of Personnel Management.

- Your librarian and school placement officer can direct you to many other sources, including many that relate to specific industries, organizations, and geographic areas. We have listed some of these resources in Figure 9.3. Much of this information is on the World Wide Web and may be linked through your library's home page.

One source you should be sure to check is the *Occupational Outlook Handbook* available in most libraries and on the Web (http://www.bls.gov/oco/). Figure 9.4 illustrates information you can

FIGURE 9.3

Most libraries subscribe to at least two of these resources. The resources provide information such as products and services, list of directors, contact names, company size, company location, and telephone and fax numbers.

Check your school's library or career placement office for the following resources:

College Placement Annual
Directory of Public High Technology Corporations
Dun's Census of American Business
Global Company Handbook
International Directory of Company Histories
Million Dollar Directory
Moody's International Manual
Occupational Outlook Handbook (stats.bls.gov/ocohome.htm)
Standard and Poor's Register of Corporations, Directors,
    and Executives
Thomas Register of American Manufacturers (thomasregister.com)
Ward's Business Directory

There are also various guides published by states. Here are only two examples:

Alabama Mining and Manufacturing Directory
Georgia Manufacturing Directory

If your are interested in listings of jobs abroad, see the sites listed in Figure 9.2 and specific sites such as JobsAbroad.com and Overseasjobs.com.

FIGURE 9.4

The Occupational Outlook Handbook provides an enormous amount of information you might find useful as you make career choices. This table identifies 10 fields that are predicted to grow and need more employees.

Source: Bureau of Labor Statistics (2003 September). Employment Projections. Retrieved September 7, 2003, from www.bls.gov/news.release/ecopro.t06.htm

The ten fastest-growing occupations in the United States, 2000–2010.

(Numbers in thousands of jobs)

	EMPLOYMENT	
OCCUPATION	2000	2010
Computer software engineers, applications	380	760
Computer support specialists	506	996
Computer software engineers, systems software	317	601
Network and computer systems administrators	229	416
Network systems and data communications analysts	119	211
Desktop publishers	38	63
Database administrators	106	176
Personal and home care aides	414	672
Computer systems analysts	431	689
Medical assistants	329	516

gather from the Handbook—information that may help you target your career search.

Finding information about jobs and employers should be part of your preparation for the job hunt. You will ask better questions in an interview if you know about the company. You will show the employer that you have a real interest in the position and want to work for the company.

It is difficult to anticipate whether prospective employers and their recruiters look at application letters or resumes first. Some read the letter, looking for motivation to move on to the resume. Some go straight to the resume. In any event, both letter and resume are important. Work hard on them.

Resumes

Resumes must be accurate, brief, and clear.

In Chapter 2, we discussed *change*. *Change* may be the key word to remember as we describe *resumes* (pronounced *rez-uh-may* and sometimes given its original French accent marks *résumé*). In the past three years, changes in technology have affected the way we produce and distribute resumes. The content of resumes has changed little, but the format and method of delivering the resume to the employer have changed. In this section, we first describe the content of a resume—that is, what information you include in a resume. We then describe current (but changing) ways to send a resume.

Spend your time on the content. Once you have the content in place, you can easily adapt the format to send the resume. You must create your resume electronically and use a laser printer or a high-quality ink-jet printer for hardcopy versions. Do not even consider submitting a typed or handwritten resume.

Concentrating on the Content

You will gather the content for your resume from your self-inventory. Select information depending on the type of resume you plan to produce and the job you are applying for. Remember that the job description establishes your purpose, and your reader is the person(s) who reviews the resume and interviews you. We include several examples of resumes in this chapter. Use the examples for ideas, but modify the content (the information) you include and the order of the content depending upon the job description.

Prospective employers around the world look for much the same characteristics as do U.S. employers: technical skills, communication skills, and good organizational skills (the ability to work well with others and to work on difficult projects until they are successfully completed). You want to show on your resume that you know how to follow instructions and to work with little supervision.

Two common types of resumes are the chronological and the functional.

Figures 9.5 and 9.6 (pages 246–249) illustrate variations on two common resume types: chronological and functional. With either resume, you must identify your purpose and audience and adapt the content and format for the specific job. Chronological resumes (Figure 9.5, pages 246–247) are the most common and familiar. They are perhaps best used when most of your education and work experience seem to point toward a specific career goal.

If you have gaps in your work or educational experience or if you decide to change careers, the functional resume (Figure 9.6, pages 248–249) may be your best choice. It allows you to list your experiences under functional categories that will best demonstrate those of your capabilities that relate to the jobs you are seeking. In the example, the student has chosen categories such as technical writing, technical editing, Web design, presentations, and creative writing. Headings on your resume might be technical support, computer programming, sales, organization, management, research, teaching, construction, and so forth.

A third type of resume that blends features of both the chronological and functional resumes is the "combined" resume (Figure 9.7, pages 250–251). Consider using it if you feel that neither the more traditional chronological resume nor the functional resume presents you the way you wish to be seen initially.

Word-processing software lets you vary your resume from employer to employer. Review the job description, and pull information from your self-inventory that will support the job description. Figure 9.8 on page 252 shows a job description with keywords highlighted. Keywords are words that you should include on your resume if at all possible. No one will be able to include all of the keywords, but you should include some. Always give an accurate, honest picture of your qualifications, and always present them in language that is familiar to your readers.

You will select information from the self-inventory and adapt headings to best describe the information you include. In the following paragraphs, we talk briefly about the types of information you probably want to include (name/addresses, education, experience, activities, and so on) and mention others you may want to consider (objective, religious or political activities). You select the information and format based on the information the reader wants. Keep the information in your resume current.

Below are the parts of a good resume (see Figures 9.5, 9.6, and 9.7).

Name and Address

Employers cannot line up an interview if they cannot reach you. In the section with your name and address(es), you might also include your e-mail address and Web address. Include the e-mail and Web address only if you check your e-mail regularly and if you want the readers to see your Web site. They will likely visit your Web site before they contact you because it is one more way to evaluate your work before interviewing you. If you move, give your new address, e-mail address, and phone number to the employers you have applied to.

Career Objective

Many people recommend you state your career objective and list those capabilities and achievements that fit you for such an objective. Remember that although a stated career objective may open some doors, it may shut others. If you plan to include a job or career objective statement, remember that prospective employers want to see a fairly specific objective. Customize it for the prospective employer so that it describes your strengths for the job for which you are applying, as shown in Figure 9.6. If you omit the career objective from your resume, you can always include it in your letter of application. On the other hand, the resume may be scanned into a database, and a letter probably will not be, so you may want to include an objective on your resume.

Education and Experience

Whether you choose the chronological or functional format for your resume, keep it brief but with good coverage of your education and experience. Be sure that resume readers can easily identify dates of schooling and work. If its focus is not clear in the name of the company or organization you have worked for, explain what the company does in a short phrase. If resume readers have not heard of the company or organization, they will not know whether it manufactures widgets, sells gizmos, or installs framzits. Use phrases and dependent clauses rather than complete sentences.

FIGURE 9.5
Chronological resume.

Kelly J. Bennett

School Address (until 12 May 06)
2011 8th Street, Apt. 10A
Boise City, ID 83700
208.111.9999
kjbennett@mail.com

Address (after 12 May 06)
1611 Wafer Lane
Marytown, ID 82200
208.456.7899

Education

Idaho Technical University, Boise City, ID
Bachelor of Chemical Engineering
Minor in Spanish
Expected graduation, May 2006

Military Training
June 2001–December 2005

- Special Forces Qualification Course, Ft. Bragg, NC 2001
- Advanced International Morse Code Course, Ft. Bragg, NC 2002
- Airborne School, Fort Benning, GA 2002
- Class A Electronics Technician School, Ft. Gilmore, NE 2003
- Class A Spanish School, Joint Service Defense Language Institute, Washington, DC, 2004
- Infantry Squadron Leadership School, Ft. Benning, GA 2005

Experience
January 2002–present

Boise City Fire Department, Boise City, ID
Firefighter II, January 2002–January 2003; *Firefighter I,* February 2003–present. Apparatus operator and unit supervisor.

January 2002–present

Idaho National Guard, Boise City, ID
Special Forces Communications Sergeant
- Operate and repair communications equipment
- Deployed to Kuwait, April–July 2003

June 1999–May 2001

ComputExperts, Boise City, ID
Computer Service Technician
- Repaired hardware for all makes of personal computers
- Managed listserv for three clients

Expertise

- Speak, write, and read Spanish fluently
- Program in C++
- Use AutoCad for design projects

References

Dr. Mervine Alioto, Professor, Department of Chemical Engineering, Idaho Technical University, Boise City, ID 83701. aliotom@itu.edu

Dr. Nathan Clarke, Assistant Professor, Department of Chemical Engineering, Idaho Technical University, Boise City, ID 83701. clarkn@itu.edu

CPT Avela Wildermuth, HQ Company, 12th Communication Battalion, Idaho National Guard, The Armory, Boise City, ID 83700. AW179@ING.ID.USA.gov

15 April 2006

About the Chronological Resume

The chronological resume emphasizes a chronological listing of education and work experience. It highlights the most recent activities and achievements. Use it when your education or employment history shows a steady progression with few or no gaps and when your employment and education are directly related to your current employment goals. The information is organized in reverse chronological order to present your current or most recent activities and achievements first. The chronological resume may not be the best if you have gaps in your employment or education or if you are changing careers and employment objectives.

Name and Address

Consider emphasizing your name by putting it in bold—and slightly larger font—but do not type your name in such a huge print that it overwhelms the rest of the resume. Bennett provides several ways to contact him, including stating the currency of addresses. Simply labeling addresses as "permanent" or "current" is not as informative.

Education

Bennett believes that his education is probably the primary qualification for the job, so he puts it first. Consider listing separately each school you attended (current or most recent first). College graduates usually do not need to include their high school education, since the chronological resume tends to emphasize the most recent history.

Be sure to include the full name of each institution and its location, the correct name of your degree or certificate, and other noteworthy credentials, such as a second major, a minor, or an area of concentration or specialization. The date of graduation (month and year are sufficient) or expected graduation provides currency of the education and helps resume reviewers see the overall chronological framework.

Bennett regards his military training as important enough to have its own heading, but it is placed after his formal college education. Many prospective employers regard military training among the best training available, so do not omit it from your resume if you have it.

Experience

Bennett's work experience is listed in reverse chronological order with beginning and ending dates indicated. Again, month and year are usually sufficient. Each entry should also include the name and location of the organization, your job title, and a brief description of responsibilities. If you received recognition or were promoted, indicate when. If you are of typical college-graduation age (perhaps from 22 to 30), list your experience, back about 5 to 10 years of employment. If you are an older college graduate, if you go back farther than 10 years, provide only minimum information about jobs, or perhaps write a brief summary of earlier jobs held. Work experience over 10 or 12 years old is much less relevant than more recent experience.

Expertise

Prospective employers seek applicants who have technical expertise to do the job but who also have other desirable skills. Although Bennett does not identify the version of AutoCad he can use, he is quite specific in mentioning the kind of programming language and application programs he uses. He also mentions his fluency in Spanish to indicate the degree of expertise. Do not overlook the procedures, equipment, and other activities that you are proficient or expert in. However, do not claim expertise in using a particular computer operating or application program if you have only seen it demonstrated or worked a school exercise or two with it.

References

We recommend that you include your references with your application—either as part of the resume or on a separate page. It lets prospective employers see the quality of persons who are willing to support your application.

Date

Although optional, dating your resume establishes the currency of the information in the resume and enables you to keep track of different versions you might have.

FIGURE 9.6
Functional resume.

Angela Maria Chang

922 Burke Place
Lubbock, TX 79401

806.697.9071
changam@tx.mail.edu
www.tx.edu/~changam

Objective   To research, design, and write descriptions for displays at museums, zoos, and entertainment parks.

Education   West Texas College, Lubbock, TX
Bachelor of Arts in English, June 2005
GPA: Major 3.50, Overall 3.21

Writing Experience

Technical Writing
- Developed documentation for file management features in Windows XP
- Performed a substantive edit on grant proposal for Plains Museum of West Texas, Lubbock, TX
- Wrote a style guide for major grant proposals
- Interviewed prospective users, compiled a user analysis, and oversaw user testing
- Designed page layouts in WordPerfect

Technical Editing
- Performed a substantive edit on grant proposal for Plains Museum of West Texas, Lubbock, TX
- Developed style guidelines including font, justification, and spacing for grant proposals
- Completed numerous copyediting and proofreading tasks using standard symbols

Web Design
- Created a personal Web site containing online resume and portfolio
- Self-taught basic- and intermediate-level HMTL codes
- Researched Web page layout and design

Research
- Researched guidelines for entertainment park information for customers
- Investigated the use of symbols, such as $, %, and & in technical documents
- Interviewed the chief editor for *Phi Kappa Phi,* a national scholarly magazine

Presentations
- Developed a 20-minute/12-slide presentation on Plains Museum of West Texas information signs for visitors (used Corel Presentations)
- Created a 15-minute/10-slide presentation on online editing (used Microsoft PowerPoint)

Creative Writing
- "Sweet and Sour Reverie," poem published in *Thistle and Thorn,* the college student literary magazine (Winter issue, 2004)

Computer Knowledge   Windows XP; WordPerfect 11; Microsoft Word 2002; Corel Presentations; Microsoft PowerPoint; Intermediate HMTL; Basic Microsoft Excel; Basic Microsoft Access

Honors
- Sigma Tau Chi, national honor society of the Society for Technical Communication
- Sigma Tau Delta, English national honor society
- Dean's List, Fall 2003, Spring 2004, Fall 2004, Spring 2005

Volunteer Activities
- Plains Museum of West Texas College, Children's Group Leader
- Buddy Holley Museum, Lubbock, TX, Student Docent

Work Experience

Summer 2004   Camp Greylock, Becket, MA, Junior Counselor, Soccer Instructor
Summer 2003   Auntie Ethel's Pizza, Lubbock, TX, Driver

References   See attached sheet.

11 April 2005

About The Functional Resume

The functional resume emphasizes clusters of skills and de-emphasizes chronological order. However, although the highlighted skills, experience, and accomplishments are not connected to specific places and dates, those are included in the education and work experience sections. Consider using the functional resume when your education and experiences are so diverse and interrupted that they do not reflect a clear-cut education or career path. However, it is just this lack of easy-to-follow paths that causes some prospective employers to dislike functional resumes. They suspect that the applicant is unfocused (what is he or she interested in this year?), is unsettled (a job hopper), or has made little progress in a career.

Fortunately, though, in today's economic world, prospective employers are becoming aware that the straight chronological resume, which years ago was standard, does not present applicants well who are re-entering the workforce after a period of unemployment, who are making career changes—either voluntarily or not, or who have little experience other than volunteer work or their college education. For those applicants, the chronological track record just is not there. But the skills may well be, and that is what the functional resume is good at presenting.

Name, Address, Education, Experience, References, and Resume Date

These parts of the resume are almost identical to those of the more standard chronological resume (see Figure 9.5 and pages 245 and 253–255). They are, however, subordinated by being placed later in the resume. In Chang's resume, the section heading *Computer Knowledge* (see Figure 9.5) is similar to Bennett's *Expertise* section. The functional resume should still enable the reader to see references to chronology, as in Chang's sections on *Education, Honors,* and *Work Experience.* There should never be an attempt to omit references to time or place. It is just a matter of de-emphasizing them in functional resumes. It is the description of skills that is emphasized. If you wish to limit your resume to one page, place the names and addresses of your references on a separate sheet (see Figure 9.8) and include it with the letter and resume.

The Sections Highlighting Functional Skills

Chang's functional resume highlights the skills that most relate to her job or employment objective. She is interested in becoming a professional communicator (researcher, writer, designer), so she categorizes her special skills into categories that align with the important functions of those who hold such positions. It takes considerable familiarity with that kind of work and careful scrutiny of job descriptions to be able to show how her skills line up with the major responsibilities and qualifications of the job. Achieving this counters those questions that some prospective employers may have about her focus, her attention, and the applicability of her skills to the prospective employer's needs.

Chang uses categories such as technical writing, technical editing, Web design, and research to give resume readers a clear idea of how her skills match those needed for the job. In addition to such functional skills, you might also consider such categories as leadership, team work, sales, and service.

Notice the use of verbs to begin the description of her work performance. In each, the bullet is followed immediately by a verb that introduces the work activity.

FIGURE 9.7
Combined chronological/functional resume.

ANGELA MARIA CHANG

822 Burke Place
Lubbock, TX 79401

806.697.9097
changam@tx.mail.edu

EDUCATION Bachelor of Arts in English, West Texas College, Lubbock, TX. Date of graduation, 10 May 2005. GPA in major, end of Fall 2004 Semester, 3.50. Overall GPA, end of Fall 2004 Semester, 3.21.

COMMUNICATION EXPERIENCE

Technical Writing Developed documentation for file management features in Windows XP; Performed substantive edit on grant proposal for Plains Museum of West Texas, Lubbock, TX; Wrote style guide for major grant proposals; Interviewed prospective users, compiled user analysis, and oversaw user testing; Designed page layouts in Corel WordPerfect 11.

Technical Editing Performed substantive edit on grant proposal for Plains Museum of West Texas; Developed style guidelines including font, justification, and spacing; Completed numerous copyediting and proofreading tasks using standard symbols.

Web Design Created personal Web site containing online resume and portfolio; Self-taught basic- and intermediate-level HMTL codes.

Research Researched guidelines for entertainment park information for customers; Investigated use of symbols, such as $, %, and &, in technical documents; Interviewed the chief editor for *Phi Kappa Phi,* a national scholarly magazine.

Presentations 20-minute/12-slide presentations on Plains Museum of West Texas information signs for visitors (used Corel Presentations); 15-minute/10-slide presentation on online editing (used Microsoft PowerPoint).

Creative Writing "Sweet and Sour Reverie," poem published in *Thistle and Thorn,* the college student literary magazine (Winter issue, 2004).

IMPORTANT COURSE WORK Document Design, Proposal Writing, Project Management, Professional Editing, Information Architecture, Writing User Guides, Interviewing, Web Writing.

HONORS Sigma Tau Chi, national honor society of the Society for Technical Communication; Sigma Tau Delta, English national honor society; Dean's List Fall 2003-Spring 2005.

EXPERIENCE (LAST 3 YEARS)

Volunteer docent, Plains Museum of West Texas, Lubbock, TX, August 2003–May 2004; November 2004–present. Worked on grant proposals, prepared informational signs for museum visitors, conducted tours and classes for public-school children.

Editorial intern, Lubbock County Prairie Dog Sanctuary, Lubbock, TX. August 2004–November 2004. Prepared guidelines for visitors to the sanctuary. Approximately 2,000 visitors a month.

Junior counselor, soccer instructor, Camp Greylock, Becket, MA. Summer 2004. Counseled 8 youths and led soccer instruction for approximately 30 campers.

Student docent, Buddy Holley Museum, Lubbock, TX. August 2002–May 2003. Conducted tours for individuals and small groups.

Delivery Driver, Auntie Ethel's Pizza, Lubbock, TX. Summer 2003. Drove approximately 200 miles each week and handled $500 weekly with accident-free driving and no errors in cash accountability.

REFERENCES See attached list

11 April 2005

About the Combined Chronological and Functional Resume

You should design your resume so that it represents your strongest qualifications for being considered for the position to which you are applying. Either the traditional chronological resume or the newer functional resume is sometimes the best resume to use. However, if you want to consider a resume that combines features of both types of resumes, think about designing one that strikes a balance between the chronological and the functional resume, one that has the best features of both: emphasis on skills that relate to job functions and robust chronological description of work experience.

Purpose of the Combined Resume

Angela Maria Chang, a soon-to-be-graduate entering the professional workplace for the first time, has little professional experience outside volunteer work and an internship. Her services as a docent and an intern have helped her develop important professional skills. Prospective employers are more interested in those professional skills than whether she gained them in a paid or unpaid job. In addition, emphasizing her volunteer work also shows her commitment to social service activities—something that an organization that wants to be known as a good corporate citizen in its community is interested in.

In an attempt to reframe her functional resume to emphasize her experience as well as her skills listed under the heading *Writing Experience* in her strictly functional resume (Figure 9.6), Chang reorganized and reformatted her resume to include another major section titled *Experience (Last 3 Years)*. This section, which includes not only her volunteer and internship work but also brief descriptions of her job performances, enables prospective employers to see more clearly the nature of her experience and—at least with her work as camp counselor, delivery driver, and restaurant server—the skills that while not directly related to the work of a communicator are transferable skills (careful, meticulous work and communicating and teaching and generally having assumed important job responsibilities) that employers value. This information—the so-whats—enables prospective employers to evaluate her experiences and commitment in those jobs.

Format of the Combined Resume

In this version of her resume, Chang avoids the table and bulleted-list format of the functional resume in Figure 9.6. Although Chang does not use bullets in this version, she uses headings, bold headings, subheadings, and short paragraphs to facilitate scanning.

FIGURE 9.8

As you write your letter of application, review the job description. Incorporate some of the words used in the description into your letter and resume. Include only those that apply to your experience or education. Prospective employers will review your letter and resume looking for three things: (1) how well your qualifications match those required or preferred in their job description, (2) the details of your education and experience you provide in your letter of application and resume that are evidence that you can perform the duties described, and (3) how well you have responded to the information requested in the job ad. We have bolded some of the phrases that an applicant for this advertised job might include. Notice that the ad calls for applicants to provide their salary requirements. In Figure 9.13 on page 266, we illustrate the application letter for a student responding to this job description.

Chemical Marketing: Assistant Manager

ErthSphere seeks an **energetic, self-motivated, hands-on individual** to **promote our chemical sales.** Top applicants for this expansion position will have a **strong scientific background** that includes **a degree in chemistry or chemical engineering and an overall GPA of 3+.** Some **chemical industry experience is desirable.**

We have targeted **the Phoenix area** for the location of our new Southwest marketing office. The company has experienced tremendous growth in recent years due to the success of our products in nuclear, beverage, and ultrapure water applications. We anticipate similar growth with the addition of our new line of fire suppressant products and a chemical marketing team that can **effectively represent the products to corporate clients.** The position of **assistant manager** will work out of the Phoenix office and **provide leadership to our dedicated marketing and sales staff and work with our R&D division.** The position of assistant manager will **require 50% travel throughout the American Southwest to ensure customer satisfaction and increased sales.**

If you would like to join our winning team, please send your resume and cover letter, including **your salary requirements,** to Leanne Roemer, ErthSphere Laboratories, Inc., 22000 Moursund Avenue, Houston, TX 77072.

Provide more than a mere list of your courses and job titles. Rather, describe what you have actually learned, done, and accomplished in school and on the job. If you have little or no work experience that is directly related to the job you are applying for, then describe and explain your work experience in terms of the transferable skills you have learned. Show how your work experience reflects a job skill and an achievement; that is, provide the so-what information that we discuss in Chapters 1 and 3 and throughout other chapters. For instance, if you are applying for a position as an agronomist and you previously worked part time for a local landscape company, a prospective employer can easily see the connection between your work and the position you are applying for. However, the question is how do you relate your part time work to the potential of being a good manager of a retail outlet? What you need to do is explain the significance of your experience and its potential to success in retail management. For instance, here is a bare-bones statement

Performed light landscape work.

This statement does not tell the prospective employer much about the significance of the experience and fails to show skills that can transfer to retail management. The so-what is not provided. Write

Performed light landscape work for a company that has been featured recently in the *Mulholland Outdoor Gazette* and *Coastal Living*. Quality of work resulted in several new landscaping accounts and favorable comments from customers.

You have now provided the so-what. Now your reader sees the significance of the job skill and the work achievement.

Begin descriptions of your work experience with nouns and action verbs. Use plenty of nouns to refer to your education and experience because most database scanners are keyed to nouns. If you have experience designing things, be sure to use the noun *designer* to increase the chances of a resume scanner picking up the key word. The order on the page and where you boldface information affect what the reader will see. Create several versions of your resume, and ask others to critique them.

Activities

You must set yourself apart from others with similar training. Your activities and other interests do this. Employers want to see this side of you. As you select information from the self-inventory, think about how others will interpret the information. Your religious and political activities may or may not be appropriate information. For example, if you are applying for a position with a service organization such as United Way, you might include your volunteer activities with the Girl Scouts and Sunday school class. Always consider including your volunteer activities—they illustrate that you have a sense of service to others. If you are applying for a position as a computer programmer at an international company, you might omit the church-related activities unless you can phrase them in a way that shows they relate to the position. After all, most positions are secular and most prospective employers are concerned about references to religion, for they do not want to be dragged into those "you didn't hire me because . . ." lawsuits. By doing your research, you will be able to avoid political and social pitfalls and still tailor your resume to the job and the employer.

Your computer skills may be important to include if they go beyond the basic office software. (College graduates are expected to understand basic word processing and file management.) Use the space to identify expertise in software and programs that members of your profession use, such as AutoCAD, Java, Flash, or C++.

References

Do a little legitimate name-dropping. Solid references—professional references—will strengthen your application considerably. Provide a personal or character reference only if it is requested. Although space is tight in a resume, we recommend that you include your references either in the resume or on a separate sheet of paper attached to your resume. That way, if a prospective employer becomes interested in you, he or she does not have to request the references and then wait until you provide them. Also be sure to give references plenty of lead time to prepare letters of recommendation—do not approach potential references a few days before you need a letter sent. Here are some additional tips on selecting references:

- Choose three to five people who are in a position to say something positive about your professional skills. If the job ad you are responding to specifies three references, consider providing an additional one—just in case a prospective employer cannot reach one of the people. References should be people who know the quality and value of your work and can write or talk positively about you and your work. Former or current teachers and former and current work supervisors who have previously rated your work, either by assigning your student work a grade or by evaluating your work at a job, are good prospects as references. People who were leaders in volunteer projects you worked on can also serve as good references. Prospective employers believe nobody else has much credibility in providing a professional reference.

- No reference should be a member of your own family, clergy, a personal friend, or a worker subordinate to you. Prospective employers are generally skeptical of such references. They consider such people too personal in their relationship with you to provide an objective professional opinion. Even if you have worked for a family member, do not include that person as a reference. Most prospective employers will assume that they will have only wonderful things to say about you.

- Have reference letters that are not more than three years old. Most prospective employers consider anything older as being outdated and a sign that you have not been in school or at work. It makes them wonder what you have been doing the past few years.

- Get permission from each person before you list him or her as a reference. It is only common courtesy to do so, and it gives that person an opportunity to decline if she or he prefers to do so, for whatever reason. You want references who are comfortable in supporting your application.

- Provide your references with a copy of your updated resume, and explain to them the type of work you are looking for.

- Make it easy for prospective employers to contact the references by providing the name, position, mailing address, e-mail address, and phone number for each. Do not include references who are difficult to contact, such as those who are working abroad or are on an extended vacation and cannot be contacted easily.

Figure 9.9 illustrates an acceptable list of references page, just in case you cannot fit the list into your resume.

Designing Your Resume

Document design options for your resume are unlimited. Just keep your reader in mind. We have several recommendations to start you off:

- Do not crowd elements on the page.

- Leave plenty of white space.

- Keep bold and italic text, typeface changes, and border lines to a minimum. (Faxed and scanned resumes should have no lines and no unusual spacing or characters. The machines have trouble "translating" the characters.)

- If you must, do not be afraid to go to a second page. However, most employers will be more attracted to a well-organized, brief summary than to a long, detailed discussion of everything you have ever done. They are busy people. A one-page resume works for most situations. But if you have experiences and achievements that are related to the job you are applying for, go on to a second page. If you go to two pages, be sure to fill the second page. You want the reader to think you have more to say.

Most word-processing software has a resume template. That is, you can open a resume-formatted file that establishes the document's design. All you must do is fill in an area as you are prompted. Resume templates can be useful, but they restrict your ability to adjust the content. You must follow the established format, and your experience might not fit neatly into the assigned categories. Resume database forms also are structured such that you may have trouble matching your qualifications with the established categories. Do the best you can.

Sending Your Resume

You have several options for delivering your resume to a potential employer. You can fax the resume or send a hard copy through the mail. Or you can

FIGURE 9.9

List of references. When you cannot incorporate your references into your resume without making the resume seem too long, list your references on a separate sheet and include it with your application. Arrange the references alphabetically or by some other order. If there are several, you might consider listing academic references in one group and work supervisors in another. Keep the list updated. It is a good idea to date the list of references, as it is to date the resume, so prospective employers know the currency of the information and you know the version you are sending.

**References for
Angela Maria Chang
922 Burke Place
Lubbock, TX 79401
changam@tx.mail.edu**

Dr. Elizabeth Lu
Assistant Professor
Department of English
West Texas College
Lubbock, TX 79411
806.344.5250
Elizabeth_Lu@tx.mail.edu

Jeremy Moosadi
Assistant Director
Plains Museum of West Texas
1114 West 36th Street
Lubbock, TX 79411
806.841.2000
moosaj@pmwt.org

Dr. Jessie Nichols
Assistant Professor
Department of English
West Texas College
Lubbock, TX 79411
806.344.5286
Jessie_Nichols@tx.mail.edu

Dr. Jody M. Offutt
Associate Professor
Department of Communication
West Texas College
Lubbock, TX 79411
806.344.5252
Jody_Offutt@tx.mail edu

March 2005

send your resume electronically as an e-mail attachment, post it on the Web, or enter it into a database. You cannot go wrong in sending a traditional, hard-copy resume. In fact, we recommend that no matter how else you send the resume, you should also send a copy laser printed on good quality paper. On the Disney Web site, you find the following advice:

> For certain positions, you may want to have two versions of your resume:
> 1. For the computer to read—with a scannable format and detailed information. Submit this one.
> 2. For the recruiter to read—possibly with a creative layout, enhanced typography, and summarized information. Carry this one to the interview.[1]

Not only does the Disney description distinguish between how you submit the versions, it also notes the extent of the information to submit. The length of the scannable resume does not matter. What matters is that you give "detailed information" with keywords (nouns) that the search engine of the database will pick up. The resume for the recruiter "summarizes" information about you. You should still use descriptive nouns, but keep your description to one to two pages.

Traditional Hard-Copy Resumes

You must have a hard copy of your resume. When you go to the interview, have several copies with you even though you know the person interviewing you has one. You may meet others who do not have a copy.

You must send

- A perfect resume, with no spelling errors or incorrect information. It must look good.

- A resume that is on the same paper stock and in the same font as the letter of application. Although you might have to adjust the size of margins or slightly adjust the size of fonts, you want your application package to have a finished look and have one basic design.

- A clean copy. Your resume will be copied and passed around the company. (We have seen several examples of resumes printed on paper that, when copied, shows streaks of cotton or other marks. These marks will distract the reader.)

- The resume in a large enough envelope that you do not have to fold it. The folds may fall in the wrong place and make some lines harder to read. If the resume is faxed or scanned, the fold lines may create problems for the fax machine or the scanner.

- A resume that will fax and scan cleanly. Large companies scan resumes. The recommendations for designing scannable resumes change with each improvement in scanning technology. Many of the formats you use for the traditional resume will work if you (1) remove any

---

[1]http://Disney.go.com/disneycareers/tips.html 16 September 2003.

lines, (2) use a 12-point sans serif font, and (3) remove unusual graphics and typefaces other than bold. If you send the traditional resume and a resume formatted for scanning in your letter of application, be sure to note that you have enclosed two resumes. (Most human resources managers will recognize what you are doing.)

Figure 9.10 shows the Tennessee Valley Authority's (TVA) guidelines for sending in a scannable resume. Applicants are advised to avoid using many of the format features that are so desirable in hard-copy resumes that are designed for human readers. Note that length is of little concern because for a computerized scanning program, length is not an important factor. The TVA guidelines resemble recommendations given by other companies and organizations.

Figure 9.11 is an example of a resume prepared for scanning. Note the 12-point sans serif font, no unusual spacing or characters, and no lines. Use bold and all-capital letters for emphasis, but keep these to a minimum. Make sure your name is the first item on the page, and list phone numbers on separate lines.

The scanned resume is designed to be searched by a database search engine, not be printed out and evaluated for how it looks. However, sometimes the scanned resume is printed out and circulated so that your qualifications can be reviewed. Figure 9.12 illustrates the problems that can occur when a resume is scanned. One of our students reported that the person interviewing him had a copy of his scanned resume, but all of his work experience had been omitted. Always have copies of your traditional resume with you. You will then have a complete version of your resume with good document design if you need it.

Electronic Resumes

You can distribute your resume electronically in several ways without generating a hard copy. You can (1) send your resume as a file in the body of your e-mail or as an attachment, (2) post your resume on your Web site, (3) submit your resume through a database, or (4) follow other instructions given by the employer. Rapid technology changes demand that you adapt your submission to the requested format of the employer (Figure 9.10). When submitting your resume electronically, you should verify that it was received. We recommend following an electronic submission with a traditional hard-copy version of your resume if you cannot confirm that your resume was received or if you want to make sure the interviewer sees a complete and well-formatted version of your resume.

When e-mailing your resume, keep two things in mind. First, apply only for jobs that you are realistically qualified for. The mass mailing of electronic resumes is creating problems for prospective employers who receive resumes that are not tailored to the job opening and lack a cover letter. Second, do not send an attachment that is difficult to open. It will help if you know how the receiver will handle it. If the receiver will print the e-mail message directly, most likely you should convert and adjust your resume to a Rich Text File

FIGURE 9.10

TVA suggestions for producing a scannable resume.

Source: TVA (2003 September). How to apply. Retrieved September 10, 2003, from http://www.tva.gov/employment/scaninstruct.htm

TVA
TENNESSEE VALLEY AUTHORITY

site help   contact us

search

TVA Home   About TVA   Power System   Environmental Stewardship   River System   Economic Development   Investor Resources   TVA Newsroom

- Current Job Opportunities
- College Recruitment
- Operations & Maintenance Training Program
- Why TVA
- How to Apply
- Return to Employment Main

Instructions for Creating a Scannable Resume

Scannable resumes, which can be read by computers, are a must in today's business environment. TVA uses the latest electronic technology to track applicants. That makes it possible for us to consider you for more jobs because the computer can quickly search your resume and identify your skills. A scannable resume has standard fonts, uses crisp, dark type, and offers plenty of facts for the computer to extract—the more skills and facts you provide, the more opportunities you have to be matched to available positions.

Preparing a scannable resume is like preparing a traditional resume: you focus on format and content. Here are some hints about getting the most mileage out of your resume.

Enhance your resume's scannability
- Use white or light-colored paper printed on one side only.
- Provide a laser-printed original.
- Use standard fonts (e.g., Helvetica, Geneva).
- Use a large-enough type size (12 to 14 points).
- Avoid fancy treatments like italics and underline.
- Avoid vertical and horizontal lines, graphics, and boxes.
- Avoid two-column formats that look like newspapers or newsletters.

Structure the content to maximize "hits"
- Use plenty of key words that define your skills, experience, education, and professional affiliations.
- Detail your experience with concrete, active words rather than vague descriptions.
- Use more than one page if necessary.
- Use keywords and acronyms specific to your industry.

TVA is an equal opportunity and affirmative-action employer. TVA ensures that the benefits of programs receiving TVA financial assistance are available to all eligible persons regardless of race, color, sex, national origin, religion, disability, or age.

Non-U.S. residents should read TVA's Citizenship Policy.

Individuals interested in Veteran's Preference eligibility should read the Veteran's Handbook.

▲ top of page

Contact Us | Search | Legal Notices | Privacy Policy | Employment | FOIA
TVA Home | About TVA | Power | Environment | Rivers | Economic Development |
Investors | News

FIGURE 9.11

Portion of chronological resume prepared for scanning. Compare this version with the traditional chronological resume in Figure 9.5. Notice the sans serif font, use of bold, and placement of text along the left margin. Figure 9.12 shows the results of scanning this resume.

Kelly J. Bennett

School Address (until 12 May 06)
2011 8th Street, Apt. 10A
Boise City, ID 83700
208.111.9999
kjbennett@mail.com

Address (after 12 May 06)
1611 Wafer Lane
Marytown, ID 82200
208.456.7899

Education

Idaho Technical University
Boise City, ID
Bachelor of Chemical Engineering
Minor in Spanish
Expected graduation, May 2006

Military Training

June 2001–December 2005

Special Forces Qualification Course, Ft. Bragg, NC 2001

Advanced International Morse Code Course, Ft. Bragg, NC 2002

Airborne School, Fort Benning, GA 2002

Class A Electronics Technician School, Ft. Gilmore, NE 2003

Class A Spanish School, Joint Service Defense Language Institute, Washington, DC, 2004

Infantry Squadron Leadership School, Ft. Benning, GA 2005

Experience

January 2002–present
Boise City Fire Department
Boise City, ID
Firefighter II, January 2002–January 2003; Firefighter I, February 2003–present. Apparatus operator and unit supervisor.

January 2002–present
Idaho National Guard
Boise City, ID
Special Forces Communications *Sergeant*
Operate and repair communications equipment
Deployed to Kuwait, April–July 2003

FIGURE 9.12

Compare the results of scanning the resume in Figure 9.11. Some of the spacing has collapsed, and some of the boldfacing has disappeared. The information is intact, however, and a search using keywords such as *chemical engineering*, *Spanish*, *electronics*, and *supervisor* will bring up this resume. We cannot explain why our test also put sevens at the top of the resume.

Kelly J. Bennett   7777777

School Address (until 12 May 06)
2011 8th Street, Apt. 10A
Boise City, ID 83700
208.111.9999
kjbennett@mail.com

Address (after 12 May 06)
1611 Wafer Lane
Marytown, ID 82200
208.456.7899

Education
Idaho Technical University
Boise City, ID
Bachelor of Chemical Engineering
Minor in Spanish
Expected graduation, May 2006

Military Training
June 2001–December 2005

Special Forces Qualification Course, Ft. Bragg, NC 2001

Advanced International Morse Code Course, Ft. Bragg, NC 2002

Airborne School, Fort Benning, GA 2002

Class A Electronics Technician School, Ft. Gilmore, NE 2003

Class A Spanish School, Joint Service Defense Language Institute, Washington, DC, 2004
Infantry Squadron Leadership School, Ft. Benning, GA 2005
Experience
January 2002–present
Boise City Fire Department
Boise City, ID
Firefighter II, January 2002–January 2003; Firefighter I, February 2003–present. Apparatus operator and unit supervisor.

January 2002–present
Idaho National Guard
Boise City, ID
Special Forces Communications *Sergeant*
Operate and repair communications equipment
Deployed to Kuwait, April–July 2003

(RTF) or an Adobe™ Acrobat (PDF) file that is inserted into the e-mail message. With current e-mail software, you can use the attachment feature to attach the electronic file in which you created your resume to an e-mail message. The receiver opens the attachment and has a clean copy of your resume with all of the formatting in place. If the receiver prints the attachment, he or she will have a hard copy of your resume just as if you sent a copy through the mail. Be aware that this does not always produce a perfect transfer—keep in touch with the person receiving your resume.

Sending a resume as an attachment is becoming a popular way to send the resume. Recent developments allow the database you use to create a resume for your school's career placement service to send your resume as an attachment that pulls directly from the data. The receiver simply double-clicks on an attachment icon to open the resume information directly into word-processing software. The receiver has a good-quality resume without your printing a copy and mailing it. If your school's career placement service has this capability, be sure to send a couple of practice attachments with your resume to friends to make sure you know how and to make sure the resume arrives in good shape.

You may put your resume on your Web site. Most likely, you cannot simply convert your word-processing file to an HTML file and place it on the Web. You will need to adjust the spacing and other features. You will probably want to take advantage of the color and graphic options available to you on the Web. You can link to pages from your resume that show projects you have done, to organizations you are active in, or to companies and organizations you have worked for. (You should obtain permission from the organizations or companies that you link to.) We suggest that you review other resumes on the Web before posting yours. Remember, once your resume is posted, your information is public and accessible to everyone. For security reasons, you might choose not to list your address and telephone number; you may just give an e-mail address.

Submitting your credentials through a database such as one established by your school's career placement office is common. Many Web-based career services (such as the ones listed in Figure 9.2) provide an electronic form. You may have some trouble fitting your credentials into the categories. Do the best you can. Use descriptive nouns—words that an employer will likely use as keywords to search the database.

The recommendation now is to use more nouns in your resume than action verbs. Employers tend to enter nouns as keywords. For example, instead of computer *programming,* use *programmer* and list the programs you work with, COBOL, AutoCAD, and Java. A teacher's aide might use nouns such as *phonics in reading groups, student evaluation,* and *parent contact.*

Letters

In this section, we describe several types of letters you may write during your job search, and we give some examples. You must adapt the letters to your

All job-search-related correspondence should be succinct and to the point.

situation. You may find that some of the letters will actually be e-mail messages. More and more, we hear from our students that employers are contacting them at some point in the interview process by e-mail. The e-mail message may simply be confirmation of the interview time, or it may include a list of questions that the applicant needs to be prepared to answer. Whether you send a letter by mail, fax, or e-mail, you must take special care in writing and sending the letter. The letters and e-mails you write and the phone conversations you have are as much a part of the evaluation process as the resume and interview.

Letter of Application

The letter of application is a way of introducing yourself to an employer. When accompanied by your resume, it should present a picture that is complete enough that prospective employers can decide whether or not they want to find out more about you. Your desire, of course, is for the letter to result in an interview. The letter of application, therefore, is a sales letter.

Selling yourself effectively is an essential requirement for landing a good job. You are a salesperson, whether you like it or not, so be a successful one. Here are some suggestions on how to make the letter of application an effective sales letter.

Features of All Good Letters of Application

- Letters of application should be neat, correct, and well written. They should be created on a computer and printed on good bond paper of about 20-pound weight. You may be short of cash when you are job hunting, but letters and resumes are not the places to be cheap. They represent you, and they should represent you well.

- Do not even think about using stationery that has the letterhead of your school, place or work, or fraternity or sorority. Using such stationery for personal purposes is not acceptable business practice. However, the heading should include your complete return address. Prospective employers cannot contact you unless they have your address.

- If possible, address the letter to a specific person, and use the person's name in the salutation. If necessary, you can acquire such names through telephone calls and Web sites.

- The introduction of your letter names the job you are applying for (including relevant position levels and job or position numbers it carries) and tells the prospective employer how you learned about the job. Avoid tricky openers. One of us recently received a letter that began, "If you don't want to hire a well-educated, fine, industrious instructor, stop right here." Unfortunately for the writer, his reader took him at his word and stopped. Courtesy, tact, and solid information will take you farther.

- Make your current status clear—such as where you are in your schooling or your professional career and when you will be available to begin work. Make sure that your availability fits into the prospective employer's time frame.

- Make it clear that you know something about the company or organization, thus letting the reader know that you have been doing your homework. Prospective employers assume you are applying to other organizations, but they do not like feeling as if they are just anonymous target number 16 or so.

- Knowing something about the prospective employer helps you choose appropriate facts. Stick to the facts. Do not express opinions about yourself. Let your references make value judgments about your work and education, and the prospective employers form their own opinions. If you have the right facts and choose them well, the opinions will be favorable. Dig into your self-inventory, and produce facts that should interest the employer. Normally, these will concern past work and educational experiences, but do not overlook the value of referring to extracurricular activities that relate to the job you seek. This portion of the letter may repeat information from the resume, but try to include additional information that backs up the entries on the resume.

- If you are responding to a job ad, have the job description (Figure 9.8) next to you as you write the letter. Use keywords from the description in your letter and resume when possible. Be sure you relate your education and experience to the required qualifications stated in the job description or advertisement. Prospective employers do not like to receive applications from people who clearly do not have the required qualifications. If the job requirements include the ability to use the latest version of AutoCad and Lotus Notes and strong interpersonal, teamwork, communication, and problem-solving skills, provide information to show that you fit the desired profile. Do not just claim you have them. Match your credentials with what the prospective employer is looking for, but do not stretch the truth. Be honest. These days, prospective employers check credentials.

- In the closing part of the letter, refer the reader to your resume for additional information. Finally, attempt to set up an interview—almost always the object of a letter of application. Make scheduling the interview as easy and convenient for the employer as possible.

- Never send out duplicated letters of application. You may have one standard letter that you modify only slightly from employer to employer, but each letter must be an original and printed on good-quality paper using a high-quality laser or inkjet printer.

Your letters of application and resumes should be perfect. Have a friend read them before you send them out.

There are two basic kinds of letters of application: the invited or solicited letter (Figure 9.13) and the uninvited, prospecting, or query letter (Figure

9.14). Both letters have all the parts of a standard business letter (see Chapter 8), and both serve as cover letters for the resume. Resumes by themselves are little more than bare-bones listings of your credentials. Always accompany your resume with a letter of application that targets and personalizes the application for the prospective employer.

The Invited or Solicited Letter

Use the invited or solicited letter (Figure 9.13) when you are responding to an advertised job opening. Invited letters of application are good-news letters, for they are welcome sights for readers who have developed plans to hire, have added funds to their operating budget for hiring, and have written and placed job advertisements. They are pleased to receive applications and have set aside ample time to read and respond to them. So you can use a direct approach: Apply for the position, explain why you are interested in the position, match your qualifications to the advertised requirements of the position, refer to your resume and other relevant items connected with the application, and request an interview.

The sample invited letter shown in Figure 9.13 is written in response to the job advertisement in Figure 9.8.

The Uninvited, Prospecting, or Query Letter

You are not limited in your job search to just responding to job advertisements. If you know the kind of organization or company you want to work for, you can write a prospecting or query letter. Use the uninvited or prospecting letter (Figure 9.14) when you contact an organization to see if there is a job opening or one that will soon be open. Your main purposes are to match your qualifications to the needs you believe a prospective employer has and find out whether a position is available. This letter is similar to the invited letter. The main difference is that in the uninvited, prospecting letter, you do not know whether an opening exists, and you are writing to introduce yourself as an applicant in case an opening exists or develops soon. Since uninvited letters are sometimes not acknowledged, it is a good idea to follow up your prospecting letter with a phone call to ensure that it was received and that somebody has seen it.

The uninvited or prospecting letter shown in Figure 9.14 is accompanied by the functional resume or the combined resume illustrated in Figures 9.6 and 9.7.

Other Letters

Several other letters are either necessary or desirable during the job hunt: requests for recommendation, interview follow-up letters, acknowledgments of job offers, job refusals, and job acceptances. Always be as courteous as possible in workplace correspondence and especially in employment letters. The sample letters in Figures 9.15 to 9.17 illustrate how to proceed in each of these matters. As you examine them, consider the following additional points.

FIGURE 9.13

Invited letter of application. This writer is responding to the job description in Figure 9.8.

2011 8th Street, Apt. 10A
Boise City, ID 83700

22 March 2006

Ms. Leanne Roemer
ErthSphere Laboratories, Inc.
22000 Moursund Avenue
Houston, TX 78910

Dear Ms. Roemer:

I am applying for the position of Assistant Manager, Chemical Marketing in your Phoenix office, which was listed on your Web site.

I will graduate from Idaho Technical University on 10 May with a Bachelor of Chemical Engineering degree and an overall GPA of 3.4 on a 4.0 scale. My GPA in chemical engineering and supporting course work in chemistry is 3.55.

After visiting your Web site and reading an article about ErthSphere in a recent issues of *CHEMTECH,* I am eager to join your new Southwest marketing team. Your company's plan to expand by promoting new fire-suppressant chemical products is particularly interesting to me. My formal education in chemistry and chemical engineering, my training in the U.S. Army and Idaho National Guard, and my three years of experience working for the Boise City Fire Department with fire suppressant chemicals should give me the specializations you call for in this position. As a graduate of the Infantry Leadership School in Fort Benning, Georgia, and as a unit supervisor for the BCFD, I believe I have both the training and hands-on experience to provide leadership for sales and service representatives and to work with other marketing and R&D people. Fluent in Spanish, I believe I can be very effective in developing and maintaining corporate-client relationships in Arizona, California, New Mexico, and Texas. I am a native of San Diego, and I am quite familiar with the American Southwest. The travel requirements are no obstacle for me.

Please see my enclosed resume for additional information about my qualifications and the names of persons who are willing to provide recommendations for me. If interviewed, I can also bring a portfolio of my major school projects, including a marketing research paper that reports the results of my research on how John's Condiments Company of Atlanta, Georgia, introduced a new line of Southwest-oriented goods, including John's New Chili Mixings and John's Southwest Seasoned Salt. Part of the background research also involved researching the impact of the growing Hispanic population on the U.S. economy.

I am fairly flexible on beginning salary, although I expect compensation in line with what others in similar positions are paid. Given that, I will be happy to discuss my salary requirements with you during an interview. I am, quite frankly, more interested in discussing the opportunity to contribute to ErthSphere's future. I look forward to meeting with you to discuss this opportunity.

Sincerely,

Kelly J. Bennett

Kelly J. Bennett

Enclosure: resume and list of references

About the Invited Letter of Application

Bennett's invited letter of application is also a cover letter for his resume (see Figure 9.5). He is responding to the job description in Figure 9.8.

Heading and Salutation

The letter is addressed to a specific person by name. If you do not have a name to address the letter to, consider calling the organization for the name of the person to whom you should address the letter. If none is available, address the letter to the company—"Dear ErthSpere Laboratories," or consider omitting the salutation. Do not use "To Whom It May Concern," which sounds old-fashioned. Be sure to include your complete mailing address so the prospective employer will not have to look on your resume for it.

Body of the Letter

Keep the letter fairly brief, although full of information that elaborates on the bare-bones lists of the resume. Four or five paragraphs should do it. Notice how Bennett structures his letter.

Paragraph 1. Begin by stating your purpose clearly—that of applying for a specific position. Remember that you need to be specific about the position (including grade level or position or job number) because the prospective employer may be running several job advertisements for several positions. Explain how you learned of the position. Employers sometimes do research on how prospective applicants can best be reached—by a publicized advertisement, through networking, or through using an external hiring agency.

Paragraph 2. Early in the letter, describe your current educational or employee status. If there are educational requirements, briefly state your qualifications to satisfy the prospective employer that you have the requisite education. If appropriate, explain when you will be available to begin work. Be sure that your schedule also fits the prospective employer's timetable. If you feel that this paragraph or the first one is too short, briefly explain why you are interested in this position.

Paragraph 3. If you have not done so in one of the earlier paragraphs, explain why you are interested in applying for this position. Prospective employers already know you are interested in getting a job. They want to know why you want to work for *them*. Notice how Bennett explains how he learned about the organization and why he is interested in the position. Likewise, you need to show that you have researched the organization and explain how your qualifications fit the requirements for the job.

Bennett's third paragraph is the real heart of his letter. Here is where he discusses his qualifications. You might decide to devote the third paragraph of your letter to your educational achievements and a fourth paragraph to your work experience. The important thing is to elaborate on your strongest qualifications for the job. Remember that the resume is primarily a list. The cover letter is where you elaborate, providing details to show that you really do possess those qualifications. Notice how Bennett attempts to relate his qualifications to the job responsibilities.

Paragraph 4. When referring to additional information in the resume, be sure that you have provided the primary information in your letter. The resume is to be read for *additional* information. It does not mindlessly repeat what you have said in the letter. Also this is the place to indicate that you can provide additional materials, such as a portfolio of work, if the prospective employer is interested.

Paragraph 5. Typically, close by requesting an interview. However, Bennett uses the end of his letter to respond to the employer's request for his salary requirements. He opts to deflect the request as tactfully as he can, in effect putting the ball back in ErthSphere's court. It is a calculated gamble, but he is interested enough in the position that he does not want to risk being rejected because he ignored the request.

Signature and Enclosure Notice

Always sign the letter and refer to the enclosed materials.

FIGURE 9.14
Uninvited or prospecting letter of application.

922 Burke Place
Lubbock, TX 79401
20 April 2005

Michel DeLoss, Executive Director
Pine Tree State Tourism Commission
1400 Passamaquoddy Drive
Bishopsville, ME 01234

Dear Mr. DeLoss:

I am writing to inquire about available full-time positions with the Pine Tree State Tourism Commission. I will be graduating in June with a degree in English, specializing in technical communication and supporting course work in museum studies. After graduation I plan to return to Maine (my home town is Kennebunkport), and I am interested in pursuing a career in which I can use my research, writing, and design skills and my experience as a museum technician.

In visiting the Commission's Web site, I was impressed by the broad array of functions covered by the Commission. Many of its new initiatives involving displays and interpreting art works, cultural objects, and other artifacts of Native American Indians, the American Revolutionary War, and the early years of maritime commerce appeal to my interests in working as an exhibit specialist, museum technician, and technical communicator.

My experience as a volunteer docent at the Plains Museum of West Texas in Lubbock, Texas, ranges from working on grant proposals to procure external funding for expanding the pioneer ranch section to preparing informational signs for museum visitors to leading tours and classes for public-school children. The grant proposal led to a $15,000 grant from the Clint Travis Foundation of Fort Worth, Texas to purchase and relocate two large windmills to the museum's external exhibition area.

Although my university education and training have been in West Texas, I spent two summers during my high-school years working on research projects for the Kenneth Lewis Roberts Foundation in Kennebunkport and was an associate member of the Maine Historical Society. My research on the illustrations of Newell Converse Wyeth in Roberts' novels culminated in a presentation to the City Council of Kennebunkport, which partially funded a research trip for me to Chadds Ford, Pennsylvania—Wyeth's home and the location of the Wyeth Gallery—to work further on the topic.

In the course of my education and experience, I have developed a portfolio of documents and presentations, which includes grant proposals, style sheets, guidelines for visitors to the Lubbock County Prairie Dog Sanctuary, an article based on my interview with the chief editor of the *Phi Kappa Phi* magazine, and a MS PowerPoint presentation on online editing. This material may be accessed by going to my Web site, www.tx.edu/~changam. Doing volunteer work and major class projects, I have learned to work within guidelines and also to work independently on projects. I can work under tight deadlines and with limited resources to accomplish goals.

I would welcome the opportunity to contribute to the work of the Pine Tree State Tourist Commission and will call you during the first week of May to discuss that possibility. If you would like to contact me sooner, you can reach me at 806.697.9071 or changam@tx.mail.edu.

Sincerely

Angela Marie Chang

Angela Maria Chang

Enclosure: Resume and List of References

About the Uninvited or Prospecting Letter of Application

Chang's uninvited letter of application is a cover letter for her functional resume (Figure 9.6) or her combined resume (Figure 9.7). This type of letter—sometimes referred to as a prospecting or job inquiry letter—is similar to the invited letter of application except that instead of applying for a position that is advertised, the writer inquires about the availability of a position that has not been advertised.

Heading and Salutation

Be sure to provide your complete mailing address and other ways to be contacted in case the reader becomes interested in your availability. Address the letter to a specific person by name and, if possible, by position or title. Uninvited letters are often easy to ignore, so try to ensure that somebody will receive your letter.

Body of the Letter

As with the invited letter of application, keep the uninvited letter brief—four to six paragraphs should do it. Notice how Chang structures her letter—it is a good model to follow.

Paragraph 1: Begin by stating your purpose clearly: You are inquiring about the availability of a position. Your letter is arriving uninvited. However, avoid sounding apologetic. Do not use such downer openers as "I realize that I may be imposing, but . . . ." Or "I apologize for taking your valuable time . . . ." These are red-flag openers that are too humble. Instead, tell the reader why you are making the inquiry. Describe your status and your plans.

Paragraph 2: Make a connection with the reader by showing that you have done your homework on the organization. Notice how Chang refers to the activities and publicized accounts of the Commission and explains why they interest her.

Paragraphs 3 and 5: Although Chang is at something of a disadvantage in not knowing exactly what work is done at the Commission, she has done enough research about it that she can line up her strongest skills with what she perceives has the Commission's activities. If you have done your research well, you will impress the reader that you have a good understanding of the work the organization does. Emphasize those areas in which you believe you can contribute.

Paragraph 4: As part of her discussion of her strongest skills, Chang reminds the reader of her earlier work in Maine and mentions names and organizations that her reader knows and respects. Use such information to begin creating a connection between you and the organization you are interested in.

Paragraph 6: Close by restating your interest in the organization should a position be open or come open soon. Since the letter is uninvited, remain positive by telling your reader when you would like to follow up on your initial inquiry. Make it easy for the reader to contact you should he or she wish to do so.

Signature and Enclosure Notice

Always sign the letter and refer to the enclosed materials. Even though you do not know whether an opening exists, include your resume and list of references. For uninvited letters, the functional resume is probably best because it emphasizes your strongest skills and not the chronology of your work record.

FIGURE 9.15

Interview follow-up and thank-you letters are proper business etiquette. If you believe a hiring decision is likely to be made quickly, express your thanks by e-mail and follow up with a traditional letter through the postal service.

[A] Begin by thanking the interviewer for his or her time and consideration. Mention the position interviewed for, and express continued interest in the position.

[B] Follow up on points or issues raised during the interview. Refer to specific people you met and to points discussed during the interview.

[C] If the interviewer or others provided important information about the job or gave you some insights into the organization or company and its culture, be sure to say how much you appreciated it. Your purpose is to let the interviewer know that you were paying attention to what was said.

[D] If appropriate, provide information about your availability or other details.

2011 8th Street, Apt. 10A
Boise City, ID 83700

24 April 2003

Ms. Leanne Roemer
ErthSphere Laboratories, Inc.
22000 Moursund Avenue
Houston, TX 77072

Dear Ms. Roemer:

[A]Thank you for the opportunity to interview with ErthSphere for the assistant manager, chemical marketing position. My visit with you and Rosa Martinez and Eugene Pertillo has increased my interest in becoming part of the ErthSphere Southwest marketing team.

[B]I enjoyed the tour of ErthSphere's headquarters building and the opportunity to talk with Rosa Martinez and Eugene Pertillo about the new fire-suppressant chemical products. If I am hired, I would like to follow up on Eugene Pertillo's suggestion that I consider enrolling in ground school for pilots at the Phoenix Flying Service. I can see how flying rental aircraft to visit the many clients throughout the Southwest is a real time- and money-saver. A few years ago I thought seriously about taking flying lessons as part of my emergency responder training for the Boise City Fire Department. I would welcome the chance to take them now.

[C]Your comments about building a new network of knowledge culture in which everybody in the organization, not just the R&D people, would be expected to contribute ideas were especially exciting to me. I have read about, but I have never visited an organization where all employees were introduced to all the different areas of the organization—until my visit to ErthSphere. And I appreciate your suggestion that I read Brown and Duguid's *The Social Life of Information*. I have already checked out a copy from our library and have begun reading it.

[D] I am in classes until 3 May. After that I will be taking exams through 7 May. I am scheduled to go backpacking on 8 and 9 May and be back for graduation on the 10th. On 8 and 9 May, I can be reached by cell phone, 208-266-3384.

I look forward to hearing from you.

Sincerely,

Kelly J. Bennett

Kelly J. Bennett

FIGURE 9.16
Request for a recommendation.

[A] Make your request
clear at the beginning.

[B] Remind the reader why
he or she should know you
and your work.

[C] Provide specific
information about the kind
of employment you are
seeking. If appropriate,
provide a deadline by which
you need the
recommendation.

[D] Refer to any document
you have enclosed with your
letter.

922 Burke Place
Lubbock, TX 79401

1 March 2005

Mr. Jeremy Moosadi, Assistant Director
Plains Museum of West Texas
1114 West 36th Street
Lubbock, TX 79411

Dear Mr. Mossadi:

[A]I am writing to request permission to use you as a reference during my current
job search.

[B]I have served as a volunteer docent at the Plains Museum since August 2003,
leading tours and classes for public-school children. In addition, during the school
year 2003–2004, I edited a grant proposal that was successful in procuring $15,000
for the purchase and relocation of two windmills from the old Post Merchant Ranch
to the museum's external exhibition area. I also developed a slide show presentation
on the Plains Museum of West Texas and created many of the informational signs
used throughout the museum.

[C]I will graduate from West Texas College with a B.A. in English in May. I hope to
find a position in a museum or state or national recreation area or park where I can
design and write descriptions for the displays.

[D]I have enclosed a copy of my resume to bring you up to date on my activities. I
will call you next week to confirm that I may use you as a reference, or if you want
me to send you an e-mail before then I can be reached at changam@tx.mail.edu.

Thank you,

Angela Maria Chang

Enclosure: Resume

FIGURE 9.17

Thank-you note for a recommendation. Thanking people who provide you with letters of recommendation is as important as thanking those who interview you. Let them know you appreciate their support.

---

922 Burke Place
Lubbock, TX 79401
21 May 2005

Mr. Jeremy Moosadi, Assistant Director
Plains Museum of West Texas
1114 West 36th Street
Lubbock, TX 79411

Dear Mr. Moosadi:

[A]Thank you so much for providing letters of recommendation for me.

[B]I have accepted a position as Communication Specialist with the Pine Tree State Tourism Commission in Bishopsville, Maine. I will be working with the Commission's Display Coordinator in designing and writing the information boards for all the displays at historical sites in the State Resort and Recreation Areas in Maine.

I begin work next week, and I am looking forward to relocating back to my home state.

[C]Again, thank you for the recommendation.

Sincerely,

Angela Marie Chang

Angela Marie Chang

[A] Begin by thanking the reader for the assistance he or she has provided.

[B] Update the reader on the situation.

[C] End by restating your appreciation for the reader's help.

Thank-You Letters

Sending a thank-you letter following an interview will set you apart from other applicants. The letter will be appreciated and will make a strong impression. It will help make you stand out from other applicants who did not bother to write thank-you letters. Your name will become that much more familiar to the employer. You simply thank the interviewers for their time and courtesy (see Figure 9.15 for an example). You can also use the thank-you letter to follow up on questions or to clarify issues that might have surfaced during the interview. The thank-you letter is the one letter you can hand-write on nice notepaper. (Most campus bookstores stock note cards with the school emblem.) In most instances, an e-mail thank-you note is acceptable. Send the thank-you letter or e-mail shortly after the interview—preferably within a day or so after the interview. It will show those who interviewed you that you are seriously interested in the position and have good follow-up skills.

Request for Recommendation Letters

As you begin the job search, you may need to write letters or e-mails to former teachers or employers requesting a letter of reference. Figure 9.16 shows one example of a request for a recommendation. The letter is not a long one. In it, you should give a specific date when the recommendation is needed and give any special instructions. Enclose a stamped and addressed envelope and your resume so that the person is reminded of your activities. Afterward send the person a thank-you note, and keep him or her posted on your job search (see Figure 9.17).

Application Forms

Even when you have a resume, fill out application forms when requested.

Look briefly at Figure 9.18, a company application form. Most employers will ask you to complete such a form before they hire you. Notice that it covers many of the same areas we have urged you to cover in your self-inventory. Most often you must complete the application at the employer's office. Be sure to have all the needed information with you—from your social security number to specific details of education and experience. Your self-inventory is a good source for this information. Use a pen with black ink, and print your answers neatly. (Black ink is preferred because it duplicates better than blue ink or pencil. Your application will be copied and distributed to those interviewing you.)

More and more companies and organizations ask applicants to complete the application form online in the office. You will also find application forms on the Web, for example, at http://www.usajobs.opm.gov/forms.asp. Fill out the forms just as you would a paper copy, providing accurate and complete information. The Web site www.opm.gov/forms/html/of.asp has several different inquiry and application forms for government positions. They are easy to download and complete using Microsoft Word.

FIGURE 9.18

Sample application form. Most application forms require the same information and ask similar questions. Be prepared when you go for an interview to complete an application form. You may want to take your self-inventory so that you have information about the jobs you have had: dates of employment, salary, employer's address and telephone number. Give accurate information about how to contact references. You need not say much in the Reason for Leaving section. Phrases such as "returned to school," "moved," or "took a better job" are sufficient.

Source: Chick-fil-A Employment Application, reprinted by permission of Chick-fil-A, Inc., 5200 Buffington Rd., Atlanta, GA 30349.

Chick-fil-A®

APPLICATION FOR EMPLOYMENT

PLEASE TELL US ABOUT YOURSELF

Name (print): Last _____ Middle I. _____ First _____ Date _____

Present Address: _____ City _____ State _____ Zip _____

Home Phone: _____ Work Phone _____

In case of an emergency, please notify: Name _____ Phone (H) _____ (W) _____

Address: _____ City _____ State _____ Zip _____

Do you have a reliable means of transportation to work? ◯ Yes ◯ No   What wage are you expecting? _____

If you are younger than 18 years old, how old are you? _____ Social Security # ___ ___ / ___ ___ / ___ ___ ___ ___

Are you eligible to work in the U.S.? ◯ Yes ◯ No (PROOF OF ELIGIBILITY IS REQUIRED UPON EMPLOYMENT)

Have you ever been convicted of a felony? ◯ Yes ◯ No

AVAILABILITY

	MON	TUE	WED	THU	FRI	SAT
FROM						
TO						

Summer _____ School Year _____ All Year _____

Minimum number of hours needed to work: _____

Maximum number of hours able to work: _____

PREVIOUS EMPLOYMENT HISTORY

PLEASE LIST YOUR THREE MOST RECENT JOBS (Including babysitting, lawn care or volunteer work):

Have you ever worked for Chick-fil-A? ◯ Yes ◯ No   If YES, which Unit? _____

Employed From	To	Name & Address of Employer	Phone #	Supervisor	Earnings	Reason for Leaving

Job skills acquired: _____

EDUCATION

High School (Last attended) _____ Location _____ Did You Graduate? ◯ Yes ◯ No

College & Vocational Schools _____ Location _____ Did You Graduate? ◯ Yes ◯ No If yes, Degree & Major _____ Grade Pt. Average _____

PERSONAL BACKGROUND

What are your interests and activities? _____

Please list awards and/or leadership positions held (work or school): _____

FIGURE 9.18
(continued)

MILITARY SERVICE

◯ Yes ◯ No   Branch: _____   Rank: _____   Start Date: _____   End Date: _____

Please describe your duties: _____

_____

PERSONAL REFERENCES

PLEASE PROVIDE FOUR REFERENCES TO WHOM YOU HAVE BEEN ACCOUNTABLE. PLEASE INCLUDE NO MORE THAN TWO FAMILY MEMBERS.

Name	Address	Phone	Relation	Years Known

PLEASE READ THE FOLLOWING STATEMENTS CAREFULLY AND SIGN

I understand that completion of this application does not indicate that there are any positions currently open and does not obligate the Chick-fil-A Operator to hire me. I certify that all of the answers given in this application are true and complete to the best of my knowledge and are subject to confirmation by Chick-fil-A.

Chick-fil-A may make such investigations and inquiries of my personal, employment, financial, academic history and other related matters as may be necessary in determining whether I can perform the essential functions of the position which I seek. I hereby release past employers, schools, and all persons contacted from all liability in responding to inquiries in connection with my application.

If I am employed, I understand that false or misleading information given in my application or interview(s) may result in termination. I understand that I am required to abide by all employer rules and regulations.

_____   _____
Date   Applicant Signature

THIS SECTION TO BE SIGNED BY EMPLOYEE ONLY AT THE TIME OF HIRE

I understand that it is the objective of Chick-fil-A, Inc. and the Chick-fil-A Operator to provide the highest quality of food at competitive prices with the highest caliber of employees possible. I also understand that one of the hardest things to prevent is the mishandling of cash and store property from within. Therefore, I acknowledge the reasonableness of and consent to the following:

1. Chick-fil-A and the Chick-fil-A Operator reserve the right to use any lawful method of investigation which either one of them may deem necessary in determining whether any person has engaged in conduct which either Chick-fil-A or the Chick-fil-A Operator feel interferes with or adversely affects the business of either one of them.

2. Persons entering and leaving any Chick-fil-A premises are subject to questioning and searches. All packages, bags, purses, coats, containers, accessories, or possessions of any sort brought onto or taken from any Chick-fil-A premises are subject to thorough inspection.

3. Chick-fil-A or the Chick-fil-A Operator may engage in a variety of security procedures, as deemed necessary by either one of them. These may include, but are not limited to, surveillance of employees or premises. I understand that these security procedures may be conducted in secrecy, unannounced to me or other persons.

I understand each of these provisions and consent to each and every provision. I also understand that cooperation with any action encompassed by these provisions is expected of all employees, and failure to cooperate may result in termination of employment.

_____   _____
Date   Employee's Signature

**Chick-fil-A, Inc. is an equal opportunity employer and considers all applicants equally
without regard to race, sex, age, religion, national origin, color, disability, citizenship, or veteran status.**

©1998 Chick-fil-A, Inc., CT002, Rev 7-98

PLANNING AND REVISING CHECKLIST: THE JOB HUNT

Think about the following at the beginning of your job hunt, and review the timetable in Figure 9.1.

The Self-Inventory

The first step in preparing for the job hunt is to inventory your education, experience, interests, and abilities. Why not create a file in your word-processing program called *self1*? Using the headings below, list everything you can think of that might be relevant to your job search. If the file grows to several pages, that is fine. You are brainstorming—an early part of the writing process.

As you write a resume, letter, e-mail inquiry, or other document, select information from the self-inventory that describes you to a specific employer (the reader) for a specific job (your purpose). Have at least two files open: the *self1* and the *resume1*, for example. Copy and paste between the two. As you update each file, change the name to show the update: *resume1, resume2, ..., self1, self2. ...* You can always go back to an earlier version if you do not like the change, and you always have a backup if something happens to the current version. ALWAYS save your files in at least two locations (on a disk and on a hard drive). Update the files as you gain work experience or add to your educational credentials.

Education

For each school and program you have attended since high school or are attending, provide the following information:

- Name, location, and dates of attendance

- Kind of degree or certificate (for example, B.S. or A.A.)

- Major or emphasis

- Courses most relevant to the job you seek and grades for these courses

- Internships or co-op programs

- Grade point average

- Academic awards (explain if necessary)

- Courses that might not appear to be relevant but that taught transferable competencies

- Courses in your education that you enjoyed the most and the least

- Courses in which you earned the highest and lowest grades
- Name, position (and academic rank if relevant), postal and e-mail addresses, and telephone number of people you think might be willing to provide a reference

Organizations

List any organizations you have belonged to, both in and out of school. For example, have you been a part of student government, student clubs, athletic teams, or civic groups? Identify political and religious activities as well. (We discuss how to represent these activities in the section of this chapter on resumes.) State the purpose of the organization. For each organization, list any positions you held, such as secretary, and define your responsibilities in the organization. Be sure to include any committee work you have done.

Work and Military Experience

List all the jobs, full time and part time, you have held, including any military experience. You may go as far back as you like, but for jobs held during and before high school, you need provide only summary information. For each job held since high school, provide the following information:

- Name, location, and Web address of the company or organization
- Business of the company or organization (for example, restaurant, trucking, computer, or medical laboratory)
- Name, address, telephone, and e-mail address of your supervisor
- Dates of employment
- Job title
- Description of your activities and responsibilities
- Description of any special training you received
- Important accomplishments, including promotions
- What you enjoyed most and least about the job
- Name, position, postal and e-mail addresses, and telephone number of people you think might be willing to provide a reference

Hobbies

List the hobbies that you have for relaxation and enjoyment. Explain the transferable skills that you learned from engaging in the hobbies.

Skills

Look back over your experience in education, organizations, jobs, and hobbies. What skills have you gained through these experiences? Think not only of specialized professional and technical skills, but also of supporting skills in areas such as teamwork, leadership, communication, and problem solving. List and describe any such skills, and tell how you achieved them. Pay particular attention to the skills that are relevant to the jobs you seek.

Honors and Recognition

List and describe any honors or recognition you have received from school, work, or organizations.

References

List those people you may want to attest to your abilities, skills, and character. Think about employers, teachers, and family friends who know you well enough to provide a reference for you. For some positions, you will be asked to provide work-related references (people who can describe your work habits and skills) and personal references (people who can comment on your character). Choose several who not only think well of you, but also have enough skill in speech and writing to convey their thoughts about you to a potential employer. List their job titles, telephone numbers, and postal and e-mail addresses.

Employer Inventory

On pages 239–243, we describe ways of gathering information about potential employers. Here are some of the things you should find out about them:

- Telephone number, e-mail address, and Web address for the location where you want to work

- Size (by number of people employed, financial strength, annual sales, and so forth)

- Products or services

- Position of organization within its field (by reputation, sales, financial strength, and so forth)

- Kinds and numbers of positions open

- Training and educational possibilities

- Technology important to company

- Growth potential

- Names of officers

- Management philosophy

- Names and addresses of human resources managers and people for whom you might work.

PLANNING AND REVISING CHECKLIST: JOB-HUNT COMMUNICATION

Think about the following when planning and revising the communications for your job hunt.

Planning the Resume

- What type of resume best fits your needs? Chronological? Functional? Combined?

- Do you want to state your job objective firmly?

- Do you have all the information you need about your education and experience, including dates, names, locations, courses, grades, job descriptions, and so forth?

- Can you explain your work experience and education in terms of carry-over skills; that is, can you provide the so-what?

- If you want to use a functional resume, which categories will best display your skills and experience?

- What capabilities and achievements in your background fit you for your job objectives?

- Will your list of references be incorporated into your resume, or will they be on a separate page?

Revising the Resume

- If you have included a job objective, is it stated specifically and succinctly?

- If you have produced a chronological resume, have you listed your education and experience in reverse chronological order?

- Is all the information in your resume accurate?

- Have you included experiences, achievements, honors, and skills relevant to the job sought?

- Have you explained the *so-what?* of your work experiences, hobbies, and education that at first glance do not seem to be related to the position for which you are applying?

- If you were an employer, would the resume interest you? Would you want to interview the person who wrote it?

- Have you used phrases and dependent clauses rather than complete sentences?

- Is the information on the page uncrowded?

- Do the headings reveal the organization?

- Does your list of references contain three to five people who have agreed to provide letters? If your college education is the most important credential, is at least one or two of your references a faculty member? Have you included information on how a prospective employer can contact them?

- Is your resume absolutely free of errors of any kind, whether of content, spelling, or grammar?

Planning the Letter of Application

- Remember the goal of your letter: to obtain an interview.

- How did you learn about the job?

- How well does the job meet your job objectives?

- How well do your skills and attributes match the job?

- Can you describe the transferable skills and the significance of your work experience and aspects of your education that at first do not appear to be relevant to the job?

- What can you do for the employer?

- How can you make it easy for the employer to schedule an interview with you?

Revising the Letter of Application

- Is your letter addressed to someone by name?

- Have you clearly stated the job you want and how you heard about it?

- Have you briefly discussed the skills and attributes that fit you for the job?

- Have you described the transferable skills and the significance of your work experience and aspects of your education that at first do not appear to be relevant to the job?

- Have you shown that you know something about the organization and the job?

- Have you made it easy for the employer to reach you to schedule an interview?

- Is the letter professional in all aspects? Tone? Style? Appearance? Format? Grammar?

Planning Other Written Correspondence

You also will write letters or e-mail messages that request recommendations, follow up on interviews, thank people for help, and accept or reject a job. In planning them, take care with the following:

- Obtain accurate names and addresses. Spell names correctly.

- Be accurate about any dates you refer to, whether in the past or in the future.

- Answer any questions that need answering.

- Furnish any requested information.

Revising the Other Written Correspondence

- Have you included all the information needed for your purpose?

- Is your tone courteous and professional?

- Is your letter or e-mail correctly formatted and error free?

Suggestions for Applying Your Knowledge

All job-hunting communications are potential assignments: self-inventory, letters of application, resumes, interview follow-up letters, and so forth. All should be completed on a computer using word-processing software and printed using a high-quality printer and should have a thoroughly professional look, with good document design and no errors.

Individual Activities

1. The employment situation, with its correspondence and interviews, is one place where your practice can approach or even be the real thing. The facts you must work with are the real facts of your own life along with information you can gather about real employers you might want to work for.

   Begin with a self-inventory. Keep it as reference material for the other assignments you may write, such as letters of application and resumes.

   With the help of your school placement officer or advisor, make a list of potential employers for people with your skills and interests. Using the resources available in your library, on the Web, and in your school's placement office, look up companies and organizations you might want to work for. Check Web sites for information on the companies. Check with friends and relatives. In other words, you can obtain a good deal of information about employers from many sources. Gather as much as you can.

2. Choose two advertisements of part-time or full-time positions or internships that appeal to you and are suited to your qualifications at present. Prepare a memo for your instructor that discusses your educational and career goals and the procedure you used to locate advertisements and the criteria used to select the two advertisements you chose. Analyze the two advertisements, comparing the differences between the two positions. Construct a table in your memo to make the points of comparison easy to see. Explain which position you regard as the more desirable for you.

3. Read the following job advertisement carefully, and write a memo to your instructor or your fellow students explaining what keywords in the job advertisement you believe an applicant would need to include in his or her application letter and resume. Identify the kinds of information an applicant would need to provide to show that he or she meets the qualifications. Explain other information an applicant might include.

Field Forester Position

Job Description: Perform a variety of tasks including timber cruising, timber management, and site preparation prescriptions. GPS mapping, harvest process auditing, tree planting quality control, and data summarizing and reporting.

Location: Task will cover west Louisiana and east Texas geographic region.

Timing: Position is currently available and will remain open until position is filled.

Skills Required:
Technical Skills—Timber cruising and biometrics
Elementary statistics
Silviculture

Computer knowledge—Spreadsheet applications, handheld computers
Problem solving and project management
Mapping and navigation

Interpersonal Skills—Self-motivated and directed
Good written and oral communications
Ability to work well with others in a team environment
Dedication to task completion and success-oriented
Practiced successful decision maker

Other Desirable Skills:
Computer programming, GIS/GPS operations, aerial photo interpretation
Contact: Call or write:
Chuck Simmons or Bonita Jurgensmeyer
Professional Foresters, Inc.
P.O. Box 105
LouTex, TX 79550
1.800.245.9986

Collaborative Activity

It almost always is helpful to have others critique our work—writing or otherwise. Pair off with another student in your class, and exchange drafts of your application letter, resume, and list of references (if it is separate from the resume) and a copy of the ad or job notice to which you are responding. (A copy of the ad or job notice helps the other student more accurately critique your draft materials.)

After reviewing your partner's application letter, resume, and list of references, write a memo to him or her assessing the drafts. Your instructor may or may not want to receive a copy of the assessment memo. Remember that the memo is written to your partner, not to the instructor. Your objective is to help improve the letter, resume, and list of references. You are not critiquing your partner; you are critiquing the materials.

Organizing your memo can present problems, since there are so many things that you are critiquing: the letter, resume, and list of references. Here are some tips for organizing your assessment memo:

- Begin with an introduction that states the purpose and previews the organization of the memo. Remember to use the preview list to create headings in the memo.

- Arrange your comments into three major sections: (1) a section on the application letter, (2) a section on the resume, and (3) a section on the list of references. Even if the list of references is included in the resume, it is important enough to treat separately in your critique.

Divide each major section into appropriate subsections, perhaps using the same subheadings in each major section. The first subsection presents your overall impression of the document (its general strengths and weaknesses) in terms of how it relates to the information in the job ad or notice. Subsequent subsections would present specific comments on such features as format, organization, style, accuracy, completeness, consistency, and ease of understanding. Since the resume is likely to be the longest and most complex of the three documents, consider developing a third level of discussion (sub-subsections) to comment on the resume heading, the education section, the work experience section, the special skills section, and so on.

Portfolios and Interviews

I
f your resume and letter have been successful, you now must prepare for your interview with potential employers. Employers want to interview you to make sure you will fit their team. They know that the future of their organization relies on new-hires who will be the solid-performing workers who make up the heart of the organization in a few years. They want to confirm that you have the knowledge and special abilities they are looking for and that you can work with others. In today's job market, they want to see samples of your work.

Think of a portfolio as a way to market your skills and talent that many other applicants will not think of using. With a well-designed portfolio, you can differentiate yourself from the rest of the applicants. In this chapter, we describe portfolios for showcasing your special abilities, your accomplishments, and your communication activities.[1] We also provide guidelines for interviewing with an employer.

Portfolios

A portfolio is an important component of your job-search materials.

Whatever your training, you will need to show your work to future employers. One way to do this is with a portfolio. A portfolio collects samples of your work in a notebook, on a Web site, on a CD-ROM, or in a form your field expects. We describe portfolios, in which you carry hard-copy documents, and electronic portfolios, which are becoming more and more prevalent—particularly CD-based and Web folios. Whatever format you use, the purpose is the same: to show your best work to a reader who is gathering information about the quality of your work.

Portfolios give you an effective means of gathering samples of your work and showing your communication activities to employers and clients. Develop the habit of collecting your work and putting it in an electronic portfolio that becomes an evolving collection of your best work. Put your best work in your portfolio to show your range of communication experience and the extent of your talent.

Future employers and clients can see how your abilities match their needs. Both in your letters of application and on your resume, you should mention that you have a portfolio. In the letter, you might add the following sentence: "I will bring a portfolio containing samples of my work to the

---

[1]The description of portfolios that appears here was first presented at the 1997 Society for Technical Communication East Tennessee Chapter's Practical Conference on Communication and more recently at the 2003 STC@50 conference in Dallas, Texas. Students in Auburn University's technical communication classes have helped develop the description, and in fall 2002, students in a graduate course on document design explored electronic portfolios. Alise Chabaud and Nathan Meier have contributed significantly to the development of the materials.

interview." On your resume, you might replace the overused phrase "References upon request" with the phrase "Portfolio available."

You collect samples of your work in a portfolio to

An effective portfolio shows samples of your work, providing evidence—not mere claims—of your achievements, skills, and abilities.

- Demonstrate your special skills, abilities, and subject matter knowledge

- Show your communication activities—particularly written and visual communication

- Show your experience in working with several types of documents and media

- Illustrate your organization and presentation skills

- Distinguish yourself from others applying for the same position

Take your portfolio with you to interviews. When the interviewer asks about your class and work projects and other communication activities, you will have examples to show.

Contents

The documents included in the portfolio should represent a cross section of your work. Be sure to present your best work. If you are a student majoring in graphic art or architecture, you would show several of your major design projects (including photographs of models and prototypes); a technical communicator would include documents written and edited in different media for different readers; an education major would include lesson plans and course materials; an engineer would include his or her senior project and, for example, a proposal written to solicit funding for a solar car project; a medical technician would include lab reports and work done on a practicum; an accountant would select writing from accounting classes, such as an analysis of a financial statement.

Most job descriptions include the phrase "must have good communication skills." With your portfolio you can proudly (and selectively) display your writing and presentations. Do not overlook your extracurricular activities, such as president of a student organization or volunteer for Big Brothers/Big Sisters. Flyers you have created and distributed, letters you have written to guest speakers, the Web site you developed—all show your communication activities.

Electronic documents such as computer-generated slide presentations or Web pages create special problems for presenting in hard-copy format. You may want to print the presentation as a handout, and you might print a portion of your Web site. If you have access to a color printer, you can display the presentation or Web page more effectively. If you give your Web address, be assured that reviewers will look at your Web site.

You may want to revise assignments and documents so that the best possible document is included in the portfolio. Have someone with a critical but friendly eye review your portfolio.

A copy of your updated resume will also help the reader. If the resume is first in the portfolio, you give the reader an overview of your education and work history. The reader then moves on to the documents that show what you have developed. If the resume is placed at the end of the portfolio, you assume that the reader has already reviewed your resume. Putting the resume in the back ensures that you have a copy available if one is needed. Not everyone who interviews you will have seen your resume, and some who have may want to refresh their memory about your education and experience.

Design and Organization

The reader should readily understand the organization of your portfolio. Some readers will work through the portfolio carefully, but most will flip through it, stopping at items that catch their attention. Here are the major parts of a portfolio:

- A *title page* with your name and address provides the reader with a clean, crisp opening to the portfolio (Figure 10.1, for example).

- A *list of the contents* provides a guide for the reader and an overview of the organization of the portfolio. The list should show how you have grouped the documents. Section dividers distinguish the different sets of documents. Placing your best work at the beginning of the portfolio may help to call attention to your strongest work. With the hypertext feature of electronic portfolios, you do not have control of the way readers access contents. However, the way you list contents suggests a default pattern that readers can follow. Do not overlook the entire picture of the portfolio. The portfolio represents you—the type and color of notebook and dividers you select and the organization and display of your work say something about you.

- A *description of each document* or section of the portfolio will help the reader. The description may be a cover sheet for each document or section. Figure 10.2 shows the description for a set of instructions on a feature of WordPerfect and the first page of the instructions. Figure 10.3 describes an oral presentation that was presented as part of a student contest before a national organization. The descriptions reflect the different writers' experiences and document design preferences. Describe the context for the document. Some questions to answer are:

  Why was the project developed?

  Who is the intended audience for the project?

  How was the project developed? What software and hardware were used?

  When was the project developed? What was the time frame for development?

  Who created the project? Was it an individual- or a team-developed project?

FIGURE 10.1

Sample title page. Your title page establishes the design for the rest of your portfolio. Instead of a vertical line, you can use a horizontal line, a different color, or another graphic feature to introduce your portfolio. Do not clutter the title page with unnecessary information or visual effects. Your name is the most important information. You may want to put a date on the page or information about how to contact you.

Portfolio

Kelly J. Bennett

School Address (until 12 May 2006)

2011 8th Street, Apt. 10A
Boise City, ID 83700
208.111.9999
kjbennett@mail.com

Address after 12 May 2006

1611 Wafer Lane
Marytown, ID 82200
208.456.7899

Instructions

Instructions for downloading an e-book were developed as a project for Document Design in Technical Communication. Each member of the class received a new pocket PC to use for the semester. We were challenged because we first had to become familiar with the new work environment. No one in the class had experience with the Windows CE environment. I was one of only two class members who had experience with a PDA.

I worked with another class member to develop these instructions.

Design Decisions

To create user-centered instructions, we incorporated screen shots to illustrate the steps for downloading an e-book. We formatted the instructions to fit on 3 cards (with steps on each side) to fit into the pocket PC carrying case for easy reference. We also created a PDF version to load on to the pocket PC.

Learning how to use the pocket PC to download an e-book did not take much time. The challenges came in writing the instructions to fit into the limited space we had allotted and in constructing the screen shots and placing them in the space. Our first drafts had too many steps and words to fit on the cards. We shortened the wording in each step and omitted steps. We tested our revisions on different class members to make sure we were not eliminating essential information.

Creating the screen shots and placing with the text proved to be the most difficult part of this project. We had to find and learn how to use software to capture the screen shots. We discovered that screen capture software was available on the utilities disk that came with the pocket PC. We found this by accident—and let everyone in the class know. We had problems getting the screen shots to stay in the location we placed them on the card. With every adjustment in wording, we had to adjust the screens. We constructed these instructions in MS Word.

Project Review

We shared the work on this project. My team member was primarily responsible for working on the text side of the instructions, and I was responsible for the screen shots and getting the text and visuals together on the card.

The usability testing helped us identify the essential steps. I do not think we eliminated too much. Most PDA users develop a sense of how to work in the Windows CE environment. Our audience, class members, had no problems downloading an e-book.

FIGURE 10.2

Sample description and instructions for the portfolio. The description identifies the content and design challenges faced by the authors.

Source: Unpublished student project, modified and printed with permission of Angela Woods and Paul Wamsted, the authors.

Downloading an e-book

1 Sync your Pocket PC. Leave your Pocket PC connected to your desktop computer.

2 On your Pocket PC select **Start→ Internet Explorer**

3 In Internet Explorer, go to an e-book source.

Downloading an e-book

4 Scroll to the **Browse By Author** section of the page. Select a letter to explore e-book titles by author's last name.

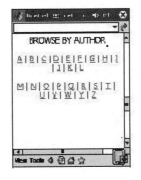

Downloading an e-book

6 Select **Yes** to complete the download.

7 After the download is complete, Microsoft Reader will open and load the title page of the e-book.

Reading an e-book

8 Once Microsoft Reader has loaded the title page, select **Go to→ Begin reading**

Reading an e-book

9 Hold the stylus on the arrow to the right of the page number for 3 seconds. The page navigation bar will open at the bottom of the screen.

Use the arrow and page bar to navigate through the e-book.

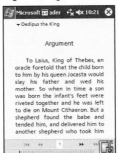

Reading an e-book

10 Select **Start→ Programs→ Microsoft Reader** to open the Library. Select a title to open and repeat steps 8 and 9 to begin reading.

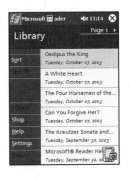

FIGURE 10.3

Sample description for an oral presentation. The description identifies the purpose and audience for the oral presentation. A copy of the presentation is included in the portfolio immediately after this description. The presentation is printed as a handout with six slides on the page.

Portfolio of Nate Hubbard

Oral Presentation

This oral presentation began as a component of my senior marketing project. For my marketing project, I developed a marketing plan for an agricultural product assigned by Professor Jonathan Fenwick. I was encouraged by my professor to enter my marketing plan in a contest for student professionals sponsored by the National Agri-Marketing Association. I presented my plan and this presentation at the national conference in San Francisco in April 2004.

Purpose	Present a marketing plan for the agricultural product *FastGrow*, a fertilizer developed for increasing soybean growth.
Audience	Judges for National Agri-Marketing Association. The judges were marketing directors from three international corporations.
Information	Described how I did a market analysis for introducing *FastGrow* as a new product. Presented the proposed marketing plan for *FastGrow*.
Specifications	20-minute computer-generated slide show
Software Used	Microsoft PowerPoint XP
Special Features	Incorporated three visuals captured from the Web and two graphs created in Microsoft Excel.
Results	Earned an Honorable Mention among the 49 students competing.

I had never created a computer slide show before this. At first I struggled with the software and had some trouble getting access to a computer, but once I learned how to add and delete slides, I created the slides in about 45 minutes. A friend then showed me how to insert pictures from the Web and the graphs.

After seeing the presentations of the winner, I now know that I probably should have used fewer slides. I included so many I had to rush through the slides to finish in 20 minutes. My visuals seemed to impress the judges.

If the project was team-developed, what was your contribution?

What are the special features of the project?

What unusual difficulties, if any, did you have in researching and creating the document or presentation?

If there were unusual difficulties, how did you overcome the difficulties?

Presentation of the Portfolio

Your portfolio should take two forms:

- The traditional paper version
- An electronic version

Keep your portfolio manageable and easy to access and navigate.

In this section, we describe the development of each. How you display your work is as much a part of the evaluation of the portfolio as what you put in the portfolio. We encourage you to develop both paper and electronic portfolios.

The Traditional Paper Portfolio

The paper-based portfolio allows the reader to see the document in its final form—if it is a paper document. You have complete control of the presentation of the documents. You do not have to worry about the format of the document shifting. You do not have to worry about somebody changing your portfolio.

You can display your work in a three-ring notebook or in a leather-bound, zippered case specially designed for portfolios. The case must securely hold the material but also allow the material to be easily reviewed. Clear plastic sheet covers, dividers, disk holders, and envelopes are aids that may also display the material effectively. You may want to use color on the title page, the description pages, and the color dividers. How you display your work is as much a part of the evaluation of the portfolio as what you put in the portfolio.

An Electronic Portfolio

Portfolios are easy for prospective employers to access and navigate if they are on the Web or put on a disk.

E-portfolios are delivered on a CD, as an e-mail attachment, or displayed on a Web site. They give you multiple design options and compact, efficient delivery for presenting your communication activities to prospective employers. You can easily include documents that only appear in electronic format—presentations, help files, Web pages, and so on. You are demonstrating immediately the sophistication of your communication activities and your technical ability, and you are setting your application materials apart from the many received.

There is one major disadvantage of electronic portfolios: You cannot control all possible views of the documents (for example, changes in format depending on the viewer's browser for Web pages or software needed to open a document).

Readers will click through the e-portfolio and stop at documents that catch their attention. The opening screen introduces the portfolio; the links provide a guide for the reader and an overview of the organization of the portfolio. You can create the page in almost any software that gives you the option for creating hyperlinks. Microsoft Word, Adobe Acrobat, Freelance, and RoboHelp are just a few examples.

Figure 10.4 illustrates the opening screen of a portfolio created in FrontPage; Figure 10.5 illustrates how the navigation system continues throughout the portfolio. As you read Figure 10.5, notice how the various projects are described. Keep in mind you can use color and features such as animation, but take care that you do not overdo the presentation and overshadow the documents.

When you create a CD- and Web-based e-portfolio, you must make these decisions:

- Where will the e-portfolio be based? For example, it might be on a password protected Web space or an autorun CD.

- What file types will be used? PDF, HTML, Microsoft Office, or FrameMaker are a few of the possibilities.

FIGURE 10.4

Opening screen of portfolio created in FrontPage. The links are the guides to the contents. Indicating the last update provides the currency of contents in the portfolio.

Source: Unpublished student project. Modified and printed with permission of the author, Alise Chabaud.

FIGURE 10.5

Print Documents overview. Notice how the navigation system operates throughout the portfolio. Clicking on the Print Documents link on the opening screen of the portfolio (see Figure 10.4) takes reader to this page. The links to the portfolio contents are displayed across the bottom of the screen.

Source: Unpublished student project. Modified and printed with permission of the author, Alise Chabaud.

Print Documents

How to Replace the Upper Radiator Hose:
Instruction Manual

The 8-page instruction manual for replacing the upper radiator hose was created as a collaborative class assignment. The brochure details for any 1986 Honda Civic owner the procedure of replacing his or her upper radiator hose in approximately 90 minutes.

Before drafting the document, my colleagues and I completed the process of removing a radiator hose and replacing it with another. Because I had never performed the task before, I took copious notes of the visual and verbal process. Digital images were also taken and later included in the manual. In this manner, we were able to generate questions, identify areas of confusion, and determine the appropriate vocabulary for the replacement process.

Radiator Hose -- View the instruction manual in Adobe

International Institute of Marketing and Sales:
Informational Brochure

As the Editorial Assistant for the *International Journal of Marketing and Sales* (*IJMS*) under Dr. Jean Smith, Executive Director of the International Institute of Marketing and Sales, I created an informational brochure to promote the Institute. 7,000 copies of the brochure were printed and distributed to members and potential members of the Institute at the annual international conference and in future mail-outs.

After gathering information from *IJMS* journals, the Institute's Web site, and interviews with IIMS members, we determined the brochure's purpose was threefold: to provide information about the Institute, to recruit members to the Institute, and to highlight the refereed journal *IJMS*. Using MS Word, I developed the content and designed the layout. The brochure was then brought to a local printing company to incorporate the photographs, background images, shading, and color schemes. At a glance, the final product looks drastically different from my original. However, my two contributions of content and layout remain intact.

IJMS brochure -- View the brochure created using MS Word (in Adobe)
Printed brochure -- View the final brochure

NewWestern, Inc.: Corporate Analysis

Collaborative project with a team of three to analyze the business strategies of and publishing trends for *NewWestern, Inc.* in Montgomery, Alabama. The 20-page report combines information on national book publishing trends and comparable markets and publishing houses. This data provided the basis for our recommendations and analysis. We gathered research from reference librarians, online, and personal interviews, and completed the report using MS Word and MS Projects.

Corporate Analysis -- View the report in Adobe

Portfolio Purpose	Web Documents	Print Documents	Presentation	Resume	Home

Last updated February 2005

- What software does the reader need to open and read the documents (for example, Adobe Acrobat Reader or Macromedia Flash)? Can you provide the software, or will it have to be downloaded?

- What is the best software to use for the opening screen and description pages to create effective navigation and design?

Your readers' needs determine the answers to these questions. We recommend testing your e-portfolio on several computers (both PC and Macintosh) and in several versions of the popular browsers. If you think it is appropriate, ask the prospective employer what platform and software are available for reviewing your e-portfolio.

Two cautions:

- Readers can see the coding behind the documents you create. For example, readers can see if you used a style sheet or evaluate how clean and documented the HTML code is. In fact, some prospective employers will be more interested in how you built your document than in the content.

- Readers can change or copy your work if it is not protected. Other effective deterrents include creating read-only files, using PDF files, or requiring a password for the Web site. We have used the PDF format in our successful job searches. Include the Adobe Acrobat Reader on the CD or on your Web site.

The e-portfolio is easy to deliver. You may send it as part of your initial application with your resume, or as an e-mail attachment or a link to the Web site. The CD and CD case should have a label with your name, contact information (e-mail address), and instructions for opening the CD. Having a hard copy of the portfolio with you at an interview will ensure that your work will be available to show, but also leave behind the e-portfolio on a CD.

You may want to have with you a sample of your work that you can leave. A three- to six-page sample, called a *leave-behind* by graphic artists, should illustrate your best work and the type of work you want to do. If you want to move into another area, the leave-behind should include a description of how the material shows you can handle a new assignment. Do not leave your complete portfolio unless you are sure you will get it back.

One last point: Show confidence in your work and enthusiasm for it during the interview. You will be presenting the portfolio to potential employers, clients, or supervisors as part of your annual review. Know the material in the portfolio, and be prepared to discuss each document.

Interviews

If your letters of application succeed, the next stage of the job hunt is the interview. If the company is large enough to have a human resources depart-

Interviews are opportunities for you to communicate your potential value to prospective employers.

ment, you may first be interviewed by someone there before you meet with someone in the department where you will work. If the company is small, you will likely meet with the people with whom you will work. Alternatively, you may be interviewed in an interactive video conference where you sit in front of a computer with a camera and microphone and meet with one or more interviewers at another location who are also sitting before a computer. Just as technology has affected how we send resumes so has it opened up the possibilities for interviews.

When you are asked for an interview, you probably will be told what to expect. If you are not told, ask whom you will be seeing and how long you should expect the interview to last. Also ask whether you will be tested (for example, on how to use a special piece of equipment such as an oscilloscope) or whether you will need to make a presentation (common for training and sales positions). Interviews frighten a great many job hunters, probably more than they should. The more you know about the interview process planned for you, and the more you know about the company, the more comfortable and confident you will be during the interview. Use the guidelines we gave in Chapter 9 for finding out information about potential employers before the interview.

Preparing for an Interview

Plan ahead. Research the company or organization— and the position, if possible.

You have certain responsibilities for the interview as well. You should prepare for the interview beforehand. Here again, your self-inventory is good preparation (see Chapter 9). Look through it, and select those items from your background that demonstrate those characteristics employers value, such as loyalty and initiative. Also look for jobs, education, and extracurricular activities that relate to the job you are seeking. If you did your job exploration thoroughly, you'll already know something about the employer. If you have not, find out what you can before the interview.

Interviewers from the human resources department, recruiters who visit college campuses, and others who may meet with you are not out to trap you. Their job is to evaluate you, to find someone that their employers need, and to help you find out for what position you are best suited. Experienced interviewers know how to assess your qualifications. They ask questions to determine if you are a responsible person. They want to see whether you are friendly and good humored, someone who will work well with other people. They examine your vocational and professional skills. You will find most professionally trained interviewers helpful and friendly.

Dress appropriately for the interview.

Make sure your nonverbal communication says the right things about you. How should you dress for the interview? Like it or not, first impressions are important. Studies show that interviewers are more favorably inclined toward suitably dressed people. For men, this means shined shoes, sport coat, slacks, shirt, and tie. For some positions, particularly office work, a suit is probably even better. It does not matter that you may wear informal clothes on the job if you get it; dress well for the interview. For women, a dress or suit appropriate for business use is the best attire. However, if a tour of the plant is part of the interview process, you might be told to wear casual slacks and shoes with low heels. Follow the guidelines. Avoid extremes of all sorts: For men, hair that is too long and beards that are too bushy are extremes, as are sloppy, ill-fitting, or unclean clothes. Excessive makeup or perfume, many jangling bracelets, or flashy, dressy clothes are extremes for women. Naturally, you should be well groomed. Dirty knuckles and fingernails have lost as many jobs for people as low grades. Do not chew gum during the interview. Do not smoke even if invited to—in fact, avoid smoking before the interview so that you will not smell of smoke.

Being Interviewed

The interview is the opportunity to sell yourself face-to-face with the prospective employer.

Arrive at the place of the interview at least 10 minutes early. Be polite and professional with every person you meet, including security personnel, receptionists, and secretaries. Any of them could have a say, albeit a small one, in how you are ranked as a candidate. When you meet the interviewer, get his or her name straight and shake hands firmly but comfortably—avoid bone crunchers or limp-as-a-fish shakes. Offer a copy of your resume if the interviewer doesn't already have one. If you have a portfolio, mention it. More than likely, other candidates for the position will not have a portfolio, so you will begin the interview with one advantage. Sit down erectly but comfortably.

Interviews with individuals within a company usually last about 30 to 45 minutes, but you may meet with more than one person separately or at the same time. After introductions are over, interviewers usually spend a few minutes setting you at ease. They do not want you to be tense. The best interviews are relaxed and friendly, even a bit casual. Neither party should dominate. After some casual talk, perhaps about sports or current events, the interviewer may shift into telling you something about the company or organization. If so, listen closely, and be prepared to come in at natural pauses with intelligent questions, but do not interrupt the interviewer while he or she is talking. Ask questions that demonstrate you have done your research on the company. Keep steady eye contact with the interviewer during all this.

Sometimes this talk about the employer comes later in the interview. In any event, questions and answers about you are the heart of the interview. Frequently, testing is part of the interview. The questions may be deliberately vague to see whether you can develop ideas on your own, or they may be quite specific and penetrating.

Responding to Typical Questions

Typical questions you may be asked.

Here are some samples:

- Why do you want to work for us?

- Tell me something about yourself.

- What sort of summer or part-time work have you had?

- What were your responsibilities?

- Why did you leave your last job?

- Do you enjoy _____ (sales), (office), (experimental), (manual), (troubleshooting) work? Why?

- Can you take criticism?

- Why have you chosen your vocation?

- What subjects did you enjoy most in school? Why?

- How have you paid for your education?

- What are your strong (weak) points?

- What do you want to be doing five years (10 years) from now?

- If you were rich enough not to have to work, how would you spend your life?

Use these questions as opportunities to show interviewers that you would be an asset to their organization or company. To questions like "What are your strong points?" or "Do you enjoy _____ work?," recount specific experiences that illustrate the quality of your work and your attitude. Refer to specific items in your portfolio that display evidence to support your statements.

Responding to Surprising Questions

Surprising questions you may be asked.

An interviewer might ask you questions that catch you momentarily off guard. Be prepared to say something. Above all, do not respond with a blank stare, even if the question puzzles you at first.

Sometimes an interviewer might ask you questions about some aspects of your education or work experiences that at first seem unrelated to the job for which you are interviewing—questions such as

"Did you enjoy working as an advertising sales representative the summer between your freshman and sophomore years?"

or

"I notice on your resume that you took three history courses. That seems a bit odd for someone who majored in economics. Tell me why you took those courses and what you learned in them?"

There is, of course, no one answer that is "correct." However, interviewers are interested in how you answer such questions. They learn several things from your answers, such as whether you are able to identify transferable skills or knowledge from previous experience, how much you retain from earlier experiences, and how you respond to an unexpected question. Be prepared for such questions—they provide you with those opportunities to provide the so-whats of your education and work experiences.

A recent book by William Poundstone entitled *How Would You Move Mount Fuji?*[2] describes interviewing techniques in which the interviewer asks purposefully puzzling questions or presents problems for the applicant to solve. Here are just three:

How many piano tuners are there in the world?
Why are beer cans tapered at the end?
How long would it take you to move Mount Fuji?

Some of the questions have correct answers. However, the real test here is to convince the interviewer that the applicant has a *credible* answer. What the interviewer is looking for is the way the applicant arrived at the answer or conclusion. Some questions—such as the last one—do not have one right answer or correct solution. The purpose of the question or problem is to test the applicant's thought process and ability to remain poised while handling an unexpected question.

Responding to Illegal Questions

Be aware that in the United States, various state and federal laws prohibit interviewers from asking you for information that is not job related or that could be discriminatory—for example, "Are you married?" or "Do you have children?" In general, all questions about race, color, creed, national origin, religion, sex, age, ethnic background, marital status, family relationships, and political beliefs are off limits to interviewers. You should not provide such information on resumes or in letters of application.

What do you do if interviewers ask improper questions? (Most will not.) You can refuse to answer, of course, but that would likely guarantee you will not get the job. One expert suggests that a wiser choice is to deflect the question by getting at the real concern of the interviewer. For example, if the interviewer asks, "Are you a U.S. citizen?" or "What country are you from?," you've been asked an illegal question. However, you could respond with "I am authorized to work in the United States." Similarly, let's say the interviewer asks, "Who is going to take care of your children when you have to travel for the job?" You might answer, "I can meet the travel and work schedule that this job requires."

If in doubt about how to answer such questions, ask a question of your own, such as "How does that relate to working for your corporation?" The interviewer's answer may lead you to a response that allays the interviewer's concern without violating your privacy and legal rights. Or it may give you further information that will help you evaluate whether the company is a good fit for you. Whatever you do, don't lie.

---

[2]William Poundstone. *How Would You Move Mount Fuji?* Boston: Little, Brown, 2003.

Asking Questions Yourself

Questions you may want to ask the interviewer.

At some point in the interview, the interviewer will discuss with you the job or jobs the employer has to offer. Here you should be able to display your professional knowledge about jobs for which you are suited. You should be fairly firm about your goals but flexible enough to discuss a related job if it looks good. Avoid the appearance of being willing to take any job at all. Ask job-related questions, such as these:

- What qualities (or skills) does this job require?

- How does the position fit in with the rest of the unit or organization?

- What is the experience of the person I would work for?

- How many people are in the office or unit?

- Is there orientation or training for the job? Is the training formal or on the job?

- Does the job offer opportunities for professional growth?

- How will I be evaluated on the job?

- Is there a probationary period?

When the interviewer discusses salary and job benefits, such as hospitalization insurance, pensions, and vacations, you are free to ask questions about these items. But do not ask about them until the interviewer brings them up. You will rarely be offered a job at a first interview. Sometimes this will occur at a second interview. Normally, however, the job offer will come at some later time.

Ending an Interview

Do not try to extend interviews. When the interviewer closes up your folder and indicates that the interview is over, it is—for better or worse. Stand up, shake hands once again, thank the interviewer, and leave.

A Recap on Interviewing

What characteristics should you display to have a successful interview? According to many interviewers, the following rank high on the list:

- Be neat and well groomed.

- Be natural, friendly, and relaxed, but not sloppy or overly casual.

- Be more interested in the work involved on the job and in its potential than in salary and benefits.

- Important: Have definite goals. Know your abilities and what you want to do. Be ready to articulate these goals.

- Use your portfolio to back up statements about your abilities and skills—experience and education.

Like athletic events, no two interviews are exactly alike. But certain situations and questions do recur. Good answers prepared for the questions listed here will go a long way to get you ready for any interview. And you can practice. Get together with friends, and interview each other. Practice talking about yourself and your accomplishments and articulating your desires. Learn how to be assertive about your qualifications.

Planning the Portfolio

CONTENTS

- Have you selected items that showcase the abilities and skills you have to offer?

- Do those abilities and skills match up with the stated or assumed qualifications and responsibilities that the employer is looking for?

- Are the items in your portfolio copies? Never include the originals.

- Have you included at least three or four items in the portfolio?

- If appropriate in applying for positions in other countries, have you included copies of your birth certificate, health records, passport or citizenship papers, driver's license, and so forth?

DESIGN AND ORGANIZATION

- Although the contents of your portfolio may range from formal reports to creative works to visuals and electronic presentations, do the portfolio navigational elements (title page, contents page, cover pages, divider pages, etc.) have a consistent design?

- Is the portfolio organized in a way that serves your purpose and is easy for reviewers to use? By chronology? By type of document or presentation? By type of project? By type of skill? Is it possible to organize the contents according to the key skills and responsibilities called for in the job description (such as communication skills, computer skills, management experience, etc.). There will, of course, be some overlap in these categories, but the categories should be rational and easy to understand.

- Is your portfolio designed in a way (using a three-ring binder or electronic files in which the items can be changed easily) that makes it easy for you to add, delete, or move items around easily as your portfolio develops? Is it easy to copy an item that an interviewer might like to have?

- Do the navigational aids (table of contents, divider pages, tabs, etc.) display the structure of the portfolio to help reviewers scan contents or locate an item quickly?

PRESENTATION

- Your portfolio itself is a document or presentation that displays your ability to present information. Is it organized and formatted well, and does it contain the items you hope will help you achieve your objective of receiving a job offer?

- Are the contents easy to access and read?

- If the portfolio is electronic, does the reader have the software needed to view the documents? Can you provide software such as Adobe Acrobat Reader or software for sound files?

- If the portfolio is electronic, do the documents open in the location within the document to best present the information? Is the document sized and oriented to open so the reader does not have to make too many adjustments? (For example, Excel files open to the location where the cursor was last placed, and PDF files can be set to open at 50% of the screen size.)

- If the portfolio is electronic, have you hidden table lines in documents? Have you used style sheets? Is the code clean in the documents?

- If the portfolio is hard copy, have you placed odd-sized or irregularly shaped items in plastic sleeves or pockets?

Revising the Portfolio

- Review the contents of the portfolio to ensure that they are the most up-to-date and pertinent selections.

- Check for typos, misspellings, odd and inconsistent spacing, and so forth.

- To ensure that your electronic portfolio works as you intend, do Collaborative Activity 1.

PLANNING AND REVISING CHECKLIST: THE INTERVIEW

Planning for the Interview

- Have you done your homework? Do you know yourself and the organization with which you will interview?

- Are your career goals well defined? Can you speak easily about them?

- Have you thought about where you would like to live and work? How flexible are you about this matter?

- Are you realistic about your goals?

- Do you know what people really do in the job you seek?

- Are you truly interested in and enthusiastic about the job you seek? If not, should you rethink your career goals?

- Have you thought about yourself from the employer's point of view? Can you show how your interests and skills will benefit the employer?

- Can you speak easily about your strengths and weaknesses?

- Have you thought about how you would answer the questions listed on pages 298–299?

- Have you thought about how to answer unexpected, puzzling, or improper questions?

- Have you examined your wardrobe and obtained the right kind of clothes?

- Are you neat and well groomed?

- Do you have extra copies of your resume to give to the interviewer?

- Does your portfolio contain your best work?

Revising the Interview

It may seem strange to speak of revising an interview, but it is entirely possible. First, you should practice interviews with your friends. Sit down with them and role-play interviewee and interviewer in turn. If you have access to video equipment, record at least three or four practice interviews. View each practice interview analytically, looking for successful responses and poor responses. Watch for the improvement that will come with practice.

Second, you will certainly have a number of interviews during your job hunt. After each one, take time to analyze objectively how well you did. Jot down interview questions for which you were unprepared, and be prepared if they come up again. In analyzing both practice and real interviews, think of these questions:

- Was the interview relaxed and friendly? Did you appear good humored?

- Did you make your career goals clear?

- Were you able to consider alternatives to your goals yet maintain the impression that your goals are well thought out?

- Did you exhibit enough knowledge about the kind of work you feel best suited for?

- Did you know enough about the organization you were interviewing with?

- Did you have enough evidence of your abilities to be convincing?

- Did you come across as being either too passive or too aggressive?

- Did you look at the interviewer during the conversation?

- Were your expressed expectations realistic?

- Did you sit comfortably during the interview?

- How did your manner of dressing compare to the interviewer's?

- Did you seem more interested in money than the job?

- Did you ask questions of your own about the organization and the job? Did you get satisfactory answers?

- Do you think you and the organization are a good match?

- Do you really want to work for the organization as represented by the interviewer?

- What do you do next? What points can you raise or answer in a follow-up letter to the interviewer?

Suggestions for Applying Your Knowledge

Individual Activity

Visit the Web site of professional associations with which you are familiar, especially those of which you are a student member, or the Web site of your school's career development or job placement office. Do any of them contain advice or have links to sites that provide information and guidelines on developing professional portfolios? Prepare a brief memo to your instructor or your classmates that reports the results of your research.

Collaborative Activities

1. Have several friends and classmates with critical (but friendly) eyes read your portfolio. Watch as they read and navigate your portfolio. Note what they read, where they stop, and whether they have problems navigating or opening the documents. Make adjustments as needed.

2. To practice interviewing, pair up with a classmate. Interview each other, developing important information about the interviewee, as mentioned in this chapter—favorite courses, job experience, hobbies, and so forth. You and your partner should show your portfolios and answer questions about the work in the portfolio. This interview relaxes students who are unfamiliar with the process and gets them talking freely about themselves. Some people have difficulty drawing attention to their own strong points but can do it easily for others. A good follow-up to this interview is to have the interviewer write a letter of application for the interviewee.

3. Conduct mock interviews before the entire class. You can even role-play in these interviews. One student can play an ill-prepared, unsuccessful interviewee; another can play a well-prepared, successful one. If your school has the necessary equipment, video-record interviews for later study.

4. Students who have participated in real interviews should tell the class about their experiences. Outside of class, you can practice interviews with friends until you are familiar with the process and totally at ease with it.

Communicating News: News-Release Publications, Brochures, and Web Sites

Organizations quickly recognize good communicators and will develop opportunities for employees to use their communication skills. The more writing you do, the better you will become and the more opportunities you will have to use your communication skills—and the more opportunities you will have for advancing in the organization. The opportunities for writing will develop into a diverse set of documents that will expand your portfolio. In this chapter, we describe three types of documents you may find yourself writing: publishing news through news releases and newsletters, developing brochures to distribute information, and contributing information to Web sites.

For each of these writing opportunities, the writing process described in Chapters 1 and 2 and the guidelines given in Chapters 3, 4, and 5 apply. You are communicating specific information to a specific audience for a specific purpose. The format and document design will change and the delivery method may be paper, electronic, or both—but you are still getting the information to readers so that they may use the information.

We will describe news-release publications, brochures, and web documents using *information*, *audience*, and *purpose* to guide the discussion. We add three additional considerations for these documents: space, schedule (timeliness), and costs.

Space How much room do you have to get the information to the reader? This will tell you the amount of information you need to get before writing. It gives you an idea of how many visuals you need to include and what other document design issues you must consider.

Schedule News-release publications, brochures, and Web sites generally have a limited life. The news is outdated at some point, brochures need changing to reflect new information, and Web sites need refreshing (if not complete updating) frequently. How often they need updating influences the document design. The design must allow easy updates.

Cost Development time and production costs must be considered in publishing news-related publications, brochures, and Web sites. Web sites require technical skill (for example, writing HTML code or JavaScript), and brochures often incorporate color or require special paper.

Adapt the documents to meet the needs of the audience.

When you write news-release publications, brochures, and Web sites, you often know ahead of time how you want to deliver the information. For example, suppose you are asked to serve as the editor of the company's weekly newsletter for employees and the newsletter will be delivered by e-mail and be available on the Web. Your client has charged you with developing a tri-fold brochure that describes the services of the counseling center. In the following sections, we describe news-release publications, brochures, and Web documents and give examples. The genre (the type of document) identifies certain expected features for each, although the features are not required and are not so restrictive that only one format appears. Keep in mind that you need to be flexible as you develop the documents, adjusting to the needs of the audience and the purpose of the document.

One scenario illustrates the flexible nature of the documents described in this chapter:

> The student services office on a college campus wants to promote development of Web sites by campus offices that are accessible to all students, including students with disabilities. The office decided to sponsor a one-day workshop and a contest to encourage the development: the Campus Accessibility Initiative (CAI). The office asked a graduate student to develop the publicity for the workshop and contest.
>
> First she gathered the information to answer the questions *who*, *what*, *when*, and *where*. She discussed with the client developing a brochure to get the information to Web developers on campus. Figure 11.1 shows an early draft of the brochure: an 8 1/2- × 11-inch sheet of paper folded in half to give four sides for the information, with the key information inside. The caption for Figure 11.1 points out several problems with the brochure.
>
> As the project developed, the supervisor of the graduate student decided to develop a Web site. The Web site promotes the event, illustrates good design principles for accessibility, and collects the registration information for the workshops. However, the brochure colors did not complement the Web site. In addition, the cost and distribution of the brochure were questioned, and the organization of the information was not effective.
>
> Figure 11.2 shows the revised announcement for the CAI. The brochure became a flyer with the colors and design matching those of the Web site. The one-page, 8 1/2 × 11 inch flyer is relatively easy to print, distribute, and post on doors and bulletin boards around campus. A poster may also be developed. The format gives readers all the information on one page with headings signaling the purpose, the workshop content, and the rules for the contest.

audience
purpose
information
space
timeliness
cost

This example illustrates the flexibility needed in developing news-release documents, brochures, and Web sites described in this chapter. The audience, purpose, and information are identified and the space, timeliness, and cost influence the document's development. The example also illustrates the use of more than one document to get the information out. There is overlap among the news documents, brochures, and Web documents we describe here. News documents are delivered in print form and via the Web now; brochures may be printed and mailed or the same information formatted for distribution on the Web; and Web sites are used for more than displaying information.

We close the chapter with another scenario description to illustrate the interrelationship among workplace activities and the different documents needed.

Knowing your audience, understanding your purpose, and developing specific information are key to the documents featured in this chapter (as they are in all documents). But because the space is limited (almost restricting), timeliness is crucial, and development and publication costs are significant factors, you must adapt to the circumstances you face.

FIGURE 11.1

The 4-panel brochure is the *first draft* of information for a workshop and competition promoting Web accessibility on a college campus. After meeting with her client, the writer decided that a flyer would better display the information and would be less expensive to produce. Figure 11.2 shows the revised announcement.

Source: Unpublished student project, modified and printed with permission of Rachel Kennedy, the author.

Competition

Who can participate?

Both faculty and students of the university are encouraged to become involved wih thte CAI Website Competition.

How do I participate in the competition?
Form a team of one to five people who have responsibility of a campus website—the site can be academic, administrative, or a student organization site.

The site must be created by the members within each group, outside design collaboration is not allowed.

Redesign your site to comply with current accessibility standards.

You may begin work at anytime on your new site. All work must be completed turned in on **June 27, 2004**.

Your site will then be entered and judged by a panel of experts.

For more information. . .

If you are interest in finding out more about CAI, please contact:
D. Tracy
999-123-4567
tracy@university.edu

S. Reign
999-123-9876
reign@university.edu

CAMPUS
accessibility
initiative

[insert graphic here]

Take the challenge!
February 20, 2004

Questions

What is the Campus Accessiblity Initiative?
CAI is a challenge to university faculty and students to create websites that are accessible to *all* users.

What does accessibility mean?
A method of coding a site to ensure that all site visitors can access the information contained within the site.

Why is accessibility a big deal?
- According to the CNET Special Report by Sally McGrane, approximately 98 percent of existing websites are not accessible to people with disabilities, such as visually impaired users.

- As a result of the large inaccessibility of websites, most of the 54.7 million Americans do not have the same awareness of the Internet as people without disabilities.

- According to San Franciscoís Disability Statistics Center, disabled Americans are less than half as likely to won a computer than their non-disabled counterparts—*why would you worry about the Internet if it isn't accessible to you?*

How can I become involved in the CAI challenge?
- Form a team and start redesigning your website for the CAI Website Competition.

- By registering for and attending the CAI Seminar, February 20, 2004 at the Conference Center.

Seminar

A day-long seminar will be given **February 20, 2004** at the Conference Center. The seminar will give attendees the most current information on accessibility issues. The courses offered include:

General Access– an introduction to access issues in the design of websites. Includes an overview of the industry-accepted guidelines and standards.

Macromedia– Macromedia's MX Suite has been released and it offers the latest accessibility tools. Explore these new features and start applying this new found knowledge in websites you are currently developing.

Java script and Accessibility– Java script is a tool and can be used to make content accessible—or inaccessible. Learn how to do the right thing within your website.

JAWS from the User's Perspective– Listen to the web and learn more about the challenges and how to use this software as an accessibility testing tool.

Accessible Web Templates– Making web templates is one of the most important steps in building a website usable to all. Learn to develop a solds foundation for your website from the beginning.

The *CAI WEBSITE DESIGN CONTEST* kicks off at the close of the seminar. The contest will give seminar attendees a chance to use the skills they have just learned in the offered seminar courses.

Registration

The deadline for registering for the seminar is **Friday, January 16, 2004**. Please register by visiting the CAI website at www.university.edu/cai and completing a registration form.

FIGURE 11.2

Compare this flyer to the first draft, the brochure shown in Figure 11.1.

Source: Unpublished student project, modified and printed with permission of Rachel Kennedy, the author.

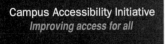

Campus Accessibility Initiative
Improving access for all

Spring 2004

Questions...

What is the Campus Accessibility Initiative?
CAI challenges university faculty and students to create websites
that are accessible to *all* users.

How can I become involved in the CAI challenge?

- Form a team and start redesigning your website for the CAI Website Competition.

- Register for and attend the CAI Seminar, February 20, 2004 at the Conference Center.

What does accessibility mean?
A method of coding a website to ensure that all site visitors can access the information contained within the site.

Why is accessibility a big deal?

- Approximately 98 percent of existing websites are not accessible to people with disabilities, such as visually impaired users (CNET Special Report.)

- Most of the 54.7 million disabled-Americans do not have the same awareness of the Internet as people without disabilities.

- 193 AU students possess disabilities hindering them from regular Internet use. It is our job to ensure all of students have the same advantages as non-disabled students when using auburn.edu sites.

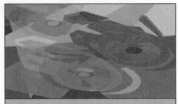

Seminar...

Attend a day-long seminar, February 20, 2004 at the Conference Center. The courses offered include:

General Access–
An introduction to access issues in the design of websites. Includes an overview of the industry accepted guidelines and standards.

Macromedia–
Macromediaís Flash MX Studio has been released and it offers the latest accessibility tools. Explore these new features and start applying this new found knowledge in websites you are currently developing.

JavaScript and Accessibility –
JavaScript is a tool and can be used to make content accessible–
or inaccessible. Learn how to do the right thing within your website.

JAWS from the User's Perspective –
Learn more about this mouse less browser and screen reader and how to use this software as an accessibility testing tool for your own web sites.

Accessible Web Templates–
Making web templates is one of the most important steps in building a website that is usable to all. Learn to develop a solid foundation for your website from the beginning.

The CAI WEBSITE DESIGN CONTEST kicks off at the close of the seminar. The contest gives seminar attendees a chance to use the valuable skills learned in the courses

Seminar Registration...

The deadline for registering for the seminar is Friday, January 16, 2004.

Please register by visiting the CAI website at www.university.edu/cai and completing a registration form.

Help make our university a more accessible campus for its students and take the CAI challenge!

Contest...

Who can participate?
AU faculty and students of are encouraged to become involved with the CAI Website Competition.

How do I participate in the competition?

- Form a team of one to five people who have responsibility of a campus website – the site can be academic, administrative, or a student organization site.

- Redesign your site to comply with current accessibility standards.*

- You may begin work at any time on your new site. All work must be completed and turned in by June 27, 2004

- Your site will then be judged by a panel of experts.

Please note that outside design collaboration is prohibited.

For more information...

If you are interested in finding out more about CAI, please contact:
D. Tracy
999-123-4567
tracy@university.edu

S. Reign
999-123-9876
reign@university.edu

News-Release Publications

Organizations want to get information about their activities to internal and external audiences. Members of the organization and others in the community use the news to participate in the activities of the organization. The newsletters and news releases promote the organization.

News Releases

Guidelines for writing a news release.

News releases answer the questions *who, what, when, where,* and *why.* Organizations want to publicize the key information for an event, promotion, award, or other newsworthy activity. Organizations often have a public relations or communications department that gets the information out. The department has a close working relationship with newspapers, radio and television stations, and other organizations. However, you may find it is your responsibility to promote your organization's activities or to get the news about your department's activities to the corporate communication office. What do you do?

1. Gather accurate information. You will need to answer the questions

   Who is the newsworthy person(s) or the event?

   What is the person doing or *what* is the purpose of the event?

   When is the event? (date, time)

   Where is the event? (location)

   Why is this event important?

2. Review your purpose after you have the answer to these questions. Your purpose will establish what the audience will need and the information to provide. News releases are informative, more than persuasive, documents, although you want to provide the information to persuade the readers to go to the event.

3. Write the news release. Often, news releases are less than one page. You may submit either on your organization's letterhead stationary or electronically. Rarely will you submit more than one page or one screen of information.

   - Use concise sentences and *double-check* the details about the date, time, and location (when relevant). Sentences and paragraphs are relatively short, providing the essential information without unnecessary descriptions. You want to get the specific information out to the news organizations.

   - Organize the release with the most important information first (commonly described as an inverted pyramid). The news editors may need to cut the release to fit the space, and often they begin cutting at the end of the release.

4. Have someone else read the press release before you send it. It is much easier to catch errors before the information goes out than it is to send out corrections.

5. Send the news release to the newspapers, radio and television stations, and other organizations. *Timeliness* is crucial for news releases. You need to get the news release to the media in advance. You may e-mail or send a print copy of the news release. For information that is dated, check with the news department to see how far in advance they need the information.

Cost The cost is minimal. The media want the information; there is no cost to submit the information.

The news release in Figure 11.3 announces the opening of a new branch office. Figure 11.4 is an example of a news release posted on the NASA Web site and also sent by e-mail to subscribers. Government agencies and corporations use news releases to keep citizens and clients informed of the organization's activities.

FIGURE 11.3

A news release provides information for news organizations to publish. You may be asked to write news releases to publicize the activities of your organization.

FOR IMMEDIATE RELEASE

11 May 2005

Solution Specialists, Inc.   Contact: Jane Reynolds
5006 Moursund Boulevard   615-222-2345
Ft. Worth TX 78000

Fort Worth, TX—Solution Specialists, Inc. (SSI), a Fort Worth-based firm specializing in providing professional-grade software for construction management for over ten years, announces the opening of a new branch office in the Houston area. Grand opening ceremonies are planned for Wednesday, June 11 at 3 pm.

The branch office is at the intersection of the Bee-Line Highway and Moffett Road in the Delmara Industrial Park.

Specializing in providing software solutions for small- and medium-sized builders and contractors, Solution Specialists brings to the Houston area some of the construction and building industries' most comprehensive up-to-date tools for developing construction estimates and contracts, project scheduling, and bidding and invoicing packages.

SSI was founded in 1992 by Juanita Juaret and Robert McKinley.

FIGURE 11.4

NASA issues news releases to keep citizens informed about its activities. Visit the Web site to see the variety of topics and the type of information released. An example of the brief description of the news item is shown above the line. *Read More* links to the news article.

Source: NASA News Releases (2003, December 11). NASA. Retrieved December 13, 2003, from http://www.nasa.gov/audience/formedia/archives/index.html

Newsletters

Newsletters inform readers of events for an organization and publicize the organization's activities. They serve to persuade the readers that the organization is healthy and active in its community.

What features make a newsletter, a newsletter?

- timely reporting of information

- concise, brief articles

- inexpensive delivery: mailed, e-mailed, or posted on the Web (or all of these delivery methods). You will find newsletters in many formats, and you will find more and more delivered across the Web.

For example, the U.S. Department of Agriculture publishes *Amber Waves: The Economics of Food, Farming, Natural Resources, and Rural America* (www.ers.usda.gov/AmberWaves) 5 times a year (see Figure 11.5 on page G in the first color insert). Online it appears as a newsletter with links to current news, *Now Featuring*, as well as links to *Findings* from research sponsored by the U.S. Department of Agriculture and the Economic Research Service. As with other newsletters published by the U.S. government, you can view the news on the Web site, download it as a PDF document, print it (in the print-friendly format), or subscribe to receive it by e-mail or postal mail.

If you are put in charge of a newsletter, the format may be established or you may need to design the first issue. You need to consider the following as you develop a newsletter.

Audience Newsletters are frequently intended for internal audiences, members of the organization. For example, the newsletter in Figure 11.6 is published each morning electronically for members of the Auburn University community. Short announcements for 5–7 items alert the university community to events and activities. Submissions are similar to the news releases—sent electronically to the editor of the *AUDaily* 3–5 days ahead of time.

Newsletters also are sent to external audiences to provide information on the organization's activities. Figure 11.7 is an example of a newsletter from the National Center for Biotechnology Information (NCBI). It is available online or as a PDF file that can be printed or as a Web-formatted (HTML) file.

Purpose The purpose of the newsletter will determine the content, length, and format of the newsletter. The *NCBI News* publishes articles related to molecular biology and genetics (Figure 11.7). The primary audience is molecular biologists and other scientists in related fields; however, journalists, medical professionals, lawyers, and others may also use the information for their work.

Information The information in newsletters (like that in all documents) depends on the needs of the audience. Getting information for the newsletter may be the most difficult part of developing a newsletter. The editor is always looking for information and relying on individuals to submit the information under the pressure of a deadline.

FIGURE 11.6

The *AUDaily* is an example of an internal newsletter. Sent each morning by e-mail to Auburn University employees, the newsletter announces campus events and other newsworthy items. Readers can skim the *Headlines* section for the contents and can move to the *Features* section for more information.

Source: *AUDaily* (December 19, 2003). Auburn University, Office of Communications and Marketing. Retrieved December 21, 2003, from http://gwcal.duc.auburn.edu/audaily/

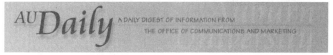

December 19, 2003

Good morning! Here's a look at what's happening at Auburn:

HEADLINES
* Campus gains 214 B-zone parking spaces
* Commencement exercises scheduled for 2 p.m.
* Engineering racers capture international award
* Women's Basketball hosts Faculty/staff Appreciation Day
* Calendar of Events

FEATURES
CAMPUS GAINS 214 B-ZONE PARKING SPACES
AU Parking Services has converted 214 west campus parking spaces to a B-zone. Effective Jan. 5, a portion of the Max Morris lot (corner of Donahue Drive and North Thach Circle) will be available for drivers with B-zone hangtags. Signs will be in place after the holiday break to designate this area as a B-zone. Students with C-zone hangtags will also have a new parking area: the site previously occupied by the hangar building (just west of Thach Circle), which will accommodate 200 vehicles. For more information contact Parking Services at 844-4143.

COMMENCEMENT EXERCISES SCHEDULED FOR 2 P.M.
Auburn will confer a total of 1,421 degrees on new graduates at a 2 p.m. ceremony today at Beard-Eaves-Memorial Coliseum. A live stream of video can be seen by clicking to http://www.auburn.edu/communications_marketing/graduationlive beginning at 1:45 p.m.

ENGINEERING RACERS CAPTURE INTERNATIONAL AWARD
The AU Society of Automotive Engineers (SAE) student chapter in the Samuel Ginn College of Engineering has been selected by SAE International to receive its 2003 Outstanding Collegiate Branch Award. This is the second time Auburn has received the award--the first being bestowed in 2000--placing it in the top one percent of branches worldwide. Only four such awards are given annually. Established in 1963 to encourage branches to excel in their technical programs and activities, the award recognizes exemplary performance in the areas of technical meetings, projects, membership continuity, and recruitment. In addition to a plaque and certificate, the Auburn branch will receive a $500 award. The Auburn SAE student chapter includes the Auburn University SAE Mini Baja and Lady Tigers Mini Baja all-terrain vehicle teams and the Auburn University Formula SAE team. In this month's FSAE Australasia competition in Australia, the Formula team, which qualified for the event by placing fifth overall out of 140 teams in the Detroit FSAE competition in May, placed third in the acceleration event, fourth in the skid pad and endurance events, and fourth overall out of a field of 21.

WOMEN'S BASKETBALL HOSTS FACULTY/STAFF APPRECIATION DAY
All AU faculty and staff members are cordially invited to AU Faculty/staff Appreciation Day with the Auburn Women's Basketball Team. On Monday, Dec. 29, employees are invited to a pre-game chalk-talk with Coach Joe Ciampi at 11:45 a.m. in the Doyle Haynes Scholarship Room located inside Beard-Eaves-Memorial Coliseum. All faculty and staff members will be admitted to the game free of charge with a valid AU ID.

CALENDAR OF EVENTS
December 19
2 p.m. - Fall Semester Commencement, Beard-Eaves-Memorial Coliseum

For events during the holiday break, click to the Web Calendar of events at http://gwcal.auburn.edu/calendar/

ABOUT AUDAILY

AUDaily is a service of the AU Office of Communications and Marketing and is distributed each weekday to faculty and staff. To read archived copies visit http://gwcal.duc.auburn.edu/audaily

For more in-depth news about Auburn University, visit the news page at http://www.ocm.auburn.edu/toppage/topnews/

TO SUBMIT INFORMATION for possible inclusion in future issues of AUDaily or to get answers to your questions, please contact Mike Clardy at 844-9996, or by e-mail at clardch@auburn.edu

To read the policy for submission, click on http://www.ocm.auburn.edu/audailypolicy.html

To view the AU Web Calendar of Events, go to http://www.auburn.edu/calendar

TO SUBSCRIBE OR UNSUBSCRIBE from this list, browse to http://www.ocm.auburn.edu/audaily

Posting of events or news items in AUDaily does not necessarily signify or imply endorsement by Auburn University.

FIGURE 11.7

The first and last page of the *NCBI News* illustrates a newsletter with articles for a specific audience, molecular biologists and geneticists. Current newsworthy items reach scientists quickly and with enough details to give them information that may apply to their research.

Source: *NCBI News* (Summer 2003). National Center for Biotechnology Information. Retrieved December 18, 2003, from http://www.ncbi.nlm.nih.gov/Web/Newsltr/Summer03/index.html

NCBI News

National Center for Biotechnology Information
National Library of Medicine
National Institutes of Health
Department of Health and Human Services

Summer 2003

The Reference Human Genome at NCBI

The Human Genome Project, a 13-year international collaborative effort, reached a major milestone in April 2003 with the release of the first reference sequence for the human genome. This finished sequence follows the working draft, completed in 2001, and described in the February 15 edition of *Nature*.[1] Over the period of the genome sequencing effort, sequencing centers from around the world deposited billions of letters of human DNA sequence into GenBank® and its collaborating databases, DDBJ and EMBL, where the data was immediately made available to researchers.

Between the appearance of the draft sequence and the release of the finished reference sequence, NCBI maintained interim assemblies of the data to ensure access by the research community to the most complete genome draft. Now, the finished reference human genome sequence, along with the results of NCBI analysis and annotations, is available for viewing and downloading.

The Genome and its Genes

The reference human genome, a small portion of which is shown in Figure 1, consists of 24 finished chromosomes of 2.9 billion bases and covers about 99 percent of the gene-containing DNA. The sequence is accurate, on average, to the level of one error per 10,000 bases. Small updates to the assembly will continue as complex regions are further refined and the small number of remaining gaps between the large stretches of contiguous sequence, or "contigs", are closed.

NCBI identifies known genes in the genome by aligning Reference Sequence (see RefSeq below) and GenBank mRNAs to the assembled

continued on page 3

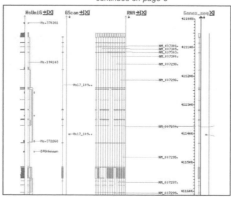

Figure 1. Map Viewer display for the human BRCA1 gene showing, from the right, the NCBI gene model, 13 transcript variants, a GenomeScan predicted gene model, and UniGene cluster sequences that map to the region.

SARS Coronavirus Resource

The first complete sequence of the SARS Coronavirus, determined by the BC Cancer Agency Genome Sciences Centre in Canada, was submitted to GenBank prior to publication as an unannotated nucleotide sequence and assigned GenBank accession number AY274119. The sequence was subsequently processed through the NCBI viral genome annotation pipeline and made available in Entrez Genomes under RefSeq accession NC_004718 as the *SARS-CoV* reference sequence within about 24 hours of its submission. The results of this computational analysis can be accessed from the

continued on page 4

In this issue

FIGURE 11.7
(continued)

Gene Expression Omnibus
continued from page 2

stage, disease state, and others. The relative abundance of a particular molecule and the degree of measurement variability are also search parameters in GEO. Results are returned as a set of pre-computed molecular abundance profiles such as that shown in Figure 1 for human synaptopodin 2. Results are returned in order of most-interesting-first, based on a scoring scheme which considers statistically significant differences, expression level, outliers, and variability.

Entrez GEO may also be queried for sequences of interest based on nucleotide sequence similarity, thus facilitating the identification of sequence homologs of interest, e.g., related gene family members or for cross-species comparisons across all GEO datasets. The "Sequence BLAST" search function on the

GEO Home Page accepts either a FASTA sequence, GI number or accession number as input and performs a BLAST search against all the sequences represented on microarray platforms or SAGE libraries in GEO.

Within Entrez GEO results, following the "Profile Neighbors" link from selected expression profiles will display those probes within the same dataset that show an expression profile that is similar to the one selected.

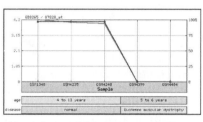

Figure 1. Expression profile for human synaptopodin 2 from GDS265 showing decreased expression in tissues taken from muscle biopsies of Duchenne muscular dystrophy patients relative to controls.

When the "Sequence Neighbors" link is selected, the results will be those sequences that are similar or identical to the query probe over all GEO datasets. Entrez GEO and Entrez GDS retrieval results are fully integrated with each other as well as other Entrez databases including Nucleotide, UniGene, MapViewer and PubMed.

All original GEO records as well as GDS data are available for download at:

ftp.ncbi.nih.gov/pub/geo/data/

Questions regarding the submission of data to GEO may be sent to:

geo@ncbi.nlm.nih.gov

General inquiries about GEO may be sent to the geo alias or to the NCBI Help Desk:

info@ncbi.nlm.nih.gov

—*TB, SD*

Department of Health and Human Services
Public Health Service, national institutes of Health
National Library of Medicine
National Center for Biotechnology Information
Bldg. 38A, Room 3S308
8600 Rockville Pike
Bethesda, Maryland 20894

Official Business
Penalty for Private Use $300

FIRST CLASS MAIL
POSTAGE & FEES PAID
PHS/NIH/NLM
BETHESDA, MD
PERMIT NO. G-816

NCBI News

Summer 2003

A table of contents, bulleted list, or some other feature introduces the newsletter so that readers can locate and read only the information they are interested in. The articles are relatively short, often giving the highlights.

Space Print-based newsletters are most frequently printed on 11- × 17-inch paper folded so that there are 4 pages or, with additional sheets of paper, 8, 12, or 16 pages. Frequently, the pages are formatted for 2 or 3 columns to allow for more than one feature on the page. Print-based newsletters have a portion of the back cover set aside for the mailing address (often formatted so that the newsletter is folded in half, stapled or taped, and mailed without an envelope).

Electronic newsletters are not limited by space, but that does not mean they should expand. Their purpose remains getting news out quickly. Use links to provide more information if necessary.

Schedule Newsletters are successful when they are published on a regular schedule (daily, weekly, monthly, or quarterly, for example). Members of the community expect the timely delivery of information.

Cost The cost of producing and mailing a newsletter depends on the media used and the length of the newsletter. More and more organizations are sending electronic newsletters via e-mail to members and others interested in the information. The costs of printing and mailing are saved—a significant saving. However, electronic newsletters require not only an editor responsible for the content, but also someone with technical expertise to maintain the electronic mailing list and/or to develop the Web site.

Guidelines for writing a newsletter.

Once you have established the parameters, write the articles. As you write, refer to *Amber Waves* (Figure 11.5 on first color insert page G), *NCBI News* (Figure 11.7), or a newsletter you receive for models.

- *Identify the contents* with a list, clearly defined headings, or a table of contents.

- *Use shorter paragraphs and vary your sentence length* to fit the column width and the online environment—know your audience.

- *Incorporate visuals.* Newsletter readers expect a visually appealing document and information displayed in visuals.

- *Provide links to more information*, when appropriate, that clearly identify sections and navigation links.

- *Establish the method of delivery.* For a paper-based newsletter, set aside a portion of the back page for the address label and postage. For an online-based newsletter, establish the mailing list (and keep it clean) and an online format that works in the environment of your readers.

Brochures

Brochures are a relatively inexpensive means of getting information on a specific topic to a specified audience. The information targets the needs of the specific audience. For example, brochures are distributed

- in a doctor's office to describe a disease

- to new employees to describe the company benefits

- to provide a description and map of a wildlife area

- to explain to parents the importance of flu shots for children

- for introducing new students to the options for living on campus

- as support materials the salesperson can hand the potential buyer for the digital camera

- in the hardware store as how-to information for building a deck and so on

Like newsletters, brochures are produced relatively quickly and at less cost than producing a book or lengthy report. They do, however, require more time to produce than a news release or newsletter. Brochures require tightly written information because *space* is limited. Space is the key controlling factor for brochures. You have to work within the structure your client wants (see Chapter 5).

Guidelines for writing a brochure.

First identify the *audience* to determine whether a brochure is the best way to deliver the information. Your audience picks up a brochure because it has information they want and can read quickly. Readers can skim for the information they need. Brochures are written for very specific audiences: the patient with glaucoma, the new parent purchasing a child booster seat (see Figure 11.8 on first color insert page H), or the consumer using an electronic check (Figure 11.9).

Purpose and *information* tie into the needs of the audience. Brochures get very specific information to the identified audience. Because the space is limited, you need to define your purpose and collect the necessary information. The child booster brochure (Figure 11.8) identifies four age groups for children and identifies the position of the child safety seat and the seat belt. The brochure shows through illustrations the positions and relies on drawings and other visuals with limited text to get the information to parents. The brochure *When Is Your Check Not a Check?* uses a question-and-answer format to get information to the consumer (using limited visuals). The information requires explanations, not shown in visuals. The question-and-answer format is not unusual for brochures.

FIGURE 11.9

When Is Your Check Not a Check? is a 4-panel brochure printed on 8 1/2- × 11-inch paper. The brochure may be found at banks and stores that use electronic checks. The brochure provides answers to the most frequently asked questions about electronic checks. Which panel is the back panel? How might a store use the back panel?

Source: *When is your check not a check?* (November 13, 2003). Board of Governors of the Federal Reserve System. Retrieved December 15, 2003, from http://www.federalreserve.gov/pubs/checkconv/checkconv.pdf

Suppose you're at a store making a purchase and decide to pay by check— at least, that's what you believe you're doing. The clerk asks you for a check that is completely filled out, partially filled out, or even blank. The clerk then runs the check through a machine and hands the voided check back to you with your receipt.

What just happened? Did you pay by check? Why did the clerk return the check to you? The answer is, you just experienced electronic check conversion.

What is electronic check conversion?

Electronic check conversion is a process where your check is used as a source of information—for the check number, your account number, and the number that identifies your financial institution. The information is then used to make a one-time electronic payment from your account—an electronic fund transfer. The check itself is not the method of payment.

How will I know that my check is being used for electronic check conversion?

When you provide your check, you must be given notice that information from your check will be used to make an electronic payment from your account. The notice is required by the federal law that applies to electronic fund transfers, the Electronic Fund Transfer Act and the Federal Reserve Board's Regulation E. Notice may be provided in different ways. For example, a merchant may post a sign at the register or may give you a written notice that you'll be asked to sign.

What are some of the differences between electronic check conversion and using my check as payment?

■ Your electronic transaction may be

processed faster than a check. Be sure you have enough money in your account at the time you make the purchase.

■ You have different consumer rights with an electronic check conversion transaction than when you use your check as payment. For example, with electronic check conversion, you have the right to an investigation by your financial institution when an error occurs.

What are my rights in electronic check conversion transactions?

■ You have the right to receive notice when you provide your check telling you that information from the check will be used to make an electronic payment from your account.

■ When you provide your check, you have the right to a notice telling you of any fee that the merchant will collect from your account electronically if you do not have enough money in your account to cover the transaction. This fee is similar to a "bounced check" fee.

■ You have the right to receive a receipt when you make a purchase at a store. The receipt will contain information about the transaction, including:
■ Date
■ Amount

■ Location
■ Name of merchant

■ You have the right to have this same information included as part of the regular account statement from your financial institution.

■ You have the right to ask your financial institution to investigate any electronic fund transfers from your account that you believe are unauthorized or incorrect.

What should I do if I have a problem with an electronic check conversion transaction?

Always review your regular account statement from your financial institution. You should immediately contact your financial institution if you see a problem. Were you charged the wrong amount? Were you charged twice for the same transaction? You have only 60 days (from the date your statement was sent) to tell the financial institution about the problem. Depending on the circumstances, the financial institution may take up to 45 days from the time you notify it to complete its investigation.

With electronic check conversion, may I use the same check more than once?

No. An electronic check conversion transaction is a one-time electronic pay-

Space You are writing the information in a brochure for the space. What you write is influenced by

- the amount of information needed

- the display format for the paper size: for example, 1-page (a flyer), 2-panel, 3-panel—whatever is appropriate for size of the paper. Do not forget to check how the organization will display and distribute the brochure. For example, the brochure may be placed in a display stand designed for trifold brochures.

- the need for a title panel and an address (distribution) panel

FIGURE 11.9
(continued)

ment from your account. If you were to use the same check for more than one transaction and you had a problem with one of the transactions, your financial institution might have difficulty investigating the problem because the same check number would appear more than once on your statement.

Can electronic check conversion occur if I mail a check to pay a bill?

Yes. For example, let's assume that each time you get your insurance bill there is a notice. It tells you that when you mail a check, information from that check will be used to make an electronic payment from your account. If you then send a check, you have agreed to electronic check conversion. Unlike what happens when you make a purchase at a store, however, you won't receive a receipt. Your check won't be returned to you with your account statement from your financial institution because the transaction was processed as an electronic fund transfer, not as a check transaction.

As with electronic check conversions in stores, be sure you have enough money in your account when you mail your check, keep records of your payments, and check your account statements from your financial institution

to make sure the amounts charged are correct.

What if I don't want my check to be used for electronic check conversion?

If you don't want your check to be used for electronic check conversion, you may have to provide another form of payment (for example, cash, debit card, or credit card).

Where can I get more information?

Contact your financial institution directly.

Where can I file a complaint?

Contact:

Federal Trade Commission
Consumer Response Center
600 Pennsylvania Ave., NW
Washington, DC 20580

877-FTC-HELP — toll free (877-382-4357)
www.ftc.gov

Please also send a copy of your complaint to:

Board of Governors of the Federal Reserve System
Division of Consumer and Community Affairs
Washington, DC 20551
202-452-3693
www.federalreserve.gov

For information on state laws that may apply to electronic check conversion, contact your state's consumer protection agency or attorney general's office.

Remember . . .

Before you agree to electronic check conversion, you should first ask yourself
■ Do I understand that the information from my check will be used to make an electronic payment from my account?
■ Do I have enough money in my account to cover the payment?

Before you leave the store, you should ask yourself
■ Did I receive a receipt?
■ Does the amount on the receipt match the amount of my purchase?
■ Was my check returned to me and voided?

When you receive your statement from your financial institution, you should
■ Make sure that the charges on your statement match your records
■ Contact your financial institution right away if you notice a problem

FRB-0302

When Is Your Check Not a Check?

John Doe

Hometown Bank

Electronic Check Conversion

Board of Governors of the Federal Reserve System

Cost Using standard size paper—in the U.S., 8 1/2 × 11 inches or 11 × 17 inches—costs less than a format that requires cutting a larger sheet of paper or creating a different fold. Color is now expected although you have choices. Full color (access to the full range of color) is expensive; 2-color uses two colors, but shades of these colors give you more options. Graphics designers and printers can show you the options available.

Schedule The life of a brochure will depend upon the life of the information.

The process of writing a brochure is similar to that for any document (Chapter 1): brainstorm, gather information, draft, revise, and revise again. Be sure to have several people review the brochure carefully.

Web Pages

The Web is now a primary source for information. As was shown above, news releases, newsletters, and informative brochures are published on the Web.

Reports, proposals, and job announcements are found on the Web (for example, review the Environmental Protection Agency reports shown in Chapter 13). In this section, we offer advice for writing for the Web as you contribute to an organization's Web site. We also illustrate the connection of documents that a Web site initiates.

As with the news-release publications and brochures we have described, you need to identify the audience, the purpose, and the information needed. And you need to consider space, schedule, and cost. Your *audience* for Web documents is the world, although realistically, you target a primary audience (those you want to read the Web site, for example, breeders of basset hounds) and a secondary audience (others who might be interested in the information, for example, owners and potential owners of basset hounds). The *purpose* and *information* fall into place as you determine what specific information you need to get to the audience and why (your purpose).

The *schedule* for delivering information is key for Web sites. Readers expect current information—for example, the latest football scores, the most current product description for the pocket PC, current requests for proposals, accurate instructions for troubleshooting a gas grill, up-to-date printer drivers, and so on. If your site is not up to date, the reader will move quickly to another site.

Your *space* limitation is the size of the screen. Once the information goes beyond a screen, you need to consider (1) how much scrolling your reader will do and (2) when to create a link to another page. Do not be fooled by space. Yes, the only space limitation is that of the server hosting your Web site, and this can seem unlimited. Pages can go on forever, but that does not help the readers of the Web page.

Professional Web sites now require technical experts and content developers. Technical development (including writing) *cost*. Even a small business must contract with a Web developer to provide a professional, credible site that provides information, products, and services for those who visit the site. The Web writing we describe here focuses on you contributing to a site, not developing a site. Often you will be asked to provide information for a site.

Writing for the Web

Writing for the Web has evolved from simply transferring documents to the Web or writing a document and saving it as a Web page. While this is easy to do, it does not take into account the Web environment and the needs of the readers. Even though many people have been reading online material for 10–15 years, we have the same problems reading online as in print: difficulty following from line to line and difficulty keeping our place in the many layers of material. We have developed techniques for reading and writing online (Chapter 2).

Suggestions for writing Web pages

Writing for the Web requires attention to details so the reader will stay on the site. As you develop materials for the Web, consider the following suggestions for writing online materials:

- Use tightly written, concise sentences and paragraphs. We suggest you write the information—but then, revise, revise, and, revise again before you have others read the material. You will revise after you get their feedback and feedback from usability testing (Chapter 17). Errors become very obvious once a Web page is posted.

- Use shorter sentences and paragraphs. Readers find the smaller chunks of information easier to read online.

- Group the information on individual pages, using headings and lists— either ordered (numbered) lists or unordered lists (bullets). Review Chapter 5, "Design and Development of Documents," for guidelines that apply to print and Web-based documents.

- Provide links to the information; however, avoid too many layers (too much drilling down through the Web pages). Work with the technical members of the team to provide a site map, bread crumbs, and other navigational features to help the reader.

- Provide clear organization and navigation guides to establish the hierarchy of the information. Use document design features such as headings, color, visuals, page layout, and other features to display the information (review Chapters 2, 5, 6, and 7).

- Know the environment the majority of your audience works in. For example, do most have high-speed access, 17-inch monitors, and software for opening multimedia files? Many of the U.S. government sites provide multiple access options to accommodate most environments— text, HTML, PDF, Excel, Word, PowerPoint are examples of the format provided.

- Incorporate features that help make the Web site accessible for those with visual, hearing, and mobility disabilities. We suggest you review the U.S. government resource page DisabilityInfo.gov (http://disability-info.gov) for the guidelines and check with the technical experts on the team about such features as alt tags to identify visuals or alternatives to tables for formatting text.

- Provide several language options if you have an international audience. Most of the U.S. government sites offer a choice of languages. Unless you are fluent in a language, you will not be responsible for the translation. However, you need to be aware that the configuration of a language may affect the page layout—for example, the amount of white space available. Google (www.google.com) and AltaVista (www.altavista.com) are among the Web sites that provide translation services for small amounts of text.

We suggest you review two resources for web development and writing for the Web: Jakob Nielsen's *Designing Web Usability*,[1] particularly Chapter 3, "Content Design," and Jonathan Price and Lisa Price's *Hot Text: Web Writing That Works*.[2]

Web Connections

Organizations use the Web beyond simply providing information. The Web offers opportunities to collect information and simultaneously distribute the information. The following is an example of the writing associated with the development and use of one Web site:

> Students visit the Resource Center for help with writing and reading projects. At the beginning of the fall semester, the staff decided to automate the procedures in the center. To track students, the Resource Center developed an online form that students complete at the beginning of each session. A number of documents associated with the initial Web page and database evolved:
>
> - A form collects the sign-in information from students (Figure 11.10). The information is collected into a database.
>
> - Instructions posted at the workstation guide students through completing the sign-in form (Figure 11.11). Parallel documents exist for the consultants in the Resource Center.
>
> - Letters are sent to the students' instructors using the mail-merge feature of MS Word to pull information from the database (Figure 11.12).
>
> - Instructions were developed for the database users and letter writers. The instructions are needed because responsibilities change in the Resource Center.

Every one of these documents, from the initial Web form to the letters, is undergoing changes as the process is being refined. The need to refine the tracking process and the dynamic nature of the Web make the changes relatively easy to make. As a member of a team working with Web documents (or almost any other document), collaborate and cooperate in the document development process—expect changes.

---

[1] Jakob Nielsen. *Designing Web Usability*. Indianapolis: New Riders, 1999.

[2] Jonathan Price and Lisa Price. *Hot Text: Web Writing That Works*. Indianapolis: New Riders, 2002.

FIGURE 11.10
Web-based forms provide an easy way to collect information from visitors to a website. Content and technical developers must work together to build the form. Writing the information requires carefully chosen words and format to avoid confusion. The form shown collects information from students visiting the Resource Center.

Source: Auburn University, Department of English.

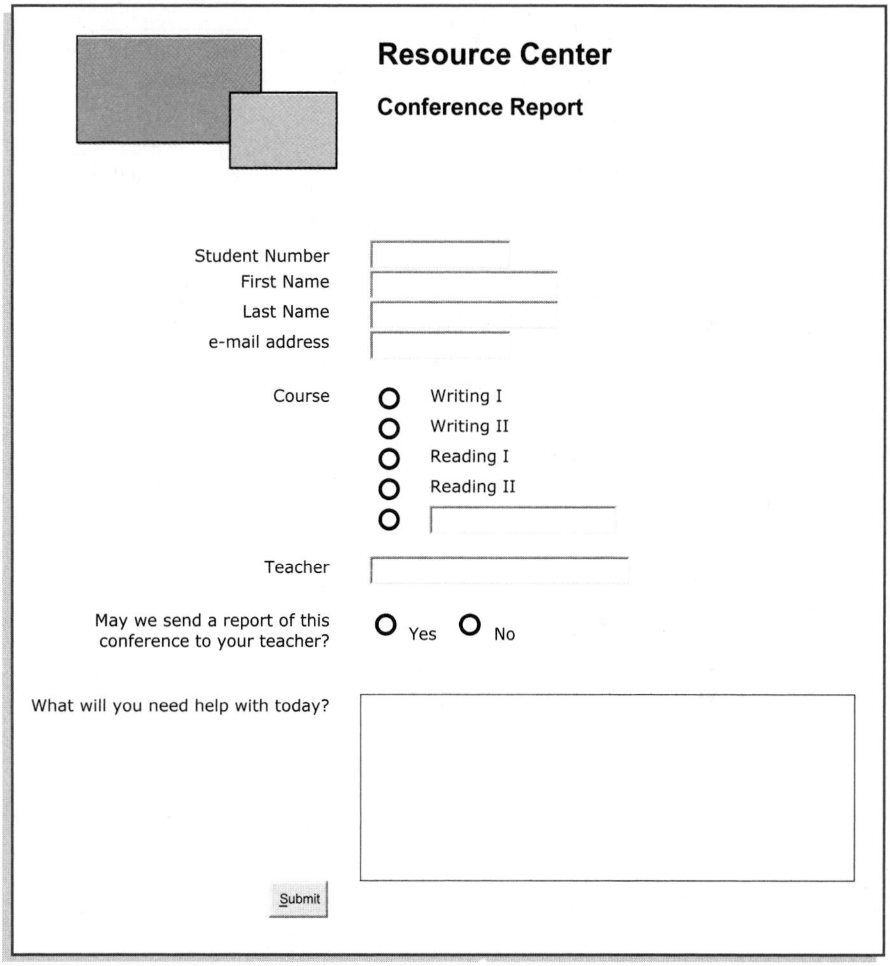

Resource Center

Conference Report

Student Number

First Name

Last Name

e-mail address

Course
- ◯ Writing I
- ◯ Writing II
- ◯ Reading I
- ◯ Reading II
- ◯

Teacher

May we send a report of this conference to your teacher?   ◯ Yes ◯ No

What will you need help with today?

Submit

FIGURE 11.11

The instructions guide students through completing the web-based form shown in Figure 11.10.

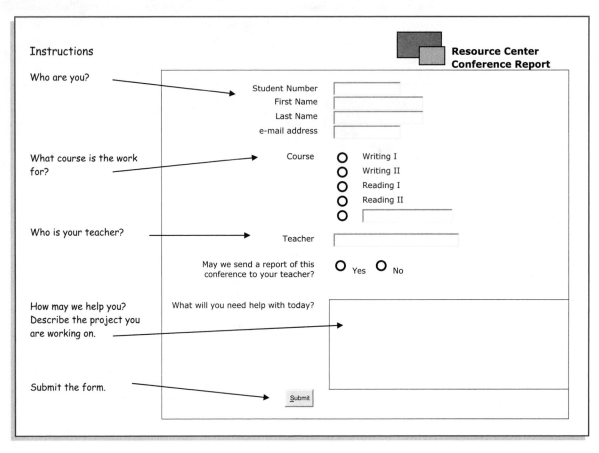

FIGURE 11.12

The web-based forms collect information that may be used in other documents. For example, information from the form shown in Figure 11.10 is collected into the web-linked database fields. The fields are merged into the letter as < <field name> >.

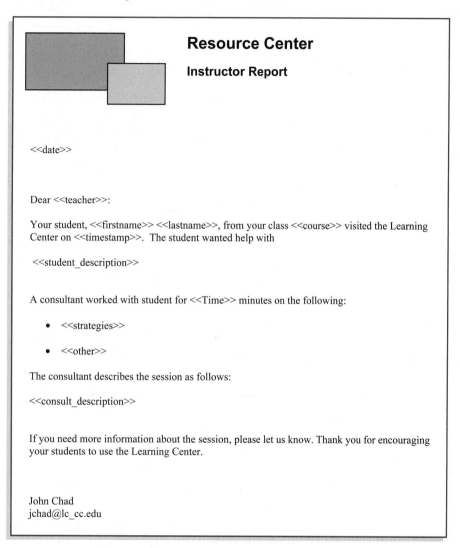

Resource Center

Instructor Report

<<date>>

Dear <<teacher>>:

Your student, <<firstname>> <<lastname>>, from your class <<course>> visited the Learning Center on <<timestamp>>. The student wanted help with

<<student_description>>

A consultant worked with student for <<Time>> minutes on the following:

- <<strategies>>

- <<other>>

The consultant describes the session as follows:

<<consult_description>>

If you need more information about the session, please let us know. Thank you for encouraging your students to use the Learning Center.

John Chad
jchad@lc_cc.edu

Suggestions for Applying Your Knowledge

Individual Activities

1. Write a news release for an organization you are active in to publicize an upcoming event. Submit the news release to the campus newspaper.

2. Develop information about your school or an organization. Write the information for publication to the Web site.

3. If you are fluent in a language other than English, translate a page from your college or organization's Web site. If you are not fluent in a language other than English, go to google.com or another Web portal. Look for the language tools area. Input the text you plan to use on the Web page. What design issues did you have to consider as you adjusted the text?

Collaborative Activities

1. With a partner, visit the U.S. government Web site contacts.gsa.gov/ listgov.nsf/FirstGovEmailListDistribution. Compare the design features and content of 3 or 4 of the newsletters (either in the same topic or the across topics). The topics include:

   Business and Finance

   Defense

   Education, Employment, and Benefits

   Environment and Agriculture

   Foreign Affairs

   Health, Safety, and Consumer Protection

   Taxes

   Travel

2. Locate 4 or 5 examples of brochures. In small groups, identify the primary audience, the purpose, and information the brochures targets. Select one brochure to show the class, and describe the features that make it an effective brochure.

3. Compare the Web site of an organization that offers the information in more than one language.

Oral Presentations

o matter what kind of job you have, you are likely to be called upon to give oral presentations. Four brief scenarios identify the range of possible occasions for oral presentations:

- A creative director and chief graphic designer make an oral presentation on their firm's capabilities and attempt to win a prospective client's next project.

- A product development specialist presents orally her innovative control system for machine tools to her company's production managers and assistant production managers and answers their questions about its implementation.

- A forester researching the types of pollution caused by local industries explains her preliminary findings to a meeting of environmental and safety engineers from local industry, government officials, and a committee of local citizens.

- As part of a health promotion campaign, an occupational nurse speaks at an employee meeting to inform production workers in his company's factories how to prevent repetitive-motion injuries.

An oral presentation is a highly effective way of communicating to colleagues, clients, and other audiences. Presentations are necessary in almost every profession, and with laptop computers and easy-to-use software, audiences expect to be shown the information. In some professions, the presentation format (Microsoft PowerPoint or Lotus Freelance slides, for example) has such widespread use that it is replacing the more formal written report.

Our purpose in this chapter is to guide you from the moment you know you must give an oral presentation in a workplace setting to the moment you sit down after completing your successful presentation. We talk about preparing for an oral presentation, building the presentation (writing and integrating the visuals), and delivering the presentation. Our focus is on presentations using presentation software such as Corel Presentations or PowerPoint; however, the description of the presentation development applies to most oral presentations using the technology available.

Preparing for Oral Presentations

One of the keys to a successful oral presentation is the conviction that you are well prepared. Preparation is much more than gathering material for an oral presentation and even more than organizing that material. Successful preparation involves, first, considering your audience and where you are talking. What is the context for your presentation? After you know the audience and the context, you can consider your purpose. When you know the context, audience, and purpose, you can select the right material to satisfy all three and organize the material.

Analyzing Context

Conversations differ depending on where you are, what you are doing, and whom you are with. A conversation with a potential employer is not the same as a conversation with a close friend. As the context changes, so do the content of your conversation and the manner of its delivery.

When you learn that you are to make a presentation, find out as much as you can about the meeting and location for your presentation. Knowing the answers to these questions can help you avoid embarrassing situations:

What is the purpose of the meeting?

Are you the only presenter?

If there is a program of presenters, where do you fit in?

Why were you invited to present?

What is expected of you?

Where is the meeting and what technology is available?

The type of meeting will influence the mode of presentation you prepare for: planned or impromptu.

Planned Presentations

- *Planned.* The most suitable oral presentation for the widest variety of occasions is the planned presentation. You organize, outline, and rehearse it, but you do not write every word or memorize it. You know what ideas and facts you are going to work with and have them well in hand. The major points of your presentation are literally at hand, on either the computer screen, handouts, or notecards.

  You want to rehearse the presentation several times but want to avoid memorizing or writing each word. If you memorize your presentation, you run the risk of forgetting the presentation if you are interrupted. Written presentations are suitable for some occasions. But reading a presentation will bore audiences. In addition, as you read, you will not be able to maintain good eye contact with your audience, and you may miss some of their reactions. However, you also have to be careful that you do not read the computer screen.

  A well-planned presentation with notes has proven to be the most effective for most presenters and audiences.

  You form the actual wording of a well-planned presentation with each delivery. It is a good presentation mode—sound, safe, and flexible.

Impromptu Presentations

- *Impromptu.* Impromptu oral presentations cannot be prepared. Rather, you cannot plan the specific presentation. Your best preparation is knowledge of the subject matter. You may be called on to stand up and discuss an arrangement, a contract, or the operation of your shop or office. At a meeting, you may stand up to question or support an action.

  You must know your subject thoroughly—keep in mind that you were invited to participate in the meeting because you are the subject matter expert.

Your confidence in the information presented will go a long way toward making a successful presentation.

Analyzing Audience

Know your audience.

Find out as much about your audience beforehand as you can. Most of your decisions based on audience, regardless of its size, will be based on the context and the audience's knowledge and expectations.

- *How many people will be in the audience and do they want to be there?* For 20 people, you might plan an informal presentation that is mainly discussion—a short presentation followed by an extensive question-and-answer period. For a large group meeting in an auditorium, discussion might be unwieldy, so you would plan for a longer, well-organized presentation.

  Audiences will give you a chance, but if it is a required meeting, you may have to work harder to keep the audience's attention.

- *How closely do you relate to your audience?* For instance, is the audience composed mainly of coworkers? Is it an audience with which you have many shared interests? Are you a student talking to students? A computer programmer talking to computer programmers? If so, in some ways your job is easier. Your language can be a bit casual, your speech patterns relaxed. You can leave some things unsaid because everybody knows them anyway. On the other hand, speaking to such a group can be tough. They are likely to question your expertise. You may need more evidence to prove your points.

  Groups that do not share your experiences present different kinds of problems. They may expect more structure and more formal language from you. When you move out of your normal workplace context, expect difficulties. Your presentation must be well prepared to overcome them. For instance, if you were an inspector for an environmental agency presenting to chemists or chemical engineers employed by pulp mills, you would undoubtedly discuss some safety measures and environmental regulations toward which some of the listeners will be sympathetic. But you could expect several who would not agree with some of your viewpoints. You should be aware of likely resistances and know what to do to overcome them.

- *What adaptations should you make for multicultural audiences?* You may need to make adjustments for audiences whose English is limited or whose culture prefers a different approach from your normal one. Although you may not always be able to determine the particular needs and interests of culturally diverse audiences, you can take certain steps to respond to diverse audiences:

  - Repeat key points and have the key points on visuals.

  - Use visuals that contain captions and labels in both English and the language of the audience.

  - Define or explain phrases or words that may be misunderstood.

- Distribute translated handouts of crucial passages.

- Be aware of cultural differences in body language. For example, be careful not to appear too aggressive for audiences that might regard a strong gaze as disrespectful.

- *What does the audience know about your subject?* We all learn a specialized vocabulary with the jobs we are educated to do. Sometimes we forget that others do not share that vocabulary. A highway engineer speaking about horizontal and vertical curves may forget that nonengineers would call the first simply *curves* and the second *hills*. When you can, use simple expressions for a nonexpert audience. If you cannot, define the needed terms. But judge your audience carefully. An audience that does not need background, simple language, or definitions will feel talked down to if you speak at a low level.

- *What does the audience expect of you?* Most workplace audiences can be classified as management, technical, or nontechnical. By technical, we mean those people who work closely with whatever it is you are talking about.

    Suppose you develop a new process in an auto shop for taking off old tires, putting new ones on, and balancing the wheels.

    If you were talking to the *management* about this new process, they would expect cost data. Will this new process cost more or less than the old? Will it require fewer or more technicians? Are safety problems involved?

    The *technicians* would also want to know some of these same things, but they would also want more details about the process itself. How do you do it? What are the major steps in the process? Does it require new equipment?

    The *nontechnicians* primarily expect to be told how the process relates to them. In the case of new tire-changing techniques, the nontechnical customers would want to know two things: Will the new process be cheaper, and will it get cars in and out of the garage faster?

To do your best, you must know your audience—the audience is in control, not you. But do not despair if you cannot always analyze an audience perfectly. Most audiences will listen carefully if they sense that what you have to say is important to them and that you have their interests in mind.

Defining Purpose and Developing Content

Purpose and content are closely related, and both relate closely to context and audience. Most presentations involve speaking to inform or to persuade—or some mixture of the two. For a specific presentation to a specific audience, you would narrow a broad purpose down to a specific one:

- To inform 20 visiting salespeople how the new billing system works.

- To persuade 20 visiting salespeople that the new billing system is better than the old.

- To inform 20 visiting salespeople about the new billing system and to persuade them that it is better than the old.

When you have your specific purpose clearly in mind, you have completed the criteria you need to choose your content. You should ask three questions about anything you intend to include in your presentation:

- Will it meet the needs and expectations of my audience?

- Will it move my purpose forward?

- Does the meeting (context) call for it?

Leave out any item that fails to meet at least one of these criteria. Your best items will meet all three. The more criteria each item meets, the more economical you will be of both your and the audience's time. Time is always a problem. Accuracy may say to include an item. Time may say to leave it out. It is a conflict that goes on in all speaking and writing.

What you include and how you show it will depend on the specific information that you need to get to the specific audience for the specific purpose you have identified.

Developing Oral Presentations

Developing the presentation involves coordinating the text (your words), the visuals, and the technology. Simplicity, clarity, consistency, and visibility apply to how you present the information through the text and visuals. The technology allows you to show your audience the information.

Visual impact holds the audience's attention.

The visual impact you gain by using technology will support, clarify, and expand your points. It can bring a wandering audience back. It helps the audience understand and retain your information. The visuals you include help audiences understand the information being presented. Graphs, drawings, tables, and photographs illustrate for the audience the points you are making. You can use animation, or you can include audio or video clips. You can show models or simulations; you can link to a Web site. And you can use objects, people, and animals.

In this section, we give some criteria for developing the presentation so that the text and visuals work together and for selecting the appropriate technology. We focus on the computer-generated presentations because of the widespread use of PowerPoint, Freelance, and other presentation software in the workplace. You can adapt the guidelines to the technology available to you (such as whiteboards or overhead projectors).

Selecting the Presentation Technology

You have a wide range of technologies to choose from—computers with presentation software, videotapes, movies, 35-mm slides, models, chalkboards or whiteboards, flannel boards, and many others. Figure 12.1 identifies several technologies. Because we are focusing on the use of presentation software, please take a few minutes to review other presentation technologies. You may not need to use or may not have the computer and projection system to use presentation software. In fact, the widespread use of PowerPoint and other presentation software has numbed some audiences.

You want to use the appropriate technology for the presentation. A whiteboard or flipchart may be all you need to note a few key points. (You can write them ahead of time.) You can prepare beforehand a handout (for example, on an 8 1/2- x 11-inch sheet of paper using front and back) to distribute key information for the audience. The audience will have a place to make notes as you make your points and they can review the information after the meeting. We do not recommend creating a handout of the presentation slides. You want the audience's attention on you and the information you are presenting, not on locating the slides on the handout.

Know the technology and how to control it. Properly made and used, visuals can increase an audience's concentration and keep attention focused on your subject matter.

Because of their effectiveness, computer and LCD projectors and overhead projectors are used in many schools and businesses. You almost certainly have seen them in action. Observe carefully how they are used. Learn what to do from the people who use them well—and what not to do from those who use them poorly. In preparing your presentation slides or transparencies, keep our criteria in mind: Keep visuals simple, clear, consistent, and visible.

Know the technology and how to control it.

Coordinating the Text and the Visuals

Your presentation needs well-thought-out words and visuals—and effective use of the technology you choose. You need to outline the presentation but, as was noted earlier, not write out every word. You want to include visuals and you also want to use the visual features of the technology effectively (in our examples, presentation software).

Text First, you want to begin as you begin other communication projects (review Chapters 1 and 2). You want to brainstorm and gather the information. You want to develop an outline (either formal or informal) and create a draft, and then you want to revise. For the oral presentation, add rehearsing as the final step before the presentation.

Presentation software supports (encourages to some extent) outlining with the outline option alongside the slide development. The Notes feature gives you the option of writing the support you want to give with each point you are making without showing the audience your notes. Figure 12.2 gives the outline for a presentation that is going to answer three questions about ISO 9000. Figure 12.3 shows the notes pages associated with Figure 12.2. You may find it helpful to write out the points you want to make while you are creating the slide. Most presentation software provides this feature.

Figure 12.4 is a presentation found on the U.S. Department of Labor, Occupational Safety & Health Administration (OSHA) Web site. The notes

FIGURE 12.1

Technologies. Select the best technology for your audience and the context and purpose of the presentation. This is a partial list of the available technologies.

Technology	Advantages	At the Presentation
Chalkboard Whiteboard	• Easy to use • Easy to control • Low cost	• Have markers in different colors and an eraser • Write neatly • Make sure your audience can see the board
Flipchart	• Easy to use • Easy to control • Low cost	• Have markers in different colors • Check for enough paper • Write neatly • Make sure your audience can see the chart
Handout Poster Model of project	• Prepare ahead of time • Easy to use • Easy to control	• Check visibility from all parts of the room • Use lettering 1″ high for 25′ distance • Confirm you have enough handouts
Overhead projector TV—VCR/DVD Slide projector	• Prepare ahead of time • Low cost to create	• Know how to run the equipment • Check the tape, slides, or DVDs • Check control of lights
Computer Document camera	• Prepare ahead of time • Low cost, if you have the projector • State-of-the-art—many audiences expect you to use this technology	• Know how to run the equipment (for most laptops, you need to press one of the function keys) • Test your presentation before the audience arrives • Check Internet access • Check control of lights

Know your audience.
Know your topic.
Know the room.

Be prepared and be flexible.

FIGURE 12.2
Slide that presents an outline for both the speaker and the audience.

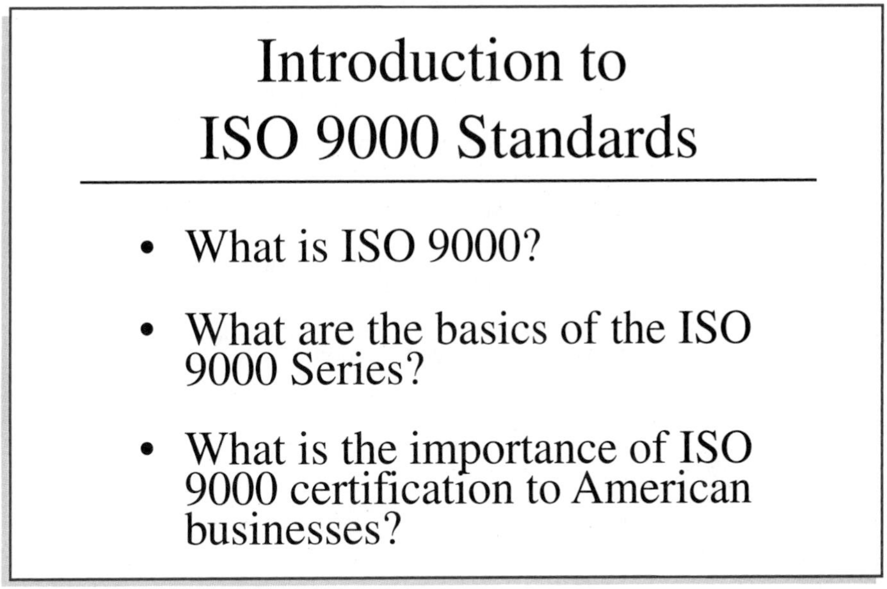

Introduction to
ISO 9000 Standards

- What is ISO 9000?

- What are the basics of the ISO 9000 Series?

- What is the importance of ISO 9000 certification to American businesses?

are included as part of the presentation. In this example, the notes indicate the presenter scripted (wrote out) the presentation. We caution you not to read your notes page but to know it very well and use the notes as prompts to you on the topic.

Visuals As you develop the presentation, use the visual features of the technology to hold the audience's attention and to help them understand your purpose. The design features you incorporate in your presentation contribute to the visual impact of the presentation. Presentation software gives you many options for design templates, color, animation on slides, and transitions between slides. Templates are the preset structures used to build presentations. The templates include title pages, text-only slides, and content slides (text and visuals). The title and body area are clearly defined with prompts such as "click to add title" and "click to add text" and preset fonts and color. The body area may be simply formatted text, bulleted lists, text and visuals, or some other combination of formatted texts and visuals. We suggest you stay with the preset colors and fonts on your first few presentations because the software developers have tested the effectiveness of the template. But know that you can change any of the visual features.

Help your audience understand your purpose with visuals. Include graphs, photographs, videoclips, Internet links—any visual you can put into digital format can be incorporated into presentation software. Keep the visuals simple and clear so they will be visible. For example, use graphs to show the shapes of trends without worrying too much about the actual numbers. Break up tables and extract only needed information. The table in Figure

FIGURE 12.3
Note page created in computer-generated presentation software.

Introduction to
ISO 9000 Standards

- What is ISO 9000?
- What are the basics of the ISO 9000 Series?
- What is the importance of ISO 9000 certification to American businesses?

← Reduced image of the slide or screen.

Notes that remind speaker of important points to elaborate.

Notes:

What is ISO 9000?

- Clarify that ISO 9000 applies not to products and services but to the processes that create them.
- Give brief history of ISO as offspring of the International Organization for Standardization, founded in 1947 in Geneva, Switzerland.
- Point out that current ISO 9000 core series was first published in 1987 and has been adopted by more than 100 nations. (U.S. represented in ISO by the American National Standards Institute.)

What are the basics of the ISO 9000 series?

- Explain that ISO 9000 is a guidance standard. It is ISO 9001, 9002, and 9003 for which companies must be certified.

What is the importance of ISO 9000 certification to American businesses?

- Empahsize the importance of achieving ISO 9000 for businesses that plan to compete seriously in a global economy.
- Point out that the European Community already mandates ISO certification for makers of certain types of products (telecommunications terminal equipment, industrial safety equipment, gas appliances, commercial scales, etc.).

12.5a on page 342 shows the data for the graph. Eliminate all unneeded features from maps. Use block diagrams rather than schematics.

Creating Simple, Clear, Consistent, and Visible Presentations

In oral presentations, the listener has only a limited amount of time to take in the information and the visual before the presenter moves on to the next point. Therefore the rule for a presentation is to simplify and then to simplify

FIGURE 12.4

The notes accompanying the presentation "Quartz-Analytical Methodologies" give detailed information to support each slide. The notes are helpful when viewing the presentation online. Visit OSHA's Web site, www.osha.gov/SLTC/multimedia.html, to view the complete presentation and additional examples of presentations.

Source: U.S. Department of Labor. Office of Occupational Safety & Health Administration. Retrieved December 2, 2003, from http://www.osha.gov/SLTC/silicacrystalline/quartz/slides/slide01.html

again. Text and visuals that are suitable in printed documents may be too complicated for use in presenting. After all, the reader can stop and study a statement or a visual in a printed document but not during a presentation. (It is common practice now to make presentations available on the Web so audience members can view them later.) Two examples illustrate the simplicity, clarity, and consistency needed in presentations.

FIGURE 12.5

Use simple visuals for presentations. The audience does not need the data shown in part (a). They need to see the trend, the line graph in part (b).

Source: *Science and Engineering Indicators 2002.* April 2002. National Science Foundation. Retrieved December 2, 2003, from http://www.nsf.gov/sbe/srs/seind02/mmslides/mm08-03/mm08-03.htm

(a)

Computer price declines
Index log scale
1996 = 100

Year	Quarter			
	1st	2nd	3rd	4th
1987	369.7	347.7	332.6	333.8
1988	330.6	322.0	317.6	315.3
1989	312.3	301.5	297.8	288.8
1990	276.1	272.6	272.2	268.1
1991	261.9	253.0	237.0	226.6
1992	224.3	213.4	202.9	196.2
1993	190.5	181.5	174.2	167.2
1994	164.0	160.9	155.8	148.4
1995	141.3	135.6	128.0	120.2
1996	111.0	101.9	96.3	90.8
1997	85.2	79.7	74.5	70.1
1998	64.3	58.9	54.4	50.3
1999	47.0	44.3	42.1	40.6
2000	39.6	38.2	37.0	35.8
2001	32.6	31.1		

(b)

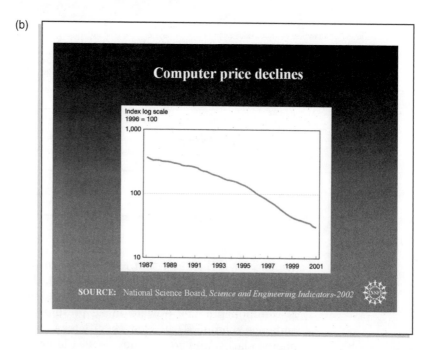

Example 1

Figure 12.6 shows a basic presentation. The information presented is specific to one parking location on a college campus, Parking Lot C, and the audience is the vice president for facilities and the supervisor of the three members of the Traffic and Parking Office. The purpose is well-defined: describe changes needed to the parking lot to get the budget approved. The first slide gives the title and identifies the presenters with their affiliation and the date included to establish the context. The second slide outlines the presentation. Each bullet is repeated as one of the headings for upcoming slides. Bulleted lists on each slide provide short phrases of information. The presenters will use the bulleted points to talk from; they will fill in the information and make the transitions between the ideas.

The presentation in Figure 12.6 does not include visuals, although it is easy to imagine visuals that might be included. Photographs of the congestion in the parking lot and a line drawing that shows the increase in spaces with 45-degree angle spaces are two possible visuals. You do not need many visuals because the audience knows the problem. This is a 20-minute presentation focused on getting the budget approved.

The presentation, as basic as it is, does have features that add visual impact to hold the audience's attention: each slide is clearly titled, the headings are consistent in size, the font and point size are consistent, and short bulleted lists display the information.

Example 2

Figure 12.7 (see pages I and J in the second color insert) shows a portion of a presentation made before the *Columbia* Accident Investigation Board. The title page gives the title (with a date), identifies the presenter, G. Scott Hubbard, and his position. The second slide gives an overview, identifying questions to be answered by the tests. The next slides briefly describe the tests and give the results. Photographs of the test equipment and results are given. One slide features a brief videoclip of the test. The conclusions and "Next Steps" are the final slides.

As in Figure 12.6, each slide provides a consistent frame for the information. Each has the NASA logo with a title for the slide. The fonts and point size are consistent, as is the background color. Photographs provide content that would require too many words to explain.

While these examples are relatively basic presentations, they illustrate the features needed for successful presentations. You should include the following slides:

Title Slide The title slide, similar to the title page of a report, identifies the topic in a brief but descriptive title, the presenter and the organization she or he represents, and the date.

Second Slide For most presentations, the next slide should briefly outline the presentation. Often, the topics identified on this slide become the headings for subsequent slides. You are telling the audience what you plan to cover.

FIGURE 12.6

Set of screens or slides for a computer-generated presentation.

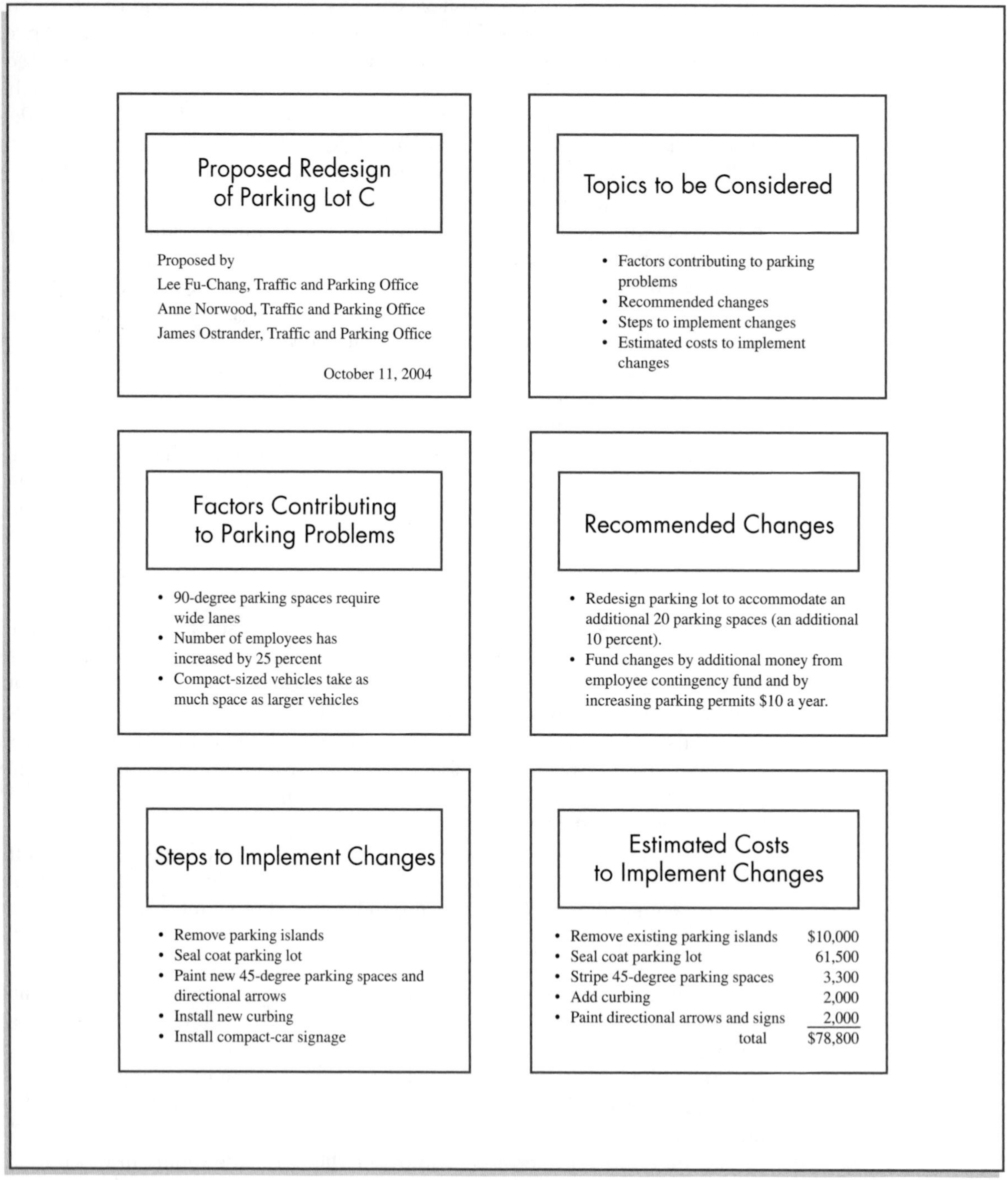

Proposed Redesign of Parking Lot C	**Topics to be Considered**
Proposed by Lee Fu-Chang, Traffic and Parking Office Anne Norwood, Traffic and Parking Office James Ostrander, Traffic and Parking Office October 11, 2004	• Factors contributing to parking problems • Recommended changes • Steps to implement changes • Estimated costs to implement changes
Factors Contributing to Parking Problems	**Recommended Changes**
• 90-degree parking spaces require wide lanes • Number of employees has increased by 25 percent • Compact-sized vehicles take as much space as larger vehicles	• Redesign parking lot to accommodate an additional 20 parking spaces (an additional 10 percent). • Fund changes by additional money from employee contingency fund and by increasing parking permits $10 a year.
Steps to Implement Changes	**Estimated Costs to Implement Changes**
• Remove parking islands • Seal coat parking lot • Paint new 45-degree parking spaces and directional arrows • Install new curbing • Install compact-car signage	• Remove existing parking islands $10,000 • Seal coat parking lot 61,500 • Stripe 45-degree parking spaces 3,300 • Add curbing 2,000 • Paint directional arrows and signs 2,000 total $78,800

Topic (Body) Slides Develop the presentation using your outline to cover the information needed for your audience and purpose.

Final Slides A summary slide that reviews and allows you to restate your purpose closes out the presentation. You may have an additional slide on which you acknowledge your resources and help you received from colleagues.

As you build the slides, aim for simplicity, clarity, consistency, and visibility. That is, you want to limit the amount of information on each slide so the audience can quickly grasp the information. We suggest that you include the following features in your computer-generated presentation:

- **Pick the design template and use it throughout the presentation.** Mixing templates disrupts the information. Using a template with too much texture or design will interfere with the text. The information is what you want readers to focus on, not adjusting to a different background with each slide.

- **Choose colors carefully for the text and the background.** Consider the amount of light in the room. There should be good contrast between the text color and the background so the audience can read the information.

- **Use consistent fonts and point size throughout.** Viewers do not want to work at reading the slides; consistency makes it easier to focus on the information.

  Presentation software makes it easy—and not so easy—to select an appropriate point size. The software will adjust the point size automatically each time you add to a slide; the more information you put on the slide, the smaller the point size. When the point size decreases, that is your signal to stop and make sure you do not have too much on a slide. Point sizes between 30 and 40 points are a good starting point.

- **Provide consistent headings.** Do not forget parallel grammatical construction.

  Use headings and bulleted lists, restricting texts to no more than 6 or 7 lines and no more than about 40 words. Any more will make screens too dense. Figure 12.6 and Figure 12.7 (see pages I and J in the second color insert) use an appropriate amount of white space and text.

- **Consider carefully any blocks of text you include.** The audience needs a few keywords or phrases. You are going to provide most of the words as you speak.

- **Be consistent in how you present your points.** You do not have to use a bulleted list on every screen. You can include short blocks of text and visuals.

- **Use transitions and animation only if needed.** When you want the audience to focus on one point, have each point come in separately. You then are focusing the attention on you and the point you are making.

The audience will listen to you rather than read the screen. The audience is distracted when the information flies in from the left or bounces in from the right. Whatever you do, do not mix the transition or animation features in a presentation.

- **Use visuals.** Show your points with graphs, photographs, and other digitally available material. Review the guidelines in Chapters 6 and 7 for visuals and develop simple, clear visuals.

The audience should be able to take in a screen's meaning at a glance. The oral presentation is a visual presentation. Keeping the text and visual features relatively simple, clear, and consistent are vital, and you also need to make sure the audience can see your presentation. If your audience cannot read or see the features of your presentation, it is worthless.

Delivering Oral Presentations

Once you have developed the oral presentation, you now must make a presentation that will achieve your purpose. Assume that you have made all the preparations we have suggested. You have organized your presentation and have your outline and notes ready. You have planned your presentation and integrated the text and visuals. You now have only one task left: delivering the oral presentation.

An oral presentation is a performance. Whether you choose a low-key conversational style or a more formal style, you are giving a performance. In this section, we talk about the preparation period, the delivery of your presentation, and the question-and-answer period that often follows a presentation.

Preparation

No matter whether you plan to give your oral presentation from notes and a flipchart or as a well-planned computer presentation, you must

- Rehearse, if only in front of a mirror and, if possible, to a tape recorder. Play back the tape, and listen critically to your pace and delivery.

- Tailor your presentation to fit precisely into whatever time is allotted you. Timing is critical. Running seriously under or over your allotted time can greatly inconvenience a good many people and gain you nothing but bad marks from your audience.

- Pay attention to the pronunciation of words. Rehearsal is the time to discover the words that you cannot pronounce or that you feel shaky about. Look them up; practice them until you have mastered them. Rehearse several times; your confidence will increase as you become more familiar with what you will cover.

- Never assume, however, that you can walk up to a computer, insert your presentation disk, and begin running it. Make sure the software on the computer has full compatibility with your presentation file. We cannot overemphasize the importance of running through your computer presentation ahead of time—on the computer and projector you will be using, if at all possible. Make sure the computer you use has the type and version of software that will run your presentation file.

- Know how to work the technology and how to work with the technology. Face the audience; a common mistake is to turn your back to the audience to read the screen.

- Dress for the occasion, whatever it is. The more comfortable you are with how you look, the more confident you will be, and the more effective your presentation will be.

Delivery

The moment has arrived. You have done all you can to get ready. You are introduced, and it is time to make your way to the front of the audience. For many people, this is an absolutely terrifying moment. For others, it is a stimulating, enjoyable experience. In either case, however, the right delivery techniques will enable you to do a better job. Let us consider here the beginning of an oral presentation, some general techniques, and the ending.

Know beforehand what you are getting into and plan accordingly.

Be familiar with the site of your presentation as well as the purpose of the meeting. If you have any control over the situation, ask for needed changes. Do the following:

Be flexible and adapt to the environment.

- *Know how to use the equipment.* Computer-driven projection systems all work about the same; however, you cannot set one up at the last minute. Arrive early and check your presentation. An overhead projector is easy to use, but you must check its position to project your whole slide on the screen and in focus.

- *Check all materials and equipment.* Having a dry-erase pen that will not write, a burned-out projector light bulb, and a screen that will not lower is frustrating and is likely to hinder an effective presentation. Check the flipchart to make sure you will have enough paper.

- *Check the view of visuals from different parts of the room.* Stand that far away yourself and see whether you can read the material presented. If you cannot, it is too small. Do not use it. It is frustrating to an audience to have a speaker point knowingly to a visual that they cannot see well enough to comprehend.

- *Remove any distractions.* You do not want to be competing with a previous presenter's material, exhibits, or drawings on a whiteboard or flipchart.

- *Rearrange the seating if necessary.* If possible, arrange the seating so that everyone is facing you and can see you and your visuals or exhibits.

- *Position yourself away from the entrance.* If possible, present from a place where latecomers or people who must leave early will not distract you and others by walking in front of you to find a seat or to leave the room.

- *Set a comfortable temperature in the room.* Check the room temperature and whether sunlight is streaming in through unshaded windows. If possible, keep the room comfortable but cool.

Beginning the Presentation

Give an overview of the information.

Rule number one: Do not hurry your beginning. Walk slowly to the podium or to the location in the room where you will begin your presentation. You will be in a brief transition period. This movement will help relax your muscles and give you a few seconds to adjust from sitting to being on the verge of presenting.

Pause and survey your audience pleasantly. If water is available, pour some and take a sip. All this business may take only 20 seconds, but if you are an inexperienced presenter, it can seem like an hour. However, this unhurried approach is essential. It gives you time to prepare yourself, and it relaxes your audience. It tells them they are about to listen to a calm, composed individual, and they will be happy for that.

Begin by greeting your audience in whatever manner is appropriate for the occasion. Perhaps a simple "Good afternoon" will do. If appropriate, express your appreciation for the opportunity to make your presentation. On more formal occasions, you may need to acknowledge the person who introduced you and greet important people in the room: "Thank you, Ms. Robinson, for that kind introduction. Mr. Weaver, Ms. Juarez, coworkers, ..."

Now begin firmly and authoritatively with your introduction. At this moment, your adrenaline will be pouring into your bloodstream. Often, introductions come in two parts: the *icebreaker* and a statement of your purpose. An *icebreaker* allows you to slip gracefully to the introduction of your presentation. You may not need the icebreaker if you are presenting to coworkers (for example, Figure 12.6) or to a group that knows you and time is limited. If you need an icebreaker, various devices can be used. You can open with a quotation or an anecdote that illustrates your major point.

You can get audience participation in some manner. Ask for a show of hands: "How many people visited the company's exhibit at last week's trade show?" You can compliment the occasion or the audience. You have many options. We have only two warnings. Your quotations and stories should apply to your topic. Do not let them seem dragged in.

Second, although some people use a joke to put people at ease, be careful of humor. If you cannot handle it, do not touch it. And if the occasion for the presentation is a serious one, humor would likely be seen as inappropriate.

Your introduction should match the occasion. Humor can be a minefield of difficulties with a multicultural audience—some members of the audience may not understand the humor (which is always based on mutual understanding), and others may fail to find the humor funny. Sometimes, more substantive problems arise. Some people of other cultures do not share what we might hold as American values. By the same token, as Americans, we might fail to appreciate fully the values of another culture.

After your icebreaker or brief opening remarks, get to your main points quickly. State your purpose and plan plainly and clearly:

> In the next 20 minutes, I will explain to you why the speed limit on our state's highways should be rolled back to 60 miles per hour. It saves gasoline, highway maintenance, and lives.

In this statement, the audience is told the main purpose and the major subdivisions of the presentation.

An introduction can accomplish two other tasks as well. If your presentation is to include several key terms or theories unknown to your audience, explain them at the beginning of your talk. Also, in a persuasive presentation, the introduction is often a good place to seek common ground with your audience:

> I am sure we all agree on the need to conserve energy, money, and lives. Where we perhaps do not agree is on how to go about it. Consider . . .

At the beginning of a presentation, never apologize for conditions or set up a rationale for failure: "If I had a little more time, I could have prepared better charts" or "At the last minute, I was unable to get my printer to ...." Instead, have your icebreaker and the rest of your introduction well in hand and get on with your presentation. Show confidence in yourself and in the information you are presenting.

During the Presentation

Present the information.

To create good rapport with your listeners:

- *Show enthusiasm for the occasion and conviction for your ideas.* There is no substitute for being eager and excited about your presentation. An audience will give their attention to a presenter who appears genuinely interested in his or her topic. But an audience that detects a presenter who is weary of or bored by the subject will quickly lose interest. Deliver your presentation with self-confidence. Having an organized presentation, showing attention to details, and using only the best tools can improve your ability to hold people's attention.

- *Feel comfortable in your place before the audience.* Move around if possible and appropriate so that you appear relaxed. Your audience will follow you as you gesture and move. Motion is important in convincing people—and even yourself, for that matter—that you are relaxed and assured. Use all the normal body motions while you are speaking.

The use of visuals is important here; they encourage natural movement as you draw, write, or move a poster or transparency. If you work with a chalkboard, whiteboard, or flipchart, make sure you do not turn your back on the audience. Stand slightly to the side as you write or draw. Move away from the screen and projector to be sure that your audience can see the information on the screen.

- *Maintain eye contact.* Eye contact is an important part of body language for two reasons. First, people are not really persuaded that you are speaking to them unless they see your eyes on them. They will think you are insincere if you fail to meet their eyes. Second, if you look at people, you get feedback. Read their body language: People sitting alertly with faces pleasantly composed are giving you positive feedback. You can continue as you are. People slumping, yawning, or looking away from you are giving you negative feedback. If that happens, do not panic, but recognize a need for change, perhaps a different speech rate, more motion, or more explanation.

  You might try addressing one statement to a person on the first row, another point to someone to your left, another point to someone to your right and farther back, and so on until you have looked at most of the audience.

- *Speak vigorously but normally.* The very sound of your voice carries part of your message. Obvious as it may seem, pay attention to whether or not you are being heard. If possible, arrange to have someone farthest from you to signal if you need to speak louder. If people are frowning, stop and ask them whether they can hear you. If they cannot, speak up or use a microphone. Practice varying your volume, pitch, and rate to get the effects you want.

  Be careful to say your words clearly. Again, practice your presentation and make sure you can pronounce each word clearly and correctly and that you know the meaning of the words. In short, stand up straight, move freely, speak loudly and clearly, and look directly at the faces of the people in front of you. If you appear enthusiastic and confident, you will keep your audience's attention.

Ending the Presentation

Give a quick review of the information.

Conclusions come in two parts, sometimes three—all short. Once you move into a conclusion, move through it quickly. It should take no more than a minute, even for a long presentation.

Summarize your major points in a sentence or two:

> Driving at 60 instead of 70 miles per hour cuts gasoline use by 10 percent and cuts down highway maintenance statewide by as much as $14 million a year. Most important of all, reducing the speed limit to 60 miles per hour will, according to projections provided by the Department of Transportation's Office of Highway Safety, save more than 200 lives a year in our state.

Note the repetition of the key points of the introduction but with the addition of some important support data.

If your presentation has been persuasive, you may wish to add a call to action to the summary:

> If I have persuaded you of the need for a 60-miles-per-hour speed limit on our state highways, write your state representative or senator today. You can be sure that the truck lobbies are bringing pressure to bear to keep the limit at 70 miles per hour.

You may also want to close your presentation with a memorable quotation or story—something like an icebreaker. If you do close with a story, keep it *very* brief.

It is important that you stop speaking before your audience stops listening. If you are one of several speakers at a meeting, do not take up more than your allotted time. If you have planned to give a 15-minute presentation, stick to it. Before you begin to speak, take your watch off and place it on the podium or table where you can see it.

Once you suggest you are going to end, end quickly. Have your final summary or quote or whatever firmly in mind or handy on the screen so that you will not miss a beat when it is time to conclude. Close firmly, but do not hurry from the podium. As you did at the beginning, pause. Hold eye contact with your audience for five seconds.

Question-and-Answer Period

Many presentations conclude with a question-and-answer period. In some business situations the entire talk, after a brief introduction, could be questions and answers. Sometimes a chairperson or moderator will take the questions; in other situations, you will. In any case, pay attention to your audience. Be sure everyone in the audience understands the question before you begin your answer. We can sum up your goals during the question-and-answer period with five Cs. You should be *courteous, correct, complete, concise,* and *confident.*

Courteous

Give everyone in the audience a fair chance to hear the questions and to ask questions. When you have a large audience, always repeat the question so that everybody can hear it. Rephrase a long, involved question.

Look around and answer questions from different parts of the room. Be polite and objective in your answer—even to the hostile questions.

Correct

Be sure your answers are accurate. Answer a question only if you can do so accurately. If you cannot, do not be afraid of saying, "I don't know." Or get the questioner's name and address, and promise to send the information. If you do, keep your promise.

Complete and Concise

Complete and *concise* are somewhat in opposition. Answer as fully as time allows and the question deserves. Questions often indicate that major points in your talk have not been understood or, worse, have been misunderstood. Elaborate as needed until you reach a correct understanding. Be complete, but keep your eye on the clock. Stop when you really have answered the question.

In many situations you would be wise to bring additional material with you for the question-and-answer period—reports, tables, charts, and so forth. Take enough time if you have such material with you to look up the answers needed.

Confident

Be prepared and answer confidently. Be careful not to let playing the expert lead you into inaccurate answers or into giving authoritative answers to questions outside your field. Be ready to say, "My opinion on that matter would be no better than anyone else's." Be prepared.

If you are confident in yourself and the information you are presenting, you should have a successful presentation.

✓ PLANNING AND REVISING CHECKLIST: ORAL PRESENTATIONS

Think about the following in planning and revising oral presentations.

Planning

- What is the context for your oral presentation? For example, is it a business meeting with coworkers or with clients?

- Where are you talking? What kind of facilities and technologies will you have?

- Will a planned or impromptu presentation serve the occasion best?

- Who are your audience? What is their level of knowledge?

- What is your audience's attitude toward your purpose, subject matter, and you? Why is the audience there?

- Are there special adjustments you must make for a multicultural audience?

- What is your purpose: informative and/or persuasive?

- How much time do you have?

- How can you support your generalizations? Examples? Anecdotes? Appeal to authority? Research?

- Do you have an interesting fact or anecdote to begin your presentation?

- What visuals are available for your presentation? Are they simple, clear, consistent, and visible enough for the context?

- What technology will you use? Chalkboard or whiteboard? Poster? Flipchart? Overhead projector? Computer and LCD projector? Other? If you plan to use a computer presentation package, are compatible hardware and software available at the site of the presentation?

Revising

For true revision, you must practice your oral presentation, preferably in front of an audience, before you deliver it. You can also "revise" in the sense that you can analyze oral presentations after they are given to aid you in preparing a better one on the next occasion. Consider the following:

- Are you within your allotted time?

- Is your purpose clearly stated?

- Does your introduction preview your presentation?
- Does your content
  - meet the needs and expectations of audience?
  - move your purpose forward?
  - satisfy the purpose?
  - provide needed, accurate information?
- Are the visuals and visual features simple, clear, consistent, and visible?
  - Consistent design template?
  - Appropriate font and point size?
  - Effective use of color?
  - Good use of animation and transitions?
  - Effective coordination of the text and visuals?
- Are you unhurried at the beginning and end of your presentation?
- Do you have good body movement? Eye contact?
- Are your gestures suitable to your subject and audience?
- Is your speech clear and distinct?
- Do you have information to handle questions that may come?

Suggestions for Applying Your Knowledge

Individual Activities

1. Locate a presentation on the Internet. One place to start is the U.S. Department of Labor's Occupational Safety and Health Administration's multimedia site: www.osha.gov/SLTC/multimedia.html. View 2 or 3 of the most recent presentations and evaluate their effectiveness.

2. If you have time, oral presentations can be tied into many of the course writing assignments. A sales letter can easily be made into a persuasive talk. Descriptions of mechanisms can be given orally as well as in writing. Proposals are often accompanied by briefings that cover their major points.

Collaborative Activities

1. Edward Tufte and others have critiqued the use of presentation software. Locate a copy of his essay "The Cognitive Style of PowerPoint"

or visit his Web site for an excerpt. Discuss the Tufte's critique of presentation software.

Alas, slideware often reduces the analytical quality of presentations. In particular, the popular PowerPoint templates (ready-made designs) usually weaken verbal and spatial reasoning, and almost always corrupt statistical analysis. What is the problem with PowerPoint? And how can we improve our presentations?[1]

2. Because the major report is usually based on the information of a specific discipline, it furnishes a good opportunity for cooperation with other departments of your school. Instructors who are experts in the subject matter can be brought into the class to help evaluate the oral presentation. Their presence in the classroom ensures a combined audience of experts and nonexperts, a situation that is common in real life.

3. Create a context for the talk, such as a sales meeting, a proposal briefing, a demonstration of a new process or mechanism to its users. Role-play as an executive, technician, member of a community group, and so forth.

---

[1]Edward Tufte, from essay "The Cognitive Style of PowerPoint." (www.edwardtufte.com) November 26, 2003.

Reports

Principles of Workplace Reports

Successful business and industrial organizations and government agencies get their jobs done by gathering information and moving it to those who need it or to those whom they want to have it—employees, suppliers, customers, sponsors, government regulators, and so on. They transfer all kinds of information in all forms of print and electronic correspondence and reports. They store these documents in easily accessible forms because correspondence and reports are usually the most permanent record of their valuable work. Unsuccessful organizations fail to keep records or transfer information efficiently. Productivity decreases. Ignorance and guesswork replace knowledge and information. The idea is simple:

> The effectiveness of an organization is tied to its reporting—it will thrive on its successful reporting of information.

Because good reporting is so important to an organization's functioning, all organizations are in the business of communication. Whether your job is in accounting, engineering, production, sales, research, or service, as a professional in the workplace, you can expect report writing to be an important part of your work. Our ability to inform and persuade is critical to our success. No one works in a vacuum:

> Every form of employment requires us to work with and through other people and to communicate with them.

The basic principles that apply to all your writing and speaking were discussed in Unit I of this text. The major types of correspondence that you might be expected to write were covered in Unit II. In Unit III, we cover the more complex task of writing reports and discuss choices you must make while planning and preparing reports.

But before we take up those tasks and choices as they relate to different types of reports in Chapters 14, 15, 16, and 17, we present helpful ways for you to look at specific types of reports and at your obligation to make the information in your reports easy to access, read, understand, and use.

Types of Reports

Reports present specific information to a specific audience for a specific purpose.

Reports carry information to those who want it or need it. The information is usually expected or requested by those receiving the report.

When you prepare a report—regardless of its length, content, and form and whether it is primarily written or oral—you will be presenting specific information to a specific audience for a specific purpose. The information you include and the relationship you establish with your audience will depend largely on your reason for reporting. Exactly what information does your audience need or expect? Of what use will the information be? In what order should the information be presented to provide the most help? The answers to these questions will give you a good idea of your purposes and your audience's purposes.

Purpose, in the most general sense, refers to the intentions that both you and your audience bring to the report. The informational report informs the audience what you have found out, and it usually includes a minimal amount of commentary and interpretation. The analytical report presents the facts together with an analysis of them. The persuasive report seeks to influence the audience's belief or action. However, keep in mind that seldom are there pure examples of such reports. Most reports have a combination of purposes.

Most reports either inform; inform and analyze; or inform, analyze, and persuade.

Purpose is only one way to classify reports, but it is a good way to begin thinking about what suits you and serves your audience. Learn to think about the purpose or function of the information in your report, and you will know what to put in your report. You will be better able to decide what information to include, what information to emphasize, and how to organize your report.

How beneficial your report is to your audience depends on how well you meet their interests, purposes, and needs, and how accurately you estimate their ability to understand what you are trying to tell them. So get to know your audiences and their needs, and keep them in mind while you plan and prepare your report. If you know your audience well, you have a leg up on the job. If you do not, you will fail to prepare a good report—no matter how much you hack away at it.

Work closely with your client (your audience) as you develop the report.

Two important points to remember when considering your audiences: They are real people like yourself and they likely will be eager to gain the information you offer.

An eager audience, however, is not necessarily a captive audience. Do not let your knowledge of the subject and your personal convenience totally govern how you prepare the report. In the heat of on-the-job reporting, always remember the courtesy that you naturally owe your audiences. You must get the report to them in plenty of time—when *they* need it or want it. By all means, if you have doubts about any aspect of the report and if you have access to your audience, ask them if they have any special requests concerning the report. They may give you information that will help you cut down on their reading or listening time and increase their comprehension. At times, your audience may make the conditions for the report and establish specific requirements concerning the content, organization, format, and publication procedure or delivery.

At other times, your organization or agency may have its own established specifications. In such situations, your anticipation of the audience's desires or your adherence to prescribed specifications is relatively easy. Sometimes, though, in the case of written reports, you may be unable to consult your readers, or your organization or agency may have no specifications. In the absence of such clear identification of the readers' needs or specifications, there are still several principles you can follow to make your reports easy to read and to make your information easy to find and understand.

Think about the audience for each report as you review each report element.

Here, we discuss the formal elements of a written report—such as a title page, a letter of transmittal or preface, an abstract or executive summary, a table of contents, a list of visuals, the introduction, and so on—and provide you with strong and simple principles that help guide you as you design a report for readers who need information to perform their work.

We will show the elements using two reports by the U.S. Environmental Protection Agency: *Draft Report on the Environment 2003* and *EPA's Draft Report on the Environment: Technical Document.* The reports are in their final form. The word *draft* is included in the titles to indicate an ongoing national dialogue on the environment (Figure 13.1 on page K in the second color insert). We will refer to the first one as the *Draft Report* and to the second as the *Technical Document.* The *Technical Document* contains the research and data that supports the *Draft Report.* We encourage you to also visit the EPA Web site www.epa.gov/indicators/ for the HTML and the PDF versions of each report.

Formal Elements

Reports can take many forms: 4 or 5 sentences scribbled on a notepad, the preliminary results of a laboratory experiment, a dozen paragraphs on how to identify phytoplankton, or perhaps a 22-volume feasibility study on the development of a supersonic transport. No clear-cut distinction exists between informal and formal reports:

- Simple problems and situations require only simple reports, perhaps most closely resembling letters, memos, and e-mail messages.

- Complex and lengthy reports, those with audiences that are distanced from the reported project, and reports that have value as long-term references, have a greater need for formalized presentation to save readers time and effort and to prevent confusion.

Well-designed reports form a series of modules—related but also independent at the same time—where closely related information is usually in one place and does not necessarily require reading other parts of the report. The formal elements help readers (1) keep in view the big picture of the main ideas of the report and (2) recognize the various units of a report, consequently speeding up the retrieval process by highlighting important information and leading readers to the specific information they want. The EPA reports have parallel modules.

The number and type of formal elements of a report vary with its size and purpose. Short reports designed to be read from beginning to end may have a brief introduction and use some headings. Other reports may add a title page and table of contents. Others designed to provide selective access to information may have these elements and a letter or memo of transmittal, an abstract, and an index. In short, formalizing certain elements of a report fights against the loss of meaning, however slight, that inevitably takes place when a message is transmitted. Some companies and organizations use a rigid, standardized plan for long reports; others are more flexible. Our advice is that you learn whatever plan you are expected to follow. If your organization or agency has an established plan, you should follow it. It probably has been developed and evolved into standard practice because it serves writers and readers well. Still, no one plan is best for all purposes. Design reports to fit the subject matter, purpose, and audience. Well-designed reports help to reduce the work of reading. Readers focus on using the information contained in the report.

Here is a list of formal elements. Long reports may have any or all of them. Compare the features of the EPA *Draft Report* and the *Technical Document* and discuss the choices the authors made.

Prefatory Elements

- Cover (Figures 13.1 and 13.2, see page K in the second color insert)
- Title page
- Letter or memo of transmittal or preface (Figures 13.3 and 13.4)
- Table of contents (needed for all except short reports) (Figures 13.5 and 13.6; and Figure 13.7, see color insert page L.)
- Lists of figures and tables (usually needed when the report contains three or more formal visuals)
- Abstract or executive summary (Figure 13.8)

[handwritten margin note: 10-12 pages can only do last after report]

Main Elements

- Introduction (Figures 13.9 and 13.10)
- Body (with headings and subheadings) (Figures 13.11, 13.12, and 13.13, see color insert pages M, N, and O)
- Ending (which may include a summary, conclusions, and recommendations)

Supplemental Elements

- May include endnotes, lists of references (Figures 13.14 and 13.15), a glossary (Figures 13.16 and 13.17), appendixes, and more

Prefatory Elements

The prefatory elements present the contextual information of the report—the author(s), audience, date, subject, coverage, and organization—to readers before they begin to read or scan the report. This context helps a diverse group of readers begin to activate their prior knowledge about the topic and occasion of the report and to begin integrating what they already know with what they will read. Prefatory pages are usually numbered in small roman numerals—iii, iv, v, and so on.

Cover

The cover (Figure 13.1), title page (Figure 13.2), and Web page (Figure 2.2) set the tone for the report. Figure 13.1 (see page K in the second color insert) illustrates the four areas of the report: air, water, humans, and ecology. Figure 2.2 (see pages A and B in the first color insert) gives you the color, or go to the PDF version of the report to see the color. The title page for the *Technical Report* even on the Web is a simple black and white page.

The cover text may be in a typeface that is larger and different from that of the text of the report. It may be in color and include the company logo or visuals appropriate for the topic (Figure 13.1). A cover/title page combination (Figure 13.2, see page K in the second color insert) is standard, but it is regarded by most graphic designers as overly formal and a trifle dull looking. The cover is not included in the numbering of pages in the prefatory section of the report.

Determine the delivery format for the report: paper, electronic, or both. The format will control how much color to use and how to format the report. In this chapter we will focus on reports delivered by paper (see Chapter 12 for discussion of Web-based reports). That said, you may want to incorporate color for your cover, section dividers, and selected areas of the report. Color printing is still expensive. If you bind the report, use a heavy stock of paper, plastic cover, or 3-ring binder

The cover may contain the same information as the title page, or it may be more like Figure 13.1, an attractive entry into the report with only the title and selected information.

Title Page

The title page (Figure 13.2 on color insert page K) gives identifying information about the report:

- the title
- the name (and, if appropriate, the position) of the person or group for whom the report is prepared
- the name (and, if appropriate, the positions or job titles) of the person or group who prepared the report
- the date of the report
- occasionally a brief table of contents

The title page is

- the same weight paper as all the other pages of the report.
- usually in the same font as that of the text of the report.
- understood to be page i of the prefatory elements, although it is not numbered.

The information is important because it introduces the subject, identifies the primary audience and author, establishes the currency of the information, helps in filing and retrieving the report, and makes the report easy to refer to. Here are some suggestions on providing the necessary information for the cover.

Title

Think of the title as a one-phrase summary of the report. It should indicate the subject as briefly and specifically as possible. Avoid unhelpful expressions like *A Report on ...*, *A Study of ...*, *An Investigation ....* Four to eight words are usually enough. One or two words often are vague; more than ten words work against easy comprehension. Here are some acceptable titles that describe succinctly the purpose and subject of reports:

- Proposed Changes in the Traffic Patterns at Lockwood Mall
- Recommendations for Preventing Workplace Violence in Late-Night Retail Establishments
- Comparative Merits of Copy Machines on the Market
- Tooth Transplantation in Pediatric Dentistry
- Battery Eliminators Save Money in the Shop
- Recommendation for Providing Accounting Support to SBDC Clients

Such key terms as *Proposed Changes*, *Traffic Patterns*, *Lockwood Mall*, *Recommendations*, *Preventing Workplace Violence*, *Late-Night Retail Establishments*, *Copy Machines*, *Tooth Transplantation*, *Pediatric Dentistry*, *Battery Eliminators*, *Recommendation*, *Accounting Support*, and *SBDC Clients* identify and emphasize the topic, purpose, and scope of the report. Equally important, they facilitate indexing and cross-referencing reports in files and databases.

Name and Position of Primary Reader

Identify the reader or group of readers of the report and, if appropriate, add their positions and organizations. If the report is distributed to a large group, identify the group or groups (for example, *Current HBK Investors* or *Prospective Environmental Sciences Majors*).

Name and Position of Author

Identify yourself by name and organization. If appropriate, give your position or job title, too. If the report has been written by a team, the authors' names should be in alphabetical order or in some other customary order, such as listing the principal investigator, team leader, or senior author first.

Date of the Report

Date the report according to when it is submitted to the reader. Never abbreviate the date; give the month, day, and year: March 17, 2005 or 17 March 2005.

Letter of Transmittal

The letter of transmittal (Figure 13.3, on page 367) officially presents the report to the readers. The letter of transmittal may be in memo, letter, or some similar form. Addressed to the readers, it provides sufficient background by

- explaining the authorization or occasion of the report (readers in the workplace are subject to many distractions and pressures, and they need to know whether the report is important enough to commit the time to read it).

- restating the title of the report (in case the letter is mailed separately from the report).

- stating the purpose of the report (readers in the workplace want to focus immediately on the task at hand).

- pointing out features of the report that may be of special interest (all readers look for this information, but this information is especially important when certain parts of a report are of significance to different segments of a diverse audience).

- acknowledging special assistance in performing the study or preparing the report, especially from those who funded the project or provided materials, equipment, or information and advice.

This background information establishes a base from which all readers—regardless of their interests or needs—can start reading the report. Close the letter or memo politely by stating your willingness to provide similar services in the future or to provide further information if the readers desire it, whichever is appropriate.

Like any good workplace correspondence, the letter or memo of transmittal should be in a format that makes it easy to read (see Chapter 8 for letter and memo formats). If the letter or memo is bound with the report, it is understood to be a page of the prefatory elements, though it usually is not numbered. If it is placed in front of the title page, it is not regarded as part of the report and is not counted as a page of the prefatory elements.

Preface

The preface (Figure 13.4, on pages 368 and 369) contains introductory material similar to that in the letter or memo of transmittal. It usually contains statements about the background, purpose, scope, and content of the report and acknowledgment of assistance received. If you include a letter or memo of transmittal, a preface usually is unnecessary (although it is common to see both in formal reports). The preface may be placed before the table of contents (especially if the preface takes the place of the letter or memo of transmittal) or after the table of contents. If it follows the table of contents, it is included in the table of contents. Whether you use the letter or memo of transmittal or the preface depends on the audience:

- Use the letter or memo of transmittal when the audience is one person or a well-defined group.

- Use the preface when the audience is more general and you do not know specifically who will be reading the report.

Compare the tone of the letter introducing the Draft Report and the Preface of the Technical Document.

The tone of the preface is often less personal than that of the letter or memo of transmittal.

When the preface takes the place of the letter or memo of transmittal, number it as a page of the prefatory elements. Center the lowercase roman numeral at the bottom of the page.

Table of Contents

Compare the table of contents of the Draft Report and the Technical Document.

The table of contents (Figures 13.5 and 13.6; and Figure 13.7 on color insert page L) lists:

1. the prefatory elements that follow it
2. the major headings and subheadings in the report, including appendixes

The table of contents provides a handy overview of the report that helps readers understand the organization of the report as a whole and also locate any major section or sections quickly. More than any other elements of formal reports, the table of contents provides a map of the contents that enables readers to make choices of what to read.

Format the table of contents to mirror the sections of the report and give the readers an easy-to-read entry into the report:

- Center and make prominent the words *Contents* or *Table of Contents* at the top of the page.

- List the headings in the report to reflect the hierarchy of the sections of the report.

- Match exactly the wording, capitalization, and order of the headings in the report.

- Indent the subheadings under each main heading to show their subordination, and indent progressively subordinate subheadings under their headings. If you numbered the chapters or major sections of the report, those numbers should be placed before the main headings in the table of contents (Figure 13.6).

- Arrange the information into three columns:

  - The left column contains capital roman numerals as major divisions or chapter numbers.

  - The center column contains the main headings and subheadings of the report. Remember to indent to show subordination of subheadings.

FIGURE 13.3

Letter of Transmittal for the EPA's *Draft Report on the Environment 2003*. The letter of transmittal introduces readers to the report. Typically, it identifies the occasion, authorization, topic, and major findings. The author acknowledges any assistance received and encourages the recipients of the report to ask questions. In this example, the Message from the Administrator, Christine Todd Whitman, serves as the letter of transmittal. Whitman's photograph personalizes the presentation.

Source: From *Draft Report on the Environment 2003,* by Environmental Protection Agency, 2003. Retrieved October 24, 2003, from http://www.epa.gov/indicators/

EPA's Draft Report on the Environment 2003

Message from the Administrator

I am pleased to present the U.S. Environmental Protection Agency's *Draft Report on the Environment*, a key step toward building a set of environmental indicators that will help answer the important questions Americans have about the environment, and that will guide our environmental decision-making in the future. This draft report provides a frank discussion of what we know—and what we don't know—about the condition of our nation's environment.

As we look over the past three decades, we see a real record of success in cleaning up and protecting our nation's environment. By many measures, our environment is healthier today than it was in 1970. The nation's commitment to environmental protection has produced cleaner air, safer drinking water for more Americans, and a much improved approach to managing wastes. Where we once took our environment for granted, we now intuitively understand the importance of environmental quality for our future. Much work remains to be done, however, and we must continue to build on our record of progress.

With this draft report, we begin an important national dialogue on how we can improve our ability to assess the nation's environmental quality and human health, and how we use that knowledge to better manage for measurable environmental results. I invite you to participate in this dialogue with us and our partners. Your comments and feedback are essential to our future efforts.

The President has called for a government focused on priorities and dedicated to excellence in public service. His Management Agenda is designed to improve the ability of the federal government to manage for results.

I thank the many EPA staff members from every program and region, our federal, tribal, state and local government partners, and the independent scientists and research institutions that contributed to this draft report.

We are all stewards of this shared planet, responsible for protecting and preserving a precious heritage for our children and grandchildren. As long as we work together and stay firmly focused on our goals, I am confident we will make our air cleaner, our water purer, and our land better protected for future generations.

Christine Todd Whitman

Administrator

FIGURE 13.4

Preface for the *EPA's Draft Report on the Environment: Technical Document.* The preface contains similar information to the letter of transmittal or abstract. It provides readers with the background and purpose for the report and may include a brief summary of the report. The preface in this example has many of the characteristics of a letter of transmittal. The signatures of EPA's Science Advisor and Chief Information Officer appear at the end of the preface.

Source: From *EPA's Draft Report on the Environment: Technical Document 2003.* Retrieved October 24, 2003, from http://www.epa.gov/indicators/

Technical Document ■ EPA's Draft Report on the Environment 2003

Preface

From EPA's Science Advisor and Chief Information Officer

The Environmental Protection Agency (EPA) has been a world leader in developing and implementing solutions to the environmental problems in our air, water and land. Through the years, working together with other Federal Agencies we have built a significant body of science and knowledge that has influenced national and international public policy, and has raised our awareness of the value of our environment. Yet, even with the enormous wealth of understanding and information that we have today, there are still gaps in our ability adequately monitor many key indicators in the cascades of events that link our efforts to protect the environment to the ultimate outcomes we seek: cleaner air, purer water, better protected land, and better human health or and ecological condition. To close that gap, we need both scientifically sound indicators and the national data to support them.

With the publication of the EPA Draft Report on the Environment, including this comprehensive Technical Document, EPA has launched a multi-year effort to improve the state of the science and our knowledge of the state of the environment. This effort addresses indicators, monitoring data and models for better tracking the impacts of our activities on the environment. This document includes indicators that EPA has monitored for many years, including ambient levels of pollutants in air, water and land. However, we recognize that protecting the environment ultimately is achieved in terms of human health and ecological condition, and these two chapters serve as anchors for the entire report.

The last sections of each chapter of this report describe challenges and data gaps associated with its particular subject area. Several general issues have emerged that we will address in the coming months and years.

Shifting to an "Outcomes" Framework

Identifying environmental "outcomes" such as better human health and ecological condition requires a significant shift in how the Agency frames questions and issues about environmental quality. The first three chapters of this report; Cleaner Air, Purer Water, and Better Protected Land, ask questions that tend to follow traditional Agency efforts to prevent, control, or remediate the effects of pollution. For example:

■ What is the quality of outdoor air in the United States?

■ What are pressures to water quality?

■ What is the extent of developed land?

The final two chapters on human health and ecological condition, ask questions about outcomes, for example:

■ What are the trends for cancer?

■ What is the ecological condition of coasts and oceans?

To understand how EPA's mission affects these outcomes, both directly and indirectly, requires indicators not only of pollutant releases and ambient conditions, but indicators that span the chain of events between the release of a pollutant, exposure of people, plants and animals, and the chain of events from dose to effects. In the case of human health, factors such as level of health care, natural disease rates, and actual human exposures must be factored into an indicator strategy. For ecosystems, indicators are needed that track hydrology, features of the landscape, natural disturbances, ecological processes, and other factors that interact with pollutants to ultimately determine ecosystem condition.

Availability of Indicators

For a few of the questions in the report, indicators were identified that are available at the national level. More frequently, however, we found that promising indicators have been developed and measured for limited geographic areas, or for a part of the causal chain. Further exploration of the relationship between measurements used for assessments and measurements used for diagnosis of causal factors also is needed. Development and testing of national indicators has been a high research priority for EPA's Office of Research and Development.

Preface   v

FIGURE 13.4
(continued)

EPA's Draft Report on the Environment 2003 ■ Technical Document

Availability of Data

For each of the indicators, we attempted to gather data of sufficient quality and coverage to support national reporting, both within and outside the Agency. Generally, the available data were too limited in place and time to describe national trends, or even to provide a national snapshot of conditions. Because the data from different organizations often serve a broad range of purposes, even when data are available nationally, gaps remain in the spatial, temporal and phemonenological coverage needed to track the outcomes of many of EPA's programs. Monitoring networks established to address specific issues must be better integrated through common definitions, designs, methods, and information systems.

Collaborating for the Future

With this draft as a starting point, we look forward to collaborating with federal and state agencies to promote integrated and coherent approaches and mechanisms for reporting on the state of the environment. Following the release of this report, we will be working closely with scientists from other federal and state agencies and the academic community to explore how best to improve our ability to measure and assess environmental conditions.

We invite all of our stakeholders to lend their creativity and commitment in the months and years ahead as they join us in meeting Administrator Whitman's challenge to focus our resources on the areas of greatest concern and to manage our work to achieve measurable results.

Paul Gilman, Ph.D.
Science Advisor and Assistant Administrator for Research and Development

Kimberly T. Nelson
Chief Information Officer and Assistant Administrator for Environmental Information

vi

Preface

Set the tab in the word processor you use to create the leaders automatically.

- The right column identifies the page numbers, aligned right, where the headings appear. Use double-spaced dots, called *dot leaders,* to connect the headings with the page numbers.

- Double-space between entries and single-space any heading that is too long for one line.

- Number the table of contents page as a prefatory page.

FIGURE 13.5

Table of Contents for the EPA's *Draft Report on the Environment 2003*. The table of contents provides quick access to various parts of the report. The entries match the headings in the report in content and should reflect the same hierarchy of topics as the headings in the report. The periods (dot leaders) lead the reader from the main headings and subheadings to the page numbers in the right margin. The words *Table of Contents* or *Contents* are usually centered at the top of the page. Often the table of contents page contains the first visible page number (a roman numeral), although it is not the first page.

Source: From *Draft Report on the Environment 2003,* by Environmental Protection Agency, 2003. Retrieved October 24, 2003, from http://www.epa.gov/indicators/

EPA's Draft Report on the Environment 2003

Contents

FIGURE 13.6

Table of Contents for the *EPA's Draft Report on the Environment: Technical Document*. Compare the tables of contents. See Figure 13.7 (color insert page L) for the Web-based version. The Contents for the *Draft Report* is one page. The Table of Contents for the *Technical Document* is three pages. The chapter titles and section headings are almost the same as those in the *Draft Report*. The second-level heading is given in the *Technical Document*. Why do you think more detail is identified in the *Technical Document*? Why do you think the *Draft Report* has the section "Limitations of Air Indicators" but the *Technical Document* has the section "Challenges and Data Gaps"?

Source: From *EPA's Draft Report on the Environment: Technical Document*. Retrieved October 24, 2003, from http://www.epa.gov/indicators/

Technical Document ■ EPA's Draft Report on the Environment 2003

Table of Contents

Table of Contents   i

FIGURE 13.6
(continued)

EPA's Draft Report on the Environment 2003 ■ Technical Document

ii   Table of Contents

FIGURE 13.6
(continued)

List of Figures and Tables

The page that lists figures and tables shows readers the location of visuals and tables. You should include it only if the report makes significant use of visuals—say, more than three figures or tables. If your report includes many figures and tables, you may group them into separate categories: *List of Figures*, *List of Tables*, and so on. Neither EPA report includes lists of figures or tables, although both contain many visuals (for example, Figure 2.2).

The list of figures and tables is set up just like the table of contents. Center at the top of the page and make prominent the words *Figures and Tables* or whatever is appropriate.

Arrange the information in three columns, similar to the table of contents: The left column contains the figure or table number (normally, tables are given capital roman numerals and figures are given arabic numbers, but the practices are not universal); the center column contains the title of the figure or table; the right column contains the number of the page it is on or is facing. Use dot leaders to connect titles of figures and tables with the page numbers.

Abstract or Executive Summary

The abstract or executive summary (Figure 13.8) is a brief, condensed statement of the most important ideas of the report. It provides the readers with a compressed overview of the report by mirroring both its content and organization. The length of the abstract or executive summary depends primarily on the length of the report. Center and make prominent the word *Abstract* or *Executive Summary* at the top of the page, double-space, and begin the abstract

The typical abstract is a paragraph of 150 to 200 words. But longer reports, say 20 or more pages, probably would require additional paragraphs. A good working estimate for the length of an abstract of a longer report is that it should not be more than 5 percent of the whole report. Thus, a 40-page report would have an abstract of approximately two pages at most. The abstract for a longer report might consist of a series of brief paragraphs, each paragraph summarizing a major section of the report. Although the abstract is a compressed version of the report, you should not write it in a telegraphic style. Its words and sentences must be in a good prose style.

An executive summary is similar to an abstract, although it tends to be longer. The EPA *Draft Report* executive summary clearly identifies the purpose of the report (first page) before giving the conclusions reached in each section of the report. The conclusions are the first sentence (bolded) of each paragraph. You can read the executive summary and understand the major points of the report. You can quickly locate areas of the report you want to read.

Main Elements

The main elements of the report follow the prefatory elements and consist of three parts: the introduction, the body, and the ending. These elements are often referred to as "the report proper."

The Introduction

The introduction (Figures 13.9 and 13.10) attracts attention, sets the context, and presents a general idea of the topic of the report. The quality of the introduction can make or break your report's success.

When busy readers turn to your report, they will start looking for answers to several questions as they try to settle into the report. They will want to know or be reminded why you are writing to them now, what you have to say, how you are going to say it, and how difficult or time-consuming it will be to read what you have written. They will also want to know the importance of the report to them and their work. And they will want the answers to these questions right away.

To hold the readers' attention and prevent mental wandering, you must pave a road that is easy to follow, build an entrance that is unavoidable, and close the gates to the sides. These are the jobs of the introduction, the first main portion of the report.

The introduction may consist of a few paragraphs or perhaps several pages. When it is lengthy, you should consider using subheadings to indicate its subparts. Whether the introduction is short or long, it should perform the following functions:

- **Explain the subject or research problem.** Readers need to know what they are going to read about. The title, the letter or memo of transmittal or preface, and the abstract or executive summary give them some information but might not provide adequate orientation. Often it is necessary to define the subject, state the research problem, explain some of the key terms used in the discussion, or give historical and other background information about the subject or research problem—including a review of the literature. Finally, you should comment on the significance of the information—the so-whats. Why is the subject important? Why should readers want to know about it?

- **Explain the purpose.** Although the purpose of the report should be self-evident to you, make sure it is equally evident to readers. Your purpose might be to report on a study requested by the readers. If so, review the facts of the request or authorization: When did they make the request? How did they make it? Did somebody else make it? Such a review is especially important if you include no letter or memo of transmittal. If the report is unsolicited, explain thoroughly the situation that led to your writing the report.

Figure 13.8

Executive Summary for the EPA's *Draft Report on the Environment 2003*. The executive summary presents an overview of the report for busy readers who must make decisions or act on information contained in the report. It may replace the letter of transmittal. The length depends on the length of the report. The EPA report executive summary begins with an overview page (shown) and includes the key statement setting the context for the report: "EPA is issuing this report as a draft to stimulate dialogue and invite input into developing and improving environmental indicators in the future" (i). This statement is also found in the letter of transmittal, preface, and introductions.

Source: From *Draft Report on the Environment 2003*, by Environmental Protection Agency, 2003. Retrieved October 24, 2003, from http://www.epa.gov/indicators/

EPA's Draft Report on the Environment 2003

Executive Summary

In this *Report on the Environment*, the U.S. Environmental Protection Agency (EPA) presents its first-ever national picture of the U.S. environment. The report describes what EPA knows—and doesn't know—about the current state of the environment at the national level, and how the environment is changing. The report highlights the progress our nation has made in protecting its air, water, and land resources, and describes the measures that can be used to track the status of the environment and human health. Key conclusions from this report are summarized below.

This report is the first step in EPA's Environmental Indicators Initiative. Launched in November 2001, this initiative seeks to develop better indicators that EPA can use to measure and track the state of the environment and support improved environmental decision-making. As a first step in developing this report, EPA identified a series of key questions about the environment—questions such as: What is the condition of waters and watersheds in the United States? What is the quality of outdoor air in the United States? The Agency then carefully examined data sources, including those from other federal agencies, to identify indicators (e.g., the extent of wetlands and the concentrations of criteria pollutants in air) that could answer these questions on a national level.

These indicators provide the basis for this report. They also reveal that there is much we don't know about the status of our environment because we currently lack sufficient information to provide a more complete picture. An important next step in EPA's initiative will be working closely with other federal agencies, tribes, states, local governments, non-governmental organizations, and the private sector to create a long-term strategy for developing an integrated system of local, regional, and national indicators. This work will involve a number of challenges, including developing better data to support better indicators, making indicators more understandable and usable, and more fully elucidating the linkage between the causes and effects of environmental pollution and stressors.

EPA is issuing this report as a draft to stimulate dialogue and invite input into developing and improving environmental indicators in the future. EPA welcomes your suggestions about how well this report communicates environmental status and trends and how to better measure and manage for environmental results. To learn more about the Environmental Indicators Initiative, to access the Technical Document that provides the detailed scientific foundation for this report, or to provide comment and feedback on this report, please visit **http://www.epa.gov/indicators/**.

Executive Summary

i

FIGURE 13.8 (continued)

Executive Summary for the EPA's *Draft Report on the Environment 2003*—continued. The remaining five pages identify the key points from the chapters on air, water (shown), land, human health, and ecological conditions. Each paragraph begins with a key point.

Source: From *Draft Report on the Environment 2003*, by Environmental Protection Agency, 2003. Retrieved October 24, 2003, from http://www.epa.gov/indicators/

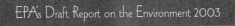

EPA's Draft Report on the Environment 2003

Purer Water

Pristine waterways, safe drinking water, lakes for swimming and fishing, and aquatic life habitat are treasured resources. The nation has made significant progress in protecting these resources in the last 30 years. For example, concerted action to protect the nation's waters has reduced discharges of pollutants to surface water and improved safety of drinking water supplies. Challenges remain, however, including polluted runoff, landscape modification, changes to water flow, airborne pollutants settling into surface water, and the aging of both wastewater and drinking water infrastructures. The precise scope and scale of these challenges—at the local and the national scale—are uncertain.

Waters and Watersheds

We know a great deal about the condition of the nation's waters at the regional, state, tribal, and local levels, but we do not have enough information to provide a comprehensive picture at the national level. The way in which the nation collects water quality data does not support a comprehensive picture of watershed health at the national level.

The nation's estuaries are in fair to poor condition, varying from poor conditions in the northeast, Gulf, and Great Lakes regions to fair conditions in the West and Southeast, based on measurements of seven coastal condition indicators.

Rates of annual wetland losses have decreased from almost 500,000 acres a year three decades ago to a loss of less than 100,000 acres averaged annually since 1986. Nevertheless, in key parts of the U.S., we continue to lose valuable wetlands.

Drinking Water

An increasing number of people are served by community water systems that meet all health-based drinking water standards. In 2002, states reported that 94 percent of the population served by community water systems were served by systems that met all health-based standards, up from 79 percent in 1993. Underreporting and late reporting of data affect the accuracy of this information.

Recreation in and on the Water

The number of beach closings has increased, but this likely reflects more consistent monitoring, reporting, and use of state-wide advisories over time, rather than a decline in the condition of recreational waters. From 1997 to 2001, the percentage of beaches affected by advisories or closings rose from 23 to 27 percent. During that same period, the number of agencies reporting to EPA on beach advisories and closings rose from 159 to 237.

Consumption of Fish and Shellfish

The percentage of U.S. fresh waters under fish consumption advisories has increased in recent years. Similar to beach closings, these increases may be the result of more consistent monitoring and reporting, so they do not necessarily indicate that conditions are getting worse. An estimated 14 percent of river miles, 28 percent of lake acreage, and 100 percent of the Great Lakes and their connecting waters were under fish consumption advisories for at least some portion of 2001. Following the U.S. ban in the mid-1970s, PCB concentrations significantly declined in Lake Michigan fish and concentrations of PCBs in lake trout declined consistently through the year 2000 in Lakes Ontario, Huron, and Michigan.

Executive Summary

FIGURE 13.9

First page of the Introduction for the EPA's *Draft Report on the Environment 2003*. The introduction identifies the purpose of the report and identifies the order the material will be presented in the report. The 5-page introduction to the *Draft Report* establishes the purpose of the report, explains the purpose of the indicators to monitor the environment, include a graphic entitled "Hierarchy of Indicators" and maps of the United States showing the "statistical context for understanding environmental progress."

Source: From *Draft Report on the Environment 2003,* by Environmental Protection Agency, 2003. Retrieved October 24, 2003, from http://www.epa.gov/indicators/

EPA's Draft Report on the Environment 2003

Introduction

How clean are our nation's air, water, and land? How healthy are its people and ecosystems? How can we measure the success of policies and programs to protect health and the environment?

This report provides the U.S. Environmental Protection Agency's (EPA's) response to these questions, with the aim of sparking a broader dialogue and discussion about how to answer them in the future. The report has two key purposes:

■ To describe what EPA knows—and doesn't know—about the current state of the environment at the national level, and how the environment is changing.

■ To identify measures that can be used to track the status of and trends in the environment and human health, and to define the challenges to improving those measures.

This report is the first step in EPA's Environmental Indicators Initiative. Launched in November 2001, this initiative seeks to develop an improved set of environmental indicators that will enable EPA to better manage for results and better communicate the status of the environment and human health. These indicators will provide critical tools for EPA to define environmental management goals and measure progress toward those goals. Early drafts of this report have already been helpful in developing EPA's strategic plan for 2003 to 2008.

An important next step in EPA's initiative will include working closely with partners—other federal agencies, states, tribes, local government, non-governmental organizations, and the private sector—to create a long-term strategy for developing an integrated system of local, regional, and national indicators. This report is issued as a draft to stimulate dialogue and invite input into developing and improving environmental measures in the future. EPA welcomes your suggestions about how well this report communicates environmental status and trends and how to better measure and manage for results. To learn more about the initiative and to provide your comments and feedback, please visit **http://www.epa.gov/indicators/**.

Using Indicators to Measure Results

This report uses the lens of environmental and health indicators to bring the current state of the U.S. environment into focus. Environmental indicators are measures that track environmental conditions over time. For example, they help measure the state of air, water, and land; the pressures on those resources; the status of human health; and the integrity of our nation's ecosystems. Examples of environmental indicators include concentrations of criteria air pollutants in ambient air, the extent of wetlands, and the levels of lead in the blood of Americans.

Environmental and human health indicators focus on outcomes—actual environmental results, such as cleaner air and

Working with Partners

Protecting the environment and human health is not EPA's task alone. Many federal departments implement legislation and manage programs that contribute directly to those goals. State, local, and county governments, along with federally recognized tribes, administer environmental programs as well. Many other factors influence human and environmental health: individual choices, collective actions by citizens, and decisions made by industry all contribute to the health of society as a whole, and of its surrounding environment.

In developing this draft report, EPA learned much from the experiences of others: the White House Council on Environmental Quality, other federal departments and agencies, tribes, and states; The H. John Heinz III Center for Science, Economics and the Environment; NatureServe; the EPA Science Advisory Board; and the National Research Council. This draft report is much stronger as a result of the comments, advice, and data they made available to EPA.

Introduction

vii

FIGURE 13.10

Introduction for the *EPA's Draft Report on the Environment: Technical Document*. Introductions begin the report; arabic page numbering begins for most reports. Because the EPA reports are six chapters long, the authors chose to include the introductions as part of the prefatory section of the report. Each chapter also has a brief introduction. The *Technical Document* introduction is one page, no graphics. Does it provide the same information as the *Draft Report*? What are the differences and how do these differences respond to the audiences for each report?

Source: From *EPA's Draft Report on the Environment: Technical Document 2003*. Retrieved October 24, 2003, from http://www.epa.gov/indicators/

Technical Document ■ EPA's Draft Report on the Environment 2003

Introduction

"When I leave office, I want to be able to say that America's air is cleaner, its water is purer, and its land better protected than it was when I arrived. As we seek to achieve this goal, EPA needs to be accountable for our stewardship."
Christine Todd Whitman, Administrator, U.S. Environmental Protection Agency

In November 2001, EPA Administrator Christine Todd Whitman directed the Agency to bring together its national, regional and program office data to produce a report on the "state of the environment." The report would represent the first step of the Environmental Indicators Initiative, a multi-year process that would ultimately allow future EPA administrators to better measure and report on progress toward environmental and human health goals and to ensure the Agency's accountability to the public.

To produce this report, EPA's Office of Research and Development (ORD) and Office of Environmental Information (OEI) led a collaborative effort to identify the key questions to be answered by the report, to identify an initial set of indicators, and to develop a process for reviewing and selecting the indicators and supporting data to be included in the final report. This task was accomplished thanks to the efforts of numerous EPA staff, representatives from other federal agencies, representatives from the states and tribes, and external advisors and reviewers. The indicators and supporting data used in this report were generated by EPA and other federal, state, tribal, regional, local, and non-governmental organizations. The Council on Environmental Quality in the Executive Office of the President was helpful throughout in coordinating interagency contributions to the project.

EPA's *Draft Report on the Environment* (ROE) consists of this *Technical Document* and a version of the report for general reading. These reports pose national questions about the environment and human health and answer those questions wherever scientifically sound indicators and high-quality supporting data are available. The reports both pose questions and present indicators related to:
■ Cleaner Air
■ Purer Water
■ Better Protected Land
■ Human Health
■ Ecological Condition

This *Draft Technical Document* discusses the limitations of the currently available indicators and data, and the gaps and challenges that must be overcome to provide better answers in the future.

For a few indicators, data are available that are truly representative of the entire nation. For other indicators, data currently are available for only one region (such as the East Coast or the Northwest), but the indicator could obviously be applied nationally if the data were available. Based on the availability of supporting data, indicators that were selected and included in this report were assigned to one of two categories:
■ **Category 1** –The indicator has been peer reviewed and is supported by national level data coverage for more than one time period. The supporting data are comparable across the nation and are characterized by sound collection methodologies, data management systems, and quality assurance procedures.
■ **Category 2** –The indicator has been peer reviewed, but the supporting data are available only for part of the nation (e.g., multistate regions or ecoregions), or the indicator has not been measured for more than one time period, or not all the parameters of the indicator have been measured (e.g., data has been collected for birds, but not for plants or insects). The supporting data are comparable across the areas covered, and are characterized by sound collection methodologies, data management systems, and quality assurance procedures.

This report is part of EPA's continuing effort to identify, improve, and utilize environmental indicators in its planning, management, and public reporting. EPA's specific strategies and performance targets to protect human health and the environment are presented in the Agency's strategic and annual plans. These planning and performance documents, together with the questions, indicators and data presented in these reports, will allow EPA to better define and measure the status and trends in environment and health, and to better measure the effectiveness of its programs and activities.

This technical report is a draft, intended to elicit comments and suggestions on the approach and findings. To learn more about EPA's *Draft Report on the Environment* and the Environmental Indicators Initiative, and to provide comments and feedback, please visit http://www.epa.gov/indicators/.

Introduction

xi

The value of the report and the objectives and purposes of your reporting should be clear to the readers. Be sure that you are clear on the purpose of the report and on the problem to which it relates. For instance, say you are working on a project to redesign a piece of machinery to reduce the vibration when it is operating and to prevent material jams caused by misalignment of the machine parts. The purpose of your report might be to persuade your readers that your redesign will solve the problem and will be within the budget of the project.

- **Explain the scope.** Let the readers know the extent of the presentation or the limits of the study. In other words, explain just how much ground the report is covering. The statement of scope tells readers what you see yourself responsible for reporting.

- **Explain the plan and order of presentation.** Always preview the report for readers. Tell them the order of topics. This statement usually is the last function of the introduction and serves as a transition to the body of the report.

Almost every important or long report will need a formal introduction that fulfills these four functions. For special circumstances you may need to do any of the following:

- Discuss in detail the problem or problems the project and report are designed to solve.

- State a hypothesis and explain how it was or will be tested.

- Review the literature relevant to the problem or hypothesis.

- Explain the nature of the investigation—the sources and methods of collecting data.

- Define important terms used in the report that you think readers might be unfamiliar with.

- Summarize your significant findings or recommendations and point out the limits of the validity of your conclusions, if the purpose of the report is to communicate your position on a set of issues.

In short, the introduction should include whatever is needed to prepare readers for the information they are about to receive.

The Body

The body, the longest section of the report, presents the detailed message. The EPA reports have 6 chapters. Figures 13.11, 13.12, and 13.13 (see pages M, N, and O in the second color insert) show pages from Chapter 2. It has no set organization, but its contents should be arranged in some logical, unified order. Regardless of the content and arrangement of the report, you must help readers to skim the report, to read it thoroughly, or to refer to specific parts of it by using headings and subheadings, which separate the text into major divisions (similar to chapters in books) and divide each major division into sections. The outline of the report is a good source for headings and subheadings.

Probably no other scanning aid will help readers more than the liberal use of headings. To test this claim, find any report, article, or manual more than two or three pages long; remove the headings; and see how suddenly the text appears to be tediously uninterrupted and how the major topics disappear into the text. (See Chapter 5.)

For those who read the entire report, the headings will be a reminder of the readers' progress. However, most readers read selectively, and headings provide them with easy reference to the parts they seek by indicating key topics. The headings and subheadings should agree with the entries in the table of contents; in fact, the headings are an expanded table of contents inserted at appropriate places throughout the text. Each heading and subheading should be worded to convey the topic of the section it heads. For example, in a section about medical needs of elderly prison inmates, the heading *Section II* or *Analysis of Medical Facilities* is too general and uninformative. A heading such as *Medical Needs of Elderly Prison Inmates* is far more informative.

Although slight variations exist in the use of headings, their format may be handled as shown in Figures 13.11, 13.12, and 13.13 or Figure 5.11. In addition to making sure that their positions clearly indicate the levels of importance of the headings, you should make sure of the following:

- Headings are worded so that they point to the text that follows and relate to each other grammatically.

- Headings are not followed immediately by a pronoun that refers to a word or phrase in them.

- Headings have written text between them, even if it is only an explanation of subdivisions to come.

- Headings have at least two lines of text between the last heading and the bottom of the page.

Remember that headings serve as excellent clues to the content and arrangement of material. Think three times before you submit a report that does not have headings.

As readers begin to read a major section of a report, they need an introduction to that section similar to the kind that they needed at the beginning of the report—an introduction that gives them at least a brief overview of the contents of the section and its purpose, scope, and organization. They have the same desire to grasp the overall picture, to find the information they need quickly, and to understand the information immediately as they did when they began reading the report. Major sections that do not adequately introduce readers to content and organization can be difficult and frustrating to work through.

The Ending

The last major part of the main elements of the report is the ending. Like the introduction, the ending should emphasize the most important ideas in the report, so make it as strong as the introduction. Some typical functions of formal end sections are (1) to summarize the major points of the report, (2) to state conclusions, and (3) to state recommendations.

Depending on the type of report and the readers' needs, the ending may contain any one or a combination of these functions. You may at times want to provide up-front visibility for the conclusions and recommendations—for instance, when readers are primarily interested in results, conclusions, and recommendations and regard the body of the report secondarily. In such instances, you should move them to the front of the report. Long sections of reports usually have their own formal ending as well as an introduction.

- **Summarizing major points:** Reports that are primarily informative usually end with a summary that helps readers make sense of the mass of details presented in the body by recalling the essential ideas covered. Just as the introduction offers readers a preview of the body, a summary at the end offers readers a postview.

- **Stating conclusions:** Reports that are primarily analytical end with a conclusion, which lists the logical implications of the findings—the so-whats. Sometimes the formal end section combines a statement of the major points and the conclusions reached. When it is appropriate to present several precise conclusions, they should be numbered.

- **Stating recommendations:** Reports that are primarily analytical and persuasive usually end with recommendations, which fulfill the advisory function of the report. That is, the recommendations tell the reader what to do or not to do. The recommendations should be laid out in a series of parallel statements, each paragraphed separately.

Supplemental Elements

After the main elements of the report come the supplemental elements, which contain information related to the report that may be of interest to readers but is not important enough to interrupt the main line of discussion. You must decide what information can be placed in the supplemental elements to help reduce the length and complexity of the main body of the report.

- **The list of references** (see Figures 13.14 and 13.15) provides complete publication information for each citation in the report. Although there is universal agreement that credit must be given to sources of borrowed information, there is no universal agreement on how to do it. See Chapter 21 for information on documentation.

- **A glossary** (see Figures 13.16 and 13.17) is included if the report contains many technical terms or words that many of the readers may not know. Arrange the words or phrases alphabetically, beginning each entry on a separate line.

- **Appendixes** contain information or documents that, although useful, might hamper easy reading of the text. Although it is not always easy to decide what material to put in appendixes, we suggest material that has direct—but secondary rather than primary—importance to the reader. Appendixes often include glossaries, copies of questionnaires, related correspondence, reports, the text of speeches or interviews, samples, exhibits, and all kinds of supplemental tables, figures, and case histories. A glossary or list of symbols that may be too lengthy to place in the introduction of the report could be placed in an appendix. Review the table of contents for the EPA *Draft Report* (Figure 13.5) and *Technical Document* (Figure 13.6).

FIGURE 13.14

References for the EPA's *Draft Report on the Environment 2003*. Readers want to know the resources so they can better understand the findings in the reports. The documentation style provides a consistent description of the author, title, and publication information so readers can locate the information.

Source: From *Draft Report on the Environment 2003*, by Environmental Protection Agency, 2003. Retrieved October 24, 2003, from http://www.epa.gov/indicators/

EPA's Draft Report on the Environment 2003

People

National Oceanic and Atmospheric Administration. NOAA Backgrounder "Working for America's Coasts: An Introduction to the National Ocean Service." January 2002. (February 25, 2003; *http://www.publicaffairs.noaa.gov/grounders/pdf/nos.pdf*).

Pastor, P.N., D.M. Makuc, C. Reuben, H. Xia, et al. *Chartbook on Trends in the Health of Americans. Health, United States, 2002,* Hyattsville, MD: National Center for Health Statistics, 2002.

U.S. Census Bureau. *Statistical Abstract of the United States 2001: The National Data Book.* Washington, DC: U.S. Census Bureau, 2001.

Water Resources

Dahl, T.E. *Status and Trends of Wetlands of the Conterminous United States 1986 to 1997,* Washington, DC: U.S. Department of the Interior, U.S. Fish and Wildlife Service, 2000.

Dahl, T.E. *Wetland Losses in the United States 1780's to 1980's,* Washington, DC: U.S. Department of the Interior, U.S. Fish and Wildlife Service, 1990.

Environment Canada and U.S. Environmental Protection Agency. *The Great Lakes: An Environmental Atlas and Resource Book,* Toronto, Ont: Government of Canada and Chicago, IL: U.S. Environmental Protection Agency, 1995.

U.S. Environmental Protection Agency. *National Water Quality Inventory: 1998 Report to Congress,* EPA-841-R-00-001. Washington, DC: U.S. Environmental Protection Agency, Office of Water, June 2000.

U.S. Geological Survey. *Strategic Directions for the U.S. Geological Survey Ground-Water Resources Program, A Report to Congress,* Reston, VA: U.S. Geological Survey, November 30, 1998.

Energy and Economy

Marlowe, Howard. Assessing The Economic Benefits Of America's Coastal Regions. October 2000. (February 25, 2003; *http://oceanservice.noaa.gov/website/retiredsites/natdia_pdf/13marlowe.pdf*)

U.S. Department of Commerce, Bureau of Economic Analysis. GDP and Other Major NIPA Series, 1929-2002:1. August 2002. (February 25, 2003; *http://www.bea.gov/bea/ARTICLES/2002/08August/0802GDP_&Other_Major_NIPAs..pdf*).

U.S. Department of Energy, Energy Information Administration. Annual Energy Review 2001. December 2002. (February 25, 2003; *http://www.eia.doe.gov/emeu/aer/overview.html*).

U.S. Environmental Protection Agency. *Latest Findings on National Air Quality: 2001 Status and Trends,* EPA-454-K-02-001. Washington, DC: U.S. Environmental Protection Agency, Office of Air Quality Planning and Standards, September 2002.

Appendix E - Sources for Environmental Protection in Context

 E-2

FIGURE 13.15

References for the *EPA's Draft Report on the Environment: Technical Document.* Compare the documentation style and the location of the documents cited in the *Draft Report* (Figure 13.14) and the *Technical Document.*

Source: From *EPA's Draft Report on the Environmental: Technical Document 2003.* Retrieved October 24, 2003, from http://www.epa.gov/indicators/

EPA's Draft Report on the Environment 2003 ■ Technical Document

Cowardin, L.M., V. Carter, F.C. Golet, and E.T. LaRoe. *Classification of Wetlands and Deepwater Habitats of the United States,* FW/OBS-79/31. Washington, DC: U.S. Fish and Wildlife Service, 1979.

Dahl, T.E. *Status and Trends of Wetlands in the Conterminous United States 1986 to 1997,* Washington, DC: U.S. Department of the Interior, U.S. Fish and Wildlife Service, 2000.

Dahl, T.E. *Wetland Losses in the United States 1780's to 1980's.* Washington, DC: U.S. Department of the Interior, Fish and Wildlife Service, 1990.

Dahl, T.E., and C.E. Johnson. Status and *Trends of Wetlands in the Conterminous United States, Mid-1970s to Mid-1980,* Washington, DC: U.S. Department of the Interior, U.S. Fish and Wildlife Service, 1991.

Danielson, T. J. *Wetland Bioassessment Fact Sheets,* EPA 843-F-98-001a-j. Washington, DC: U.S. Environmental Protection Agency, Office of Wetlands, Oceans, and Watersheds, Wetlands Division, July 1998.

Davis, D.G. North American Birds - A Rough Assessment of Wetland Dependency., unpublished. Preparation for a presentation given at the Wetlands, Migratory Birds, and Ecotourism Workshop in Newburyport, Massachusetts, October 24, 2000.

Day Boylan, K. and D.R. MacLean. Linking species loss with wetland loss. *National Wetlands Newsletter* 19 (6). (Nov/Dec 1997).

Diaz, R.J. and R. Rosenberg, Marine benthic hypoxia: a review of its ecological effects and the behavioural responses of benthic macrofauna. *Oceanography and Marine Biology Annual Review* 33: 245-303 (1995).

Duda, A.M. Municipal point source and agricultural nonpoint source contributions to coastal eutrophication. *Water Resources Bulletin* 18: 397-407 (1982).

Environment Canada and U.S. Environmental Protection Agency. *The Great Lakes, An Environmental Atlas and Resource Book,* Toronto, Ont: Government of Canada and Chicago, IL: United States Environmental Protection Agency, Great Lakes National Program Office, 1995.

Fisher, S.G. Stream ecosystems of the western United States. In C.E. Cushing, K.W. Cummings, G.W. Minshall (eds.), *River and Stream Ecosystems, Ecosystems of the World 22,* New York, NY: Elsevier Press, 1995.

Frayer, W.E., T.J. Monahan, D.C. Bowden, and F.A. Graybill. *Status and Trends of Wetlands and Deepwater Habitats in the Conterminous United States, 1950's to 1970's,* Fort Collins, CO: Colorado State University, Department of Forest and Wood Sciences, 1983.

Gilliom, R.J., D.K. Mueller, J.S. Zogorski, and S.J. Ryker. A national look at water quality. *Water Resources Impact* 4: 12-16 (2002).

Houser, L.S. and F.J. Silva. *National Register of Shellfish Production Areas,* PHS Publication No. 1500. Washington, DC: U.S. Department of Health, Education, and Welfare, Public Health Service, Division of Environmental Engineering and Food Protection, Shellfish Sanitation Branch, 1966.

Hoxie, N.J., J.P. Davis, J.M. Vergeront, R.D. Nashold, and K.A. Blair. Cryptosporidiosis - associated mortality following a massive waterborne outbreak in Milwaukee, WI. *American Journal of Public Health* 87 (12): 2032-2035 (1997).

Kaufmann, P.R., P. Levine, E.G. Robison, C. Seeliger, and D.V. Peck. *Surface waters: Quantifying Physical Habitat in Wadeable Streams,* EPA 620-R-99-003. Washington, DC: U.S. Environmental Protection Agency, Office of Research and Development, July 1999.

National Atmospheric Deposition Program, Mercury Deposition Network. Total Mercury Wet Deposition, 2001. 2001. (March 25, 2003; *http://nadp.sws.uiuc.edu/mdn/maps/2001/01MDNdepo.pdf*)

National Atmopheric Deposition Program, National Trends Network. Nitrate ion wet deposition, 2001. 2001. (March 25, 2003; *http://nadp.sws.uiuc.edu/isopleths/maps2001/no3dep.pdf*)

National Atmopheric Deposition Program, National Trends Network. Ammonium ion wet deposition, 2001. 2001. (March 25, 2003; *http://nadp.sws.uiuc.edu/isopleths/maps2001/nh4dep.pdf*)

National Oceanic and Atmospheric Administration. *The 1990 National Shellfish Register of Classified Estuarine Waters,* Rockville, MD: ORCA Strategic Environmental Assessments Division, 1991.

National Oceanic and Atmospheric Administration. *The 1995 National Shellfish Register of Classified Growing Waters,* Silver Spring, MD: ORCA, Office of Ocean Resources Conservation and Assessment, Strategic Environmental Assessments Division, 1997.

National Oceanic and Atmospheric Administration. *Population: distribution, density and growth, NOAA's State of the Coast Report.* Silver Spring, MD. 1998. (February 2003; *http://state-of-coast. noaa.gov/bulletins/html/pop_01/pop.html*).

National Research Council. *Clean Coastal Waters: Understanding and Reducing the Effects of Nutrient Pollution,* Washington, DC: National Academies Press, 2000.

Nixon, S.W. Coastal marine eutrophication: a definition, social causes, and future concerns. *Ophelia* 41: 199-219 (1995).

FIGURE 13.16

Glossary for the EPA's *Draft Report on the Environment 2003*. Definitions and descriptions of terms will help readers understand the report. Many readers will look for clarification of only 2–3 terms, but you need to provide as many terms as needed. You might conduct an informal usability test to make sure you have included the terms needed. Terms in glossaries are presented alphabetically.

Source: From *Draft Report on the Environment 2003*, by Environmental Protection Agency, 2003. Retrieved October 24, 2003, from http://www.epa.gov/indicators/

EPA's Draft Report on the Environment 2003

A complete glossary reference list can be found in EPA's Report on the Environment Technical Document, Appendix E.

A

acid deposition: A complex chemical and atmospheric phenomenon that occurs when emissions of sulfur and nitrogen compounds are transformed by chemical processes in the atmosphere and then deposited on earth in either wet or dry form. The wet forms, often called "acid rain," can fall to earth as rain, snow, or fog. The dry forms are acidic gases or particulate matter.

advisory: A nonregulatory document that communicates risk information to those who may have to make risk management decisions.

aerosol: 1. Small droplets or particles suspended in the atmosphere, typically containing sulfur. They are emitted naturally (e.g., in volcanic eruptions) and as a result of human activities such as burning fossil fuels. 2. The pressurized gas used to propel substances out of a container.

agricultural waste: Byproducts generated by the rearing of animals and the production and harvest of crops or trees. Animal waste, a large component of agricultural waste, includes waste (e.g., feed waste, bedding and litter, and feed-lot and paddock runoff) from livestock, dairy, and other animal-related agricultural and farming practices.

air pollutant: Any substance in air that could, in high enough concentration, harm man, other animals, vegetation, or material. Pollutants may include almost any natural or artificial composition of matter capable of being airborne. It may be in the form of solid particles, liquid droplets, gases, or a combination thereof. Generally, they fall into two main groups: (1) those emitted directly from identifiable sources and (2) those produced in the air by interaction between two or more primary pollutants, or by reaction with normal atmospheric constituents, with or without photoactivation. Exclusive of pollen, fog, and dust, which are of natural origin, about 100 contaminants have been identified. Air pollutants are often grouped in categories for ease in classification; some of he categories are: solids, sulfur compounds, volatile organic chemicals, particulate matter, nitrogen compounds, oxygen compounds, halogen compounds, radioactive compound, and odors.

air pollution: The presence of contaminants or pollutant substances in the air that interfere with human health or welfare or produce other harmful environmental effects.

air quality criteria: The levels of pollution and lengths of exposure above which harmful health and welfare effects may occur.

air quality standards: The level of pollutants prescribed by regulations that are not to be exceeded during a given time in a defined area.

air toxics: Air pollutants that cause or may cause cancer or other serious health effects, such as reproductive effects or birth defects, or adverse environmental and ecological effects. Examples of toxic air pollutants include benzene, found in gasoline; perchloroethylene, emitted from some dry cleaning facilities; and methylene chloride, used as a solvent by a number of industries.

algal blooms: Sudden spurts of algal growth, which can degrade water quality and indicate potentially hazardous changes in local water chemistry.

ambient air: Any unconfined portion of the atmosphere; open air, surrounding air.

ambient air quality standards: See criteria pollutants and National Ambient Air Quality Standards.

anthropogenic: Originating from humans, not naturally occurring.

Appendix D - Glossary of Terms

D-2

FIGURE 13.17

Glossary for *EPA's Draft Report on the Environment: Technical Document*. Compare the content and design of one page from the glossary for the *Draft Report* (Figure 13.16) written for the nontechnical audience with the glossary for scientists, the primary readers of the *Technical Document*.

Source: From *EPA's Draft Report on the Environmental: Technical Document 2003*. Retrieved October 24, 2003, from http://www.epa.gov/indicators/

EPA's Draft Report on the Environment 2003 ■ Technical Document

accretion: The gradual build-up of sediment along the bank or shore of a river or stream.

acid deposition: A complex chemical and atmospheric phenomenon that occurs when emissions of sulfur and nitrogen compounds are transformed by chemical processes in the atmosphere and then deposited on earth in either wet or dry form. The wet forms, often called "acid rain," can fall to earth as rain, snow, or fog. The dry forms are acidic gases or particulate matter.

adipose tissue: Fatty tissue.

advisory: A nonregulatory document that communicates risk information to those who may have to make risk management decisions. (EPA, December 1997)

aerosol: 1. Small droplets or particles suspended in the atmosphere, typically containing sulfur. They are emitted naturally (e.g., in volcanic eruptions) and as a result of human activities (e.g. burning fossil fuels). 2. The pressurized gas used to propel substances out of a container. (EPA, December 1997)

agricultural waste: Byproducts generated by the rearing of animals and the production and harvest of crops or trees. Animal waste, a large component of agricultural waste, includes waste (e.g., feed waste, bedding and litter, and feedlot and paddock runoff) from livestock, dairy, and other animal-related agricultural and farming practices.

air pollutant: Any substance in air that could, in high enough concentration, harm man, other animals, vegetation, or material. Pollutants may include almost any natural or artificial composition of airborne matter capable of being airborne. They may be in the form of solid particles, liquid droplets, gases, or in combination thereof. Generally, they fall into two main groups: (1) those emitted directly from identifiable sources and (2) those produced in the air by interaction between two or more primary pollutants, or by reaction with normal atmospheric constituents, with or without photoactivation. Exclusive of pollen, fog, and dust, which are of natural origin, about 100 contaminants have been identified. Air pollutants are often grouped in categories for ease in classification; some of he categories are: solids, sulfur compounds, volatile organic compounds, particulate matter, nitrogen compounds, oxygen compounds, halogen compounds, radioactive compounds, and odors. (EPA, December 1997)

air pollution: The presence of contaminants or pollutant substances in the air that interfere with human health or welfare or produce other harmful environmental effects. (EPA, December 1997)

air quality criteria: The levels of pollution and lengths of exposure above which harmful health and welfare effects may occur. (EPA, December 1997)

air quality standards: The level of pollutants prescribed by regulations that are not to be exceeded during a given time in a defined area. (EPA, December 1997)

air toxics: Air pollutants that cause or may cause cancer or other serious health effects, such as reproductive effects or birth defects, or adverse environmental and ecological effects. Examples of toxic air pollutants include benzene, found in gasoline; perchloroethylene, emitted from some dry cleaning facilities; and methylene chloride, used as a solvent by a number of industries.

algal blooms: Sudden spurts of algal growth, which can degrade water quality and indicate potentially hazardous changes in local water chemistry. (EPA, December 1997)

ambient air: Any unconfined portion of the atmosphere; open air, surrounding air. (EPA, December 1997)

ambient air quality standards: See *criteria pollutants* and *National Ambient Air Quality Standards*.

animal waste: Byproducts that result from livestock, diary, and other animal-related agricultural practices.

anthropogenic: Originating from humans, not naturally occurring. (EPA, MAIA, August 2002)

aquatic ecosystems: Salt water or fresh water ecosystems, includes rivers, streams, lakes, wetlands, estuaries and coral reefs.

aquifer: An underground geological formation, or group of formations, containing water; source of ground water for wells and springs. (USGS, 1996)

arsenic: A silvery, nonmetallic element that occurs naturally in rocks and soil, water, air, and plants and animals. It can be released into the environment through natural activities such as volcanic action, erosion of rocks, and forest fires or through human actions. Approximately 90 percent of industrial arsenic in the U.S. is used as a wood preservative, but arsenic is also used in paints, dyes, metals, drugs, soaps, and semiconductors. Agricultural applications (used in rodent poisons and some herbicides), mining, and smelting also contribute to arsenic releases in the environment. It is a known human carcinogen.

arteriosclerosis: Hardening of the arteries.

asbestos: Naturally occurring strong, flexible fibers that can be separated into thin threads and woven. These fibers resist heat and

D-2   Glossary of Terms   Appendix D

**PLANNING AND REVISING CHECKLIST:
FORMAL ELEMENTS OF WORKPLACE REPORTS**

Think about the following while planning and revising formal elements of reports.

Planning

- What is the purpose of the report? If it is to be used as a reference work, does it have a detailed table of contents and plenty of headings and subheadings?

- What formal elements are appropriate for the report?

- Is a cover required?

- Does the report require a letter or memo of transmittal or a preface?

- Is an abstract required or preferred?

- What is the format for headings and subheadings?

- What, if any, material will be placed in an appendix?

Revision

- Are the required elements present?

- Is the overall design attractive, effective, and consistent?

- Do the entries in the table of contents agree with the headings?

- Do the lists of figure and table captions agree with the captions and page numbers of the visuals?

- Does the report provide direct access to information through a table of contents, headings and subheadings, and other cues?

- Are the elements mechanically correct, consistent, and accurately typed?

Suggestions for Applying Your Knowledge

Individual Activity

At the end of Chapter 1, "The Process of Workplace Communication," we suggest that you start gathering examples of workplace writing. Examine one of the more formal, but relatively brief, examples you have collected, and write a report for your instructor and classmates that explains the following:

- what type of report it is

- its intended audience

- what features aid or hinder legibility

- what features provide clues to its organization

- what formal elements it contains

- correctness of spelling, grammar, and punctuation

Evaluate what the writer has done well. What additional strategies and techniques were available that the writer could have used?

Collaborative Activity/Multicultural Activity

Working in teams, go to the U.S. government portal site firstgov.gov (see Figure 19.5 on page P in the second color insert) or to another country's portal site (for example, Canada's www.canada.gc.ca). Locate a government report. Prepare an informal oral presentation to show class members the key parts of the report, where it follows the guidelines presented in this chapter, and where it is different.

Recommendation Reports

frequent task for people in the workplace is reporting and explaining recommendations and decisions. Such recommendations and decisions, usually growing out of a problem-solving situation, must be explained and justified. The resulting reports present the results using practical logic. Before we get to the reports themselves, pause for a moment and think about what we mean by practical logic.

Practical Logic

You may or may not have taken a course in formal logic, but you have been practicing practical logic and coming to decisions since you were a child. When you stood before a candy counter weighing the merits of buying four licorice sticks for $1.00 against buying five jawbreakers, also for $1.00, you were analyzing a problem. You were comparing and contrasting alternatives. You were doing a cost analysis: 4 for $1.00 versus 5 for $1.00. You remembered the flavor of the two candies and realized that the licorice in your estimation was superior. You weighed quantity versus quality. You reached a series of conclusions:

- The jawbreakers were cheaper.

- Each piece of candy lasted 10 minutes.

- The jawbreakers would give you 50 minutes of pleasure.

- The licorice would give you 40 minutes of pleasure.

- However, the flavor of the licorice was superior.

- For you, 40 minutes of superior pleasure were better than 50 minutes of inferior pleasure.

- Therefore, for you, the licorice sticks were a better buy.

If you proceeded to buy the licorice, you were backing your conclusions with a decision.

As you grew older, your analyses became bigger and more complicated. Perhaps you wanted to buy a bicycle. You considered cost, naturally. You also considered the comparative weights of bicycles. You compared 10-speed bikes against 12-speed bikes. You made these comparisons not in an abstract way but by considering them against your own needs. If you were a serious biker who planned long trips through hilly country, a lighter, expensive 12-speed might be the answer. On the other hand, if you were an occasional bike rider who simply wanted to combine some exercise with transportation around the flat streets of town, you probably would have chosen a heavier, less expensive, 10-speed bike.

In such analyses, you were following the processes of induction and deduction that we describe for you on pages 67–69. You were drawing on information that you already possessed or that was easily obtainable. Analyses you will conduct in the workplace are different in degree but not in kind. That is, the process will be more complex and involve more information but will still draw on essentially the same practical logic you have frequently used. We will look at the process in more detail. With some variations, practical logic is likely to follow a course similar to this:

- Defining the problem

- Creating solutions

- Testing solutions

- Choosing a solution

Defining the Problem

A problem can be either a question or a situation. In the candy and bike examples, the problem is a question: Should I buy licorice sticks or jawbreakers? What sort of bike should I buy?

A problem situation is always a situation that deviates from the norm. For example, you are cruising smoothly down an interstate highway. Your car is performing in its normal manner. Suddenly, you hear a loud whooshing sound and see clouds of steam pouring out through the hood. You have a problem.

In defining the problem, the approach is approximately the same whether you are dealing with a question or a situation. In defining a problem, you must both relate the problem to its environment and break the problem down into its components. You must be clear-eyed about your objectives in solving the problem. Finally, you must recognize any limitations set upon you in solving the problem. We will illustrate these points by using a problem that a student, Scott Pahl, dealt with.[1]

Scott looked at a problem in the Minnesota Department of Transportation. In the past few years, the department's grass-mowing budget has been getting out of hand. In a recent year, mowing costs totaled almost $25 million. What is to be done?

Relating to the Surrounding Environment

Where does grass mowing fit into the total picture of the department's responsibilities? As big a chore as mowing the grass on the state's highways is, it is only one of the department's many responsibilities. It is a small part of a budget that exceeds $600 million. Considerably more important to the state

---

[1]All excerpts are from "The Feasibility of Using *SlowGrowth* Plant Growth Regulator Instead of Mowing to Maintain Grassy Areas Along Minnesota's Highways," an unpublished student report, printed with the permission of Scott Pahl, the author. We have modified the report slightly to update the information and to emphasize the points we want to make about recommendation reports.

are the maintenance of existing highways and the construction of new ones. Although the citizens of the state expect the grassy areas near their roads to be kept neat, they do not want money taken away from road building and maintenance to achieve this neatness. Solving the grass-mowing problem is important, but it is not a problem of crisis proportions.

In this manner, Scott looked at the grass-mowing problem in relation to the surrounding environment of the department's other tasks and problems. Any problem must be seen in proper perspective before you begin seeking its solution. Consider again the loud whooshing sound coming from your car. If that occurred at 3:00 a.m. on a lonely country road, it would be a totally different problem than if it occurred at 3:00 p.m. at a spot 100 feet from a full-service gas station.

Breaking Down the Problem

In defining your problem be specific about its elements. What are its components? If you do not analyze your problem carefully at the beginning, you will find yourself out of your depth when you try to find a solution. In analyzing your problem, you must look beneath the surface problem—high costs in Scott's problem—and search for its causes. The solution almost certainly will attack these subproblems and not the surface problem. In breaking down your problem, you will often find valuable the journalist's questions of *who*, *what*, *when*, *where*, *why*, and *how*. Using these questions, Scott came up with such facts as these:

- *Mowing season:* 15 May to 1 October

- *Total miles mowed:* 9,910 miles, broken down into metro areas, the interstate system, and the nonmetro state highways

- *Number of mowings per season:* 10 in metro areas, 6 on interstates, 3 on state highways

- *Cost:* $24,855,000 in 2004. Costs include wages, equipment operation and maintenance, equipment replacement, storage, worker's compensation, and insurance.

- *Associated problems:* The work is tedious and dangerous. Mowers tip over on steep slopes; motorists throw things at the mower operators. Every year workers are seriously injured, and over the years several have been killed.

The U.S. Geological Survey Web site is an excellent source for maps: http://ask.usgs.gov/maps.html

Scott found much more, but you get the idea. Look at all the possible causal factors in your problem. Make a list of related problems: for example, the danger to the mower operators. As you examine these factors, use the software on your computer to record your findings and help you to analyze the information. For example, you might use a spreadsheet program to develop the cost analysis or find a map on the World Wide Web that shows the area affected by the mowing. The more you document early, the better off you will be later.

Setting Objectives

Knowing your objectives is an important key to solving the problem. The solution to our bicycle-choosing problem above rests on the objectives. The objective of cross-country travel calls for a different solution from the objective of riding a few miles to work each day. You must be absolutely clear-eyed about what you want as the outcome of the solution. You should have one major objective. You may have other objectives of lesser importance. State them all clearly, preferably in writing. Know the priority you set on each.

Scott's major objective was clear: Lower the cost of grass management on the state's highways. He had lesser objectives as well, including lowering the operators' accident rate and freeing the operators for other kinds of maintenance work.

Knowing the Limitations

Almost always, there are limitations you must observe in solving a problem. They might include available funds and technology, people's attitudes, environmental problems, time, and so forth. One test for any solution is that it can be accomplished within the limitations.

The limitations in the grass-maintenance problem were these:

- Citizens expected grass bordering the highways to be maintained neatly.

- Any solution had to be ecologically safe.

Creating Solutions

Creating solutions and the next step, testing solutions, are understandably closely related. Given the speed with which the human mind makes connections, it is likely that most of us, at least some of the time, test a solution almost as quickly as we form it in our minds. However, we separate the steps here for two reasons. First, we want to suggest that if you make snap decisions about solutions, you may overlook the solution that would ultimately be best. Second, if you are seeking solutions in a group, you may do better if the group creates solutions without the pressure of immediately testing them. By doing so, group members can present solutions, even silly-sounding ones, without fear of someone immediately jumping on their ideas. It is not at all unusual for a solution that at first glimpse seems ridiculous to prove to be the best one.

Obviously, creating solutions calls for the problem solver to possess knowledge relevant to the problem. Someone with no knowledge in the appropriate subject matter will have difficulty in forming solutions. For example, a problem solver who did not know about the various kinds of bikes available would be in no position to frame an answer to the question, "What bike should I buy?" If you lack the needed knowledge from your education and experience, you must seek it as part of the problem-solving process. If you want to buy a bike, you might first go to the manufacturers' Web sites to read about the bikes, or you might check with friends to see what bikes they have and ask to ride them, after which you would go to the bike shop with questions to ask. As you will see, Scott's knowledge as an agronomy student enabled him to come up with the solution that he ultimately chose.

Wherever your knowledge comes from, begin creating solutions. Write down all your ideas, even the outlandish ones. Scott's possible solutions were these:

- Leave the situation as he found it.

- Stop mowing the grass.

- Mow the grass at less-frequent intervals.

- Pave over some or all of the grassed areas.

- Stop the grass from growing.

When he was satisfied that he had thought of all the possible solutions, Scott was ready to test them.

In the workplace, you will rarely work alone on a problem. You may come up with a list of possible solutions, but you will meet with others and probably modify some of the solutions and more than likely add to the list. If you find yourself working alone on a problem, seek out the advice of others. Scott interviewed members of the department of transportation and the sales representative from AgriHighway. Almost everyone likes to talk about his or her work.

One of your authors recently had the responsibility of building a computer classroom. After identifying 10 to 12 specific questions about the computers to buy and how to set up the environment, she met with seven other faculty members on campus responsible for computer classrooms. She came back with suggestions that made setting up the new classroom easier. She learned about the best way to give every workstation access to sound without having a room full of computers with speakers, how to add locks to each computer, and how to ensure a stable desktop environment with an image-creating software program.

Testing Solutions

Solutions may be tested logically and empirically. To test a solution logically, you will work with the objectives and limitations you have already stated. These objectives and limitations lead you to the criteria—the standards of judgment—you will use to measure the effectiveness of the proposed solutions. In the bike example, consider the major objective as buying a bike suitable for cross-country travel. Assume a cost limitation of $1,000. Such an objective and limitation might lead to these criteria:

The bike should

- be lightweight

- have gearing suitable for long hills

- have an effective braking system

- be sturdy and easily maintained

- not cost more than $1,000

Think your criteria through carefully. Without proper standards of comparison, you will be unable to test your solutions. You should also set priorities for your criteria. Which of the preceding criteria is the most important? It may well be the $1,000 limitation. If that is the case, no matter how lightweight a bike is and how effective its gearing system, if it costs more than $1,000 it will not be considered.

Once the criteria are set, testing the solution becomes fairly simple. You gather information on the relevant attributes of bikes in the below-$1,000 range. You compare their weights, gearing systems, and so forth. The bike that best meets the criteria will emerge as the choice.

In Scott's grass-management problem, his objectives and limitations led him to several criteria. A proposed solution had to

- lower the exposure of workers to danger and free them for other jobs

- lower the cost of grass management

- be ecologically safe

- be aesthetically pleasing

His first priority was lowering the cost. However, the solution had to meet the other criteria to be seriously considered. Scott was then ready to examine his solutions against his criteria:

- Leaving the situation as it was, although it met all the lesser criteria, obviously did not lower the cost or reduce the exposure of workers to danger.

- Stopping the grass mowing lowered the cost but would not be aesthetically pleasing.

- Mowing the grass at less-frequent intervals lowered the cost but also failed the aesthetic test.

- Paving all the grass areas was too expensive to consider and would not be aesthetically pleasing.

- Stopping the grass from growing was possible. Scott was an agronomy student and knew of a product manufactured by the AgriHighway Company, *SlowGrowth*, that would retard grass growth. He examined this solution thoroughly and found that it passed all his criteria. It lowered costs. It left the grass in good enough condition to be aesthetically pleasing. It was ecologically safe. The necessary spraying took much less time than the mowing; therefore, workers would be less exposed to danger and would be free for other work.

empirical testing

Logically, Scott had his solution. He also considered empirical testing. By empirical testing, we mean testing a solution's effectiveness through either physical means or social scientific means such as polls or questionnaires. For example, the directions that come with a carpet-cleaning fluid tell you to test the fluid in some inconspicuous place. If the cleaner removes all the color from your carpet under the couch, you will know not to use it on the rest of the carpet. That is the empirical physical test. If your solution might affect people, perhaps the workers in some section of a plant, a questionnaire polling their attitudes toward the change might be advisable. This would be an empirical social scientific test. You systematically ask a group of people the same questions and analyze their answers.

Choosing a Solution

Scott knew that *SlowGrowth* had been empirically tested by AgriHighway and had proven effective. That fact had entered into his logical testing. However, he was not prepared to recommend on the strength of AgriHighway's testing that the state spray the grass along 9,910 miles of highway. Obviously, further large-scale testing was called for. Scott decided that his recommendation would be that the department conduct a major test of *SlowGrowth* on several hundred miles of state highway. Furthermore, the testing should be in several spots in the state. Parts of the state are warmer and drier than others, and cities have microclimates of their own, different from the nearby suburbs and rural areas. If the testing proved successful, the state could consider a grass-management program that included the use of *SlowGrowth*.

Scott had arrived at his recommendation. It was time for him to report it.

Reporting the Solution

If you have followed a reasoning process similar to the one just described, most of your work has been done when it is time for you to write your report. You have defined your problem. You know what solutions you have seriously considered and the criteria you have used to compare them. You know your conclusions and the recommendations they lead to. Your tasks now are to plan the organization and format of your report and to write it so that it is understandable and acceptable to your readers. Before beginning, however, you would be wise to think about your objective and your audience.

In Scott's case, his objective was clear: to persuade his audience that his proposed solution was the appropriate one. His primary audience was well defined. It consisted of several department of transportation managers, a neutral if somewhat skeptical audience. They were engineers by education and experience. They were an educated audience who, at the most, might need a few agronomic concepts explained. Secondary readers might be members of citizen groups, particularly those concerned about ecological effects, or OSHA or union representatives concerned about the safety of workers.

Review Chapters 3 and 4 for help with setting up your recommendations and persuading your audience. Chapters 5, 6, and 7 suggest ways to design and present the text and visuals so that the reader can easily review the information

As you will see, Scott kept his objective and readers in mind as he planned and wrote his report. For example, he knew that his report would have to provide specific information to support his recommendation. He would provide AgriHighway's test results; he would include a spreadsheet that showed the comparison of costs. The order in which he presents the information and how he presents the information (in bulleted lists or in paragraphs, for example) will influence what information the readers gather from his report.

Like other workplace documents, recommendation reports have similar features. A complete recommendation report may consist of all of the following:

Prefatory Elements	Letter of Transmittal
	Title Page
	Table of Contents
	List of Illustrations
Main Elements	Introduction
	Body
	Summary and Conclusions
	Recommendations
Supplemental Elements	List of References
	Appendix

In this chapter, we discuss only the introduction, body, summary and conclusions, and recommendations. For the other parts we refer you to Chapter 13, "Principles of Workplace Reports," where they are thoroughly discussed. Keep in mind that you will follow the conventions established by the company or organization you work for. Your report may be a 3- to 5-page memo without a list of references or an appendix, or it may be a 300-page report, presented in a 3-ring binder with a computer-generated slideshow summarizing the key points and also available on your organization's Web site in HTML and PDF format. You must adapt your presentation to meet the purpose of the report, to meet the needs of the audience, and to provide the information needed.

Introduction

In describing a typical introduction in Chapter 13, we tell you to explain your subject, purpose, scope, and plan to your readers. The introduction to a recommendation report follows this basic format. In a recommendation report, your subject is the problem you are working with. Your purpose is to present your solution and show how you have arrived at it. Your scope includes the definition of the problem, the solution or solutions you are considering, the evaluation of the solutions, your conclusions, and your recommendations. Your plan is how you intend to present your material. Scott's introduction demonstrates all the basic parts of a successful introduction.

Introduction

Last year, the Department of Transportation spent almost $25 million, out of a total budget of slightly over $600 million, on mowing the grass areas along the state's highways. This grass mowing is a major summertime chore for state highway crews. In the struggle to keep the many miles of highway medians, ditches, and embankments mowed, other important projects are delayed, and limited budgets are depleted.

Under contract to the Department, I studied the problem. I considered four possible solutions:

- Leaving the situation as is.
- Lowering the frequency of mowing or stopping it altogether.
- Paving over the grass.
- Retarding the growth of the grass.

The major criteria used to evaluate the solutions were that the acceptable solution had to lower the cost of grass management, be aesthetically pleasing, and be ecologically safe. Lesser criteria were lowering the exposure of the workers to danger and freeing them for other jobs.

Only the solution of retarding the growth of the grass met all the criteria. Therefore, it is the only one considered in this report.

Immediately following this introduction, I present a summary of my data and major conclusions followed by my recommendations. Following my recommendations are three sections in which I describe the problem fully, present a solution to it, and evaluate the solution.

We draw your attention to several things in this introduction. First of all, Scott disposes of all his solutions but one. This is advisable only when one solution clearly stands out as the best. When the solutions are more balanced, you may have to carry over a consideration of the alternative solutions to the body. We will discuss that further in a moment. Second, Scott's plan reveals that he has chosen what is frequently called an *executive format* for his report. That is, he presents his summary, conclusions, and recommendations *before* he presents the body of his report. We discuss the rationale for doing so when we discuss the summary and conclusions.

Body

The body of your recommendation report should display your reasoning in enough detail to allow your readers to judge for themselves if your analysis has been adequate. You should in your report, as in your reasoning, describe the problem, present your solution or solutions, and evaluate them. With only one solution, your organization might look like this:

- Definition of problem

- Presentation of solution

- Evaluation of solution by criteria

If the problem can be simply defined, that task may sometimes be done in the introduction. In that case, the body would consist of only the last two items on the list: presenting and evaluating solutions.

When you have two or more solutions to evaluate, your organization will be slightly more complicated:

1. Definition of problem

2. Presentation of solutions

3. Evaluation of solutions

   a. Criterion A

      i. Explanation of criterion A

      ii. Evaluation of solutions 1 and 2

   b. Criterion B

      i. Explanation of criterion B

      ii. Evaluation of solutions 1 and 2

(And so forth.)

You can also organize the evaluation of solutions by solution rather than by criteria, in this manner:

1. Definition of problem

2. Explanation of criteria

3. Solution 1

   a. Presentation of solution 1

   b. Evaluation by criteria

4. Solution 2

   a. Presentation of solution 2

   b. Evaluation by criteria

We find that most people can demonstrate the differences among their solutions more sharply when they organize by criteria. No matter which plan you choose, be sure both criteria and solutions are carefully explained before you begin your evaluation. Scott's table of contents, reproduced in Figure 14.1, illustrates how he used the general plans we have shown you for his purposes.

In **defining his problem**, Scott discusses the existing mowing program, its costs, and its associated problems. Here is Scott's description of the mowing program:

The Mowing Program

The state normally starts its mowing season May 15, about one month after the grass be-gins to green up, and ends it on October 1. The state's mowing responsibilities can be di-vided into three major groups of roads: the metro area roads, the nonmetro interstate highways, and the nonmetro highways. The crews attempt to mow the metro highways every 2 weeks. Some metro areas will be mowed 10 times during a season. The areas along the nonmetro interstates are mowed, on the average, 6 times per season. The non-metro highways receive 3 mowings per season.

In **presenting his solution**, Scott begins with a clearly stated overview of his solution to the grass management problem:

SlowGrowth Grass-Management Program

SlowGrowth, a plant-growth regulator, developed and released by the AgriHighway Company, shows a good deal of promise in the area of chemically-assisted turf grass

FIGURE 14.1.
Table of contents. The headings in the table of contents match the headings in the report in wording and in typeface. You want to show the reader the hierarchy of information in your report and help the reader easily locate the information.

Table of Contents

management. *SlowGrowth* works by suppressing cool-season grasses' vegetative and re-productive development. The plants remain a healthy, normal green color. With proper application, grass growth can be suppressed for up to eight weeks, reducing the need to mow.

The overview allows the readers to grasp the solution in its entirety before they are hit with the details. It is a good technique. Scott follows the overview with technical descriptions of *SlowGrowth*'s chemistry and mode of action. He concludes by describing how *SlowGrowth* would be applied.

In describing your solution, you must be careful not to provide too much detail. Executives, the usual readers of recommendation reports, are unlikely to want the same level of detail that someone implementing the solution would need. In other words, executives would not need a full set of instructions, but they would need enough detail to understand how the solution will work. As you construct your report, be careful to use language that your readers can understand. Define any technical terms that you must use and your readers are unlikely to know. Here is how Scott explained the application of *SlowGrowth*:

Proper Application

The product should be applied after the grass greens up and is actively growing but before the seedheads start to emerge. This normally occurs in late April. Applied in this manner, *SlowGrowth* will give vegetative and reproductive growth suppression for up to 8 weeks.

In situations in which full-season grass suppression is needed, *SlowGrowth* may be applied more than once per season. To avoid plant injury, there should be a 6-week wait between applications.

As you will see when we discuss the summary and conclusions section, Scott included material useful in supporting his conclusions.

In **evaluating his solution**, Scott applies his criteria of cost, aesthetics, ecological safety, and solution of associated problems. Here is a piece of his evaluation of the ecological safety of *SlowGrowth*:

Ecological Safety

SlowGrowth is a safe compound. It is nonirritating to either whole or abraded skin and only slightly irritating to eyes. Its toxicity to fish and birds is quite low. However, it should not be sprayed on lakes or streams, and animals should not be allowed to graze on treated areas. As with any chemical, care should be taken to avoid prolonged or unnecessary contact with *SlowGrowth*.

Mefluidide, the chief component of *SlowGrowth*, is unstable in the soil, with a half-life of only 2 days. It is rapidly broken down by soil microbes. Therefore, it will not build up in the soil or cause serious problems for birds or other wildlife.

In evaluating your solution, you are using practical logic to make your argument. You need not show your reasoning in every detail, but you must show enough so that readers can judge the validity of your argument. Also, if your solution involves any risks, you should draw them to your readers' attention. They will need to weigh them in their decisions. Scott, for example, pointed out that, despite *SlowGrowth*'s safety, animals should not graze on grass treated with it. Also be careful to point out so-whats to your readers as Scott has done in his statement, "Therefore, it will not build up in the soil or cause serious problems for birds or other wildlife."

Summary and Conclusions

overview of the report

The summary and conclusions section is often the only part of the report many readers read. Therefore, it must be well done. Also, most of the time, executive readers will find the summary and conclusions and read them before they read anything else in the report. When read in this sequence, the summary and conclusions become the overview of the report that helps readers understand the report. Furthermore, this section helps the readers to select those parts of the report they may wish to read more thoroughly.

For example, an executive reader might be satisfied with Scott's summary statements concerning ecological safety. Consequently, she might not bother to read the body section, where greater detail about ecological safety can be found. On the other hand, she might doubt Scott's cost figures and choose to read the section on cost with great care. Many reports place summaries, conclusions, and recommendations immediately following the introduction on the principle that if executives are likely to read them early anyway, these parts will serve best up front where they are easily found. As you see in Scott's table of contents, Figure 14.1, that is the format he chose.

To write a good summary, you must read through your report body, selecting those key facts that have led you to your conclusions. Generally, such key facts will be surrounded by supporting details. To summarize, you leave out the details and report only the key facts. Do not merely pile up facts in a random way. Rather, place facts together in a context that allows you, through induction and deduction, to demonstrate how you reached your conclusions. Figure 14.2 illustrates the sequence that leads you from facts through conclusions to recommendations. We can illustrate these principles by comparing the material in several sections of Scott's reports with his use of the same material in his summary and conclusions.

In his evaluation, Scott showed some of his cost calculations:

> The per-gallon cost of *SlowGrowth* is $79.00. At the recommended application rate of 1.5 pints per acre, the chemical costs per acre would be $14.80. To this must be added the average application cost of $5.00 per acre, for a total cost per acre of $19.80. By comparison, mowing costs, on average, are $13.00 per acre for each mowing. One mowing costs less than one application, but two mowings at a total cost of $26.00 exceed the cost of the application by $6.20.

While describing the state's grass-mowing program, Scott described the different number of mowings used in the state, depending on the type and location of the highway. In his section on the solution, Scott, in discussing the application of *SlowGrowth*, said that one application would retard grass growth for up to eight weeks. Now read through Scott's summary and conclusions, and see how these key facts and others are condensed and properly

FIGURE 14.2
Logic sequence.

SUMMARY
Key facts drawn together in a related context
↓
CONCLUSIONS
The implications of the facts—the *so-whats*
↓
RECOMMENDATIONS
The actions that follow as a result of the conclusions

related to one another, allowing Scott to reach his conclusions and state them in a convincing way.

Summary and Conclusion

The state's current highway grass-management program is costly at $24,855,000 a year. It is also dangerous. Every year workers mowing grass are injured, and fatalities have occurred. A possible solution to this problem of high costs and injuries is the use of *SlowGrowth*, a plant-growth regulator manufactured by the AgriHighway Company. A single application of *SlowGrowth* retards the growth of grass for up to 8 weeks. Although its growth is retarded, the grass retains its natural healthy green color. *SlowGrowth* is ecologically safe. It is noncorrosive to machinery and, if used properly, nontoxic to human beings and wildlife. However, the manufacturer does recommend that animals not be allowed to graze on grass sprayed with *SlowGrowth*. *SlowGrowth* breaks down quickly in the soil, having a half-life of only 2 days. Because *SlowGrowth* is rapidly broken down by soil microbes, it will not build up in the soil and cause serious problems for wildlife.

A comparison of the costs involved in mowing and in applying *SlowGrowth* shows that a grass-management program using *SlowGrowth* can be worked out that will lower costs. Currently, the mowing season runs from May 15 to October 1. During that time, the metro roadways are mowed, on average, 10 times, nonmetro interstates 6 times, and nonmetro highways 3 times. Each mowing costs, on average, $13.00 per acre. The comparable cost for each *SlowGrowth* application is $19.80 per acre. The break-even point in cost for using *SlowGrowth* thus comes between the first and second mowing. Given the 8-week period of retardation following each *SlowGrowth* application, two applications—one before the spring grass-growing season and one before the late summer grass-growing season—would be cost effective on the metro and interstate areas. For the highway areas, a single *SlowGrowth* application in early spring coupled with a fall mowing would be the most cost effective. Because the combined number of mowings and applications under the *SlowGrowth* program would be considerably lower than under the current all-mowing program, the workers' exposure to danger would be greatly reduced, and they would be free for other maintenance work.

AgriHighway Company's testing of *SlowGrowth* has been thorough, but it would seem prudent for the Department to run a series of tests of its own before launching a statewide program. Climatic conditions vary throughout the state. Also, metro areas have microclimates different from surrounding areas. Therefore, any testing should include both metro and nonmetro areas and enough locations in the state to test *SlowGrowth*'s performance under the state's various climatic conditions.

Notice that Scott's final conclusions form a bridge to the recommendations that follow. In fact, your conclusions should always be written so that the reader can anticipate the recommendations. The recommendation section of a report is no place for surprises.

Recommendations

Recommendations are action steps. The recommendation section is the place in your report where you tell the readers what they *ought* to do. (If you are writing a decision report rather than a recommendation report, this is the place where you tell your readers what is going to be done.) The recommendation section should be short. Your reasoning has been displayed elsewhere in the body and in the summary and conclusions. You need not repeat any of it in the recommendations. Confine yourself to action statements.

The first recommendation should always answer the key question of the problem. What is the solution to the problem, the answer to the chief question asked? Later recommendations, if any, will supplement the first recommendation and show how it should be implemented. In our bicycle example, the first and only recommendation might be simply, "Buy Brand-X bicycle." In Scott's report, the recommendation section is necessarily more complex, but it demonstrates the principles stated here.

Recommendations

1. The Department of Transportation should begin a statewide test on the state's highways of the effectiveness of AgriHighway's *SlowGrowth* in grass management.
2. The testing should be conducted in both metro and nonmetro areas. Enough test areas should be chosen to reflect the varied climatic conditions in the state.
3. The test grass-management program should be as follows:
   a. Apply *SlowGrowth* twice per season, spring and late summer, on interstate and metro right-of-ways.
   b. Apply *SlowGrowth* once in the spring on nonmetro highway right-of-ways, and follow with a late-summer mowing.

When the recommendations are stated, your report is done. You have studied your problem, found a solution for it, and reported both your reasoning and your solution.

Recommendation Reports as Correspondence

Recommendation reports that do not exceed 4 or 5 pages are frequently given a letter or memo format. In Figure 14.3, a report by Donna Smith

FIGURE 14.3

Recommendation reports may be presented in a memo format. You are recording the information for others to read once and make a decision.

Date: 20 March 2005

To: Mary A. Young
              Director
              Tribble Residence Hall

From: Donna Smith *D.S.*
              Committee Chair
              Tribble Hall Improvements Committee

Subject: Recommendation for the Purchase of 200 Study Lamps for
              Tribble Residence Hall

At your request the Tribble Hall Improvements Committee investigated the purchase of two study lamps each for the 100 student rooms in the Tribble Residence Hall. The available ceiling lighting in the rooms is insufficient for studying, and no lamps are provided. In this report, I explain the criteria used by the Committee in this investigation, describe our method of gathering information about the lamps, and present our findings followed by our comparison of the lamps and our recommendations.

Features Compared

You set a price limitation on the lamps of $25 each. Another major criterion was that the lamps could be used at night by one roommate without disturbing the other roommate. We did not consider halogen lamps. The university has banned halogen lamps from the campus because of the fire hazard. For this reason, only lamps using high-intensity bulbs were considered.

A high-intensity bulb is an incandescent bulb that gives a highly concentrated light over a small area, thus lessening the effect on anyone outside the circle of its light. High-intensity bulbs have an additional advantage of long life and, therefore, require fewer replacement bulbs than regular incandescent bulbs.

The Committee found several high-intensity lamps within the $25 limit and compared them by the following criteria, arranged in order of priority:

1. *Size*—to fit available space, lamps must be 12 inches or less in height, and lamps with folding arms must have a reach of 20 inches or less.

2. *Price*—low price (under $25) is an important consideration.

FIGURE 14.3
(continued)

Page 2
Mary A. Young
20 March 2005

> 3. *Availability of special features*—features such as a high/low switch and a swivel
>   shade are desirable.

Stores Visited

The Committee visited two major office supply stores (The Carson Company and
Warner's Office Center), two major discount stores (K-Mart and Walmart), two
bookstores (Varsity Bookstore and Anderson's Books), and two merchandise warehouses
(Best Products and Service Merchandise).

The office supply stores, bookstores, and discount stores did not have high-intensity
lamps within the price limitation. Best Products and Service Merchandise had the best
selection within the price limitation. Committee members talked to sales representatives
about special features, reviewed catalogs, and examined the lamps. We also asked about
a special price for the purchase of 200 lamps.

Comparison of the Lamps

Store	Model	Unit Price[a]	Total Price[a]	Special Features
Best Products	Ledu	$14.97	$2994	• all metal
	Mobilite	9.99[b]	1998	• all metal • folding arm • high/low switch • swivel shade
Service Merchandise	Mighty Mite	9.92	1984	• all metal • folding arm • high/low switch
	Tensor Asteroid	19.97	3994	• all metal (brass) • cool inner reflector • folding arm

[a]Price does not include sales tax.
[b]Mobilite's regular unit price is $14.93. However, Best Products will offer a special
unit price of $9.99 for the purchase of 200 lamps.

Because all lamps compared met the size criterion, the Committee compared special
features available against price. As shown in the table, all the possible lamps have several
special features. The cool inner reflector (the inner wall of the shade) absorbs heat and
keeps the shade from getting hot. Folding arms and swivel shades give versatility to
setting the angle of the lamp and its distance from the desk top. The advantage of a

FIGURE 14.3
(continued)

Page 3
Mary A. Young
20 March 2005

high/low switch is that the high setting can be used for studying and the low setting for lighting the room just enough to move around without bothering a sleeping roommate.

The Mobilite has the greatest number of special features for the price. While it does not have the brass finish and cool inner reflector of the Tensor Asteroid, the advantage of its low price and high/low switch outweigh the disadvantages of not having these features.

Recommendation

The committee recommends the purchase of the Mobilite from Best Products.

illustrates a recommendation report written as a memo. Donna organized her report using the comparison mode of argument. Her introduction establishes the purpose, occasion, and plan of the report. She establishes her criteria and puts them in priority order. She takes time to define a term, *high-intensity bulb*, that her reader will need.

After describing the committee's investigation, she gives the key findings in a table. Drawing on the table, she presents her conclusions and recommendation. Although the memo format does not call for a table of contents, she provides enough headings to guide the reader through the report. All in all, the report is an excellent example of a short recommendation report.

✓ PLANNING AND REVISING CHECKLIST: RECOMMENDATION REPORTS

You and members of your team should think about the following as you plan and revise a recommendation report.

Planning

Recommendation reports report the solutions to problems. You must therefore begin by defining the problem, creating solutions for it, testing the solutions, and choosing a solution. In doing so, you will create a good deal of information. After you have reached your conclusions and recommendations, you must report them and, as well, report as much of your reasoning as is necessary to be credible to your readers.

Defining the Problem

- Describe the problem.
- Describe the components of the problem.
- Relate the problem to the surrounding environment.
- State your objectives in solving the problem.
- List any limitations you have in solving the problem.

Creating Solutions

- State as many solutions to the problem as you can. Brainstorm; put down every solution that occurs to you.
- Inventory your information. Do you have enough to solve the problem? If not, where can you get the needed information?

Testing Solutions

- Using what you know about your objectives and limitations, form criteria to use in testing your solutions.
- If appropriate, set priorities for your criteria.
- Test your solutions against your criteria.
- Conduct any available and appropriate empirical tests on your solutions.

Choosing a Solution

- Step back from the testing and review the results.
- On the basis of your reasoning and testing, choose the best solution.

Planning the Report

- Who are the readers of your report?

- What is their purpose in reading it?

- Will they have problems with any of the technical vocabulary or concepts involved?

- Are they likely to want a fully detailed report or a summary?

- Do you have several readers, perhaps some with different needs?

- What will be your reader's likely reaction to your recommendations? Enthusiastic? Indifferent? Hostile?

- What organization and format will present your report the best?

- Will an executive format, placing the conclusions and recommendations before the body of the report, be an appropriate choice?

- Can you dispose of some or all of the unacceptable solutions quickly, perhaps in the introduction, or must you treat some of them fully?

- Would it be best to organize by solution or by criteria?

- Are there visuals such as tables or charts that would be useful?

- Are there so-whats of your information that need special emphasis?

- Should you answer some of the special questions that executives frequently have? How big is the problem? How important is solving it? Who should carry out the solution? When should the solution be implemented?

Revision

In revision, pay attention to organization, content, style, format, and grammar.

Organization and Content

- Does your introduction make the problem clear?

- Does your introduction make clear the solutions you considered?

- If appropriate, does your introduction state your criteria clearly and succinctly?

- Does your introduction give the plan of your report?

- Does the body of your report display your reasoning well enough to allow your readers to judge your work?

- Are your criteria and solution(s) adequately explained?

- Does your organization sharply illuminate how your proposed solution(s) is (are) measured by your criteria?

- Could some of your data be better displayed in a visual?
- Have you displayed your organization with appropriate headings?
- Can your summary, conclusions, and recommendations stand alone?
- Do your conclusions prepare the way for your recommendations?
- Is your chief recommendation clearly stated?
- Have you stated needed supplementary recommendations?
- Do you provide any needed details about implementing your recommendations?

Style

- Are your sentences active?
- Is your vocabulary appropriate for your audience?
- Have you achieved clarity and conciseness?

Format and Grammar

- Have you chosen an appropriate format—report, letter, or memo?
- Does your report follow good document design conventions and present the information so the reader can find what he or she needs?
- Have you proofread carefully, eliminating all grammatical and typographical errors?
- Will your work present a good appearance to your reader?

Suggestions for Applying Your Knowledge

Individual Activity

Think about the next big purchase you plan to make—for example, a DVD player, a sewing machine, or a chain saw. Identify the features you want and the cost limitations. Research the product and write up your recommendation in a memo similar to the one in Figure 14.3.

Teamwork is an important part of recommendation reports. Members of the team offer different perspectives on the problem and solutions; members share the work in developing recommendations.

Collaborative Activity

Problem-solving and recommendation reports lend themselves particularly well to collaborative efforts, and community and school problems provide excellent opportunities to develop a report and contribute to solving a problem. A glance at a local paper will reveal community problems ranging from potholes in the streets to curbside pickup of recyclables. Most schools perennially have problems such as inefficient use of energy, poor food service, and delays in phone registration.

Working in teams, choose a problem. Be sure to choose a problem that suits the interests and knowledge of team members. Narrow the problem to a manageable study for the time frame the team is working in. For example, the team cannot solve the recycling problems for the entire campus, but team members can certainly study paper recycling in a computer classroom. After a preliminary study of the problem, submit a proposal to your instructor describing the problem and outlining the team's research plans. (See Chapter 15 for advice on writing proposals.)

Once your instructor approves the project, begin analyzing the problem by using the method described in this chapter. When the analysis is complete, present the results in a recommendation report. Depending on the length of the report, use either a report or a correspondence format.

Proposals

Proposals are made for many purposes and come in many lengths and formats. An insulation contractor, for example, called in to examine an old house, may submit a proposal to the house's owner. He may outline the quantity and type of insulation needed and describe how the job will be done. He will estimate how soon the job can be done and set a price for it. If he is a good salesperson, he may provide the names and phone numbers of satisfied customers. He may provide an incentive for quick action: "For the rest of August, we offer a summer discount of 10 percent. In September our prices go back up." The whole proposal, or bid, as it may be called in this instance, may be on one page. At the other end of the scale, an aircraft manufacturer, proposing to build a new aircraft for a large airline, may submit a proposal that fills several books. The aircraft proposal will contain information on plans, facilities, schedules, costs, key engineering and management personnel, and much more.

A proposal contains specific information: the work you or your organization wants to do for someone, including details about the need for the work, how the work will be done, schedule, price, and personnel. In other words, you answer the questions *who, what, when, where, how,* and *why.* Figure 15.1 illustrates the questions you should ask and answer as you write a proposal. The answers appear in the appropriate section of the proposal identified in the request for proposal (RFP) or in headings similar to the ones identified in Figure 15.1. The specific audience is members of the company or organization you are trying to convince to have the work done. Your purpose is to get your audience to select and pay you to do the proposed work.

The proposal is a persuasive document. Achieving credibility will help you as much in a proposal as it does in a sales letter. Adopt the *you-attitude*. Focus on how your proposal will benefit the company or organization paying you for the work. Clearly state your so-whats in a proposal. Usually, the major so-what is the relevance of your work in solving some problem of concern to the organization to which you are making the proposal.

solicited proposals

Proposals fall into two general categories: solicited and unsolicited. A *solicited proposal* is in answer to a request for a proposal—commonly referred to as an RFP. The RFP is usually developed and published by some branch of government, a company, or an organization. Individuals or other companies or organizations respond to the RFP with a proposal for how they will complete the work.

If you or your organization wants to work with the National Aeronautical Space Administration (NASA) or the Environmental Protection Agency (EPA), for example, go to the agency's Web site, and you will find the link to information for research grants or calls for proposals for work that these agencies need done. For example, the National Science Foundation publishes funding opportunities—the RFPs—on the website www.nsf.gov/home/grants.htm.

Most organizations now publish their RFPs on the Web. For example, the FedBizOpps (formerly *Commerce Business Daily*) lists contracts greater than $25,000 for the federal government. The RFP identifies whom to contact for more information on submitting a proposal or requesting a form for

FIGURE 15.1

Questions to ask as you respond to a Request for Proposal. Your answers will be placed in the proposal in the section calling for the information. In the right column, we identify section headings that might be used; the order will depend upon the RFP requirements. Open a file on your computer, put in the headings, and begin writing (making notes).

Organizations issue an RFP when they cannot complete the work themselves. Your proposal describes how you can do the work in a reasonable amount of time at a reasonable cost.

Questions		Possible Section Headings
Who?	Who will do the work? Who will solve the problem? Identify their qualifications and the special skills and qualifications they bring to the task that others cannot provide.	**Personnel** **Consultants** **Technical Support**
What?	What is the problem? What work will be done? Identify the problem (or restate it to make it clear you understand the problem) and describe the work that will be done to solve the problem. Answer the so-whats.	**Introduction** **Problem** **Solutions**
When?	When must the work be completed? Establish a time line of events for completing the work. Depending upon the size of the project, you may identify completion dates for individual tasks leading to the final completion date.	**Schedule** **Time Line** **Calendar of Events**
Where?	Where will the work be done? Describe the location and work environment for the project or where the final product will be delivered.	**Facilities** **Location** **Work Sites**
How?	How will the work be completed? How much will the project cost? Identify and describe equipment and supplies needed. Provide a detailed budget.	**Work and Management Plan** **Budget** **Equipment and Supplies**
Why?	Why will you or your organization be the best choice for completing the work.	**Overview** **Executive Summary** **Services Provided**

submitting a quote or bid on a job. The example in Figure 15.2 identifies the project: renovation of a psychiatric ward at the Veterans Affairs Medical Center in Muskogee, Oklahoma. Proposers (bidders) can get an idea of the size of the project from the budget range given: $500,000 to $1,000,000. Bidders must meet the criteria "within 100 mile radius of Muskogee, OK." The time schedule and a source for more information on the project are identified. This is just one example of how companies find work to bid on.

FIGURE 15.2

Example of an RFP (Request for Proposal) from the U.S. government's Web site fedbizopps.gov. The RFP identifies specific requirements for a psychiatric ward: for example, giving the square footage of the area to be remodeled and identifying what needs to be removed. We changed the format slightly to get all the information on one page. The original description was in all capital letters and very difficult to read.

Source: From RFP623-04-04, October 23, 2003, by FedBizOpps.gov (Federal Business Opportunities). Retrieved November 16, 2003 from http://www.fedbizopps.gov/

C -- RENOVATE 5 EAST FOR INPATIENT PSYCHIATRIC WARD

General Information

Document Type: Sources Sought Notice
Solicitation Number: 623-04-04
Posted Date: Oct 23, 2003
Original Response Date: Dec 02, 2003
Original Archive Date:
Current Archive Date:
Classification Code: C -- Architect and engineering services

Contracting Office Address

Attn: Department of Veterans Affairs Medical Center, 1011 Honor Heights Drive, Muskogee, Oklahoma 74401

Description

The Muskogee VA Medical Center, 1011 Honor Heights Drive, Muskogee, OK4401 is requesting 254s and 255s for A/E service for project 623-301, renovate 5 east, building 53 for inpatient psychiatric unit. Request A/E firm to provide all required labor, material and equipment to develop construction documents to include contract drawings and specs, site investigations for the development of contract documents. Construction period services and site visits. Project design consists of remodeling 12,500 square feet of vacated space, on the 5th floor, east wing of building 53 for acute general psychiatric ward to accommodate 15 patient beds (this includes 1 restraint/seclusion room). The project includes demolition, architectural changes to existing space, mechanical, electrical, plumbing and modification of HVAC systems. This project will also provide clinical facilities consisting of patient bedrooms with bathrooms, communication center (nurses stations), nursing unit support, exam and treatment rooms, and education area. This ward will be unlocked ward, and all the functions in the existing space will be changed and replaced to meet the safety and security of the new inpatient mental health unit. The complete area will be remodeled with patient privacy issues, ADA, NFPA, Life Safety and NEC codes. The project shall be designed (drawing and specification) according to VA design criteria, construction standard and life safety codes. Detailed cost estimate and construction period services of the entire project should be included. The contractor will also need to provide construction period services to ensure the design meets applicable criteria. The construction design shall include planning/phasing to ensure that patient care during construction is not impeded. Additionally, continual access to the medical center must be maintained for all handicapped, patients, visitors, and employees. A/E firms are to submit 254s and 255s to Muskogee VAMC, 1011 Honor Heights Drive, Muskogee, OK 74401. Attention: 90(c). 254s and 255s must be hand carried or mailed and delivered to the above office by 4:30p.m. Tuesday, December 2, 2003. Faxed copies will not be accepted. Time for completion of design is 210 days. NAICS code is 541310 and the business size is 4 mil. Estimated value of construction contract is $500,000-1,000,000.00 A/E firms must be within 100 mile radius of Muskogee, OK

Additional Information   RFP 623-04-04

unsolicited proposals

An *unsolicited proposal* is made on the initiative of the proposer. The proposer sees an opportunity or a need to solve a problem and proposes a solution that will fulfill the need or solve the problem.

In this chapter, we look at both types of proposal and at a useful classroom project: the proposal for a paper.

Solicited Proposals

A request for a solicited proposal will state carefully what goods or services are wanted. The RFP will specify how the proposal should be organized and what information to include.

You can learn a good deal about how to organize and write a proposal by looking at such requests. We reproduce part of a National Science Foundation (NSF) solicitation that requests proposals from colleges and universities to provide scholarship activities for students earning a degree in computer science, engineering, or mathematics. The NSF provides the funds for the scholarships; the school provides the activity for the student to earn the scholarship.

In the following pages, we will intermingle portions of the request for proposals (set between the horizontal lines) with comments on the sections of the RFP and margin notes to call attention to features of the proposal. We use ellipsis dots (. . .) to show where we left out information. We encourage you to go to the NSF Web site, www.nsf.gov, to view the complete proposal: NSF Computer Science, Engineering, and Mathematics Scholarships (CSEMS), NSF 04-506. Following is the first page of the RFP.

NSF Computer Science, Engineering, and Mathematics Scholarships (CSEMS)

Program Solicitation

Reference number identifies the RFP.

NSF 04-506
Replaces Document 03-501

National Science Foundation
Directorate for Education and Human Resources
Division of Undergraduate Education

Letter of Intent Due Date(s) *(optional)*:
December 03, 2003

Deadlines are firm—no exceptions.

Full Proposal Deadline(s) (due by 5 p.m. proposer's local time):
January 28, 2004

SUMMARY OF PROGRAM REQUIREMENTS
General Information

Program Title:
NSF Computer Science, Engineering, and Mathematics Scholarships (CSEMS)

Synopsis: a succinct
statement of purpose.

Synopsis of Program:

This program supports scholarships for academically talented, financially needy students, enabling them to enter the high technology workforce following completion of an associate, baccalaureate, or graduate level degree in computer science, computer technology, engineering, engineering technology, or mathematics. Academic institutions apply for awards to support scholarship activities, and are responsible for selecting scholarship recipients, reporting demographic information about student scholars, and managing the CSEMS project at the institution.

. . .

Award Information

- **Anticipated Type of Award:** Standard or Continuing Grant
- **Estimated Number of Awards:** 90
- **Anticipated Funding Amount:** $30,000,000 for FY 2004, pending availability of funds. Awards are normally not expected to exceed $100,000 per year for up to four years.

The first page identifies the sponsoring organization (NSF) and the office (Division of Undergraduate Studies). The title identifies the purpose of the RFP. Deadlines are clearly identified on the RFP. To be fair to all who submit proposals, there are no exceptions to the deadline. A proposal will not be accepted at 5:01 p.m.

The first section of the RFP is the *Summary of Program Requirements*. The synopsis succinctly gives an overview. A synopsis is very similar to an abstract or preface although it is usually shorter—a brief overview. The one paragraph clearly identifies the purpose of the scholarship program. Watch for phrases from the synopsis to appear in other sections of the RFP.

The remaining sections of the *Summary* give the key points from each section of the RFP (see the Table of Contents below). We have included the *Award Information* so you will see the number of awards planned and the amount of funding available. The *Summary* section may be the only part of the report some reviewers read. They get an overview of the project and see quickly if the minimum requirements are met by the proposer. Often several hundred proposals are received for grant money. Judges may use the *Summary* to eliminate those who do not meet the minimum requirements or who do not state their purpose clearly.

TABLE OF CONTENTS

This RFP is long enough that it has a table of contents. You will want to read the entire RFP carefully to make sure you understand all the requirements. You also will find significant guidance throughout the RFP identifying the information needed. For example, even though the *Proposal Review Information* is buried in the middle of the RFP, you will want to read it and be able to respond to the questions it asked before you begin writing the proposal.

In this example, we include portions of sections I, II, III, V, and VI. The *Introduction* (I) and *Program Description* (II) give the details of the RFP. The *Introduction* expands on the information in the synopsis. The *Program Description* gives the goals and objectives of the scholarship program.

Compare the Introduction and the Synopsis.

I. INTRODUCTION

The NSF Computer Science, Engineering, and Mathematics Scholarship (CSEMS) program provides institutions with funds for student scholarships to encourage and enable academically talented but financially needy students to enter the high technology workforce following completion of an associate, baccalaureate, or graduate degree in computer science, computer technology, engineering, engineering technology, or

The purpose is stated again.

mathematics. The program was established by the National Science Foundation (NSF) in accordance with the American Competitiveness and Workforce Improvement Act of 1998 (P.L. 105-277) as modified by P.L. 106-313. The Act reflects the national need to increase substantially the number of American high technology workers and to develop high-quality professionals in these fields.

II. PROGRAM DESCRIPTION

The CSEMS program emphasizes the importance of recruiting students to high technology disciplines, mentoring and supporting students through degree completion, and partnering with industry to facilitate student career placement in the high technology workforce. Participating institutions are expected to support the goals of the CSEMS program including:

- Increased numbers of well educated and skilled employees in technical areas of national need;
- Improved educational opportunities for students in the named disciplines;
- Increased retention of students to degree achievement;
- Improved student support programs at institutions of higher education;
- Strengthened partnerships between institutions of higher education and high technology industry.

The goals are presented in a bulleted list.

Student eligibility is determined, in part, by demonstrated financial need as defined by the U.S. Department of Education to be the difference between the institutional Cost of Attendance and the Estimated Family Contribution (see http://www.ed.gov/prog_info/SFA/StudentGuide/2002-3/need.html or http://www.fafsa.ed.gov). CSEMS scholarship funds may be used for expenses included in the institution's Cost of Attendance as calculated according to U. S. Department of Education guidelines. Refer to Section III. C. (Scholarship Recipients) in this Solicitation for details.

It is expected that scholarship recipients will achieve one of the following by the end of the scholarship award period:

- Receive an associate, baccalaureate, or graduate degree in one of the CSEMS disciplines;
- Transfer from an associate degree program to a baccalaureate degree program or from an undergraduate program to a graduate program in one of the CSEMS disciplines;
- Successfully complete a stage within an associate, baccalaureate, or graduate degree program in one of the CSEMS disciplines that, in the particular institution, is documented and described as a point of unusually high attrition.

Specific outcomes are established.

CSEMS grants may be made for up to four years and may provide individual scholarships of up to $3125 per year. Awardee institutions may elect to support individual student scholars for four years or may elect to support several cohorts of students for a shorter duration within the award period.

. . .

The *Program Description* establishes the framework for the grant, in this case, the scholarship program. It is at this point that you and your organization determine if you can meet the goals (the first set of bullets). This section also defines the terms and establishes the outcomes (the second set of bullets). The scope of the program is identified: "grants may be made for up to four years . . . up to $3125 per year."

When you respond to an RFP, you want to use some of the same phrasing as the RFP. Reviewers of RFPs do not have time to look for responses; they look for keywords and phrases. You need your best persuasive writing—your best sales skills. You want to show the proposal reviewers that you and your organization provide a unique product or service—something your competition cannot duplicate.

One significant "selling point" is the principal and co-principal investigators (the PIs) and, in this case, the university or college. The reputation of the investigators and the strength of the school influence the reviewers' decision. They know the work of the PI and that he or she has a team and organization to support high-quality work and successful completion of the proposed project.

III. ELIGIBILITY INFORMATION

A. Institutions

Institutions of higher education (as defined in section 101 (a) of the Higher Education Act of 1965) in the United States and its territories that grant associate, baccalaureate, or graduate degrees in computer science, computer technology, engineering, engineering technology, or mathematics are invited to submit proposals. An institution may submit no more than one proposal per competition.

B. Principal Investigator

The Principal Investigator must be a faculty member currently teaching within one of the CSEMS disciplines who can provide the leadership required to ensure the success of the project. Projects involving more than one department within an institution are eligible, but a single Principal Investigator must accept overall management responsibility. Other members of the CSEMS project management team may be listed as Co-Principal investigators.

C. Scholarship Recipients

CSEMS scholarship recipients will be selected by the awardee institution, but must:

criteria for students

- be citizens of the United States, nationals of the United States (as defined in section 101(a) of the Immigration and Nationality Act), aliens admitted as refugees under section 207 of the Immigration and Nationality, or aliens lawfully admitted to the United States for permanent residence;
- be enrolled full time in computer science, computer technology, engineering, engineering technology, or mathematics degree programs at the associate, baccalaureate, or graduate level. Enrollment must be full-time for each semester or quarter a student receives a scholarship;
- demonstrate academic potential or ability; and
- demonstrate financial need, defined for undergraduate students by the US Department of Education rules for need-based Federal financial aid, or, for graduate students, defined as financial eligibility for Graduate Assistance in Areas of National Need (GANN).

Financial need is defined for undergraduates . . . [this section continues with the specific details for determining financial needs, including websites and other resources to go to]

A principal investigator (PI) is identified for all grants. The PI is the one who manages the resources awarded and is held accountable for the success or failure of the program. The organization making the award carefully reviews the credentials of the PI and, in many cases, the credentials of other members of the project. Proposal reviewers then check to make sure the person(s) making the proposal are eligible. In this example, the criteria for the institution, principal investigator, and the students are clearly identified.

The longest section of the RFP, *Proposal Preparation and Submission Instructions,* identifies each part needed in the proposal and gives instructions for what to include and how to format the proposal. Take no shortcuts and do not get creative when responding to a solicited proposal's guidelines. The reviewers have a lot to read so you want to make it easy for them. Remember, reviewers are looking for ways to eliminate proposals.

Preparing a proposal requires research and time. You need to research the products and services your organization can provide. You also need to research your competition. What do you think they will propose? Part of the research time should be spent learning about the review process and the review board—the context and your audience. What does the review board expect? Why is what you are proposing worthwhile? Answer the so-what question.

You will need to judge your time for writing the proposal, working backward from the deadline to establish a schedule for researching and gathering information for the proposal and then actual time to write the proposal. Adapt the questions identified in Figure 15.1 to help you develop the proposal. Present your facts and the implications of those facts in a thorough and attractive manner.

V. PROPOSAL PREPARATION AND SUBMISSION INSTRUCTIONS

A. Proposal Preparation Instructions

Letters of Intent *(optional):*

Letters of Intent are encouraged, although optional. What would you do if you wanted this grant?

Optional Letters of Intent are encouraged and should be sent by electronic mail to csems@nsf.gov by December 3, 2003. Letters should indicate only the intent to submit a proposal along with the institution and Principal Investigator's name. The letter should not discuss the substance of the project.

Full Proposal Instructions:

Read the Grant Proposal Guide.

Proposals submitted in response to this program announcement/solicitation should be prepared and submitted in accordance with the general guidelines contained in the NSF *Grant Proposal Guide* (GPG). The complete text of the GPG is available electronically on the NSF Website at: http://www.nsf.gov/cgi-bin/getpub?gpg. Paper copies of the GPG may be obtained from the NSF Publications Clearinghouse, telephone (301) 947-2722 or by e-mail from pubs@nsf.gov.

The following instructions supplement or deviate from the GPG guidelines.

Full Proposal Content

1. Cover Sheet.

Most RFPs establish the format expected.

While filling out the cover sheet in FastLane, it is important to choose the program solicitation number indicated on the cover of this document "NSF Computer Science,

Engineering, and Mathematics Scholarship Program" from the list of programs in the "NSF Unit Consideration" section. This choice must be specified in order to have access to the DUE Project Data Form, which is required for CSEMS proposals.

An informative title for the proposed Computer Science, Engineering and Mathematics Scholarship project must be provided on the appropriate line. Please use the full project title and refrain from using the CSEMS acronym, NSF, or the institution's name in the project title.

2. Project Data Form.

A Project Data Form must be completed for all proposals. The information on this form is used to direct proposals to appropriate reviewers and to determine the characteristics of projects supported by the Division of Undergraduate Education. In Fastlane, [online application form] . . .

3. Project Summary.

Provide a brief (500 words or fewer) description of the CSEMS project including the number of scholarships to be provided, the discipline areas to be served by the scholarship funds, the objectives of the project, and basic information about the student recruitment, selection, support, and career placement services to be provided as part of this CSEMS project.

The project summary **MUST** address both Merit Review Criteria (Intellectual Merit and Broader Impacts) in separate statements. See Section VI. A., Proposal Review Process, for a statement of the two criteria. NSF will return without review proposals that do not address both criteria in the Project Summary.

4. Table of Contents.

The Table of Contents is generated by FastLane and cannot be edited.

5. Project Description.

The Project Description must not exceed 15 single-spaced pages of 12-point type. Proposals that exceed the page limit will be returned without review. The Project Description should contain the following information:

a. Results from Prior NSF Support.

Please report on the results from related prior NSF support. . . .

b. Project Objectives and Plans.

The project should have specific objectives that reflect the objectives of the CSEMS program and local needs, as well as specific plans to select students, encourage them to achieve their best academic performance, and enable them to enter the workforce in their fields.

c. Significance of Project and Rationale.

The proposal should address how the goals of the CSEMS program (see Program Description, Section II), will be met. In addition, it should include information on the demographics of the departments or programs affected by the scholarships, including

---

When you respond to an RFP, you want to use some of the same phrasing. Reviewers of RFPs look for keywords and phrases.

number of majors and number of graduates per year, as well as information on enrollment and retention within the institution and programs involved. A rationale for the number of scholarships and the scholarship amount requested should also be provided.

d. Activities on Which the Current Project Builds.

. . . . Proposals should discuss existing support structures and projects that are relevant to the CSEMS project . . . .

e. CSEMS Project Management Plan.

CSEMS projects should be guided by a management plan in which the key personnel, the strategic plan, and project logistics are defined. The roles and responsibilities of the personnel involved should be clear. . . .

Plans should be in place for activities such as advertising and recruitment of students, selection of students, maintenance of CSEMS records, reporting responsibilities, oversight for student support services, and implementing a process by which students who lose CSEMS eligibility will be replaced by new students.

The management plan should indicate how students' eligibility will be determined, the mechanisms by which scholarships for students will be provided (up to a maximum amount of $3125 per year per student), and how scholarship program outcomes will be evaluated and disseminated. . . .

f. Student Selection Process and Criteria.

The proposal should include a plan for the process by which students will be selected to receive the CSEMS scholarship award. Included in this plan should be a description of the eligibility criteria to be used in selecting scholars. . . .

The selection process for scholarship recipients should include indicators of academic merit and other indicators of likely professional success. Multiple indicators may be appropriate in gauging both academic merit (e.g., grade point average, placement test results) and professionalism (e.g., motivation, ability to manage time and resources, communication skills). Selection criteria should be flexible enough to accommodate applicants who come from diverse backgrounds and with diverse career goals. The program encourages efforts to increase the number of members of underrepresented groups (e.g., women, minorities, and persons with disabilities) in STEM fields, but it aims broadly to assist any student with financial need.

g. CSEMS Student Support Services and Programs.

It is expected that awardee institutions will have or develop support programs and services designed to enhance student learning, confidence, performance, retention to graduation, and career or higher education placement. Examples of student support include:

- Recruitment of students to higher education programs and careers in the CSEMS disciplines;
- Support and mentoring of students by faculty and industry representatives;
- Academic support services such as tutoring, study-groups, or supplemental instruction programs;

- Industry experiences or internship opportunities;
- Community building and support among CSEMS scholars within the institution;
- Participation in local or regional professional, industrial or scientific meetings and conferences;
- Access to appropriate technology and technological support personnel; and
- Career counseling and job placement services for CSEMS scholars.

. . .

h. Quality Educational Programs.

Institutions should provide evidence of the high quality of their educational programs, including those in the targeted disciplines. For example:

- External accreditations held by the institution, especially accreditations in the CSEMS disciplines; and
- Academic courses of study that are well-defined, current, and academically rigorous.

Institutions should also provide student performance data that documents the success of the academic programs. For example:

- Percentage of enrolled students who are retained through completion of the targeted degree;
- Percentage of students who continue their education at higher degree levels; and
- Data on student placement in employment or further higher education upon graduation.

i. Assessment and Evaluation.

As with all NSF projects, CSEMS projects must have clear and specific plans for assessment and evaluation. . . .

j. Special Program Features.

There are several considerations related to special features of the CSEMS program that may need to be considered and addressed in CSEMS proposals. These include:

CSEMS projects should provide student support structures that help the scholarship recipients succeed as students and, later, as working professionals. Ideally, CSEMS scholars are part of a cohort that is managed and supported as part of an active learning community. . . .

CSEMS projects often include enhancements such as research opportunities, tutoring of others, and internships for scholarship recipients. . . .

The CSEMS disciplines—computer science, computer technology, engineering, engineering technology, and mathematics—are legislatively determined. Scholarships are used to enhance our national workforce and productivity needs in these areas. . . .

. . .

k. Project Description Content Checklist.

. . . The proposal should include, within the project description (limited to 15 single-spaced pages), the following:

- Results from prior NSF support, with particular emphasis on any prior CSEMS awards made to the institution;
- [9 bullets]

6. References Cited. If applicable.

7. Biographical Sketches.

Show the proposal reviewer you have the knowledge and skills to do a good job.

Include a 2-page biographical sketch for the Principal Investigator and each listed Co-Principal Investigator and/or Senior Personnel.

8. Budget, Budget Justification, and Allowable Costs:

Provide a budget for each year of support requested. The maximum CSEMS request is normally not to exceed $100,000 per year. The $100,000 per year limit includes all funds (scholarships, administrative costs, and student support costs). . .

9. Current and Pending Support.

Provide a list of Current and Pending Support for the Principal Investigator and each Co-Principal Investigator. Investigators with no prior support should list the CSEMS proposal as a pending project.

10. Facilities, Equipment, and Other Resources.

See GPG Section II. D.9.

11. Supplementary Documentation.

Evidence of the high quality of academic programs or excellence in student recruitment, support, or career placement may be included as supplementary documentation. . . .

These *Submission Instructions* give very specific guidelines—for example, "refrain from using the CSEMS acronym, NSF, or the institution's name in the project title" and "provide a brief (500 words or fewer)" project summary. NSF provides FastLane, a set of forms online. Online completion of forms is becoming commonplace. Organizations issuing RFPs want the standard cover sheets, data forms, table of contents, budgets, and other information to come in the same for all applications. Again, proposal reviewers find this standardization of information easier to work with. They will spend less time looking for information and more time focused on the details of the proposal.

In this example, the reviewers will spend most of their time reviewing the *Project Description*. The *Project Description* consists of 11 sections (a–k). The section headings provide the headings for the project description you provide. The *Project Description* "must not exceed 15 single-spaced pages of 12-point type." That is not a lot of space when you have 11 areas to provide detailed information for that will persuade the proposal reviewers. Do not overlook the sentence immediately following: "Proposals that exceed the page limit will be returned without review."

Your writing skills will be put to the test because you need to answer the questions—the Merit Review Criteria: What is the intellectual merit of the proposed activity? and What are the broader impacts of the proposed activity? Section VI, *Proposal Review Information*, explains the review process and the criteria the reviewers use to judge proposals. You will find a similar section in all RFPs—a statement of the criteria for judging the proposals. What are the criteria in the RFP in Figure 15.2?

VI. PROPOSAL REVIEW INFORMATION

A. NSF Proposal Review Process

. . .

Be sure to address all the questions in this section of the RFP you respond to.

The two National Science Board approved merit review criteria are listed below (see the Grant Proposal Guide Chapter III.A for further information). The criteria include considerations that help define them. These considerations are suggestions and not all will apply to any given proposal. While proposers must address both merit review criteria, reviewers will be asked to address only those considerations that are relevant to the proposal being considered and for which he/she is qualified to make judgments.

What is the intellectual merit of the proposed activity?

How important is the proposed activity to advancing knowledge and understanding within its own field or across different fields? How well qualified is the proposer (individual or team) to conduct the project? (If appropriate, the reviewer will comment on the quality of the prior work.) To what extent does the proposed activity suggest and explore creative and original concepts? How well conceived and organized is the proposed activity? Is there sufficient access to resources?

What are the broader impacts of the proposed activity?

How well does the activity advance discovery and understanding while promoting teaching, training, and learning? How well does the proposed activity broaden the participation of underrepresented groups (e.g., gender, ethnicity, disability, geographic, etc.)? To what extent will it enhance the infrastructure for research and education, such as facilities, instrumentation, networks, and partnerships? Will the results be disseminated broadly to enhance scientific and technological understanding? What may be the benefits of the proposed activity to society?

NSF staff will give careful consideration to the following in making funding decisions:

Integration of Research and Education

One of the principal strategies in support of NSF's goals is to foster integration of research and education through the programs, projects, and activities it supports at academic and research institutions. These institutions provide abundant opportunities where individuals may concurrently assume responsibilities as researchers, educators, and students and where all can engage in joint efforts that infuse education with the excitement of discovery and enrich research through the diversity of learning perspectives.

Integrating Diversity into NSF Programs, Projects, and Activities

Broadening opportunities and enabling the participation of all citizens—women and men, underrepresented minorities, and persons with disabilities—is essential to the health and vitality of science and engineering. NSF is committed to this principle of diversity and deems it central to the programs, projects, and activities it considers and supports.

Additional Review Criteria:

Reviewers will be asked to consider the above two merit review criteria with emphasis placed on the CSEMS program components (see "Program Description"). Those elements include:

- Student-support infrastructure for the successful graduation of scholarship recipients,
- Management and administration plan that is effective and clearly articulated,
- Evidence of faculty participation and support from the appropriate financial aid and student services personnel,
- Justification of the number and amount of scholarships requested based on current student demographics, and
- Educational program of high quality.

Most of the information found in proposals of any size at all is requested in this NSF solicitation—information on cost, people, facilities, and schedule. NSF wants to know precisely what will be done and why, and it is particularly interested in the value and significance (the so-whats—the Merit Review Criteria) of what is to be done.

Remember that the proposal is a persuasive document. Emphasize the value and quality of your organization's products and services. Point out the unique advantages offered by the experience and education of the members of your organization. If possible, provide testimonials covering your previous work or the work of the organization you work for. Use a persuasive argument and problem-solving techniques in the proposal. Provide information that shows you understand the problem and what is expected from you and your organization to solve the problem.

Unsolicited Proposals

Unsolicited proposals are much like solicited ones. Essentially, they require the same information, with one major difference. In a solicited proposal, the solicitors recognize a need. Therefore, you do not have to sell them on the need, only on your ability to understand and interpret the need and to meet it. In an unsolicited proposal, you must first convince the audience that the need exists. If you cannot, they will have no particular interest in your goods or services.

For example, a roofing contractor called in by a homeowner to bid on re-shingling a roof does not have to establish the need for the job; however, the contractor might have to justify that a more expensive (but longer lasting) shingle be used. But an enterprising contractor who sees a roof in need of repair may have to convince the owner that reshingling is necessary. Often, establishing a need calls for a problem-solving organization. The problem establishes the need. Your goods or services supply the solution.

When preparing an unsolicited proposal, you can devise your own organization. A small, simple, unsolicited proposal might fall into six parts:

1. *Summary*—provides a concise statement of the proposal
2. *Introduction*—establishes need
3. *Overview section*—defines the process to be followed or describes the goods to be furnished, or both
4. *Work and management plan*—outlines the tasks to be done and schedules their accomplishment
5. *Detailed budget*—gives precise information on costs
6. *Personnel section*—briefly gives the relevant qualifications of the people involved

Often, short proposals are drafted in the form of a letter or memo. Even so, headings and applicable visuals should be used, particularly easy-to-read informal lists and tables.

The proposal in Figure 15.3, modeled after an actual successful proposal, follows the six steps just outlined. Take the time to read it now. The letters next to the headings in the model proposal correspond to the following comments.

A. *Project Summary.* The proposal is set up in a memo format commonly used for short proposals. It includes, as do most proposals, a summary of the proposal. Executives like to have a concise statement of a proposal before they study it in detail. You will impress them favorably if you compress the major points of your proposal into a short summary.

B. *Introduction.* The beginning of the introduction defines the subject, peer advising, and points out its successful use elsewhere. The survey presented shows that early and careful planning has taken place. The results of the survey do not show that an outright problem of student dissatisfaction exists. The results do show that students might feel more comfortable with another approach. The survey results also set to rest the thought that the faculty might object. The statement about more faculty time and possible innovative advising techniques presents significant so-whats.

C. *Description of the Program.* A description of the program, the methodology, outlines the strategy and some of the timing of the operational experiment. Again it shows that a good deal of thought has gone into the proposal. The final paragraph again suggests that the money spent for the proposal may result in a new and more desirable advising procedure than currently exists. Such a development is likely to please the Center for Educational Development, an organization charged with developing innovative methods to improve the college's educational process.

D. *Facilities.* Facilities must be explained somewhere. In a simple report like this one, the work and management plan is a good location. If facilities were extensive, they would rate a section of their own.

FIGURE 15.3
Example of a proposal.

Battle Creek College

Kellogg MI 48108
                        Department of Criminal Justice Studies
                                      www.battlecreekc.edu/cjs

DATE: December 10, 2004

TO: Janice H. Grumbacher, Director
          Center for Educational Development
          317 Clark Library

FROM: Martin A. Doyle   **M.D.**
          Student, Criminal Justice Studies

RE: Request for Funding a Peer Advising Program for Criminal Justice Studies Students

Project Summary (A)

A survey shows that students and faculty in Criminal Justice Studies (CJS) favor the concept of peer advising. Peer advising is being successfully used in other colleges in the United States. This proposal requests $3,926 to set up a pilot program in peer advising in CJS. The pilot program would run for 13 months from May 2005 through May 2006. The pilot program will be monitored by senior CJS faculty. Evaluative reports will be written and disseminated at the end of the pilot program.

Introduction (B)

A new development in many two- and four-year colleges is the successful use of students for advising their fellow students regarding course registration, program development, and job opportunities. Called peer advising, this new development supplements but does not replace normal faculty advising.

In the Fall of this year, I surveyed the faculty and students in Criminal Justice Studies regarding their opinions about peer advising. A complete copy of the survey results, "Response to Peer Advising in the Department of Criminal Justice Studies," is available from me upon request. The results can be summarized briefly:

- Rightly or wrongly, many students feel they are imposing upon their advisers' time by seeking assistance. Some students view their advisers as having more important matters to contend with.
- Students feel that peer advisers will be better able to relate to the problems of their fellow students.
- Students stated frequently that they would feel freer and more comfortable in bringing their problems to peer advisers.
- Faculty acceptance of peer advising was high. Most felt it would be a welcome addition for both faculty and students.

The study showed such strong support for peer advising among faculty and students that such a program seems to have a good potential for success. If successful, peer advising will remove a significant burden from the CJS faculty, freeing them for additional time to pursue their teaching and professional development. The program may lead to similar innovative advising techniques in other departments of the college.

In the remainder of this proposal, I describe the program and how it will be established (the methodology), a work and management plan, a detailed budget, and the qualifications of the key personnel involved.

FIGURE 15.3
(continued)

Description of the Program (C)

If instituted, peer advising will be conducted for 13 months as a pilot program. A peer advising unit of two students will be set up in Spring 2005. William Morrell, Chief Adviser for CJS, has agreed to train the two peer advisers and to supervise the program through the year. Beginning in Fall 2005, regular office hours will be maintained with one or both peer advisers present at all times.

The advising unit will deal with

- registration and scheduling difficulties
- guidance on classes and instructors
- sequence of classes and prerequisites
- recommended classes
- questions on the CJS program
- information for potential majors
- information on jobs and placement
- information on University services and agencies

The peer advising unit will work closely with

- current faculty advisers
- the director of CJS
- Admissions and Records

The peer advising unit will collect statistics and information on

- number of students helped
- types of problems dealt with
- where and who solved the problems
- feedback from CJS students and faculty

In the Spring of 2006 the peer advisers will prepare a full evaluation consolidating all the data collected and presenting conclusions concerning the potential of peer advising in CJS. William Morrell will prepare a separate evaluation of the program. Both evaluations will be submitted to Dr. Carlos Montoya, Director of CJS; Dr. Mary Albrecht, Dean of the College of Arts and Sciences; and your office.

Dr. Montoya and Dean Albrecht will decide whether to continue the peer advising in CJS or not. Dean Albrecht will also consider the possibility of peer advising in other departments of the College.

Work and Management Plan

This section provides details on the facilities, the task breakdown, and management of the peer advising program.

Facilities (D).   Dr. Montoya has agreed to provide an office for the peer advising unit. The office will be located in an area easily accessible to CJS students. CJS will furnish the office with a desk, telephone, filing cabinet, bookshelves, a swivel desk chair, three straight chairs, a computer, and a computer table. The peer advisers will have the use of CJS office supplies, including stamps and stationery.

FIGURE 15.3
(continued)

Page 3
Janice H. Grumbacher
December 10, 2004

Task Breakdown (E).   There will be three major tasks: training, holding office hours, and evaluating the program. The chart shows the task timetable:

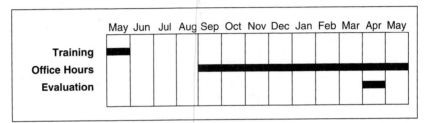

Training.   In May 2005, William Morrell will give the two peer advisers 10 hours of training in advising procedures to include filling out registration forms and procedures for adding and dropping courses. He will provide information concerning other college programs, particularly those that provide aid in needed study skills such as note taking, reading, listening, and library research. He will aid the peer advisers in learning the interpersonal communication skills needed for effective advising.

Office Hours.   September 7, 2005–May 26, 2006. Office hours will be scheduled from 11 a.m. to 2 p.m., Monday through Friday, holidays and school breaks excluded. During each of the heavy advising months of September and January, an additional 20 hours of advising time will be scheduled and two advisers will be present during peak hours.

Evaluation.   April 1–30, 2006. During April 2006, the two peer advisers will consolidate the information they have gathered throughout the year and write their evaluation report. A total of 16 hours is scheduled for this task.

Management (F).   William Morrell will supervise the entire peer advising experiment as part of his duties as Coordinator of Advisers for the CJS program. He will be readily accessible to the peer advisers. He will monitor their procedures and provide advice and counsel when needed. Throughout the year he will provide informal reports to Dr. Montoya. At the end of the experiment he will provide an evaluation of the peer advising program.

Budget (G)

Because CJS is furnishing office space, office supplies, and clerical help, the entire budget needed is for salary for the two peer advisers. The normal student hourly wage of $6.50 per hour is requested. The budget breaks down in the following manner:

Training Time	Salary for 2 peer advisers	20 hours	$130.00
Office Hours	Salary for 3 hours of advising a day for 176 days	528 hours	3,432.00
	Salary for additional advising time in September	40 hours	260.00
Evaluation Time	Salary	16 hours	104.00
	TOTAL	604 hours	$3,926.00

FIGURE 15.3
(continued)

Page 4
Janice H. Grumbacher
December 10, 2004

The budgeted $3,926 will be divided approximately equally between the two peer advisers. If this grant request is approved, your office is requested to transfer $130 to the CJS budget in April 2005 and the remaining $3,796 in September 2005. Normal college accounting procedures will be used by CJS to account for expenditures.

Personnel (H)

I request that I be one of the peer advisers. In March 2005, the other peer adviser will be chosen from among applicants for the job by a secret ballot of the CJS students.

My qualifications are as follows. After graduation from high school in 1999, I served four years in the U.S. Air Force as a police officer. I left the service with the rank of sergeant. From November 2003 to the present I have been a sheriff's deputy in Battle Creek County. I am currently working half-time while I complete my CJS studies. I have a special interest in counseling. To develop myself in this area, I have taken Social Science 1104, Dynamics of Small Groups, and I am currently taking Social Science 2111, Interpersonal Communication. My current grade point average is 3.2.

William Morrell, who will supervise the program, is Coordinator of Advisers for CJS. Before taking his degree in Criminal Justice Studies at the University of Washington, he was a police officer with the Seattle, Washington, Police Department for eight years. He also has a Master's degree in Educational Administration from the University of North Dakota. With Battle Creek College for the past eleven years, Morrell has been Coordinator of Advisers since 1995.

Conclusion (I)

Evidence gathered at other schools indicates that peer advising is successful—a positive benefit to students, faculty, and the school. I have reports concerning established programs at two major universities that I will send to you at your request. Preliminary studies here indicate that both faculty and students favor peer advising in CJS.

I will be happy to discuss this proposal with you at your convenience. I will be open to any modifications in the plan you might suggest.

cc: William Morrell
   Dr. Carlos Montoya
   Dean Mary Albrecht

E. *Task Breakdown.* The tasks to be accomplished are presented in a chronological sequence. A simple visual shows the time relationship of the tasks.

F. *Management.* Proper management is always a concern. People want to know that the spending of their money will be overseen by experienced, responsible managers.

G. *Budget.* The budget is presented in a simple table form. Do not overlook any possible expenses. If appropriate, specify the time and method of payment. Tell how the money will be accounted for.

H. *Personnel.* In a simple proposal, a short narrative biography that gives relevant education and experience is usually enough. Use your sales skills here. The facts chosen for the student's biography emphasize his maturity and experience. The two courses listed establish an interest in counseling that is a strong selling point for the project. The information on William Morrell establishes his credibility as a supervisor and points out that the project will have high-level direction.

I. *Conclusion.* The conclusion resells the proposal. It emphasizes previous successes for peer advising and offers to provide evidence for this claim. Indicating flexibility and the willingness to negotiate is also important. Often proposals cannot be carried out exactly as proposed.

Proposals are unique documents. They combine the skills needed for information giving, analysis, and persuasion. Remember, too, they are legal documents. Whatever you say you will do, you must do. You can be held legally accountable. More than likely, you have signed a contract confirming the cost of the project and the work to be done. The satisfaction of writing a successful proposal is considerable. When someone gives you money on the strength of a proposal you have written, you have direct evidence of your writing and persuasive skills.

Proposal for a Paper

Frequently, instructors ask students to propose what they intend to do for their major term report. Many of the principles used in writing business proposals can be applied equally well in such proposals for papers. Such a proposal will assure you and your instructor that you know where you are heading and will not waste time and energy following dead-end paths. Also, it is an excellent rehearsal for the larger proposals discussed in this chapter.

Review the example of a proposal for a paper in Figure 15.4 before reading the rest of this chapter.

FIGURE 15.4

Student's proposal for a paper—a recommendation report.

Date: February 2, 2005

To: Professor Richard Cohen
          302 Haecker Hall

From: Ann Osborn   *A.O.*
          Campus Box 342

Subject: Proposal for a report on the feasibility of protecting the Technical Communication Computer Center from
          computer viruses and worms

I propose to conduct and report on a study on how to best protect the Technical Communication Computer Center
(TCCC) from destructive computer viruses and worms

The viruses and worms enter the lab through the campus network and through student and faculty disks that have
been contaminated. While the campus network administrators, students, and faculty take precautions, we can do
more in the TCCC to protect the computers.

The audience for my report will be Carole K. Yang, the Director of TCCC. Yang has an M.S. in Management of
Information Systems and 5 years experience working in computer labs.

Plan and Resources

My preliminary research indicates that to be feasible any protection plan will involve at least four stages:

1) Gather information on the new viruses and worms: how they operate, how they can be detected, and what
   detection programs protect most effectively against them.

2) Train the TCCC technical support staff on installation and management of the virus protection programs
   and develop instructions for users of the computers in TCCC.

3) Develop an action plan that will go into effect the instant a virus or worm is detected in the TCCC.

4) Submit a plan for routine monitoring and upgrades to the virus and worm protection system.

For this study and report, I will gather information needed in the first stage. I will then use the information to
prepare ways of accomplishing the second, third, and fourth stages.

In my initial search, I have found good sources in the library as well as people with knowledge that will be helpful.
My sources include:

- Ann Mendocino, Director, University Computing Services

- Andrew Rosenberg, Associate Professor, Management of Information Systems

- jonesallprotection.com, a Web site with hourly updates on virus and worm infections

- smithcatches.com, source for software to combat infections

FIGURE 15.4
(continued)

2

Schedule

Week of Semester	Task
5th week	Complete research and planning
6th week	Submit organizational plan for report
7th–9th weeks	Draft report
10th–11th weeks	Revise report
12th week	Submit final report

Credentials

I am a Management of Information Systems major. My course work has made me familiar with computer programming and the problems of computer viruses. I have worked parttime for both Computer Information Services and the TCCC. I have experience in detecting and destroying computer viruses and worms.

cc: Carole K. Yang

Subject, Purpose, and Audience of the Proposed Paper

A proposal for a paper should clearly state the subject, purpose, and audience for the paper. To introduce her subject and purpose, Ann Osborn briefly defines the problem she proposes to address. For a different kind of paper, a set of instructions, for example, the writer might describe the paper to be written and explain its purpose. Ann next specifies her audience, in this case the Director of the Technical Communication Computer Center. For a class project, the audience may be fictional or, as in Ann's case, a real person with use for the proposal. If at all possible, a real audience is best because you can identify the specific information your reader needs. Rarely, the audience will be the instructor to whom the proposal is addressed.

Methodology and Resources for Researching and Producing the Paper

Your reader will want to know how you plan to carry out your work and what your resources are. In her methodology and resources section, Ann describes the results of her preliminary research into the problem and proposes the solutions she intends to examine. She does not suggest that one solution might be superior to another. If, in preparing the proposal for your paper, you have done enough research to suggest a favored solution, you may do so. However, be careful not to eliminate options that further research may prove better than the one chosen.

The writer's resources are a list of articles and people that her preliminary research show to be valuable. Some instructors like an annotated bibliography that describes what information each source provides. In any case, the resource section must be complete enough to convince the instructor that you have made a good start on your study and that you know where to find relevant information.

Schedule of Work

In most proposals for a paper, the schedule of work need not be elaborate. As Ann has done, indicate the major milestones in your work and propose a completion date for each. If there are some complications to the schedule, you might consider showing it in a table or other visual, such as a flow chart (see Chapters 5, 6, and 7).

Credentials for Doing the Paper

Finally, you should state why you are qualified to carry out the work proposed. Ann states both the academic and work credentials that provide evidence that she can do what she proposes to do. Credentials should not be overblown, but they should be complete enough to convince the instructor that you will not get bogged down for lack of knowledge, skill, or experience.

Proposal writers are valuable members of organizations. They describe and "sell" the products or services of the organization. When the proposal is accepted, the proposal writer and the organization are successful.

✓ PLANNING AND REVISING CHECKLIST: PROPOSALS ·

Think about the following as you plan and revise a proposal.

Planning

Proposals, like recommendation reports, often deal with problems and their solutions. Therefore, you must frequently begin your planning by defining the problem and creating several solutions for it, much as we describe the process in the recommendation report checklist on pages 410–412. If your proposal is a solicited proposal, be sure to read and follow the RFP directions carefully. Plan answers for all the questions asked and note carefully the format required.

- What problem(s) does your proposal aim to solve?

- What solution or solutions are you proposing? What are the so-whats of your solutions? In what ways do they benefit your readers?

- Who are the readers of your proposal? What is their purpose in reading it? Do you have several readers, perhaps some with differing needs?

- Will the readers have problems with any of the technical vocabulary in the proposal?

- What will be the readers' reaction to the proposal? Enthusiastic? Indifferent? Skeptical? What can you do to counteract negative reactions and reinforce positive ones?

- What will be your methods in carrying out the work proposed? How will you do the work?

- What facilities and equipment will you need? Who will furnish them? Are needed equipment and facilities readily available?

- What is your schedule of work? Can you show your schedule in a visual?

- How will the project be managed? Who will be the manager?

- What is the cost of what you are proposing? Who pays what? What are the details of the budget?

- Who will do the work proposed? Why are they fitted to do the work?

Revising

In revision, pay attention to organization, content, style, format, and grammar.

ORGANIZATION AND CONTENT

- Have you provided a summary that can stand by itself for a busy reader?

- Does your introduction make clear the problem you propose to solve?

- If appropriate, does your introduction describe your proposed solutions?

- Does your introduction define any terms or concepts your readers may find difficult?

- Does your introduction state a few significant so-whats to interest your readers in reading further?

- Does your methodology section make clear the strategy and timing of the methods you will use? Can any significant so-whats be mentioned here?

- Is your work schedule clear? Would a visual help?

- Is your budget complete? Are all expenses accounted for and justified?

- Will the facts presented convince your readers that the people proposed to carry out the work will do a competent job?

STYLE

- Have you achieved clarity and conciseness?

- Is your vocabulary appropriate to your subject and audience?

FORMAT AND GRAMMAR

- Have you chosen the most appropriate format: report, letter, or memo?

- Is your proposal neat and free from errors?

- Have you used an effective document design to obtain a good layout with some typographical interest?

- Have you provided sufficient headings to guide the reader through the proposal?

- If you have used a report format, do your table of contents and headings match?

- Have you completed all the online forms?

Suggestions for Applying Your Knowledge

Proposals provide a rich field for both long and short writing assignments and for class discussion.

Individual Activities

You could submit a proposal for a paper such as the one illustrated in Figure 15.4.

Short proposals can be bids. You can bid to furnish products or services in construction, research, interior design, food service, health services, and so forth. You could bid to build a porch, install track lighting, furnish carpets or drapes, or cater a party. The possibilities are enormous. The proposals can come from schoolwork, off-campus work, or some combination of the two. Include only information that is absolutely relevant to the bid, such as what is to be furnished, by whom, and at what cost. You might also include a few sales touches such as experience and testimonials.

Long proposals could be a term project. Like short proposals, they could relate to major fields of study or to off-campus work. They could relate to community problems. They could involve extensive research in the area involved, perhaps even including surveys and interviews, as in the model proposal about peer advising. In long proposals, you would have more sections, such as facilities, equipment, schedules, and personnel. You would establish the need for the product or service offered. You would promote your ability to fulfill the terms of the proposal. You would devise an organization and a format that present your proposal in the best way possible.

Collaborative Activities

1. Long proposals can also be team or even class projects. There are certainly enough sections to go around. You could even try a proposal that is real and not just an exercise. Most colleges have an office that deals in grants. You could go to the grants office in your college and find out whether they have any student-oriented requests. The NSF solicitation used as an example in this chapter was just such a request. Or search the World Wide Web for requests for proposals. If you find such an RFP, it might be a stimulating group project that could end in real accomplishment.

2. Long proposals frequently have to be sold with an oral presentation as well as a written document. They provide good applications of persuasive speaking skills.

3. A good deal of material can be gathered for class discussion. The grants office at your college or university will likely have on hand out-of-date requests for proposals they would be happy to let you have. These requests can furnish material for good class discussions as you analyze the types of information, organization, and format they call for. They provide fine examples of our constant theme: Workplace writing provides specific information to a specific audience for a specific purpose.

   In teams, develop a chart that shows a comparison and contrast of the organizational plans and formats called for. You can learn from all of them, but decide which ones are best and why. If you cannot obtain actual proposals submitted by various units of your college or by companies in your area, go to Web sites for government agencies, companies, and organizations to find current requests for proposals. Discussion of how they were researched, organized, and written will help you learn how to do your own proposals. The originator of the proposal might be willing to participate in the discussion.

Mechanism Descriptions

We define mechanism very broadly.

Mechanism description explains the purpose, appearance, physical structure, and sometimes the operation or behavior of a mechanism. The word *mechanism,* as used here, refers to any object that takes up space and behaves in a predictable manner or performs work. In this sense, a driver's license is as much a mechanism as is a clutch or an automobile. A mechanism or object can be small or large, simple or complex, artificial or natural. It can be so large that we cannot see it in its entirety with our naked eye. It also can be so small, so fleeting, so far away, so deeply hidden that we cannot see it without the assistance of special cameras and recording devices used with computers, electron microscopes, and powerful telescopes. Hand tools (scissors, pen, nail punch), devices (oil pump, artesian well, deep-sea camera, electric dust extractor, geodetic satellite, Tesla coil, laser printer), natural objects (egg, knee joint, flower, kidney, meteor, volcano, paramecium), and synthetic objects (the molecular arrangement of fluorocarbons, olean, the plastic in milk cartons) suggest the wide range of mechanisms. In addition, the layout of a wastewater treatment plant or the floor plan of an office complex or an abstract entity such as the Federal Reserve System might also be regarded as mechanisms.

The world we live in is highly artificial and engineered—from crossbreeding and cloning of animals and plants to improved roadways and measuring systems. Mechanisms may even be otherwise unseeable until they are described. Scientists often work with entities that cannot be seen by optical means, especially in the world of astronomy, physics, and molecular biology. The shape and size of atoms, the double-helix structure of DNA, the synaptic ends of nerves, the existence of black holes, and many concepts of modern physics and molecular biology cannot be seen directly, but they can be objectified and visualized from data that convince us that they are present. Mechanism description is an important means of conveying evidence of their presence and of making visible to the mind what might not be visible to the eye.

At work, at home, and at leisure, we are surrounded by mechanisms and objects. To evaluate them or use them, we need to know all their functions, their features, and how their parts work together or relate to one another. Mechanism descriptions help to meet our need to know.

Regardless of the mechanism or object to be described, the main problems confronting you when you describe it are (1) how much information to provide, (2) how best to create an image of the mechanism or object in your readers' minds, and (3) how to arrange the details of the description.

Deciding How Much Information to Provide

Focus your description on what is important to you and your audience.

One of the universal problems of mechanism description is the decision of how much information to provide. You can potentially include so much in the description that it becomes unacceptably long and provides information that readers cannot use. You must select what information to include and what to leave out. Two familiar considerations face you immediately when you prepare to describe a mechanism or object:

1. Determining the purpose of your description
2. Understanding your audience's needs

Determining the Purpose of Your Description

Mechanism description is always selective. You probably will never describe a mechanism or object just to describe it. The information about it you include depends on whether you are describing it to readers and listeners who will approve its manufacture, make it, buy it, ship it, store it, operate it, evaluate it, repair it, or in some instances, identify it well enough to locate it. Sometimes the purpose is to compare features of different models of the same product or to explain the improvements of a new model with an earlier one. So the obvious first step in planning your description is to determine your purpose in describing it. You must focus on what is important to your purpose.

A special purpose of mechanism description is the detailed description required in patent applications, conventionally referred to as the "description of the preferred embodiment."[1] A major part of a patent application is a description of an invention in "full, clear, concise, and exact terms" that "distinguish the invention from other inventions and from what is old" and describes "completely the process, machine, manufacture, composition of matter, or improvement invented."[2]

Understanding Your Audience's Needs

Be sure to explain the importance or significance of the features you describe—the so-whats.

An obvious second step in planning your description is to determine what your audience needs to know to understand your description. Mechanisms have specially designed features and functions built into them that are important to readers and listeners. Describing these is one of your most important tasks. You do not want to burden readers with unnecessary information, but you also do not want to omit meaningful information. After a few attempts at describing mechanisms, you will learn the ways in which many a mechanism—which is clear and easy for you to understand—can be difficult and confusing to those to whom you are describing it. Sometimes it is difficult to determine when simply to state a feature and when to explain its significance. You must estimate how familiar your readers are with the concepts you are describing. For instance, if it is important to point out that a certain

---

[1]From *A Guide to Filing a Utility Patent Application* (p. 5) by Patent and Trademark Office, March, 1998, Washington, D.C.: U.S. Department of Commerce.

[2]From *A Guide to Filing a Utility Patent Application* (p. 5) by Patent and Trademark Office, March, 1998, Washington, D.C.: U.S. Department of Commerce.

element is made of tungsten, is it also necessary to explain the so-what—that tungsten is used because of its hardness and its capability to withstand corrosives and high temperatures? Or, in another example, if there must be a clearance of 18 inches above a device, is it important to explain that this much clearance is needed to open the top cover of the device? In a way, you walk the tightrope between the legal maxim that "the fact speaks for itself" and the often-proclaimed scientific principle that "a fact in itself is nothing."

Because you know so well the features of the mechanism you describe, it may be difficult for you to remember that such knowledge might appear isolated and unimportant to your readers unless you explain the importance of the feature. How many readers do you think would have the technical background to understand the significance of the following information?

> The protective shroud is made of 3003 aluminum and is flared to the outer edges as shown in Figure 7.

Providing a couple of additional sentences explains the so-whats, the significance, of the features (the composition of the material and the tapered design):

> The 3003 aluminum is used because it is malleable, resists corrosion and is lightweight. Flaring the outer edge of the shroud extends the heating surface to the outer edge of the shroud.

Of course, you might need to elaborate further and explain why the material should be malleable and lightweight and resist corrosion and why the heating surface should extend to the outer edge of the shroud. You need to know this level of detailed information in case it is important to provide it for your audience. So as you plan your description, ask yourself whether you know the significance, importance, or implications of such features. If you do not, then you need to research those matters.

Let us look at an example of how you can be sure you know enough about the features to explain them to readers. Assume that you are describing an electric paper shredder that reduces paper to unreadable 1/4-inch strips and that you want to point out several important features. In preparing your notes, you might find the two-column format in Figure 16.1 handy. The left column identifies the feature, and the right column identifies the significance of the feature: the so-what.

When you mention the features in your presentation, immediately explain the significance of the feature so that it has meaning to your readers and listeners. The two-column format shown in Figure 16.1 will do, or you can combine the information into a bulleted list, such as the one shown in Figure 16.2.

When you review and revise your description, keep asking yourself whether your intended reader is likely to need certain features translated into more meaningful terms. By doing so, you will ensure that your readers will take in the full meaning of what you say about the mechanism. Concern about insulting your readers' intelligence by providing information that they

FIGURE 16.1

Two-column format for listing major features of a mechanism and the significance of those features. The Significance column translates the features into meaningful concepts for readers.

Feature	Significance
Built-in shredder continuously feeds through the shredder	Works automatically, without supervision.
3/4 hp motor	Has 70 percent more shredding power than most other models, shreds 14 sheets of 20-lb. bond paper at one time.
12″ throat	Accepts computer printout pages and other large-size paper.
Hardened cutter blades	Cannot be damaged by conventional staples and paper clips.
10″ high × 21″ wide × 22″ deep	Compact and small enough to use on table or desk top.
Soft rubber feet	Will not mar furniture.
Brown, gray, or beige finish	Fits most office decors and color schemes.

FIGURE 16.2

Bulleted list of major features of a mechanism and the significance of those features.

The Shredmaster 180 has seven major features:

- Built-in shredder continuously feeds forms through the shredder. Works automatically and without supervision.
- 3/4 hp motor has 70 percent more shredding power than most other models. Shreds 14 pages of 20-lb. bond paper at one time.
- 12″ throat accepts computer printout and other large-size pages.
- Hardened cutter blades cannot be damaged by conventional staples or paper clips.
- Size: 10″ high × 21″ wide × 22″ deep—small enough to use on a table or desk top.
- Soft rubber feet won't mar furniture.
- Brown, gray, or beige finish matches most office decors and color schemes.

already know is often overemphasized. Even readers who understand the significance or importance of a feature will likely appreciate the reminder and proceed to skip over the material they know. However, readers who do not know the significance or importance of a feature will need the information if they are to understand fully the concept you are describing.

Describing a Familiar Mechanism

If your purpose is to remind readers of the major features and parts of a mechanism with which they are somewhat familiar, you can rely on visuals to describe its appearance and on a few words to describe its materials, connections, and functions. Figure 16.3 is a description of a device provided by the manufacturer to acquaint customers with their purchase. The description, appearing at the front of the customer's manual for the blender, is brief yet sufficient for its purpose and well organized. The mechanism is described in terms of its major parts and their functions.

Describing an Unfamiliar Mechanism

Often your purpose will be to acquaint readers with mechanisms or objects with which they are unfamiliar. In such cases, you will need to explain more thoroughly the purpose, physical structure, and use or operation of the mechanism. Let us assume, for instance, that you are introducing a group of students or field assistants to a device they must know forward and backward—the Berlese funnel, a common collection device used by entomologists to collect and test samples for insect habitation (Figure 16.4).[3]

The purpose of your description—and your audience's purpose in using the description—determine the amount of detail you include.

The description of the Berlese funnel provides more detail than does the description for the Oster liquefier-blender in Figure 16.3. The extent to which a mechanism or object is to be described (and consequently, the length of the mechanism description) depends on what readers need to know about the mechanism. If your purpose were to provide specifications so that someone could make the mechanism, you would need to include detailed information that would provide a pattern to be copied. Not even the most minor dimensions or features could be omitted. Once you have established in your mind the purpose of your description and what your readers need to know of the mechanism or object, you will know what and how much to include in your description.

---

[3]From an unpublished student report, used with permission of the author, Jim Johnson.

FIGURE 16.3

The first page of a manufacturer's booklet describing a product (Courtesy Oster Corporation). The description is brief, yet sufficient for its purpose, and is well organized. The two-column format, placing an exploded view of the blender to the right of the written description, enables readers to move back and forth from the writing to the pictures with ease. The headings and numbered parts help readers identify parts.

Source: From *Know Your Osterizer Liquefier-Blender*, 203287-Rev-N (p. 1). Reprinted with permission of Sunbeam Oster Corporation.

Know Your
Osterizer.
LIQUEFIER-BLENDER®

This Osterizer blender is designed for household use only.

cover

The cover for your Osterizer blender consists of two parts, the plastic feeder cap (1) and the vinyl cover (2). The cover is self-sealing and is made of vinyl and resistant to absorption of odors and stains. The feeder cap is removable for use as a measuring cap and provides an opening for the addition of other ingredients.

container

The 5-cup container (3) for the Osterizer blender is graduated for easy measurement and is molded of heat and cold resistant material. The convenient handle and pouring lip permit easy removal of liquid mixtures, while thicker mixtures are more easily removed through the bottom opening.

agitator or processing assembly

Consists of three parts: (4) a sealing ring of neoprene used as a cushion between the container and the agitator; (5) agitator of high-grade stainless steel; (6) a threaded container bottom.

motor and motor base

The powerful multi-speed motor is the heart of the appliance and designed just for this unit. It is completely enclosed within the housing (7).

The Osterizer blender motor uses a "free-floating" feature to reduce noise and wear. This feature allows the square post which protrudes from the motor base to move slightly from side to side.

Your Osterizer blender contains a powerful food processing motor, but it can be overloaded. To avoid this possibility, closely follow the instructions and the quantities specified in the recipes in this book.

The illustration and photography of Osterizer blenders found in this book do not necessarily depict the particular model Osterizer blender that you have purchased. These photographs are merely a guide to illustrate the versatility of your Osterizer blender.

care and cleaning of your Osterizer blender

Never store foods in your Osterizer blender container. Always remove the agitator assembly and wash and dry container and agitator assembly thoroughly after you have finished blending. Re-assemble container after cleaning so it will be ready for future use. Never place processing assembly on motor base without the container. See page 2 for proper assembly and tightening instructions.

Osterizer blender parts are corrosion resistant, sanitary, and easily cleaned. Wash in warm, soapy water and dry thoroughly. DO NOT WASH ANY PARTS IN AN AUTOMATIC DISHWASHER.

NEVER IMMERSE THE MOTOR BASE IN WATER. It does not require oiling. Its outside can be cleaned with a damp cloth (unplug cordset first).

203287-Rev -N   [1]

FIGURE 16.4

Description of a mechanism involves both written and visual description. For such description, you will have to select the details to include and what to omit, based primarily on what you believe readers will need or want to know. Notice the placement of visuals and the references and labeling of the parts.

Source: An unpublished student report, used with permission of the author, Jim Johnson.

The Berlese Funnel

You have several methods for sampling soil, leaves, or trash for insect habitation. You can simply pick out insects from a sample by hand, use a sieve to separate insects from a sample, or "bake" insects from a sample by using the Berlese funnel. The first two methods are not always satisfactory, because some insects will probably be overlooked. When an absolute count of the insects is required, use the Berlese funnel, named after the Italian entomologist who invented it in 1912. The Berlese funnel uses heat from an incandescent bulb to dry the sample and force the insects to burrow away from the heat source and ultimately drop through a funnel into a collection jar. Although Berlese funnels vary in size, depending on how large a sample needs testing, they all have the same parts and appearance and work the same way. As shown in Figure 1, the three main parts of a workbench-sized Berlese funnel capable of holding up to a half gallon sample are (1) the cover, (2) the container, and (3) the stand. Its overall height is 15 inches.

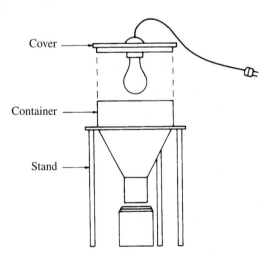

Figure 1. The main parts of the Berlese funnel
and the collection jar

FIGURE 16.4
(continued)

The Cover

The metal cover (Figure 2) resembles a miniature trash can lid. It covers the container and serves as a mount for the 100-watt bulb. Air vents in the cover allow excess heat to escape and enable you to observe the sample without removing the cover. A 1/2-inch flange holds the cover in place.

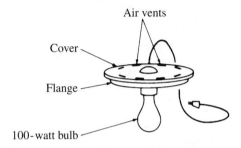

Figure 2. The cover

The Container

The container (Figure 3), which fits into the steel retaining ring of the stand, is divided into an upper and a lower section. The upper section is the 4-1/2-inch deep plastic reservoir that holds the sample, and the lower section is the plastic funnel through which the insects drop into the collection jar. A galvanized screen with a 1/4-inch mesh, upon which the sample is placed, separates the two sections. The container has an overall height of eleven inches and a diameter of 8-1/2 inches before narrowing to a diameter of 1 inch at the bottom of the funnel.

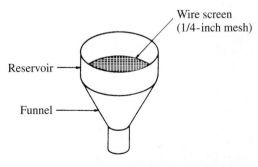

Figure 3. The container

FIGURE 16.4
(continued)

The Stand

The stand (Figure 4) supports the container and allows room for the collection jar to be placed beneath the funnel. It is composed of a 1/2-inch steel retaining ring with a 9-inch diameter into which the sample container is placed and of three legs made of 1/2-inch steel cylinders 11 inches long. The legs are attached to the retaining ring by screws, allowing the stand to be disassembled for storage or transportation.

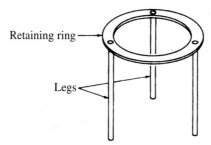

Retaining ring

Legs

Figure 4. The stand

Using the Berlese Funnel

The Berlese funnel works like an oven. The heat from the 100-watt bulb "bakes" the sample, forcing the insects to seek a moister area. As the top of the sample dries, the insects burrow down toward the remaining moist sample. When the entire sample is dry, the insects have passed through the wire screen and dropped through the funnel into the collection jar.

Helping Readers Visualize the Mechanism

One of the major aims of mechanism description is to create for readers a clear mental picture of the mechanism or object you are describing. Therefore, it is natural for you to want to show readers what it looks like. The four common ways of doing this are to use pictorials, adjectives and other modifiers, analogies, and geometric shapes.

Using Pictorials

Your ability to lead your audience to an understanding of the mechanism depends on your ability to visualize important features. For more information on visuals, see Chapters 6 and 7.

When visual understanding is involved, pictorials (photographs and drawings) are the most exact method of communication. Verbal language, written or spoken, simply does not measure up to visual language in showing physical appearance and spatial relationships. Look once again at the visuals in Figure 16.3 and 16.4, and consider how many additional words and sentences would be required to describe the devices as fully as the visuals do.

However, the old saying that "one picture is worth a thousand words" is true only if the picture is a good one and if it communicates better than words. Unless you are skilled in photography and drawing, you will need help in making pictorials. Digital cameras and graphics programs give you the tools to create pictorials, but consider your level of proficiency and your time as well as your audience's expectations and the purpose of the document. If you have any doubts, have a professional graphic artist create the pictorials. If you work for an organization that has a presentations department that will do your artwork for you, count your blessings. If you do not, you must hire someone to do them. You may find an appropriate visual on the World Wide Web. Remember, though, to acknowledge your source if it is for a school paper. If you include borrowed visuals in a document that you plan to publish, you must get written permission to use the visuals, including those from sources on the World Wide Web. However, even when others prepare pictorials for you or you borrow a pictorial, you should know what defines a good one. You may be required to supply preliminary sketches to be made into finished pictorials. And, of course, as author of the document, you are also responsible for the quality of the pictorials.

The choice, execution, and placement of pictorials should be given at least as much importance as text is when you plan your description. Determine what aspects of the object you want to convey so that you can decide which type of pictorial best illustrates that information. Use as many visuals as necessary to show the mechanism or object: exploded views, sectional views, partial views, and separate views to show alternative positions of mechanisms or objects. For information about using visuals, see Chapters 6 and 7.

Using Adjectives

Using adjectives, analogies, and geometric shapes are other ways to describe features.

As useful as visuals are, words (especially adjectives and other modifiers) are also essential in description. Adjectives describe visual appearance: *narrow, short, curved, round*. They also describe texture and other tactile features: *dry, sticky, bumpy, smooth, rough, dimpled, sharp*. They describe sounds: *squeaky, screeching, hissing, high-pitched, humming*, and so forth. They also describe taste and odor: *acrid, sweet, sour, smoky*. When using adjectives, keep two goals in mind. First, be as specific as necessary to reduce ambiguity. For instance, *curved, crooked, undulating, wavy*, and *bent* are adjectives that describe lines or planes that are not straight. Because they are not synonyms, you should select the adjective that most accurately depicts the configuration you mean. Second, use adjectives that are familiar to your readers. For instance, *saw-toothed, serrated, crenelated, dentate*, and *dentiform* refer to tooth-shaped features or objects. *Oval, ovoid, elliptical*, and *ellipsoidal* refer to egg-shaped features or objects. Use adjectives that most readers are likely to recognize. *Coin-shaped* is a lot more familiar to most readers than are *nummiform* and *nummular*.

Using Analogies

Suppose we want to describe something that we have seen for the first time or that our readers have never seen. How do we describe the unknown? Usually, the best way is by comparing it to the known.

Can you remember the tremendous excitement you felt when you first looked at objects under a microscope? Those magnified images revealed a world previously hidden from you. In 1665, Robert Hooke, a 17th-century English scientist, constructed a microscope that allowed him to examine many objects never before seen by the human eye. Following is part of his description of what he saw when he looked at a piece of outer bark of the cork oak with the microscope as he recorded it in *Micrographia* (1665). We have modernized the spelling.

> I took a good clear piece of cork, and with a pen knife sharpened as keen as a razor, I cut a piece of it off, and thereby left the surface of it exceedingly smooth, then examining it very diligently with a microscope, I thought I would perceive it to appear a little porous; but I could not so plainly distinguish them, as to be sure that they were porous, much less what figure they were of. But judging from the lightness and yielding quality of the cork, that certainly the texture could not be so curious, but that possible, if I could use some further diligence, I might find it discernible with a microscope, I with the same sharp pen knife, cut off from the former an exceedingly thin piece of it, and placing it on a black object plate, because it was itself a white body, and casting the light on it with a deep plano-convex glass, I could exceedingly plainly perceive it to be all perforated and porous, much like a honeycomb, but that the pores of it were not regular; yet it was not unlike a honeycomb in these particulars.
>
> First, in that it had a very little solid substance, in comparison of the empty cavity that was contained between, as does more manifestly appear by the Figure A and B of the XI scheme, for the *interstitia*, or walls (as I may so call them) or partitions of those

pores were nearly as thin in proportion to their pores, as those thin films of wax in a honey-comb (which enclose and constitute the sexangular cells) are to theirs.

Next, in that these pores, or cells, were not very deep, but consisted of a great many little boxes, separated out of one continued long pore; by certain diaphragms, as is visible by the Figure B, which represents a sight of those pores split the long-ways.

Although Hooke's style may seem strange to modern readers (especially his long sentences), he used two conventional methods to convey impressions of what he saw. As his references to "Figure A and B" indicate, he used drawings. His comparison of cells to "honeycomb" and "little boxes" shows that he relied on analogies to describe what the cells looked like.

Take a lesson from Hooke. When an object resembles something else your readers are more familiar with, analogies can be helpful in explaining its shape, size, and structure. A common way to do this is to use metaphors of shape based on the letters of the alphabet: A-frame, C-clamp, I-beam, O-ring, S-hook, T-square, Y-joint, and so on. Another way is to name parts of objects after parts of anatomy: head, eyes, ears, mouth, teeth, lip, throat, tongue, neck, shoulder, elbow, arm, leg, foot, and heel. Gears and saws have teeth; pliers and vises have jaws; needles have eyes; and so on. A third way is to use resemblances to other well-known objects: a mushroom-shaped anchor; a barrel-shaped container; a canister the size of a tube of lipstick.

Analogies also can be used to suggest structure, shape, and size:

Each stair tread on an escalator is like a small four-wheel truck.

Some bearing sleeves are porous and under a microscope look like very fine sponges but are rigid.

The simplest portable hair dryer looks a little like an oversized handgun in which a small fan blows hot air out of a screened nozzle.

The tape-recording head is a small C-shaped electromagnet the size of a dime.

The barometer case looks like a small metal shoe box with a glass lid.

The islands hang like a loose necklace from the entrance of the bay.

The combustion chamber is shaped like a fat figure eight.

Our galaxy may be surrounded by an ultraviolet halo emitted by neutrinos.

If you cannot make the comparison by using a well-known and easily visualized analogy, you can often compare a new mechanism with an older one or a more complex one with a simpler one.

Disposable syringes are just like rubber ones except they are made of plastic and can be discarded after use.

A compact disc is a secondary storage medium for computer data and programs. It is identical in shape and size to the compact discs used for recording music.

An automobile battery is a much larger and chemically different version of the battery that powers a flashlight.

How good an analogy is depends on how well the comparison clarifies the object being described. It would not do to describe something as resembling a pair of dividers or a lemur unless your readers could be expected to know what a pair of dividers or a lemur looks like. You would be using one unknown to describe another unknown. Furthermore, an analogy can mislead rather than clarify if it does not suggest the right features. For instance, comparing an object to a circle is ineffective if the object looks more like a wheel or a doughnut. Likewise, comparing an object to a funnel is misleading if it is only cone-shaped. Everyone knows what a tree is, but to refer to an object as "tree-shaped" does not take into account the differences between oaks, pines, palms, and weeping willows. Be sure your analogy is familiar, is appropriate, and reveals as many specific characteristics as possible.

Using Geometric Shapes

When an object has an easily identifiable geometric shape, you can refer to that shape—assuming that you and your readers know basic geometrical terminology. However, if your readers cannot be expected to know what a rhombus or a parallelepiped is, do not refer to them. And if the object you are describing is three dimensional, do not refer to a two-dimensional shape. For instance, if your readers look at a two-dimensional drawing of a three-dimensional object, they might mistake a cone for a triangle. You must either provide a three-dimensional view or explain that the object is conical. Following is a brief review of terms from your geometry class that can be greatly useful in mechanism description.

Two-Dimensional Shapes

Two-dimensional shapes include angles, polygons, and circles.

Angles Angles are shapes formed by two straight lines that meet. When two straight lines meet at a 90° angle, the angle is said to be a *right angle*. Angles less than a right angle are called *acute* angles. Angles greater than a right angle are called *obtuse* angles.

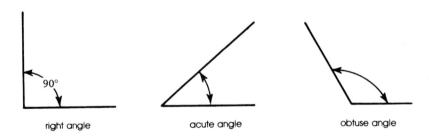

right angle   acute angle   obtuse angle

Polygons Polygons are two-dimensional shapes bounded by straight sides. The most usual kinds of polygons are illustrated in Figure 16.5. Most of these shapes exist around us. The face of an Egyptian pyramid is a triangle. A musical percussion instrument, the triangle, is an example of an equilateral triangle. If you fold a square sheet of paper diagonally so that its opposite corners meet, you have made a right triangle. The courthouse squares in traditional county seats are laid out on a square parcel of land. The face of a length of board is a rectangle if the length exceeds the width. Home plate on a

FIGURE 16.5

References to geometric shapes are important in describing mechanisms.

NUMBER OF SIDES	NAME OF SHAPE	SHAPES
3	triangle	△ equilateral △ isosceles ◿ right
4	quadrilateral	□ square ▭ rectangle ▱ parallelogram ⬦ rhombus
5	pentagon	⬠
6	hexagon	⬡

baseball diamond and the five-sided building in Arlington, Virginia, that is the headquarters for the U.S. armed services are pentagons. The cells in a honeycomb are hexagons.

Circles A circle is a shape bounded by a curved line that is at all points at an equal distance from its center. A hula hoop, the face of a coin, and wedding rings are circular.

A half-circle, or semicircle, is half a circle with a diameter line connecting the end points. Half a circle without a diameter line is a type of arc.

An oval is a shape that looks like a stretched-out circle. The orbit of a satellite and the layout of a race track are examples of ovals.

Three-Dimensional Shapes

Technically speaking, a three-dimensional shape is a solid object. For our purposes in mechanism description, however, the object need not be solid— we are concerned with the shape. For example, a container or housing for a piece of machinery may be referred to as cubical or cylindrical even though the object is not solid. The most common three-dimensional shapes are polyhedrons, cylinders, cones, spheres, and ellipsoids.

Polyhedrons Polyhedrons are "solid" objects bounded by plane surfaces. The most familiar type of polyhedron is the cube. Children's blocks, dice, and even some kinds of ice "cubes" are cubes.

Cones Cones are shapes that come to a point at one end with the opposite end a circle. The upper part of a funnel, the nose "cone" on a space capsule, cinder-coned volcanoes, and even some kinds of ice cream "cones" are examples of cones.

Cylinders Cylinders are shapes that look like jars, drinking glasses, cans, rods, dowels, and tubes.

Spheres Spheres are "solid" objects bounded by a surface that is at all points the same distance from its center. Tennis balls, globes, and marbles are examples of spheres. A hemisphere is half a sphere. Domes are typically hemispherical.

Ellipsoids Ellipsoids are egg-shaped objects. An egg, a football, and various seeds and pills are shaped like ellipsoids.

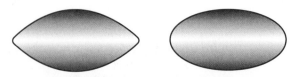

Arranging the Details of the Description

Descriptions of mechanisms typically have a three-part arrangement: overall description, part-by-part description, and explanation of the mechanism's operation.

Because you have multiple details to tell readers about a mechanism or object, and because a mechanism or object has more than one part, it is impossible to describe it all at once. Therefore, you must lead readers through a particular order of presentation. The following three-part arrangement will usually be satisfactory:

- An introductory overall description of the function and appearance of the entire mechanism

- A description of the function and appearance of each major part of the mechanism

- An explanation of how the mechanism operates or is used

What you are doing, in effect, is explaining what the mechanism does and looks like, what each part does and looks like, and how the mechanism as a whole works. Proportions of the description usually work out this way: For a mechanism of five major parts, the presentation will have seven main sections—an introduction, five sections describing the five functional parts, and a concluding section describing the operation of the mechanism. Figure 16.6 is the basic organizational pattern.

The title is usually no more than the name of the mechanism being described: Multipurpose Police Vehicle, Field-Effect Transistor, Underground Storage Tanks, Microprocessor Chip, Gradiometer, Buckminster Fullerenes, and so on.

The Introduction

Your readers must have an understanding of the overall mechanism or object and a mental framework in which to fit all the details before they get to the details, or they will be swamped. The introduction provides this kind of frame of reference and overview for the entire mechanism or object. It names the mechanism or object again (in many cases explaining the origin of its name when it is not obvious), explains its function or behavior, describes its overall appearance, and lists its individual parts. Here is an introductory paragraph that does these things:

> A volcano is a cone-shaped mountain with a crater in the top that from time to time erupts, spewing gases, rock, ash, and molten lava. The main features are its crater (the opening in the earth's surface) and the conduit connecting the opening to the interior of the earth, which contains magma (hot, molten lava). The largest active volcano in the world is Mauna Loa in the Hawaiian Islands, which towers more than 13,500 feet above sea level.

See also the introduction to the description of the Berlese funnel (Figure 16.4). Following are some principles to keep in mind when you introduce a mechanism or object.

FIGURE 16.6

Basic organization pattern of mechanism description. The introduction provides an overview of the purpose, appearance, and major parts of the mechanism. The body describes each major part of the mechanism. The ending explains how the mechanism works or is used, if this information is not provided in the introduction.

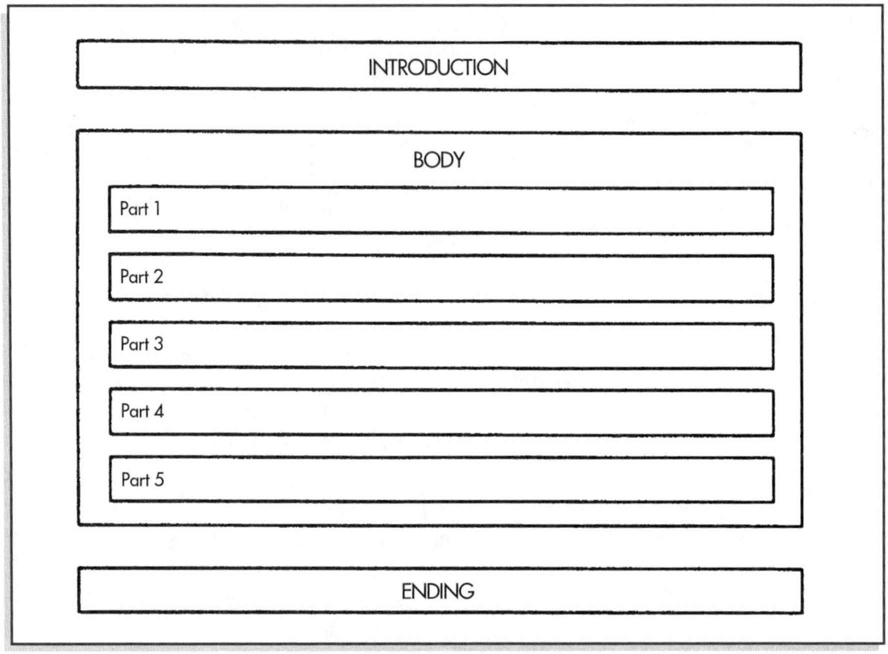

- **Explaining its name helps readers develop a richer conception of the mechanism or object.** Although much current nomenclature is unnecessarily abstract and jargonistic (for example, the tendency to call a container a "functional storage and transportation module" or a stairwell a "vertical egress and exit area"), several traditional methods exist for naming things, and you should be aware of them and use them. Here are just a few of the more frequently used methods.

  One of the most common sources of names is to add the suffix *-er* or *-or* to a verb to indicate its function. Thus, *engraver, opener, propeller, recorder, sprinkler, trimmer, circuit breaker* and *elevator, modulator, oscillator, refrigerator, antenna rotator,* and *sensor* are named for their functions. As long as it is clear what is being accelerated, trimmed, oscillated, and so on, you need not elaborate on the significance of the name. However, when the function is not obvious, you need to clarify. For instance, a *multiplexer* and *demultiplexer* (obviously things that create a "multiplex" or perform multiplexing and "demultiplex" or perform demultiplexing) are components of modern telephone systems. These devices convert voice into digital sounds, a process called *multiplexing*. The conversion allows multiple communications to travel simultaneously on an individual line. Demultiplexing, as you can imagine, is the conversion of the digital signal back into the sound of a human voice.

When Latin or other foreign words are incorporated into a name, some explanation may be necessary: For instance, the word *meter* refers to a measuring device (*measure* = meter) as in *thermometer* (*thermos* = heat, *meter* = measurer). Do you have any idea what a *sphygmomanometer* measures? In some instances, the suffixes -*er* and -*or* are omitted, as in *cruise control* and *brake*—instead of *cruise controller* and *braker*.

A second method of naming items is to shorten and combine words, as in *ammeter* (am[pere] + meter), *altimeter* (alti[tude] + meter), *transistor* (trans[ference] + [re]sist[ence] + or), and *maglev train* (mag[netic] + lev[itation] + train). Acronyms are another form of shortening and combining words, especially using only the initial letter or two of a series of words to form another word. For instance, *radar* comes from *radio detection and ranging*; *scuba* from *self-contained underwater breathing apparatus*.

A third common method of naming, especially in physical, natural, health, and social sciences, is to name items after their inventor, developer, or discoverer, or to honor someone. The *Wangensteen suction* is named after the nineteenth-century American surgeon who invented a suction machine to use in the treatment of gastric and intestinal disorders. The *Mercator* grid is a type of map projection that is named after its inventor, Gerhardus Mercator, a 16th-century Danish cartographer. The *Furbish loutwort* is a plant named after Kate Furbish, the botanist who discovered it. The *Maginot Line,* a defensive line built in the late 1920s on France's eastern border, was named after Andre Maginot, the French Minister of War at the time. *Halley's Comet* is named after the astronomer who predicted its return. The rover that sent back so many photographs of the Martian terrain in the summer of 1997 is named *Sojourner*, partly in honor of the abolitionist Sojourner Truth and partly as an allusion to its primary mission of conveying truth about the Martian surface.

Most relevant to description, many items are named for some aspect of their appearance: alligator clamp, programming comb, mushroom anchor, mouth of a river, bottlenose whales and dolphins, and a c-strap on a motorcycle seat or saddle.

- **The most important statements you make about a mechanism or object early in your description relate to its function, parts, and appearance.** If you are familiar with the mechanism or object, it is easy to assume that your readers share your knowledge. But you must remind yourself that most readers will need information about what the mechanism or object does (if known), what it looks like, and what its major parts are. Here are a few sample explanations of the function and listing of the major parts of mechanisms and objects:

A hand hacksaw is a metal-cutting saw of three parts: a handle, a C-shaped frame, and a thin, narrow blade fastened to the open side of the frame.

An amoeba, a one-celled animal found in fresh water, consists of a nucleus, the surrounding protoplasm, and an enclosing outer membrane.

A cantaloupe is a small melon with a ribbed, netted rind; delicately flavored orange flesh; and seeds.

A microwave oven consists of a housing, power unit, magnetron, wave guide, and oven cavity.

The steering system on a sailboat consists of the rudder, the rudder post, and the tiller.

Venetian blinds, horizontally slatted window shades that can be adjusted to control the amount of sunlight that enters a room, from unimpeded sunlight to nearly complete darkness, consist of the following parts:

1. control cords to lift and lower the blinds,

2. control cords to adjust the tilt of the blinds, and

3. slats resting on crosspieces between pairs of tapes.

A miter box is a device used to guide a saw in cutting stock to form angle joints. The simplest form consists of a wood or plastic trough with saw cuts through the sides, usually at angles of 45° and 90°.

The heart consists of four chambers (two atria for receiving blood and two ventricles for pumping blood), valves to prevent a back flow of blood, and numerous vessels that help this part of the circulatory system to work.

These examples partition the mechanism or object into main parts. You can provide a more extensive forecast of the parts and subparts by "nesting" the subparts with each main part, as in these examples:

The UJ1000 Printing Calculator has three main parts:

1. the upper panel (composed of the display screen and the printer),

2. the control board (composed of the power, decimal, and printer switches), and

3. the keyboard (composed of the function pad, the number pad, and the memory pad).

The cell, as shown in a magnified cross section in Figure 1, includes three principal parts:

1. the membrane, which holds the cytoplasm together and separates the cell's internal parts from the external environment;

2. the cytoplasm, the substance between the nucleus and the membranes; and

3. the organelles, which are highly specialized components such as the nucleus, mitochondria, endoplasmic reticulum, Golgi complex, and lysosomes.

Such extended partitioning gives readers an outline of the main parts and subparts of the mechanism or object. Occasionally, such detailed forecasting can be done, provided that it does not present too much information too fast. In general, you should identify only the main parts in the introduction and introduce the subparts later.

Explaining the function of a mechanism requires thinking as the inventor thought.

- **Every mechanism is designed or has the form to fulfill a particular function.** The question to answer is: Why is the mechanism designed as it is? or why is the object shaped as it is? Sometimes you can explain this in the first sentence of the introduction, as in several of the examples given earlier. Other times, you will have to devote a sentence or more to explaining the function:

  > A drafting compass is designed for drawing circles, arcs, and ellipses.
  >
  > A torque wrench is used to tighten bolts to a specified degree of tightness.
  >
  > A joystick is a lever that can be tilted any direction (360°) to control the position of the cursor on the display screen. It is used primarily in computer graphics and games.

  In explaining the function, be sure to describe all the important functions the mechanism is designed to perform. For instance, an air conditioner has more functions than to cool a space. Most air conditioners also circulate the air, remove moisture from the air, and filter the air. An explanation of the function of an air conditioner should fully reveal the kinds of "conditioning" it is designed to do.

- **When the mechanism or object you are describing is part of a larger mechanism or object, you should explain how the mechanism or object relates to the larger whole.** An ammunition clip or magazine is part of a rifle; a distributor is part of the ignition system of an automobile; a speaker is part of a stereo system. Providing a larger context for the mechanism or object helps readers understand it better.

- **Your readers always need a notion of the size, shape, and general appearance of the mechanism or object.** Size can be explained by giving dimensions (the metal plate is 20 × 30 × 1/4 inches) or by comparisons (the film canister is about the size of a tube of lipstick). Shape can be expressed by geometric shapes (the bookend is shaped like an equilateral triangle) or comparison to shapes of the letters of the alphabet and numbers. A drawing that shows the entire mechanism or object is often placed in the introduction to give readers some idea of its general appearance as a whole and to orient them to the physical viewpoint from which they are viewing it.

- **Every mechanism or object has at least two parts.** Partitioning the mechanism or object into its major parts usually presents no problems unless it is extremely simple or complicated. In either instance, you must make some arbitrary decisions. Try to come up with no fewer than two parts and not more than five or six. Something as simple as a piece of chalk, when thought of as a mechanism, has two ends for marking on a chalkboard and a cylindrical body used for a handle (unless some kind of handle or holder is provided). Just because the mechanism or object is in one piece is no sign that you should not look for at least two parts.

Do not confuse a physical piece with a part. Similarly, if a mechanism or object has lots of pieces, you should group several of them under one large part. For example, an adjustable beam compass can be separated into as many as 30 pieces, but it can be regarded as having only three major functional parts: the writing head, the center pin, and the adjustable beam. The 30 or so pieces are grouped as subparts of these major functional parts.

- **The list of parts indicate the order in which the parts will be discussed.** The order may be one of three sequences:

  1. Function: The parts are described in the order of their activity—Part A moves Part B, which moves Part C, and so forth.

  2. Space: The parts are described from left to right, top to bottom, outside to inside, front to back, and so on.

  3. Importance: The parts are described from the most significant to the least significant.

  Random order is seldom satisfactory.

The Body

The part-by-part description explains the function and appearance of each part of the mechanism and how each part contributes to the operation of the mechanism.

The body of a mechanism description explains each major part in the order indicated by the list of major parts in the introduction. The parts description provides much the same information for each part that the introduction does for the mechanism or object as a whole. Simply think of the parts as a miniature mechanism or object. Give at least one section of details for each major part. The following example describes a bolus gun, which is used by veterinarians and other persons who work with livestock to administer medication in pill or tablet form.[4] In the introduction (which is not included here), the writer explains the function of the bolus gun, compares it to a hypodermic syringe in design and use, indicates the different sizes it comes in, provides an overview of the instrument by listing its three main parts (the plunger, the barrel, and the pill chamber), and provides the following drawing:

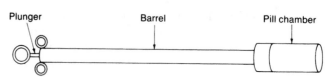

Figure 1. The bolus gun

---

[4]From an unpublished student report, used with permission of the author, Don Bowles.

FIGURE 16.7
Description of the main parts of a bolus gun, an instrument used to administer medication in pill (bolus) form to large animals.

Source: An unpublished student report, used with permission of the author, Don Bowles.

THE PLUNGER

The plunger (Figure 2) fits inside the barrel and pushes the bolus out of the pill chamber into the animal's throat. It consists of a ring grip, stem, and knob. Located at the back of the plunger, the ring grip is used to maneuver the plunger. The stem is that part of the plunger between the ring grip and the knob. When the stem is pushed forward in the barrel, it causes the knob to move forward and eject the bolus from the pill chamber into the animal's throat. The knob is attached to the front of the plunger and fits inside the pill chamber. It is the knob, shaped like a disc measuring 3/16 inch thick and 7/8 inch in diameter, that ejects the bolus.

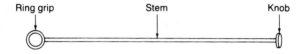

Figure 2. The plunger

THE BARREL

The barrel (Figure 3), which is 10-3/4 inches long and 1/2 inch in diameter, is long enough to insert the pill chamber well into the animal's mouth and is large enough to enclose the plunger. Two ring grips, through which the operator's forefinger and middle finger are inserted, provide the necessary grip on the gun while administering the medicine.

Figure 3. The barrel

THE PILL CHAMBER

The pill chamber holds the bolus before it is ejected into the animal's throat. As shown in Figure 4, it consists of a base, clip, and cover. The base connects the pill chamber to the barrel and supports the clip and the cover. The clip holds the bolus steady while the gun is being positioned in the animal's mouth. It is 2 inches long and 1/4 inch wide to accommodate large pills. The cover is made of pliable plastic to protect the animal's mouth and throat.

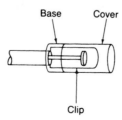

Figure 4. The pill chamber

In the body of the description (see Figure 16.7), the writer devotes a section of details to each main part, explaining the part's function and appearance and identifying its subparts. In the rest of each section, the writer gives the details of material, finishes, weight, connections, and use needed to give readers a visual and functional understanding of the part.

The Ending

The ending explains how the mechanism works or is used. Here, you divide its function or behavior into meaningful stages and explain what happens in each. For instance, if the writer who described the bolus gun had not provided such information in the introduction, he might have described its use like this:

> The bolus gun, designed like a hypodermic syringe, can be used with one hand. The operator grips the gun with one hand, opens the animal's mouth with the other, and inserts the end of the gun deep enough into the animal's throat to prevent the pill or tablet from being coughed up.

Another way to end your description is to explain briefly the principles involved in its action. For instance, a toaster broils thinly sliced materials, such as bread; or an air conditioner cools a space by removing heat from it. If you have included this information in your introduction, you need not write a separate ending.

PLANNING AND REVISING CHECKLIST: MECHANISM DESCRIPTIONS

Think about the following when planning and revising a mechanism description.

Planning

- How familiar are your intended readers or listeners with the mechanism? Will some terms need to be defined? Should any so-whats be explained?

- What is the purpose of the description? Is it to help your intended audience to understand the function, appearance, and parts of the mechanism or object? Is it to help them manufacture, pack, store, ship, unpack, assemble, or service it? Is it to help them identify it?

- Does your audience need to know why the mechanism was developed? What it replaced? How it differs from earlier models or versions?

- What visuals, adjectives, analogies, and geometric shapes enable your audience to visualize the mechanism or object?

Revising

- Is the description complete and accurate for your and your readers' purposes?

- Have you provided a clear initial overview of the function, appearance, and parts of the mechanism or object?

- Are the function, appearance, and components of each major part explained clearly?

- Have you explained the significance of the purpose, features, and operation of the mechanism?

- Are details, measurements, adjectives, analogies, and references to geometric shapes clear and reasonably specific?

- Are the visuals clear and easy to understand, considering the intended readers?

Suggestions for Applying Your Knowledge

Individual Activities

1. Explain the visual analogy behind the name of each of the following:

A-frame	chip
alluvial fan	claw hammer
band saw	cradle roof
bottle-nosed dolphin	deadman
caterpillar gate	death's head moth
dining ell	kidney bean
disk brake	leaf spring
dovetail joint	malleus, stapes, incus (the three small bones in the inner ear
fiddlehead fern	of humans)
fiddler crab	monkey wrench
forklift	needle-nose pliers
foxhole	organ pipe cactus
gateleg table	pineapple
hairspring	rocker arm
hammerhead shark	sea cucumber
hip roof	T-hinge
J-stroke	U-bolt
kangaroo rat	wing nut
kettledrum	

2. Explain the visual analogy behind the names of five items from your field of study (excluding any that are listed above).

3. Analyze the description of the bolus gun or the Berlese funnel for its use of so-whats. Divide a sheet of paper into two columns and list the features and their so-whats. If you find instances in which additional so-whats would be helpful, include them, too.

4. Choose a mechanism, object, entity, or system with which you are familiar and you believe that most of your fellow students are not. Explain its function and overall appearance, partition it into no fewer than two and not more than six major parts, and explain the order of parts that you would use to arrange your description. Explain the visuals that you would use.

5. Write a description of some mechanism, object, entity, or system with which you are familiar and you believe that most of your fellow students are not. Be prepared to explain to other students in the class the intended audience, the purpose and the arrangement of the description, and the methods to help readers visualize the mechanism or object and its parts.

Collaborative Activities

1. Form a panel with two other students in your class to give an oral description of a mechanism, object, entity, or system with which the three of you are familiar. Arrange to have a visual or visuals of the mechanism or object or the thing itself in class. Decide who will make the initial introduction of the mechanism or object, who will describe its major functional parts, and who will describe the way it operates or behaves. Time: 10 to 15 minutes.

2. Analyze and discuss in class the description of the field sprayer in Figure 16.8.[5]

---

[5]From *Field Sprayer Equipment and Calibration* (pp. 3-15) by William Mayfield, n.d., Auburn, AL: Alabama Cooperative Extension Service.

FIGURE 16.8

Sample description of a mechanism titled *Field Sprayer Equipment and Calibration.*

Source: Permission granted by the Alabama Cooperative Extension System to use Filler Sprayer Equipment and Calibration, Circular R-11, as an example. Information may be out of date.

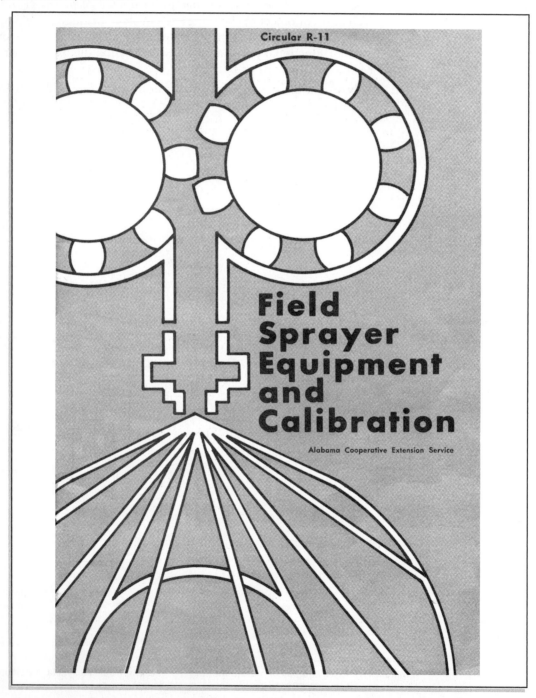

FIGURE 16.8
(continued)

by
WILLIAM MAYFIELD
Extension Agricultural Engineer

THE MODERN FARMER has many good chemicals to use, but they must be applied properly to be effective. Many of these materials are toxic to crops, animals or humans, and it is absolutely necessary that they be delivered only to the target area.

Study and carefully follow the instructions from equipment and pesticide manufacturers. All spraying equipment should have instruction manuals when you buy it. Keep these manuals in a safe and convenient place.

EQUIPMENT

Conventional sprayers usually consist of a pump, a pressure regulator and gauge, strainers, a tank cut-off valve, nozzles and agitators (Figure 1).

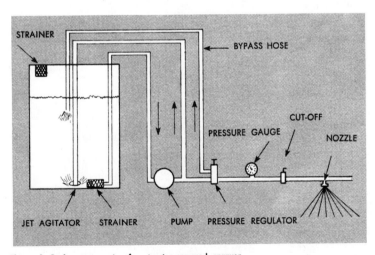

Figure 1. Basic components of a tractor-powered sprayer.

—3—

FIGURE 16.8
(continued)

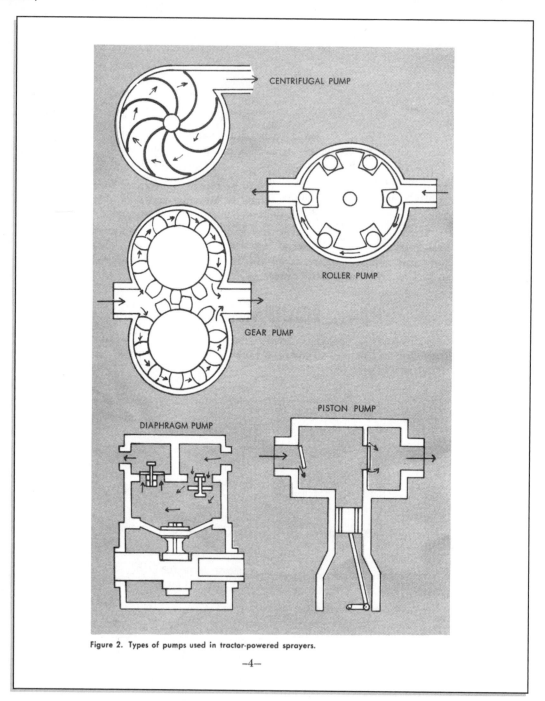

Figure 2. Types of pumps used in tractor-powered sprayers.

—4—

FIGURE 16.8
(continued)

PUMPS. Types of pumps that are normally used for sprayers are shown in Figure 2, and the advantages and disadvantages of each are listed in Table 1. Gear and roller pumps are satisfactory for emulsions and solutions. Piston and diaphragm pumps are satisfactory for all materials including wettable powders. You can also use roller pumps to apply wettable powders, but wettable powders are abrasive and pump rollers must be replaced often. The pump should be able to supply the required volume of spray (and some bypass volume for agitation) at 100 pounds per square inch when operating at 550 revolutions per minute. This will insure enough capacity under spraying conditions.

Table 1. ADVANTAGES AND DISADVANTAGES OF PUMP TYPES

Pump Type	Operating Pressure	Advantages	Disadvantages
Piston	0-1000	Adaptable to all spray formulas. High pressure. Resistant to wear. Parts easily replaced.	Expensive. Heavier than most.
Gear	0-200	Inexpensive. Medium pressure.	Low volume. Short life. Unsatisfactory for wettable suspensions.
Roller	0-350	Durable when made of noncorrosive steel and plastic. Medium volume and pressure.	Rollers must be replaced frequently when spraying wettable suspensions.
Diaphragm	0-100	Low wear from abrasive materials. Parts are easily replaced. Medium price. Medium pressure.	Low volume. Synthetic rubber diaphragm is nonresistant to some pesticides.
Centrifugal	0-65	Adaptable to all spray formulas. Low wear from abrasive materials.	Expensive. Low pressure. High speed is necessary but not always available on tractor PTO.

—5—

FIGURE 16.8
(continued)

STRAINERS. There should be a strainer at the tank opening, on the suction hose and at each nozzle. Line and suction strainers should be 50- to 100-mesh screen. Nozzle strainers should be 50- to 200-mesh screen, depending on the size of the nozzle's orifice. The strainers should always have smaller openings than the orifice or nozzle opening with which it is used.

PRESSURE REGULATOR AND GAUGE. The pressure regulator lets enough material return to the tank to keep the desired pressure on the boom (Figure 3). The regulator should be a bypass type with a screw adjustment. The gauge should be mounted near the pressure regulator and have a capacity of at least 100 pounds per square inch.

NOZZLES. The nozzles determine the spray distribution pattern and affect the volume of spray delivered. Therefore, the nozzles must be the correct size and must deliver the best distribution pattern for the job to be done. The parts of a spray nozzle are illustrated in Figure 4. Nozzles are classified by capacity, type and angle of spray pattern. Some common spray patterns are shown in Figure 5.

Nozzles are commonly available in brass, stainless steel, aluminum, plastic, nylon and ceramic. Usually, brass, aluminum and

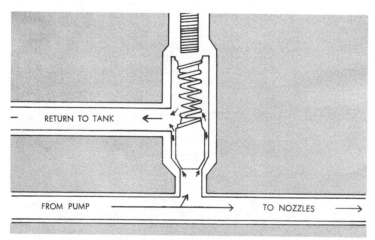

RETURN TO TANK

FROM PUMP

TO NOZZLES

Figure 3. The pressure regulator. It lets the flow from the pump return to the tank when there is enough boom pressure to compress the spring. The load on the spring adjusts the boom pressure.

—6—

FIGURE 16.8
(continued)

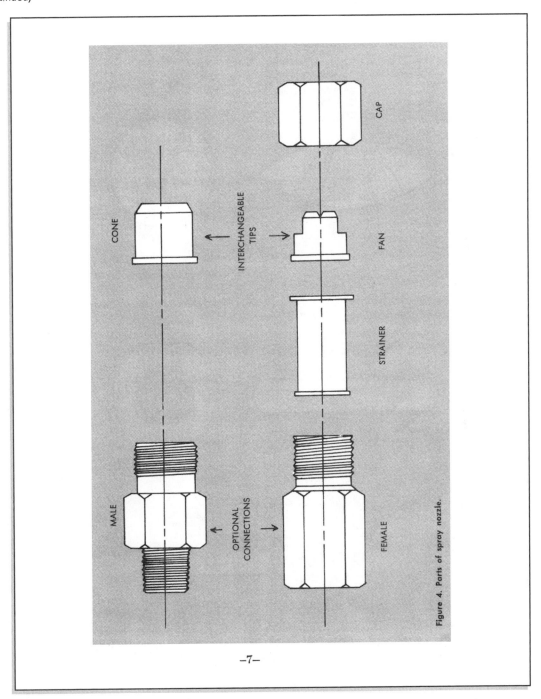

Figure 4. Parts of spray nozzle.

FIGURE 16.8
(continued)

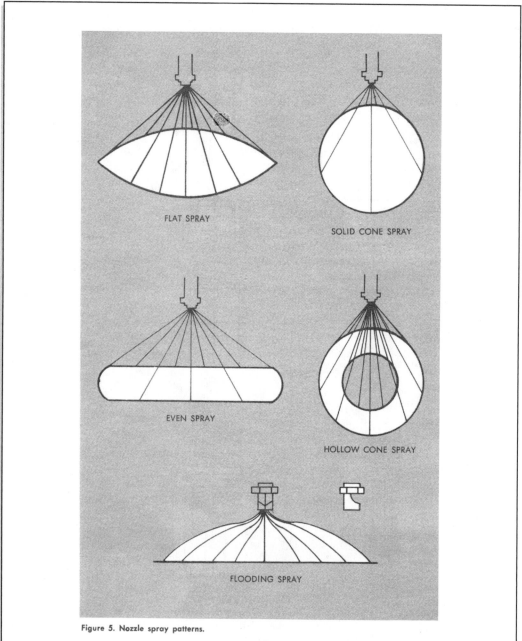

Figure 5. Nozzle spray patterns.

FIGURE 16.8
(continued)

plastic nozzles have about the same life. Stainless steel should last about 3 times as long as brass; hardened stainless steel about 10 to 15 times, and tungsten carbide about 180 to 200 times as long.

FOR PREEMERGENCE HERBICIDE APPLICATION, fan-type nozzles with 65- to 110-degree angles are used. The 80-degree angle is most used. With the common 20-inch boom spacing, operate 80-degree nozzles 18 inches above the ground (Figure 6). Use a pressure of 20 to 50 pounds per square inch. *Even-flow fan-type nozzles* are best for band application.

FOR POSTEMERGENCE HERBICIDE APPLICATION, use 65- to 95-degree fan-type nozzles at a pressure of 15 to 40 pounds per square inch under most conditions. Directed spray equipment may use a combination of fan-type and cone-type nozzles but must be equipped according to the manufacturer's recommendations.

FOR LAY-BY, flooding-type wide-angle nozzles are usually operated at pressures between 10 and 40 pounds per square inch. Check instructions and charts carefully for speed, pressure and nozzle capacity.

FOR INSECT CONTROL, arrange cone-type nozzles with the required number per row to give complete coverage of plants. One or two nozzles per row may be enough for smaller plants, but for large plants, three nozzles per row may be needed.

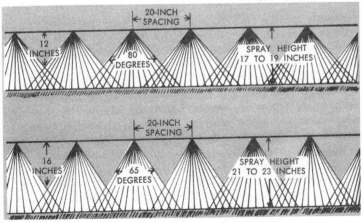

Figure 6. Nozzles with different angles need different boom heights.

—9—

FIGURE 16.8
(continued)

FOR FUNGICIDE APPLICATION, arrange three *hollow cone nozzles* per row to give complete foliar coverage. Use pressure of at least 70 pounds per square inch. It is important to use as much water per acre as recommended on the fungicide label.

TANK. Select a tank with a large opening for easy filling, inspection and cleaning. The opening should have a strainer. Be sure the tank can be completely drained. You can get tanks of corrosion-resistant metals, plastic linings and fiber glass. A tank can be mounted in many positions, but the tractor balance and ease in filling should be considered.

AGITATOR. Liquid concentrates, emulsions and soluble powders need very little agitation. The return flow in the bypass usually gives enough agitation for these materials. However, wettable powders need vigorous agitation; jet agitators are needed in addition to the bypass agitation. Connect the jet agitator between the pump and the pressure regulator so that full pump pressure can be used for agitation (Figure 1).

CUT-OFF VALVE. Be sure you have a quick acting, cut-off valve between the pressure regulator and the boom where it can be easily operated from the tractor seat.

HOSES AND FITTINGS. Select hoses that resist sunlight, oil and chemicals, and are flexible and durable.

Nozzle Arrangement on Boom

Nozzle spacing and alignment on the boom are important for uniform coverage. The height of the nozzle tip above the area to be sprayed, nozzle spacing and the angle of spray patterns are all related and should be carefully considered when spraying. Figure 6 shows two types of nozzles and the relationships between spray angles and nozzle heights. Notice that with different spray angles the height has to be adjusted to give uniform coverage. Manufacturers' spray manuals give you the boom heights for various spray angles and nozzle spacings.

Figure 7 shows other boom and nozzle relationships. The top illustration shows that if you let the boom droop, you get uneven coverage and skips. The middle illustration shows what happens when nozzles with different spray angles are used along the boom. The bottom illustration shows skips that occur when nozzles are plugged or when operating pressure is higher or lower

—10—

FIGURE 16.8
(continued)

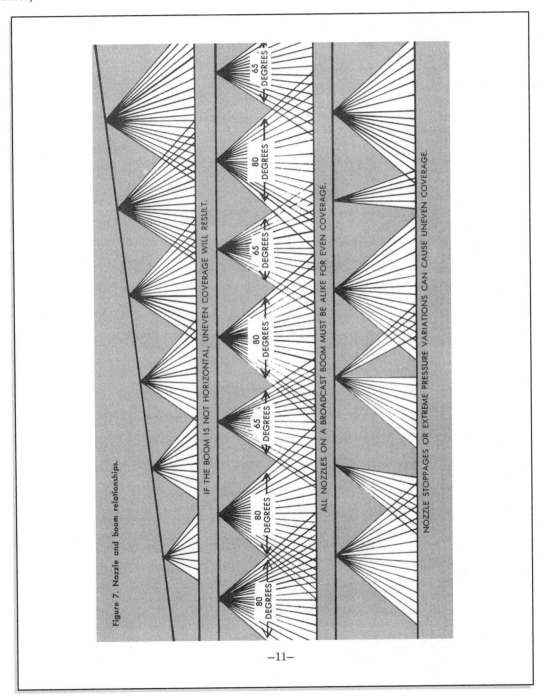

Figure 7. Nozzle and boom relationships.

IF THE BOOM IS NOT HORIZONTAL, UNEVEN COVERAGE WILL RESULT.

ALL NOZZLES ON A BROADCAST BOOM MUST BE ALIKE FOR EVEN COVERAGE.

NOZZLE STOPPAGES OR EXTREME PRESSURE VARIATIONS CAN CAUSE UNEVEN COVERAGE.

65 DEGREES
80 DEGREES
65 DEGREES
80 DEGREES
65 DEGREES
80 DEGREES
80 DEGREES

–11–

FIGURE 16.8
(continued)

than recommended. Although the required amount of material per acre may be discharged, the coverage is not uniform.

Misalignment of nozzle tips is a common cause of uneven coverage (Figure 8). Be sure fan-type spray patterns are parallel with the boom when installing nozzle tips. Figure 9 shows four arrangements of nozzles on a boom; parts B, C and D are drop-nozzle arrangements.

When you need a band application of herbicides, apply spray with an even-spray nozzle. The nozzle height can be adjusted to give the desired band width.

Boomless or Broadcast Sprayers

A boomless or broadcast sprayer is different from other sprayers because of its nozzle arrangement. A cluster of nozzles or a special nozzle is used to give a wide spray path. This sprayer has fewer nozzles and is better adapted to rough or steep terrain than a boom type. However, it is harder to get uniform coverage and accurate placement with a broadcast sprayer because the spray material simply falls onto the plants while the conventional boom-type sprayer forces the material into the plant foliage. The slightest wind disrupts the spray pattern of the broadcast sprayer, causing drift and uneven distribution.

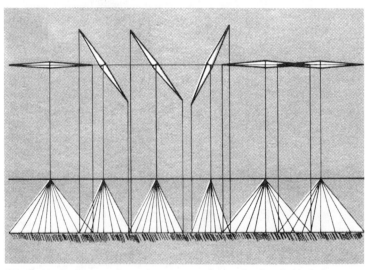

Figure 8. Nozzle alignment. For good coverage, nozzles must be aligned with the boom.

—12—

FIGURE 16.8
(continued)

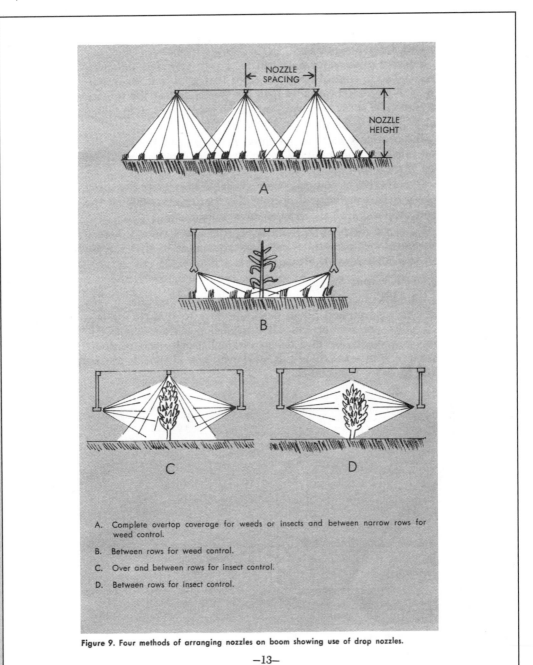

A. Complete overtop coverage for weeds or insects and between narrow rows for weed control.

B. Between rows for weed control.

C. Over and between rows for insect control.

D. Between rows for insect control.

Figure 9. Four methods of arranging nozzles on boom showing use of drop nozzles.

—13—

FIGURE 16.8
(continued)

Directed Spray Equipment

Directed spray equipment can be a very effective and inexpensive way to control weeds in crops that grow tall fairly rapidly. The crop must be taller than the weeds so that the nozzles can direct the spray material toward the base of the crop plants and strike the foliage of the weeds (Figure 10).

The nozzles must be mounted below and to the side of the crop foliage and must be supported and directed toward the base of the plant.

Several types of equipment are available to support the spray nozzles. Select, mount and operate the nozzles according to the recommendations of the equipment manufacturer.

Using a directed spray with sweeps on a cultivator is a very economical way to control weeds, but this must be used as a single part of a total weed control system.

Ultra-Low Volume Sprayers

Ultra-low volume (ULV) application of a pesticide means applying concentrated liquid pesticides in a total spray volume of ½ gallon per acre or less. ULV-applied pesticides are faster, more convenient, and give longer residual toxicity and wash-off resistance with some chemicals. However, few chemicals are labeled for ULV application.

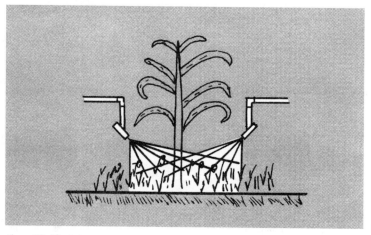

Figure 10. Directed spray.

—14—

FIGURE 16.8
(continued)

ULV sprayers have many problems, especially with ground equipment. Calibration, distribution, flow rate, drift and safety are some of the more serious.

The physical properties of each pesticide formulation are different and flow rates are not the same; therefore, calibration must be done with the pesticide itself. Flow rates often are so low that the volume of spray caught for measurement in the short calibration time is too small for accurate measurement and calibration. Low flow rates and the small-orifice spray nozzles often result in nozzle stoppage. And, because of the low flow rate, it is difficult to detect a stoppage.

Distribution studies have indicated that it is very difficult to get a uniform distribution pattern across the spray swath. The extremely small particles delivered from a ULV sprayer drift easily. This is true with both the multirow, mist-blower-type sprayer and those with a single spray orifice for each row.

Special safety precautions must be followed when applying concentrated ULV insecticides. The potential dangers to the operator during calibration, nozzle cleaning, filling and spraying are greater because of the greater concentration of toxic material.

Instructions

L earning how to do something new can be either enjoyable or frustrating. Often, the key is how clear and complete the instructions are. Some instructions, written by people who do not know how to perform the procedure, are full of misinformation. Other instructions, written by people who know the procedure thoroughly and who assume that everybody else does too, contain directions that are too general or incomplete. Good instructions are written by people who know the procedure inside out and who know how much detailed instruction their readers need—whether the readers are novice learners or experienced and highly skilled learners who want more conceptual understanding and more opportunities to explore and experiment on their own.

Whatever work you specialize in, you are certain to have to produce instructions. When you become good at producing instructions, you also become one of your organization's most valuable members, because good instructions can aid your organization in three ways:

1. Good instructions are effective customer-relations tools that help customers use the products and services they lease or purchase. If products and services are difficult to learn and use, customers will not lease or buy. On the other hand, good instructions enhance an organization's reputation by helping customers and clients get maximum value for their purchases and leases.

2. Good instructions—especially those that accompany a company's products or services—not only are a marketing plus but also protect the company from some product liability lawsuits. This is an important matter. If a customer, using the company's instructions, damages equipment or material or injures himself or herself or others, the company is subject to possible legal liability.

3. Good instructions are also useful in helping employees learn to do many jobs quickly and easily—from assembling, stocking, and shipping to operating, repairing, overhauling, and storing.

Your instructions should present straightforward help in solving problems for either customers or employees. Instructions can be oral, written, or, as shown in Figure 6.1 (see page 131), visual, but they should be put in writing and visuals when a mistake in the procedure is likely to be serious or when it is inconvenient, unfeasible, or impossible to communicate orally with your audience.

Written instructions come in all sizes and for different purposes and for different users. In this chapter, we discuss the more common classifications of written instructions:

- Brief instructions presented in correspondence, on panels on packages, on sheets and leaflets

- Longer instructions presented in booklets and manuals

- Troubleshooting and error-management procedures

Instructions and troubleshooting and error-management procedures may be prepared to be read on paper or on a computer screen. Our discussion covers collecting information, writing brief and lengthy sets of instructions, creating troubleshooting guides, and testing instructions for usability.

Collecting the Information to Write Instructions

When providing instructions for an untrained audience, you need to spell things out.

Because readers of instructions expect you to write with authority, you must know the procedure inside out before you try to tell others how to do it. But knowing how to perform a procedure does not automatically mean you can produce good instructions. Beginners who will use your instructions often lack the background or technical skills to perform what you may regard as commonly understood procedures. You must have the additional abilities to (1) put yourself in the shoes of the beginner so that you can predict their difficulties and (2) express to others what you know and do intuitively.

To conduct a comprehensive analysis of the procedure and your readers, you must consider eight topics—eight kinds of information that you need to collect:

- reader's goal(s), which identify what the user of your instructions should be able to do after reading the instructions

- materials and equipment needed to perform the procedure

- major stages of the procedure

- duration of the procedure (how long it will take to perform the procedure)

- step-by-step activities of each major stage

- precautions to be observed when performing the procedure

- visuals that illustrate situations, equipment, actions, and other aspects of the procedure

- degree of difficulty that users of your instructions might experience in learning or performing the procedure

Use a plan sheet to record the information you need to create clear, specific instructions.

To gather this information, you must spend time learning the procedure and analyzing your readers and their goals and the environment in which they will use the instructions. To record the essential information you will need in working with these topics, we suggest that you use the Plan Sheet for Instructions (Figure 17.1), which is similar to those used by directors of training in preparing training manuals and other instructional material.

FIGURE 17.1

Plan Sheet for Instructions. This form is good for handwritten plans. You can modify the form for a computer-generated draft.

Plan Sheet for Instructions

(A) **Reader's Goal or Goals:**

(B) **Materials:**

Equipment:

(C) **Major Stages:**

(D) **Duration of the Procedure:**

(E) Step No.	(F) Steps in Performing the Procedure	(G) Precautions	(H) Notes about Visuals	(I) Notes about Learning and Performance Difficulties

Reader's Goal or Goals

(A) **The statement of the reader's goal or goals (Figure 17.1) defines what the reader should be able to do when he or she finishes using the instructions.** A good goal statement should complete a how-to statement:

[How to] replace a fuel pump.

[How to] check the credit rating of a customer.

[How to] send an attachment by e-mail.

[How to] identify igneous rock.

[How to] conduct a presentence investigation.

[How to] calibrate a centrifuge using a tachometer.

[How to] evaluate a long-term health-care insurance policy.

[How to] install a peripheral device on a computer, such as a modem, digitizer, or switcher.

[How to] inspect an oil cooler for cracks, damaged threads, and evidence of wear.

[How to] determine moisture content in textiles.

The reader's goal(s) should be stated quite specifically, such as "[How to] unjam a Bunscomb Bob Cat Chipper/Shredder, Model No. 1464." The goal(s) can also be developed into quantitative statements. For instance, a goal can be stated as "The reader will be able to replace the fuel pump in 30 minutes." Such a concrete, specific goal helps you clarify your objectives and write instructions that will aid the reader in achieving that goal. Identifying the reader's goal(s) is a good starting point because it focuses on yours and the reader's purposes and will be reflected in the title of the instructions. Focus early and continuously on what the reader hopes to achieve in using the instructions.

Materials and Equipment

(B) **The materials and equipment lists (Figure 17.1) specify the items needed to perform the procedure.** Materials are those items consumed during the procedure. Equipment is the hardware. In baking bread, the ingredients (flour, yeast, water, salt, etc.) are the materials; the measuring cup, mixing bowl, spoon, bread board, loaf pans, and oven (or bread machine) are the equipment. You must know your reader's needs as best you can so that you can decide how much the reader knows and understands and whether the reader needs to be motivated to assemble the materials and equipment you list. To make the list as useful as possible, place it in the introduction, be as specific as the reader and the situation call for, and, if necessary, try to persuade the reader to use the equipment, tools, and materials you specify.

- *Put the list in the introduction.* Tell the reader exactly what to use so that he or she will know, before starting the procedure, the exact tools, parts, and test equipment required to complete the job. Do not wait until the middle of the procedure to tell the reader that an essential part is needed to finish the job. It is conventional to list materials and tools in the order in which they are used in the procedure.

Exact dimensions and quantities are both necessary and reassuring to your audience.

- *Be specific. Be complete.* In explaining to somebody how to ice-fish, do not say to use a fishing pole, line, and hook if the person needs a 2-foot pole, 15 feet of 2-pound-test monofilament line, and a size 10 hook. If raw sunflower seeds are part of a recipe, be specific, or the chef may procure salted, roasted, barbecue-flavored, or garlic-flavored sunflower seeds. If a high-intensity candling light of 80 to 100 ohms is needed, do not simply state that a light source is required. If a specific part is needed, include the manufacturer's part number or acceptable replacement stock number. Even people who are familiar with a procedure can benefit from a friendly reminder of specificity, such as to use an insulated-handle screwdriver when working on electrical circuits.

- *Use consistent terminology.* Be consistent in choosing nomenclature and labeling equipment and material. It is difficult to produce a good set of instructions—and even more difficult for readers to follow instructions—for procedures in which units, functions, and features have been inconsistently labeled. One of your authors, for example, has used software in which a feature is labeled *tone presentation* on one screen and *present* on another. How many readers, do you suppose, would know that a feature labeled an antenna in one section of a report is the same as an item labeled air terminal in another section?

Sometimes you need to motivate your audience to perform actions in a specific way.

- *If necessary, try to persuade the reader to use the material and equipment you specify.* You must take into account the tendency of some readers not to believe it necessary to use the precise material or equipment you specify. Too many readers have an appalling lack of knowledge about the necessity for wearing protective eyeware when performing certain procedures. Others will not understand why the latest, more expensive version of a software program is needed instead of an older, less expensive version. To respond to the reader's belief that "it does not seem necessary to use that . . . ," consider adding parenthetical statements. For example, in Figure 17.4 on page 498, "one sheet of medium grit sandpaper to smooth the wood frame" explains to users of the instructions why that particular item is needed and might motivate them to use it.

Major Stages of the Procedure

(C) **The overview of the major stages of the procedure (Figure 17.1) provides important conceptual information.** For instance, assume that we are explaining how to change the points in the distributor of an automobile. Our overview of the major stages might look like this:

The three major stages in changing the points in a distributor are (1) removing the old points, (2) installing the new points, and (3) adjusting the new points.

In online instructions, the major stages are represented as links.

Removing the Old Points
Installing the New Points
Adjusting the New Points

The links enable readers to locate the part of the instructions they want.

This highly condensed version of the procedure presents three ways to help readers grasp the big picture before they become immersed in the details of the procedure.

First, because the overview organizes the procedure into three major stages, it reduces the amount of information the reader needs to process at any given time. For example, the process might well involve 50 or more individual steps, which at first might appear intimidating to a beginner. However, organizing the work into three major stages makes the procedure appear more manageable. Thinking initially about accomplishing three major actions is less overwhelming than thinking about performing 50+ steps and will reduce the tendency of readers to worry in advance about whether they are going to fail.

Second, because each of the major stages in the overview identifies the task to be accomplished in each stage, the overview enables the reader to:

- Create a mental model of what is involved in each stage

- Identify the major subgoals of that part of the procedure: At the end of the first stage, the old points will have been removed; at the end of the second stage, the new points will have been installed; at the end of the third stage, the new points will have been adjusted.

These status descriptions help to reassure the reader that the action can be accomplished, perhaps even easily and confidently, by following the instructions.

Third, because the major stages are listed in the order in which they are to be completed, the overview is a content map that helps the reader read selectively or predictably. Sometimes, of course, readers attempt to perform a procedure without even bothering to look at the instructions. Few readers will deliberately read a set of instructions from beginning to end. But for those who do, each major stage is the core of a heading, and the two (the overview list and the headings) help the reader keep the big picture in mind.

Instead of following a set of instructions from beginning to end, many readers are likely to start trying to do the procedure, figuring things out as they go along, and to resort to the instructions only when they are stuck. Or they may want to review only the steps in a particular stage—for example, adjusting the points. Such a chronological overview provides nonlinear access to specific parts of the procedure, enabling some readers to read ahead if they wish. But all readers will have one thing in common: the desire to find quickly just the information they need.

When a major stage turns out to be long and complicated, consider providing an overview of it, just as you do for the entire procedure:

Estimating Storm Runoff

After determining the adequacy of drainage needed to maintain water in the pond during droughts, you need to estimate the potential storm runoff. To do this, you must identify (1) the kind of soil in the drainage area, (2) the types of vegetation in the drainage area, and (3) the steepness and shape of the watershed. Tables I through III show a range of runoff computations for different pond sizes.

A table of contents (see pages 366 and 369) might be appropriate for longer sets of instructions. Listing the major stages of a procedure or major steps of a stage responds to the diverse needs of different readers. Not including these kinds of overviews is likely to be a major flaw in the design of your instructions.

Duration of the Procedure

(D) **The duration of the procedure (Figure 17.1) is the amount of time necessary to perform the procedure.** Stating the duration of the procedure might not seem important to you, but beginners need to know approximately how much time a procedure requires. For instance, if we rewrote our earlier overview statement about replacing points in a distributor as follows, the reader could estimate the amount of time he or she should set aside to perform the procedure:

If you have never changed the points in a distributor, it will take you approximately one hour to (1) remove the old points, (2) install the new points, and (3) adjust the new points.

When a major stage in a procedure is long and complicated or you anticipate your reader not knowing how long it might take to complete, you can provide a similar overview for that stage:

Installing the Pool Liner

Before installing the liner, check the pool bottom to be sure there are no stones, twigs, or sharp objects that might damage the liner. After the liner is unboxed and placed at the deep end of the pool, it will take four to six people (see Figure 4) approximately 25 to 30 minutes to pull it into position and adjust it properly.

Remember that you should estimate the approximate amount of time it takes beginners to do the work, not you and other experts. In time, as readers become more proficient in performing the process, they will be able to reduce the time needed.

Step-by-Step Procedure

Every step is developed, no matter how simple it might seem to you.

(E) (F) The step-by-step part of the instructions explains the process in detail for novice readers. **State each step in terms of what the reader *does* when performing the step (see Figure 17.1).** This is where you must think through the process in detail, sequencing steps logically. What does the user do first? Second? Third? As you develop the steps, keep these three matters in mind:

- Sequence the steps in the best order for the reader to complete the instructions.

- Use imperative verbs.

- Avoid ambiguities.

For online instructions, if possible, present each step on its own screen to cut down scrolling.

- **Sequence the steps in logical order.** Your instructions should state explicitly the sequence of steps (1, 2, 3, and so on) and should clearly distinguish instructional material from conceptual or background material. Numbering the steps is important because readers typically switch back and forth between instructions and work, reading a bit, then performing an action, then reading some more. The numbered steps make it easier for readers to find their place in the instructions. Numbering the steps makes clear the order in which steps are performed, which may or may not be a crucial consideration. Even in situations in which the reader can choose the order of action (for instance, it makes no difference in cleaning a double-barrel shotgun which barrel is cleaned first—assuming that they are of the same gauge), you should set the sequence based on your experience of what is the best recommended practice. Show the reader one good way to perform the step.

- **Use imperative verbs.** To present instructions in short, distinct steps, use a single imperative verb and as few words as possible to tell the reader exactly what to do. An imperative verb will usually be the first word of the instruction:

  1. *Disengage* the clutch.

  However, you will often begin an instruction with an adverbial phrase:

  4. Before cutting the first strip, *check* to ensure that the pattern is straight.

  or

  2. Using the wire feeler gauge, *set* the gap between the electrodes to the correct clearance (see Figure 2A).

  Use a specific imperative verb (one that states a command) to tell the reader the statement is *instructional:*

  Instructional: 1. Disengage the clutch. (Use this style for instructions.)

  Descriptive: The clutch is disengaged.

  Subjunctive: The clutch should be disengaged.

  The descriptive and subjunctive verbs are not instructional in that they do not tell the reader explicitly to do anything.

- **Avoid ambiguous statements.** Be aware that statements can have multiple meanings that confuse and befuddle readers. For instance, it is

Avoid confusion by explaining each step clearly.

essential that the user of instructions for mixing concentrated sulfuric acid and water know the precise way to do it. The statement: "Mix the concentrated sulfuric acid and water" sounds simple enough, right? However, the reader must decide how to mix the two. Is the acid added to the water? Is the water added to the acid? Are the acid and water poured simultaneously into a third container? The instruction is unclear, ambiguous, which can lead to poor or, as in this case, potentially dangerous results. Pouring the water into the acid or pouring the two simultaneously into a third container creates a volatile gas that can be messy and perhaps even cause an explosion. The safe procedure is to pour the acid into the water. Thus, to reduce ambiguity, the instruction should read: "Pour the concentrated sulfuric acid into the water." If necessary, explain why it is done that way.

Write instructions so that it will be difficult for someone to misunderstand them. To prevent costly errors in instructions and to check the clarity of the instructions, try them out yourself. Better yet, find an inexperienced person (but one who is a reasonable representative of the intended audience) to try the instructions while you watch and take notes for possible revisions. (See pages 513–515 for information about conducting usability tests.)

Precautions

Precautionary statements alert your audience about delicate operations and potentially dangerous situations.

(G) Identify precautions (Figure 17.1) that readers should observe while performing the step. According to the National Safety Council, approximately 3.7 million disabling accidents occurred on the job in the United States in 2002. There were also 4,900 fatalities in the workplace in the United States during 2002.[1] Because learners make many mistakes, giving precautions to help reduce the risks of personal injury and property damage are among your most important responsibilities. Place precautions into one of three categories:

- *Caution:* To prevent damage to tools, equipment, and materials
- *Warning:* To prevent injury to the person performing the procedure or to others nearby
- *Danger:* To warn of life-threatening situations to the person performing the procedure or to others nearby

Use headings, bold print, color, and other typographical features to highlight precautions and make them visibly distinct from surrounding text. Any of the forms shown in Figure 17.2 may be used.

You must be on the lookout for points in the procedure where a precaution might be helpful. It is not easy to foresee when users of instructions will have a problem, a question, are likely to make a mistake, or might need to recover from an error. Relying on your own memories of the difficulties you

---

[1] *Injury Facts, 2002.* www.ncc.Org/library/report_injury_usa.htm (23 October 2003).

FIGURE 17.2

These are sample cautions and warnings statements. The word *caution, warning, danger,* or other suitable words are highlighted to make the statements visually prominent. Warnings and cautions are usually amplified with statements that explain the importance of observing the precaution, the consequences of not following the caution or warning, and the preventive or corrective action to be taken.

CAUTION!

Tighten the nut to 25-30 pounds per inch. If you tighten the nut too hard, you will strip the threads.

CAUTION!
Oil rags are combustible. Wash or destroy them immediately.

CAUTION!

If the old gasket is not completely removed from the engine block, the new filter will not seal properly and will result in oil leaks and possible engine damage.

WARNING

Do not get under vehicle held up by a jack or by concrete blocks. The jack might slip and a concrete block will not hold the car's weight. Use jack stands or ramps.

 **DANGER!**

High frequency electromagnetic **radiation can cause fatal internal burns.** If you feel the slightest warming effect while near the equipment, **move away quickly.**

ELECTROMAGNETIC RADIATION

WARNING

Before making adjustments, shut off the engine, allow the cutting blades to come to a complete stop, and disconnect the spark plug.

had as a novice, the experience of others, and data derived from user testing will help you target places where probable problems and errors are most likely to occur.

Ideally, readers should follow instructions exactly. Unfortunately, many readers ignore instructions because the readers fail to understand the implications of not doing things exactly the right way or underestimate the potential problems in performing a task. Be aware of many readers' tendencies to think that precautions really do not seem necessary. When writing caution, warning, and danger statements, keep these three principles in mind:

- Use a consistent format for precautions throughout the set of instructions so that all warnings have the same look and are easy to spot.

- Place precautions where they seem most appropriate. General safety information needed to establish a safe and secure environment for performing the procedure or that applies throughout the procedure should go in the introductory section of the instructions. Specific safety information that pertains to a specific step should be included within the instruction for performing that step.

- To encourage readers to do exactly as the precaution says and to help them avoid making a mistake, explain the potential difficulty or danger:

Extinguish all cigarettes and flames. A spark can ignite hydrogen gas from the battery.

"Extinguish all cigarettes and flames" is the precaution. "A spark can ignite hydrogen gas from the battery" describes the potential consequences of making a mistake and explains the importance of following the precaution. Adding this so-what provides the supplementary conceptual information that some readers need.

Visuals

Visuals help your audience see the entire process and the specific steps. For more information on visuals, see chapters 6 and 7.

(H) Identify the visuals that will help readers develop a mental picture of what they are to do in the step (Figure 17.1). Visuals are important enough in instructions to be regarded as equal partners with words. Decide early in your planning the visuals that will be helpful to your reader. Sometimes, as exemplified in Figure 6.1, visuals are the only medium of instructions. Keep the following questions in mind when you write instructions. Have I *told* the reader *what* to do? Have I *shown* the reader *how* to do it? Use column H in the Plan Sheet for Instructions to remind yourself of visuals you will want to use to illustrate the written instructions. Notice the use of visuals in instructions in Figures 17.2, 17.6, 17.7, and 17.10.

Learning and Performance Difficulty

(I) Estimate the degree of difficulty readers might experience in learning or performing the step (Figure 17.1). The degree of difficulty refers to the

Analyze your audience so that you present instructions at the level they can absorb.

time and effort it takes to learn how to perform an action. Some tasks, of course, are more difficult to learn and perform than others. As you fill out this column in the Plan Sheet for Instructions, try to indicate how easy or difficult the task is to learn, remember, and perform by using words such as *difficult, moderate to difficult, moderate, moderate to easy,* and *easy.* Just remember that you are considering the degree of difficulty for users of your instructions, not for you.

Do not fall into the trap of assuming that because you know how to do certain things, your reader also will know how to do them and will be bored by elementary instruction. A good way to learn the reader's needs is to recall your own experiences in learning the task. This might take some real memory work, because now that you can perform the procedure well, you have probably forgotten the difficulties you encountered as a learner. Another reliable way to learn the reader's needs is to conduct a user testing of the set of instructions (see pages 513–515).

Such analysis will help you decide how detailed your instruction for the task should be. You can also use column I to remind yourself of any prior knowledge or special skill that the reader may need to perform the task. For instance, if the reader is to check the electrolyte level in a battery, you must decide whether you can simply assume that the reader has the prior knowledge to do it or whether you must provide step-by-step instructions. If the reader at some point in a procedure has to transfer a file to another computer, you must decide whether the reader already knows how to do it or whether you must explain the process. Keep asking yourself: Now that I have told the reader *what* to do, should I tell the reader *how* to do it? Column I in Figure 17.1 is where you make notations about adding supplementary material for readers who may require more information about performing a troublesome step.

Sometimes the primary information in the instructions fails, and the reader needs supplemental information to perform a task successfully. For instance, it may not be enough to state: "Disconnect the main electric cable from the generator outlet." This direction, as clear as it seems, omits a great deal of information that the reader must supply:

- The location of the main electric cable and generator outlet

- The identity of the main electric cable

- The tools needed to disconnect them

- The correct way to disconnect them

- The importance of disconnecting them correctly

A reader who lacks this necessary information risks making mistakes. A note, such as the one shown in Figure 17.3, is the best way to walk the reader through a task that is unfamiliar, that is difficult or dangerous to perform, or that results in an unexpected or undesired outcome. Learners need help both on what to do and why to do it.

FIGURE 17.3

Sample versions of a note that provides information that can help users of instructions perform an unfamiliar task. The first version is more effective because the reader sees the how and why sections labeled.

Step 4. Disconnect the main electric cable (the large cable with the shiny green protective cover) from the generator outlet (located just behind the large air vent). See Figure 2.

How? Pull the cable boot straight out to disconnect the cable.

Why? Do not pull on the cable itself. Doing so may damage the carbon conductor inside the cable and increase the chance of an electrical short or spark, which might result in an electrical shock or fire.

Or

Step 4. Disconnect the main electric cable (the large cable with the shiny green protective cover) from the generator outlet (located just behind the large air vent). See Figure 2.

Note: Pull the cable boot straight out to disconnect the cable. Do not pull on the cable itself. Doing so may damage the carbon conductor inside the cable and increase the chance of an electrical short or spark, which might result in an electrical shock or fire.

Figure 17.4 is an example of a completed Plan Sheet for Instructions. Moving from the completed plan sheet to the first draft of your instructions should go fairly smoothly. The statement of the reader's goal or goals, the list of materials and tools or equipment, the duration of the procedure, and the list of the major steps give you the core of the introduction. The numbered steps, safety precautions, and notations give you the blueprint for the step-by-step procedure. In fact, your entries for Steps in Performing the Procedure (F) will use language much like that you will use in writing the instructions. As you examine the examples of different kinds of instructions in the rest of this chapter, you will notice that the completed plan sheet gives you the important information in the order in which you will most likely use it in writing the instructions.

Once you have completed the plan sheet, review it carefully to make sure it contains no misinformation, irrelevant information, vague instructions, or logical gaps. Leave nothing to chance.

Now let us analyze the first of the three types of instructions listed earlier: brief instructions presented in correspondence, on packages and panels, and in sheets and leaflets.

FIGURE 17.4

Sample of a completed Plan Sheet for Instructions.

Plan Sheet for Instructions

Reader's Goal or Goals: *Build a silkscreen frame (the first of six stages in printing your own t-shirts)*

Materials: *Two 20" lengths of 2" x 2" pine (to make the frame)*
Two 16" lengths of 2" x 2" pine (to make the frame)
One sheet of medium grit sandpaper to smooth the wood frame
Eight corrugated fasteners to secure the corners of the wood frame
Wood glue (such as Elmer's)

Equipment: *Carpenter's square and pencil to mark wood pieces*
Handsaw to saw wood
Miter box to cut 45° angles at the ends of the wood pieces
Table saw with dado blade to make grooves in the wood pieces
Hammer to drive corrugated fasteners into the wood frame

Major Stages: *1. Cutting and grooving the wood pieces*
2. Sanding the wood pieces
3. Gluing the wood pieces together
4. Fastening the corners together

Duration of the Procedure: *Approximately one hour (if the reader already knows how to use a miter box and saw with a dado blade)*

Step No.	Steps in Performing the Procedure	Precautions	Notes about Visuals	Notes about Learning and Performance Difficulties
Stage 1.	*Cutting and Grooving the Wood*			
1.	*Using the handsaw and miter box, cut the ends of the wood pieces to make miter joints.*	*Cut the wood at the correct angles so that….*	*drawing to show how each corner should be cut*	*must know how to use the miter box*
2.	*Using the carpenter's square and pencil, draw a line down each piece of wood 3/8" from the edge away from the print or long side of the wood.*	*none*	*drawing to show where the line is to be drawn*	*easy*
3.	*Using the table saw with a dado blade, carefully cut a 3/16" groove in each piece of wood as shown.*	*Wear safety goggles to protect eyes from flying wood particles. Make sure the….*	*drawing to show cross-sectional view of the board*	*must know how to use table saw with dado blade*

Writing Brief Sets of Instructions

Correspondence

You will often write letters, memos, and e-mail that provide brief but specific instructions to clients, potential clients, and coworkers. Such a letter is shown in Figure 17.5. The letter instructs guests on how to use a hotel's express checkout service. Though brief, the letter contains a lot of information:

- The first two paragraphs introduce the instructions. The first paragraph contains statements designed to create goodwill.

- The second paragraph explains why the reader is receiving the instructions and introduces the instructions that are presented in the numbered, displayed list that follows.

- The list presents the instructions simply and directly, with sufficient detail that the reader will know what to do.

- The third and fourth paragraphs provide additional useful information.

- The fifth and final paragraph resells the hotel's services and attempts to continue the goodwill established with the reader.

The instructions also illustrate the following five conventional strategies for explaining step-by-step actions:

1. **The reason for performing the procedure is explained.** The reader is motivated to perform the procedure by having the so-what explained (here is a way to avoid the wait at the front desk at checkout time). Once the reader realizes how the procedure is useful or important, he or she is likely to follow it.

2. **The instructions are written in the imperative voice.** That is, the reader is told to perform some action, as in "*tune* the guest room television" and "*Select* Account Review/Checkout." Notice that the imperative is simply the you sentence form—"You turn the guest room television to the Menu Screen"—with the "you" missing. Imperative statements sound a bit brusque when taken out of context as we have done here, but they do not really trouble anyone. You have read imperative sentences many times in instructions, we suspect, and we are sure you have never been disturbed by them. Remember that instructions tell how to do something. Readers rely on you to tell them what to do and how to do it.

3. **The instructions are short and to the point.** They run from a low of four words to a high of 17, averaging about 11 words each. From 10 to 14 words is average in instructions.

4. **The instructions are presented in an uncluttered, simple format.** Each step is emphasized by being separated from the others and

FIGURE 17.5
Sample instructional letter.

Wunderbar Haus
Rhinelander Park, WI 54529-5204

Dear Guest:

Thank you for staying at the Wunderbar Haus. We hope that you enjoyed the fine facilities, programs, and services provided for your convenience.

Because we are expecting a large number of people to depart the guesthouse tomorrow, you are encouraged to use our express check-out service. If you have left a major credit card imprint upon registration, simply use our express video checkout (available from 6 a.m. to 12 noon). The procedure takes only a minute or two.

1. Using the remote control, tune the guest room television to the **Menu Screen** (channel 1).

2. Select **Account Review/Checkout**.

3. Select **Account Review** to view the current charges posted to your room account.

4. If you agree, and wish to check out, select **Check Out**. Or, if you disagree, please contact the Front Desk by dialing 7 on your guest room telephone.

When you select **Check Out**, the charges are applied to your credit card and a copy of your bill is available at the Concierge Desk in the main lobby.

The hotel check-out time is 12 noon. Departures after 12 noon may be subject to a half-day room charge. Should you require assistance with luggage carrying or storage, please press the Belldesk button on your guest room telephone.

We hope you have enjoyed your stay with us. We have certainly enjoyed serving you and look forward to accommodating you in the future whether you are traveling on business or pleasure.

Sincerely,

Hans Kroeber

Hans Kroeber, Assistant Manager
Guest Relations

displayed in a numbered list, each in its own paragraph, surrounded by white space.

5. **Important words are emphasized.** Bold print highlights the menu items.

These strategies serve equally well in memo, e-mail, or online instructions.

Instructional Sheets and Leaflets

Instructions also appear on sheets and leaflets enclosed with goods, as shown in Figure 17.6, which explains how to mount decorative ceiling hooks for

FIGURE 17.6
Step-by-step procedures. Note the contingent instructions depending on the type of ceiling into which the hooks are to be installed.

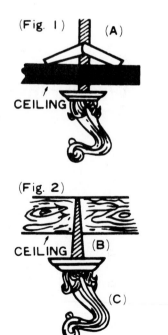

HOW TO INSTALL CEILING HOOKS

CAUTION: Do not use hooks on radiant-heating ceiling. Do not drape electrical wire on the hook. Slide the chain link only over the hook. Weight of object should not exceed 15 pounds.

FOR PLASTER OR PLASTER BOARD CEILINGS (Fig. 1)

1. Drill hole in the ceiling to the same diameter as the closed flaps of the enclosed toggle bolt assembly (A).
2. Insert flaps and bolt into the ceiling with the toggle bolt protruding through the ceiling.
3. Lock the assembly by screwing on the hook as shown.

FOR WOOD OR ACOUSTICAL TILE CEILINGS (Fig. 2)

1. Screw steel screw (B) into hook (C).
2. Screw the assembly into the wood.

(Fig. 1) (A)

CEILING

(Fig. 2)

CEILING (B)

(C)

hanging flowerpots, chimes, or chains for swag lamps. Here are some guidelines for developing instructional sheets and leaflets:

- **Use a title that is specific enough to assure readers that they have the right instructions for the right job.** Usually, the first thing readers look for on an instruction sheet is the title. The title should specifically link the right information to the right job. Words such as *directions, instructions, procedures,* and *how to . . .* confirm what type of document it is. Naming the procedure in the title also helps: "How to Install Ceiling Hooks." Readers feel even more assured when the title refers to specific brands and models. "How to Control the Flight Path in the XSG-3 Sounding Glider" is better than "Controlling Flights of Experimental Gliders." The more specific title lets readers know that they and the writer have the same procedure and machine in mind.

- **Emphasize precautions.** Warnings and cautions should be placed where they cannot be overlooked easily.

- **If the instructions contain several steps or series of steps, use a numbered system instead of bullets, dashes, or other marks.** As readers look over the instructions, they should see down the left margin each instruction beginning with an arabic numeral and period (or some other mark).

- **Use visuals to help readers understand and follow an instruction.** The visual should be placed as close as possible to the instruction. Include captions and call-outs (references to visuals in the text) to identify visuals and relate them to the instructions. Otherwise, readers may not refer to them at all.

Writing Instruction Booklets and Manuals

As you can see from the samples in this chapter, the design of instructions is important. You must think carefully about several features:

- The amount of space they will occupy. Some instructions must be squeezed into a small panel on the side of a box; others fill a manual.

- Instruction booklets and manuals share many characteristics with briefer forms of instructions: directions are given in short imperative sentences; are separately paragraphed; are emphasized by surrounding white space, numbering, and different fonts; and are supported by visuals.

- Longer instructional booklets and manuals include features that help readers quickly find a particular section that contains needed information for a specific action. Such guides include a table of contents; an overview statement and flowchart that map the contents verbally, visually, or both; an index; tabs to mark the beginning of major sections; and sometimes even a different colored paper for each section.

Increasingly, instructions are presented online. See Chapter 2 for more suggestions on designing online documents.

Read the instructions for building an accident-free tree stand (Figure 17.7), and then analyze its format, arrangement, and style.

Format Layout and design of instructions are quite important. Notice the heavy reliance on visuals, bold type, and headings. Visuals *show* the reader how to do the work. The two-column format beginning on page 3 places the visuals next to the written instructions they illustrate. (One common fault in preparing instructions is failing to place visuals where they are immediately useful.) Headings and subheadings help readers keep their place as they look back and forth between their work and the instructions.

Arrangement Many instructions contain only the steps of the procedure, as illustrated in Figure 17.5. However, instructions for complicated procedures may contain an introduction, a body (the step-by-step instructions), and an ending section—essentially the same arrangement as for describing a mechanism.

At the beginning of the instructions for assembling the accident-free tree stand are a title page that illustrates the finished product (the accident-free tree stand as it will look when fully assembled) and a one-page introduction. The one-page introduction explains the problem for which the stand is a solution, reassures the reader that the procedure will be easy and fairly inexpensive, lists the major stages in the procedure, and lists the equipment and materials for the job.

The body of the instructions—the step-by-step procedure for making the tree stand—is on the next six pages. Here, the writer and readers narrow their focus from an overall view of the procedure to the individual steps. Each step is emphasized by a numbered heading and by being stated in the imperative. These instructions require no formal ending. They end after the instructions for completing the last step on page 7.

Style Keep two stylistic considerations in mind when you write instructions.

- **Avoid writing in a telegraphic style.** As we mentioned earlier, you should keep your sentences short and to the point but write with natural, grammatical expression.

Natural Expression Used in Accident-Free Tree Stand Instructions	Telegraphic Style
Place the ladder on its side and nail one of the 4-1/2 foot long sections above the last step on the inside of the ladder . . .	Place ladder on side and nail one 4-1/2 foot section above last step on inside of ladder . . .

As you can see, the telegraphic style omits most articles and conjunctions. But even when readers can understand a telegraphic style, many

FIGURE 17.7
Instructions.

Source: Unpublished student report, printed with permission of T. Peyton Ashmore, the author.

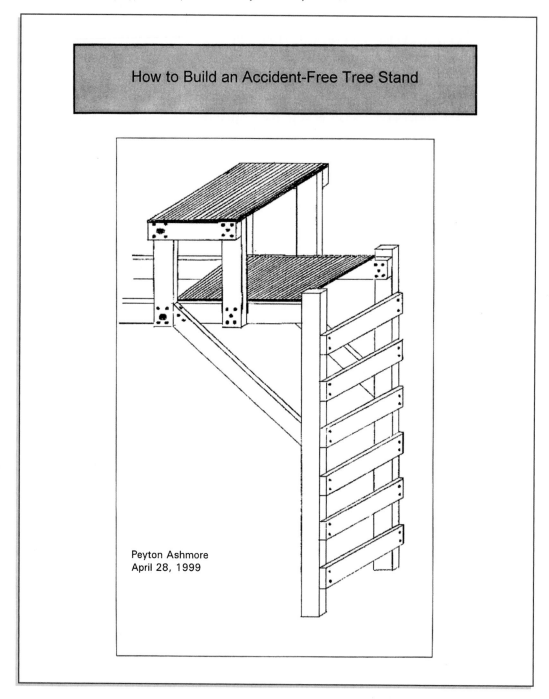

How to Build an Accident-Free Tree Stand

Peyton Ashmore
April 28, 1999

FIGURE 17.7
(continued)

How to Build an Accident-Free Tree Stand

Many hunting accidents occur due to inadequate tree stands. These tree-stand accidents can be attributed to rotted wood, rusted nails, and stress failures. These instructions explain how to construct a tree stand that should prevent all types of accidents caused by faulty construction or inadequate materials. The assembly, which should take approximately two hours, consists of five major stages: 1) constructing the ladder, 2) constructing the foot platform, 3) constructing the seat platform, 4) attaching the chain to the foot and seat platforms, and 5) chaining the tree stand to a tree.

Materials Needed

The materials will cost approximately $50.

Quantity	Unit	Material
1	box	#8 galvanized penny nails
1	sheet	½" treated exterior plywood
2	each	twist tight fasteners
2	each	8' link chain (⅝" diameter)
2	each	2"x4"x14' treated wood
4	each	2"x4"x12' treated wood
3	each	1" hex head bolts

Tools Needed

- Hammer
- Adjustable wrench
- Pliers
- Hand saw or power saw
- 45° triangle
- Tape measure

1

FIGURE 17.7
(continued)

Stage I Constructing the Ladder

Step 1   Cut one of the 2"x4"x12' boards into 6 equal lengths of 2 feet. These pieces form the steps of the ladder portion of the tree stand.

Step 2   Place the two 2"x4"x14' boards parallel to one another on the ground. Be sure to position the boards so that the 2" side is facing up. Leave approximately 2 feet spacing between the two 2"x4"s.

Step 3   Beginning at the bottom of the ladder, nail the steps of the ladder to the 2'x4'x14' boards, spacing the steps 14 inches apart. The 4" side of the steps face up (Figure A). Two nails on each side should be sufficient.

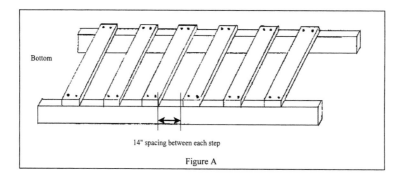

Bottom

14" spacing between each step

Figure A

Stage II Constructing the Foot Platform

This stage consists of making the supports (steps 1, 2, and 3) and braces (steps 4, 5, and 6) for the foot platform and making the foot platform itself (steps 7 and 8).

Making the Supports . . . . . .

Step 1   To make the supports for the foot platform, cut one of the 2"x4"x12' boards into three lengths: each piece 4 feet long.

2

FIGURE 17.7
(continued)

Step 2   Place the ladder on its side and nail one of the 4-foot-long sections above the last step on the inside part of the ladder (Figure B). The maximum distance between this brace and the last step should be 14". Use 5 nails to secure the foot support.

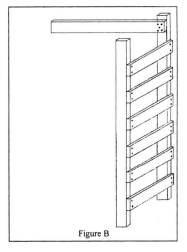

Figure B

Step 3   Repeat step 2 for the opposite side of the ladder at the same end (Figure C).

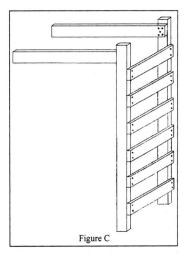

Figure C

3

FIGURE 17.7
(continued)

Making the Braces . . . .

Step 4   Take one of the 2"x4"x12" boards and cut two 3-½-feet sections.

Step 5   Trim the ends of the two 3-½-feet sections to a 45° angle (Figure D). Be sure to cut the ends so that they are both parallel.

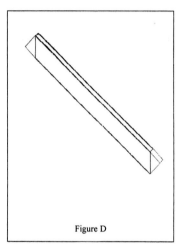

Figure D

Step 6   Nail the braces to the ladder as shown in Figure E. The portion of the braces that connect to the ladder should be toe-nailed.

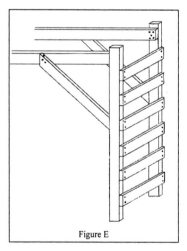

Figure E

4

FIGURE 17.7
(continued)

Making the Foot Platform . . . .

Step 7   Cut a 2-½'x2-½' section from the
sheet of treated plywood. Be sure
there is enough plywood left to cut a
1'x1-⅛' seat.

Step 8   Nail the plywood to the top of the
4-feet long support boards. Be
sure that plywood is placed flush with
the ladder (Figure F). Nail the
plywood at each corner and at a
couple of places along the support
boards.

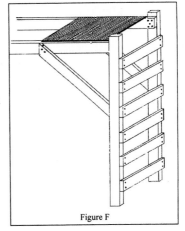

Figure F

Stage III Constructing the Seat Platform

This stage consists of making the seat braces (steps 1, 2, and 3) and the seat itself (steps 4 and 5).

Making the Seat Braces . . . .

Step 1   Cut four 2-feet lengths from
another 2"x4"x12" board. Place
two of these 2-feet lengths flush
with the 45° brace and the 4-
feet sections.

Step 2   Place the other 2-feet lengths one
foot from the rear of the plywood
(Figure G). Use 5 nails to secure
the front posts to the foot support.
Use only four nails for the back
posts arranged as shown in
Figure G.

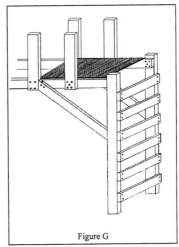

Figure G

5

FIGURE 17.7

(continued)

Step 3 Cut two more lengths from the 2"x4"x12" board and apply them horizontally to the tops of the previously placed braces. These are the supports for the seat of the tree stand (Figure H). Use 5 nails to secure the seat brace to the front vertical supports. Use only 4 nails, arranged as shown in Figure G, for the back supports.

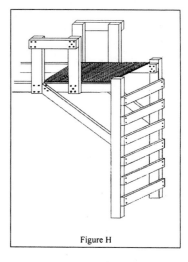

Figure H

Making the Seat . . . .

Step 4 Cut a 1'x2-½'-feet piece from the plywood.

Step 5 Place the piece of plywood on the two horizontal braces (Figure I). Place nails at each corner and at several places along the brace.

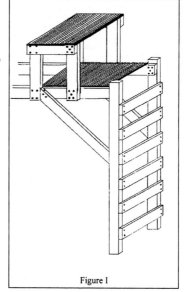

Figure I

6

FIGURE 17.7
(continued)

Stage IV Attaching the Chain to the Foot and Seat Platforms

If you are uncomfortable with the chain attachment, you can use the extended foot platform boards to nail the stand to the tree.

Step 1   Using a 1" hex head bolt, attach the link chain on the foot platform (Figure J).

Step 2   Using a 1" hex head bolt, attach the link chain on the seat platform (Figure J).

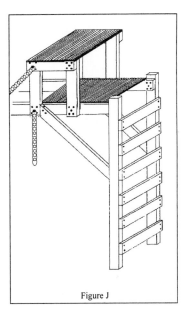

Figure J

Stage V Chaining the Tree Stand to a Tree

Step 1   Using a 1" hex head bolt, attach the twist tight fastener to the platforms on the opposite sides of the platforms from the chains.

Step 2   Place the tree stand parallel against the tree.

Step 3   Bring the chains around the tree and connect them to fasteners.

Step 4   Twist the fasteners to take up the slack in the link chain to secure the tree stand to the tree.

7

will avoid it because it looks different from natural prose. Telegraphic styles are too choppy and do not save all that much space anyway.

- **Know when to use the imperative voice.** Use the imperative when you are writing an instruction. For example, you should write

  > Nail the braces to the ladder.

not

  > You should nail the braces to the ladder.

not

  > The braces are to be nailed to the ladder.

not

  > The braces must be nailed to the ladder.

  Only the first sentence is imperative. The other three do not tell the reader what to do, and the reader may fail to recognize them as instructions.

Troubleshooting and Undoing Errors

When something goes wrong during a procedure, the reader will likely look for troubleshooting procedures to aid in isolating and correcting the problem. Troubleshooting information contributes greatly to a set of instructions, because being able to recognize and correct errors successfully reduces the frustration and problems of learning how to perform new procedures. Readers want to be able to diagnose the problem, bring about the desired result, and get on with completing the task.

User testing your instructions will help you predict difficulties that readers might experience and help you identify the kinds of information readers need to identify problems and take corrective actions.

Troubleshooting guides must be context sensitive and brief and uncluttered, as illustrated in Figure 17.8, and placed where they are needed. They may accompany a specific step, come at the end of a major section of the procedure, or at the end of the instructions. A three-column table with headings such as *Problem, Probable Cause,* and *Solution* is apt to be the easiest way to lead readers quickly from the symptom of the problem to the solution with a minimum amount of information. List the most frequent or most likely problems first. Any one problem may have several possible causes. List the possible causes and solutions in order from the most frequent to the least frequent occurrence.

FIGURE 17.8

A troubleshooting table is an effective way to present information on how to solve problems associated with performing a procedure.

	TROUBLESHOOTING TABLE	

Note: Many video cassette problems are caused by defective cassettes. Check the cassette by substituting a known good cassette.

Problem	Probable Cause	Solution
Motor does not run when cassette is inserted	1. Power is not on.	Check to see if power is on. If not, turn on.
	2. Micro-actuating arm is bent or broken.	Bend the actuating arm (Fig. 2) far enough to actuate the micro-switch (Fig. 3) when the cassette is inserted, or replace.
	3. Micro-switch is defective.	Replace.
	4. Motor is defective.	Replace.
Poor visual or audio quality	1. Cassette is defective.	Check by inserting a known good cassette.
	2. Drive surfaces are dirty.	Using isopropyl (rubbing) alcohol, clean and wipe dry the outer edge of the flywheel, motor drive pulley, capstan shaft, and tape head (Fig. 4 A, B, C, and D).
	3. Drive belt is defective or incorrectly installed.	If the drive belt (Fig. 5) is stretched, replace. If the belt is not installed with the stripes on the outside (Fig. 5), reinstall. If the drive belt rides too high or too low on the motor pulley (Fig. 6), readjust.

Testing Instructions for Usability

As with any document, your instructions are doomed to almost certain failure if you

- Slap them together quickly in the haste of meeting a deadline (either to get a product or service out or to make the instructions available)

- Rely on your own ability to follow the instructions to determine whether the instructions are clear and understandable for the eventual user

Do not select experts to test your instructions. Select people who are representative of those who will actually be using your instructions.

To avoid both mistakes, (1) schedule the project to allow time for testing the instructions, and (2) test the instructions in an operational context (instead of sitting at your desk going over the procedure for the umpteenth time). Testing for usability requires careful thought and disciplined review.

As you create a set of instructions, work through the procedure several times, attempting to put yourself in the user's shoes, walking through the steps and trying to anticipate problems. Look for statements that are too general, for inconsistencies between written and visual material, for insufficient clues on how to access specific information, or for places where information has been omitted. Remember, the more knowledgeable you are about the procedure, the more difficulty you will have predicting problems for users. Ultimately, to see whether your careful and thorough consideration for the eventual user has been adequate and whether your instructions will work, you must test them on people who can represent the eventual user.

Testing for usability takes time, but doing it right will save time and money and will prevent trouble later on. Here are some guidelines for testing your instructions for usability:

- **Maintain a positive attitude about testing your instructions.** Assume that you have lots of opportunities to improve them. Once you make the psychological commitment to conduct user testing, you will likely receive plenty of help. Here is what one of our students recently wrote about her experience with user testing:

  > The user test helped me a lot. I admit that when I first learned that we were required to have another student test our sets of instructions, I was more than a bit skeptical—I assumed the testing was busywork to keep the project on our minds. Now, I know nothing could be further from the truth. The user test gave me the opportunity to see my own writing being used for something, which I thoroughly enjoyed. The tester's assessment memo to me gave me a solid basis for revisions that I needed to focus on. In my own testing of another student's set of instructions, I was put in the place of a learner, and I realized how much I looked for clarity. The difficulty I had in attempting to use another person's set of instructions helped me identify ways to improve my own.[2]

  Listen carefully to what your tester says, and if the tester provides a written report, read it carefully. Do not argue with the tester or take issue with the tester's findings. Instead, pay careful, respectful attention to the opinions of the tester, who represents the opinions of the eventual users of your instructions. Be willing to make changes.

- **Estimate the time it takes to prepare, arrange, and administer a user test** and, if necessary, to repeat the test or to retest certain parts of the

---

[2]Used with permission of Anne L. Casey.

instructions after they have been revised. Sometimes testing results only in minor tweaking of the instructions. At other times, extensive revision is required and corrections can be time consuming.

- **Prepare the test carefully.** Decide whether you will test the entire set of instructions or just certain parts. You may decide to test only those steps that you are not sure you explain well. But it is usually better to test the entire set of instructions to see whether users have difficulty even where you think there will be none. If the instructions are to be used by several groups of users—say systems analysts, applications programmers, and computer operators—design tests to see if the instructions are usable by them all.

  The quality of the test is extremely important. Have a specific plan for the test to help you and the tester of the instructions stay organized and focused. Developing a checklist will help. If you use a check sheet, introduce the tester or testers to it to see whether they understand what they are to do. Figure 17.9 is an example of testing guidelines that are easily formatted into a checklist.

- Prepare the tester or testers. Testers are collaborators with you on the project, and if they are to assist you, they need to know the objectives of the test. Some who agree to test your instructions may be a bit apprehensive about what they are to do and unsure about the objectives of the test. Explain to them that you are testing the instructions, not them, and that you want them to point out problems when they encounter them. Review the checklist with them, and remind them that the test is not to be performed perfunctorily.

- Observe closely while the tester uses the instructions. Watch the user go through each step, noticing where he or she works with ease and where he or she has difficulties. When problems arise with the instructions, ask the user what he or she believes is the source of the difficulty and solicit suggestions about how to correct it.

FIGURE 17.9

Sample checklist for user testing.

Title of the instructions _____

Name of author(s) of instructions _____ Name of user/tester _____

Location, date, and time of user test _____

The Title Page (if there is one)

Feature   *Tester's comments*

Is the title of the instructions clear?

Are the author's name, affiliation, and date given?

Are the elements placed attractively on page?

Is there a visual to interest reader in using the
instructions?

The Introduction

Feature   *Tester's comments*

Is it clear when the procedure is performed?

Is it clear how long it will probably take to perform
the procedure?

Is there an attempt to motivate the reader to perform
the procedure?

Are equipment and material specified?

Are special precautions given on creating safe environment to perform the procedures?

The Step-by-Step Procedure

Feature   *Tester's comments*

Are headings used to indicate sections?

Do the headings repeat the wording in the overview
statement?

Are the instructions numbered and in the correct order?

Are imperative verbs used in the instructions?

Does each instruction explain how to perform the
step—and why, if appropriate?

Are visuals adequate and placed where the reader
can read the instruction and visualize the action at the
same time?

The Format

Feature   *Tester's comments*

Are the pages numbered?

Are page margins sufficient and consistent?

Are the type fonts and sizes appropriate?

Mechanics, grammar, and style

Feature   *Tester's comments*

Are there grammar, punctuation, or spelling errors?
If so, identify.

Are there abbreviations, words, symbols, etc. that
you believe should be defined? If so, identify.

✓ PLANNING AND REVISING CHECKLIST: INSTRUCTIONS

Think about the following while planning and revising instructions.

Planning

- Who is the intended audience? Are there special considerations to keep in mind? Do readers need to be motivated to perform the procedure the way you have explained? Should theory, terminology, and other background information be presented and explained? How detailed should information and instructions be, considering the audience?

- Are there places in the procedure where cautions, warnings, and notes should be provided?

- What equipment and materials are required to perform the procedure? What special materials or equipment might be needed under certain circumstances?

- What actions in the procedure should be illustrated? What visuals are most appropriate, and where should they be placed in the instructions?

- Will you need to include any routine maintenance, repair, or troubleshooting procedures that the intended audience could be expected to perform?

Revising

- Is the introduction to the instructions adequate, considering the audience?

- Is it easy to follow the chronology of steps and, if necessary, the substeps? Is it clear why one section follows another?

- Are the instructions written in the imperative voice?

- Are steps adequately explained? Is enough information given that readers require? Has anything been left out that might help readers?

- Is nomenclature consistent throughout the instructions?

- Are the instructions free of jargon?

- Are the cautions, warnings, and notes presented clearly and formatted appropriately?

- Are appropriate visuals used and are they positioned effectively?
- Are maintenance, repair, and troubleshooting procedures within the area of expertise of the intended audience?

Suggestions for Applying Your Knowledge

Individual Activities

1. Your textbooks, especially lab manuals, probably contain many examples of instructions. Bring one example to class to examine in the light of the information provided in this chapter.

2. Elaborate on each of the following safety precautions in instructions on how to jump-start a car. Be sure that your so-whats would be clear to the intended readers.

   Make sure the vehicles do not touch.
   Do not jump-start unless both batteries are the same voltage.
   Do not jump-start if the battery is frozen.
   Wear goggles.

3. Complete a Plan Sheet for Instructions for a procedure from your field of study, from your work, or from one of your hobbies.

4. Using the filled-out plan sheet from suggestion 3, write a set of instructions for either a do-it-yourselfer or a technician.

Individual or Collaborative Activities

1. Either as an individual or as a member of a group, discuss a hobby procedure that you recently learned. Who instructed you? Were the instructions written? Oral? Visual? A combination of the three? Did you have any initial problems in following the instructions? If so, what were they and how could they be corrected? What were other weaknesses or particular strengths in the instructions?

2. Either as an individual or as a member of a group, analyze the instructions in Figure 17.10. Prepare a user-test report to help guide revisions that you or your group believe should be made.

FIGURE 17.10

Instructions for following the "rules of the water road."

Source: From *(Almost) Everything You Ever Wanted to Know about Boating—But Were Ashamed to Ask* by U.S. Coast Guard, February, 1972, Washington, D.C.: U.S. Coast Guard.

Over half of the boats that got into an accident did so by smashing into another boat or some immovable object. If you think that's bad news — then how about the fact that most of these accidents happened because the operator of the boat *wasn't even looking ahead!* It would seem that these people, from the time they stepped into their boats were no better than an accident going somewhere to happen. In other cases the operator was looking ahead but he *didn't know what to do!*

It can be truly said that there are old boatmen.....and there are bold boatmen.....but there ain't no old, bold, boatmen. Not for long anyway.

To keep from running into things with your boat you must learn and use the "Rules of the Water Roads". In this little program we can only give you the smallest amount of all those things you need to know about the rules. For the rest, take an advanced boating course from the Coast Guard Auxiliary. OK, here we go.....

There are many different sets of rules of the road. Which set *you* use depends on *where* you are going to use your boat. You must understand that conditions are often very different on various water areas. The Coast Guard Auxiliary course, and other advanced courses will give you the straight scoop and we can promise you it *all* makes good horsesense.

There are three *general* situations where you will be meeting, crossing, or overtaking another boat. By learning these rules the rest should be easy. OK then, case number one....

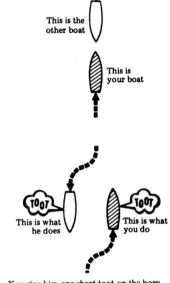

1. Meeting head-on

This is the other boat

This is your boat

This is what he does

This is what you do

You give him *one short* toot on the horn
and
He gives you *one short* toot back

FIGURE 17.10
(continued)

OR, as in this case....

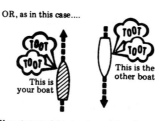

This is
your boat

This is the
other boat

You steer straight ahead.....so does he,
and
You give him *two short* toots on the horn
and
so does he.

How about that?

2. Crossing

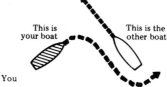

This is
your boat

This is the
other boat

You

1. Slow down
2. Turn right
3. Pass well behind the back of the
    other boat.

    This means that you are *BURDENED*
with the responsibility of slowing down, steering to the right, and passing to the rear of the
other boat. The other boat is *PRIVILEGED*
and *must* hold the same direction and speed.

3. Overtaking and passing.

OK, here's the situation

This is the
other boat

This is
your boat

    If you want to pass *you* are called the
overtaking boat and you are *BURDENED*
with the responsibility of making the signals,
making the steering changes, and passing the
other boat. You can pass him on either side.
    The best side is the safe side. Suppose
that his right side is best....
You
    give one short toot on the horn
This
    tells him you want to pass on his right
    side....
He
    looks ahead for you and if clear and safe
    he gives you one short toot on the horn..

This
    means the way ahead is clear and he will
    hold his course and speed....
You
    turn to the right, increase speed, cross his
    wake *carefully*, and pass on his right side
    like this....

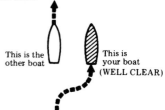

This is the
other boat

This is
your boat
(WELL CLEAR)

    To pass on the left side you give *two*
toots on the horn.....he gives two toots back.
You increase speed, turn out to the left, cross
his wake carefully and pass well clear on his
left side.
    Finally, always stay well clear of sail-
boats. In almost every case they have the right
of way.

Research

Research Strategies

Y ou conduct research in whatever workplace setting you find yourself. The research may be as easy as locating a vendor to supply a video splitter. You go to the company's Web site to get ordering information and the telephone number. The research may be as involved as conducting a 2- to 4-year on-site study of the migration patterns of gray wolves. The research may require you to use the library, interview subject matter experts, and visit sites; or you may search the Web from your office or send out a questionnaire to employees.

The chapters in this unit suggest effective research strategies (Chapter 18, "Research Strategies") and identify several of the many research sites for gathering information (Chapter 19, "Research Sites and Sources: Library and Internet Research," and Chapter 20, "Research Sites and Sources: Field Research"). Chapter 21, "Documenting Sources," provides guidelines for showing the source of your research.

Identifying the Problem

In the workplace, you solve problems daily: situations that require a solution so that you can do your job more efficiently and the organization you work for can stay in business. You take some sort of *action* to change the current situation for the better. You are solving practical problems.[1]

In Chapter 14, "Recommendation Reports," we described several ways to report problems and solutions. For example, in Scott Pahl's study of the problem of mowing grass along Minnesota highways, the cost had increased so significantly that the Minnesota Department of Transportation began to look for an alternative to mowing.

We will refer to Pahl's study in the following pages (see Chapter 14).

Describe the Current Situation

For practical problems, you must study the current situation, identify the problem, and provide a timely solution. You do not know what might change in the future. Technology changes, our perceptions change, scientists develop a more effective solution, the seriousness of a problem grows. For example, a community's landfill can hold no more solid waste, or airplanes built in the 1970s and flown without major accidents for 35 years now begin to have serious and even fatal accidents. Fifteen years ago, in his original report, Scott Pahl recommended testing *Embark,* a plant-growth regulator; however, *Embark* is no longer available because of environmental concerns that

---

[1]Carolyn D. Rude, in "The Report for Decision Making: Genre and Inquiry," classifies problems as theoretical ("problems of values, principles, and concepts"), empirical problems ("facts that can be observed or tested"), and practical problems ("require choice about action"). *Journal of Business and Technical Communication* 9 (1995): 177. We focus on practical problems in the workplace, although you will certainly encounter theoretical and empirical problems as well.

showed up with its use over several years. When Scott did his research and wrote his report, *Embark* was the best product available. Fifteen years later, it is not. (We adjusted the report slightly so that we could continue to use it as an example.)

As you describe the current situation, you explore the problem in depth. You probably will discover that there is more to the problem than you thought. As you talk with different people familiar with the problem, you will get different perspectives on the problem and suggestions for possible solutions. Note the different perspectives and suggestions as you look for solutions. The need for a video splitter (mentioned in the first paragraph) evolved out of a need to solve a problem. Finding a video splitter was not the problem. The problem was that every time the projection system was hooked to the computer, the monitor cable had to be unplugged and the LCD cable had to be plugged into the computer. The computer was positioned such that it was difficult to reach the back of the computer. Setting up the LCD soon resulted in bent pins on the monitor cable and costly repairs. In addition, users complained of spending 10 minutes before and after the presentation to set up and take down the LCD. The technician saw the problem only as the bent pins; the end user saw the problem as the setup time. The video splitter solved both the problem of bent pins and set up time. Users now run the projection system without unhooking the monitor from the computer.

Identify the Criteria for Studying the Problem

Carolyn Rude identifies criteria to consider when solving problems:

> Criteria are those factors that predict whether a decision will yield desirable consequences. They are the reasons for making a decision. Criteria vary with problem and context. Establishing criteria is part of constructing the reality of the community—what is possible, true, and important in a particular context.[2]

She identifies three broad areas of criteria: technical, managerial, and social:

technical criteria

- **Technical criteria** provide a way to judge whether it is possible to solve the problem. For example, are the equipment, the laws, and the resources available? Is it possible to have one video input and two video output signals? Is there enough room to install the workstation? Can the fence be placed inside the property line without removing trees?

managerial criteria

- **Managerial criteria** focus on such issues as cost, personnel, and schedules. Managers look at feasibility: The technical aspects of the problem can be solved, but is the solution cost effective? Are there enough work crews and support staff to take on the new client and meet the deadlines?

---

[2]Rude 195.

social criteria

- **Social criteria** respond to issues such as should the solution be implemented? What will its effect be on the environment? How many deaths can be expected?

Only a few criteria for selecting a video splitter required attention: the cost (managerial criteria) and the availability of and sources for the feature to create two video outputs from one video input (technical criteria). There are no social considerations here—a simple problem, a simple solution.

Among the criteria Scott Pahl considered in the recommendation report on mowing Minnesota highways are

technical criteria	*SlowGrowth* plant-growth regulator works; available equipment can be adapted to spread the product
managerial criteria	cost of application; number of crew needed to apply the product
social criteria	low risk to workers; environmentally safe chemical; aesthetically pleasing results

Spend time identifying the criteria. The criteria provide you with specific points to compare as you look for a solution to a problem.

Generate Possible Solutions and Follow the Leads

After you identify a problem, generate several possible solutions. Rarely will you look for solutions by yourself. You will meet with others affected by the problem; you will study the history of the problem. The list of possible solutions provides a starting point for your research. You will eliminate some of the solutions immediately. For example, constructing a new building just so a more effective presentation room is available is not a solution (too costly). Renovating the current room is a possibility, but even that requires decisions that limit the extent of the renovation, for example, whether to replace current furniture or work with the current furniture.

Your research will lead you to other possible solutions. Follow the leads. For example, in interviewing the manager of a computer classroom about security concerns, you learn that the use of fiber-optic cables is not enough assurance that the computers will be secure. You must also padlock the computer case to prevent access to the chips, boards, and drives inside the computer. Or suppose you need to improve the yield for your cotton crop. One of the works cited at the end of a government report looks like it might discuss the advantages and disadvantages of using a fertilizer developed from telephone books and chicken manure. You go to your library's Web site and locate the report.

Locating the Information

You have identified solutions and have a list of leads to follow. Now you must locate the information that will help you make decisions and recommend a solution to the problem. The list of possible solutions will direct where you go for the information you need to solve the problem. Either the information will exist because others have solved the problem or a similar problem or the information must be gathered because the problem is unique. If others have already done the research on a portion of the problem or if the solution exists, you need only locate the solution.

If the problem is unique, you may have to gather information firsthand using interviews, questionnaires, or direct observations. These sources are frequently referred to as *primary sources*.

Secondary sources are those you go to for help or information rather than developing the information on your own. These might include sources inside your organization (for example, the accounting department), on the Web (such as a site that publishes government reports), or a publication located in your school, company, or local library.

More than likely, you will have to locate information from both primary and secondary sources. For example, assume that you have just been promoted to Web coordinator for your organization and that you have been given $40,000 to purchase the computer, software, and other peripherals you and your assistants will need to create the Web site. You have some experience with designing Web sites, so you can list fairly quickly what you need; however, you have also heard about some new technology and software. First, you decide to call a friend in a similar position at another company. She suggests you join an online discussion group for Web site developers. You also attend the monthly meeting of the local chapter of the Society for Technical Communication and meet others doing similar work. You ask several software and hardware vendors for demonstrations, or you visit colleagues who are using some of the products you need. You locate the current prices and specifications online at vendors' Web sites. You are gathering information firsthand—interviews, networking, hands-on experience. You also go to your library or go online and read the latest reviews on the products in publications such as *PC World* or Web sites such as cdnet.com or internet.com. You gather this information from others and rely on their thorough research to help you evaluate the products.

In the Minnesota highway study, Scott Pahl used on-site visits, interviews with Minnesota Department of Transportation workers and vendors of products, and library research to find reports of experiments on controlling grass in medians. The research for a video splitter required less diverse sources. A visit to a classroom equipped with the splitter, the recommendation by a colleague of a source for the splitter, and a visit to the Web site of the company selling video splitters yielded a quick, inexpensive solution.

In the next two chapters, we describe some of the common locations for gathering information. Chapter 19, "Research Sites and Sources: Library and Internet Research," focuses on library and Internet research—research we think of as text-based and in most cases research that someone else has done (secondary sources). You are borrowing from the work of others. For example, say you cannot possibly remember the hurricanes and their level of intensity that have moved through your region in the past 10 years, but you need this information because you manage the emergency supply inventory. You locate the information on the National Weather Service Web site. Or you need to know what experiments have been conducted in the past 20 years on cigarette smoking. You search the library database for scientific journals that publish the results. Chapter 20, "Research Sites and Sources: Field Research," describes research methods you most likely will use to gather information. For example, you will conduct interviews with the campus police and the locksmith shop to explore the best security system for the computer classroom. Or you will count the cars that move through a busy intersection and observe how many line up waiting to turn left before you recommend a turn lane and turn light. You are going outside the environment you normally work in, that is, your classroom or office, to gather information—you are in the field.

Consider locating the information a challenge—a challenge that involves detective work in the library, on the Internet, or in the field. When you are thorough, you will be successful in finding a solution to the problem.

Taking Notes

It is important to take notes on the information you are gathering. You cannot possibly remember all of the details you need to make the final report (even if it is a simple memo identifying the computer and software you need for a Web production workstation). You need to record the information from the articles and books you have found. Careful notetaking is essential. Our memories are simply too short to hold the information we have found, and we need to transform what we read into our own words. We need to adapt the information gathered to the problem we are researching.

See Chapter 21, "Documenting Sources."

Good notetaking also assures you that you have the necessary bibliographic information to attribute the information gathered to the original source. You must acknowledge the sources of the information in your reports—avoid plagiarism. Readers much prefer knowing the source of the information you gather rather than finding out later that what you produced as your own was originally someone else's idea. Taking careful notes on your sources helps when you write the report.

How to Take Notes

How you take notes will depend on how you gathered the information and where you found the information. You will take notes whether you gather the information through firsthand observations or from secondary sources. And you will need to note more than just the information you need to solve the problem. You need to note who or what was your source, where to go if you need to refer back to the information, when the information was gathered, and when you located the information. Always note the source and the date you collected information whether you are recording information from primary sources or secondary sources.

You have several options for taking notes:

- Write notes on the source

- Make electronic notes using a laptop or handheld

- Record notes using an audio or video recorder or a handheld

- Use notecards

In the following paragraphs, we suggest ways to be an efficient notetaker for each of these options. You may use several of these methods depending on the type of sources you will consult and how many sources you use. As you gather the information and take notes, refer back to the problem frequently. If you have worked through our suggestions in the earlier section, "Identifying the Problem," you have drafted a problem statement and brief history of the problem and have listed the solutions you are researching. If you have written the problem and history in a computer file, you can add to it and modify the problem statement and solutions as you proceed through your research.

Notes on the Source

Do you annotate your
textbooks?

Frequently, when you find information in a periodical or on an organization's Web site, you make a copy of it or you print out a copy from the Web. You can read the source and make notations on the copy as you read—annotations. In working with a source, you might number and underline the major points, mark unfamiliar terms and provide synonyms, highlight statements that you agree or disagree with, cross-reference related ideas, and record ideas that occur to you as you read the material. Use the annotations to interact with the source. Figure 18.1 illustrates one way to be an active reader and make annotations.

Here are some suggestions for making useful notes on the copy and for keeping track of the information so you can use it to write up the solution to the problem.

Identify the source.

- Immediately after you copy the information or print it from the Web, write on the source all the information you need to document it. You must identify the title of the work, the author(s), and the publication date. For material from the Web, be sure to get the address (if it does not show on the printed version) and note the date you collected the information. You can lose a lot of time going back to sources for missing documentation information. Some magazines and journals include bibliographical information on each page, but many do not. Refer to Chapter 21, "Documenting Sources," for a complete description of what you need to record and the format to use.

Skim first to review the
organization.

- Skim the source to get an idea of how the information is organized. Be an active reader—that is, interact with the material by making notes

FIGURE 18.1

Handwritten annotations on a photocopied article. You will create your own system of making notes on your sources. In this example, we make notes in the margins to call attention to important information. The notes at the end are ideas that occurred while reading the article.

Source: "Bike Helmets: A New Safety Standard." *Consumer Product Safety Review* (Spring 1998). Retrieved September 23, 1998 from http://www.spsc.gov/cpscpub/pubs/cpsr_nws8:pdf

CONSUMER PRODUCT SAFETY REVIEW

SPRING 1998
VOL. 2, NO. 4

U.S. Consumer Product Safety Commission

Ann Brown, *Chairman*
Mary Sheila Gall, *Commissioner*
Thomas H. Moore, *Commissioner*

Includes recalls from the National Highway Traffic Safety Administration

Bike Helmets: A (New) Safety Standard

To help protect bikers, the U.S. Consumer Product Safety Commission (CPSC) recently issued a new federal safety standard for bicycle helmets. This standard will provide, for the first time, one uniform mandatory safety standard for all bike helmets, as well as special requirements for young children's helmets.

By March 1999, all bike helmets manufactured or imported for sale in the U.S. must comply with the CPSC standard. A bike helmet will carry a label or sticker stating that it meets CPSC's new safety standard. Bike helmets currently conform to several different voluntary standards.

CPSC's new bike helmet standard includes requirements for helmet performance during a crash, greater coverage for young children's heads, and chin strap requirements to help keep helmets on the head during a fall or collision.[1] This new standard was developed as a result of the Children's Bicycle Helmet Safety Act of 1994.

Injury Data

In recent years, about <u>900 people were killed</u> annually in bicycle-related   *bikes and*
incidents.[2] Most (90%) of these deaths were associated with <u>motor vehicle</u>   *cars*
<u>collisions.</u>

Bike-related injuries took an especially high toll on children. More youngsters, ages 5 to 14, went to U.S. hospital emergency rooms for bicycle-related injuries than for injuries associated with any other sport. For children under age 5, bike-related injuries were number two for sports-related injuries, behind playground injuries.[3]

In 1996, among all age groups, an estimated 566,000 people were treated for bike-related injuries in U.S. hospital emergency rooms. About 356,000 of those injured were children under age 15. A CPSC study of bicycle hazards indicated that the injury risk for children under age 15 was more than five times that for older riders.[4]

children under 15 –
most accidents

Head Injuries

Approximately 60% of all bike-related deaths involved head injuries. For   *most*
children under age 5, about 64% of the deaths involved head injuries.   *were*
Of total injuries, approximately 30% involved the head and face. Young   *head*
children incurred almost twice the proportion of head and facial injuries as   *injuries*
older victims.

In the CPSC study, about one-half of the injuries to children under age 10 involved the head, compared with one-fifth of the injuries to older riders. This may have been partly due to the fact that only 5% of the victims younger than 15 in that study were wearing a helmet, compared with 30% of those 15 and older.   *helmet not used by younger riders*

Continued on page 2

FIGURE 18.1
(continued)

Consumer Product Safety Review Spring 1998

In several studies, bike helmet usage has been associated with dramatically reducing the risk of head and brain injury. One widely-cited study puts this reduction at 85% for head injury and 88% for brain injury.[5]

Major Provisions of the Standard

CPSC's new bike helmet safety standard mandates several important safety requirements. These include the following: *the new standard requires* ↓

✓ ■ *Impact protection in a crash:* The standard establishes a performance test to ensure that helmets will adequately protect the head in a collision or fall. This test involves dropping a helmet attached to a headform from specified heights onto a fixed steel anvil. Three shapes of anvils (flat, hemispherical, and curbstone) are used to represent different surfaces that may be encountered in actual riding conditions.

  The impact tests are performed on different helmets of each model being evaluated. Each is subjected to one of four differing environmental conditions. These include high, low, and room temperatures, as well as immersion in water for several hours.

  Test helmets are impacted at several different points to ensure that the helmet provides protection all around the head.

✓ ■ *Children's helmets and head coverage:* The new bike helmet standard specifies an increased area of head coverage for young children, ages 1 to 5. This additional coverage is to account for the different characteristics of young children's heads and will provide added head protection for this age group.

greater head coverage

■ *Chin strap strength and stability:* The performance tests for chin straps measure whether they are strong enough to prevent breakage or excessive elongation, and whether they work to resist a helmet's rolling off the head during a collision or fall.

✓

  In the strength test, the chin strap, when subjected to a weight falling a specified distance, must remain intact and not elongate more than a certain amount.

stronger strap

  In the roll-off test, a helmet is secured onto a test headform. A falling weight is attached to the edge of the helmet shell to attempt to pull the helmet off the headform. The helmet must remain on the test headform to pass the test.

prevents roll off

Additional Requirements

In addition to the provisions above, the new bike helmet standard includes requirements for the following:

look for ↓ also

■ *Peripheral vision:* The standard requires that a helmet allow a field for vision of 105 degrees to both the left and right of straight ahead. ✓

■ *Labels and instructions:* Helmets must carry labels including information on, among other things, how to care for the helmet, what to do if the helmet is damaged, and how a helmet should be fitted and worn. ✓

■ *Certification labels, testing, and recordkeeping provisions:* To help ensure that bicycle helmets meet the CPSC requirements, manufacturers must have a certification test program and maintain test records. Bike helmets must have a label stating that they meet the CPSC standard. ✓

— *Scott Heh, Directorate for Engineering Sciences*

more info ✓ follow up

For More Information

To obtain a copy of the Safety Standard for Bicycle Helmets briefing package, contact: Office of the Secretary, U.S. Consumer Product Safety Commission, Washington, DC 20207/ 301-504-0800.

The *Federal Register* notice with the final CPSC bike helmet standard is posted on the CPSC web site a www.cpsc.gov. Click on "Business," then "Official Federal Information," and then "CPSC Federal Register Notices of Interest." The web site also lists numerous CPSC brochures on bikes and bike helmet safety. Click on "Consumer," then "CPSC Publications," then "Recreational Safety."

---

need to find out —
  what state law is for Illinois?
  helmet required??
might poll class members —
see who uses?
  have children — do children use?

---

or signaling with lines or other marks key areas of the text. If you find your mind wandering, stop reading. You probably will not have time to reread the material, so pay attention as you read, and make notes and other marks that will direct you to the information when you refer back to it to write your report.

Use different colors for different types of notations.

• Have 2 to 3 different color marking pens and paper or notecards with you as you begin to read. You will come up with your own system of notation as you read. You might highlight key information as you read through the article and then go back with a different color pen and place a star by the information you will need for your report. Or you might write notes in the margin as you read and then go back and highlight the most important information. Because you most likely will find more than one bit of information in the article, you may want to note on the front of the copy, on a separate piece of paper or notecard, or in a computer file the information you want to refer back to. Be sure to cross-reference this additional sheet with the source in case it gets separated. For the example in Figure 18.1, the cross-reference might be *Bike Helmets, CPSR,* Spring '98. Note the page number with a brief description to remind you of the content.

Review the notes when you write.

- Have the copy and your notes with you when you sit down to write your report.

You need to be careful with this method of notetaking. You can easily overlook or forget relevant information if you do not review the source as you write your report. As you outline your report, you may need to make notations where you plan to insert the information. When you write the section, the notation will point you to the source.

Electronic Notes

You will use a computer to send and receive information and to write your report. If you also use a computer to gather and record your research notes, your notes will already be in a form that you can move into your document file, and you will not need to retype or recopy them. Laptop computers and handhelds (such as Palm Pilots or Dell Axim pocket PCs) make this easy. Most likely, you can find a computer to record your notes as you gather information. Many libraries now have workstations available for you to write up your findings, particularly for sources that cannot leave the library. Some libraries lend laptops and handhelds for use in the library. Here are a few suggestions for taking notes electronically:

Save your file immediately.

- Establish a file-naming convention (for example, last name of the author or *bikehelmet*) and create a folder (a keyword from the problem, for example, *SecurityLocks*) to hold your notes.

Identify the source.

- Once you create a file for each source, immediately identify the source. If you use the documentation format (Chapter 21) you plan to use in your report, you can copy and paste this information straight into your report and avoid rekeying it.

Use white space and different color fonts to distinguish each notation.

- Read the source and then type your notes. Be sure to identify page number(s) for each selection. You might want to double-space the notes to allow plenty of white space in your electronic word-processing file. By doing so, you can more easily review the information and cut and paste it quickly into the final document. You may find it helpful to print a copy of your notes and use scissors to cut the notes so you can order them with the other information you have gathered.

Identify the source for each note.

- Tag each block of information with a brief identifying keyword that links the note to the source. The tag identifies the source in some abbreviated format—either formally, using one of the documentation styles described in Chapter 21, or informally with an abbreviated name for the source. For example, (Bike 2) identifies the *Consumer Report* information on bike helmets, or use author and the page number (Pahl 6) for the sample report in Chapter 14.

Keep your electronic files organized.

- More and more, you will find yourself gathering information electronically. For example, you can copy a passage from the Web, or a colleague might send you an electronic file with information to incorporate in your report. The same general guidelines apply: Establish a file-naming convention and a folder to store the information. Open the file and document the source, using the appropriate bibliographic entry.

Notes Recorded

Important: If you are just developing your electronic notetaking strategies, here are a few suggestions: (1) be consistent in naming the files, (2) always save your electronic notes in at least two places, and (3) do not hesitate to print a hard copy if you need one.

Frequently, the notes you take on primary sources will be recorded either using videotape or audiotape or digitally on a handheld. Or you will develop survey forms or logsheets for an experiment and need to take notes. More than likely you will develop a form to record direct observations. We discuss field research in Chapter 20. Here we suggest some basic procedures for recording notes using equipment and forms.

Equipment

- If you use any type of equipment such as a laptop, handheld (Palm or Pocket PC), video recorder, or audio recorder, check the equipment at least three separate times to make sure it works. Know how to use the equipment and be prepared to troubleshoot any problems that may occur. Have additional batteries, power cords, disks or CDs, tapes, and other supplies.

- Get written permission to record an interview or visit a site. Identify the source of the information in your research notebook or an electronic file on your laptop and on each tape used (see Chapter 21, "Documenting Sources").

- If possible, survey the site before you begin recording so you can adjust how you will record the information. Prepare for interviews and rehearse questions if necessary.

- Save the notes on the handheld, transfer them to your computer, and label the audiotapes, videotapes, or disk you use with the date and keywords (such as the location or the name of the person you interview).

Forms

- Develop a systematic collection process guided by a form you complete to record observations. The form will probably need to be revised several times before it is tested and revised again after it is tested. You want to develop a format that is easy to use but that provides enough options to gather all the relevant information.

- Know the form and rehearse the questions before you try to gather information. Practice on others in your organization before conducting the survey, for example, in a busy mall or as visitors leave a theme park.

Notecards

Notecards are the traditional method for keeping track of information, particularly library research. Notecards are portable and easy to use and are relatively inexpensive. Here are some suggestions for using notecards:

- Buy a couple of packs of 3- × 5-inch notecards for keeping track of your sources and 4- × 6-inch notecards for information from the sources. The size of the card identifies the purpose of the card immediately. Take notes as you read. Use a pen to make notes because the ink will hold up to the use you are going to give the information on the cards. Notecards are easy to handle and rearrange, and they withstand multiple handling better than pieces of paper.

- When you compile a list of potential source material, make a bibliography card for each source. Use the 3- × 5-inch cards for this. The format should be similar for all of your resources: author's name, title, publisher, location, date. As Figure 18.2 shows, you can divide the bibliographical information for a periodical into four parts: (1) author's name, (2) title of the article, (3) title of the periodical, and (4) volume number, date, and page numbers. Figure 18.3 shows a bibliography card for a government document. Do not forget the Web address and date if you get something from the Web. If you interview someone, make a notecard so you will not forget to include the bibliographic information in your list of resources. Review Chapter 21, "Documenting Sources."

- When you take notes during your reading, create a notecard for each note and write on one side of the card only. Use the 4- × 6-inch cards for this purpose because you can get more information on the card. As shown in Figure 18.4, you should put three kinds of information on each notecard: (1) a brief descriptive heading at the top to help you with sorting and arranging notecards as you organize your material, (2) the note itself, and (3) the author and page(s) used at the bottom to identify the source of the note. If you note more than one work by the author or more than one author with the same last name, indicate the title and author's initials as well as the author's last name and pages.

- Write down all the information you will need, so you will not have to go back to the source. The source may not be there. Keep informed

FIGURE 18.2

A bibliography card for a periodic article should have the author's name on the first line, the title of the article on the second line, followed by the title of the periodical, the volume number (and issue number, if available), date, and page numbers. Limit yourself to one source per card so you can arrange the cards easily.

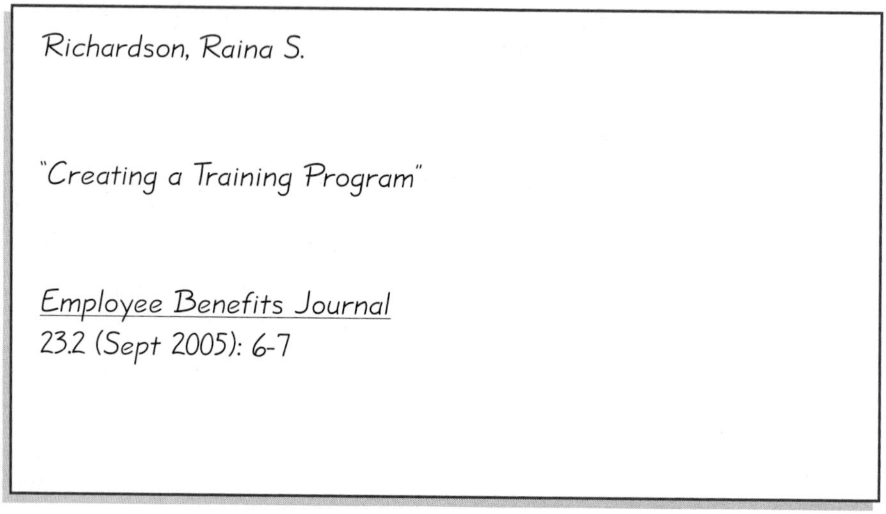

Richardson, Raina S.

"Creating a Training Program"

Employee Benefits Journal
23.2 (Sept 2005): 6-7

FIGURE 18.3

A bibliography card for a government document should have the name of the agency on the first line, the title of the publication on the second line, and the city, publishing organization, and date on the final lines. The publication identifies Mel Martinez as secretary of HUD, but he is not the author. He represents HUD. (Use italics for the title instead of underlining when you create the bibliography in your computer-generated report.)

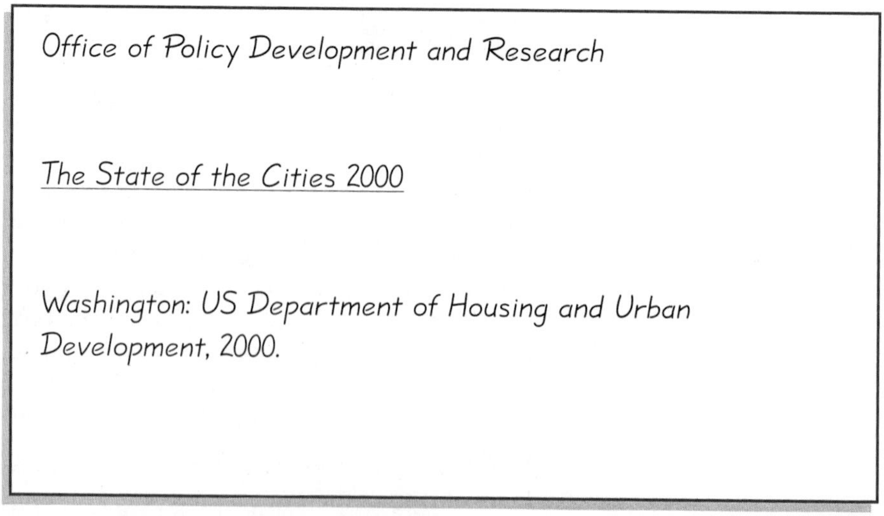

Office of Policy Development and Research

The State of the Cities 2000

Washington: US Department of Housing and Urban
Development, 2000.

FIGURE 18.4
Limit yourself to one note per card so you can arrange them easily. A typical notecard has a topic heading at the top, the note itself, and enough bibliographical information to identify the specific source without having to write it all out.

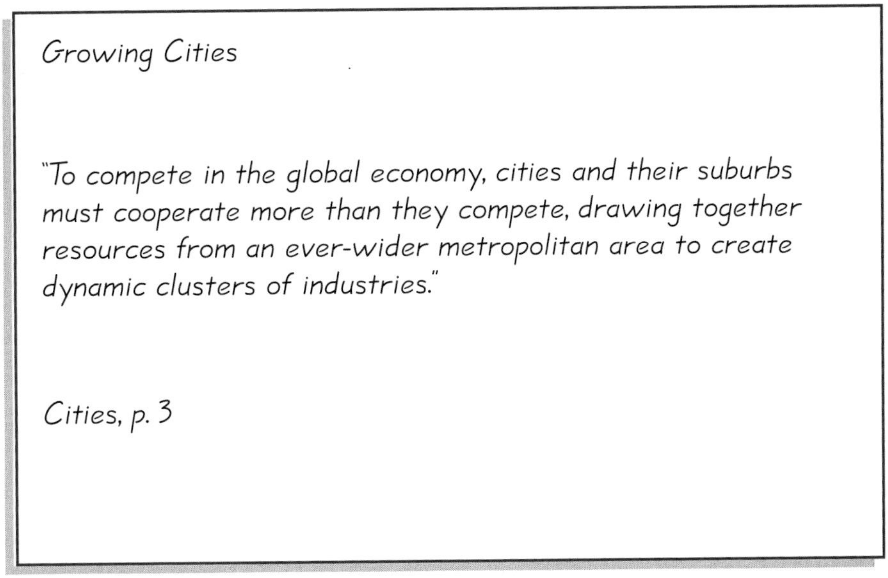

> *Growing Cities*
>
> *"To compete in the global economy, cities and their suburbs must cooperate more than they compete, drawing together resources from an ever-wider metropolitan area to create dynamic clusters of industries."*
>
> *Cities, p. 3*

about the topic you are researching. Be alert for changes in information and update if possible.

- Write legibly so you can read your own handwriting.

Types of Notes

You will probably take three kinds of notes using any of the methods described above:

- quotations
- paraphrases
- summaries

The type of notes you make depend on how you plan to use the information, who is going to read the information, and the source of the information.

Quoting

Quotations are appropriate when you need to record the exact words of the original source. Figure 18.4 is an example of a quotation note.

- Quotations are fairly easy to note. Copy the passage word for word exactly as it is printed, and put quotation marks around the passage to remind you that the passage is a direct quotation.

- Indicate the exact page(s) where the quotation appears. Or if you have transcribed the quote from audiotapes, note the source and date.

- If you want to omit part of the source's words, indicate the omitted part with ellipsis points. (See "Ellipsis Points" in Unit V, "Writer's Guide.")

- If you want to insert some explanatory word or phrase of your own inside the quotation, indicate the insertion by putting it inside brackets. (See "Brackets" in Unit V, "Writer's Guide.")

Do not hesitate to include quotes in your report; however, review the report to make sure your own words provide a substantial amount of the report. Quotes from sources should support your ideas, not be the only ideas you present.

Paraphrasing

Paraphrases are appropriate when you want to state facts taken from another person's writing. They require you to put the author's ideas or statements in your own words.

- Rephrase the original passage to fit the context of your report. That is, use your own words and sentence structure to relay the information. However, that does not mean that you can distort or change the gist of the original passage. An original passage and the paraphrased note are shown in Figure 18.5.

- If you want to jot down a personal note that occurs to you while you are making a notecard, do so below the quotation or paraphrase (Figure 18.5). Making such personal notes is an excellent practice, for it helps you recall the ideas you had about the topic when you were working on it. Bracket the personal note to keep it separate from the quoted or paraphrased material.

You will paraphrase or summarize much of the research you gather in the workplace.

Summarizing

Summaries consist of a few sentences in your own words to condense the essence or major ideas of what you have read. Knowing how to paraphrase also equips you to write summaries of longer passages—a useful way to jog your memory about research materials or to provide readers with a usable condensed version of a longer document. An original two-paragraph passage and a summary of that passage are shown in Figure 18.6.

- Read the author's opening and closing statements, and condense and reword them into your own words, making sure not to distort the author's intended meaning.

FIGURE 18.5

Compare the original information (top) with a paraphrase of the information (bottom). The important information is captured in the paraphrase, but the sentence structure and the words are changed.

Original passage

Increase the Federal Housing Administration (FHA) loan limit so that more middle-income city residents and minorities, who have traditionally tended to rely on FHA mortgage insurance, can enjoy the benefit of FHA single-family mortgage insurance, including down payments of less than 5 percent, and more flexible underwriting criteria. Raising the loan limit to a single nationwide threshold of $227,150 would also provide borrowers more room to finance housing rehabilitation costs under FHA's purchase rehab program—an important consideration in older urban housing markets.

Increase FHA Loan Limits

The FHA provides two incentives that encourage middle-income wage earners and minorities to purchase a home in the city. First, the FHA offers low down payment (less than 5%) and mortgage insurance. Second, the FHA increased the loan amount to $227,150 in part to encourage the refurbishing of older city homes.

[Will this help the River Edge area of the city?]
[Get an estimate of how many potential buyers.]
Cities, p. 31

FIGURE 18.6

Compare the original information (top) with a summary of the information (bottom). The important information is captured in the summary, but the sentence structure and words are changed.

Source: *Mission to the Solar System: Exploration and Discovery: A Mission and Technology Roadmap* (Pasadena, CA: Jet Propulsion Laboratory, National Aeronautics and Space Administration, 1997).

Original passage

The Prebiotic Chemistry in the Outer Solar System Campaign seeks to identify and map the distribution of organic compounds, assay and understand details of organic chemical processes, and search for evidence of prebiological or protobiological activity on satellites of the gas giants. Europa and Titan, the two most likely sites for life, can be used as natural biological laboratories to understand how planetary environments can lead to life. Figure 3-2 illustrates activities related to the Campaign.

Europa, one of Jupiter's four major satellites, is a Moon-sized body. Its high albedo and spectral characteristics indicate the presence of surface water ice or frost. *Galileo* spacecraft observations indicate liquid water or even oceans under the surface. Water appears to be a critical precursor to life, and furthermore, internal heating of Europa by Jupiter's gravity may produce hydro-thermal vents, similar to those on the terrestrial sea floor that support living communities by chemosynthesis rather than photosynthesis. Thus, detection and characterization of any Europa oceans is an integral part of our search for evidence of any life outside of Earth.

Titan, Saturn's largest satellite, has a thick nitrogen-methane atmosphere with a surface pressure 1.5 times that of the Earth. Laboratory simulations and *Voyager* data strongly suggest prodigious atmospheric organic chemistry powered by sunlight. The Cassini/Huygens mission will provide an initial survey of the nature of the surface and how the surface and atmosphere interact chemically. Then, advanced missions will provide detailed characterization of Titan's surface and atmosphere. These data may provide clues to the conditions on early Earth that led to the emergence of life.

Organic evidence in the gases of Europa and Titan

Scientists want to focus one part of space research on Europa and Titan, satellites of Jupiter and Saturn, respectively. Each has at least two significant features that provide a favorable environment for organic activity. Evidence of water and significant internal heat have been found on Europa. Saturn's nitrogen-methane atmosphere and surface pressure provide an environment suitable to initiate life.

Solar System, p. 34

- Write the topic sentences of each paragraph or block of paragraphs. If the document is long, identify the main points of each major section. Condense and reword these, adding whatever transitions are necessary to make the relationship among the ideas clear.

- Check to see that you have reconstructed the main ideas or the line of thought in the original.

In Chapter 21, "Documenting Sources," we give several formats for acknowledging sources.

Frequently in workplace reports, you will use information gathered from a number of sources within the company. Whether you quote, paraphrase, or summarize the information, always acknowledge your source. The acknowledgment will frequently be phrases used within the report such as "Susan DuBois, Chief Information Officer, provided . . ." or "the Facilities Management Committee is the source . . . ." The acknowledgment in such phrases might appear less structured and somewhat informal. It is not. Your reader needs to know where you found your information and the authority behind the information. In the last section of this chapter, "Evaluating the Information," we discuss this further.

Evaluating the Information

You have identified the problem and completed some of the research. Now you need to step back from the research and evaluate what you have found and what you still need to do to resolve the problem.

You can adjust the standard questions—*Who?, What?, When?, Where?, Why?,* and *How?*—to evaluate the sources of your information. Figure 18.7 summarizes how these standard questions are applied to evaluating the information.

Authority and Source

Knowing who the source is lends authority to the information. That is, readers evaluate how much they trust the information as accurate and usable for their needs in part by knowing who the source is. You probably trust a medical doctor's recommendation about the best way to clean a wound more than you do that of the person you sit next to in the doctor's office. However, if the doctor recommends an ointment that he helped develop, and he is now paid by the pharmaceutical company for each sale, you might question the impartiality of his advice. If an organization promotes its product as the only (or best) solution, you should compare its claims with those of its competitors. You compare different makes and models of cars before you buy; as a researcher, you should do the same thing when comparing solutions to a problem.

Review Chapter 2 on Web sources and Chapter 19 for guidelines for evaluating the location of information.

Sources of information give readers of reports, memos, and other workplace documents one more way to evaluate the information. For example, professional journals earn credibility by having experts in the field review an

FIGURE 18.7

Evaluate information before you include it in your report. You can use the 6 questions (left column) or remember the 3 areas: source, information, and place in report (right column). Include only information that applies to the problem you are solving.

Who?	Who is the source of the information?	Authority	Source
Where?	Where can the reader locate and verify the information?	Source/Location	
What?	What is the information?	Content	Information
How?	How valid and reliable is the information? How is the information developed? Is it believable?	Worth of Info Valid/Reliable	
When?	When did the information originate?	Timeliness	Place in your report
Why?	Why are you including the information? Do you need the information?	Relevance	

author's work before printing the article. Publications such as *Consumer Reports* or *PC Magazine* describe the test procedures and criteria used when they make recommendations about products and services. Their reputation for fair evaluations gives you some assurance that you can rely on their recommendations. Just as there are reliable and unreliable sources in print, there are reliable and unreliable sources on the Web. Regardless of the location, you should read critically and evaluate the information before incorporating it into your report, memo, or other workplace writing.

Content: Reliable and Valid

As you research your topic, you need to evaluate the information you find. Have the technical, managerial, and social criteria been researched thoroughly? What methods were used to develop the information? What sources did the producers of the information rely on?

You must evaluate the content of the information to make sure it is accurate and reliable. Statisticians use the terms *reliable* and *valid* to evaluate the research methods used. Simplified to suit our purposes here:

- *Reliable* data means that the procedures used have been done correctly and another researcher can duplicate the process and expect similar results.

- *Valid* data means the procedure tests what it is intended to test.

As you collect information, you should make sure that the information was developed in some systematic way. For example, the cost accountant used standard accounting procedures to determine production costs for the tennis racquets, and you can rely on those costs to establish the wholesale and retail price. If the accountant provides production costs that are too low, most likely you will price the tennis racquets too low and lose money. However, you cannot rely just on the production costs figures. You must know what your competitors charge and what consumers will pay. If the accountant provides you with production costs for racquetball racquets, you cannot use these costs to establish pricing for tennis racquets. The comparison is neither valid nor relevant, and production costs will be only one of several factors you must consider.

Timeliness and Relevance

The immediacy of problems you encounter in the workplace requires timely and relevant information. Production costs for tennis racquets produced 10 years ago has little relevance if you are establishing pricing now. Computer prices hold for maybe a month. Technology changes rapidly, and consumers' perceptions and needs change. For example, concern for the environment prompted a shift from pull-off tabs on soft drink cans to the pop-top tab that stays attached to the can. Drugs that were once thought safe have been pulled from the market when shown as unacceptably harmful.

Be aware of the development and publication dates of the information you gather. Note that the dates might not coincide. It may take awhile to get the information published. You have to evaluate whether the time frame is appropriate and whether the information is still reliable and valid.

You probably will not have much trouble collecting enough information. Actually, the hard part is selecting relevant information from the vast amount of information available. For example, if the environmental impact studies on *SlowGrowth* do not report on conditions similar to those in Minnesota, Scott Pahl would not be able to make any argument for *SlowGrowth*'s impact there. Likewise, rather than including a visual showing the rainfall across the United States, Pahl would prefer a visual that targeted rainfall in Minnesota.

As you read Chapters 19 and 20, evaluate the information you are gathering for your report, memo, or other workplace document. Chapter 21 provides examples of widely accepted formats for identifying your sources. Identifying your sources in a standard way gives your readers a way to evaluate the information you provide for solving the problem. They can readily see who originated the information and where they can locate this source, and they see from the date when the information originated.

Suggestions for Applying Your Knowledge

Individual Activities

Choose a problem to research. Write a one-paragraph description of the problem. After you have described the problem, do the following:

1. Find an article in a periodical and try 2 of the 3 notetaking types: write on the source, make electronic notes, and use notecards. Which process worked best for you? Do you need to modify how you made your notes? How? Why?

2. Select a passage from an article. Paraphrase the passage. Summarize the passage.

3. Locate a source on a U.S. government Web site that might have information to solve the problem you are researching. Describe your search process and the information found.

4. Use the search engines available on the World Wide Web to locate information related to the problem. What did you find? How easy or difficult was it to find timely and relevant information?

Collaborative Activities

Choose a local problem to research—one that 3-5 members of the class can find local resources and conduct observations. Write a one-paragraph description of the problem. After you have described the problem, do the following:

1. Discuss with team members how information will be gathered and recorded (electronic notes, notes on source, notecards); establish file-naming conventions.

2. Have half the team locate a source on your college Web site that might have information to solve the problem you are researching. Describe the search process and the information found.

    Have half the team use the search engines available on the World Wide Web to locate information related to the problem. Share the findings with all members of the team. How easy or difficult was it to find timely and relevant information?

3. Gather the notes in one location so that all members of the team have access to the notes. Review the problem and identify what each member needs to do next to find a solution.

CHAPTER 19

Research Sites and Sources: Library and Internet Research

T ake a tour of your school or community library, or, if you are employed, check to see whether your company has a library (many do). Tours are frequently part of your orientation to school or company resources. Listen carefully and note areas you most likely will use in your research. If you visited the library your freshman year, you probably should take a refresher tour if you are now a junior or senior. You will view the library from a different perspective because more than likely, your interests are now more focused and specialized. You probably have a better idea of what you need to locate in the library.

You will also see how technology has changed the library and how you look for information. Library catalogs are online, giving you access to the library through the World Wide Web. The Web also gives you access to databases, often called knowledge bases, developed by corporations, organizations, and governments. *Google, Yahoo,* or many Internet service providers (ISPs) are among the many Web portals that have search features. Almost every professionally developed Web site for companies, organizations, and governments has a search feature.

Effective search strategies are an important skill to have.

You must develop effective search strategies for the electronic environment to make the best possible use of the vast amount of information available.

In this chapter, we first describe library and Internet sources. We provide examples; you must explore the library sites. In the second section, we focus on search strategies. We suggest strategies for finding information to help you solve the problem you are researching. You must select and evaluate the sources to make sure they are worthwhile, reliable sources that provide relevant and timely information.

Library and Internet Sites

You can now visit a library without going there in person. You can find the complete texts of many articles from periodicals and government reports on the Web. Books are available in electronic form—no paper version. In this section, we describe the traditional library (the building) and online libraries available to you. We encourage you to visit all of the sites.

Traditional Libraries: The Buildings

The traditional library offers a good place to start for understanding the resources in a library and how to locate information in a library. Plan to visit your school or local library and orient yourself to its organization so that your research trips are efficient searches for information.

On your first trip to the library, pick up a map of the library. You will soon learn which areas you will frequent most, but on your first trip look for the following areas:

- online catalog access to the library's holdings and/or card catalog (a rare sight now)

- newspapers and current periodicals

- the stacks—location of most of the books that can be checked out

- reference section(s)—location of publications such as dictionaries and handbooks that must be used in the library

- circulation desk—where you check out materials

- microfilm section

- specialized databases available on CD-ROM (if they are not part of the online catalog)

As you look for these sections, you may see other parts of the library that interest you: music-listening rooms, computers to use for writing papers, a children's book section, a section for government documents, and so on. Explore.

You need to understand the classification system the library uses to organize the material. Many libraries have adopted the Library of Congress (LC) classification system. Figure 19.1 identifies the major divisions of the LC system. The series of numbers associated with the major division pinpoint the topic and location. As you work with your research problem, you will find yourself returning to the same sections of the library. However, you should also follow leads to other sections of the library. You might be surprised at what you find. You will probably find a discussion of the problem you are researching that brings in information that you had not considered.

Understanding the physical layout of the library and the organization of the information in the library may make it easier for you to understand and locate information online. The physical layout places related sources together. For example, a library may house all reference sources (sources such as indexes, handbooks, and dictionaries) in one central location apart from the materials that can be checked out. Another library may place related reference sources and circulating material on the same floor. Learn the general organization and layout of the library you use.

Online Libraries

Libraries have certain areas of the online catalog open for anyone to visit, but other areas require a username and password for library members.

Most libraries now not only have the holdings online for users, but also give users access to databases electronically. The access may be limited to the holdings of the library only, but again, libraries are changing. Few libraries remain that rely on the card (hard-copy) catalog. At the very least, most have their holdings cataloged in a database that you access at terminals throughout the library. Libraries are sharing databases. When you access the holdings of the library, you may be connecting to the Internet and using databases shared by several libraries. The library is a part of a consortium of libraries (often organized by states, for example the Alabama Virtual Library, www. virtual.lib.al.us), and the databases for the libraries are on the Web.

FIGURE 19.1

Library of Congress call numbers. Each general heading is broken into categories with letters and numbers assigned such that each work has a unique call number.

Library of Congress Call Numbers	
General Works	A
Philosophy and Religion	B
Auxiliary Sciences of History	C
History: General and Old World	D
History: America	E-F
Geography. Maps. Anthropology.	G
Economics and Business	H-HJ
Sociology	HM-HX
Political Science	J
Law (General)	K
Education	L
Music	M
Fine Arts	N
Language and Literature	P
Science	Q
Medicine	R
Agriculture	S
Technology	T
Military Science	U
Naval Science	V
Bibliography. Library Science.	Z

User interfaces for the online "card catalog" look different for each library, but the information is the same. Figure 19.2 is an example of the information for the 6th edition of this textbook, *How to Write for the World of Work,* found in the Library of Congress catalog. Not only do you get the publication information (author, title, publisher, and publication date), but you also get the call number, the book's location in the library, and whether the book is on the shelf or checked out.

The links (the underlined text) take you to other books by the author(s), related subjects (Figure 19.3), and publications with a call number (HF 5721.P39) in the example in Figure 19.4). The **previous** and **next** buttons (Figure 19.3) allow you to move to the next set of entries or back to the earlier set. You have the option of saving the information to a disk, printing the information, or sending the information to an e-mail address. You might save the information to disk when you want to gather a lot of information and need time to carefully review the sources.

FIGURE 19.2

The Library of Congress has the 6th edition of this textbook, *How to Write for the World of Work.* The online catalog provides the following information—and more:

search information and search results	for example, *cunningham, donald h* yielded 16 possibilities
type of material	book, in this example, but microfilm, electronic, e-book are other possibilities
bibliographic information	title, author(s), edition, publisher; the lead author's name links to other works by the same author
call number	unique number assigned to the source; the link leads to a list of sources with similar call numbers (a good way to find additional sources on the topic)
location	where to find the source in the library
status	indicates whether the source is available or, if it is checked out, when it is due

Source: Library of Congress Online Catalog. Retrieved October 19, 2003, from catalog.loc.gov/

FIGURE 19.3

Selecting the Subjects/Content tab (see Figure 19.2) yields a list of links to related subjects. For this textbook, the related subjects are *commercial writing* and *business writing*. A partial list of the *business writing* links is shown with subcategories given, such as *business writing— Finland*.

Source: Library of Congress Online Catalog. Retrieved October 19, 2003, from catalog.loc.gov/

The Library of Congress   >> Go to Library of Congress Authorities

LIBRARY OF CONGRESS ONLINE CATALOG

Help | New Search | Search History | Headings List | Titles List | Request an Item | Account Status | Other Databases | Start Over

DATABASE: Library of Congress Online Catalog
YOU SEARCHED: Subject Browse = business writing
SEARCH RESULTS: Displaying 1 through 25 of 25.

◀ Previous   Next ▶

#	Hits	Headings (Select to View Titles)	Type of Heading
[1]	498	Business writing	LC subject headings
[2]	1	Business writing Automation.	LC subject headings
[3]	1	Business writing Awards.	LC subject headings
[4]	1	Business writing Bibliography.	LC subject headings
[5]	1	Business writing Case studies.	LC subject headings
[6]	5	Business writing China.	LC subject headings
[7]	1	Business writing Computer-assisted instruction.	LC subject headings
[8]	5	Business writing Computer programs.	LC subject headings
[9]	1	Business writing Computers programs.	LC subject headings
[10]	2	Business writing Cross-cultural studies.	LC subject headings
[11]	13	Business writing Data processing.	LC subject headings
[12]	1	Business writing Databases.	LC subject headings
[13]	1	Business writing Finland.	LC subject headings
[14]	1	Business writing Germany.	LC subject headings
[15]	1	Business writing Great Britain.	LC subject headings
[16]	73	Business writing Handbooks, manuals, etc.	LC subject headings
[17]	1	Business writing Handbooks, manuals, etc. Software.	LC subject headings
[18]	1	Business writing History Sources.	LC subject headings
[19]	42	Business writing Problems, exercises, etc.	LC subject headings
[20]	4	Business writing Programmed instruction.	LC subject headings
[21]	2	Business writing Research.	LC subject headings
[22]	2	Business writing Self-instruction.	LC subject headings
[23]	1	Business writing Simulation methods.	LC subject headings
[24]	1	Business writing Software.	LC subject headings
[25]	11	Business writing Study and teaching.	LC subject headings

◀ Previous   Next ▶

Help - Search - History - Headings - Titles - Request - Account - Databases - Exit

The Library of Congress
URL: http:// www.loc.gov/
Mailing Address:
101 Independence Ave, S.E.
Washington, DC 20540

Catalog/authority record errors?
Use our Error Report Form
Questions about searching?
Ask a Librarian

Library of Congress Online Catalog
URL: http://catalog.loc.gov/
Library of Congress Authorities
URL: http://authorities.loc.gov/

FIGURE 19.4

Resources with call numbers close to HF 5721.P39, *How to Write for the World of Work,* can be found by following the link from the call number. Shown is a partial list of resources that you might find helpful if you want more information. *Business communication* is in many of the titles found.

Source: Library of Congress Online Catalog. Retrieved October 19, 2003, from catalog.loc.gov/

DATABASE: Library of Congress Online Catalog
YOU SEARCHED: Call Number Browse = HF5721 .P39 2000
SEARCH RESULTS: Displaying 1 through 25 of 25.

◀ Previous   Next ▶

#	Call Number	Name: Main Author, Creator, etc.	Full Title	Date
☐ [1]	HF5721 .P39 2000	Pearsall, Thomas E.	How to write for the world of work / Thomas E. Pearsall, Donald H. Cunningham, Elizabeth O. Smith.	2000
☐ [2]	HF5721 .P4	Perry, Sherman. [from old catalog]	Principles of good correspondence covering points of vital importance to the correspondent and the stenographer	1922
☐ [3]	HF5721 .P5	Picken, James Hamilton.	Business correspondence handbook, edited by James H. Picken.	1926
☐ [4]	HF5721 .P5 1926a	Picken, James Hamilton. [from old catalog]	Business correspondence handbook,	1926
☐ [5]	HF5721 .P5 1927	Picken, James Hamilton. [from old catalog]	Business correspondence handbook,	1927
☐ [6]	HF5721 .P53	Picken, James Hamilton.	Principles of selling by mail, by James Hamilton Picken.	1927
☐ [7]	HF5721 .P6	Poe, Roy W., 1915-	Business communication; a problem-solving approach [by] Roy W. Poe [and] Rosemary T. Fruehling.	1973
☐ [8]	HF5721 .P6 1978	Poe, Roy W., 1915-	Business communication : a problem-solving approach / Roy W. Poe, Rosemary T. Fruehling.	1978
☐ [9]	HF5721 .P6 1984	Poe, Roy W., 1915-	Business communication : a problem-solving approach / Roy W. Poe, Rosemary T.	1984
☐ [23]	HF5721 .R58 1984	Robbins, Jane E. (Jane Elizabeth), 1948-	Contemporary business letters with Apple Writer II for the IIe / Jane E. Robbins, Kate Lee Johnson.	1984
☐ [24]	HF5721 .R59 1983	Robbins, Jane E. (Jane Elizabeth), 1948-	Contemporary business letters with WordStar / Jane E. Robbins, Dennis P. Curtin.	1983
☐ [25]	HF5721 .R66 1985	Rooney, Pamela S., 1944-	Business and professional writing : a problem-solving approach / Pamela S. Rooney, Roberta M. Supnick.	1985

Clear Selected

◀ Previous   Next ▶

Save, Print and Email (Help Page)		
Select Records	**Select Format**	**Print or Save**
○ All (this page only) ◉ Selected (this page only) ○ Selected (across pages)	◉ Text Format (Save, Print or Email) ○ MARC Format (ONLY Save)	Print or Save Search Results
Email Search Results	Enter email address:	

Help - Search - History - *Headings* - *Titles* - Request - Account - Databases - Exit

Many libraries also provide other services online. If you find a source but it is checked out, you can have it recalled. Or if it is available electronically such as an e-book or article, you may download the file for the source. You also can view your account and see which books you have checked out and when they are due.

Electronic access to library holdings and electronic connections to data-bases give us access to such a vast amount of information that it becomes difficult to focus our search on the information we need. We suggest how to search online catalogs, databases, and the Web in the section "Electronic Search Strategies."

Commercial and Organization Sites

International organizations give their clients access to resources through several languages.

The Web has revolutionized how companies and organizations transmit information about products, services, and activities to their customers and members. Some companies have created knowledge databases to store information about products, company procedures, employment opportunities, reports, instructions, membership forms, directories, shipping information, and so on. The information may be text, photographs, drawings, audio or video files, pictures of events as they happen, slide presentations, weather maps, and satellite feeds. The electronic environment is constantly changing and expanding.

The organization you work for may also have information available to only those in the organization. For example, financial records, customer order records, information on product prototypes, and other proprietary information may provide you with the information you need to solve the problem you are researching. You must be careful with proprietary information—information that belongs to the organization you work for. If your report will be read outside of the company, check with others (e.g., your supervisor and the legal department) before releasing the information.

Locating information on company and organization Web sites requires you to read carefully and follow the links (leads) to other information. Site maps help (see Figure 2.2 on pages A and B in the first color insert, for example), but you must be alert, patient, and careful to keep track of your search paths.

While electronic access generally makes locating information easier and gives you access to more information, you should also check your organization's library. The library specializes in the interests of the organization and often stores the company archives. For example, you might review the report completed 10 years ago on providing an on-site daycare center to employees before you propose a daycare center now. Reviewing the older report may suggest issues you have not thought of. Like other libraries, corporate libraries are moving to electronic databases.

Do not overlook the small collections of information in companies and organizations that tend to build as they are needed. The collections may start with one person's interest and research into a problem or a department may start a library of frequently used resources and reports published by the department. Search out these areas and the people who are building them.

Government Sites

Government sites for U.S. city, state, and federal governments and for other countries contain a wealth of information. You find such information as the demographic, economic, and geographic features of the population the government represents. You can also find out information about the government, such as who to call if you have a question about the city recycling activities, how to contact your state legislator, or a report from NASA on the latest mission.

U.S. government Web sites are phenomenally rich sources of information. Throughout this textbook, we have used examples from government sites in part because of the variety and ease of locating information and in part because the information is public information, not copyrighted (although we still must acknowledge the source). You might start at one of these U.S. government sites:

- web portal: www.firstgov.gov (see Figure 19.5 on page P in the second color insert)

- Library of Congress: www.loc.gov

- one of the many agencies, for example: www.nasa.gov (National Aeronautics and Space Administration), www.epa.gov (Environmental Protection Agency), www.hud.gov (Department of Housing and Urban Development)

Larger libraries around the country serve as federal depositories for U.S. government publications. That is, they receive many of the government publications and make them available for anyone to borrow. State governments have similar libraries that house state publications such as the laws of the state, brochures published by the agricultural extension agency, or reports from the state's board of education. Web sites for other countries offer similar information; for example, visit Canada's Web site canada.gc.ca. The sites often provide access through a language other than English (see Figure 2.5 on pages D and E in the first color insert).

You have access to physical sites—library buildings, corporate libraries, and government agencies—and you have access to online libraries and companies, organizations, and government Web sites. The amount of information is overwhelming. To make the best possible use of these vast resources, you must define the problem you are researching as clearly and distinctly as possible. Focus on your immediate task: reporting a solution to a problem (specific information) to a specific audience for a specific purpose. In the next section, we describe search strategies that will help you locate information.

Electronic Search Strategies

Search strategies require patience and methodical digging through information. The complete version of much of the information you find will be in a traditional format such as a book or magazine article or a videotape or photograph; however, you will probably do most of your searching for information online. We provide search strategies that begin in an online environment. As you dig for information, refer back to your problem and the criteria you identified (see Chapter 18).

Searching Electronic Databases

Your search for sources to complement your field research (Chapter 20) begins with a search using an online database. The database may be the holdings of a library, a database that focuses on a topic or field (for example, *Health and Safety Science Abstracts* and *Textile Technology Digest*) or on selected publications (for example, *InfoTrac* or *NewsBank NewsFile Collection*), or a company's knowledge base (for example, Hewlett Packard's Web site for printer drivers at www.hp.com). Each database has its own user interface (what you see on the screen), and each requires you to enter the search in a slightly different way. However, the behind-the-scenes search process is similar for all of the databases.

The search strategy and process rely on Boolean logic. Boolean logic is shown graphically using Venn diagrams in Figure 19.6. You will not see the process, but you will use *and, or,* and *not* in the corresponding phrases *all of these* or *as a phrase* for *and* and *any of these* for *or.* Using *as a phrase* looks for words in the same order used in the phrase. You may also use the symbols ?, *, or $ for truncating terms. The symbol used depends on the database; look for instructions. You truncate a term to broaden the search; for example, *financ?* will locate *finance, finances, financial,* and so on.

You provide the keywords in the appropriate fields; sites construct the search for you.

Figures 19.7, 19.8, and 19.9 illustrate what the search might look like as you progress through a search for information on Web accessibility. Beginning at the firstgov.gov portal (see Figure 19.5 on page P in the second color insert), you can use the search field in the top right of the Web site to locate information. Figure 19.7 shows a portion of the list of over 1,000 sources available when the keywords *web accessibility* are entered. Figure 19.8 shows the advanced search Web page, and Figure 19.9 shows the results of the more focused search.

Your responsibility is to select keywords, words that signal the database what to look for. The keywords you select will depend on the purpose of your search and the information you are trying to gather. You might begin with specific keywords. For example, if you are searching a company's knowledge base for information about printers, you can enter the model number of the printer you are interested in. If you are searching a library's database, you enter the title of a book. If the printer and book are in the databases, you will have a successful search. However, if you lack specific information on the printer or, instead of locating one book by an author, you want all of the books by one author, you must modify your search. Entering the type of the printer will give you a list of models to select from. If you want to locate all of the books by an author in a library, you enter the author's name.

Searching using a subject keyword requires you to either expand or narrow your search depending on the results. For example, the keyword *golf*

FIGURE 19.6

If you could *see* the Boolean logic behind the search process, you might see this. You identify the sets of data using key-words. The ovals represent a set of data, a keyword. When you provide more than one keyword or set, more than one oval, you must identify how you want to relate the sets. The *and* and *or* establish the relationship. *Not* is used to limit the search further.

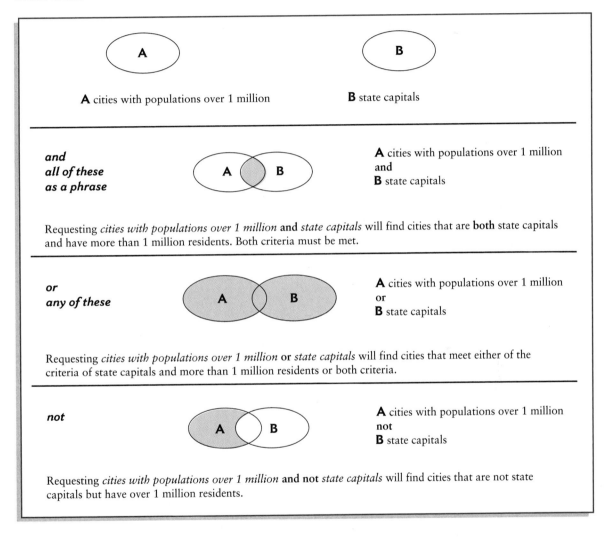

A cities with populations over 1 million

B state capitals

and
all of these
as a phrase

A cities with populations over 1 million
and
B state capitals

Requesting *cities with populations over 1 million* **and** *state capitals* will find cities that are **both** state capitals and have more than 1 million residents. Both criteria must be met.

or
any of these

A cities with populations over 1 million
or
B state capitals

Requesting *cities with populations over 1 million* **or** *state capitals* will find cities that meet either of the criteria of state capitals and more than 1 million residents or both criteria.

not

A cities with populations over 1 million
not
B state capitals

Requesting *cities with populations over 1 million* **and not** *state capitals* will find cities that are not state capitals but have over 1 million residents.

might produce 482 entries, but when the keyword *women* is added to the search, only 29 entries appear. When you begin with a narrow topic, *graphite golf clubs* (as a phrase) you might find no entries. But changing the search strategy to treat *graphite* and *golf clubs* separately with *golf clubs* as a phrase, you might find only 1 entry. You might want to look through 482 entries if you are doing thorough research, or 29 entries or 1 entry might be enough for your purpose.

Review the database screen before you begin your search. Most provide suggestions and options for conducting an efficient search. You can modify

FIGURE 19.7

Entering *web accessibility* into the firstgov.gov search field yields over 1,000 sources.

Source: Federal Citizen Information Center. Office of Citizen Services and Communications. Retrieved October 21, 2003, from www.firstgov.gov

FIGURE 19.8

The advanced search feature on the firstgov.gov Web site helps you to focus the search for information. Notice on this Web page the options for narrowing a search.

Source: Federal Citizen Information Center. Office of Citizen Services and Communications. Retrieved October 19, 2003, from www.firstgov.gov/fgsearch/index.jsp

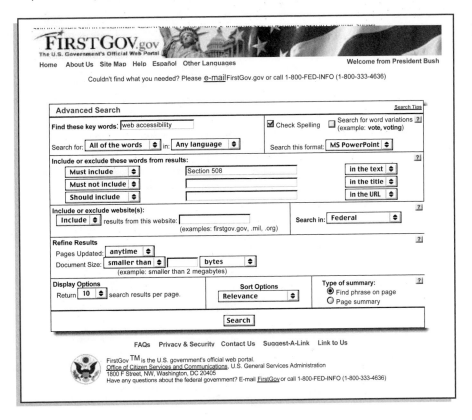

your search strategies in most databases without reentering the keywords. Before you give up on a search, double-check the keyword(s) you entered. A misspelled word or name will result in no matches or unintended matches.

Many library databases first prompt you to select whether the keyword(s) are part of the title, journal title, author's name, subject, or call number. This selection narrows the area of the database, the field, for the search (Figure 19.8). The search for the keyword will be quicker because it assumes, for example, that the words you enter for the title must appear in that order with *and* or *as a phrase* assumed. When you go into a company's knowledge base through a series of links on the Web site, you are narrowing the search. Hewlett Packard, for example, sells more than printers. A series of choices will take you from the home page to printers and eventually to printer drivers.

FIGURE 19.9

Adding the words *section 508* and a requirement that the format be *PowerPoint* (see Figure 19.8), narrowed the results to 2 possible sources of information for Web accessibility.

Source: Federal Citizen Information Center. Office of Citizen Services and Communications. Retrieved October 21, 2003, from www.firstgov.gov/fgsearch/index.jsp

Using Web Portals and Search Engines

Yahoo!, MSN Search, and *Excite* are just a few of the currently available Web portals. Other sites such as *Google* and *AltaVista* are powerful search engines. Each has its own interface, organization, and areas it specializes in. Read the screen to begin your search. For most Web portals, you will find the search most efficient if you first select one of the categories given on the opening screen. After you go to that category site, enter the keyword(s) you want to search for. The results identify Web sites that match the keyword(s) in some way and many list the possibilities in descending order of probable match. You can also customize the search process so that you will be prompted when a new Web site appears that covers topics in which you are interested.

Gathering the Information

Searching the Web and Web sites requires patience. You do not want to stop and write down every path you take. Navigation aids such as the breadcrumbs or links on the Web pages and the Back key and Home key on the browser toolbar help. Links change color if you activate them, so you can retrace your steps to some extent. Using the bookmark feature in your Web browser helps once you find a site. However, searching sites until you find the information you need takes time.

When you find the information, record the Web site address. You can open a file in your word-processing software (perhaps the file with your notes on the problem you are researching) and copy and paste the address, with notes from the site. It is easy to copy text and visuals from Web sites directly into word-processing or other software files; just be sure to acknowledge your source (see Chapter 21, "Documenting Sources"). You can print out the information and include the Web address on the page (an option under print).

For many sources you will find several options for viewing, saving, and printing the information. See Figure 19.2 for options from the Library of Congress online catalog. Options you may find include

- **PDF**   Adobe's Portable Document Format retains the original formatting of the document; it can be viewed with Adobe Acrobat Reader.

- **full text**   The complete text of the article is provided; however, the visuals might not be included or might be included but not in the original format.

- **text**   Text is provided with most of the formatting removed so that the information can be viewed through almost any software; the text and some visuals are available but not in their final form.

- **HTML**   Text and visuals are formatted to be viewed on the Web.

- **e-mail**   Information from the online catalog or database or files from a Web site may be sent (so you can keep all your research notes electronic).

- **print page**   For Web pages such as product information sheets, you may select Print Page to get the information shown on the Web in a format that is better suited for printing on 8 1/2- × 11-inch paper than simply printing the Web page.

Reference Sources

In this section, we provide an overview of commonly used and readily available reference sources: periodical and abstract indexes, directories, and online periodicals and news media. (Periodicals are magazines, newspapers, journals, and other publications published at regular intervals—daily, weekly, monthly, quarterly, for example.) The reference sources we identify represent only a few of the many sources available. The sources you use will depend in part on what is available. Some of the reference sources will be in electronic form only and others are published in hard-copy and electronic form. The hardest part of using reference sources is locating the information in them. Frequently, the sources have more than one way to access the information.

Know the overall content and purpose of the reference source, and be aware of what it covers and what it does not cover. Read the description of the electronic database or the hard-copy source before you begin your search. The following is the description for *InfoTrac's Expanded Academic ASAP:*

> InfoTrac OneFile (Gale) A 'mega-content' database indexing over 6,000 periodicals, newspapers, and newswires with backfile coverage from 1980 to present, updated daily. The database includes full text articles for 3,000 periodicals, 89 wire services and business press releases. OneFile offers single source searching for news and periodical articles on a wide range of topics: business, computers, current events, economics, education, environmental issues, health care, hobbies, humanities, law, literature and art, politics, science, social science, sports, technology, and many general interest topics. Audience: middle school through college, general public.[1]

Ask yourself if the topic you are researching falls into one of these subject areas. The topic areas are broad, so even if you can place your topic in one of these areas, you may not find anything in the database. Try another database. If you know the title of the magazine you want to search, enter the title. If you receive no results, try another database. If you do find material using the title or keywords, do not assume you have found all or even the most important information on the topic. The periodicals indexed by *InfoTrac,* for example, represent only a small number of the thousands of periodicals published.

Recognize the gap between the time an article is published and the time it is picked up by a database. The time span advertised by the publisher of the database does not mean that every article published in the periodicals has been indexed in the database. For example, a search in *ERIC* (the leading electronic database for periodicals related to education) in October 2003 found the latest issue of *College English* indexed to be October 2002; however, a search of *Academic Search Elite* had *College English* through September 2003. You may have to go to another index with more recent issues cataloged, visit the Web site of the publisher of the periodical (in this case, www.ncte.org, National Council of Teachers of English), or go to the library's current periodicals section and look at the periodical.

Reference sources vary in how much information they provide and in what form the information is presented. The following references are examples of the types of sources available.

---

[1]From the Alabama Virtual Library site. Retrieved October 4, 2003, from http://www.virtual.lib.al.us/databases/index.html

Periodical and Abstract Indexes

Periodical and abstract indexes catalog together related publications and topics. These electronic indexes were once separated into indexes, bibliographies, and abstracts, but technology has given publishers the ability to combine the information into one form. The database entry has some or all of the following features: the bibliographic citation for the source, an abstract, the complete article (referred to as *fulltext*), and options for saving the information to a disk and ordering information if you want a hard copy of the article. You search using keywords, titles, authors, or other descriptors.

Visit your library online for a list of periodical and abstract indexes. Here are a few to look for:

- *ABI/Inform* (*American Business Information*)
- *ERIC* (education-related sources)
- *InfoTrac* (see the description on the preceding page)

Directories

Directories give brief, concise information on companies, organizations, and people. Search them to find such information as who owns Xerox, what is the largest advertising agency in the world, when Joe Camel was introduced, or which automobile was first in U.S. sales last year. If you need to locate companies in a certain industry or companies that manufacture a certain product, a good business directory will provide the names, addresses, and telephone numbers. Check your library for electronic versions of the directories or use a search engine on the Web to go directly to the company or organization's site. Here are a few of the most popular directories:

- *Directory of Foreign Manufacturers in the United States*
- *Standard & Poor's Corporate Records*
- *Thomas Register of American Manufacturers*
- *U.S. Government Periodicals Index*

Other reference sources include almanacs, atlases, dictionaries, encyclopedias, handbooks, and yearbooks. Some focus on a particular topic or field of study; others provide a broader coverage of topics. Reference librarians know how to search the library's print material, Web sites, and other electronic sources. You can help by clearly stating the problem you are researching and being familiar with the organization of the library.

Online Periodicals and News Media

News services and publications have Web sites. Some require you to subscribe, others limit what information you receive at no charge, and others provide the full text. For example, *cnn.com* or *msnbc.com* provide clips from the television broadcast and other information that complements the content of the television broadcast. The Web sites for popular magazines such as *www.forbes.com* or *time.com* present information from the print versions as well as additional information. You can print the articles and often you can download the articles.

Go to the original source whenever possible. The online versions of periodical, magazine, and newspaper articles often do not include the visuals in the abstracts or fulltext versions. Also seeing the surrounding articles (and advertisements) may provide additional information for your research project and visiting the location in the library will yield new resources.

Evaluation of Information

As you collect sources from the library and Internet, you will probably quickly evaluate the source to help narrow the search for information. In Chapter 18, we describe three factors to consider as you evaluate sources: (1) authority and source, (2) content reliability and validity, and (3) timeliness and relevance (see Figure 18.7). In Chapter 2, we provide guidelines for evaluating a Web site (see page 51 and Figure 2.5 on pages D and E in the first color insert). Review both chapters before you read the rest of this chapter. In this section, we provide several quick ways to evaluate information as you collect it. You will be using your critical thinking skills. You may incorporate these suggestions into your notetaking strategies.

Use the suggestions to help you narrow your search and evaluate the sources. Review the sources closely before incorporating information into your report.

Authority and Source

As you collect information from library and Internet resources, you must be aware of who or what organization has produced the information. If you cannot find the author or sponsoring organization on the information, do not use it. Ask yourself these questions:

Authority and Source

- Who is the author and/or sponsoring organization?

- Does the author or organization specialize in this area?

- How do I contact the source to verify the information?

- Who or what led me to this source?

Content: Reliable and Valid

Collecting information and evaluating the information sometimes overlap. Although you will spend most of your time synthesizing the information you collect, first you must collect enough information to evaluate the problem. In the collection process, you will do a quick evaluation as you go. To confirm most information, you want at least two sources that say the same thing. Review your notetaking strategies (Chapter 18), but you might also find it helpful to develop mental notes. Say, for example, that you hear a brief news story about AIDS on CNN. You search out a confirmation and clarification of the story by going to the Centers for Disease Control and Prevention's Web site, and you make mental notes and notes in your report draft to find out why. The notes you collect look like the following:

Content: Reliable and Valid

Information	**Mental Notes**	**Source**
Biotechnology advances offering hope for vaccine	Still developing— not there yet	CNN news 10/7/2003
Increase in exposure to AIDS for women	Excellent line graph to use in report	www.cdc.gov, 6/1/01
	Find information on local AIDS resources	Interview specialist at local hospital

Next, you will spend time with the notes developing the report and applying critical thinking strategies as you evaluate all of the information. Taking notes and developing the notes into a report take time; allow enough time to think about your findings and to write the report.

Timeliness and Relevance

Each research problem will have an appropriate time frame from which to draw information. If the problem is computer-related, you might need to pull from sources no more than 3 months old for software development issues, no more than a week for pricing, and across 19 years for historical information. As you first make notes about the problem and establish the criteria to research (Chapter 18), you will develop an idea of the time frame for relevant information.

Date Final Report Due	March 12, 2005
Date of Publication of Information	June 2004
Difference in days/months/years	9 months
Will the reader consider this information up-to-date?	less than a year old—ok

Suggestions for Applying Your Knowledge

Individual Activity

Tour your school, community, or company library, and pick up a map. Locate the section(s) of the library where the majority of the information for your area of specialization is found. Spend half an hour browsing through that area(s) of the library and make a list of 5 to 10 reference sources you think will help you in your course work or in finding solutions to a problem you are studying.

Collaborative Activities

1. Visit the Web sites of 3 U.S. government agencies. Compare the sites, and describe the type of information you found.

2. Select a topic (if possible, related to a problem you are researching). Conduct a search of articles on the topic using 3 to 5 electronic databases. Write a brief report comparing the results of your search across the databases. Be prepared to report your findings in class.

Research Sites and Sources: Field Research

R esearch frequently requires firsthand knowledge. That is, you must collect the information instead of relying on the reports of others. Field research requires you to leave your desk to collect information outside your office. In this chapter, we describe three methods for collecting information from the field: interviews, surveys, and direct observations. As a researcher, you may interview *subject matter experts* (SMEs). The SMEs may be within your organization or outside the organization. You may interview face to face or by telephone. When you must collect information from a number of people but lack the time to interview each one, you might develop a set of questions—a survey—to collect the information. You may distribute the survey electronically by e-mail or on the Web, or you may send the survey by mail. Alternatively, you may find that a visit to the site of the problem or setting up a comparison test may provide helpful information for solving the problem. More than likely you will use several methods for gathering information to solve a problem.

Seek help from others in your organization who have experience in conducting field research.

We begin by suggesting ways to prepare for collecting the information. We review suggestions first made in Chapter 18 for evaluating the information gathered. We provide guidelines for conducting interviews, developing surveys, and using direct observations to gather information to help solve workplace problems. Every discipline has its own methods for conducting field research (and library research).

Preparing for Field Research

Before you begin to collect information, you must establish some collection procedures. You will probably have only one opportunity to interview the person or a limited amount of time to visit the site or conduct the experiment. Be prepared. Plan carefully. Here are five suggestions for preparing to do your research:

Review the problem.

1. **Review your notes on the problem you are researching.** State the problem in specific language and figure out what sort of information you need to solve the problem. In the example in Chapter 14, Scott Pahl studied the problem of increased costs of mowing highway medians. In reviewing his notes on the problem, Pahl determined that he needed to know more about the existing process and to research alternatives to mowing and their costs and impacts.

Identify tasks to gather information.

2. **Establish objectives for collecting the information.** The objectives should identify specific tasks you must complete. For example, Scott Pahl knew he needed to interview the supervisors of the work crews mowing the grass to get a better understanding of how frequently the crews had to mow and what sort of problems they encountered. He knew he needed to find environmental experts and agronomists who specialized in grass. He also thought it would be helpful to visit at least some portions of the highways to identify the type of grass growing

and to consider the aesthetic issues raised in letters of complaint from commuters. His initial objectives were to interview the work crew supervisors and locate and interview SMEs on grass control.

You will add to your objectives at each stage of collecting the information. For example, after visiting the site, Scott Pahl decided he needed to return to the site with an environmental engineer to evaluate the safest application procedure for *SlowGrowth*.

Schedule the tasks to gather information.

3. **Set up a schedule for completing each task identified in your objectives.** You might find a large wall calendar or an electronic calendar that alerts you to due dates. Project management software has features that allow you to schedule and coordinate multiple tasks. Many of your projects will have a fixed due date. The date when the work must be complete should be the first date you put on your calendar. You then work back from the due date to schedule the tasks. If you do not have a specific due date, impose one on yourself. As you build the schedule, allow some extra days for tasks that require more time than expected.

Test your research instruments.

4. **Test your interview questions, survey, and direct observations procedures before you implement them.** Draft questions, surveys, and observation procedures, and ask others to review them before you go to the source. Some of the major trouble spots you might encounter while conducting field research include the following:

- *Selecting the Wrong Subjects to Interview* Will a 21-year-old want the same features in a car as a 35-year-old or a 60-year-old? Probably not. Will surveying mall-goers about improving access to the planned sports complex give the same results as polling sports fans leaving the basketball arena that the proposed sports complex will replace? The mall-goer may not attend sporting events at the arena.

  Before you select the target population, review the research problem and describe the characteristics of the subjects. Age difference is an obvious factor to consider in selecting subjects to research; however, you should look at other factors—many that cannot be directly observed. For example, you may need to consider level of education, income level, hand-eye coordination, desire to learn a new skill, and so on.

- *Selecting the Wrong Sites to Visit* A successful test of *SlowGrowth* in the Southeast will not ensure that it will retard the growth of weeds in Minnesota (Chapter 14). You might find different factors affecting the problem if you visit a site in the morning instead of in the afternoon. As you develop the problem statement and focus on the problem(s), you must take into account where the problem occurs most frequently and whether you can get to that site for direct observations or must simulate the problem in another location.

- *Observing Factors That Do Not Apply to the Research Problem* Pinpointing criteria to analyze the problem will help establish what and what not to observe. For example, the make and model of a vehicle that enters a parking lot may be unimportant in analyzing traffic flow and congestion. A simple count of vehicles or axles may be enough. A simple count can be collected easily using a machine, but identifying vehicles requires a member of the research team to observe and record each car's make and model or to analyze the videotapes of the traffic and note the types of vehicles.

- *Asking Ambiguous and Irrelevant Questions* You have limited time to ask questions; make every one count. Ask the SME who developed a new bulletproof vest about the material used in the vest, the construction of the vest, and the types of bullets it will repel. Do not ask the SME to list the advantages of using a vest. The advantages have been established, and you can gather the statistics that support the use of bulletproof vests before interviewing the SME. However, it would be appropriate to ask the SME's prediction for an improved rate of survival with vests made with the new material.

- *Using Inconsistent Collection Procedures* Work with other members of the team to develop the research procedures. Depending on the problem, several members of the team may be doing the same tasks. Each member may have to administer the survey, interview SMEs, or make a site visit. Team members should be using identical research procedures. For example, one team member cannot read the survey questions to a respondent while another member lets the respondent read the questions and still another e-mails the questions. The different environments may affect how the responses are given. You will need to discuss each team member's responsibilities and ensure consistent gathering of information.

Report your progress.

5. **Evaluate your progress throughout the project and make adjustments as needed.** Few projects go so smoothly that you complete the tasks and solve the problem without interruptions to the schedule. Often you must rely on and adjust to others whose schedule may not fit yours.

Progress Reports

You may have to make progress reports to your supervisor or client. Progress reports may be informal memos to the project coordinator in your organization or more formal reports to the client. In progress reports,

- Review the problem. How much review you provide will depend upon your reader's familiarity with the problem. Simply identifying the problem in the subject line of a memo may be enough, or you may need to give a 1- to 2-page summary of the problem.

- Report on current activities and the status of the research tasks. You might include a calendar that shows which tasks are on schedule and which have fallen behind. You might include a summary of the current expenses and project future expenditures.

- Alert your supervisor and the client if the project research is running into problems. You should also assure them that the problem is under control. Supervisors and clients expect a few problems. Keep them informed.

- End the progress report with a short conclusion or summary or end with a list of objectives to guide the work both in the short term (until the next progress report is due) and long term (until the project is completed).

Evaluating the Information

In Chapter 18, "Research Strategies," we describe three areas you should review as you work through the problem and look for solutions. Field research requires the same type of scrutiny as library and Internet research even though you are collecting information firsthand rather than relying on the reporting of others. You must evaluate your field research sources, the information, and the place it has in your report. Ask the questions given in Figure 18.7 and reviewed below:

- **Source** Who are the sources of the information? What is their area of expertise? Why are they the authority on the problem?

- **Information** How valid and reliable is the information gathered? Have I asked the right questions in interviews and on surveys? Does the information gathered on-site provide the information needed?

- **Place in report** How is the information gathered contributing to solving the problem? Did I gather the information in a timely manner?

In the remaining pages, we provide guidelines for conducting interviews, administering surveys, and making direct observations.

Interviews

You know the problem. You have a good idea of some of the information you need. You have identified the SMEs you need to meet with to discuss the problem or a portion of the problem. The SMEs may be a part of your organization: for example, the customer service department that provides you a list of the most frequent troubleshooting questions or the bench technicians who explain how the new microprocessor will work. Or you may have to locate an SME. Library and Internet resources can help you here, or ask others.

Prepare for the interview.

The key to conducting effective interviews is *preparation*. You must prepare for interviews whether the interview is an informal telephone call to a vendor to get a price quote or a more formal meeting with the lead scientist of a research project. Start with library and Internet resources. For example, in choosing how to configure the computer system you need, you can begin at the Web site of a computer vendor. Your call to the vendor may be unnecessary, or you may need help deciding which combination ethernet and modem card to put in the laptop. To get a better understanding of a lead scientist's expertise before your visit, you might search the *Applied Science and Technology* electronic database and read the complete text of her reports.

Make a list of questions.

Before the interview make a list of questions. The questions will evolve out of your preliminary research in preparation for the interview. Design the questions to gather the information you need. *Ask direct questions:* What steps do you take to process the travel voucher? or How long does it take the work crew to mow a mile of highway median? Of course, at times, you will want to elicit the opinion of the SME: What options do we have for managing the software environment in the computer classroom? or How do you think the traffic should be rerouted? (A question requiring only a yes or no response, such as Do you think the traffic should be rerouted? doesn't help you explore solutions to the problem.)

Listen to responses and ask follow-up questions.

Effective questions will get you a long way toward conducting a productive and informative interview, but you also must *listen to the responses*. You may need to ask follow-up questions to clarify responses and to extend the responses further. Often factors you have not considered come out in the discussion. You must be adept at adjusting your questions. For example, in discussing with the locksmith the problem of security in the textile research lab, the supervisor learned about a fiber-optic system that can be installed, which is comparable in cost to a combination lock system yet secures the equipment as well as the room. The supervisor asked many follow-up questions to learn about the fiber-optic system.

Stay focused on the topic and areas related to your original purpose for the interview. The person you interview will appreciate your efficient use of time and your understanding of the problem.

Be professional: arrive on time for interviews and thank the SME when you leave.

You also must *be considerate* of the SME. Be on time for the appointment and stay only as long as needed to gather the information. If you want to tape the interview, request permission and be prepared to take notes if the person does not want to be taped. You might follow the interview with a short thank-you note or return the favor and answer the SME's questions when she or he calls.

Review your notes as soon as possible.

Finally, *review your notes* as soon as possible after the interview to fill in information that you did not write down as you discussed the problem with the SME. If you have to go back to the SME for more information, think through your questions carefully before you go back. If you taped the interview, review the tape and transcribe the conversation so you can review the information easily.

Surveys

In this section, we describe the type of survey you develop in response to an immediate, local problem. Surveys (also referred to as *questionnaires*) provide you with a tool for collecting information from individuals you cannot interview easily. Donald Zimmerman and Michel Lynn Muraski caution that the survey "should not be the sole source of information. In gathering information, social scientists suggest triangulation—gathering data in different ways to validate the information . . . ."[1] You will want to take courses in statistics and survey development before you conduct a large-scale survey. We suggest guidelines for surveys you might conduct for local problems.

For example, say you want to offer health benefits to your employees. You need to know how many of your 45 employees currently have health insurance. You send out an e-mail to everyone asking for a simple yes or no response. In this instance, you should probably offer a brief explanation of your plans and invite suggestions. The main purpose of your e-mail is to find out who has insurance. You can track who responds with the return address on the e-mail message.

For most surveys you will have several questions to ask. Your audience will probably give you only a few minutes to gather the information. We suggest you do the following before distributing your survey:

- **Review your notes on the problem you are researching.** If you have a clear understanding of the problem, you will develop a survey focused on getting the information from respondents.

- **Draft and test a set of questions that will gather the information you need.** Testing surveys goes beyond passing it around to others in your office. You must test it on a group similar to the population you plan to survey. Expect revisions and changes.

See Chapter 18 for a discussion about reliability and validity.

A reliable survey may be given to a similar population and similar results will be found. A valid survey gathers the information that it is designed to gather. You need to know two other terms used in survey research: sample and population. In most cases, you cannot possibly ask everyone, the population, affected by the problem to respond to your survey. Instead, you select a representative sample from the population to ask the questions. The size of your sample will depend on the size of your population.

Figure 20.1 summarizes the types of questions you can use. The type you select will depend on the topic, the amount of information you need, the decisions you must make based on the questions, and factors such as the

---

[1]Donald Zimmerman and Michel Lynn Muraski, *The Elements of Information Gathering: A Guide for Technical Communicators, Scientists, and Engineers* (Phoenix: Oryx, 1995) 123. You should review this source. The authors provide guidelines for conducting a survey.

FIGURE 20.1

Invest time in constructing the questions for your surveys. Select questions that will give you a meaningful response that can easily be totaled and evaluated.

yes/no	Quick and easy to respond to and to tally, but may not supply appropriate or complete information.
	Will the voice recognition software help? A yes or no answer will not give you an idea of how it will or will not help the employee.
	Will the voice recognition software run on the laptops the sales staff use? A yes or no response is all that is needed here.
multiple choice	Quick and easy to respond to and to tally. The options must be designed so the choices cover the possible options without conflict in meaning.
	How many special classes have you attended at the City Zoo? ___ *no classes* ___ *1–2 classes* ___ *3–4 classes* ___ *more than 4*
ranking	Ranking gives a list of items and the respondent identifies his or her preference.
	Indicate your preference for health insurance (1 most preferred, 4 least preferred) __ *$30 a month hospital stays only* __ *$50 a month routine medical bills and full hospital coverage* __ *$80 a month full coverage ($20 deductible per visit)* __ *$99 a month full coverage with dental plan ($20 deductible per visit)*
rating	Rating questions ask the respondent to select from a range of choices.
	Strongly Agree Agree No Opinion Disagree Strongly Disagree *1 2 3 4 5* *My chair is comfortable.* *1 2 3 4 5* *My chair provides me with adequate back support.* *1 2 3 4 5* *My work area has adequate lighting.* *1 2 3 4 5*
open-ended	Asking questions that allow respondents to write freely or to fill in a blank gives you a lot of information. The information, however, may or may not be easy to analyze. The amount of space you provide will influence the answer you receive.
	If you could design a software program to help you in your job, what features would you like?
demographic	You need to find out about the person answering the survey. Ask only the personal questions that matter. For example, when surveying accountants about the method of accounting they use, you probably don't need to know their gender; however, their job title and age may help you determine their level of experience.

budget for the survey, how you will reach the target population, and the amount of time respondents are willing to give you. We include an example of a survey (Figure 20.2).

- **Design a survey form that is quick and easy to respond to.** An e-mail message, a Web-based form, a postcard, a sheet of 8.5 × 11-inch paper are some of the formats you might use. Start with an introductory paragraph that identifies the purpose of the survey or omit an introduction. If you include an introduction, be careful not to influence your reader's responses by giving away your position on the topic.

  Responses to 1 or 2 questions may be all you can get from customers entering a store. If your sample population receive the survey in the mail, they may be willing to spend 20 to 30 minutes on responding. Testing your survey will give you an idea of how much time most people will need. Know your audience and how long you can expect them to spend answering the questions. You might want to state in the introduction how long the survey will take.

- **Include in your report the size of your sample and a copy of the survey.** As you analyze the responses, focus on the trends you see in the data rather than isolating individual questions. Use the responses as one part of the information you gathered to solve the problem. Report the margin of error for the survey results, if appropriate. The margin of error indicates the range of percentage points the final results may vary. For example, if 46 percent respond "yes" and the error is ±5, as few as 41 percent or as many as 51 percent could vote yes in the population.

Two examples of surveys illustrate the range of possibilities for collecting information from a large number of people. This method of field research has developed in recent years into an effective and efficient means of gathering information from a sample of the population in order to make decisions that will affect the population.

Figure 20.2 is an example of a survey distributed through the campus newspaper of a university in the Southwest. The target population is students of the university. Students have more than likely stopped to read the newspaper, so they may also take the time to respond to the survey. The survey is designed to fill the front of one sheet of paper that can easily be distributed through the newspaper. Each question is important because of the limited time to get information from the students and the limited space available on the sheet of paper. The survey sheet can be folded with the return address showing and dropped in campus mail.

This survey was designed to gather information from a cross section of the student population. The cost of developing, distributing, and collecting the survey was minimal, but some problems arose. Lack of control after distribution led to such problems as who responded (faculty and staff also read the newspaper) and how many times a person responded. How might the survey developers change the distribution to control for who responds without

FIGURE 20.2

A survey such as this one allows you to get information from a large group of people without a lot of expense. However, it is not a scientific survey. Because the survey was inserted in a campus newspaper, the controls for who responds and how many respond limit the usefulness of the results. The results yield general trends and provide a starting point for a more focused study.

Survey for Public Transportation on Campus

The West River County Council, the City of Levelland, and University of South Plains are studying the feasibility of public transportation for the area. Please take 5–10 minutes to complete the survey.

1. Are you a _____ full-time student or a _____ part-time student?

2. Are you a _____ Freshman _____ Sophomore _____ Junior _____ Senior _____ Graduate Student?

3. Do you have a driver's license? _____ Yes _____ No

4. Do you live in a _____ single family home
   _____ apartment or condominium
   _____ trailer park
   _____ on-campus housing (including dorm, fraternity, or sorority)

5. Identify the closest intersection to where you live while attending USP:

   _____ and _____

6. How do you get to classes most of the time?   Please check only one.
   _____ drive alone   _____ carpool   _____ bicycle   _____ motorcycle
   _____ apartment shuttle bus   _____ taxi   _____ bus   _____ walk
   _____ other_____ (please identify)

7. Which USP building do you spend most of your time in? _____

8. If you drive to campus, where do you usually park? Please check only one.
   _____ university parking lot   _____ public parking lot
   _____ private parking lot   _____ other

9. How much do you pay to park on campus? $_____ per _____ (day, month, semester, year)

10. If free public transportation were available from your residence to campus, would you use it?
    _____ every day   _____ 1 day/week   _____ 2–3 times/week   _____ never

11. If a free campus shuttle were available, would you use it?
    _____ every day   _____ 1 day/week   _____ 2–3 times/week   _____ never

12. If you had to pay for public transportation from your residence, how much would you be willing to pay?
    _____ up to 25¢ _____ 26¢–50¢ _____ 51¢–75¢ _____ no more than $1

13. **Optional** Age ____ under 18 ____ 18–22 ____ 23–35 ____ 36–50 ____ 51–64 ____ over 65

14. **Optional** If you have a disability, please check the term that best describes your disability.
    _____ mobility _____ visual _____ hearing _____ speech _____ health _____ other

Comments?

Please fold the survey so the address for the Campus Police shows. Drop the form in any campus mail box.

increasing the cost of collecting the information? What changes do you suggest in the questions? Do the questions' formats yield useful responses (review Figure 20.1)? What additional questions might be asked if the front *and* back of the paper were used?

In the second example of a survey, we have included selections from a survey conducted by the National Science Foundation and reported in *Science & Engineering Indicators—2002.* Figure 20.3 describes the survey method developed to poll the attitudes of a sampling of U.S. citizens about science and technology. If you go to the Web site, you can get the questions asked. Figures 20.4, 20.5, and 20.6 illustrate how the survey results are interpreted and presented.

Figure 20.3 describes the methodology, the design of the survey and the variables measured. Note the descriptors for the target population ("noninstitutionalized adults, age 18 or older, residing in the United States. Residential households with working phones . . . ."), the sample size (2,000), and the section describing errors that might occur in the sampling. Figure 20.4 illustrates a small portion of the data collected. The data is reported in a table found in the appendix of the report. Discussions and interpretation of data are found in the body of the report. In Figure 20.5, a portion of the data shown in Figure 20.4 is illustrated in the pie charts. The researchers use this and other data to interpret and report on the attitudes of U.S. citizens toward science and technology. The conclusions for a portion of the report are shown in Figure 20.6. Can you see how the survey developed from a methodology, to collected data, to interpretation of data, to conclusions? (We found these documents on National Science Foundation Web site, www.nsf.gov.)

Direct Observations

For many practical problems in the workplace, a firsthand look at the problem will give you a better understanding of contributing factors. Visiting the site, testing the product with those who will use the product, and running comparison tests provide opportunities to see the problem. Review the first two sections in this chapter on preparing and evaluating your research project.

Site Visits

A site visit might involve walking down several floors to see the room you have been given to convert to a Web development office for you and two assistants, or it might involve a trip to your organization's production facilities in Brazil to witness firsthand the chicken-processing plant that is consistently 20 percent more productive than other plants. Regardless of the site, these three strategies will make your visit more productive:

- **Plan your visit.** Before you visit, understand your purpose for visiting the site. Review your notes and the problem statement. Define for

FIGURE 20.3

Every research project has methods or guidelines for conducting the research. Those projects with more rigid and formal guidelines (a methodology) can withstand the tests of reliability and validity. The results provide a level of assurance that the results will not change if a different target population is surveyed. The methodology described in this example establishes the guidelines for surveying 2,000 adults from the U.S. population to find public attitudes toward science and technology.

Source: National Science Foundation (2002, May 30). *Survey of Public Attitudes Toward and Understanding of Science and Technology.* Retrieved October 22, 2003, from www.nsf.gov/sbe/srs/spa/spameth.htm

Survey Methodology:
Survey of Public Attitudes Toward and Understanding of Science and Technology

- Overview
- Survey Design
- Survey Quality Measures
- Trend Data
- Availability of Data
- Questionnaire

Overview ▲

a. Purpose

NSF's Survey of Public Attitudes Toward and Understanding of Science and Technology is used to monitor public attitudes and understanding of science concepts and the scientific process. The survey provides information used by education policy makers and researchers. The survey has been closely coordinated with surveys in other countries to facilitate international comparisons.

b. Respondents

The survey is completed by adults residing in the United States.

c. Key variables

- Science and technology information acquisition
- Age
- Attitudes towards science and technology
- Educational level
- Geographic location (within U.S.)
- Interest in science and technology
- Occupation
- Perceived impact of science and technology
- Knowledge of science and technology
- Race/ethnicity
- Sex
- Computer access

2. Survey Design ▲

a. Target population and sample frame

The target population is noninstitutionalized adults, age 18 or older, residing in the United States. Residential households with working phones are in the sample frame.

b. Sample design

The Survey of Public Attitudes Toward and Understanding of Science and Technology calls for 2,000 completed interviews with adults residing in households with working telephones in the United States. Persons residing in group quarters and institutions (including military barracks) are excluded. Military personnel residing off-base are included. A list assisted random digit dial design is used in the study. The 2001 sample was generated using the Genesys sampling system from Marketing Systems Group (MSG) incorporating a

FIGURE 20.3

(continued)

list-assisted, one block frame. Ten thousand pieces of random sample were generated to represent the population of the United States, including those residing in Alaska, Hawaii, and the District of Columbia. The sample was divided into 50 replicates of 200. One replicate was utilized during a pretest of the survey instrument while the remaining 49 were used in the primary fielding.

Respondents within households were selected using the most recent birthday technique. The individual over the age of 18 with the most recent birthday was considered the eligible respondent at the number dialed. Interviews were conducted in English or Spanish.

c. Data collection techniques

The 2001 survey was conducted by ORC Macro (under contract to SRS). Primary data collection was done using computer-assisted telephone interviewing (CATI).

d. Estimation techniques

The Genesys random-digit sample has no design effect (a design effect of 1.0), so it is not necessary to weight for primary sampling units or any other sample stratification. The basic sample produces a national random sample of households, not respondents. At the conclusion of interviewing, a weight was created for each case in the system file. The weighting algorithm was developed to correct for two distortions: first, there are different numbers of eligible respondents in each household, and only one respondent was selected from each household. Second, differential response rates within an RDD sample produce a disproportionately high number of college graduates and a disproportionately small number of high school dropouts. To correct for differential rates of participation in the interviews, an initial 60-cell weighting matrix was used that includes five age strata, two racial-ethnic strata, two sex strata, and three educational strata. Estimates for the US population were obtained from the Bureau of the Census' *Current Population Reports*. The 60 cells were then collapsed into 32 cells to control for cells in which only a small number of respondents occurred.

3. Survey Quality Measures ▲

a. Sampling variability

The coefficient of variation for a percentage estimate of 50 percent in the total population in 2001 was approximately 2.5 percent. The coefficients of variation were larger for subgroups of the population, but *decreased* as estimates approached extremes.

b. Coverage

Households without phones are not included in the sample frame and thus are not covered. There is also some undercoverage of individuals with recently installed phones due to the time lag between the selection of phone numbers and interviewing. Adjustment was made for multiple phone lines associated with a given household, correcting for differences in the probability of selection of that household. In addition, the benchmark to the Current Population Survey is designed to correct for some of the known biases introduced by coverage errors.

c. Nonresponse

(1) Unit nonresponse - The *cooperation rate* for the 2001 survey was 51 percent using standard definitions for final outcome codes from the American Association for Public Opinion Research (AAPOR) with non-resolved records averaging 36 attempts.[1] The overall *response rate* was 39 percent utilizing the CASRO formula.

(2) Item nonresponse - There was only minimal nonresponse for non-critical items in the survey. For the vast majority of the questions included in the 2001 survey, no respondent refused to answer the question. Few questions had a non-response of greater than one half of one percent.

FIGURE 20.3
(continued)

---

d. Measurement

Opinion and attitude questions are by their nature relatively prone to measurement error, since slight changes in question wording or changes in question ordering can have a significant impact on response. A large number of items in the survey have been repeated, and analyses indicate that these items are stable and tend to correlate with other related information points, suggesting that they are measuring the same underlying constructs.

4. Trend Data ▲

Science and Engineering Indicators has contained information on public attitudes toward science and technology in every biennial edition since 1972 (except 1978). A significant restructuring of the survey was undertaken in 1979, which has provided the framework for subsequent surveys. Time trends for many of the variables can be constructed for the years 1979, 1981, 1985, 1988, 1990, 1992, 1995, 1997, 1999, and 2001.

5. Availability of Data ▲

a. Publications

The data from this survey are published biennially in Science and Engineering Indicators, available on the SRS Web site.

b. Electronic access

Data from this survey are available on the SRS Web site.

c. Contact for more information

Additional information about this survey can be obtained by contacting:

> Melissa Pollak
> Senior Analyst
> Science and Engineering Indicators Program
> Division of Science Resources Statistics
> National Science Foundation
> 4201 Wilson Boulevard, Suite 965
> Arlington, VA 22230
> (703) 292-7808
> via e-mail at mpollak@nsf.gov

6. Questionnaire ▲

- Word version 📄 *(118K)*
- PDF version 📄 *(107K)*

Footnotes

[1] The cooperation rate for this survey is defined as the number of respondents divided by the number of in-scope households for which there was a response to the phone within the allotted six tries. Note that, by definition, the response rate is lower than the coverage rate.

Last Modified: May 30, 2002 Comments to srsweb@nsf.gov

FIGURE 20.4

Science & Engineering Indicators—2002 reports the findings of the Survey of Public Attitudes Toward and Understanding of Science and Technology as well as other sources to provide "a broad base of quantitative information about U.S. science, engineering, and technology." The table in this example records responses to the question: "Where do you get most of your information about current news events?" The pie charts in Figure 20.5 show the information graphically.

Source: National Science Board (April 2002). Chapter 7—Science and Technology: Public Attitudes and Public Understanding. *Science & Engineering Indicators—2002.* Retrieved October 22, 2003, from www.nsf.gov/sbe/srs/seind02/start.htm

Appendix table 7-42.
Leading source of information about current news events: 2001
(Percentages)

Characteristic	Newspaper	Magazine	Internet	Books/other print	TV	Radio	Family	Friend/colleague	Other	Don't know	Sample size (number)
All adults	29	3	7	*	53	5	*	1	1	*	1,574
Male	29	4	10	*	48	7	*	1	1	*	751
Female	29	3	5	1	57	4	*	1	1	*	823
Formal education											
Less than high school	22	2	3	0	69	1	0	4	0	1	116
High school graduate	29	3	7	*	54	6	*	1	1	*	834
Baccalaureate degree	30	7	12	1	42	8	0	1	*	*	393
Graduate/professional degree	43	6	10	1	30	9	*	1	1	*	221
Science/mathematics education[a]											
Low	25	2	3	*	62	4	*	2	1	*	674
Middle	33	4	9	*	46	5	*	1	1	1	469
High	33	6	16	*	35	9	*	1	1	*	431
Attentiveness to science and technology[b]											
Attentive public	37	7	8	*	44	3	0	*	1	*	195
Interested public	27	4	9	1	53	6	*	1	1	*	755
Residual public	29	2	6	*	55	6	0	2	1	*	624

* = <.5

[a]Respondents were classified as having a "high" level of science/mathematics education if they took nine or more high school and college science/math courses. They were classified as "middle" if they took six to eight such courses and "low" if they took five or fewer.

[b]To be classified as attentive to a given policy area, an individual must indicate that he or she is "very interested" in that issue, is "very well informed" about it, and a regular reader of a daily newspaper or relevant national magazine. Individuals who report that they are "very interested" in an issue area but do not think that they are "very well informed" about it are classified as the "interested public." All other individuals are classified as members of the "residual public" for that issue. The attentive public for science and technology combines the attentive public for new scientific discoveries and the attentive public for new inventions and technologies. Any individual who is not attentive to either of those issues but who is a member of the interested public for at least one of those issues is classified as a member of the interested public for science and technology. All other individuals are classified as members of the residual public for science and technology.

NOTE: Percentages may not add to 100 because of rounding. A few respondents did not provide information about their highest level of education. Responses are to the following question: We are interested in how people get information about events in the news. Thinking about the kind of issues we have been talking about, where do you get most of your information about current news events?

SOURCES: National Science Foundation, Division of Science Resources Statistics (NSF/SRS), NSF Survey of Public Attitudes Toward and Understanding of Science and Technology, 2001.

See figure 7-19 in Volume 1.

Science & Engineering Indicators – 2002

FIGURE 20.5

The authors use data such as that shown in Figure 20.4 to support the discussion and conclusions found in the report. They develop the visuals that graphically display the data to help readers interpret the results. The pie charts shown on the right in this example use data from the table shown in Figure 20.4.

Source: National Science Foundation (April 2002). Chapter 7—Science and Technology: Public Attitudes and Public Understanding. *Science & Engineering Indicators—2002.* Retrieved October 22, 2003, from www.nsf.gov/sbe/srs/seind02/start.htm

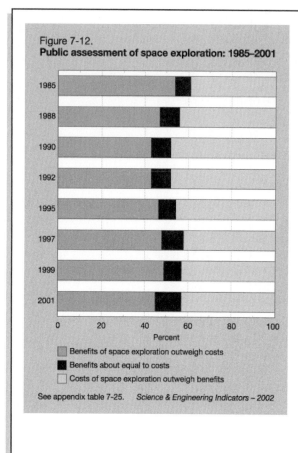

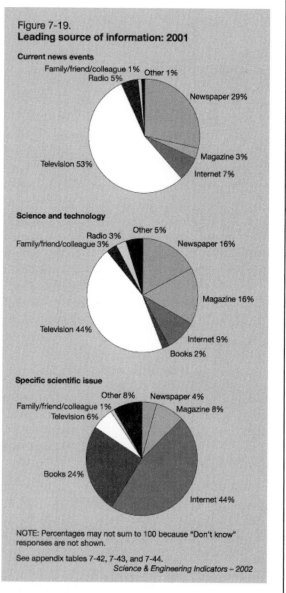

FIGURE 20.6

Each chapter in the *Science & Engineering Indicators—2002* report begins with the conclusions the researchers make from the survey of public attitudes on science and technology. This example is the first of two pages of highlights for Chapter 7—Science and Technology: Public Attitudes and Public Understanding.

Source: National Science Foundation (April 2002). Chapter 7—Science and Technology: Public Attitudes and Public Understanding. *Science & Engineering Indicators—2002*. Retrieved October 22, 2003, from www.nsf.gov/sbe/srs/seind02/start.htm

Highlights

◆ **In National Science Foundation (NSF) surveys conducted since 1979, about 90 percent of U.S. adults report being very or moderately interested in new scientific discoveries and the use of new inventions and technologies.** Those with more years of formal education and those who have taken more courses in science and mathematics are more likely than others to express a high level of interest in science and technology (S&T).

◆ **News about S&T, however, does not attract much public interest.** According to Pew Research Center surveys, only about 2 percent of the most closely followed news stories of the past 15 years were about scientific breakthroughs, research, and exploration. The leading science-related news event of 2000 was the announcement that scientists had completed mapping the human genome. However, only 16 percent of the public claimed to be following that story very closely. Twenty-eight percent said they were closely following news about the Microsoft antitrust court case, an event that may more of a business than a technology story, although the outcome could have a major impact on innovation in the software industry.

◆ **The number of people who feel either well informed or moderately well informed about S&T is relatively low.** In 2001, less than 15 percent of NSF survey respondents described themselves as well informed about new scientific discoveries and the use of new inventions and technologies; a substantial minority, approximately 30 to 35 percent, thought that they were poorly informed. People are feeling less informed than they used to. A recent downward trend is particularly noticeable for the five S&T-related issues included in the NSF survey.

◆ **Most Americans do not know a lot about S&T.** The general public's ability to answer basic questions about science has hardly changed. For instance, in 2001, only about 50 percent of NSF survey respondents knew that the earliest humans did not live at the same time as dinosaurs, that it takes Earth one year to go around the Sun, that electrons are smaller than atoms, and that antibiotics do not kill viruses. However, the number answering the last item correctly rose from 40 percent in 1995 to 51 percent in 2001, an increase that may be attributable to widespread media coverage of an important public health issue, antibiotic-resistant bacteria.

◆ **For the first time, a majority (53 percent) of NSF survey respondents answered "true" to the statement "human beings, as we know them today, developed from earlier species of animals," bringing the United States more in line with other industrialized countries in response to this question.** Although a majority (60 percent) of people surveyed in a Gallup poll were opposed to the Kansas State Board of Education's decision to delete evolution from the state's science standards (a decision that was later reversed), more than two-thirds favored teaching both evolution and creationism in U.S. public school classrooms.

◆ **A majority of Americans (about 70 percent) lack a clear understanding of the scientific process.** Although more than 50 percent of NSF survey respondents in 2001 had some understanding of probability, and more than 40 percent were familiar with how an experiment is conducted, only one-third could adequately explain what it means to study something scientifically. Understanding how ideas are investigated and analyzed is a sure sign of scientific literacy. Such critical thinking skills can also prove advantageous in making well-informed choices at the ballot box and in other daily living activities.

◆ **All indicators point to widespread support for government funding of basic research.** In 2001, 81 percent of NSF survey respondents agreed with the statement: "Even if it brings no immediate benefits, scientific research that advances the frontiers of knowledge is necessary and should be supported by the Federal Government."

◆ **Data from the NSF survey show a gradual decline in public support for genetic engineering over the past 15 years.** The shift can be seen most clearly among the college educated and those classified as attentive to S&T. In no year has a majority of Americans agreed that the benefits of genetic engineering outweighed the harmful results. In 2001, 40 percent of those surveyed thought that the benefits outweighed the harmful results, down from 49 percent in 1985. However, the number of people who think the harms outweigh the benefits has also declined in most years, from 39 percent in 1985 to 33 percent in 2001. Concurrently, the percentage saying that the benefits are equal to the harms increased from 12 percent in 1985 to 28 percent in 2001.

◆ **In the 2001 NSF survey, 61 percent of respondents reported that they supported genetically modified food production;** 36 percent said that they were opposed. In addition, 89 percent said that they supported genetic testing to detect inherited diseases (9 percent were opposed), and 47 percent said that they supported cloning animals, about the same as the percentage opposing the technology.

◆ **Anti-biotechnology sentiments are much more common in Europe than in the United States.** In addition, the number of people harboring negative perceptions of biotechnology has increased in both Europe and Canada during the past few years, especially when compared with attitudes in the United States. These latest findings are from an international study conducted in late 1999 and early 2000 in the United States, Europe, and Canada.

yourself exactly what kind of information you need and why. Make a list of what you must look for, but also be prepared to see things you do not expect. Check to make sure that you have the equipment and material you need to gather data: maps, floor plans, measuring tapes, video and sound recorders, camera, specimen containers—whatever you need to collect and record data.

- **Take careful notes and videotape the site, if appropriate.** You may ask someone to give you an overview of the problem and the site. Or you may walk around and observe before getting the opinions of those on the site. Regardless of how good an observer you are, you must record your observations, either in a notebook, on a laptop or handheld, or by voice as you record or videotape. Memories cannot be trusted to recall accurately what we observe.

- **Review your notes shortly after the visit.** You may need to clean up and add to your notes. Sometimes during a site visit, you will take notes so fast that you will be unable to write complete sentences. Immediately after the visit, fill in the gaps while the details are still fresh in your mind. When you refer back to your notes several weeks or months later, you will still clearly understand what you observed.

Firsthand knowledge of the problem provides you with the authority to make decisions about how to solve the problem. Readers of your report expect you to know all aspects of the problem and to answer their questions. Site visits contribute to your understanding of the problem.

Usability Tests

We discuss usability testing in Chapter 16.

Usability tests are a research tool that frequently save an organization from making a large investment in a product with no assurance that the product will be accepted by the consumer. Usability tests test the product with a group (a sample) of users of the product. For example, writers of software documentation have computer users with different ability levels work through the instructions for installing a printer or setting restrictions on the user access to network administration features. Or you might be asked to write a set of instructions for new employees that will show them how to log on to the company's internal online knowledge base. Before you print 50 copies, test the instructions on several people with different levels of experience in using the online knowledge base.

Before you do large-scale usability testing, read more about how to set up the tests.[2] The suggestions we provide assume you are testing a fairly simple document or product for limited and almost immediate use. That is, you are responding to an immediate problem that requires a quick solution. For

---

[2]For example, see JoAnn T. Hackos and Janice C. Redish, *User and Task Analysis for Interface Design* (New York: Wiley, 1998).

example, the company you work for just loaded new customer-order-processing software that also gives the technician the specifications for making eyeglass lenses. No instructions are provided, so the first day the customer service representatives (CSRs) and technicians use the software is chaotic. In the evening, you write instructions so that the CSRs and technicians will have less trouble. You must test the instructions because you know the software too well. You might ask the first CSR and technician who arrive in the morning to work through the instructions. You can then make changes before the others arrive and test again. To develop your instructions, follow these steps:

- **Identify the problem.** For example, customers are unhappy with the delay in processing their orders, and they would lose confidence that their order for new glasses is correct if the CSR struggled with entering the order. The CSRs and technicians need to learn how to use the software quickly with little interruption of service to the customers.

- **Meet with the product developers and other SMEs to learn about the product.** If at all possible, work with the product developers. However, if you lack either time to do this or access to the developers, you may have to learn the product on your own so that you can help others. In the above case, you knew the software.

- **Select a representative sample of users.** Remember, you can be certain of the effectiveness of the product only with the users you tested the product on. You chose to have several CSRs and technicians review your instructions.

- **Conduct the test and record the results.** Most usability test sites have more than one means of collecting information about the product. In the case of testing software, the user's keystrokes may be recorded, a video camera may capture the eye movements of the user, another camera may record posture, audiotaping could capture any comments, and so on. In our example, you will not do all of this. Either you will give the instructions to CSRs and technicians and ask them to write suggestions on the instructions as they work through them, or you might sit beside them and note where they stop and ask you questions.

- **Evaluate the results and adjust the product's features.** In the example, all you probably need to do is go back to your office, fix the problem areas on the instructions, and retest, if necessary. You cannot change the software features. However, if you encounter numerous problems, you should write a memo describing the problems. Send the memo to the source of the software and your supervisor, if necessary.

Usability testing has become an important part of product development for software, hardware, and documentation. We commonly relate usability testing to products associated with the computer industry, but all businesses and industries test their products in some way before mass producing them.

Comparison Tests

You may find that you must test a product or service before you recommend it as a solution to the problem you are researching. The test may be as simple as comparing price and durability features of a product (for example, snow plows for the company parking lots) or comparing vendor response time and length of service contracts for newly purchased oscilloscopes. Comparison tests help you focus on individual factors or criteria when you are considering more than one product or service.

The test may be a controlled experiment similar to what you would do for a chemistry or biology lab. You set up controlled experiments so that you narrow the causes of the problem. Scott Pahl's final recommendation called for testing *SlowGrowth*. He did not conduct the experiment, but if he were to construct the field test, he would probably test variables such as application season, amount of application, and rate of growth. He could not control the weather, but he could monitor the amount of rainfall as a variable that might influence the rate of growth.

As with surveys, you will need more specialized courses and experience before you can design and carry out a controlled experiment. However, for relatively simple, local problems, you can conduct comparison tests to study a relatively simple problem. Here are some suggestions for conducting comparison tests:

- **Review the problem and establish the purpose of the test.** To keep the comparison controllable, focus on reasonably small parts of the problem. You cannot test every laser toner cartridge available, but you can test the three brands of cartridges available from the local office supply store that fit your organization's laser printers.

- **Identify the variables or features to focus on.** As you select the variable to test, you are breaking the problem into small components. For the toner cartridges, you might measure features such as the ease of installation, the number of copies the cartridge makes, and the quality of the print judged by points per inch, darkness, and crispness of the letters.

- **Conduct the tests and record the results.** Using the toner cartridge example, you might ask 3 to 5 people to install the three ink cartridges you have selected for evaluation. For print quality, you first might print sample pages from several of the documents that your department produces (a memo, a letter, pages from a report with visuals) and ask 10 to 15 people to evaluate the results (possibly with a response as simple as acceptable/not acceptable).

- **Evaluate the results and make recommendations.** To compare the results for each feature side by side, you might construct a table. The comparisons will not always be easy and the best will not always be obvious. Some comparisons will require judgment calls. If you explain your decisions and back them up with test results, your audience will seriously consider your recommendations.

Acquiring firsthand knowledge takes time. Your reward will be your and your audience's greater confidence in the solutions you produce.

Suggestions for Applying Your Knowledge

Identify a problem that you and your classmates can research by site visit, interview, survey, testing, or a combination of these methods. After you have identified a problem, do the following.

Individual Activities

1. Visit the site of the problem and write a 1- to 2-page memo describing what you found. If others in your class also visit the same site, compare your description with theirs. Discuss any differences that may affect how you solve the problem.

2. Schedule an interview with an SME close to the problem. Before you conduct the interview, develop 5 to 10 questions you want to ask. Test your questions on a classmate before you interview.

Collaborative Activities

1. Develop a set of questions for a survey. Bring the survey to class and ask your classmates to complete the survey. After you have had a chance to review the responses, ask the members of your class to suggest ways to improve the survey.

2. With a team member, create a form for collecting data from a usability test or comparison test you are conducting as part of your research of the problem. Have classmates complete the usability or comparison test. Fix any trouble spots before you administer it in the field.

Documenting Sources

R eaders rely on the information provided in workplace documents to make informed decisions about the problem at hand. As a writer, you need to know how to gather information from many sources— from primary sources such as personal experiences, surveys, interviews, direct observations (Chapter 20, "Research Sites and Sources: Field Research") and from secondary sources found in the library and on the Internet (Chapter 19, "Research Sites and Sources: Library and Internet Research"). The more thorough and accurate you are in analyzing the problem and reporting your conclusions and recommendations, the more your audience will trust your solution to the problem.

In part, you project the thoroughness and accuracy of your report through the primary and secondary sources you use. However, you must identify these sources to your readers so that they can locate the sources and make independent judgments on the value of the information (see Figure 18.7). They will judge the authority of the source in part by the author's position and reputation and the quality of the periodical, Web site, or other form the information appears in. And they will note the timeliness of the information, that is, whether the information and sources are current.

Whether information is published in print format or electronically, whether it is an internal company document or a document found in a library, and whether it is a government source and considered public domain or is copyrighted or proprietary information—you must acknowledge your sources. Some readers will rely solely on your evaluation of the information, but others will want to review the original source. In most cases, the readers do not go back to the original source to discredit your report. Instead, they want more background information on the problem, or they want to use your report and that of some of your sources to conduct their own research on another aspect of the problem. Show your readers where to find the information by providing the author(s), the title or other identifying description of the work, and the publication information, including the date and location of the source.

In the following pages, we describe several methods for citing sources and how to document the source. We begin by explaining how to handle quotations, paraphrases, summaries, and other material such as visuals that you use in the document. We briefly discuss the difference between proprietary, copyrighted, and public domain information—particularly information available electronically. Finally, we describe the documentation styles of the American Psychological Association (APA) and the Modern Language Association (MLA).

Incorporating Information

In Chapter 18, we describe how to take notes so that when you are ready to write the report, you will have the information to support your ideas. Now we will discuss how to incorporate the notes into your document. An important tactic that helps readers follow your writing is the skillful handling of quoted and paraphrased material in your reports. If you make inept use of quotations, paraphrases, summaries, and other forms of information, you lose control of your report. It is therefore important to know when and how to quote, paraphrase, summarize, and incorporate nontext material. Here are some conventions that will help you stay on top of the information you have gathered and use it to support your views.

Quotations and Paraphrases

Quotations and paraphrases are used to show support from authoritative sources. Be careful about how you incorporate them into your document.

- **In general, avoid beginning and ending a report or paragraph with quotations or paraphrases.** There are two reasons for this:

    First, quotations and paraphrases in these positions produce a weak effect by drawing the focus away from *your* ideas. Because the beginning and end are the two most emphatic positions, you should place your ideas and conclusions in these positions.

    Second, quotations and paraphrases at the beginning of a report or a paragraph make you appear too indebted to the ideas of others, as if *your* writing serves only to comment on somebody else's thoughts. An important exception to these suggestions occurs when you want to use a quotation or a paraphrase as an attention-getting device.

> Use quotations for the added authority they can give to your ideas.

- **Introduce quotations and paraphrases by acknowledging them with a comment** that includes the author(s) credentials, such as "As one recent research study has found . . ." or with a specific reference, such as "Dr. Hiram Walton, head of the nuclear disposal site survey team, states that . . . ." Simply placing a quotation into the text without setting a context for it leaves readers trying to figure out the relevance of the quotation to what you are discussing.

> The authors' credentials give the reader a good idea of the authors' connection to the topic and why you are citing the authors.

- **Make sure that all quotations correspond exactly to the original wording, spelling, and interior punctuation.** Departures of any kind should be explained. If you choose to omit words from a quoted passage, you must indicate the omitted words by using ellipsis points (three spaced periods; four spaced periods if between sentences). See "Ellipsis Points" in Unit V, "Writer's Guide." If you add a word or short phrase within a quotation, enclose the added words in brackets. Do not use parentheses because readers will assume that the parenthetical statement exists in the original passage.

- **Except as noted in the next item, enclose all quotations inside quotation marks.** A quotation within a quotation is enclosed in single quotation marks (typed by using the apostrophe). See Unit V, "Writer's Guide," page 647.

- **Indent quotations longer than three lines and omit the quotation marks.** See Unit V, "Writer's Guide," page 646 and Figure 21.1 and Figure 21.3.

Summaries

The guidelines for summaries are not as specific as those for quotations and paraphrases because the information is usually gathered and synthesized from several sources. Just as the summaries from your notes have helped you review information and tie together key points, the summaries in your report should tie together key points for your readers. You may or may not be able to point to specific sources. Summaries are stronger if you use your own words rather than quoting or paraphrasing others (except, as we noted above, to grab readers' attention).

- **Include summaries at key places in the document to help the reader review your main points.** Depending on the length of the document, you may summarize the information at the end of sections of the document as well as at the end of the document. You may begin the document with a summary. If the summary is part of a report or research article, it may be identified as an Executive Summary or Abstract.

- **Do not introduce new information in the summary.** A summary reviews information that has already been presented. Because you have already cited the source of any new information in the body of the document, you need not cite it again in the summary—unless it is a quotation or paraphrase.

Visuals, Audiotapes and Videotapes, Electronic Text, and Other Sources

Information gathered from a variety of media sources such as visuals, audiotapes and videotapes, unrecorded interviews, and text from electronic sources such as e-mail and Web sites require special attention in incorporating and documenting the information. You need to acknowledge the source regardless of the form it takes. The following suggestions cover only a few possible forms. You will adapt how you acknowledge the source to the documentation style you choose and the special features of the material.

- **For visuals, identify the source immediately after the caption or in an acknowledgment section at the end of the document.** Provide enough information for the reader to locate the source. We have done this throughout the textbook for visuals that we have used, with permission, from other sources.

  Review Chapters 6 and 7 for information on types of visuals. In most cases, if you give the complete documentation information with the visual (in the caption), you need not list the source in the list of works cited or references. If you abbreviate the source in the caption, give the complete information for the source in the list of works cited or references.

- **Acknowledge audiotaped and videotaped material as you do text or visuals, but note in the documentation the format (for example, videocassette, slides).** If you add taped material to a Web site, be sure to get permission to use the material.

- **Incorporate a phrase into the document that acknowledges particular contributions gathered in an interview.** For example, you might use the phrase "Dr. Karl Lawler, director of IMON's research and development, suggested . . . ." If you follow MLA format, document the interview in the works cited section. If the interview is an informal discussion or with someone within your organization, you may not need to include it in your works cited.

  APA format does not require you to document the interview because it is considered unrecoverable information. You should include the date and initial and surname of the person you interview at the first location you cite the person (for example, A. Lawler, personal communication, February 18, 2005). Do not include the interview in the list of references.

Take careful notes as you gather information from electronic sources.

- **Document information you have gathered electronically such as e-mail and electronic mailing list discussions and text from the Web or electronic databases.** Follow the guidelines for using quotes and paraphrases. It is easy to copy the material and easier still to lose track of the source. Review the suggested APA and MLA formats for this type of information in the following pages.

Using Proprietary, Copyrighted, Public Domain, and Internet Information

You will gather information from sources that may be proprietary, copyrighted, within the public domain, or easy to access on the Internet. Broadly speaking, these categories distinguish the extent to which you can use the information and the type of acknowledgment you must provide.

Have permission before you release the information to someone outside the company.

Proprietary information belongs to a company or organization. The company or organization you work for more than likely has information (frequently recorded in internal documents such as memos or reports) that should not be released to clients or others outside of the company. Even if you developed the information, you developed it as an employee of the company, and the company must give you permission to release it.

Obvious examples of proprietary information include software programs, financial statements, and marketing plans. However, memos and reports on issues such as security, travel reimbursements, or the description of a product development process also belong to the organization. You cannot include the information in a packet to a client or in your portfolio without permission.

Get permission to use copyrighted material.

Copyrighted work may be published or unpublished; it may be registered with the U.S. Copyright Office, but it does not have to be; it may carry the copyright symbol © or not. Works copyrighted in the United States do not automatically carry an international copyright; copyright laws vary among countries. The work belongs to the author(s) or organization that created the work. You must ask permission to use the work or information you gathered from the work, particularly if you will profit from using the material.

For example, we asked permission for some of the material used in this textbook because we did not create the material originally and because multiple copies of this textbook will be published, and we may benefit from the sale of the textbook.

For more information about copyright laws, go to the Library of Congress Web site: www.loc.gov/copyright.

Acknowledge sources that are part of the public domain.

Public domain documents belong to the public. U.S. government documents are in the public domain. You do not need permission to use them; however, you must acknowledge any information you use. Remember, your reader may want to go to the original source to do further research. In the next section, we describe how you cite a document published by a government agency either in print or in electronic form.

If you plan to use documents from a country other than the United States, check the copyright laws of that country. The information we provide here covers only U.S. copyrighted material.

Acknowledge Internet sources.

Internet resources provide access to a wide range of information. We use the term *information* broadly here to mean images and audio and video clips as well as text. Some of the information is part of the public domain. You can use it without permission, but you must provide the Web address and the date you located the information. Other information found on the Web is copyrighted material, for example, articles published in periodicals or news accounts. Many pages may have the copyright symbol ©, but the symbol is not required.

You must obtain permission to use the information whether you use it in a printed document or in an electronic document such as your Web site. This includes obtaining permission to create a link to a Web site that is copyrighted or inserting an image from another site onto your page. You can create links and borrow images from the Web for your documents easily, but do not let the ease of use create a false sense of ownership.

Acknowledge all your resources: proprietary information, copyrighted sources, public domain materials, and Internet resources.

Two points to make about information that is so readily available:

1. Acknowledge the source, whether it is copyrighted or not. You want your reader(s) to know where you found the information. The reader will know you have gone to experts on the problem and based your recommendations on research gathered from library, Internet, and field research.

2. Make every effort to obtain permission to use a copyrighted source. If you cannot secure permission, *do not use the source*. Find another source that has the same information and that will give you permission. You do not need permission from the holder of the copyright for class assignments, but for workplace assignments, you must have permission.

Documenting Sources

To acknowledge the sources you use, you must identify the source. This acknowledgment is call *documentation* (literally meaning that you lead readers to other documents). Good documentation includes enough information about the source for readers to locate it. The following are two of the many style manuals giving guidelines for documenting sources.

APA *Publication Manual of the American Psychological Association,* 5th ed. Washington, DC: American Psychological Association, 2001.

MLA *MLA Handbook for Writers of Research Papers,* 6th ed. New York: Modern Language Association, 2003.

We describe APA and MLA in this chapter, but you should check with the technical communicators in your company or organization for guidelines on which style to use. Or select the style commonly used in your field. You must make informed decisions about the format based on knowing the accepted format for commonly referred documents in your field of study or organization and the information needed for the documentation.

Most provide essentially the same information so that the reader can locate the source: **author information, title information,** and **publication information:**

- **Author information** comes first in all documentation styles used. The author may be one or several individuals who developed the material or an editor who collects material from others and publishes a document. The editor's name appears first as the editor of the document if the entire work is cited. Sometimes a committee or defined group develops the document and does not single out individual authors, for example, a government agency. The group's name appears in the author position.

  APA   initials are used for the authors' first names (E. S. Overman)

  MLA   the name is identified as it is published (E. S. Overman or E. Samuel Overman, whichever is shown on the title page)

- **Title or other descriptive identifier** pinpoints the specific document. Accuracy is especially important when documenting the title. Many authors publish more than one document. The title identifies one document.

  APA   *How to write for the world of work* (only the first word of the title is capitalized unless a proper noun is included)

  MLA   *How to Write for the World of Work* (each word in the title is capitalized except articles, prepositions, and conjunctions)

A reference code is assigned to almost every document; however, the code is rarely included in the documentation. A Library of

Congress classification system (see Figure 19.1), the SuDoc number for government documents, or a classification system developed by an organization to track specific documents are examples of reference codes. An ISBN (International Standard Book Number) is assigned to books. The classification is unique to the document. The reference code is found on the copyright page (immediately following the title page in most cases).

- **Publication information** identifies where the document can be found. Publication information includes

  - the original publisher, including the city or Web site where it is published.

  - the date of publication. The date of publication is important because it allows the reader to judge the document's timeliness and relevance to the information presented.

    APA the date follows the names of the authors in parentheses

    MLA the date follows the name of the publisher

  - information on the larger document if the resource is part of a larger document, such as a journal, anthology, or Web site.

  - a brief descriptive phrase may be included to identify the format of the interview, taped source, some electronic text, or other unpublished material.

  - page numbers, editions, and any other information needed to help the reader locate the source and acknowledge the producers of the information.

Study the following examples for a better understanding of the type of information you must provide. We first give examples following the American Psychological Association's (APA) recommendations (Figures 21.1 and 21.2). We then use the same examples to illustrate the Modern Language Association's (MLA) recommendations (Figures 21.3 and 21.4). Your library Web site may have the most frequently used documentation styles, or visit www.apa.com and www.mla.com for current guidelines (particularly for electronic sources).

APA: American Psychological Association

The Publication Manual of the American Psychological Association (5th edition) recommends using in-text parenthetical citations and a list of references at the end of the report to document sources.

See Figure 21.1

In-Text Citations An in-text parenthetical citation always identifies the author and the year of publication so readers can find it in the list of references at the end of the document.

If referring to a specific part of a source, cite the page numbers for all documents with page numbers, including PDF files. For electronic sources without page numbers, give the paragraph number, using the ¶ symbol or the abbreviation *para.* to indicate paragraph. If the paragraphs are not numbered, identify the section and then count to the paragraph. The paragraph symbol is found in most word-processing software on the menu for Insert—Symbol.

(Morton, 2005, ¶4)
(Matterson, 2004, Introduction, para. 4)

When paraphrasing, you do not have to identify the specific location (the page or paragraph number). However, it will help your reader if you do provide the location.

See Figure 21.2

Reference List A reference list at the end of the report provides the publication information necessary to locate the source referenced. Arrange the reference list alphabetically.

Figures 21.1 and 21.2 show how the references in the text are accounted for in the reference list. Readers can go to the original source for more information. The following examples demonstrate the various ways to present

FIGURE 21.1

The in-text parenthetical citations on this page follow the APA style. Note where page numbers are placed and when the author or authors' names are included inside the parentheses. In the center of the page, the direct quotation is indented because it is longer than three lines. Quotation marks are not necessary when quotations are set off.

Researchers seem to agree that the survey should be as simple as possible. McKinney and Oglesby (2004) suggest testing the survey for readability level "to insure that the content is appropriate for the respondents" (p. 322).

Recent studies (Griffey, 2002; Peavey & Abernathy, 2003) show that the survey should be personalized, as well as easy to complete. Every attempt should be made to get responses from all subjects. According to Griffey, who returns the survey can affect results:

In a Wisconsin study with 45.9% response, it was discovered that 78% of the former students in the top percentile of their class returned the survey, while only 28% from the bottom percentile returned the survey. Students in the top percentile responded within 3 days of receiving the survey while most other students responded only after a second request to complete the survey. (p. 85)

The tendency for successful students to return more surveys than their less successful classmates can invalidate finds and conclusions (Martin, 2004, ¶ 11).

Snelling (2004b) suggests that a high response rate is possible from all segments of the population if the survey is completed online. To develop an online survey, she suggests . . .

FIGURE 21.2

Following APA style guidelines, the list of references for a report contains full publication information on each work cited in workplace reports. Guidelines for formatting the documentation on the reference page include:

- Single-space entries for a workplace report.

- Use a hanging indent so that the first line is against the left margin but lines following are indented about 1/2 inch.

- Use author's initials and invert the first and last names.

- Use capital letters only for the first word and proper nouns of titles and subtitles for books and articles.

- Use capitals and italics for the titles of periodicals; italicize the volume number.

- Italicize the title of the work for workplace reports; do not use quotation marks around the article or essay found within the work.

- Give the date the information was retrieved from the Internet source as well as the Web address, which is not followed by a period.

References

Griffey, R. L. (2002). The personalization of surveys. *Journal of Survey Techniques, 14,* 83-93.

Martin, G. M. (2004). *Developing online surveys.* Retrieved June 5, 2004, from
http://www.surveying.org/students.htm

McKinney, J., & Ogelsby, F. (2004). *Designing surveys.* New York: Acme.

Peavy, J. M., & Abernathy, M. (2003). High-rate response: The standards set in a pilot study of HMO users and private health care users. *Studies in Research Techniques, 22,* 120-128.

Snelling, B. (2004a). Phrasing open-ended questions. *Journal of Survey Techniques, 14,* 106-107. Retrieved November 2, 2004, from EBSCO database.

Snelling, B. (2004b). Designing questionnaires. *Studies in Research Techniques, 6,* 99-103.

---

in-text parenthetical citations according to APA documentation style. We then illustrate format for entries in the reference list.

APA: In-Text Parenthetical Citations

- **One work by one author.** Place the author's name, year of publication, and page number(s) in parentheses:

  Installing firewalls has caused some problems, most due to the intricate nature of the programs already running on the server (Mahem, 2003, p. 119).

Notice the use of commas between the author's name, the year of publication, and the page number. When you use the author's name as part of your sentence, cite the year after the author's name and the page number(s) in parentheses after the information you are citing. Because the date was given earlier, there is no need to repeat the date for the reference in the last sentence.

> Mahem's study (2003) revealed that while service providers paid only a nominal fee for protection against worms and viruses, the installation process is costly and cumbersome (p. 119). The study also revealed serious breaches in the firewall. Because of the vulnerability of the network, Mahem recommended a 10-step protocol for configuring servers.

- One work by two authors. When citing a work that has two authors, always cite both names. Use the ampersand & when the authors are cited parenthetically; use *and* when the authors' names are part of the sentence.

> Researchers have succeeded in producing antibodies with a cell from an animal primed with a known antigen (Kohler & Janus, 2002).

> Kohler and Janus (2002) succeeded in producing antibodies with a cell from an animal primed with a known antigen.

- One work by three, four, or five authors. When citing a work that has three to five authors, cite all the authors the first time you refer to the work. After the first reference, include only the surname of the first author followed by *et al.* for the other authors:

> During the past decade several projects have used laser delay resourcing (Johnson, Martin, & Azziz, 2002, p. 247).

> Kleinmann, Morgan, Fenwick, and Dean (1999) discovered new evidence for changing the procedure. Recent tests show that although the main sail is effectively stabilized during launch, it tends to drift to the right from its maximum ordinate (Kleinmann et al., 2003, p. 254).

- Work by a corporation or organizational author. Use the name of the corporation or organization as the author:

> According to a recent study (Northeastern Commission on Higher Education [NCHE], 2004, p. 9), more and more adults are returning to college.

Use the abbreviation for the source if you cite it more than once.

- Work with no identifiable author. Place the first main words of the title of the article or book in the author position. Enclose titles of articles and chapters in quotation marks:

> No agricultural developments will yield results without parallel developments in water management ("Afghanistan resources," 2004, p. 3).

Italicize the title of books, periodicals, brochures, and reports:

> There are three important sources for server administrators: (1) graduates from schools and colleges, (2) server administrators currently in the work force as

contractors, and (3) technicians working as administrators but not receiving the recognition or equivalent pay (*Technical people*, 2004, p. 29).

- **Authors with the same surname.** If you cite works by two or more authors who have the same surname, include the author's initials in all in-text citations:

    C. D. Fulweiler (2004) reports that the average payload on the X-RD 70 is . . . (p. 117).

- **Two or more works within the same parentheses.** Use a semicolon to separate two or more references in the same parenthesis. They should be listed in alphabetical order:

    A slightly etched surface has better capillary action for the flow of the copper (Delong & Shinoda, 2004; Uhlig, 2000).

- Add *a, b, c,* and so on to the date when there are two or more works by the same author with the same date:

    A recent study (Timmons, 2004b, p. 22) shows that . . .

    The letters are assigned to work in the order they appear in the alphabetical listing of references.

- **Personal communications:**

    Rose McClure of the University of Guelph, Ontario, Canada, believes that "contrary to popular opinion, electronic communication has generated more paperwork, not less" (personal communication, April 11, 2004).

    In a recent research project on the social dynamics of Barnacle geese, investigators tested the relationship between "facial expressions" of the geese and dominance patterns (J. Probst, personal communication, July 16, 2003).

See Figure 21.2

APA: Reference List

At the end of the report all the sources referenced are grouped in a reference list.

Every source must appear except personal communications. Each entry in the list must be cited in the report.

APA: Forms for Print-Based Documents

- Book by one author:

    Moustakas, C. E. (1990). *Heuristic research: Design, methodology, and applications.* Newbury Park, CA: Sage.

- Book by two authors:

    Volino, P., & Magnenat-Thalmann, N. (2000). *Virtual clothing: Theory and practice.* New York: Springer.

- Book by three or more authors:

    Horn, G. A., Scheremet, W., & Zweiner, R. (1999). *Wages and the euro.* New York: Physica-Verlap.

- Book by corporate or organizational author:

  Oakland Athletics. (2001). *2001 Oakland Athletics information guide.* Oakland, CA: Author.

- Book with an editor:

  Strate, L., Jacobson, R. L., & Gibson, S. B. (Eds.). (2003). *Communication and cyberspace: Social interaction in an electronic environment.* Creskill, NJ: Hampton.

- Articles or chapters in a book:

  Levine, A. S., & Billington, C. J. (1994). Dietary fiber: Does it affect food intake and body weight? In J. D. Fernstrom & G. D. Miller (Eds.), *Appetite and body weight regulation: Sugar, fat, and macronutrient substitutes* (pp. 191-199). Boca Raton, FL: CRC Press.

- Document by a government agency:

  U.S. Environmental Protection Agency, Center for Environmental Research Information. (2001, June). *Guide to industrial assessments for pollution prevention and energy efficiency.* Washington, DC: U.S. Government Printing Office.

- Journal article:

  Dragga, S., & Voss, D. (2003). Hiding humanity: Verbal and visual ethics in accident reports. *Technical Communication, 50,* 61–82.

- Popular magazine article. Give the date as shown on the magazine (month or month and day); give all the page numbers when the article appears on discontinuous pages:

  Kluger, J. (2003, November 3). Medicating young minds. *Time, 162,* 48–53, 55–56, 58.

- Newspaper article:

  Acohido, B. (2003, October 27). Amazon opens pages to perusal. *USA Today,* p. B2.

- Interviews and other personal communications are not included in the list of references in APA style.

APA: Forms for Electronic and Other Information

- Electronic articles based on a print source and retrieved from a database. The first date is the date of publication; the second date is the date the information was accessed:

  Brown, B., & Brown, M. (2003, November 25). Pocket PCs get more versatile, less expensive. *PC Magazine, 22,* 38. Retrieved November 8, 2003, from EBSCO database.

  Kalina, R. (2003, October). Gee's Bend modern. *Art in America, 91,* 104–09, 148–49. Retrieved November 8, 2003, from EBSCO database.

- Online articles from an Internet-only periodical:

  Certicom. (n.d.) The next generation of cryptography: Public key sizes for AES. *Code & Cipher, 1.* Retrieved November 8, 2003, from http://www.certicom.com/resources/codeandcipher/

- Abstract from an Internet database:

  Jiang, L., Keman, Y., Tielin, H., Yunfeng, L., Shipeng, L., & Zhang, Y. (2003). Scalable portrait video for mobile video communication. *IEEE Transactions on Circuits & Systems for Video Technology, 13.* Abstract retrieved November 8, 2003, from EBSCO database.

- E-mail is cited in the text only since it is considered personal communication:

  (D. Nash, e-mail to D. Font, August 15, 2004)

- Electronic mailing list postings are cited in the reference list only if they are archived and have scholarly content; otherwise, treat them as a personal communication and cite them in the text. When citing them in the reference list, include the name of the mailing list and the archive address:

  Hamilton, W. (2003, September 18). Early-onset diabetes in children. Message posted to Ref-Links electronic mailing list, archived at http://www.dia.org/mail-archives/ref-link/msg00384.html

- Television:

  Boyd, D. (Executive Producer). (2004, April 1). *Your local news in Vermont* [Television broadcast]. Burlington, VT: WVTT.

APA: Writing the APA Reference List

Entries in the reference list for APA documentation are arranged in alphabetical order by the surname of the first author or editor (Figure 21.2). A work that has a corporate or organizational author is alphabetized by the first word of the corporation or organization (excluding *A, An, The*). A work that has no identifiable author is alphabetized by its title (excluding *A, An, The*).

When several works by the same author are listed, arrange them chronologically, starting with the earliest. The author(s)' names are given for each entry in APA style.

Parrish, H. M. (1955). Early excision and suction of snakebite wounds in dogs. *North Carolina Medical Journal, 16,* 93-102.

Parrish, H. M. (1963). Poisonous snakebite. *New England Journal of Medicine, 269,* 524-610.

Parrish, H. M. (1969). Seven pitfalls in treating pit viper bites. *Resident Physician, 67,* 108-120.

Parrish, H. M. (1970). Hospital management in pit viper envenomations. *Clinical Toxicology, 3,* 501-502.

List one-author entries before multiauthor entries beginning with the same surname. Repeat the author's name.

Parrish, H. M. (1953). Early excision and suction of snakebite wounds in dogs. *North Carolina Medical Journal, 16*, 93-102.

Parrish, H. M. (1969). Seven pitfalls in treating pit viper bites. *Resident Physician, 67*, 108-120.

Parrish, H. M. (1970). Hospital management in pit viper envenomations. *Clinical Toxicology, 3*, 501-502.

Parrish, H. M., & Carr, C. (1967). Bites of copperheads in the United States. *Journal of the American Medical Association, 201*, 927-935.

MLA: Modern Language Association

The *MLA Handbook for Writers of Research Papers* (6th edition) recommends using in-text parenthetical citations and list of works cited at the end of the report to document sources.

See Figure 21.3

In-Text Citations An in-text parenthetical citation identifies the author and page(s) referenced so the reader can find it in the list of works cited at the end of the report.

Cite the page numbers for all documents with page numbers, including PDF files.

For electronic sources, give the paragraph, using the abbreviation *par.* or *pars.* to indicate paragraph. If the paragraphs are not numbered, use the screen number preceded by *screen*, if given. If no type of reference number is given, cite the source by title.

(Matterson par. 4)

Works Cited A list of works cited at the end of the report provides the publication information necessary to locate the source cited. Arrange the works cited alphabetically by author's surname.

See Figure 21.4

Figures 21.3 and 21.4 show how the citations in the text are accounted for in the list of references. Readers can go to the original source for more information. The following examples demonstrate the various ways to present in-text parenthetical citations according to MLA documentation style. We then illustrate format for entries in the list of references.

MLA: In-Text Parenthetical Citations

- One work by one author. Place the author's name and page number(s) in parentheses:

  Installing firewalls has caused some problems, most due to the intricate nature of the programs already running on the server (Mahem 119).

There is no comma between the author's name and the page number. When you use the author's name as part of your sentence, cite the page number(s) in parentheses after the information you are citing:

FIGURE 21.3

The in-text parenthetical citations on this page follow the MLA style. Note where page numbers are placed and when the author or authors' names are included inside the parentheses. In the center of the page, the direct quotation is indented because it is longer than three lines. Quotation marks are not necessary when the quotation is set off.

Researchers seem to agree that the survey should be as simple as possible. McKinney and Oglesby suggest testing the survey for readability level "to insure that the content is appropriate for the respondents" (322).

Recent studies (Griffey; Peavey and Abernathy) show that the survey should be personalized, as well as easy to complete. Every attempt should be made to get responses from all subjects. According to Griffey, who returns the survey can affect results:

> In a Wisconsin study with 45.9% response, it was discovered that 78% of the former students in the top percentile of their class returned the survey, while only 28% from the bottom percentile returned the survey. Students in the top percentile responded within 3 days of receiving the survey while most other students responded only after a second request to complete the survey. (85)

The tendency for successful students to return more surveys than their less successful classmates can invalidate finds and conclusions (Martin par. 11).

Snelling ("Designing") suggests that a high response rate is possible from all segments of the population if the survey is completed online. To develop an online survey, she suggests . . .

Mahem's study revealed that while service providers paid only a nominal fee for protection against worms and viruses, the installation process is costly and cumbersome (119). The study also revealed serious breaches in the firewall. Because of the vulnerability of the network, Mahem recommended a 10-step protocol for configuring servers.

- **One work by two or three authors.** When citing a work that has two or three authors, always cite all names:

   During the past decade several projects have used laser delay resourcing (Johnson, Martin, and Azziz 247).

- **One work by more than three authors.** When citing a work that has more than three authors, include only the name of the first author followed by *et al.* for the other authors:

   New evidence has been discovered for changing the procedure. Recent tests show that although the main sail is effectively stabilized during launch, it tends to drift to the right from its maximum ordinate (Kleinmann et al. 254).

- **Work by a corporation or organizational author.** Use the name of the corporation or organization as the author, abbreviating common terms:

   According to a recent study (Northeastern Commission on Higher Educ. 9), more and more adults are returning to college.

FIGURE 21.4

Following MLA style guidelines, the list of references for a report contains full publication information on each work cited in workplace reports. Guidelines for formatting the documentation on the reference page include

- Single-space entries for a workplace report.

- Use a hanging indent so that the first line is against the left margin but lines following are indented about 1/2 inch.

- If an author has more than one work on the list, use a long dash (or 3 hyphens) in place of the author's name for each entry following the first entry.

- Give authors' names as they appear on the work, and invert only the first author's name when the work has more than one author.

- Use initial capital letters for most of the words in the title and subtitle, except for the articles (*a, an, the*), prepositions (for example, *of, with, for*), conjunctions (such as *and* and *but*), and the *to* in infinitives (to play).

- Italicize the title of the work for workplace reports; use quotation marks around the article or essay found within the work.

- Give the date the information was retrieved from the Internet source as well as the Web address.

Works Cited

Griffey, R. L. "The Personalization of Surveys." *Journal of Survey Techniques* 14 (2002): 83-93.

Martin, Grace Morton. *Developing Online Surveys.* 10 May 2004. 5 June 2004. <http://www.surveying.org/students.htm>.

McKinney, Joan, and Fred Ogelsby. *Designing Surveys.* New York: Acme, 2004.

Peavy, John M., and M. Abernathy. "High-Rate Response: The Standards Set in a Pilot Study of HMO Users and Private Health Care Users." *Studies in Research Techniques* 22 (2003): 120-128.

Snelling, Barbara. "Phrasing Open-ended Questions." *Journal of Survey Techniques* 14 (2004): 106-107. EBSCO. Auburn, Ralph Brown Draughon Lib. 2 Nov. 2004 <http://www10.epnet.cm/>.

——. "Designing Questionnaires." *Studies in Research Techniques* 6 (2004): 99-103.

- **Work with no identifiable author.** Place the first word or two of the title of the article or book in the author position. Enclose titles of articles or chapter in quotation marks:

  No agricultural developments will yield results without parallel developments in water management ("Afghanistan Resources" 3).

Italicize the titles of books, periodicals, brochures, and reports:

> There are three important sources for server administrators: (1) graduates from schools and colleges, (2) server administrators currently in the work force as contractors, and (3) technicians working as administrators but not receiving the recognition or equivalent pay (*Technical People* 29).

- **Authors with the same surname.** If you cite works by two or more authors who have the same surname, include the author's initials in all in-text citations:

  > C. D. Fulweiler reports that the average payload on the X-RD 70 is . . . (117).

- **Two or more works within the same parentheses.** Use a semicolon to separate two or more references in the same parenthesis:

  > A slightly etched surface has better capillary action for the flow of the copper (Delong and Shinoda; Uhlig).

- **Two or more works by the same author.** Add enough of the title to distinguish it from other works by the author and give the relevant page number or numbers:

  > A recent study (Timmons, *Bituminous* 22) shows that . . . .

  > Timmons's recent study (*Bituminous* 22) shows that . . . .

- **Personal communications:**

  > Rose McClure of the University of Guelph, Ontario, Canada, believes that "contrary to popular opinion, electronic communication has generated more paperwork, not less."

  > In a recent research project on the social dynamics of Barnacle geese, investigators tested the relationship between "facial expressions" of the geese and dominance patterns (Probst).

When you cite publications with in-text parenthetical entries, you must include them in the list of works cited at the end of the report.

MLA: List of Works Cited

At the end of the report all the sources cited are grouped in a list of works cited (see Figure 21.4). Every work cited must appear in the works cited list, and each entry in the works cited list must be cited in the report.

Ask your instructor which he or she prefers: underlining or italics to signify titles. MLA suggests underlining because italics may be harder to read; however, we and many others recommend italics for workplace documents and the more up-to-date look.

MLA: Forms for Print-Based Documents

- **Book by one author:**

  > Moustakas, Clark E. *Heuristic Research: Design, Methodology, and Applications.* Newbury Park, CA: Sage, 1990.

- Book by two authors:

    Volino, Pascal, and Nadia Magnenat-Thalmann. *Virtual Clothing: Theory and Practice*. New York: Springer, 2000.

- Book by three or more authors:

    Horn, Gustav A., Wolfgang Scheremet, and Rudolf Zweiner. *Wages and the Euro*. New York: Physica-Verlap, 1999.

    If there are more than three authors, you may name only the first and add *et al.*

- Book by corporate or organizational author:

    Oakland Athletics. *2001 Oakland Athletics Information Guide*. Oakland, CA: Oakland Athletics, 2001.

- Book with an editor:

    Strate, Lance, Ron L. Jacobson, and Stephanie B. Gibson, eds. *Communication and Cyberspace: Social Interaction in an Electronic Environment*. Creskill, NJ: Hampton, 2003.

- Articles or chapters in a book:

    Levine, Allan S., and Charles J. Billington. "Dietary Fiber: Does It Affect Food Intake and Body Weight?" *Appetite and Body Weight Regulation: Sugar, Fat, and Macronutrient Substitutes*. Ed. Joyce D. Fernstrom and Gil D. Miller. Boca Raton: CRC, 1994. 191-200.

- Document by a government agency:

    United States Environmental Protection Agency. Center for Environmental Research Information. *Guide to Industrial Assessments for Pollution Prevention and Energy Efficiency*. Washington, DC: U.S. Government Printing Office, 2001.

- Journal article:

    Dragga, Sam, and Dan Voss. "Hiding Humanity: Verbal and Visual Ethics in Accident Reports." *Technical Communication* 50 (2003): 61–82.

- Popular magazine article. The + indicates the article was not on consecutive pages. Give the page numbers for consecutive pages, for example, 54–56, when possible. Abbreviate all months except May, June, and July:

    Kluger, Jeffrey. "Medicating Young Minds." *Time* 3 Nov. 2003: 48+.

- Newspaper article:

    Acohido, Beatrix. "Amazon Opens Pages to Perusal." *USA Today* 27 Oct. 2003: B2.

- Interviews:

> Powell, Mary. Personal interview. 6 Sept. 2004.
> Martinez, Henri. Telephone interview. 10 Jan. 2005.

MLA: Forms for Electronic and Other Information

- Online abstract or full text article from periodical that originated in print form. The first date is the date of publication; the second date is the date the information was accessed:

> Brown, Bruce, and Marge Brown. "Pocket PCs Get More Versatile, Less Expensive." *PC Magazine* 25 Nov. 2003: 38. EBSCO. Auburn, Ralph Brown Draughon Lib. 8 Nov. 2003 <http://web10.epnet.com/>.

> Kalina, Richard. "Gee's Bend Modern." *Art in America* Oct. 2003: 104+. EBSCO. Auburn, Ralph Brown Draughon Lib. 8 Nov. 2003 <http://web10.epnet.com/>.

- Online articles from an online periodical:

> Certicom. "The Next Generation of Cryptography: Public Key Sizes for AES." *Code & Cipher* 1.1 (n.d.) 8 Nov. 2003 <http://www.certicom.com/resources/codeandcipher/>.

- E-mail is cited similarly to other personal communications:

> Nash, Debra. "Re: State Report." E-mail to Dean Font. 15 Aug. 2004.

- Electronic mailing list postings should include both the posting date and the date of retrieval:

> Hamilton, William. "Early-Onset Diabetes in Children." Online posting. 18 Sept. 2003. Ref-Links. 4 June 2004 <http://www.dia.org/mail-archives/ref-link/msg00384.html>.

- Television:

> Boyd, Dan. *Your Local News in Vermont.* Burlington, VT: WVTT. 1 Apr. 1999.

MLA: Writing the MLA List of Works Cited

Entries in the list of works cited (MLA) are arranged in alphabetical order by the surname of the first author or editor (Figure 21.4). A work that has a corporate or organizational author is alphabetized by the first word of the corporation or organization (excluding *A, An, The*). A work that has no identifiable author is alphabetized by its title (excluding *A, An, The*).

When several works by the same author are listed, arrange them alphabetically by title. Using MLA style, give the author's name only in the first entry. For subsequent entries, type one long dash (or three hyphens) and a period, and cite the title.

> Parrish, Harriet. "Early Excision and Suction of Snakebite Wounds in Dogs." *North Carolina Medical Journal* 16 (1955): 93.

—. "Hospital Management in Pit Viper Envenomations." *Clinical Toxicology* 3 (1970): 501-02.

—. "Poisonous Snakebite." *New England Journal of Medicine* 269 (1963): 524-610.

—. "Seven Pitfalls in Treating Pit Viper Bites." *Resident Physician* 67 (1969): 108-20.

List one-author entries before multiauthor entries beginning with the same surname.

Parrish, Harriet. "Early Excision and Suction of Snakebite Wounds in Dogs." *North Carolina Medical Journal* 16 (1955): 93-102.

—. "Hospital Management in Pit Viper Envenomations." *Clinical Toxicology* 3 (1970): 501-02.

—. "Seven Pitfalls in Treating Pit Viper Bites." *Resident Physician* 67 (1969): 108-20.

Parrish, Harriet, and Caleb Carr. "Bites of Copperheads in the United States." *Journal of the American Medical Association* 201 (1967): 927-35.

Documenting sources pinpoints the location of the information for the reader. The examples we provide cover several widely accepted formats for identifying your sources. Identifying your sources in a standard way allows your readers to evaluate the information you provide for solving the problem. They can readily see who originated the information and where they can locate this source, and they see from the date when the information originated.

PLANNING AND REVISING CHECKLIST: DOCUMENTATION IN REPORTS

Think about the following while planning and revising documentation.

Planning

- How should the information source be acknowledged?
- Is a particular format for documentation required?
- If not, what would be the most appropriate format for documentation, considering the purpose and audience of the report?

Revising

- Have you been consistent in your use of format for documentation?
- Does every reference cited in the text of the report have an entry in the reference list (APA) or works cited (MLA)?
- Is there an in-text citation for each entry in the works cited or reference list?
- Is permission needed to use any of the information?

Suggestions for Applying Your Knowledge

1. The following sources are given in the order in which they are cited in a report. Arrange them in proper order and format them as they would appear in a list of works cited (MLA) or list of references (APA).

   Hare
   - A book published by Van Nostrand Reinhold of New York, titled Painting of Steel Bridges and Other Structures, written by C. H. Hare, and published in 1996.

   Melville
   - Bridge Pier Scour with Debris Accumulation is the title of an article appearing in the September 1992 issue of the Journal of Hydrological Engineering on pages 1306 through 1310 (volume 118). The authors are B. W. Melville and Donna M. Dongol.

   Kennedy
   - J. Beth Kennedy and Marshall Z. Soliman are authors of an article titled Dynamic Response of Multigirder Bridges, which appeared on pages 2222-2238 of volume 118 in the August 1992 issue of Journal of Structural Engineering.

Manning • A book titled Removing Concrete from Bridges published by the Transportation Research Board of the National Research Council located in Washington, DC in 1991. The author is David George Manning.

Fifth • Civil Engineering published an article titled Fifth Time Around, as California Pier Disappears, which identified no author. It appeared in the July 1997 issue on page 12 of volume 62.

Kothyari • The Journal of Hydrological Engineering published an article titled Temporal Variation of Scour Around Circular Bridge Piers, written by U. C. Kothyari and others. It appeared on pages 1091-1106, August 1999, in volume 118.

U.S. Congressional • In 1998, the U.S. Government Printing Office in Washington, D.C., published a report written by the U.S. Congressional House of Representatives Committee on Public Works and Transportation's Subcommittee on Investigations and Oversight. The report is titled Bridge Safety: Hearings before the Subcommittee on Investigations and Oversight of the Committee on Public Work and Transportation, House of Representatives, 102nd Congress, First Session, 7-8 May 1997.

Custom • ENR: Engineering News-Record contains the article Custom Forms: Bridge Work in the October 6, 2003, vol. 251, issue 14, p. 35, 1/6p, 1c. The source was found on the EBSCO host web6.epnet.com available through the Auburn University Ralph Brown Draughon Library on November 11, 2003.

① Bridge • http://www.pbs.org/wgbh/nova/bridge/ with videoclip "Bridge Band-Aids" on the NOVA Online site for PBS, produced by WGBH Science Unit. Created November 1997. Retrieved November 11, 2003. Part of the television program Super Bridge.

2. If you are planning to use a documentation system other than one recommended in this chapter, prepare a brief explanation of it for your instructor. Explain at least these three basic features:

   • The method of citation used to lead the reader from the text to the documentation (parenthetical identification of author and year or another method)

   • The arrangement of the documentation (bibliography citations arranged alphabetically or another method)

   • The form of the documentation entry in the bibliography or list of references.

Writer's Guide

Writer's Guide

his writer's guide contains a series of short descriptions of various writing techniques, conventions, and problems. We have arranged the guide alphabetically to make it easier for you to find your way around.

Whether you are a student or a company employee, you should check to see whether you are required to use a specific style guide. If you are in a writing class, your instructor may use the abbreviations on the inside front cover of this textbook in marking your papers, correspondence, and reports. In this way, your instructor will refer you to entries in this Writer's Guide that should show you how to correct a problem in your writing. In some classes, you may be required to follow the guidelines presented in such style manuals as *Scientific Style and Format: The CSE Manual for Authors, Editors, and Publishers* or the *Publication Manual of the American Psychological Association* or the *United States Government Printing Office Style Manual*. Or you may be directed toward general editing guides such as Amy Einsohn's *The Copyeditor's Handbook* and Karen Judd's *Copyediting: A Practical Guide*.

Once you are a professional in the workplace, you should also find out whether the company or organization you work for has a preferred style guide. Corporate style guides are common. They are developed to help ensure that a company's or organization's documents present information in a professional and consistent manner. A few of these style guides become a standard in their industry. For example, *The Microsoft Manual of Style for Technical Publications* has evolved from a guide for writers within Microsoft to a guide used by many professionals in the workplace on such matters as computer terms and usage, spacing after periods, and use of quotation marks and hyphens.

If you are not required to follow a particular style guide, style manual, or commercial editing book, you can use this Writer's Guide. Its guidelines are based on the most recent and best practice in workplace writing. In any event, you should decide—either for yourself or in conjunction with your teacher, supervisor, or editor—what decisions you will make about forms of abbreviations and acronyms, what to capitalize, how to express sums, and various matters of punctuation and spelling. Once those decisions have been made, be sure to use them consistently.

Abbreviation

Abbreviations are often used in workplace writing. However, they must be used with some care. Remember that abbreviations are primarily for the convenience of the writer. If they are likely to inconvenience the reader, they should not be used. Use without explanation only those abbreviations you are absolutely certain your reader will understand correctly. If you have any doubts at all, the first time you use a term, spell out the full expression and follow it with the abbreviation in parenthesis—Trunk Highway (TH)—or use the abbreviation and follow it with the full expression—TH (Trunk Highway). The abbreviation may be used alone in later references.

In preparing documents and presentations for translation, use as few abbreviations as necessary. Different languages have different abbreviations for the same expressions. For instance the World Health Organization is abbreviated as WHO in English; it is abbreviated as OMS or l'OMS (the Organisation mondiale de la santé) in French. Some languages do not have abbreviations. The added difficulty in translating abbreviations can be costly.

Practice differs on whether to capitalize abbreviations or use lowercase letters. Many abbreviations are capitalized to mark them as abbreviated forms even though they usually are written out in lowercase in text: RFP (request for proposal), REM (rapid eye movement), HEPA filters (high-efficient particulate air filters). Others are either capitalized or lowercased according to the organization or company style manual, as with psi or PSI (per square inch). Just be consistent. Proper nouns are always capitalized: Brinnel hardness number (Bhn), United States (U.S.).

It used to be that most abbreviations took terminal periods (lb.). But today the tendency is to eliminate terminal periods: sq ft, cm, kg. The period is still used for the abbreviation of *inch* (in.) to avoid confusion with the word *in*. Generally, hyphens in expressions that are abbreviated are omitted in the abbreviated form: computer-based training (CBT).

Any college-level dictionary will list the abbreviations you are likely to need. In most dictionaries, the abbreviations will be listed twice—once as an abbreviation in normal alphabetical order and once behind the word for which it is an abbreviation. Other appropriate sources for standard abbreviations are the *American Medical Association Manual of Style*, *The Chicago Manual of Style*, the Council of Biology Editors' *Scientific Style and Format: The CBE Manual for Authors, Editors, and Publishers*, and *The Oxford Dictionary of Abbreviations*.

Guidelines concerning the acceptability of abbreviations vary from place to place, but the following rules are usable unless you have instructions to the contrary.

Widely Accepted Abbreviations

Some abbreviations are generally known and accepted, even preferred in most writing. The following is a representative list of such abbreviations:

Academic Degrees

A.A.   B.A.   B.S.   M.A.   M.S.   M.B.A.   Ph.D.   D.V.M.

Abbreviations of academic and professional degrees usually have periods, but they may also be written as AA, BA, BS, MA, MS, MBA, PhD, and DVM.

Common Measurements

Commonly known measurements expressed in two or more words are usually abbreviated either in capitals or lowercase without periods, although lowercase is increasingly used:

MPG   mpg   MPH   mph   RPM   rpm   KM   km

Proper nouns are capitalized:

Btu   British thermal unit
F   Fahrenheit

Latin Terms

ca. (*circa*, about, approximately), sometimes abbreviated c.
etc. (*et caetera*, and so forth)
e.g. (*exempli gratia*, for example)
i.e. (*id est*, that is)
vs. (*versus*, against), sometimes abbreviated v.

Organizations and Countries

In most of your writing, you may also abbreviate the names of organizations and countries when names are long and unwieldy. Be careful to use a standard abbreviation and to spell out the first time if it is unfamiliar to the reader.

CBS   Columbia Broadcast System
FBI   Federal Bureau of Investigation
NASA   National Aeronautics and Space Administration
USAF   United States Air Force
ASARC   the Australia South Asia Research Centre
U.S.A.   United States of America
U.K.   United Kingdom

Although the practice is divided on using periods with abbreviations, it is quite common not to include periods for abbreviations of countries and organizations.

States and U.S. Territories

The general practice is to spell out the names of states and territories in running text:

The new transfer station will be built in Fulton, Missouri.

An exception is a mailing address:

Send the registration form to P.O. Box 319, Fulton, MO 65251.

For postal codes, use the U.S. Postal Service abbreviations: two letters, all caps, no internal or terminal punctuation:

Alabama	AL	Montana	MT
Alaska	AK	Nebraska	NE
Arizona	AZ	Nevada	NV
Arkansas	AR	New Hampshire	NH
California	CA	New Jersey	NJ
Colorado	CO	New Mexico	NM
Connecticut	CT	New York	NY
Delaware	DE	North Carolina	NC
District of Columbia	DC	North Dakota	ND
Florida	FL	Ohio	OH
Georgia	GA	Oklahoma	OK
Guam	GU	Oregon	OR
Hawaii	HI	Pennsylvania	PA
Idaho	ID	Puerto Rico	PR
Illinois	IL	Rhode Island	RI
Indiana	IN	South Carolina	SC
Iowa	IA	South Dakota	SD
Kansas	KS	Tennessee	TN
Kentucky	KY	Texas	TX
Louisiana	LA	Utah	UT
Maine	ME	Vermont	VT
Maryland	MD	Virginia	VA
Massachusetts	MA	Virgin Islands	VI
Michigan	MI	Washington	WA
Minnesota	MN	West Virginia	WV
Mississippi	MS	Wisconsin	WI
Missouri	MO	Wyoming	WY

For information about formats for business addresses in other counties, see *Merriam Webster's Guide to International Communication*, second edition, or a similar reference.

Time

A.M.   P.M.

These abbreviations may also be written as a.m., p.m. (or, less often, as am and pm, with no periods).

B.C.   A.D.

These abbreviations may also be written as BC and AD, with no periods. Generally, A.D. or AD goes before the date (e.g., A.D. 1066) and B.C. or BC follows the date (e.g., 300 B.C.). It is noteworthy that the abbreviations C.E. or CE (Common Era—equivalent to the Christian Era, commonly expressed as A.D. or AD) and B.C.E. or BCE (Before Common Era—equivalent to B.C. or BC) are beginning to be used by some in recognition that the Christian calendar is no longer used exclusively by persons of the Christian faith. Just be consistent.

C.S.T. or CST (central standard time)

Titles

Dr.   Mr.   Mrs.   Ms.   Prof.

These abbreviated titles are used only before the name, as in *Dr. Tsing*, or *Dr. Hu Tsing*. By themselves, of course, titles are spelled out: The *doctor* drove a black car.

Abbreviations Accepted in Specialized Writing

Abbreviations are widely used in workplace writing. Terms of measurement of two or more words, such as *Brinnel hardness number* (Bhn), *British thermal unit* (Btu), and *cubic foot* or *feet* (cu ft), will be abbreviated both in lists and tables and in the textual prose. Workplace writers will use such abbreviations as *C.O.D.* (collect on delivery) and *f.o.b.* (free on board, meaning the receiver pays the transportation charges).

But even in workplace writing, some restraint is called for. A document with a lot of abbreviations is likely to turn off the reader and slow understanding. Therefore, many writers in the workplace do not abbreviate one-word measurements, such as *ounce* or *pound*, in their text.

Internal consistency is important. Once you abbreviate a term a certain way, continue to do so throughout your text. A typical piece of workplace writing might look like this:

The horizontal and vertical alignment of the highway is consistent with a freeway designed for 70 mph. The maximum mainline curve is 3%. Maximum speed on the frontage roads will be 35 mph.

Abbreviations to Avoid

In any running text, general or specialized, there are many abbreviations that you should avoid. We specify running text because some of the abbreviations are suitable in displayed text such as lists, tables, illustrations, and addresses, where space may be limited. In your text, you should spell out the following words and phrases.

Chatty E-Mail Abbreviations

Although some tend to use abbreviations in their informal e-mail, such as IMHO (in my humble opinion), TIC (tongue in cheek), BBFN (bye bye for now), and FWIW (for what it's worth) most professionals in the workplace do not find them acceptable in more formal documents (including business e-mail).

Common Words and Expressions

government, not gov.   Protestant, not Prot.

First Names

Charles, not Chas.   William, not Wm.

Geographical Locations

France, not Fr.   New York, not N.Y.

Geographical Terms

street, not st.   road, not rd.   mountain, not mt.

Seasons, Months, Days

winter, not wtr.   January, not Ja. or Jan   Monday, not Mon.

Titles

Professor, not Prof.

Acronym

An acronym is a coined word formed from the initial letters or other parts of a group of words: WATS (Wide Area Telecommunication Service), UNICEF (United Nations International Children's Emergency Fund), AIDS (Acquired Immune Deficiency Syndrome), SARS (Severe Acute Respiratory Syndrome).

Like abbreviations, acronyms are created primarily as shortcuts to pronouncing or spelling out long words or phrases. Introduce them by placing them in parentheses when the spelled out term is first used:

The Alabama Department of Transportation (ALDOT) proposed the site for the new interchange. Representatives from ALDOT will be present to discuss . . . .

When overused, acronyms make a passage look like a code to outwit cryptographers. Used with care, they are acceptable.

An acronym is pronounced either like a word or like initials. NOW (National Organization of Women) is pronounced like the word *now*. Acronyms formed in part by syllables of words are usually not written in full capitals: radar (*ra*dio *d*irecting *a*nd *r*anging), centrex (*centr*alized *ex*change), Nazi (*Na*tional-so*zi*alist). NFL, GOP, and RBIs (although sometimes pronounced as *ribbies*) are acronyms that are pronounced like initials.

Long-established acronyms are sometimes called hidden or forgotten acronyms because we no longer recognize them as acronyms. They are written as common nouns: scuba (*self-contained underwater breathing apparatus*), laser (*lightwave amplification by stimulated emission of radiation*).

Apostrophe

In English, the apostrophe has three major uses: (1) to form the plurals of numerals, letters, and symbols; (2) to form the possessive case of nouns and indefinite pronouns; and (3) to replace omitted letters and numerals.

Forming Plurals

Generally, form the plurals of numerals by adding *s*.

> The 1930s were Depression years.
> The temperature was in the 90s for a week.

Forming Possessives

Keep in mind that non-English-speaking cultures do not indicate possession with an apostrophe. In writing or in preparing texts for translation to members of those cultures, instead of writing "the committee's charge" write "the charge of the committee." Also increasingly practiced these days for the possessive case of inanimate objects, writers are dropping the apostrophe and *s* and even the *of*:

> the committee charge (instead of "the committee's charge" or "the charge of the committee")
>
> company profits (instead of "the company's profits" or "profits of the company")

In English, observe the following rules in forming the possessive case.

Joint Possession

When there is joint possession, add the apostrophe and *s* only to the last name of the group:

> Sigrid and Alfred's house

When there is separate possession, add the apostrophe and *s* to each member of the group:

> Sigrid's and Alfred's houses

Plural Nouns

Form the possessive of plural nouns by adding an apostrophe plus *s* to words that do not end with *s* or an "s" sound:

> women's   alumni's

Add only the apostrophe to plural words that do end in *s* or an "s" sound:

advisors'   actresses'

Pronouns

For indefinite pronouns, add an apostrophe and *s* to form the possessive:

anyone's   everyone's   everybody's   nobody's
no one's   other's   neither's

Form the possessive of all other pronouns without the apostrophe:

my (mine)   your (yours)   his, her (hers)   its
our (ours)   their (theirs) whose

Its is the possessive indefinite singular pronoun, not *it's*. *It's* is the contraction of *it is*. *Your* is the possessive second person singular pronoun, not *you're*. *You're* is the contraction of *you are*. Do not confuse these forms.

Singular Nouns

To form the possessive of singular nouns, including proper nouns, add an apostrophe and *s*. This is true even for nouns that already end in *s* or another "s" sound such as *x* or *z*.

woman's   horse's   table's   lynx's

There are a few exceptions to this rule. When adding an apostrophe and *s* results in an *s* or *z* sound that is hard to pronounce, add only the apostrophe:

The Andersons' address   Moses'   conscience'

Try these pronunciations for yourself. Note that *lynx's* is easy to pronounce, where as *conscience's* is awkward to say.

Replacing Letters and Numerals

In contractions, we omit letters; and in numerical expressions, we sometimes omit numerals. In both these uses, the apostrophe replaces the missing element:

He doesn't work here now.
It's Mary at the door.
He graduated in '02.

Keep in mind, though, that most non-English-speaking cultures do not use contractions. Instead of using *isn't*, use *is not*; instead of *doesn't*, use *does not*. Instead of using *02* or *'02*, use *2002*.

Brackets

The major use you are likely to have for brackets is to insert material of your own into a quoted passage. Such insertion is sometimes necessary for various reasons: (1) to add a date or fact not obvious from the passage, (2) to indicate by use of *sic* (Latin for *thus* or *so*) an error of fact or usage in the original and therefore not your error, or (3) to straighten out the syntax of a sentence you may have disturbed through the use of ellipses (see the section on ellipsis points on pages 627–628). Brackets are the accepted signal to the reader that the inserted material is not part of the original. Therefore, do not use parentheses for this purpose.

In that month [January], the GNP fell.

He fell to erth [sic] from a plane.

I was encouraged to engage in others [partnerships] . . . on the same terms with those that I have in Quebec.

Bullets

Bullets (•) are used in a displayed list instead of numbers to emphasize key points or topics (see also the section on lists on pages 631–632). Various marks can serve as bullets—circles, squares, triangles, arrows, and so forth—although the standard bullet is a small square (■) or dot (·). Be sure to use the same size and type of bullet for comparable items in a displayed list, either all 12-point (●), or 10-point (•), or 8-point (•). Dashes (—) can also be used as a type of eye guide, similar to a bullet. See the section on lists on pages 631–632.

Bullets are used when sequence is not an important concern (either because all items are equally important or because the items do not constitute a complete list).

For example, use bullets if items in the displayed list are of equal importance.

Additional projects funded by the society are these:

- feasibility study for landfills in Lincoln County, New Mexico

- comparative analysis of wood and steel in the construction of domestic houses

- improved procedures for collecting data for analyzing food preferences of mourning doves in northwest Arkansas

Number items in a displayed list if the sequence is important.

The three major styles of supervision and the order in which we discuss them are as follows:

1. The autocratic supervisor

2. The democratic supervisor

3. The free-rein supervisor

Capitalization (Uppercase Letter)

Rules for capitalization vary from organization to organization, and the tendency is toward capitalizing fewer and fewer words. The current edition of one of the most widely recognized style manuals, *The Chicago Manual of Style*, is less prescriptive than its previous editions on the issue of capitalization. It identifies an "*up* style" (a tendency to use uppercase, that is, capital letters) and a "*down* style" (a tendency to use lowercase). The choice might be dictated by the organization you work for or it may be your own, but be consistent.

Writing in all capital letters in e-mail is generally considered inappropriate—akin to shouting. If you wish to emphasize something in e-mail, write it in bold type or with asterisks around the word(s) being emphasized. It is also more difficult to read a text in all capital letters than it is text in uppercase and lowercase letters. The following general practices are fairly standard.

Official Titles

Capitalize an official title when you place it before a person's name or use it to refer to a specific person:

> Congresswoman Smith
> Colonel Peter R. Moody
> The President is in her office.

Do not capitalize a title used in a general way:

> Most professors enjoy teaching.
> A field-grade officer, usually a major or a lieutenant colonel, commands the battalion.

Proper Nouns

Capitalize proper nouns and the words that derive from them.

Brand Names

> Chevrolet   Motorola   Nike   Xerox

Many brand names of computer programs, databases, and interfaces use what are referred to as intercaps. Capitalize as the providers desire:

> PageMaker   QuarkXPress   DjVu technology   PeopleSoft   neXTSTEP

Buildings and Structures

> Empire State Building   Hoover Dam
> the Golden Gate Bridge   the Eiffel Tower
> the Kremlin   the Sphinx

Companies

Southern Companies, Inc.   Nokia   Microsoft

Course Titles

CHEM 2011 Advanced Wood Chemistry
ENGL 3549 Scientific and Technical Communication

However, do not capitalize a common course reference (unless the word is a proper noun):

My curriculum requires 9 hours of chemistry.
Professor Ladendorf teaches civil engineering courses.
Four English courses will be offered this summer.

Days of the Week

Monday   Tuesday

American and German writers capitalize the days of the week. However, in many languages, the days of the week are not capitalized. In Spanish and French, for instance, the days are *lunes* and *lundi* (Monday), *martes* and *mardi* (Tuesday), *miércoles* and *mercredi* (Wednesday), and so forth.

Geographic Entities

| England, English | Texas, Texans | the Ohio River |
| The Amazon | the Persian Gulf | the Arctic Circle |

Historical Terms

Magna Carta	Revolutionary War	World War II
War of the Roses	the Napoleonic Wars	Treaty of Ghent
Hammurabi's Code	the Stone Age	

Holidays

| Easter | Independence Day | Ramadan |
| Visakha Puja | Diwali | |

Languages

French   Russian   Swahili

Months

January   February

Many languages, including English, capitalize the names of months. However, in many languages the months are not capitalized. In Czech and French, for instance, the months are *ledens* and *janvier* (January), *únor* and *fevrier* (February), *březen* and *mars* (March), and so forth.

Organizations

United States Senate   United Nations   American Red Cross
Association Expedition Polaires Francaises
Deutsches Hydrographisches Institute
South Asian Association of Regional Cooperation

People

Charles Darwin, Darwinism
Plato, Platonic
Karl Marx, Marxist

Religious Terms

God	the Bible	the Old Testament	Judaism
Jews	Jewish	Protestant	Catholic
Muslim	Nirvana	Ashura	

Seasons

Do not capitalize the names of seasons: winter, spring, summer, fall, autumn, and so forth. However, if the season is part of a proper name, capitalize it: Winter Carnival, Fall Festival, Springfest.

Scientific Terms

Capitalize and italicize the phylum, class, order, family, and genus of plants and animals. Italicize but do not capitalize the species.

Homo sapiens   *Saxifrage stolonifera*

Ships

SS Titanic   *USS San Pablo*   *HMS Dreadnought*

Notice that names of ships are also usually italicized.

Titles of Books, Articles, Plays, and Movies

Unless you are following a documentation style that requires another practice, capitalize the first word of every title. Capitalize all other words except prepositions of fewer than five letters, articles, and conjunctions:

Logical Construction: The Structure of Design
Maxims and Instructions from the Boiler Room
"Getting Inside Your Camera"
"What's a Camera for?"

Colon

The colon is a mark of introduction. You can use it to introduce lists and quotations (particularly long quotations).

Introducing Lists

There will be three final steps: a location-design hearing, a final EIS, and a design study report.

The Metropolitan Council's long-range planning indicates that expansion of the urban service limit should involve the following areas:

- existing urban service area

- addition to the urban service area

- freestanding growth centers

Do *not* place a colon between a verb or a preposition and the objects that follow. Both the colons in the following examples are *incorrect* and should be removed:

Incorrect: The three steps are: a location report, a final EIS, and a design study report.
Incorrect: Public hearings have been scheduled for: Apple Valley, Eagan, and Mendota.

Place no punctuation at all after a verb or preposition:

Correct: The three major steps are a location report, a final EIS, and a Design Study Report.

Correct: Public hearings have been scheduled for Apple Valley, Eagan, and Mendota.

You may use a capital or a lowercase letter following colons. Generally, a complete sentence would start with a capital letter:

Complete sentence: The sign provided clear directions: "Express Lane is for vehicles with two or more passengers."

Generally, a series of phrases or dependent clauses would start with a lowercase letter:

Incomplete sentence: The proposal must contain the following elements: a title page, a table of contents, an introduction that identifies the problem or objective, a description of the proposed action, a schedule for the proposed action, and a justification for the proposed action (including costs).

Introducing Quotations

The Environmental Impact Statement for I-35E clarifies the impact on wetlands as follows: "The most significant impact to water resources would be the direct displacement of wetlands. Of approximately 2,300 acres of wetlands in the study area, 28 acres would fall within the corridor of the proposed actions and would be filled or altered."

Other Conventional Uses

Dear Ms. Swearingen: (formal salutation in a letter)
6:22 P.M. (separate hour from minutes in some expressions of time)
8:4:1 (expression of proportion)

Comma

Commas have so many uses that it is little wonder people sometimes use them incorrectly. In this elementary guide, we will keep things as simple as we can and still cover the major rules.

Most comma use is connected with phrases and clauses, so let us begin by defining these terms:

Phrases are words grouped together to serve a grammatical purpose in a sentence. They do not contain a subject and a verb. Phrases are classified according to the part of speech they are formed around, such as *at the beginning* (prepositional phrase), *testing the product* (gerund phrase), *to complete a project* (infinitive phrase), and *the schedule* (noun phrase).

Clauses are words grouped together to serve a grammatical purpose in a sentence. They consist of both a subject and a verb. An independent clause is a clause that can stand by itself as a complete sentence: "The status of the two offices remained unchanged." A dependent (or subordinate) clause cannot stand alone. It must be connected to an independent clause: "Although additional people were hired, the status of the two offices remained unchanged."

Joining Compound Sentences

When two independent clauses are joined by a coordinating conjunction (*and, but, for, nor, or,* and *yet*), use a comma before the conjunction:

> Building the highway on the present alignment would have little impact on the north bluffs, *but* building it on the new alignment would create a severe impact.

See also the sections on run-on sentences (pages 647–648) and semicolons (pages 648–649).

Separating Elements in a Series

In separating the elements in a series, the comma may be used these ways: *first, second, and third* or *first, second and third.* The first way (first, second, and third) is preferred because using it reduces the risk of ambiguity:

> *Possibly ambiguous:*   The appendix contains raw data, photographs and correspondence. (It is not immediately obvious whether "photographs and correspondence" are examples of "raw data," or are parallel elements with "raw data.")
>
> *Much less ambiguous:*   The appendix contains raw data, photographs, and correspondence.

Here are additional examples of the preferred use of what is called the serial comma:

> This seepage emerges as natural springs that feed tributary streams, lakes, and marshes.

Our choices are to try to meet the deadline, request an extension, or withdraw from the competition.

Holiday schedules cannot be traded with co-workers, sick days cannot be carried over to the next fiscal year, and travel by personal vehicle cannot be reimbursed.

The components of the recreation system range from miniparks, neighborhood play-grounds, and community playfields to multipurpose parks, park reserves, and historic parks.

For lists with internal punctuation, see the section on semicolons on pages 648–649.

Setting Off Introductory Elements

We begin about 25 percent of our sentences with an introductory word, phrase, or subordinate clause. After such an introductory element, a comma is never wrong:

Unfortunately, the bridge will be seen as an artificial object.
Of the 36 Indian mounds, only 12 were well preserved.
As speed increases, foreground details fade rapidly.

Sometimes, when the introductory element is short, you may omit this comma. Either of the following is correct:

Having seniority, the senior sales representative of the district will have his or her choice of assignments.

Having seniority the senior sales representative of the district will have his or her choice of assignments.

Do be careful, however, when omitting the comma. Make sure you do not cause your reader to overread. Look at the following sentence:

Because foreground objects do not block viewing, bridge structures can provide an op-portunity for outstanding vistas.

Remove the comma after *viewing* and readers will mistakenly read that the bridge structures are being viewed. When they realize their error, they must back up and begin again.

Unless you are quite sure of what you are doing, you may always want to use the comma after introductory elements. Be careful, however, not to con-fuse a long, complete subject with an introductory element. This error could cause you to put a comma incorrectly between subject and verb. You would want no punctuation at all at the spot we have marked with brackets in this example:

Planned recreational development of the area [ ] includes a river valley trail system.

You may, however, have a parenthetical element between the subject and the verb that would call for two commas, one on each side of the element:

This game refuge, as proposed, would cross the entire area.

Setting Off Final Elements

Subordinate clauses or phrases that follow a main clause present more of a problem than do introductory elements. Generally, if they are not closely tied to the thought of the main clause, they are preceded by a comma. Definitely use a comma when the final element presents a change of thought:

Railroads and highways have contributed to the area's urbanization, although much of the area is still undeveloped.

However, when the final element is tied closely into the preceding main clause, you are better off without the comma:

I needed a hat because I would be outside all day.

Reading aloud will usually help in this situation. If you pause before the final element while reading aloud, it is a good sign that a comma is needed.

Setting Off Parenthetical and Interrupting Elements

When a word, phrase, or clause is parenthetical to the main thought of the sentence or interrupts the flow of the sentence, set commas around it:

The cultural features, mainly Indian mounds, are to the west of the highway.

The inserted phrase, *mainly Indian mounds*, adds information to the sentence, of course, but it is an aside. It interrupts the flow of the main clause.

The phrase *of course* is usually set off by commas. So are conjunctive adverbs such as *consequently*, *however*, and sometimes *nevertheless* and *therefore*:

The bridge is so high, of course, to allow river traffic to pass underneath. However, the most expansive vistas are to the east.

See also the sections on dash (page 626) and parentheses (pages 639–640).

Setting Off Nonrestrictive Modifiers

Nonrestrictive modifiers are set apart from the rest of the sentence by commas. Restrictive modifiers are not. Sometimes, determining which is which is a puzzle. A restrictive modifier is essential to the meaning of the sentence. For instance:

The design choices *for the Cedar Avenue Bridge* are all costly.

The italicized modifier defines and identifies which design choices, among all the possible design choices the writer could be talking about, are meant. The writer is not talking about the design choices for the Brooklyn Bridge or the Golden Gate Bridge. The writer is talking specifically and exclusively about the design choices for the Cedar Avenue Bridge. The modifier is therefore *restrictive*—it is essential to the meaning of the sentence. Look now at a non-restrictive modifier:

> Old Shakopee Road, *which is a two-lane highway with narrow shoulders,* in 2003 became inadequate for handling commuter traffic.

In this case, the italicized modifier adds important and useful information, but it is not essential to the sentence. The road's name provides the identification needed: It is not any road; it is Old Shakopee Road. Therefore, the modifier is *nonrestrictive*.

   If in doubt, try reading your sentence aloud. You will probably pause quite naturally at the breaks around nonrestrictive modifiers. These pauses are your clues to insert commas. See also the sections on dash (page 626) and parentheses (pages 639–640).

Other Conventional Uses

The comma is the conventional mark of punctuation in several situations.

Addresses Written in Sentence Form

> The main office address is Suite H, 1269 River Valley Drive, Eagan, IN 43911.

However, since the U.S. Postal Service has dropped the comma between the name of a city and the name of a state, it is becoming increasingly acceptable to drop the comma in addresses written in sentence form as well:

> The main address is Suite H, 1269 River Valley Drive, Eagan IN 43911.

As with other punctuation practices, be consistent in your use.

Complimentary Closing

> Sincerely,

Dates

> May 21, 1967, is my birthday.

(But *21 May 1967* and *May 1967* are both written without commas.)

Figures in Thousands

Americans separate thousands with a comma:

> The lowest bid is $72,500.00.
> The tax delinquent roll contains 1,738 names.

However, in some countries, such as in England and Germany, the thousands separator is a period, as in $72.500,00 (see page 77).

Informal Salutation

> Dear Felicia,

Titles and Degrees

Margaret E. Zhou, Vice President of International Marketing, is . . . .
Neil Soderstrom, M.D., is . . . .

Dash

The dash is essentially a mark of separation. It is a rather peculiar but also a rather useful mark of punctuation—as long as it is not overused. It is peculiar because it can be substituted for many other marks of punctuation, particularly the comma and parentheses. And, of course, it is this peculiarity that makes the dash useful.

When substituted for a comma, the dash indicates that the writer meant to be emphatic about the separation:

The table lists the total acres of wetlands within the project—all of which would be eliminated.

Placing dashes around parenthetical material indicates a degree of formal separation greater than the comma would indicate and less than parentheses:

Several protective measures—wood fiber mats, mulches, and special seed mixtures—will prevent erosion.

When the parenthetical statement interrupts rather than follows a clause, it must be set off with paired commas or paired dashes—one at the beginning and one at the close. Always check to see if the closing comma or dash is there.

You may also use the dash to emphasize items in a list or occasionally, instead of a colon, to introduce a list:

Several anti-erosion measures are available:

−wood fiber mats

−mulches

−special seed mixtures

−berms and dikes

Several antierosion devices are available—wood fiber mats, mulches, special seed mixtures, and berms and dikes.

Note that when a list is displayed with dashes, numbers, or bullets, there is no need for commas to separate the items in the list. The white space is considered to be sufficient separation.

The popularity of the dash may tempt you to overuse it, but it quickly loses its emphatic value if you substitute the dash too freely for other marks. Used discreetly, the dash is a useful—even productive—mark of punctuation.

Diction

You have good diction when you choose words and expressions suitable to the occasion and express your thoughts as simply and clearly as possible.

Most people recognize that words that are suitable for some occasions are not suitable for others. The happy slang of locker rooms and poker games would be inappropriate in an annual business report. A passage from an annual report on student housing, for instance, reads this way:

> Dormitories were full and dorm waiting lists long as students began fall classes this year. More than 250 students were waiting to be assigned rooms. In some instances, students were temporarily housed in local hotels and motels.

This language is simple and serious and quite adequate to the occasion of the report. It is neither slangy nor heavy and pompous. Do not let the desire to be more formal lead you into windy pomposities such as *viable interface* and *at this point in time* or tired clichés such as *grim reality* or *Mother Nature*. Your cleaned-up everyday language, supported by whatever professional vocabulary both you and your readers need and understand, will serve you well. You do not have to *ascertain reality* to write formally. *Finding out the facts* will serve just as well.

Your ear, once again, is a good guide. Read your work aloud. If it sounds foolish or pompous, it probably is. If you are sure you would not say something the way you have written it, do not write it that way either.

Faulty diction can also be caused by a lack of precision in choosing the words needed to express your thoughts. We once heard a newsreader speak of an accident that *decapitated* a person's leg at the knee. A moment with a good dictionary will convince you of the impossibility of that. You may say *communicating* when *talking* is the more precise word. You may have confused *enormity* with *enormousness*. Perhaps you wrote the nonstandard *irregardless* for *regardless*. Perhaps you used *good* as in "Johnny played good" instead of "Johnny played *well*." You may have windily talked about *factors* when you should have found some specific words to express what the factors really are.

You will not learn a great deal about good diction by reading about it. Rather you learn it by reading and listening to people who have it and by practicing what you have learned. And do not forget to spend time with your dictionary. See also Chapter 4.

Ellipsis Points

Ellipsis points consist of three or four spaced periods. They have several uses in workplace writing. Use ellipsis points to indicate that you have omitted something from a quoted passage. Use four periods rather than three when the omission comes at the end of the sentence, the first period of the four being the period of the sentence. For example, the preceding sentence could be quoted as follows:

Use four periods . . . when the omission comes at the end of a sentence. . . .

Notice that we have removed supplemental material from the sentence but have been careful not to change its meaning. Note also the spacing before and after each ellipsis point.

To indicate the omission of material within a sentence, replace the material with three spaced periods in a row (each period having a space before and after it):

original: An earthquake will likely occur along a boundary where the Orozco fracture zone off the coast of Mexico and Central America is sliding beneath the North American Plate.

with omitted material indicated:

An earthquake will likely occur along a boundary where the Orozco fracture zone . . . is sliding beneath the North American Plate.

The three spaced periods indicate the omission of "off the coast of Mexico and Central America."

To indicate the omission of material at the end of a sentence, replace the omitted material with four periods: one period immediately after the last word before the omission to indicate that the sentence has ended, and three spaced periods to mark the omission.

original: Unlike many forms of pollution, acid rain can fall hundreds of miles from the pollution source, often crossing national boundaries.

with omitted material and end of the sentence indicated:

Unlike many forms of pollution, acid rain can fall hundreds of miles from the pollution source. . . .

On occasion, you might use ellipsis points as an emphatic mark of separation between statements:

Be sure to get your copy . . . ORDER NOW . . . Mail the coupon below with your check, credit card number, or money order for the full amount.

Exclamation Point

The exclamation point is placed after a statement to emphasize the statement. Its presence indicates that the information in the statement is particularly impressive, unusual, or emotional:

The project engineer recommended the building despite knowing it was unsafe!

The exclamation point has limited use in workplace writing. Use it sparingly, and certainly never use more than one after a statement.

Hyphen

Hyphens are used in word division and in numbers. For these two uses, see the sections on word division (pages 658–659) and numerals (pages 634–635).

Here we are concerned with the use of the hyphen to combine two or more words to make them function as one word. Some publishers' and newspapers' style guides devote dozens of pages to the use of the hyphen. We attempt to simplify matters by considering hyphens used in compound modifiers and compound words.

Compound Modifiers

Compound modifiers are compound words also, but here our problems are somewhat eased. Most compound modifiers, whether in the dictionary or our own invention, are hyphenated when used before the words they modify. For example:

> a coarse-grained texture
> a close-mouthed man
> a light-blue coat
> the always-on-the-go executive

In informal writing, we might see all these examples and similar modifiers written without the hyphen. But in workplace writing, it is a good idea to use the hyphen to avoid confusion. Take the example of *light-blue coat*. A *light, blue coat* is light in weight. This is perhaps even more clearly stated as *A lightweight blue coat*. If the hyphens were omitted, consider the possibilities for confusion in *heavy-machinery operator*, *used-car buyer*, and *pink-skinned pig*.

Note that we have specified that a compound modifier is hyphenated when it is placed *before* the word it modifies. In constructions where the modifier appears as a predicate adjective—that is, after a linking verb—it is usually not hyphenated.

> For the always-on-the-go executive . . .
> For the executive who is always on the go . . .

In the second example, the adjective phrase *always on the go* is joined to its pronoun by the linking verb *is*. (A linking verb is used to connect a subject to another noun or modifier. *To be* is the most usual linking verb, but many verbs, such as *seem*, *feel*, and *appear* can function as linking verbs.)

If in doubt about the hyphenation of compound words, whether they are used as modifiers or not, consult your dictionary. If you do not find an entry for the compound, use your own judgment and the principles given here. Remember, your goal is to avoid confusing the reader.

Compound Words

In English, we form many new words by compounding two existing words, as in *wristband*, *wrist-drop*, and *wrist shot*. We have no trouble speaking such compounds, but we do have problems as soon as we attempt to write them. As our three examples demonstrate, sometimes they are written as one word, sometimes hyphenated, sometimes as two words. No rules are observed uniformly enough to be of much help here. Few of us will keep such fine distinctions in our heads.

What is the answer? When your piece of writing is important—perhaps a report or a letter of application—use your dictionary if you are not absolutely sure of the spelling. There is no better way. When the dictionary offers a choice of spellings, choose the first and use it consistently throughout the document. If the construction is so new that it has not made its way into dictionaries, refer to other documents in your company or organization or use what appears to be most common usage in the field you are writing in.

Italics

In print, italics are a special typeface or font, like this: *Modern Photography*. When writing in longhand, you italicize by underlining:

The use of italics in place of underlining has increased with the use of computers and software that includes effects such as italic and bold. Italics are used to emphasize a word or short phrase, to indicate a non-English word within English text, to refer to a word as a word, and to signal a title.

Emphasis

You can emphasize a word or several words by italicizing them:

> *Do not* place a colon between a verb or a preposition and the objects that follow.

Like all emphatic devices, italics quickly lose their value if you overuse them.

Non-English Words and Phrases

We sometimes incorporate non-English words into English text. When they have been completely accepted—like *rendezvous*, for instance—we do nothing to make them stand out. If they are still considered noticeably non-English, we italicize them:

> The officer in charge of a firing squad has the unpleasant task of giving the *coup de grâce*.

If in doubt how to handle a word, use your dictionary. The entry for the word will indicate whether or not you should italicize it.

Italicize scientific names and phrases:

American chars belong to the genus *Savelinus*.
The samples were examined *in situ*.

Titles

Many style manuals require titles of books, journals, magazines, newspapers, films, and television programs to be italicized:

The Compact Edition of the Oxford English Dictionary
Newsweek
CNN Headline News

Many of these same style manuals require the title of an article, chapter, or section of a work to be enclosed in quotation marks. See the section on quotation marks (pages 645–647). Do not confuse titles of books and book chapters or titles of magazines and articles.

Words as Words

When you use words as words and letters as letters, italicize them to prevent misunderstanding. There are frequent examples of such uses in this textbook, for instance:

Omitted is spelled with one *m* and two *t*'s.

List

A list is an itemized series, often arranged in a particular order. It may be part of the running text or in outline (sometimes called displayed) form.

Forming Displayed or Outlined Lists

Displayed or outline lists should be used sparingly and only when you want to emphasize the elements in the list. For example, consider the following list, which is part of the running text:

The main criteria for selecting a computer monitor should be that the display (1) supports a full assortment of characters, symbols, numbers, and punctuation marks, (2) is easy to read, (3) is comfortable to view so as not to cause operator fatigue, (4) has operator controls for brightness and contrast, and (5) minimizes high reflection.

Compare that passage with the following displayed or outline list:

The main criteria for selecting a computer monitor should be that the display

1. supports a full assortment of characters, symbols, numbers, and punctuation marks
2. is easy to read
3. is comfortable to view so as not to cause operator fatigue
4. has operator controls for brightness and contrast
5. minimizes light reflection

Many writers do not include the serial commas or the period in displayed lists (as this list does not), reasoning that the white space functions as punctuation.

The displayed or outline list is a powerful format because it pulls the attention of readers and directs their eyes toward the items in the list, heightening the list by breaking it away from surrounding text, which is normally seen as a solid block. Each item is seen completely and is not buried within the passage, enabling readers to distinguish each item clearly.

Numbering or Bulleting Items in a List

Numbering the items in a list suggests that the order is important and that the list is complete. If the sequence of the list is unimportant or if the entries in the list represent only some of the possible items, then use bullets (•) or dashes (—) instead of numbers as eye guides. See the section on bullets (page 617).

Misplaced or Dangling Modifier

Modifiers are words, phrases, or clauses that limit or restrict other words, phrases, or clauses. *Green* modifying *coat* limits the coat to that color. "The bridge *that fell down*" cannot be the bridge that remained standing. "A boy *moving downhill*" cannot at the same time also be a boy moving uphill. For the most part, we use modifiers with little difficulty, seldom thinking about them. But if we become careless in their placement, we can create sentences that are vague or misunderstood or, on occasion, accidentally funny.

Modifiers that are in the wrong position to modify the words that the writer or speaker intended to modify are called *misplaced*. Modifiers that have nothing in the sentence to modify are called *dangling*.

Misplaced Modifiers

To correct a misplaced modifier, place it as close as possible to the words it modifies. Here are some examples:

Incorrect: The report about the resident students *of 6 July 2004* reached me today.

Here the italicized modifier is located properly to modify *students* but incorrectly to modify *report*. If *report* is to be modified, move the phrase:

Correct: The report *of 6 July 2004* about the resident students reached me today.
Correct: The 6 July 2004 report about the resident students reached me today.

Another example:

Incorrect: Many researchers are attempting to identify factors that contribute to student development *in residential college life*.

If we move the italicized modifier, we have quite a different statement:

Correct: Many researchers are attempting to identify factors *in residential college life* that contribute to student development.

You are the writer or speaker in charge of the sentence. Put the modifier next to the words being modified, and say exactly what you mean.

Dangling Modifiers

Unlike misplaced modifiers, which modify the wrong word, dangling modifiers have nothing to modify:

Incorrect: *Analyzing change during the first year of college,* students who lived at home participated in fewer extracurricular activities.

At first impression, this sentence leads us to believe that the students were analyzing change. But the sentence does not make sense that way. Looking at the sentence again, we realize that the word meant to be modified by the italicized modifier is not in the sentence. Let us say the missing word is *she*. We can now correct the sentence:

Correct: Analyzing change during the first year of college, *she* found that students who lived at home participated in fewer extracurricular activities.

Any time you begin a sentence with a phrase of the type represented by "Analyzing change" or "To analyze change," be alert. Be sure you include the words you intend to modify.

Numbers (Numerals)

The point at issue in writing numbers is whether they are written as a numeral (26) or a word (twenty-six). The rules we give you are generally, though not universally, accepted. If the company or organization you work for has a style guide, check to see what it recommends. Whether you use these rules or others, be consistent throughout any piece of work.

Compound-Number Adjectives

In workplace writing, two numbers frequently function together as a compound adjective. When such is the case, to avoid confusion write one as a number and one as a word:

3 two-lane highways   two 12-foot driving lanes

Be careful about hyphenating number adjectives. There is considerable difference between *100 gallon drums* and *100-gallon drums*. In fact, it would be far safer to write the first as *100 one-gallon drums*.

Fractions

Fractions connected to whole numbers are always written as numerals:

42-3/4   6 2/3 $7\frac{1}{2}$

When fractions are formed by using full-sized numbers, a hyphen is usually inserted to ensure that 11-2/3 is not read as 112/3.

Small fractions are often written as words. If the fraction stands alone, write it as an unhyphenated compound:

one fourth   two thirds

Hyphenate a fraction written as an adjective:

one-third speed   two-fifths full

Numerals

Most style and usage books call for a number to be expressed as a numeral in the following instances:

Addresses

1262 Pater Road, Dayton, OH 45419

or

1262 Pater Road, Dayton OH 45419

Increasingly, the comma between the city and state is not used.

Dates

25 July 2003   or   July 25, 2003

Decimals

6.42 kilometers   3.5 liters

Exact Sums of Money with Monetary Unit

$106.20 USD   £26   50¢

Fractions Connected to Whole Numbers

42-1/2   6-3/4

Identifying Numbers

Her telephone number is 212.626.6934.

More and more people are using the period instead of the hyphen to separate elements in telephone number. However, it is still correct to use 212-626-6934.

The equipment inventory number is CJ293855.

Percentages

61 percent   61%

References to Pages and Figures

Page 6   See Figure 10.

Tables and Illustrations

For reasons of space and clarity, all numbers in tables and illustrations are normally written as numerals.

Time

6:20 A.M.   0620   6:20 P.M.   1820

Units of Measure

10 meters   20 amperes   42 feet   9 tons

Time (with o'clock)

We normally use the term *o'clock* (shortened form of *of the clock*) with the hour. And we generally write the hour as a word:

eleven o'clock   (not 8 o'clock)

The term *o'clock* is becoming archaic in all but the most formal writing. Increasingly, we write or say "Plan to meet at 8:00" instead of "Plan to meet at eight o'clock." But use *o'clock* in a formal announcement, such as "The Investiture Ceremony will take place at two o'clock."

Words or Numerals

A common rule about whether to spell out a quantity (sixty) or use a numeral (60) is this: Do not write any number that begins a sentence as a numeral.

The only exception is when a year, such as 2004, begins the sentence. This is a sensible rule. In certain circumstances, a hurried reader might connect the number to the period of the preceding sentence and so read the number as a decimal. If writing the number as a word will be cumbersome, revise the sentence:

Five hundred ten insurance policies were sold in September.
In September, 510 insurance policies were sold.

The general trend in workplace writing is to use figures more than words. However, in some instances, a word is still preferred or optional.

Approximate Numbers

Often, numbers used in an approximate way are written as words, regardless of their size. The notion is that written as a figure the number might imply an exactness that is not meant.

The bookstore sold more than three thousand hand calculators during the fall term alone.

Numbers over 10

In most workplace writing, the "rule of 9" still persists: All numbers 9 and below are written in words, and numbers 10 and over are written as numerals.

We have three choices in how to cross the valley.
Only 36 Indian mounds are well preserved.

If numbers under and over 10 are linked together in a series, write them all as numerals for consistency:

Historical sites in the area include 36 Indian mounds, 2 Indian villages, and 3 pioneer cemeteries.

Some organizations and publications prefer in text that numbers up to one hundred to be expressed as words and over one hundred as figures. Under this system, hyphenate the two-word numbers between twenty-one and ninety-nine.

Numbers over 100

Numbers over 100 are spelled out only if they begin a sentence. In English, large numbers are written with commas every three numerals, counting from the right:

3,125,400,000

Remember, though, that in some countries, the thousands separator is a period:

3.125.400.000.

If numbers under and over 100 are linked in a series, all are written as figures:

In 129 historical sites, only 36 Indian mounds are well preserved.

Paragraph

A typical paragraph is a central statement followed by opinions and facts that relate to or support the central statement—as in this example:

> Saint Anthony Falls, the only major cataract on the Mississippi River and the original reason for the existence of Minneapolis, is the focal point of this historic district. Father Louis Hennepin, the first European to see the falls, viewed it and named it in 1680. In 1823, soldiers from the recently established Fort Snelling harnessed its powers for grist and lumber mills. The first dam was built in 1847, and the first big sawmill in 1848. Within another ten years, four flour mills were in operation, and Minneapolis was on its way to national leadership in both lumber and flour milling.

Generally, the central statement comes first in the paragraph, as it does in this example. In this position, it fulfills two jobs. It introduces the paragraph (by signaling the influence of Saint Anthony Falls on the development of Minneapolis), and it provides the necessary transition from the preceding paragraph.

Sometimes, however, the central statement may be placed last:

> A check of deer-auto collisions recorded by the Department of Natural Resources within the study area showed 60 auto-killed deer in 2002 and 64 in 2003. Several locations had a high incident of deer-auto collisions. These locations are within linear bands of vegetation extending from the river valley to various woodlots and agricultural fields within the study area. Deer follow these vegetational bands in their movements between the valley and the higher ground. The proposed highway bisects several of these bands. Therefore, it seems likely that deer-auto accidents will continue and perhaps increase.

Placing the central statement last is useful in persuasion. You allow the facts to convince the reader before you draw the conclusion. It is a device to be used sparingly, however. Used too often, it can leave readers wondering why they have to plow through so many facts without proper guidance.

Paragraphs come in many lengths. A paragraph used as a transition between longer units might be only a sentence or two long. On the other hand, a paragraph in a scholarly book might be 250 to 300 words long.

Paragraphs also vary in length depending on where they appear. Paragraphs in newspapers and brochures run only about 50 words long, in magazines about 100 words. These lengths relate to the narrowness of the columns being used. Newspapers and magazine editors avoid long columns of print without a break. They break paragraphs at fairly slight shifts in thought. In nonfiction books of a general nature, paragraphs run 100 to 150 words long. Probably for most workplace writing, an average of about 100 words per paragraph would be appropriate. In double-spaced word-processed work, this would be about 2-1/2 paragraphs to a page. Online text also requires shorter paragraphs than are used in paper print.

Think of paragraphing as a way of guiding your reader through your material. Well-constructed paragraphs help the reader to spot your generalizations, usually the key to your organization. Normally, your generalizations are your major statements—the ideas and opinions you want your reader to retain. Do not forget the visual impact of paragraphing. Large blocks of unbroken print can turn off the reader. But too-short paragraphs may suggest a lack of organization. A document with paragraphs of varying lengths will probably present most material best.

Parallelism

When you start a series of sentence elements that serve the same function, put them into the same grammatical form. For instance, you will use many lists in workplace writing. Place all elements of the list in the same form, as in this example:

> Always consider the following factors in designing an exhibit:
>
> - distance of viewers from exhibit
> - average viewing time
> - material to be used
> - lighting conditions
> - visual acuity of viewers

In this example, each item on the list is based on a noun—*distance, time, material,* and so on. A writer who switched grammatical forms would have faulty parallelism, as in this list:

> - distance of viewers from exhibit
> - to consider viewing time
> - what material should be used?

In this faulty list, the writer went from a noun phrase to an infinitive phrase to a complete clause. Use any grammatical form in your list that is convenient for you, but stick to the same form throughout.

We have many paired constructions in English, such as *both . . . and, either . . . or, neither . . . nor, not . . . but,* and *not only . . . but also,* that call for parallel forms after each part of the pair. Look at this example:

> *Correct:* Design your exhibit *either for a* technically skilled audience *or for the* general public.

Both elements are based on prepositional phrases and are correctly parallel. You would have faulty parallelism with this next structure:

> *Incorrect:* Design your exhibit either for a technically skilled audience or to please the general public.

Here the parallelism breaks down with the introduction of the infinitive phrase *to please* in the second element.

In most compound sentences, you will be wise to keep both clauses in the same voice: active or passive (see the section on sentences on pages 651–652). In this example, both sides of the compound sentence are in the active voice:

Correct: People want to excel, construct, and imitate; and they seek pleasure, recognition, friends, and security.

The reader would be disturbed if we switched to the passive voice in the second clause:

Incorrect: People want to excel, construct, and imitate; and pleasure, recognition, friends, and security are sought by them.

The following two main clauses read easily despite their length (36 words) because all the elements in both clauses are carefully balanced:

Speeding drivers passing a billboard off the highway will be able to read nine words at most, but slow-moving students passing a sign in a cafeteria line will be able to read several hundred words.

Any time you have elements in any kind of series, take a hard look at them. Be sure you have them in a parallel grammatical form.

Parentheses

One of the three marks of punctuation used to enclose parenthetical material (commas, dashes, and parentheses), parentheses are the "heaviest." They separate the inserted material more definitely and can enclose longer elements—up to several sentences, if necessary—than other marks. Look at the following examples. Pay particular attention to the punctuation inside and around the parentheses:

Norway spruce (*Piscea abies*), a native of Europe, is similar to white spruce in most characteristics. The model tree would have a straight central stem, normal taper (forming a cone the base of which is 70 to 80 percent of its height), and foliage that would be progressively less dense going from the bottom of the tree to the topmost whorl. The primary purpose of shaping is to control the height and width and to develop uniform taper. (Other purposes are to correct deformities, to remove multiple leaders, and to prune lower branches to form a handle and a complete base whorl.) A variety of tools may be used in the shaping process.

Keep these matters of punctuation in mind when using parentheses:

- Place no punctuation before the first parenthesis.

- Delay any punctuation needed after the last word before the first parenthesis until after the second parenthesis.

- Use any capitalization and punctuation required by the sentence structure inside the parentheses.

- Use no special punctuation around parentheses placed between sentences.

A special conventional use of parentheses is to enclose figures or letters in lists. The numbering may use both parentheses or only the closing parenthesis:

> The two main steps in shearing any species with a regular whorled branching habit are (1) regulations of the terminal whorl and (2) clippings or shearing of the side branches.

> The two main steps in sharing any species with a regular whorled branching habit are 1) regulations of the terminal whorl and 2) clippings or shearing of the side branches.

For more information on setting off parenthetical statements, see also the sections on commas (pages 622–626), brackets (pages 616–617), and dashes (page 626).

Period (Dot)

Use a period for the uses illustrated in the following applications.

Abbreviations

> Mr. Ryoichi Hayata
> Clair Reynolds, M.D.
> Col. David Kern

Certain abbreviations are written without periods: HBO (Home Box Office). For more information about particular abbreviations, consult the section on abbreviations (pages 609–614) and a good dictionary.

Decimal Points

> .05 $24.88 HKD

Remember that some countries use a comma to express the decimal point.

Leaders

Leaders are spaced periods (or dots) that lead the eye; they are often used in tables and tables of contents.

> Innovations in Cleaning Up Existing Pollution 8
> Innovations in Detecting Existing Pollution 13
> Innovations in Preventing or Reducing Pollution 22
> Innovations in Turning Pollutants into Useful Products 29

People's Initials

> James S. Robertson

When using initials for both first and middle names, use open initials—that is, place an extra space between them: I. G. Bradshaw, not I.G. Bradshaw.

Period to End a Declarative Sentence

It is no longer unusual to see a woman finish ahead of many men in a marathon.

If a sentence ends with an abbreviation followed by a period, a second period is not needed:

Our new district manager worked for A. Stimmons, Inc.

Run-in Sidehead

A subheading that is on the same line as the first line of text is called a run-in sidehead. It is often followed by a period.

Types of Stars. Stars are classified according to their photospheric ("surface") temperatures or according to color, which is a direct consequence of those temperatures. Some red supergiant stars are . . . .

With Parentheses

When a period and an expression in parentheses fall together, place the period according to the logic of the sentence. If the parenthetical expression is part of the sentence, the period goes outside the closing parenthesis.

One of the new director's suggestions is to reduce the number of plays per season from six to five (a change that has already been effected for next year).

Sure enough, the screen showed oranges down from 22 drachmas a kilo to 15 (about 40 cents).

If the entire sentence is parenthetical, the period goes inside the closing parenthesis.

There is a lot to get used to. I miss the privilege of working whenever I feel like it. (This is my first 8-to-5 job.)

In Arab homes, Americans are apt to rattle around, feeling exposed and often somewhat inadequate because of too much space. (The Arab houses and apartments of the middle and upper classes that Americans stationed abroad typically occupy are much larger than the dwellings Americans usually inhabit.)

With Quotation Marks

Place the period inside the closing quotation mark.

Edwin Bayrd's book *The Thin Game: Dietary Scams and Common Sense* was extolled by a major consumer magazine as containing "the soundest commonsense diet to come along for a long time."

All of Yoshiaki's friends call him "Yoshi."

For more information on using periods as ellipsis points, see pages 627–628.

Pronoun

Pronouns substitute for nouns and function like nouns. Take care with pronouns in regard to agreement, reference, and case.

Agreement

Make a pronoun agree in number and gender with its antecedent:

> Guido monopolized the meeting, but *he* . . . .
> The woman walked through the lobby; then *she* . . . .
> Set the table down and put the lamp on *it.*
> The group members, when *they* meet . . . .

Traditionally, when we could be referring to either a man or a woman, we have used the male pronoun:

> The *student* first gets a class card, then *he* . . . .

Concern for equity in gender has made many feel that this construction is unfair or at least insensitive. English still lacks a natural pronoun for such situations, but one way around this problem is to use a plural construction when you can:

> The *students* first get a class card, then *they* . . . .

Be particularly careful with collective nouns (see the section on verb agreement on page 657). They can be considered either singular or plural, depending on meaning. Make your pronoun agree with whatever number and verb you choose for the collective noun:

> The *committee* is having *its* first meeting tonight.
> The committee are arguing intensely among *themselves*; *they* . . . .

Case

A brief lesson from the history of English is appropriate here. At one time—about fourteen hundred years ago—all nouns in English had case. A noun used as the object of a sentence was in the nominative case, an indirect object was in the dative case, and so forth. Thus, a hound eating a bone was a *hund*, but a hound given a bone was a *hunde*. Except for the possessive case—*a hound's bone*—these cases did not survive in nouns. Today, word order and prepositions tell us whether a noun is subject (S), object (O), or indirect object (IO):

> John gave the bone to the hound.
> S   O   IO

But case did survive in pronouns. Correct case is seldom necessary for understanding. If someone incorrectly says, "Annette and me went fishing," we understand that person as well as if he or she had correctly said, "Annette and I went fishing." If not necessary for understanding, however, case is still important. Quite frankly, status is involved. People who keep their pronouns sorted out correctly are considered by many other people to be more educated than those who do not.

A pronoun used as the subject of a sentence is in the nominative case: *I, he, she, we, they, who.* Pronouns used as objects of verbs are in the objective case: *me, him, her, us, them, whom.* The pronouns *you* and *it* are the same in both cases.

Let us look at some examples:

> *He* hit *me.*
> *We* are going to *him* at once.
> *He* gave *her* the credit card.
> *She* bought the car for *us* boys.
> *Who* is going to the exhibit?
> *He* gave the car to *whom*?

Many people have no trouble sorting out pronouns until they have to use a double object. Then they go to pieces and use the nominative case rather than the objective, perhaps because it sounds more elegant to them. The following forms are *correct:*

> He gave the book to *my brother and me.*
> It is a matter between *him and me.*
> She sent *them and us* an invitation.
> Between *you and me,* I think I understand it.

If in doubt about a double object, try it in the singular. Few people would say, "He gave the book to *I.*" Therefore, "He gave the book to *my brother and I*" would be equally incorrect. "He gave the book to *my brother and me*" is correct.

There is only one tricky place in the whole sorting out of pronouns: the seldom-used predicate nominative. After any form of the verb *to be* (*is, are, was,* and so on), we use the nominative case rather than the objective:

> It is *she.*
> Is it *she*?

Despite this rule, almost everyone says, "It's *me,*" not, "It's *I.*" As we say, this construction is seldom used, particularly in writing. And if you get it wrong, most people will not notice. But do pay attention to your other pronouns. They may be more important than you think.

Reference

Make sure your reader can tell without the slightest hesitation which word or word group your pronoun refers to. If you suspect any confusion, rewrite your sentence.

Despite the distance between the nouns and pronouns in the following sentence, the references are quite clear:

> The *speaker* should place *notes* on the lectern provided. *She* should not wave *them* about.

In the following sentence, the reference is unclear. It could go back to either *leader* or *secretary:*

> Both the group leader and the secretary are responsible for the proper recording of motions. *He* should keep an accurate record.

In cases like this, repeat the needed noun: "The *secretary* should keep an accurate record."

In the following sentence, *this* clearly refers to the broad concept of considering all contributions worthwhile:

> Group members should believe that all contributions are worth considering. *This* in itself will prevent many arguments and unhappy members.

However, in the following sentence, *this* is an unclear reference:

> A faulty fact can usually be identified when placed next to an accurate statement. However, *this* may not occur.

We do not know what will not occur. We have three choices: (1) a faulty fact being identified, (2) a faulty fact being placed next to an accurate statement, or (3) an accurate statement being made. A clear rewrite might be "However, *this identification* may not occur."

As the last example demonstrates, you should examine every reference for the possibility of misunderstanding. Remember that references that are clear to you might not be clear to your reader. Be particularly careful whenever you are using *this, that, which,* or *it.*

Question Mark

If you write a direct question, place a question mark at its end:

> How far must you drill to reach stable rock?

Polite requests may be punctuated with a question mark or a period:

> Will you please send me the noise analysis report before Tuesday?

or

> Will you please send me the noise analysis report before Tuesday.

Use a period, not a question mark after an indirect question:

Representatives of the Sierra Club asked what the impact of the larger dam would be.

Question Mark with Quotation Mark

When a question mark and a quotation mark fall together, place the question mark according to the logic of the sentence. If the question is part of the quotation, the question mark goes inside the quotation mark:

"When is the application due?" was the question on all the writers' minds.
The question on all the writers' minds was "When is the question due?"

If the entire sentence is a question, the question mark goes outside the quotation mark:

What do you mean when you say the program is "viable"?

If the quotation as well as the entire sentence is a question, place the question mark inside the quotation mark. That suffices for each mark:

Did you like Richard Burton's performance in "Who's Afraid of Virginia Woolf?"

Quotation Marks

Use quotation marks to set off quotations and certain titles. You may also use them to set off words used as words, although that practice is becoming outdated. (For additional information on making and documenting quotations, see Chapter 21, "Documenting Sources.")

Designating Titles

Titles of works shorter than book length, such as chapters in books, magazine articles, short stories, and poems, are set inside quotation marks:

Enclosed is the brochure "Comparing Your Options in Home Insurance," which we believe will help you decide which home insurance plan is best.

Wallerstein and Kelly's "California's Children of Divorce" presents data gathered both from individual case studies and from group questionnaires.

Designating Words as Words

Words used as words are italicized (see the section on italics on page 631) or set inside quotation marks:

What is meant by the term *annealing*?
What is meant by the term "annealing"?

Setting Off Quotations

Use quotation marks to enclose a passage repeated from an earlier statement whether written or spoken. The quotation marks signal that you have reproduced the passage word for word:

> Zoo director Sheryl Sikes stated: "The Zoo Board believes that most of the traffic will originate from the metropolitan area and will use the major freeways to reach the zoo."

You may make small, properly marked additions and omissions in quoted material, as explained in the sections on brackets (pages 616–617) and ellipsis points (pages 627–628).

If your quotation runs longer than three lines, do not put it inside quotation marks. Instead, indent it on the page in the following manner:

> In a letter to the Maine Department of Transportation, the Chairman of the Rockport Environmental Council expressed the Council's major concern about the new route:
>> The proposed route would cut a path across the marsh, destroying valuable habitat. Even though the new bridge would be supported by piers, the piers themselves and the associated construction activities would leave permanent scars and damaging effects on the landscape.

Use a colon to introduce indented quotations.

With Other Marks of Punctuation

Fairly definite rules govern the use of other punctuation marks with quotation marks.

Introductory Marks

Quotations that need an introduction are preceded by commas or, in more formal circumstances, by a colon:

> The Rockport mayor said, "No major conflicts with the plans for existing development are anticipated."

> The Rockport mayor supported alternative C with this statement: "All Rockport land-use planning has anticipated the construction of alternative C. Therefore, we strongly recommend this alternative."

See also the section on colons (page 620).

When a quotation is closely integrated into a sentence, use no introductory mark of punctuation:

> The zoo director supports the building of the freeway because she believes that "most of the major traffic will originate from the metropolitan area. . . ."

The use of the lowercase letter at the beginning of the quotation tells the reader that the preceding part of the sentence has been omitted. Therefore, no ellipsis is needed. However, an ellipsis is needed to signal the omission of the material at the end of the sentence. See also the section on ellipsis points (pages 627–628).

Quotation Marks Within Other Quotation Marks

When you use quotation marks within other quotation marks, use single quotes for the inside marks:

> In objection, the council said, "We question your use of the terms 'prudent and feasible' in this regard."

With Colons and Semicolons

When a colon or semicolon is needed at the end of a quotation, always set it outside the marks:

> The council questions our use of the terms "prudent and feasible"; we agreed that the issue is open to interpretation.

With Commas and Periods

Two basic styles apply to using quotation marks with commas and periods. Generally, these two styles are referred to as the *American style* and the *British style*. In the American style, a comma or period at the end of any words set inside quotation marks is always set inside quotation marks, even when logic indicates it should go outside:

> The council member questioned our use of the terms "prudent and feasible."

In the British style, a comma or period at the end of any words set inside quotation marks is always set outside the marks:

> The council member questioned our use of the terms "prudent and feasible".

Generally, American readers expect the American style and British readers expect the British style. However, the distinction is disappearing as globalization grows. Regardless of which style you use, be consistent.

With Dashes, Exclamation Points, and Question Marks

Dashes, exclamation points, and question marks follow the logic of the sentence. When they are part of the quotation, they go inside the marks:

> Many new tree growers ask, "Why should trees be shaped?"

When they belong to the sentence, they go outside:

> What is meant by the term "shaping"?

Note that in the first example, the question mark also serves as end punctuation for the sentence.

Run-On Sentence

The rule for avoiding run-on sentences is simple enough: Do not join two independent clauses with only a comma or with no punctuation at all. Normal punctuation between two independent clauses is one of the following: a period, a semicolon, or a comma and coordinating conjunction (*and, but, for, nor,* or *yet*). The trick is to recognize an independent clause when you see one. The following are all independent clauses, which means they have a subject and verb and can stand by themselves as complete sentences. If you have difficulty with run-on sentences, memorize these patterns:

> Overhead projection is a dramatic method of presenting facts and ideas clearly, concisely, and effectively.
>
> The instructor controls the equipment with a switch of her fingertips.
>
> Put your overhead visuals on a transparent base.
>
> Most inks can be washed off easily.
>
> They are safe to use.

Placing a conjunctive adverb (an adverb that serves both as an adverb and connective) before an independent clause does not make the clause subordinate. Nor does the conjunctive adverb serve as a strong connective. Therefore, you must use normal punctuation as defined in this section before an independent clause beginning with a conjunctive adverb. The major connective adverbs are *accordingly, also, anyhow, besides, consequently, furthermore, however, indeed, likewise, moreover, nevertheless, then, therefore.*

Observe carefully these examples of correct punctuation:

> Most inks can be washed off easily. Therefore, they are safe to use.
>
> Most inks can be washed off easily; therefore, they are safe to use.
>
> Most inks can be washed off easily, and, therefore, are safe to use.

See also the section on colons (pages 620–621), commas (pages 622–626), periods (pages 640–642), semicolons (pages 648–649), and sentence fragments (pages 652–653).

Semicolon

The semicolon is used in certain situations between independent clauses and when internal commas make it necessary in a series. It really has quite limited uses. Do not confuse a semicolon (;) with a colon (:). Do not use the semicolon to introduce lists or quotations, and do not use it after the salutation in a letter. The colon is used in these situations. See the sections on colons (pages 620–621) and run-on sentences (pages 647–648).

Independent Clauses

You can use the semicolon between two independent clauses at any time instead of the more normal period; however, the semicolon is most widely used when the link between the two clauses is one of the conjunctive adverbs: *consequently, however, nevertheless, therefore,* and so on. In this situation, the comma is not considered strong enough punctuation, and the period is perhaps too strong:

> The outlet will be below water level; therefore, it will be entirely submerged and not visible from the bank.

Sometimes, independent clauses between which you would normally use a comma and a coordinating conjunction already have strong internal commas. In this case, substitute a semicolon for the comma:

> The buildings, mainly flour- and sawmills, are gone; but foundations, penstocks, tailraces, and some machinery remain.

Series

When the elements of a series have internal commas, to avoid confusion substitute a semicolon at the breaks where you would normally use commas:

> The schools examined were Normandale, a two-year public community college; Hamline, a four-year private school; and the University of Illinois, a four-year public school.

Sentence

Elsewhere in this guide we tell you about various sentence faults. See the sections on misplaced and dangling modifiers (pages 632–633), sentence fragments (pages 652–653), run-on sentences (pages 647–648), parallelism (pages 638–639), and verb agreement (pages 657–658). In this section, we give some positive advice about writing better sentences. Specifically, we discuss choice of directness, sentence length, sentence order, and appropriate voice.

Directness

Write directly to your thought. Write to express ideas, not to line up words in a row. Do not follow old formulas that are word wasters. Do not *make application to*; simply *apply*. Do not *make contact* with people; instead, simply *see* them or *meet* them. Do you begin thank-you notes with "I want to thank you for . . . ."? Why not simply say "Thank you for . . . ."? It sounds fairly pompous to say or write *at this point in time* rather than *now*. If something happens *due to the fact that*, simply say *because*. If something *is in accordance* with regulations, it is really *under* or *by the regulation*. The list of such tired, indirect ways of saying things is unfortunately all too long. You will avoid most of them if you think about what you want to say and say it in the most direct way you can.

We also waste a good many words by not recognizing the value of the verb in English:

> *Compare:*   What is the conclusion to be drawn from this research?
> *With:*   What can we conclude from this research?

The second sentence saves three words. How was that achieved? By taking the action idea in the noun *conclusion* and putting it in the verb *conclude*, where it belongs.

Besides using fewer words when you put action into verbs, you will make your writing more vivid. This sentence is pallid and indirect:

> A blockage of debris in the conduit could cause a flood in the upper pool.

By putting action into verbs, we have this far better sentence:

> Debris blocking the conduit could flood the upper pool.

Look at the use of verbs and verb forms in the opening paragraph of an advertising letter (the italics are ours):

> *To help prevent* highway deaths, engineers *may* someday *control* traffic with computers. For long distances, the computer *may steer, accelerate, and brake* the car *as needed.* The driver *will lounge, read, play cards, even sleep* while *being whisked* down the highway.

The professional writer of this paragraph knew that verbs snap people to attention. She used verbs to express ideas vividly and directly. She did not hide her ideas behind a smoke screen of needless words. (See also pages 78–88.)

Length

Vary the length of your sentences. Let your sentences range over a spread of about 5 to 35 words. Being conscious of your sentence length will prevent the two extremes of poor writing: too-short sentences and too-long sentences. The former results in disconnected, primer-like sentences:

> The glaciers formed the topography of the study area. They left an accumulation of glacial drift. This drift is from 100 to 500 feet thick.
>
> [25 words in 3 sentences]

At the other extreme, too-long sentences are too complex for the reader to follow. Sometimes, as in this example from a government document, the writer loses control over the material:

> As of the effective date of this memorandum, projects which have received design approval (as defined by PPM 90-1) may receive PS&E approval, if otherwise satisfactory, on the basis of past state highway submissions which identify and document the economic, social and environmental effects previously considered with respect to these advanced projects, together with a supplemental report, if necessary, covering the consideration and disposition of items and not previously covered and now listed herein paragraph 4.b.
>
> [76 words in 1 sentence—depending on how you count the initialisms. That is too long.]

Order

Normal English sentence order is subject first, verb second. Following the verb, a wide range of objects, modifiers, subordinate clauses, and additional main clauses is possible:

Actual shearing *techniques differ* among growers.
                          S   V

Some prefer to begin trimming at the base of the tree and work upward to the
 S   V
terminal leader.

Professional writers begin most of their sentences with the subject. Less often, they begin their sentences with a simple adverbial opener, followed by the subject:

In the terminal whorl, the grower will encounter some common situations that require corrective action.

However, these are dangerous tools, and you should take extra precautions.

Least often of all, they begin their sentences with a subordinate clause or verbal phrase:

When the operation is repeated annually, it has the effect of developing a shorter, well-shaped, and compact tree.

To use any herbicide safely, follow the exact instructions on the label.

Sentence openers before the subject usually serve as transitional devices, linking the sentences to a previous idea.

We appreciate professional writing because it puts no roadblocks between us and the thought. Follow the professional pattern, and you will avoid the difficulties of sentences like the following:

If it appears logical to use the same shoulder width and surface type as that in place on adjacent projects, or if aspects of traffic growth or traffic assignment splits would justify a different selection, or if stage construction is a consideration, it may be desirable to deviate from standards.

This sentence, poor on several counts, puts its main idea—permissible deviation from standards—last. Readers wander through the conditions, wondering why they are reading them. Reverse the order and use a list, and the result will be a far better statement:

You may deviate from standards under these conditions:

- if it appears logical to use the same shoulder width and surface type as that in place on adjacent projects

- if aspects of traffic growth or traffic assignment would justify a different selection

- if stage construction is a consideration

Voice

English sentences that have direct objects are in either of two voices: active or passive.

Active: The glaciers *formed* three striking and different natural features.
Passive: Three striking and different natural features *were formed* by the glaciers.

In the active-voice sentence, the subject acts; in the passive-voice sentence, the subject is acted upon. Active-voice sentences use fewer words and state more directly what you have to say. With the passive voice, you run the risk of forgetting the final prepositional phrase—*by the glaciers*—and leaving the actor unknown.

For simple instructions, the imperative mood of the active voice is clearly superior to the passive. A passage in a safety brochure reads this way:

Effective: Keep your distance. Never operate a crane beneath the power lines without adequate clearance. Play it safe. Leave more than the minimum six feet required. Remember, too, a boom may rebound when a load is released.

The passage is clear and direct, and it clearly says: "This means you!" Compare the active-voice version with the passive:

Less effective: Distance should be kept. A crane should not be operated beneath power lines without adequate clearance. More than the minimum six feet should be allowed for safety reasons. It should be remembered that a boom may rebound when a load is released.

The second version is indefinite and needlessly long.

Less effective: It is requested that you send me a copy of your speech.
Effective: I would appreciate a copy of your speech.

The second, active-voice version is far closer to normal speech and far more polite than the impersonal passive-voice construction.

However, the passive voice has many uses. Use it when the person or thing acted upon is more important than the actor or when you wish to de-emphasize the actor. Do not use the passive voice by accident. Know it when you see it, and use it only when it is clearly better than the active-voice version of the same idea. (See also pages 87–88.)

Sentence Fragment

If you inadvertently punctuate a piece of a sentence as a complete sentence, you have written a sentence fragment. Sentence fragments most often lack a complete verb or are introduced by a relative pronoun or a subordinating conjunction.

Incomplete Verb

Incorrect: The glaciers *forming* three striking and different natural features.

In this sentence, *forming* is a gerund (an *-ing* form of a verb, used primarily as a noun—as in "Forming strong alliances with clients is important."). Correct the sentence by correcting the verb:

Correct: The glaciers *formed* three striking and different natural features.
Correct: The glaciers *are forming* three striking and different natural features.

Relative Pronouns

The relative pronouns are *who, that, what, which, whoever,* and *whatever.* They signal that the clause they introduce needs to be connected to a complete sentence. When you make this connection, you have corrected the error.

> *Incorrect:* The Minnesota River is an underfit river. That is too small for its valley.
> *Correct:* The Minnesota River is an underfit river that is too small for its valley.

Subordinating Conjunctions

Subordinating conjunctions, as the name implies, connect a subordinate (or dependent) clause with a main clause. Therefore, their presence at the beginning of a clause marks the clause as subordinate and unable to stand alone. Common subordinating conjunctions are *after, although, because, since, though, unless,* and *when.*

As with the relative clause, the answer here is to join the subordinate clause to the main clause.

> *Incorrect:* Although the area is largely undeveloped. It does have some light industry.
> *Correct:* Although the area is largely undeveloped, it does have some light industry.

Sometimes writers will deliberately write fragmentary sentences to gain some special effect. In the following example, the writer attempts to catch the feeling of conversation:

> Unbelievable? Not really. In *Highway to Life* you'll find out how modern, safe, and multi-lane divided highways are reducing traffic fatalities by as much as 90 percent.

The source of the example is an advertising letter, where such use is appropriate. But use this device with care; be sure your deliberate use is so obvious that it cannot be mistaken for an error.

Slash Mark

You will write for a long time before you use a slash mark, one of the more obscure marks of punctuation. But it does have its uses. If you have ever written *and/or* or addressed a letter to somebody "in care of" somebody else and used the informal abbreviation *c/o,* you have used the slash mark. If you have typed in a Web address, you may begin by typing http://.

To go along with its miscellaneous uses, the slash mark goes by a variety of names. Some persons call it a *bar;* others call it a *diagonal;* still others refer to it as a *slant sign.* Some call it a *slash.* Dictionaries refer to it as a *virgule.* The slash mark, by whatever name you call it, is a sign of separation.

To separate the elements of an address:

> The address is Sgt. Mary Newland/APO 716/New York, NY 10009.

To separate the numerator from the denominator in a fraction:

3/4   5/8   33-1/2

In some informal writing, to separate the month from the day and the day from the year in dates:

5/11/05   M/D/Y

However, remember that it is better to write out dates in long form (11 May 2005 or May 11, 2005). Some countries use month-date-year, and others use date-month-year; 5/11/05 might be read as May 11, 2005 or 5 November 2005.

Spelling

Spelling correctly is important. Many people are quick to judge your competence and intelligence by how well you spell. A misspelled word or two in a letter of application may block you from a job as quickly as would lack of experience or education. This may be unfortunate or even unwise, but it is one of the facts of life.

For many historical reasons, such as changes in pronunciation and the introduction of words from other languages, English is a difficult language to spell. Nevertheless, it has certain rules, explained in numerous books. Look for them in your library—under either *spelling* or *orthography*—or in your bookstore. The rules really do help and are worth mastering.

If you keep a dictionary handy and use it, you probably spell the difficult words correctly. If you are like most people, it is the everyday words that you misspell the most. Most of us are reluctant to lift the heavy dictionary off the shelf when we need it only to check the spelling of a common word. All too often, our confidence is misplaced. Here is another approach:

- Use the spell checker on your computer.

- Proofread. Stop at words that cause you problems. Read carefully for correctly spelled words that are the wrong words. That is, if you use *too* for *to* or *accept* for *except*, the spelling checker will not catch your error.

- Consult one of the small books that list without definition 20,000 to 30,000 of the most commonly used words. These books also divide words into syllables, so they are useful for breaking a word at the end a line if necessary.

- Ask someone else to read your work. All work going outside your company or organization should be read by more than one person.

Symbol

A symbol is a written sign (certain letters or other marks) that represents something else by resemblance or convention. When using symbols, know your audience well. Most readers are used to seeing only a few standard symbols, so we advise you to write out names of most symbols. Readers who know words like *liter, micro, angstrom, more or less* (or *plus or minus*), or *ohm* do not necessarily recognize the symbols L, μ, Å, $\pm$, and Ω.

It may be convenient for you to summarize the procedure for making common table salt with $2Na + Cl2 \rightarrow 2NaCl$. But if your reader does not understand the symbols, you will have to use other language, such as "When two atoms of sodium are reacted with one molecule of chlorine, two molecules of sodium chloride are formed." Or instead of writing $C_6H^1_2O_6 \rightarrow 6CO_2O$, you might write "The complete metabolism of glucose (blood sugar) in the human body requires six molecules of oxygen (O_2) to produce six molecules of carbon dioxide (CO_2) and six molecules of water (H_2O)."

A symbol represents the sound of speech: Fe, the symbol for iron, is pronounced as *iron*. So when you read a passage that contains *Fe*, do not pronounce the Fe as "fee" or "fay," and do not say the letters *f-e*. Say *iron*.

Be certain that your readers understand the meaning of the symbol you use, or explain the meaning in parentheses the first time the symbol appears.

Transition

Transitions move the reader from one idea to the next. More important, they show the relationships among ideas as shown in the relationship of one sentence to the next or of one paragraph to a previous paragraph. You may need a transition to tie a sentence or paragraph into the overall purpose of a report.

Transitions take many forms: headings and words within sentences.

Headings as Transitions

The use of headings, particularly when combined with a good lead-in, can provide excellent transition:

FILLING SCHEDULES

Three types of filling schedules can be used when operating a natural-air drying bin: fast-fill, layer-fill, and weekly-fill.

Fast-Fill Schedule

With the fast-fill schedule . . . .

Layer-Fill Schedule
    If filled in layers . . . .

Weekly-Fill Schedule
    The weekly-fill schedule . . . .

Notice in these last examples the repetition of key words in the sentences that follow the headings. Including the key words in the opening sentences reinforces for readers that they are in the right section. Also, avoid sentences that begin with vague openings such as "This is . . . ."

However you provide them, transitions are a key to the coherent and logical presentation of your material. Do not leave your readers without them.

Words Within Sentences

You can make a transition with words such as *however, therefore,* and *consequently,* as in this sentence:

Generally, the system adapts best to large operations; *however,* it is a flexible system and may, in some instances, fill the needs of small operations.

You can provide a transition by repeating key words from one paragraph or sentence to the next. Read the first sentence in this paragraph and in the previous two paragraphs, and you will see that we have done exactly that with the key word *transition.* Sometimes you will need a more obvious transition to move from one part of a report to the next, as in this example:

Before making specific recommendations for design and management of natural-air drying systems, we will describe the principles involved.

Underlining

About the only time you will use underlining is to indicate an active hyperlink that will take a reader from one electronic document to another or from one location to another in an electronic document. Such links typically are formatted with a different font, style, or color. They are frequently underlined, as in this example:

bupers1234@earthlink.net

When you are referring to such links in a paper document, remove the hyperlink feature (usually underlining) because the link feature is pointless. Locate the feature for turning on and off the link feature under the Format and AutoCorrect menu of your word processing program.

Verb Agreement

Make the verb agree with its subject. Normally, this will not be a problem, but some trouble spots exist.

Collective Nouns

We have a good many collective nouns in English, nouns such as *audience, band, committee, group, company,* and *class.* Collective nouns can take either singular or plural verbs, depending on the meaning of the sentence:

> The *committee is* having *its* last meeting this afternoon.
> The *committee are* arguing intensely among *themselves.*

Most Americans feel uncomfortable using a plural verb after a collective noun. The British do it naturally. Americans are more likely to say, "The *committee members are* arguing among *themselves.*" (See also the section on pronouns, page 642.)

Compound Subjects

Compound subjects connected by *and* take a plural verb:

> Hydrogen and oxygen are . . . .

When you have a compound subject in an *either . . . or* construction, the noun closest to the verb decides the form of the verb. Note the reversal in these two examples:

> Either the group members or the *leader is* . . . .
> Either the leader or the group *members are* . . . .

Intervening Prepositional Phrases

When a prepositional phrase with a plural object—for example, *of the women*—comes between a singular noun or pronoun and its verb, writers often go astray and use a plural verb:

> *Incorrect:* The *stack* of letters *are* . . . .
> *Correct:* The *stack* of letters *is* . . . .

The pronouns most likely to cause difficulty in this construction are *each, either, neither,* and *none,* all of which take singular verbs. Grammar often is at war with meaning here, but grammar decides the verb:

> *Incorrect:* If *each* of the group members *have* . . . .
> *Correct:* If *each* of the group members *has* . . . .

Plural-Sounding Nouns

Some nouns sound plural but are not—for instance, *electronics*, *economics*, *mathematics*, *physics*, and *measles*. Despite their sound, such nouns take singular verbs:

Mathematics is necessary in . . . .

Nouns of Measurement, Time, and Money

Plural nouns that express measurement, time, or money take singular verbs:

One hundred yards is the distance from goal line to goal line.
Ten years was the sentence.
Five thousand dollars is a lot of money.

Word Division

Word-processing software and laser printing technology have eliminated many word division problems. The word either fits on a line or moves to the next line. Occasionally, you may have to hyphenate a word. If so, review the following guidelines and consult a good dictionary.

In the few instances when you have to carry part of a word over to another line, break it between syllables and hyphenate it:

Even more important than the dormitory program is the . . . .

Your dictionary will show the syllabic division of words:

croc·o·dile   gum·my   gra·cious

A few standard rules cover the proper way of dividing words:

- When a vowel ends a syllable or stands by itself, break after the vowel:

    paro-chial   esti-mate (not est-imate)

- Break between double consonants, unless the double consonant appears in the root of the word:

    occur-ing
    bril-liant
    spell-ing
    toll-ing

- Do not carry over single letters or *-ed* when the *e* is silent. For instance, you would not carry over the *-y* of *busy* or the *-ed* or *bucked*. You could break *darted* before the *-ed* because the *ed* is pronounced. However, usually it is better not to carry over only two letters. Leave them on the line above, or carry the whole word over.

Break Web addresses across lines only when necessary. Simply put a space at the logical point in the address to allow a portion of the address to move to the next line. A logical point is between file names.

The English Department news is found at
www.auburn.edu/english/news/edn/091504.htm

The English Department news is found at
www.auburn.edu/english/news/
edn/091504.htm.

Index